Harvard Business Review On Management

Harvard Business Review

On Management

Harper & Row, Publishers

New York, Hagerstown, San Francisco, London

Designed by C. Linda Dingler

Library of Congress Cataloging in Publication Data

Main entry under title:
Harvard business review—on management.
    Articles originally published in the Harvard
business review during the past 25 years.
    Bibliography: p.
    Includes index.
    1. Management—Addresses, essays, lectures.
I. Harvard business review. II. Title: On
management.
HD21.H35   658.4   75-6339
ISBN 0-06-011769-9

Contents

Foreword   ix

PART I
General Management and Administration

1. *H. Edward Wrapp*   Good Managers Don't Make Policy
                            Decisions   5
2. *Robert L. Katz*   Skills of an Effective Administrator   19
3. *Roger Harrison*   Understanding Your Organization's
                            Character   39
4. *Harry Levinson*   Management by Whose Objectives?   54
5. *Robert H. Hayes*   Qualitative Insights from Quantitative
                            Methods   70
6. *John S. Hammond III*   Better Decisions with Preference Theory   86

PART II
Planning and Strategy

7. *Myles L. Mace*   The President and Corporate Planning   119
8. *John K. Shank*   Balance "Creativity" and "Practicality" in
   Edward G. Niblock   Formal Planning   143
   William T. Sandalls, Jr.
9. *Frank F. Gilmore*   Formulating Strategy in Smaller
                            Companies   156

PART III
Marketing

10. *Theodore Levitt*   Marketing Myopia   176
11. *B. Charles Ames*   Marketing Planning for Industrial
                            Products   197
12. *Derek A. Newton*   Get the Most Out of Your Sales Force   214

13. *Benson P. Shapiro*   Manage the Customer, Not Just the Sales
                               Force   238

14. *Philip Kotler*   Demarketing—Yes, Demarketing   251
     Sidney J. Levy

15. *Louis W. Stern*   Grass Roots Market Research   261
     J. L. Heskett

PART IV
Finance

16. *William W. Sihler*   Framework for Financial Decisions   287

17. *John G. McLean*   How to Evaluate New Capital
                               Investments   308

18. *Gordon Donaldson*   New Framework for Corporate Debt
                               Policy   326

PART V
The Individual and the Organization

19. *Richard E. Walton*   Improving the Quality of Work Life   357

20. *Frederick Herzberg*   One More Time: How Do You Motivate
                               Employees?   361

21. *John J. Morse*   Beyond Theory Y   377
     Jay W. Lorsch

22. *Paul R. Lawrence*   How to Deal with Resistance to Change   390

PART VI
Interpersonal Relations

23. *Fernando Bartolomé*   Executives as Human Beings   413

24. *Chris Argyris*   Interpersonal Barriers to Decision Making   425

25. *Edward W. Jones, Jr.*   What It's Like to Be a Black Manager   448

PART VII
Control

26. *Richard F. Vancil*   What Kind of Management Control Do You
                               Need?   464

27. *Cyrus F. Gibson*   Managing the Four Stages of EDP
     Richard L. Nolan   Growth   482

28. *John C. Chambers*   How to Choose the Right Forecasting Tech-
     Satinder K. Mullick   nique   501
     Donald D. Smith

PART VIII
Production and Operations

29. *Wickham Skinner*   Manufacturing—Missing Link in Corporate
                              Strategy 533
30. *William K. Holstein*   Production Planning and Control Inte-
                              grated 548
31. *Philip H. Thurston*   Requirements Planning for Inventory
                              Control 578
32. *J. L. Heskett*   Sweeping Changes in Distribution 585
33. *Theodore Levitt*   Production-Line Approach to Service 601

PART IX
Expanding Horizons

34. *Peter F. Drucker*   New Templates for Today's Organizations 623
35. *Larry E. Greiner*   Evolution and Revolution as Organizations
                              Grow 636
36. *William C. Goggin*   How the Multidimensional Structure Works at
                              Dow Corning 650
37. *Douglas S. Sherwin*   Strategy for Winning Employee Commit-
                              ment 669
38. *Kenneth R. Andrews*   Can the Best Corporations Be Made
                              Moral? 686
39. *O. A. Ohmann*   "Skyhooks": With Special Implications for
                              Monday Through Friday 698

Bibliography

John B. Bennett   The Well-Read Manager 715
Ronald L. Weiher

The Contributors 727

Index 733

Foreword

The *Harvard Business Review* is a medium for the continuing education of executives in business, industry, and government. Drawing on the talents of many of the most creative people in modern business and business teaching, it attempts to bridge the gap between academic planning and business practice.

Harvard Business Review—On Management, containing articles selected from the thousands published in the past 25 years of *HBR,* has been designed for managers and would-be managers who want to improve their skills and to learn more about the role of the executive.

The book contains some of *HBR's* most outstanding presentations of management philosophies and strategies; approaches which, we believe, every well-informed practicing businessman should understand. We have tried to cover in a systematic fashion many management functions and problems of special importance—a fairly good range of topics but, of course, still only a sample of all the ones possible. The selection of articles has been limited to include only methods and ideas which will not go out-of-date.

We hope that this book will be useful to the business community for a long time.

The Editors
Harvard Business Review

Part I
General Management and Administration

Preface

The phrase "general management" is not new in the lexicon of business, but very few top executives will give the same answer when one asks, "What is general management?" Indeed, this phrase in common usage is a catchall that covers the whole spectrum of management activities. But despite its imprecise definition and broad scope of coverage, "general management" in this section, as the following articles demonstrate, has a common thread which consists of both qualitative and quantitative judgments, methods, and decisions.

In "Good Managers Don't Make Policy Decisions," H. Edward Wrapp argues that top executives instead give their organizations a sense of direction, and that they are masters of developing opportunities. Although these and other characteristics of good managers described in this article run counter to much of the literature and teaching of management, he supports his heresies by identifying and analyzing five talents of special significance with which skillful general managers operate.

The second selection, which also discusses the talents good executives use in carrying out their job functions, focuses on administration effectiveness. When HBR first published "Skills of an Effective Administrator," by Robert L. Katz, in its January–February 1955 issue, many companies were energetically trying to identify the personality traits of the ideal executive. This HBR Classic was written to direct attention away from the effort and toward a more useful question: What observable skills does an effective executive demonstrate? To bring his discussion up to date, the author has written a retrospective commentary that appears at the end of the article.

Whereas effective management gives a business its constructive thrust and drive for success, internal fictions are destructive. Two articles, each written by a practicing psychologist, discuss the organizational climate and the psychological assumptions underlying it. According to Roger Harrison, in "Understanding Your Organization's Character," the resolution of organizational conflicts requires a knowledge of the company's basic ideological orientation. He postulates four separate ideologies that determine the compatibility of an organization's interests with those of its members, as well as the organization's ability to deal with the external environment.

Harry Levinson, in "Management by Whose Objectives?," contends that the ordinary MBO appraisal process, far from being a constructive technique, raises great psychological issues. This technique, which he says is "one of the greatest management illusions," serves simply to increase pressure on the individual. But rather than rejecting the process itself, he argues that it can be improved by examining the underlying assumptions about motivation.

To an ever-increasing extent, modern management is adopting and applying quantitative techniques originally developed in fields such as science, engineering, and economics. These techniques are certainly proving their usefulness; but, in addition to that, the clear, analytical thinking that underlies them is beginning to leaven administrative attitudes at large and to cast new light on the general processes and problems of management itself, as a kind of "intangible" bonus value. This section of the book concludes with two selections on concepts of quantitative analysis of business problems.

Robert H. Hayes, in "Qualitative Insights from Quantitative Methods," stresses the point that exact methods for solving specific problems are leading to a better understanding of the real nature of the art of management. Then, "Better Decisions with Preference Theory," by John S. Hammond III, demonstrates how such decision-making techniques can be tailored to help the executive bring his attitude toward risk into the analysis of business problems involving uncertainty.

1. Good Managers Don't Make Policy Decisions

H. Edward Wrapp

The successful general manager does not spell out detailed objectives for his organization, the author believes; nor does he make master plans. He seldom makes forthright statements of policy. He is an opportunist, and he tends to muddle through problems—although he muddles with a purpose. He enmeshes himself in many operating matters and does not limit himself to "the big picture."

The upper reaches of management are a land of mystery and intrigue. Very few people have ever been there, and the present inhabitants frequently send back messages that are incoherent both to other levels of management and to the world in general. This may account for the myths, illusions, and caricatures that permeate the literature of management—for example, such widely held notions as these:

□ Life gets less complicated as a manager reaches the top of the pyramid.

□ The manager at the top level knows everything that's going on in the organization, can command whatever resources he may need, and therefore can be more decisive.

□ The general manager's day is taken up with making broad policy decisions and formulating precise objectives.

□ The top executive's primary activity is conceptualizing long-range plans.

□ In a large company, the top executive may be seen meditating about the role of his organization in society.

I suggest that none of these versions alone, or in combination, is an accurate portrayal of what a general manager does. Perhaps students of the management process have been overly eager to develop a theory and a discipline. As one executive I know puts it, "I guess I do some of the things described in the books and articles, but the descriptions are lifeless, and my job isn't."

What common characteristics, then, do successful executives exhibit *in reality*? I shall identify five skills or talents which, in my experience, seem especially significant. (For details on the method used in reaching these conclusions, see page 18.)

Keeping Well Informed

First, each of my heroes has a special talent for keeping himself informed about a wide range of operating decisions being made at different levels in the company. As he moves up the ladder, he develops a network of information sources in many different departments. He cultivates these sources and keeps them open no matter how high he climbs in the organization. When the need arises, he bypasses the lines on the organization chart to seek more than one version of a situation.

In some instances, especially when they suspect he would not be in total agreement with their decision, his subordinates will elect to inform him in advance, before they announce a decision. In these circumstances, he is in a position to defer the decision, or redirect it, or even block further action. However, he does not insist on this procedure. Ordinarily he leaves it up to the members of his organization to decide at what stage they inform him.

Top-level managers are frequently criticized by writers, consultants, and lower levels of management for continuing to enmesh themselves in operating problems, after promotion to the top, rather than withdrawing to the "big picture." Without any doubt, some managers do get lost in a welter of detail and insist on making too many decisions. Superficially, the good manager may seem to make the same mistake—but his purposes are different. He knows that only by keeping well informed about the decisions being made can he avoid the sterility so often found in those who isolate themselves from operations. If he follows the advice to free himself from operations, he may soon find himself subsisting on a diet of abstractions, leaving the choice of what he eats in the hands of his subordinates. As Kenneth Boulding puts it: "The very purpose of a hierarchy is to prevent information from reaching higher layers. It operates as an information filter, and there are little wastebaskets all along the way."[1]

What kinds of action does a successful executive take to keep his information live and accurate? Here is an example:

□ One company president that I worked with sensed that his vice presidents were insulating him from some of the vital issues being dis-

1. From a speech at a meeting sponsored by the Crowell Collier Institute of Continuing Education in New York.

cussed at lower levels. He accepted a proposal for a formal management development program primarily because it afforded him an opportunity to discuss company problems with middle managers several layers removed from him in the organization. By meeting with small groups of these men in an academic setting, he learned much about their preoccupations, and also about those of his vice presidents. And he accomplished his purposes without undermining the authority of line managers.

Focusing Time and Energy

The second skill of the good manager is that he knows how to save his energy and hours for those few particular issues, decisions, or problems to which he should give his personal attention. He knows the fine and subtle distinction between keeping fully informed about operating decisions and allowing the organization to force him into participating in these decisions or, even worse, making them. Recognizing that he can bring his special talents to bear on only a limited number of matters, he chooses those issues which he believes will have the greatest long-term impact on the company, and on which his special abilities can be most productive. Under ordinary circumstances he will limit himself to three or four major objectives during any single period of sustained activity.

What about the situations he elects *not* to become involved in as a decision maker? He makes sure (using the skill first mentioned) that the organization keeps him informed about them at various stages; he does not want to be accused of indifference to such issues. He trains his subordinates not to bring the matters to him for a decision. The communication to him from below is essentially one of: "Here is our sizeup, and here's what we propose to do." Reserving his hearty encouragement for those projects which hold superior promise of a contribution to total corporate strategy, he simply acknowledges receipt of information on other matters. When he sees a problem where the organization needs his help, he finds a way to transmit his know-how short of giving orders—usually by asking perceptive questions.

Playing the Power Game

To what extent do successful top executives push their ideas and proposals through the organization? The rather common notion that the "prime mover" continually creates and forces through new programs, like a powerful majority leader in a liberal Congress, is in my opinion very misleading.

The successful manager is sensitive to the power structure in the organization. In considering any major current proposal, he can plot the position of the various individuals and units in the organization on a scale ranging from complete, outspoken support down to determined, sometimes bitter, and oftentimes well-cloaked opposition. In the middle of the scale is an area of comparative indifference. Usually, several aspects of a proposal will fall into this area, and *here is where he knows he can operate*. He assesses the depth and nature of the blocs in the organization. His perception permits him to move through what I call *corridors* of comparative indifference. He seldom challenges when a corridor is blocked, preferring to pause until it has opened up.

Related to this particular skill is his ability to recognize the need for a few trial-balloon launchers in the organization. He knows that the organization will tolerate only a certain number of proposals which emanate from the apex of the pyramid. No matter how sorely he may be tempted to stimulate the organization with a flow of his own ideas, he knows he must work through idea men in different parts of the organization. As he studies the reactions of key individuals and groups to the trial balloons these men send up, he is able to make a better assessment of how to limit the emasculation of the various proposals. For seldom does he find a proposal which is supported by all quarters of the organization. The emergence of strong support in certain quarters is almost sure to evoke strong opposition in others.

VALUE OF SENSE OF TIMING

Circumstances like these mean that a good sense of timing is a priceless asset for a top executive. Let me illustrate:

□ A vice president had for some time been convinced that his company lacked a sense of direction and needed a formal long-range planning activity to fill the void. Up to the time in question, his soft overtures to other top executives had been rebuffed. And then he spotted an opening.

A management development committee proposed a series of weekend meetings for second-level officers in the company. After extensive debate, but for reasons not announced, the president rejected this proposal. The members of the committee openly resented what seemed to them an arbitrary rejection.

The vice president, sensing a tense situation, suggested to the president that the same officers who were to have attended the weekend management development seminars be organized into a long-range planning committee. The timing of his suggestion was perfect. The president, looking for a bone to toss to the committee, acquiesced immediately, and the management development committee in its next meeting enthusiastically endorsed the idea.

This vice president had been conducting a kind of continuing market research to discover how to sell his long-range planning proposal. His previous probes of the "market" had told him that the president's earlier rejections of his proposal were not so final as to preclude an eventual shift in the corridors of attitude I have mentioned.

The vice president caught the committee in a conciliatory mood, and his proposal rode through with colors flying.

As a good manager stands at a point in time, he can identify a set of goals he is interested in, albeit the outline of them may be pretty hazy. His timetable, which is also pretty hazy, suggests that some must be accomplished sooner than others, and that some may be safely postponed for several months or years. He has a still hazier notion of how he can reach these goals. He assesses key individuals and groups. He knows that each has its own set of goals, some of which he understands rather thoroughly and others about which he can only speculate. He knows also that these individuals and groups represent blocks to certain programs or projects, and that these points of opposition must be taken into account. As the day-to-day operating decisions are made, and as proposals are responded to both by individuals and by groups, he perceives more clearly where the corridors of comparative indifference are. He takes action accordingly.

The Art of Imprecision

The fourth skill of the successful manager is knowing how to satisfy the organization that it has a sense of direction *without ever actually getting himself committed publicly to a specific set of objectives*. This is not to say that he does not have objectives—personal and corporate, long-term and short-term. They are significant guides to his thinking, and he modifies them continually as he better understands the resources he is working with, the competition, and the changing market demands. But as the organization clamors for statements of objectives, these are samples of what they get back from him:

"Our company aims to be number one in its industry."

"Our objective is growth with profit."

"We seek the maximum return on investment."

"Management's goal is to meet its responsibilities to stockholders, employees, and the public."

In my opinion, statements such as these provide almost no guidance to the various levels of management. Yet they are quite readily accepted as objectives by large numbers of intelligent people.

Why does the good manager shy away from precise statements of his objectives for the organization? The main reason is that he finds it impossible to set down specific objectives which will be relevant for any reasonable period into the future. Conditions in business change continually and rapidly, and corporate strategy must be revised to take the changes into account. The more explicit the statement of strategy, the more difficult it becomes to persuade the organization to turn to different goals when needs and conditions shift.

The public and the stockholders, to be sure, must perceive the organization as having a well-defined set of objectives and a clear sense of direction. But in reality the good top manager is seldom so certain of the direction which should be taken. Better than anyone else, he senses the many, many threats to his company—threats which lie in the economy, in the actions of competitors, and, not least, within his own organization.

He also knows that it is impossible to state objectives clearly enough so that everyone in the organization understands what they mean. Objectives get communicated only over time by a consistency or pattern in operating decisions. Such decisions are more meaningful than words. In instances where precise objectives are spelled out, the organization tends to interpret them so they fit its own needs.

Subordinates who keep pressing for more precise objectives are in truth working against their own best interests. Each time the objectives are stated more specifically, a subordinate's range of possibilities for operating are reduced. The narrower field means less room to roam and to accommodate the flow of ideas coming up from his part of the organization.

AVOIDING POLICY STRAITJACKETS

The successful manager's reluctance to be precise extends into the area of policy decisions. He seldom makes a forthright statement of policy. He may be aware that in some companies there are executives who spend more time in arbitrating disputes caused by stated policies than in moving the company forward. The management textbooks contend that well-defined policies are the sine qua non of a well-managed company. My research does not bear out this contention. For example:

□ The president of one company with which I am familiar deliberately leaves the assignments of his top officers vague and refuses to define policies for them. He passes out new assignments with seemingly no pattern in mind and consciously sets up competitive ventures among his subordinates. His methods, though they would never be sanctioned by a classical organization planner, are deliberate—and, incidentally, quite effective.

Since able managers do not make policy decisions, does this mean that well-managed companies operate without policies? Certainly not. But the policies are those which evolve over time from an indescribable mix of operating decisions. From any single operating decision might have come a very minor dimension of the policy as the organization understands it; from a series of decisions comes a pattern of guidelines for various levels of the organization.

The skillful manager resists the urge to write a company creed or to compile a policy manual. Preoccupation with detailed statements of corporate objectives and departmental goals and with comprehensive organization charts and job descriptions—this is often the first symptom of an organization which is in the early stages of atrophy.

The "management by objectives" school, so widely heralded in recent years, suggests that detailed objectives be spelled out at all levels in the corporation. This method is feasible at lower levels of management, but it becomes unworkable at the upper levels. The top manager must think out objectives in detail, but ordinarily some of the objectives must be withheld, or at least communicated to the organization in modest doses. A conditioning process which may stretch over months or years is necessary in order to prepare the organization for radical departures from what it is currently striving to attain.

Suppose, for example, that a president is convinced his company must phase out of the principal business it has been in for 35 years. Although making this change of course is one of his objectives, he may well feel that he cannot disclose the idea even to his vice presidents, whose total know-how is in the present business. A blunt announcement that the company is changing horses would be too great a shock for most of them to bear. And so he begins moving toward this goal but without a full disclosure to his management group.

A detailed spelling out of objectives may only complicate the task of reaching them. Specific, detailed statements give the opposition an opportunity to organize its defenses.

Muddling with a Purpose

The fifth, and most important, skill I shall describe bears little relation to the doctrine that management is (or should be) a comprehensive, systematic, logical, well-programmed science. Of all the heresies set forth here, this should strike doctrinaires as the rankest of all!

The successful manager, in my observation, recognizes the futility of trying to push total packages or programs through the organization. He is willing to take less than total acceptance in order to achieve modest progress toward his goals. Avoiding debates on principles, he tries to piece together particles that may appear to be incidentals into a program that moves at least part of the way toward his objectives. His attitude is based on optimism and persistence. Over and over he says to himself, "There must be some parts of this proposal on which we can capitalize."

Whenever he identifies relationships among the different proposals before him, he knows that they present opportunities for combination and restructuring. It follows that he is a man of wide-ranging interests and curiosity. The more things he knows about, the more opportunities he will have to discover parts which are related. This process does not require great intellectual brilliance or unusual creativity. The wider ranging his interests, the more likely that he will be able to tie together several unrelated proposals. He is skilled as an analyst, but even more talented as a conceptualizer.

If the manager has built or inherited a solid organization, it will be difficult for him to come up with an idea which no one in the company has ever thought of before. His most significant contribution may be that he can see relationships which no one else has seen. Take this example:

□ A division manager had set as one of his objectives, at the start of a year, an improvement in product quality. At the end of the year, in reviewing his progress toward this objective, he could identify three significant events which had brought about a perceptible improvement.

First, the head of the quality control group, a veteran manager who was doing only an adequate job, asked early in the year for assignment to a new research group. This opportunity permitted the division manager to install a promising young engineer in this key spot.

A few months later, opportunity number two came along. The personnel department proposed a continuous program of checking the effectiveness of training methods for new employees. The proposal was acceptable to the manufacturing group. The division manager's only contribution was to suggest that the program should include a heavy emphasis on employees' attitudes toward quality.

Then a third opportunity arose when one of the division's best customers discovered that the wrong material had been used for a large lot of parts. The heat generated by this complaint made it possible to institute a completely new system of procedures for inspecting and testing raw materials.

As the division manager reviewed the year's progress on product quality, these were the three most important developments. None of them could have been predicted at the start of the year, but he was quick to see the potential in each as it popped up in the day-to-day operating routines.

EXPLOITATION OF CHANGE

The good manager can function effectively only in an environment of continual change. A *Saturday Review* cartoonist has caught the idea as he pictures an executive seated at a massive desk instructing his secretary to "send in a deal; I feel like wheelin'." Only with many changes in the works can the manager discover new combinations of opportunities and open up new corridors of comparative indifference. His stimulation to creativity comes from trying to make something useful of the proposal or idea in front of him. He will try to make strategic change a way of life in the organization and continually review the strategy even though current results are good.

Charles Lindblom has written an article with an engaging title, "The Science of Muddling Through."[2] In this paper he describes what he calls "the rational comprehensive method" of decision making. The essence of this method is that the decision maker, for each of his problems, proceeds deliberately, one step at a time, to collect complete data; to analyze the data thoroughly; to study a wide range of alternatives, each with its own risks and consequences; and, finally, to formulate a detailed course of action. Lindblom immediately dismisses "the rational comprehensive method" in favor of what he calls "successive limited comparisons." He sees the decision maker as comparing the alternatives which are open to him in order to learn which most closely meets the objectives he has in mind. Since this is not so much a rational process as an opportunistic one, he sees the manager as a muddler, but a muddler with a purpose.

H. Igor Ansoff, in his book, *Corporate Strategy*,[3] espouses a similar notion as he describes what he calls the "cascade approach." In his view, possible decision rules are formulated in gross terms and are successively refined through several stages as the emergence of a solution proceeds. This process gives the appearance of solving the problem several times over, but with successively more precise results.

Both Lindblom and Ansoff have moved us closer to an understanding of how managers really think. The process is not highly abstract; rather, the manager searches for a means of drawing into a pattern the thousands of incidents which make up the day-to-day life of a growing company.

CONTRASTING PICTURES

It is interesting to note, in the writings of several students of management, the emergence of the concept that, rather than making decisions, the leader's principal task is maintaining operating conditions which permit the various decision-making systems to function effectively. The supporters of this theory, it seems to me, overlook the subtle turns of direction which the leader can provide. He cannot add purpose and structure to the balanced judgments of subordinates if he simply rubber-stamps their

2. *Readings in Managerial Psychology*, edited by Harold J. Leavitt and Louis R. Pondy (Chicago, University of Chicago Press, 1964), p. 61.
3. New York, McGraw-Hill Book Company, Inc., 1965.

decisions. He must weigh the issues and reach his own decision.

Richard M. Cyert and James G. March contend that in real life managers do not consider all the possible courses of action, that their search ends once they have found a satisfactory alternative. In my sample, good managers are not guilty of such myopic thinking. Unless they mull over a wide range of possibilities, they cannot come up with the imaginative combinations of ideas which characterize their work.

Many of the articles about successful executives picture them as great thinkers who sit at their desks drafting master blueprints for their companies. The successful top executives I have seen at work do not operate this way. Rather than produce a full-grown decision tree, they start with a twig, help it grow, and ease themselves out on the limbs only after they have tested to see how much weight the limbs can stand.

In my picture, the general manager sits in the midst of a continuous stream of operating problems. His organization presents him with a flow of proposals to deal with the problems. Some of these proposals are contained in voluminous, well-documented, formal reports; some are as fleeting as the walk-in visit from a subordinate whose latest inspiration came during the morning's coffee break. Knowing how meaningless it is to say, "This is a finance problem," or, "That is a communications problem," the manager feels no compulsion to classify his problems. He is, in fact, undismayed by a problem that defies classification. As the late Gary Steiner, in one of his speeches, put it, "He has a high tolerance for ambiguity."

In considering each proposal, the general manager tests it against at least three criteria:

1. Will the total proposal—or, more often, will some part of the proposal—move the organization toward the objectives which he has in mind?

2. How will the whole or parts of the proposal be received by the various groups and subgroups in the organization? Where will the strongest opposition come from, which group will furnish the strongest support, and which group will be neutral or indifferent?

3. How does the proposal relate to programs already in process or currently proposed? Can some parts of the proposal under consideration be added on to a program already under way, or can they be combined with all or parts of other proposals in a package which can be steered through the organization?

THE MAKING OF A DECISION

As another example of a general manager at work, let me describe the train of events which led to a parent company president's decision to attempt to consolidate two of his divisions:

◻ Let us call the executive Mr. Brown. One day the manager of Division A came to him with a proposal that his division acquire a certain company. That company's founder and president—let us call him Mr. Johansson—had a phenomenal record of inventing new products, but earnings in his company had been less than phenomenal. Johansson's asking price for his company was high when evaluated against the earnings record.

Not until Brown began to speculate on how Johansson might supply fresh vigor for new products in Division A did it appear that perhaps a premium price could be justified. For several years Brown had been unsuccessful in stimulating the manager of that division to see that he must bring in new products to replace those which were losing their place in the market.

The next idea which came to Brown was that Johansson might invent not only for Division A but also for Division B. As Brown analyzed how this might be worked out organizationally, he began to think about the markets being served by divisions A and B. Over the years, several basic but gradual changes in marketing patterns had occurred, with the result that the marketing considerations which had dictated the establishment of separate divisions no longer prevailed. Why should the company continue to support the duplicated overhead expenses in the two divisions?

As Brown weighed the issues, he concluded that by consolidating the two divisions, he could also shift responsibilities in the management groups in ways that would strengthen them overall.

If we were asked to evaluate Brown's capabilities, how would we respond? Putting aside the objection that the information is too sketchy, our tendency might be to criticize Brown. Why did he not identify the changing market patterns in his continuing review of company position? Why did he not force the issue when the division manager failed to do something about new product development? Such criticism would reflect "the rational comprehensive method" of decision making.

But, as I analyze the gyrations in Brown's thinking, one characteristic stands out. He kept searching for the follow-on opportunities which he could fashion out of the original proposal, opportunities which would stand up against the three criteria earlier mentioned. In my book, Brown would rate as an extremely skillful general manager.

Conclusion

To recapitulate, the general manager possesses five important skills. He knows how to:

1. *Keep open many pipelines of information*—No one will quarrel with the desirability of an early warning system which provides varied view-

points on an issue. However, very few managers know how to practice this skill, and the books on management add precious little to our understanding of the techniques which make it practicable.

2. *Concentrate on a limited number of significant issues*—No matter how skillful the manager is in focusing his energies and talents, he is inevitably caught up in a number of inconsequential duties. Active leadership of an organization demands a high level of personal involvement, and personal involvement brings with it many time-consuming activities which have an infinitesimal impact on corporate strategy. Hence this second skill, while perhaps the most logical of the five, is by no means the easiest to apply.

3. *Identify the corridors of comparative indifference*—Are there inferences here that the good manager has no ideas of his own, that he stands by until his organization proposes solutions, that he never uses his authority to force a proposal through the organization? Such inferences are not intended. The message is that a good organization will tolerate only so much direction from the top; the good manager therefore is adept at sensing how hard he can push.

4. *Give the organization a sense of direction with open-ended objectives* —In assessing this skill, keep in mind that I am talking about top levels of management. At lower levels, the manager should be encouraged to write down his objectives, if for no other reason than to ascertain if they are consistent with corporate strategy.

5. *Spot opportunities and relationships in the stream of operating problems and decisions*—Lest it be concluded from the description of this skill that the good manager is more an improviser than a planner, let me emphasize that he is a planner and encourages planning by his subordinates. Interestingly, though, professional planners may be irritated by a good general manager. Most of them complain about his lack of vision. They devise a master plan, but the president (or other operating executive) seems to ignore it, or to give it minimum acknowledgment by borrowing bits and pieces for implementation. They seem to feel that the power of a good master plan will be obvious to everyone, and its implementation automatic. But the general manager knows that even if the plan is sound and imaginative, the job has only begun. The long, painful task of implementation will depend on his skill, not that of the planner.

PRACTICAL IMPLICATIONS

If this analysis of how skillful general managers think and operate has validity, then it should help us see several problems in a better light.

Investment analysis: The investment community is giving increasing attention to sizing up the management of a company being appraised. Thus far, the analysts rely mainly on results or performance rather than on a probe of management skills. But current performance can be affected by many variables, both favorably and unfavorably, and is a dangerous base for predicting what the management of a company will produce in the future. Testing the key managers of a company against the five skills described holds promise for evaluating the caliber of a management group.

Incidentally, I believe that the manager who is building his own company and the man who is moving up through the hierarchy of a larger organization require essentially the same capabilities for success.

The urge to merge: In today's frenzy of acquisitions and mergers, why does a management usually prefer to acquire a company rather than to develop a new product and build an organization to make and sell it? One of the reasons can be found in the way a general manager thinks and operates. He finds it difficult to sit and speculate theoretically about the future as he and his subordinates fashion a plan to exploit a new product. He is much more at home when taking over a going concern, even though he anticipates he will inherit many things he does not want. In the day-to-day operation of a going concern, he finds the milieu to maneuver and conceptualize.

Promotion practices: Scarcely any manager in any business can escape the acutely painful responsibility to identify men with potential for growth in management and to devise methods for developing them for broader responsibilities. Few line managers or staff professionals have genuine confidence in the yardsticks and devices they use now. The five skills offer possibilities for raising an additional set of questions about management appraisal methods, job rotation practices, on-the-job development assignments, and the curricula of formal in-house management development programs.

One group of distinguished executives ignores with alarming regularity the implications of the five skills. These are the presidents of multidivision companies who "promote" successful division managers to the parent company level as staff officers. Does this recurring phenomenon cast doubt on the validity of my theory? I think not. To the contrary, strong supporting evidence for my thesis can be found in the results of such action. What happens is that line managers thus "promoted" often end up on the sidelines, out of the game for the rest of their careers. Removed from the tumult of operations, the environment which I contend is critical for their success, many of them just wither away in their high-status posts as senior counselors and never become effective.

Appendix to Chapter 1

Basis of Conclusions in This Article

I have reached the conclusions outlined here after working closely with many managers in many different companies. In truth, the managers were not preselected with research in mind. Never did I tell the man that he was being studied, nor was I in fact studying his behavior. Research was not the purpose of our relationship. We were collaborating to solve some real problem.

Researching the management process when the manager is aware that he is being studied sometimes produces strange results. Rarely is a good executive able to think objectively about the management process as it is exemplified in his own methods. When he tries to explain to a researcher or writer, he tends to feel compelled to develop rational, systematic explanations of how he does his job—explanations which in my opinion are largely fictional.

A manager cannot be expected to describe his methods even if he understands them. They border on manipulation, and the stigma associated with manipulation can be fatal. If the organization ever identifies him as a manipulator, his job becomes more difficult. No one willingly submits to manipulation, and those around him organize to protect themselves. And yet every good manager does have to manipulate.

My definition of a good manager is a simple one: under competitive industry conditions, he is able to move his organization significantly toward the goals he has set, whether measured by higher return on investment, product improvement, development of management talent, faster growth in sales and earnings, or some other standard. Bear in mind that this definition does not refer to the administrator whose principal role is to maintain the status quo in a company or in a department. Keeping the wheels turning in a direction already set is a relatively simple task, compared to that of directing the introduction of a continuing flow of changes and innovations, and preventing the organization from flying apart under the pressure.—*The Author*

2. Skills of an Effective Administrator

Robert L. Katz

Twenty years ago, this author pointed out that management's real concern should be for what a person can do rather than what he is. And he identified three basic skills—technical, human, and conceptual—that every successful manager must have in varying degrees, according to the level of management at which he is operating. Today, he stands by his original statement, but he refines a number of ideas in the light of his subsequent experience.

Although the selection and training of good administrators is widely recognized as one of American industry's most pressing problems, there is surprisingly little agreement among executives or educators on what makes a good administrator. The executive development programs of some of the nation's leading corporations and colleges reflect a tremendous variation in objectives.

At the root of this difference is industry's search for the traits or attributes which will objectively identify the "ideal executive" who is equipped to cope effectively with any problem in any organization. As one observer of U.S. industry recently noted:

"The assumption that there is an executive type is widely accepted, either openly or implicitly. Yet any executive presumably knows that a company needs all kinds of managers for different levels of jobs. The qualities most needed by a shop superintendent are likely to be quite opposed to those needed by a coordinating vice president of manufacturing. The literature of executive development is loaded with efforts to define the qualities needed by executives, and by themselves these sound quite rational. Few, for instance, would dispute the fact that a top manager needs good judgment, the ability to make decisions, the ability to win respect of others, and all the other well-worn phrases any management man could mention. But one has only to look at the successful managers

AUTHOR'S NOTE: This article is based on a study prepared under a grant from the Alfred P. Sloan Foundation.

in any company to see how enormously their particular qualities vary from any ideal list of executive virtues."[1]

Yet this quest for the executive stereotype has become so intense that many companies, in concentrating on certain specific traits or qualities, stand in danger of losing sight of their real concern: *what a man can accomplish.*

It is the purpose of this article to suggest what may be a more useful approach to the selection and development of administrators. This approach is based not on what good executives *are* (their innate traits and characteristics), but rather on what they *do* (the kinds of skills which they exhibit in carrying out their jobs effectively). As used here, a *skill* implies an ability which can be developed, not necessarily inborn, and which is manifested in performance, not merely in potential. So the principal criterion of skillfulness must be effective action under varying conditions.

This approach suggests that effective administration rests on *three basic developable skills* which obviate the need for identifying specific traits and which may provide a useful way of looking at and understanding the administrative process. This approach is the outgrowth of firsthand observation of executives at work coupled with study of current field research in administration.

In the sections which follow, an attempt will be made to define and demonstrate what these three skills are; to suggest that the relative importance of the three skills varies with the level of administrative responsibility; to present some of the implications of this variation for selection, training, and promotion of executives; and to propose ways of developing these skills.

Three-Skill Approach

It is assumed here that an administrator is one who (a) directs the activities of other persons and (b) undertakes the responsibility for achieving certain objectives through these efforts. Within this definition, successful administration appears to rest on three basic skills, which we will call *technical, human,* and *conceptual.* It would be unrealistic to assert that these skills are not interrelated, yet there may be real merit in examining each one separately, and in developing them independently.

TECHNICAL SKILL

As used here, technical skill implies an understanding of, and proficiency in, a specific kind of activity, particularly one involving methods, processes,

---

1. Perrin Stryker, "The Growing Pains of Executive Development," *Advanced Management,* August 1954, p. 15.

procedures, or techniques. It is relatively easy for us to visualize the technical skill of the surgeon, the musician, the accountant, or the engineer when each is performing his own special function. Technical skill involves specialized knowledge, analytical ability within that specialty, and facility in the use of the tools and techniques of the specific discipline.

Of the three skills described in this article, technical skill is perhaps the most familiar because it is the most concrete, and because, in our age of specialization, it is the skill required of the greatest number of people. Most of our vocational and on-the-job training programs are largely concerned with developing this specialized technical skill.

HUMAN SKILL

As used here, human skill is the executive's ability to work effectively as a group member and to build cooperative effort within the team he leads. As *technical* skill is primarily concerned with working with "things" (processes or physical objects), so *human* skill is primarily concerned with working with people. This skill is demonstrated in the way the individual perceives (and recognizes the perceptions of) his superiors, equals, and subordinates, and in the way he behaves subsequently.

The person with highly developed human skill is aware of his own attitudes, assumptions, and beliefs about other individuals and groups; he is able to see the usefulness and limitations of these feelings. By accepting the existence of viewpoints, perceptions, and beliefs which are different from his own, he is skilled in understanding what others really mean by their words and behavior. He is equally skillful in communicating to others, in their own contexts, what he means by *his* behavior.

Such a person works to create an atmosphere of approval and security in which subordinates feel free to express themselves without fear of censure or ridicule, by encouraging them to participate in the planning and carrying out of those things which directly affect them. He is sufficiently sensitive to the needs and motivations of others in his organization so that he can judge the possible reactions to, and outcomes of, various courses of action he may undertake. Having this sensitivity, he is able and willing to *act* in a way which takes these perceptions by others into account.

Real skill in working with others must become a natural, continuous activity, since it involves sensitivity not only at times of decision making but also in the day-by-day behavior of the individual. Human skill cannot be a "sometime thing." Techniques cannot be randomly applied, nor can personality traits be put on or removed like an overcoat. Because everything which an executive says and does (or leaves unsaid or undone) has an effect on his associates, his true self will, in time, show through. Thus, to be effective, this skill must be naturally developed and unconsciously, as well as consistently, demonstrated in the individual's every action. It must become an integral part of his whole being.

Because human skill is so vital a part of everything the administrator does, examples of inadequate human skill are easier to describe than are highly skillful performances. Perhaps consideration of an actual situation would serve to clarify what is involved:

When a new conveyor unit was installed in a shoe factory where workers had previously been free to determine their own work rate, the production manager asked the industrial engineer who had designed the conveyor to serve as foreman, even though a qualified foreman was available. The engineer, who reported directly to the production manager, objected, but under pressure he agreed to take the job "until a suitable foreman could be found," even though this was a job of lower status than his present one. Then this conversation took place:

Production Manager: "I've had a lot of experience with conveyors. I want you to keep this conveyor going at all times except for rest periods, and I want it going at top speed. Get these people thinking in terms of 2 pairs of shoes a minute, 70 dozen pairs a day, 350 dozen pairs a week. They are all experienced operators on their individual jobs, and it's just a matter of getting them to do their jobs in a little different way. I want you to make that base rate of 250 dozen pair a week work!" [Base rate was established at slightly under 75% of the maximum capacity. This base rate was 50% higher than under the old system.]

Engineer: "If I'm going to be foreman of the conveyor unit, I want to do things my way. I've worked on conveyors, and I don't agree with you on first getting people used to a conveyor going at top speed. These people have never seen a conveyor. You'll scare them. I'd like to run the conveyor at one-third speed for a couple of weeks and then gradually increase the speed.

"I think we should discuss setting the base rate [production quota before incentive bonus] on a daily basis instead of a weekly basis. [Workers had previously been paid on a daily straight piecework basis.]

"I'd also suggest setting a daily base rate at 45 or even 40 dozen pair. You have to set a base rate low enough for them to make. Once they know they can make the base rate, they will go after the bonus."

Production Manager: "You do it your way on the speed; but remember it's the results that count. On the base rate, I'm not discussing it with you; I'm telling you to make the 250 dozen pair a week work. I don't want a daily base rate."[2]

2. From a mimeographed case in the files of the Harvard Business School; copyrighted by the President and Fellows of Harvard College.

Here is a situation in which the production manager was so preoccupied with getting the physical output that he did not pay attention to the people through whom that output had to be achieved. Notice, first, that he made the engineer who designed the unit serve as foreman, apparently hoping to force the engineer to justify his design by producing the maximum output. However, the production manager was oblivious to (a) the way the engineer perceived this appointment, as a demotion, and (b) the need for the engineer to be able to control the variables if he was to be held responsible for maximum output. Instead the production manager imposed a production standard and refused to make any changes in the work situation.

Moreover, although this was a radically new situation for the operators, the production manager expected them to produce immediately at well above their previous output—even though the operators had an unfamiliar production system to cope with, the operators had never worked together as a team before, the operators and their new foreman had never worked together before, and the foreman was not in agreement with the production goals or standards. By ignoring all these human factors, the production manager not only placed the engineer in an extremely difficult operating situation but also, by refusing to allow the engineer to "run his own show," discouraged the very assumption of responsibility he had hoped for in making the appointment.

Under these circumstances, it is easy to understand how the relationship between these two men rapidly deteriorated, and how production, after two months' operation, was at only 125 dozen pairs per week (just 75% of what the output had been under the old system).

CONCEPTUAL SKILL

As used here, conceptual skill involves the ability to see the enterprise as a whole; it includes recognizing how the various functions of the organization depend on one another, and how changes in any one part affect all the others; and it extends to visualizing the relationship of the individual business to the industry, the community, and the political, social, and economic forces of the nation as a whole. Recognizing these relationships and perceiving the significant elements in any situation, the administrator should then be able to act in a way which advances the over-all welfare of the total organization.

Hence, the success of any decision depends on the conceptual skill of the people who make the decision and those who put it into action. When, for example, an important change in marketing policy is made, it is critical that the effects on production, control, finance, research, and the people involved be considered. And it remains critical right down to the last executive who must implement the new policy. If each executive recognizes the over-all relationships and significance of the change, he is almost certain to be more effective in administering it. Consequently the chances for succeeding are greatly increased.

Not only does the effective coordination of the various parts of the business depend on the conceptual skill of the administrators involved, but so also does the whole future direction and tone of the organization. The attitudes of a top executive color the whole character of the organization's response and determine the "corporate personality" which distinguishes one company's ways of doing business from another's. These attitudes are a reflection of the administrator's conceptual skill—referred to by some as his "creative ability"—the way he perceives and responds to the direction in which the business should grow, company objectives and policies, and stockholders' and employees' interests.

Conceptual skill, as defined above, is what Chester I. Barnard, former president of the New Jersey Bell Telephone Company, is implying when he says: ". . . the essential aspect of the [executive] process is the sensing of the organization as a whole and of the total situation relevant to it."[3] Examples of inadequate conceptual skill are all around us. Here is one instance:

In a large manufacturing company which had a long tradition of job-shop type operations, primary responsibility for production control had been left to the foremen and other lower-level supervisors. "Village" type operations with small working groups and informal organizations were the rule. A heavy influx of orders following World War II tripled the normal production requirements and severely taxed the whole manufacturing organization. At this point, a new production manager was brought in from outside the company, and he established a wide range of controls and formalized the entire operating structure.

As long as the boom demand lasted, the employees made every effort to conform with the new procedures and environment. But when demand subsided to prewar levels, serious labor relations problems developed, friction was high among department heads, and the company found itself saddled with a heavy indirect labor cost. Management sought to reinstate its old procedures; it fired the production manager and attempted to give greater authority to the foremen once again. However, during the four years of formalized control, the foremen had grown away from their old practices, many had left the company, and adequate replacements had not been developed. Without strong foreman leadership, the traditional job-shop operations proved costly and inefficient.

In this instance, when the new production controls and formalized

---

3. *Functions of the Executive* (Cambridge, Harvard University Press, 1948), p. 235.

organizations were introduced, management did not foresee the consequences of this action in the event of a future contraction of business. Later, when conditions changed and it was necessary to pare down operations, management was again unable to recognize the implications of its action and reverted to the old procedures, which, under the circumstances, were no longer appropriate. This compounded *conceptual* inadequacy left the company at a serious competitive disadvantage.

Because a company's over-all success is dependent on its executives' conceptual skill in establishing and carrying out policy decisions, this skill is the unifying, coordinating ingredient of the administrative process, and of undeniable over-all importance.

Relative Importance

We may notice that, in a very real sense, conceptual skill embodies consideration of both the technical and human aspects of the organization. Yet the concept of *skill,* as an ability to translate knowledge into action, should enable one to distinguish between the three skills of performing the technical activities (technical skill), understanding and motivating individuals and groups (human skill), and coordinating and integrating all the activities and interests of the organization toward a common objective (conceptual skill).

This separation of effective administration into three basic skills is useful primarily for purposes of analysis. In practice, these skills are so closely interrelated that it is difficult to determine where one ends and another begins. However, just because the skills are interrelated does not imply that we cannot get some value from looking at them separately, or by varying their emphasis. In playing golf the action of the hands, wrists, hips, shoulders, arms, and head are all interrelated; yet in improving one's swing it is often valuable to work on one of these elements separately. Also, under different playing conditions the relative importance of these elements varies. Similarly, although all three are of importance at every level of administration, the technical, human, and conceptual skills of the administrator vary in relative importance at different levels of responsibility.

AT LOWER LEVELS

Technical skill is responsible for many of the great advances of modern industry. It is indispensable to efficient operation. Yet it has greatest importance at the lower levels of administration. As the administrator moves further and further from the actual physical operation, this need for technical skill becomes less important, provided he has skilled subordinates and can help them solve their own problems. At the top, technical skill may be almost nonexistent, and the executive may still be able to perform effectively if his human and conceptual skills are highly developed. For example:

In one large capital-goods producing company, the controller was called on to replace the manufacturing vice president, who had been stricken suddenly with a severe illness. The controller had no previous production experience, but he had been with the company for more than 20 years and knew many of the key production personnel intimately. By setting up an advisory staff, and by delegating an unusual amount of authority to his department heads, he was able to devote himself to co-ordination of the various functions. By so doing, he produced a highly efficient team. The results were lower costs, greater productivity, and higher morale than the production division had ever before experienced. Management had gambled that this man's ability to work with people was more important than his lack of a technical production background, and the gamble paid off.

Other examples are evident all around us. We are all familiar with those "professional managers" who are becoming the prototypes of our modern executive world. These men shift with great ease, and with no apparent loss in effectiveness, from one industry to another. Their human and conceptual skills seem to make up for their unfamiliarity with the new job's technical aspects.

AT EVERY LEVEL

Human skill, the ability to work with others, is essential to effective administration at every level. One research study has shown that human skill is of paramount importance at the foreman level, pointing out that the chief function of the foreman as an administrator is to attain collaboration of people in the work group. Another study reinforces this finding and extends it to the middle-management group, adding that the administrator should be primarily concerned with facilitating communication in the organization. And still another study, concerned primarily with top management, underscores the need for self-awareness and sensitivity to human relationships by executives at that level. These findings would tend to indicate that human skill is of great importance at every level, but notice the difference in emphasis.

Human skill seems to be most important at lower levels, where the number of direct contacts between administrators and subordinates is greatest. As we go higher and higher in the administrative echelons, the number and frequency of these personal contacts decrease, and the need for human skill becomes proportionately, although probably not absolutely, less. At the same time, conceptual skill becomes increasingly more important with the need for policy decisions and broad-scale action. The human skill of dealing with individuals then becomes subordinate to the conceptual skill of integrating group interests and activities into a whole.

In fact, a research study by Professor Chris Argyris of Yale University has given us the example of an extremely effective plant manager who, although possessing little human skill as defined here, was nonetheless very successful:

This manager, the head of a largely autonomous division, made his supervisors, through the effects of his strong personality and the "pressure" he applied, highly dependent on him for most of their "rewards, penalties, authority, perpetuation, communication, and identification."

As a result, the supervisors spent much of their time competing with one another for the manager's favor. They told him only the things they thought he wanted to hear, and spent much time trying to find out his desires. They depended on him to set their objectives and to show them how to reach them. Because the manager was inconsistent and unpredictable in his behavior, the supervisors were insecure and continually engaged in interdepartmental squabbles which they tried to keep hidden from the manager.

Clearly, human skill as defined here was lacking. Yet, by the evaluation of his superiors and by his results in increasing efficiency and raising profits and morale, this manager was exceedingly effective. Professor Argyris suggests that employees in modern industrial organizations tend to have a "built-in" sense of dependence on superiors which capable and alert men can turn to advantage.

In the context of the three-skill approach, it seems that this manager was able to capitalize on this dependence because he recognized the interrelationships of all the activities under his control, identified himself with the organization, and sublimated the individual interests of his subordinates to *his* (the organization's) interest, set his goals realistically, and showed his subordinates how to reach these goals. This would seem to be an excellent example of a situation in which strong conceptual skill more than compensated for a lack of human skill.

AT THE TOP LEVEL

Conceptual skill, as indicated in the preceding sections, becomes increasingly critical in more responsible executive positions where its effects are maximized and most easily observed. In fact, recent research findings lead to the conclusion that at the top level of administration this conceptual skill becomes the most important ability of all. As Herman W. Steinkraus, president of Bridgeport Brass Company, said:

"One of the most important lessons which I learned on this job [the presidency] is the importance of coordinating the various departments into an effective team, and, secondly, to recognize the shifting emphasis from time to time of the relative importance of various departments to the business."[4]

It would appear, then, that at lower levels of administrative responsibility, the principal need is for technical and human skills. At higher levels, technical skill becomes relatively less important while the need for conceptual skill increases rapidly. At the top level of an organization, conceptual skill becomes the most important skill of all for successful administration. A chief executive may lack technical or human skills and still be effective if he has subordinates who have strong abilities in these directions. But if his conceptual skill is weak, the success of the whole organization may be jeopardized.

Implications for Action

This three-skill approach implies that significant benefits may result from redefining the objectives of executive development programs, from reconsidering the placement of executives in organizations, and from revising procedures for testing and selecting prospective executives.

EXECUTIVE DEVELOPMENT

Many executive development programs may be failing to achieve satisfactory results because of their inability to foster the growth of these administrative skills. Programs which concentrate on the mere imparting of information or the cultivation of a specific trait would seem to be largely unproductive in enhancing the administrative skills of candidates.

A strictly informative program was described to me recently by an officer and director of a large corporation who had been responsible for the executive-development activities of his company, as follows:

"What we try to do is to get our promising young men together with some of our senior executives in regular meetings each month. Then we give the young fellows a chance to ask questions to let them find out about the company's history and how and why we've done things in the past."

It was not surprising that neither the senior executives nor the young men felt this program was improving their administrative abilities.

The futility of pursuing specific traits becomes apparent when we con-

4. "What Should a President Do?" *Dun's Review*, August 1951, p. 21.

sider the responses of an administrator in a number of different situations. In coping with these varied conditions, he may appear to demonstrate one trait in one instance—e.g., dominance when dealing with subordinates— and the directly opposite trait under another set of circumstances—e.g., submissiveness when dealing with superiors. Yet in each instance he may be acting appropriately to achieve the best results. Which, then, can we identify as a desirable characteristic? Here is a further example of this dilemma:

A Pacific Coast sales manager had a reputation for decisiveness and positive action. Yet when he was required to name an assistant to understudy his job from among several well-qualified subordinates, he deliberately avoided making a decision. His associates were quick to observe what appeared to be obvious indecisiveness.

But after several months had passed, it became clear that the sales manager had very unobtrusively been giving the various salesmen opportunities to demonstrate their attitudes and feelings. As a result, he was able to identify strong sentiments for one man whose subsequent promotion was enthusiastically accepted by the entire group.

In this instance, the sales manager's skillful performance was improperly interpreted as "indecisiveness." Their concern with irrelevant traits led his associates to overlook the adequacy of his performance. Would it not have been more appropriate to conclude that his human skill in working with others enabled him to adapt effectively to the requirements of a new situation?

Cases such as these would indicate that it is more useful to judge an administrator on the results of his performance than on his apparent traits. Skills are easier to identify than are traits and are less likely to be misinterpreted. Furthermore, skills offer a more directly applicable frame of reference for executive development, since any improvement in an administrator's skills must necessarily result in more effective performance.

Still another danger in many existing executive development programs lies in the unqualified enthusiasm with which some companies and colleges have embraced courses in "human relations." There would seem to be two inherent pitfalls here: (1) Human relations courses might only be imparting information or specific techniques, rather than developing the individual's human skill. (2) Even if individual development does take place, some companies, by placing all of their emphasis on human skill, may be completely overlooking the training requirements for top positions. They may run the risk of producing men with highly developed human skill who lack the conceptual ability to be effective top-level administrators.

It would appear important, then, that the training of a candidate for an administrative position be directed at the development of those skills which are most needed at the level of responsibility for which he is being considered.

EXECUTIVE PLACEMENT

This three-skill concept suggests immediate possibilities for the creating of management teams of individuals with complementary skills. For example, one medium-size midwestern distributing organization has as president a man of unusual conceptual ability but extremely limited human skill. However, he has two vice presidents with exceptional human skill. These three men make up an executive committee which has been outstandingly successful, the skills of each member making up for deficiencies of the others. Perhaps the plan of two-man complementary conference leadership proposed by Robert F. Bales, in which the one leader maintains "task leadership" while the other provides "social leadership," might also be an example in point.

EXECUTIVE SELECTION

In trying to predetermine a prospective candidate's abilities on a job, much use is being made these days of various kinds of testing devices. Executives are being tested for everything from "decisiveness" to "conformity." These tests, as a recent article in *Fortune* points out, have achieved some highly questionable results when applied to performance on the job. Would it not be much more productive to be concerned with skills of doing rather than with a number of traits which do not guarantee performance?

This three-skill approach makes trait testing unnecessary and substitutes for it procedures which examine a man's ability to cope with the actual problems and situations he will find on his job. These procedures, which indicate what a man can *do* in specific situations, are the same for selection and for measuring development. They will be described in the section on developing executive skills which follows.

This approach suggests that executives should *not* be chosen on the basis of their apparent possession of a number of behavior characteristics or traits, but on the basis of their possession of the requisite skills for the specific level of responsibility involved.

Developing the Skills

For years many people have contended that leadership ability is inherent in certain chosen individuals. We talk of "born leaders," "born executives," "born salesmen." It is undoubtedly true that certain people, naturally or innately, possess greater aptitude or ability in certain skills. But research in psychology and physiology would also indicate, first, that those having strong aptitudes and abilities can improve their skill through practice and training, and, secondly, that even those lacking the natural ability can improve their performance and over-all effectiveness.

The *skill* conception of administration suggests that we may hope to improve our administrative effectiveness and to develop better administrators for the future. This skill conception implies *learning by doing*. Different people learn in different ways, but skills are developed through practice and through relating learning to one's own personal experience and background. If well done, training in these basic administrative skills should develop executive abilities more surely and more rapidly than through unorganized experience. What, then, are some of the ways in which this training can be conducted?

TECHNICAL SKILL

Development of technical skill has received great attention for many years by industry and educational institutions alike, and much progress has been made. Sound grounding in the principles, structures, and processes of the individual specialty, coupled with actual practice and experience during which the individual is watched and helped by a superior, appear to be most effective. In view of the vast amount of work which has been done in training people in the technical skills, it would seem unnecessary in this article to suggest more.

HUMAN SKILL

Human skill, however, has been much less understood, and only recently has systematic progress been made in developing it. Many different approaches to the development of human skill are being pursued by various universities and professional men today. These are rooted in such disciplines as psychology, sociology, and anthropology.

Some of these approaches find their application in "applied psychology," "human engineering," and a host of other manifestations requiring technical specialists to help the businessman with his human problems. As a practical matter, however, the executive must develop his own human skill, rather than lean on the advice of others. To be effective, he must develop his own personal point of view toward human activity, so that he will (a) recognize the feelings and sentiments which he brings to a situation; (b) have an attitude about his own experiences which will enable him to re-evaluate and learn from them; (c) develop ability in understanding what others by their actions and words (explicit or implicit) are trying to communicate to him; and (d) develop ability in successfully communicating his ideas and attitudes to others.

This human skill can be developed by some individuals without formalized training. Others can be individually aided by their immediate superiors as an integral part of the "coaching" process to be described later. This aid depends for effectiveness, obviously, on the extent to which the superior possesses the human skill.

For larger groups, the use of case problems coupled with impromptu role playing can be very effective. This training can be established on a formal or informal basis, but it requires a skilled instructor and organized sequence of activities. It affords as good an approximation to reality as can be provided on a continuing classroom basis and offers an opportunity for critical reflection not often found in actual practice. An important part of the procedure is the self-examination of the trainee's own concepts and values, which may enable him to develop more useful attitudes about himself and about others. With the change in attitude, hopefully, there may also come some active skill in dealing with human problems.

Human skill has also been tested in the classroom, within reasonable limits, by a series of analyses of detailed accounts of actual situations involving administrative action, together with a number of role-playing opportunities in which the individual is required to carry out the details of the action he has proposed. In this way an individual's understanding of the total situation and his own personal ability to do something about it can be evaluated.

On the job, there should be frequent opportunities for a superior to observe an individual's ability to work effectively with others. These may appear to be highly subjective evaluations and to depend for validity on the human skill of the rater. But does not every promotion, in the last analysis, depend on someone's subjective judgment? And should this subjectivity be berated, or should we make a greater effort to develop people within our organizations with the human skill to make such judgments effectively?

CONCEPTUAL SKILL

Conceptual skill, like human skill, has not been very widely understood. A number of methods have been tried to aid in developing this ability, with varying success. Some of the best results have always been achieved through the "coaching" of subordinates by superiors. This is no new idea. It implies that one of the key responsibilities of the executive is to help his subordinates to develop their administrative potentials. One way a superior can help "coach" his subordinate is by assigning a particular responsibility, and then responding with searching questions or opinions, rather than giving answers, whenever the subordinate seeks help. When Benjamin F. Fairless, now chairman of the board of the United States Steel Corporation, was president of the corporation, he described his coaching activities:

"When one of my vice presidents or the head of one of our operating companies comes to me for instructions, I generally counter by asking him questions. First thing I know, he has told me how to solve the problem himself."[5]

Obviously, this is an ideal and wholly natural procedure for administrative training, and applies to the development of technical and human skill, as well as to that of conceptual skill. However, its success must necessarily rest on the abilities and willingness of the superior to help the subordinate.

Another excellent way to develop conceptual skill is through trading jobs, that is, by moving promising young men through different functions of the business but at the same level of responsibility. This gives the man the chance literally to "be in the other fellow's shoes."

Other possibilities include: special assignments, particularly the kind which involve interdepartmental problems; and management boards, such as the McCormick Multiple Management plan, in which junior executives serve as advisers to top management on policy matters.

For larger groups, the kind of case-problems course described above, only using cases involving broad management policy and interdepartmental coordination, may be useful. Courses of this kind, often called "General Management" or "Business Policy," are becoming increasingly prevalent.

In the classroom, conceptual skill has also been evaluated with reasonable effectiveness by presenting a series of detailed descriptions of specific complex situations. In these the individual being tested is asked to set forth a course of action which responds to the underlying forces operating in each situation and which considers the implications of this action on the various functions and parts of the organization and its total environment.

On the job, the alert supervisor should find frequent opportunities to observe the extent to which the individual is able to relate himself and his job to the other functions and operations of the company.

Like human skill, conceptual skill, too, must become a natural part of the executive's makeup. Different methods may be indicated for developing different people, by virtue of their backgrounds, attitudes, and experience. But in every case that method should be chosen which will enable the executive to develop his own personal skill in visualizing the enterprise as a whole and in coordinating and integrating its various parts.

5. "What Should a President Do?" Dun's Review, July 1951, p. 14.

Conclusion

The purpose of this article has been to show that effective administration depends on three basic personal skills, which have been called *technical, human,* and *conceptual.* The administrator needs: (a) sufficient technical skill to accomplish the mechanics of the particular job for which he is responsible; (b) sufficient human skill in working with others to be an effective group member and to be able to build cooperative effort within the team he leads; (c) sufficient conceptual skill to recognize the interrelationships of the various factors involved in his situation, which will lead him to take that action which is likely to achieve the maximum good for the total organization.

The relative importance of these three skills seems to vary with the level of administrative responsibility. At lower levels, the major need is for technical and human skills. At higher levels, the administrator's effectiveness depends largely on human and conceptual skills. At the top, conceptual skill becomes the most important of all for successful administration.

This three-skill approach emphasizes that good administrators are not necessarily born; they may be developed. It transcends the need to identify specific traits in an effort to provide a more useful way of looking at the administrative process. By helping to identify the skills most needed at various levels of responsibility, it may prove useful in the selection, training, and promotion of executives.

When this article was first published there was a great deal of interest in trying to identify a set of ideal personality traits that would readily distinguish potential executive talent. The search for these traits was vigorously pursued in the hope that the selection and training of managers could be conducted with greater reliability.

This article was an attempt to focus attention on demonstrable skills of performance rather than on innate personality characteristics. And, while describing the three kinds of administrative skill (technical, human, and conceptual), it also attempted to highlight the importance of conceptual skill as a uniquely valuable managerial capability, long before the concept of corporate strategy was well defined or popularly understood.

It still appears useful to think of managerial ability in terms of these three basic, observable skills. It also still appears that the relative importance of these skills varies with the administrative level of the manager in the organization. However, my experience over the past several years in working with senior executives in a wide variety of industries suggests that several specific points require either sharp modification or substantial further refinement.

Human Skill

I now believe that this kind of skill could be usefully subdivided into (a) leadership ability within the manager's own unit and (b) skill in intergroup relationships. In my experience, outstanding capability in one of these roles is frequently accompanied by mediocre performance in the other.

Often, the most internally efficient department managers are those who have committed themselves fully to the unique values and criteria of their specialized functions, without acknowledging that other departments' differing values have any validity at all. For example, a production manager may be most efficient if he puts all his emphasis on obtaining a high degree of reliability in his production schedule. He would then resist any external

pressures that place a higher priority on criteria other than delivering
the required output on time. Or a sales manager may be most efficient if he
puts all his emphasis on maintaining positive relationships with customers.
He would then resist all pressures that would emphasize other values, such
as ease of production or selling the highest gross margin items. In each case,
the manager will probably receive strong support from his subordinates,
who share the same values. But he will encounter severe antagonism from
other departments with conflicting values.

To the extent that two departments' values conflict with each other,
skillful intergroup relationships require some equivocation. But compromise is often perceived by departmental subordinates as a "sellout."
Thus the manager is obliged to choose between gaining full support from
subordinates or enjoying full collaboration with peers and/or superiors.
Having both is rarely possible. Consequently, I would revise my original
evaluation of human skill to say now that internal *intragroup* skills are
essential in lower and middle management roles and that *intergroup* skills
become increasingly important in successively higher levels of management.

Conceptual Skill

In retrospect, I now see that what I called conceptual skill depends
entirely on a specific way of thinking about an enterprise. This "general
management point of view," as it has come to be known, involves always
thinking in terms of the following: relative emphases and priorities among
conflicting objectives and criteria; relative tendencies and probabilities
(rather than certainties); rough correlations and patterns among elements
(rather than clear-cut cause-and-effect relationships).

I am now far less sanguine about the degree to which this way of thinking can be developed on the job. Unless a person has learned to think
this way early in life, it is unrealistic to expect a major change on reaching
executive status. Job rotation, special interdepartmental assignments, and
working with case problems certainly provide opportunities for a person to
enhance previously developed conceptual abilities. But I question how easily
this way of thinking can be inculcated after a person passes adolescence.
In this sense, then, conceptual skill should perhaps be viewed as an *innate*
ability.

Technical Skill

In the original article, I suggested that specific technical skills are unimportant at top management levels. I cited as evidence the many professional managers who move easily from one industry to another without
apparent loss of effectiveness.

I now believe this mobility is possible only in very large companies, where the chief executive has extensive staff assistance and highly competent, experienced technical operators throughout the organization. An old, established, large company has great operational momentum that enables the new chief executive to concentrate on strategic issues.

In smaller companies, where technical expertise is not as pervasive and seasoned staff assistance is not as available, I believe the chief executive has a much greater need for personal experience in the industry. He not only needs to know the right questions to ask his subordinates; he also needs enough industry background to know how to evaluate the answers.

Role of the Chief Executive

In the original article, I took too simplistic and naïve a view of the chief executive's role. My extensive work with company presidents and my own personal experience as a chief executive have given me much more respect for the difficulties and complexities of that role. I now know that every important executive action must strike a balance among so many conflicting values, objectives, and criteria that it will *always* be suboptimal from any single viewpoint. *Every* decision or choice affecting the whole enterprise has negative consequences for some of the parts.

The chief executive must try to perceive the conflicts and trace accurately their likely impact throughout the organization. Reluctantly, but wittingly, he may have to sacrifice the interests of a single unit or part for the good of the whole. He needs to be willing to accept solutions that are adequate and feasible in the total situation rather than what, from a single point of view, may be elegant or optimum.

Not only must the chief executive be an efficient operator, but he must also be an effective strategist. It is his responsibility to provide the framework and direction for overall company operations. He must continually specify where the company will place its emphasis in terms of products, services, and customers. He must define performance criteria and determine what special competences the company will emphasize. He also needs to set priorities and timetables. He must establish the standards and controls necessary to monitor progress and to place limits on individual actions. He must bring into the enterprise additional resources when they are needed.

Moreover, he must change his management style and strike different balances among his personal skills as conditions change or as his organization grows in size and complexity. The *remedial* role (saving the organization when it is in great difficulty) calls for drastic human action and emphasizes conceptual and technical skills. The *maintaining* role (sustaining the organization in its present posture) emphasizes human skills and requires only modest technical or strategic changes. But the *innovative* role (developing and expanding the organization) demands high competence in both conceptual and intergroup skills, with the technical contribution provided primarily by subordinates.

In my view, it is impossible for anyone to perform well in these continually changing roles without help. Yet because effective management of the total enterprise involves constant suboptimizing, it is impossible for the chief executive to get unanimous or continuous support from his subordinates. If he is overly friendly or supportive, he may compromise his effectiveness or his objectivity. Yet somewhere in the organization, he needs to have a well-informed, objective, understanding, and supportive sounding board with whom he can freely discuss his doubts, fears, and aspirations. Sometimes this function can be supplied by an outside director, the outside corporate counsel, or the company auditor. But such a confidant requires just as high a degree of conceptual and human skills as the chief executive himself; and to be truly helpful, he must know all about the company's operations, key personnel, and industry. This role has been largely overlooked in discussions of organizational requirements, but in my view, its proper fulfillment is essential to the success of the chief executive and the enterprise.

Conclusion

I now realize more fully that managers at all levels require some competence in each of the three skills. Even managers at the lowest levels must continually use all of them. Dealing with the external demands on a manager's unit requires conceptual skill; the limited physical and financial resources available to him tax his technical skill; and the capabilities and demands of the persons with whom he deals make it essential that he possess human skill. A clear idea of these skills and of ways to measure a manager's competence in each category still appears to me to be a most effective tool for top management, not only in understanding executive behavior, but also in the selection, training, and promotion of managers at all levels.

3. Understanding Your Organization's Character

Roger Harrison

The character of an organization lies in the ideological differences that underlie organizational conflicts. This author argues that the failure to understand these differences often causes conflict between organizations as well as within them. After discussing the different ideologies and types of organizations they embody, he shows how to determine the fit of organizational and human interests.

The failure to recognize the ideological issues that underlie organizational conflict is common among managers and administrators. Usually the issues are recognized only when they are blatant and the lines of struggle are drawn, as in labor-management relationships. But by then the conflict may well have developed to the point where a constructive resolution is virtually impossible.

While the term "organization ideologies" is perhaps unfortunately ambiguous, it is the best name I can apply to the systems of thought that are central determinants of the character of organizations. An organization's ideology affects the behavior of its people, its ability to effectively meet their needs and demands, and the way it copes with the external environment. Furthermore, much of the conflict that surrounds organization change is really ideological struggle (an idea that is certainly not new to political science but one about which behavioral scientists have, until recently, been curiously quiet).

For example, during the commissioning and start-up stages of a U.S. chemical plant in Europe, it became apparent that the Americans and local nationals involved had rather different ideas about decision making and commitment to decisions. Consider the approach of each group:

▢ The Americans tended to operate within what I shall later describe as a task-oriented ideology. In problem-solving meetings they believed that everyone who had relevant ideas or information should contribute to the debates, and that in reaching a decision the greatest weight should be given to the best-informed and most knowledgeable people. They strove, moreover, for a clear-cut decision; and once the decision was made, they usually were committed to it even if they did not completely agree with it.

□ Some of the nationals, however, came to the project from very authoritarian organizations and tended to operate from a power-oriented ideological base (this will also be described later). Each individual seemed to be trying to exert as much control as possible and to accept as little influence from others as he could. If he was in a position of authority, he seemed to ignore the ideas of juniors and the advice of staff experts. If he was not in a position of authority, he kept rather quiet in meetings and seemed almost happy when there was an unclear decision or no decision at all. He would then proceed the way he had wanted to all along.

The task-oriented people regarded the foregoing behavior as uncooperative and, sometimes, as devious or dishonest. The power-oriented people, however, interpreted the task-oriented individuals' emphasis on communication and cooperation as evidence of softness and fear of taking responsibility.

Each group was engaging in what it regarded as normal and appropriate practice and tended to regard the other as difficult to work with or just plain wrong. The fact that the differences were ideological was dimly realized only by the more thoughtful participants. The remainder tended to react to each other as wrongheaded *individuals*, rather than as adherents of a self-consistent and internally logical way of thinking and explaining their organizational world.

In this article I shall present a theory that identifies four distinct, competing organization ideologies and their meaning for the businessman. But, first, let me attempt to further clarify the concept. Here are the most obvious functions that an organization ideology performs:

□ Specifies the goals and values toward which the organization should be directed and by which its success and worth should be measured.

□ Prescribes the appropriate relationships between individuals and the organization (i.e., the "social contract" that legislates what the organization should be able to expect from its people, and vice versa).

□ Indicates how behavior should be controlled in the organization and what kinds of control are legitimate and illegitimate.

□ Depicts which qualities and characteristics of organization members should be valued or vilified, as well as how these should be rewarded or punished.

□ Shows members how they should treat one another—competitively or collaboratively, honestly or dishonestly, closely or distantly.

□ Establishes appropriate methods of dealing with the external environment—aggressive exploitation, responsible negotiation, proactive exploration.

Values and Ideologies

An organization ideology, however, is more than a set of prescriptions and prohibitions. It also establishes a rationale for these "do"s and "don't"s. This rationale explains the behavior of an organization's members as well as the working of the external environment (in the latter case, by telling members how to expect other people and organization systems to behave).

The rationale of an organization ideology is similar to what behavioral scientists call "organization theory." The difference is that behavioral scientists try with varying degrees of success to keep their values from influencing their organization theories; people, for the most part, do not try to keep their values from influencing their organization ideologies. (This is one reason why education about organization behavior is likely to be so emotionally loaded; if you change a man's organization theory, he usually ends up questioning his values as well.)

Among people in organizations, ideas of "what is" and "what ought to be" merge into one another and are—or are made to appear—consistent. Here is an example:

The ideology of a large U.S. manufacturer of consumer products prescribed that work should be organized in the way that produced the most profit. If this meant that some organization members had boring jobs which offered little opportunity for satisfaction and pride in their work, then it was unfortunate but ideologically irrelevant. According to the rationale of this ideology, a majority of people did not have much aptitude or desire for responsibility and decision making, anyhow, and those who did would rise by natural selection to more responsible, satisfying jobs.

Some young managers, however, had rather more egalitarian personal values. They uneasily suspected that there were more boring jobs than there were apathetic people to fill them. They were very excited about a group of research studies which attempted to show that giving employees more responsibility and involvement in decision making actually led to improved performance. But in my discussions with the managers, I found that the studies' instrumental value in improving organization effectiveness was not the cause of their popularity; rather, they were welcomed because they helped the managers reconcile their personal values with the dictum of the prevailing ideology that work should, above all, be organized to produce the best economic result. (I have, in fact, found that behavioral research findings are usually accepted or rejected on such ideological grounds instead of on the probability of their being true.)

A Conceptual Framework

There is a considerable body of thought in political science which holds that attempts to resolve ideological struggle are unwarranted interferences with the natural course of history and as such are doomed to be ineffectual.

I do not feel that this theory has been adequately tested, particularly in regard to organization change and development. The first step in testing it is to develop ways of discovering and understanding ideological conflicts when they arise in organizations.

In the remainder of this article I shall present a conceptual framework for doing this. It postulates four organization ideologies: (1) power orientation; (2) role orientation; (3) task orientation; and (4) person orientation. These ideologies are seldom found in organizations as pure types, but most organizations tend to center on one or another of them. I shall describe and contrast them in their pure form to emphasize their differences, and then indicate what I believe to be the strengths and weaknesses of each. After this I shall apply the conceptual model to some common conflicts in modern organization life.

POWER ORIENTATION

An organization that is power-oriented attempts to dominate its environment and vanquish all opposition. It is unwilling to be subject to any external law or power. And within the organization those who are powerful strive to maintain absolute control over subordinates.

The power-oriented organization is competitive and jealous of its territory (whether this be markets, land area, product lines, or access to resources). It seeks to expand its control at the expense of others, often exploiting weaker organizations. Even a weak power-oriented organization takes satisfaction in being able to dominate others that are still weaker. Such organizations always attempt to bargain to their own advantage and readily find justification for abrogating agreements which are no longer self-serving.

Some modern conglomerates project images of power ideology. They buy and sell organizations and people as commodities, in apparent disregard of human values and the general welfare. They seem to have voracious appetites for growth, which is valued for its own sake. Competition to acquire other companies and properties is ruthless and sometimes outside the law. Within the organization, the law of the jungle often seems to prevail among executives as they struggle for personal advantage against their peers.

There is, however, a softer form of the power orientation that is often found among old established firms, particularly those with a background of family ownership. Here the employees may be cared for rather than exploited, especially those that are old and loyal. Externally, the proprietors may hold to a code of honor, especially when dealing with others like themselves. This is the power orientation with a velvet glove. But when the benevolent authority is crossed or challenged, from either within or without, the iron fist is very likely to appear again. In such cases, the test of power orientation is how hard a person or organization will fight for power and position when these are at issue.

ROLE ORIENTATION

An organization that is role-oriented aspires to be as rational and orderly as possible. In contrast to the willful autocracy of the power-oriented organization, there is a preoccupation with legality, legitimacy, and responsibility.

It is useful to see role orientation as having developed partly in reaction to power orientation. Competition and conflict, for example, are regulated or replaced by agreements, rules, and procedures. Rights and privileges are carefully defined and adhered to. While there is a strong emphasis on hierarchy and status, it is moderated by the commitment to legitimacy and legality. The different attitudes of the power and role orientations toward authority might be likened to the differences between a dictatorship and a constitutional monarchy.

Predictability of behavior is high in the role-oriented organization, and stability and respectability are often valued as much as competence. The correct response tends to be more highly valued than the effective one. Procedures for change tend to be cumbersome; therefore the system is slow to adapt to change.

Most commercial organizations are too constricted by market demands to afford the extreme rigidity of a pure role orientation or the worst excesses of its tendency to place procedural correctness before task effectiveness. Some businesses, however, which either control their markets or operate in areas that are highly regulated by law, exhibit a considerable degree of role orientation. The rationality, impersonality, and adherence to procedure of many banks, insurance companies, public utilities, and social work organizations are cases in point. Their role orientation leaves the customer, the public, or the client with little alternate choice in dealing with them.

TASK ORIENTATION

In the organization that is task-oriented, achievement of a superordinate goal is the highest value. The goal need not be economic; it could be winning a war, converting the heathen, reforming a government, or helping the poor. The important thing is that the organization's structure, functions, and activities are all evaluated in terms of their contribution to the superordinate goal.

Nothing is permitted to get in the way of accomplishing the task. If established authority impedes achievement, it is swept away. If outmoded roles, rules, and regulations hinder problem solving, they are changed. If individuals do not have the skills or technical knowledge to perform a task, they are retrained or replaced. And if personal needs and social considerations threaten to upset effective problem solving, they are suppressed in the interests of "getting on with the job."

There is no ideological commitment to authority, respectability, and order as such. Authority is considered legitimate only if it is based on appropriate knowledge and competence; it is not legitimate if it is based solely on power or position. And there is little hesitation to break rules and regulations if task accomplishment is furthered by doing so.

There is nothing inherently competitive about task orientation. The organization structure is shaped and changed to meet the requirements of the task or function to be performed. Emphasis is placed on rapid, flexible organization response to changed conditions. Collaboration is sought if it will advance the goal; allies are chosen on the basis of mutual goals and values; and there is little "advantage seeking" in relationships with other organizations.

The task orientation is most readily found in those small organizations whose members have come together because of some shared value, task, or goal. Examples are social service organizations, research teams, and high-risk businesses. Often, however, internal conflict and external stress drive these organizations toward power and role orientations.

Large organizations that operate in highly complex, shifting environments offer more durable examples. Companies involved with dynamic markets or fast-changing, complex technology frequently establish project teams or "task forces." These groups of specialists are selected to solve a particular problem and often operate in a very flexible and egalitarian manner until the problem is solved. The units are then disbanded, and the members join other teams to work on new problems. Although the larger organization in which it operates may be basically role- or power-oriented, the project team or task force often exhibits a relatively pure task orientation. Moreover, these groups have been so successful that some organizations are trying to install a task-oriented ideology throughout their operations.

Some of the aerospace industries have probably gone the furthest in this direction, TRW Systems being a notable example. Although I do not know of any large organization that could be classed as "pure" in its task orientation, the success of such task-oriented programs as MBO is a sign of the growing interest among managers. Parenthetically, the most frequent reason for the failure of MBO is probably that task-oriented managers try to install it in power- or role-oriented organizations.

PERSON ORIENTATION

Unlike the other three types, the person-oriented organization exists primarily to serve the needs of its members. The organization itself is a device through which the members can meet needs that they could not otherwise satisfy by themselves. Just as some organizations continually evaluate the worth of individual members as tools and accept or reject them accordingly, so the person-oriented organizations are evaluated as tools by their members. For this reason, some of these organizations may have a very short life; they are disposable when they cease to provide a system for members to "do their own thing."

Authority in the role- or power-oriented sense is discouraged. When it is absolutely necessary, authority may be assigned on the basis of task competence, but this practice is kept to the bare minimum. Instead, individuals are expected to influence each other through example, helpfulness, and caring.

Consensus methods of decision making are preferred; people are generally not expected to do things that are incongruent with their own goals and values. Thus roles are assigned on the basis of personal preference and the need for learning and growth. Moreover, the burden of unrewarding and unpleasant tasks is shared equally.

Illustrations of person orientation are small groups of professionals who have joined together for research and development. Some consulting companies, too, seem to be designed primarily as vehicles for members. It is typical of such organizations that growth, expansion, and maximization of income and profit are not primary considerations. Rather, the organizations, hopefully, are conducted to make enough money to survive and provide their members with a reasonable living as well as an opportunity to do meaningful and enjoyable work with congenial people.

There seem to be increasing pressures from the members of modern industrial organizations to move toward person orientation. Young professionals are pushing their companies for opportunities to work on interesting, worthwhile (congruent with their own values) projects. Engineers and scientists, for example, have refused to work on projects for the military and have been successful in getting transfers to nondefense-related activities. Job recruiters find that college graduates are often more interested in opportunities to learn and grow than they are in their chances for organization advancement. Such signs of social change illustrate why the person orientation must be considered an ideological force to be reckoned with, even though there are few contemporary organizations that operate in total congruence with its principles.

Strengths and Weaknesses

An organization ideology obviously has a profound effect on organization effectiveness. It determines how (a) decisions are made, (b) human resources are used, and (c) the external environment is approached. An organization ideology tends to be internally viable when the people within the system want and need the prescribed incentives and satisfactions that reward good performance. It tends to be externally viable when the organization it embodies is a microcosm of the external environment and rewards the same skills, values, and motivations.

EXTERNAL VIABILITY

Usually, as an organization increases in size, its operational environment becomes more complex. Most arenas in which large companies operate change rapidly and/or have many features that require an integrated response. World-wide markets and rapidly changing technology, for example, make heavy demands on the information-processing and decision-making capabilities of organizations.

The power-oriented organization is not well adapted to flexible response and effective information processing in such environments. Since decisions are made at the top, the information has to pass through many people who screen out the "irrelevant" data. Moreover, some may distort the message to their own advantage (aggressive competition is part of the ideology). And when conditions change rapidly, the time lag introduced by the filtering process may unduly delay organization response.

The role-oriented organization is also insufficiently flexible to easily adapt to rapid external changes. In order to achieve the security that is one of its highest values, it must perpetuate rather rigid roles and reporting relationships. This gives stability but means that even the most powerful individuals may be unable to produce needed changes quickly.

In times of change, established procedures often do not apply, and the information channels become overloaded with problems that require higher-level decisions. Consider what happened in the commissioning and start-up example referred to at the beginning of this article:

Because equipment was not working properly, many actions which ordinarily would have been dealt with by standard operating procedures required top-management decisions. But the ordinary channels would not carry the necessary volume of information, and the quality of decision making and problem solving suffered accordingly. However, when control was shifted to teams of experts clustered around each plant (a task-oriented system) the problems were handled much more smoothly.

Change-oriented structures: The task-oriented organization's greatest strength is dealing with complex and changing environments. Decentralized control shortens communication channels and reduces time lags, distortion, and attenuation of messages.

Both the power- and role-oriented organizations associate control with a *position* in the organization; neither provides for rapid and rational reassignment of appropriate *persons* to positions of influence. In contrast, the task-oriented ideology clears the way for a very flexible system of control—one that can shift rapidly over time as differing resources are required by external problems.

Probably the best example of this system in operation is the project team or task force that is formed to identify, diagnose, and solve a particular problem. Even some rather bureaucratic organizations make use of these temporary systems for emergency problem solving. The task force leader is selected for his combination of technical expertise and ability to manage a small group in an egalitarian manner.

The temporary work system is a particularly characteristic response of the task-oriented organization to environmental change. These temporary systems can be activated quickly, provided with the necessary mix of skills and abilities, and disbanded again when the need is past. Their use provides what is, in effect, a continuously variable organization structure.

The person-oriented organization, too, is well adapted to dealing with complexity and change. It also features a fluid structure and short lines of communication and control.

Coping with threat: In a highly competitive environment where organizations are frequently confronted with overt threats and hostility, the strengths and weaknesses of ideological types form a different pattern.

For example, while the power-oriented organization is not well suited to handle complexity and change, its structure and decision-making processes are admirably suited for swift decision making and rapid-action follow-through under high-risk conditions. It tends to promote tough, aggressive people who can lead the organization in a dangerous, competitive environment.

The task-oriented organization usually takes longer to respond, but the response is more likely to be based on adequate data and planning. In contrast to the power-oriented structure, which is aggressively directed from the top, it tends to enlist the full commitment of organization members at all levels.

The role-oriented organization does not deal successfully with sudden increases in threat because it relies heavily on established operational procedures. Consequently, its structure is too cumbersome to react quickly in cases of overt threat.

And the person-oriented organization has difficulty directing its members' activities in unison until the danger is so clear and present that it may be too late. The person-oriented structure, however, does offer some advantages—its members are committed and have a high concern for one another's welfare.

Probably the most viable organization in a hostile, threatening environment would have a combination of the power and task orientations. This is a difficult marriage, however, because the desire for personal power is often incompatible with the required willingness to relinquish control to those with the most knowledge and ability for the task at hand.

INTERNAL VIABILITY

The power-oriented organization is an excellent structure for attaching many eyes, ears, hands, and feet to one brain. It exercises tight internal control and integration. As mentioned earlier, the system works well when problems take the form of overt challenges that can be comprehended and solved by one or a few intelligent, courageous men at the top.

But when the power-oriented organization becomes large and complex, this control tends to break down. Under these conditions the role-oriented ideology is more effective. It provides rules and procedures that allow a high degree of internal integration with little active intervention from the top.

It is obviously more difficult to achieve internal cohesion under a task- or person-oriented ideology. For example, if the work is done by temporary project teams, how are their efforts to be coordinated to a common goal? When a problem-solving team comes up with a solution and then disbands, how is its work to be given impact and continuity in the rest of the organization? Some stable and central structure is needed to provide coordination, long-range planning, and continuity of effort. If it is too stable, however, it may become role-oriented (rigid and hard to change) or power-oriented (recentralizing control). The personal power and security needs of individual members may foster such developments.

These dilemmas of internal structure have led to various compromise solutions such as the "matrix organization." The term "matrix" is used because the actual working groups *cut horizontally across* the normal functional-pyramidal organization, bringing together selected individuals from different functions and different levels to work in a relatively autonomous, egalitarian group. Structural stability is provided by a fixed *role-oriented* framework organized on functional lines. Personnel are readily detachable from the functions for varying periods of time during which they join a *task-oriented* work unit or project team. They are directed by the work unit; but their pay, career prospects, and promotions emanate from the role-oriented part of the system.

Matrix forms of organization have been used with success in highly technical businesses operating in a fast-changing environment. Again, TRW Systems is perhaps the oldest and most comprehensive example. Considerable experimentation with matrix forms has also taken place in the chemical industry, both in the United States and abroad.

Although the matrix system can be effective, it often suffers from attempts of the role-oriented functions to overcontrol the task-oriented functions. The resulting conflict is usually won by the former, which has greater permanence and more resources. One reason for this difficulty is that organizations try to operate partially task-oriented structures without commitment to the ideology. Role-oriented people cannot be plugged into a task-oriented system without conflict.

Effective motivation: While the power-oriented organization provides a chance for a few aggressive people to fight their way to the top, it offers little security to the ordinary person. It is most viable in situations where people are deprived and powerless and have to accept a bad bargain as better than none. For example, the power-oriented organization thrives in underdeveloped countries.

The power-oriented organization also has the problem of using too much of its energy to police people. Reliance on rewards and punishments tends to produce surface compliance and covert rebellion. Where the quantity and quality of work can be observed (as on an assembly line), inspection and discipline may keep the system working. But if the power does not command loyalty as well, the system usually breaks down. A simple example is the sabotage of hard-to-test aspects of car assembly by disgruntled workers.

The role-oriented ideology tries to deal with the difficulty of supervising complex decision-making and problem-solving tasks by rationalization and simplification. Each job is broken into smaller elements, rules are established, and performance is observed. When conditions change, however, the members are likely to continue carrying out the same (now ineffective) procedures.

The power- and role-oriented organizations simply do not provide for the development and utilization of internal commitment, initiative, and independent judgment on the part of members at other than the highest levels. Nevertheless, in societies where most people's aspirations are just to get by, or at most to achieve a measure of economic security, the power- and role-oriented organizations are able to function adequately.

In affluent societies, however, where security is more widely assured, people begin to look for deeper satisfactions in their work. They attempt to change tightly controlled work assignments and rigid internal structures. When trends toward task orientation ("useful," "meaningful" work) and person orientation (interesting work, self expression, and "doing one's own thing") begin to develop in the wider society, internal pressures for change develop within power- and role-oriented organizations.

Unfortunately, not all people can function productively in a flexible and egalitarian structure. Some people *are* dependent, apathetic, or insecure. They do need external incentives to work and directives or rules to guide their activities.

Furthermore, the task-oriented ideology has its own ways of exploiting the individual. When his knowledge and skills become obsolete for the task at hand, an individual is expected to step gracefully aside to make room for someone who is better qualified. Status and recognition depend almost entirely on task contribution; if the problems facing the organization change suddenly, this can produce cruel reversals of an individual's personal fortune and work satisfaction.

The person-oriented organization seems to be specially created to fit the work situation to the motives and needs of the independent, self-directed individual. It is flexible to his demands, whereas the power-oriented organization is controlling; it gives scope for his individual expression, whereas the role-oriented organization programs every move; it is concerned about his personal needs, whereas the task-oriented organization uses people as instruments for "higher" ends. Unfortunately, as discussed above, the person-oriented organization is less likely to be effective in the external environment than organizations based on the other ideologies.

Toward Resolving Conflict

One basic tension runs throughout the ideologies and organization types discussed thus far. It is the conflict between (a) the values and structural qualities which advance the interests of people and (b) the values and structural qualities which advance the interests of organizations.

I can identify six interests, all mentioned previously, which are currently the subject of ideological tension and struggle. Three of these are primarily interests of people, and three are primarily interests of organizations. The three interests of people are:

1. Security against economic, political, or psychological deprivation.

2. Opportunities to voluntarily commit one's efforts to goals that are personally meaningful.

3. The pursuit of one's own growth and development, even where this may conflict with the immediate needs of the organization.

The three interests of organizations are:

1. Effective response to threatening and dangerous complex environments.

2. Dealing rapidly and effectively with change and complex environments.

3. Internal integration and coordination of effort toward organization needs and goals, including the subordination of individual needs to the needs of the organization.

These are obviously not all the interests at issue, but in my opinion they are among the most salient.

Exhibit I shows the position of each ideology vis-à-vis each interest and indicates, as does the preceding analysis, that the four ideologies have quite dissimilar profiles. Each ideology thus "fits" the needs of a given organization and its members differently. For example, a small organization operating in a rapidly changing technical field and employing people who desire personal growth and autonomy might find its best fit with either the task or person orientation (this depends, of course, on how competitive its markets are and what financial shape it is in). A very large organization operating a slowly changing technology in a restricted market and employing people who desire stability and security might find that a role orientation would provide the best balance.

For most organizations, however, there is no perfect fit with any one of the four ideologies. The "ideal" ideology would possess some power orientation to deal smartly with the competition, a bit of role orientation for stability and internal integration, a charge of task orientation for good problem solving and rapid adaption to change, and enough person orientation to meet the questions of the new recruit who wants to know why he should be involved at all unless *his* needs are met.

But, unfortunately, this mixture of ideologies *and their consequences* for people and organizations will inevitably result in conflict, and its subsequent wear and tear on organizations and their members. Trying to mix ideologies may also prevent each type from producing the advantages that are unique to it.

On the other hand, I do not think that the most viable organizations and the maximum satisfaction of human needs will result from monolithic structures which are ideologically homogeneous. It seems to me that we must learn to create and maintain organizations that contain within them the same diversity of ideologies and structures as are found in the complex environments in which the organizations must live and grow. This means that organizations may have to be composed of separate *parts* that are ideologically homogeneous within themselves yet still quite different from each other.

Such organizations will be very effective in dealing with complex environ-

Exhibit I. Interests of people and the organization under four orientations

A. Interests of people

	Security against economic, political, and psychological deprivation	Opportunities for voluntary commitment to worthwhile goals	Opportunities to pursue one's own growth and development independent of organization goals
Power orientation	Low: At the pleasure of the autocrat	Low: Unless one is in a sufficiently high position to determine organization goals	Low: Unless one is in a sufficiently high position to determine organization goals
Role orientation	High: Secured by law, custom, and procedure	Low: Even if, at times, one is in a high position	Low: Organization goals are relatively rigid and activities are closely prescribed
Task orientation	Moderate: Psychological deprivation can occur when an individual's contributions are redundant	High: A major basis of the individual's relationship to the organization	Low: The individual should not be in the organization if he does not subscribe to some of its goals
Person orientation	High: The individual's welfare is the major concern	High: But only if the individual is capable of generating his own goals	High: Organization goals are determined by individual needs

B. Interests of the organization

	Effective response to dangerous, threatening environments	Dealing rapidly and effectively with environmental complexity and change	Internal integration and coordination of effort – if necessary, at the expense of individual needs
Power orientation	High: The organization tends to be perpetually ready for a fight	Moderate to low: Depends on size; pyramidal communication channels are easily overloaded	High: Effective control emanates from the top
Role orientation	Moderate to low: The organization is slow to mobilize to meet increases in threat	Low: Slow to change programmed procedures; communication channels are easily overloaded	High: Features a carefully planned rational system of work
Task orientation	Moderate to high: The organization may be slow to make decisions but produces highly competent responses	High: Flexible assignment of resources and short communication channels facilitate adaptation	Moderate: Integrated by common goal; but flexible, shifting structure may make coordination difficult
Person orientation	Low: The organization is slow to become aware of threat and slow to mobilize effort against it	High: But response is erratic; assignment of resources to problems depends greatly on individual needs and interests	Low: A common goal is difficult to achieve and activities may shift with individual interests

ments and maximizing satisfactions for different types of people, but they will be subject to more internal conflict and ideological struggle than most current organizations could tolerate. For example, instead of a "company spirit" there will be several "company spirits," all different and very likely antagonistic. In this environment of conflicting but mutually interdependent parts, the management—not the resolution—of conflict will be a task of the greatest importance. One can imagine, in fact, that the most important job of top managers will not be directing the business, but, instead, managing the integration of its parts.

Concluding Note

Whether men confront or avoid them, ideological issues will continue to sharpen of their own accord, both inside and outside the organization. As long as we continue to raise and educate our children permissively, the pressure from younger members of the organization for greater person orientation will increase. As operational environments become more turbulent and more technical, the attractions of task orientation will make themselves felt. Yet every change in organizations means some degree of power redistribution and with it some shift in rewards—such shifts will always be resisted by those with the most to lose, usually the older members of the organization who have a higher status. Thus I believe that ideological conflict will increase within organizations, whether that conflict is dealt with openly or not.

By dealing with such conflict openly, however, businessmen may find ways to manage it in the service of both the organization and its members and also to use tension creatively as well as competitively. Hidden conflict, on the other hand, tends to eat away at the strength of an organization and then to erupt when it is most dangerous to organization health.

In writing this article, I have attempted to render these inevitable ideological differences more conceptually clear. The next step is to develop a common language and set of norms that support both the open confrontation of such issues and the strategies for dealing with them in our organizations.

4. Management by Whose Objectives?

Harry Levinson

*Because it is based on reward-punishment psychology, the process of manage-
ment by objectives in combination with performance appraisal is self-defeating.
Here, the author argues that the MBO technique can be improved by examining
the underlying assumptions about motivation, by taking group action, and by
considering the individual's personal goals first.*

Despite the fact that the concept of management by objectives (MBO)
has by this time become an integral part of the managerial process, the
typical MBO effort perpetuates and intensifies hostility, resentment, and
distrust between a manager and subordinates. As practiced, it is really just
industrial engineering with a new name, applied to higher managerial
levels, and with the same resistances.

Obviously, somewhere between the concept of MBO and its implementation, something has seriously gone wrong. Coupled with performance appraisal, the intent is to follow the Frederick Taylor tradition of a more
rational management process. That is, which people are to do what, who
is to have effective control over it, and how compensation is to be related
directly to individual achievement. The MBO process, in its essence, is an
effort to be fair and reasonable, to predict performance and judge it more
carefully, and presumably to provide individuals with an opportunity to be
self-motivating by setting their own objectives.

The intent of clarifying job obligations and measuring performance
against a man's own goals seems reasonable enough. The concern for having
both superior and subordinate consider the same matters in reviewing the
performance of the latter is eminently sensible. The effort to come to common agreement on what constitutes the subordinate's job is highly desirable.

Yet, like most rationalizations in the Taylor tradition, MBO as a
process is one of the greatest of managerial illusions because it fails to
take adequately into account the deeper emotional components of motivation.

In this article, I shall indicate how I think management by objectives, as
practiced in most organizations, is self-defeating, and serves simply to

increase pressure on the individual. By doing so, I do not reject either MBO or performance appraisal out of hand.

Rather, by raising the basic question, "Whose objectives?" I propose to suggest how they might be made more constructive devices for effective management. The issues I shall raise have largely to do with psychological considerations, and particularly with the assumptions about motivation which underlie these techniques.

The "Ideal" Process

Since management by objectives is closely related to performance appraisal and review, I shall consider these together as one practice which is intended:

□ To measure and judge performance.

□ To relate individual performance to organizational goals.

□ To clarify both the job to be done and the expectations of accomplishment.

□ To foster the increasing competence and growth of the subordinate.

□ To enhance communications between superior and subordinate.

□ To serve as a basis for judgments about salary and promotion.

□ To stimulate the subordinate's motivation.

□ To serve as a device for organizational control and integration.

MAJOR PROBLEMS

According to contemporary thinking, the "ideal" process should proceed in five steps: (1) individual discussion with his superior of the subordinate's description of his own job, (2) establishment of short-term performance targets, (3) meetings with the superior to discuss progress toward targets, (4) establishment of checkpoints to measure progress, and (5) discussion between superior and subordinate at the end of a defined period to assess the results of the subordinate's efforts. In *ideal* practice, this process occurs against a background of more frequent, even day-to-day, contacts and is separate from salary review. But, in *actual* practice, there are many problems. Consider:

No matter how detailed the job description, it is essentially static— that is, a series of statements.

However, the more complex the task and the more flexible a man must be in it, the less any fixed statement of job elements will fit what he does. Thus the higher a man rises in an organization and the more varied and subtle his work, the more difficult it is to pin down objectives that represent more than a fraction of his effort.

With preestablished goals and descriptions, little weight can be given to the areas of discretion open to the individual, but not incorporated into his job description or objectives.

I am referring here to those spontaneously creative activities an innovative executive might choose to do, or those tasks a responsible executive sees which need to be done. As we move more toward a service society, in which tasks are less well defined but spontaneity of service and self-assumed responsibility are crucial, this becomes pressing.

Most job descriptions are limited to what a man himself does in his work.

They do not adequately take into account the increasing interdependence of managerial work in organizations. This limitation becomes more important as the impact of social and organizational factors on individual performance becomes better understood. The more a man's effectiveness depends on what other people do, the less he himself can be held responsible for the outcome of his efforts.

If a primary concern in performance review is counseling the subordinate, appraisal should consider and take into account the total situation in which the superior and subordinate are operating.

In addition, this should take into account the relationship of the subordinate's job to other jobs, rather than to his alone. In counseling, much of the focus is on helping the subordinate learn to negotiate the system. There is no provision in most reviews and no place on appraisal forms with which I am familiar to report and record such discussion.

The setting and evolution of objectives is done over too brief a period of time to provide for adequate interaction among different levels of an organization.

This militates against opportunity for peers, both in the same work unit and in complementary units, to develop objectives together for maximum integration. Thus both the setting of objectives and the appraisal of performance make little contribution toward the development of teamwork and more effective organizational self-control.

Coupled with these problems is the difficulty superiors experience when they undertake appraisals.

Douglas McGregor complained that the major reason appraisal failed was that superiors disliked playing God by making judgments about another man's worth. He likened the superior's experience to inspection of assembly line products and contended that his revulsion was against being inhuman. To cope with this problem, McGregor recommended that an individual should set his own goals, checking them out with his superior, and should use the appraisal session as a counseling device. Thus the superior would become one who helped the subordinate achieve his own goals instead of a dehumanized inspector of products.

Parenthetically, I doubt very much that the failure of appraisal stems from playing God or feeling inhuman. My own observation leads me to believe that managers experience their appraisal of others as a hostile, aggressive act that unconsciously is felt to be hurting or destroying the other person. The appraisal situation, therefore, gives rise to powerful, paralyzing feelings of guilt that make it extremely difficult for most executives to be constructively critical of subordinates.

OBJECTIVITY PLEA

Be that as it may, the more complex and difficult the appraisal process and the setting and evaluation of objectives, the more pressing the cry for objectivity. This is a vain plea. Every organization is a social system, a network of interpersonal relationships. A man may do an excellent job by objective standards of measurement, but may fail miserably as a partner, subordinate, superior, or colleague. It is a commonplace that more people fail to be promoted for personal reasons than for technical inadequacy.

Furthermore, since every subordinate is a component of his superior's efforts to achieve his own goals, he will inevitably be appraised on how well he works with his superior and helps the latter meet his needs. A heavy subjective element necessarily enters into every appraisal and goal-setting experience.

The plea for objectivity is vain for another reason. The greater the emphasis on measurement and quantification, the more likely the subtle, nonmeasurable elements of the task will be sacrificed. Quality of performance frequently, therefore, loses out to quantification.

A *case example*: A manufacturing plant which produces high quality, high prestige products, backed by a reputation for customer consideration and service, has instituted an MBO program. It is well worked out and has done much to clarify both individual goals and organizational performance. It is an important component of the professional management style of that company which has resulted in commendable growth.

But an interesting, and ultimately destructive, process has been set in motion. The managers are beginning to worry because when they now ask why something has not been done, they hear from each other, "That isn't in my goals." They complain that customer service is deteriorating. The vague goal, "improve customer service," is almost impossible to measure. There is therefore heavy concentration on those subgoals which can be measured. Thus time per customer, number of customer calls, and similar measures are used as guides in judging performance. The *less* time per customer and the *fewer* the calls, the better the customer service manager meets his objectives. He is cutting costs, increasing profit—and killing the business. Worse still, he hates himself.

Most of the managers in that organization joined it because of its reputation for high quality and good service. They want to make good products and earn the continued admiration of their customers, as well as the envy of their industry. When they are not operating at that high level, they feel guilty. They become angry with themselves and the company. They feel that they might just as well be working for someone else who admittedly does a sloppy job of quality control and could hardly care less about service.

The same problem exists with respect to the development of personnel, which is another vague goal that is hard to measure in comparison with subgoals that are measurable. If asked, each manager can name a younger man as his potential successor, particularly if his promotion depends on doing so; but no one has the time, or indeed feels that he is being paid, to thoroughly train the younger man. Nor can one have the time or be paid, for there is no way in that organization to measure how well a manager does in developing another.

The Missed Point

All of the problems with objectives and appraisals outlined in the example discussed in the foregoing section indicate that MBO is not working well despite what some companies think about their programs. The underlying reason it is not working well is that it misses the whole human point.

To see how the point is being missed, let us follow the typical MBO process. Characteristically, top management sets its corporate goal for the coming year. This may be in terms of return on investment, sales, production, growth, or other measurable factors.

Within this frame of reference, reporting managers may then be asked how much their units intend to contribute toward meeting that goal, or they may be asked to set their own goals relatively independent of the corporate goal. If they are left free to set their own goals, these in any case are expected to be higher than those they had the previous year. Usually, each reporting manager's range of choices is limited to his option for a piece of the organizational action, or improvement of specific statistics. In some cases, it may also include obtaining specific training or skills.

Once a reporting manager decides on his unit's goals and has them approved by his superior, those become the manager's goals. Presumably, he has committed himself to what he wants to do. He has said it and he is responsible for it. He is thereafter subject to being hoisted on his own petard.

Now, let us reexamine this process closely: the whole method is based on a short-term, egocentrically oriented perspective and an underlying reward-punishment psychology. The typical MBO process puts the reporting manager in much the same position as a rat in a maze, who has choices between only two alternatives. The experimenter who puts the rat in the maze assumes that the rat wants the food reward; if he cannot presume that, he starves the rat to make sure he wants the food.

Management by objectives differs only in that it permits the man himself to determine his own bait from a limited range of choices. Having done so, the MBO process assumes that he will (a) work hard to get it, (b) be pushed internally by reason of his commitment, and (c) make himself responsible to his organization for doing so.

In fairness to most managers, they certainly try, but not without increasing resentment and complaint for feeling like rats in a maze, guilt for not paying attention to those parts of the job not in their objectives, and passive resistance to the mounting pressure for ever-higher goals.

PERSONAL GOALS

The MBO process leaves out the answers to such questions as: What are the manager's personal objectives? What does he need and want out of his work? How do his needs and wants change from year to year? What relevance do organizational objectives and his part in them have to such needs and wants?

Obviously, no objectives will have significant incentive power if they are forced choices unrelated to a man's underlying dreams, wishes, and personal aspirations. For example:

If a salesman relishes the pleasure of his relationships with his hard-earned but low-volume customers, this is a powerful need for him. Suppose his boss, who is concerned about increasing the volume of sales, urges him to concentrate on the larger quantity customers rather than the smaller ones, which will provide the necessary increase in volume, and then asks him how much of an increase he can achieve.

To work with the larger quantity customers means that he will be less likely to sell to the individuals with whom he has well-established relationships and be more likely to deal with purchasing agents, technical people, and staff specialists who will demand of him knowledge and information he may not have in sophisticated detail. Moreover, as a single salesman, his organization may fail to support him with technical help to meet these demands.

When this happens, not only may he lose his favorite way of operating, which has well served his own needs, but he may have demands put on him which cause him to feel inadequate. If he is being compelled to make a choice about the percent of sales volume increase he expects to attain, he may well do that, but now under great psychological pressure. No one has recognized the psychological realities he faces, let alone helped him to work with them. It is simply assumed that since his sales goal is a rational one, he will see its rationality and pursue it.

The problem may be further compounded if, as is not unusual, formal changes are made in the organizational structure. If sales territories are shifted, if modes of compensation are changed, if problems of delivery occur, or whatever, all of these are factors beyond the salesman's control. Nevertheless, even with certain allowances, he is still held responsible for meeting his sales goal.

PSYCHOLOGICAL NEEDS

Lest the reader think the example we have just seen is overdrawn or irrelevant, I know of a young sales manager who is about to resign his job, despite his success in it, because he chooses not to be expendable in an organization which he feels regards him only as an instrument for reaching a goal. Many young men are refusing to enter large organizations for just this reason.

Some may argue that my criticism is unfair, that many organizations start their planning and setting of objectives from below. Therefore, the company cannot be accused of putting the man in a maze. But it does so. In almost all cases, the only legitimate objectives to be set are those having to do with measurable increases in performance. This highlights, again, the question, "Whose objectives?" This question becomes more pressing in those circumstances where lower level people set their objectives, only to be questioned by higher level managers and told their targets are not high enough.

Here you may well ask, "What's the matter with that? Aren't we in business, and isn't the purpose of the man's work to serve the requirements of the business?" The answer to both questions is, "Obviously." But that is only part of the story.

If a man's most powerful driving force is comprised of his needs, wishes, and personal aspirations, combined with the compelling wish to look good in his own eyes for meeting those deeply held personal goals, then management by objectives should begin with *his* objectives. What does he want to do with his life? Where does he want to go? What will make him feel good about himself? What does he want to be able to look back on when he has expended his unrecoverable years?

At this point, some may say that those are his business. The company has other business, and it must assume that the man is interested in working in the company's business rather than his own. That kind of differentiation is impossible. Everyone is always working toward meeting his psychological needs. Anyone who thinks otherwise, and who believes such powerful internal forces can be successfully disregarded or bought off for long, is deluding himself.

The Mutual Task

The organizational task becomes one of first understanding the man's needs, and then, with him, assessing how well they can be met in this organization, doing what the organization needs to have done. Thus the highest point of self-motivation arises when there is a complementary conjunction of the man's needs and the organization's requirements. The requirements of both mesh, interrelate, and become synergistic. The energies of man and organization are pooled for mutual advantage.

If the two sets of needs do not mesh, then a man has to fight himself and his organization, in addition to the work which must be done and the targets which have been defined. In such a case, this requires of him and his boss that they evaluate together where he wants to go, where the organization is going, and how significant the discrepancy is. The man might well be better off somewhere else, and the organization would do better to have someone else in his place whose needs mesh better with organization requirements.

LONG-RUN COSTS

The issue of meshed interests is particularly relevant for middle-aged, senior-level managers. As men come into middle age, their values often begin to change, and they feel anew the pressure to accomplish many long-deferred dreams. When such wishes begin to stir, they begin to experience severe conflict.

Up to this point, they have committed themselves to the organization and have done sufficiently well in it to attain high rank. Usually, they are slated for even higher levels of responsibility. The organization has been good to them, and their superiors are depending on them to provide its leadership. They have been models for the younger men, whom they have urged to aspire to organizational heights. To think of leaving is to desert both their superiors and their subordinates.

Since there are few avenues within the organization to talk about such conflict, they try to suppress their wishes. The internal pressure continues to mount until they finally make an impulsive break, surprising and dismaying both themselves and their colleagues. I can think of three vice presidents who have done just that.

The issue is not so much that they decide to leave, but the cost of the way they depart. Early discussion with superiors of their personal goals would have enabled both to examine possible relocation alternatives within the organization. If there were none, then both the managers and their superiors might have come to an earlier, more comfortable decision about separation. The organization would have had more time to make satisfactory alternative plans, as well as to have taken steps to compensate for the manager's lagging enthusiasm. Lower level managers would then have seen the company as humane in its enlightened self-interest and would not have had to create fearful fantasies about what the top management conflicts were that had caused a good man to leave.

To place consideration of the managers' personal objectives first does not minimize the importance of the organization's goals. It does not mean there is anything wrong with the organization's need to increase its return on investment, its size, its productivity, or its other goals. However, I contend that it is ridiculous to make assumptions about the motivations of individuals, and then to set up means of increasing the pressures on people based on these often questionable assumptions. While there may be certain demonstrable short-run statistical gains, what are the long-run costs?

One cost is that people may leave; another, that they may fall back from competitive positions to plateaus. Why should an individual be expendable for someone else and sacrifice himself for something that is not part of his own cherished dreams? Still another cost may be the loss of the essence of the business, as happened in the case example we saw earlier of the manufacturing plant which had the problem of deteriorating customer service.

In that example, initially there was no dialogue. Nobody heard what the managers said, what they wanted, where they wanted to go, where they wanted the organization to go, and how they felt about the supposedly rational procedures that had been initiated. The underlying psychological assumption which management unconsciously made was that the managers *had to be made* more efficient; ergo, management by objectives.

Top management typically assumes that it alone has the prerogative to (a) set the objectives, (b) provide the rewards and targets, and (c) drive anyone who works for the organization. As long as this reward-punishment psychology exists in any organization, the MBO appraisal process is certain to fail.

Many organizations are making this issue worse by promising young people they will have challenges, since they assume these men will be challenged by management's objectives. Managements are having difficulty, even when they have high turnover rates, hearing these youngsters say they could hardly care less for management's unilaterally determined objectives. Managements then become angry, complain that the young people do not want to work, or that they want to become presidents overnight.

What the young people are asking is: What about me and my needs? Who will listen? How much will management help me meet my own requirements while also meeting its objectives?

The power of this force is reflected in the finding that the more the subordinate participates in the appraisal interview by presenting his own ideas and beliefs, the more likely he is to feel that (a) the superior is helpful and constructive, (b) some current job problems are being cleared up, and (c) reasonable future goals are being set.

The Suggested Steps

Given the validity of all the MBO problems I have been discussing to this point, there are a number of possibilities for coping with them. Here, I suggest three beginning steps to consider.

1. MOTIVATIONAL ASSESSMENT

Every management by objectives program and its accompanying performance appraisal system should be examined as to the extent to which it (1) expresses the conviction that people are patsies to be driven, urged, and manipulated, and (2) fosters a genuine partnership between men and organization, in which each has some influence over the other, as contrasted with a rat-in-maze relationship.

It is not easy for the nonpsychologist to answer such questions for himself, but there are clues to the answers. One clue is how decisions about compensation, particularly bonuses, are made. For example:

□ A sales manager asked my judgment about an incentive plan for highly motivated salesmen who were in a seller's market. I asked why he needed one, and he responded, "To give them an incentive." When I pointed out that they were already highly motivated and apparently needed no incentive, he changed his rationale and said that the company wanted to share its success to keep the men identified with it, and to express its recognition of their contribution.

I asked, "Why not let them establish the reward related to performance?" The question startled him; obviously, if they were going to decide, who needed him? A fundamental aspect of his role, as he saw it, was to drive them ever onward, whether they needed it or not.

□ A middle-management bonus plan tied to performance proved to be highly unsatisfactory in a plastic-fabricating company. Frustrated that its well-intentioned efforts were not working and determined to follow precepts of participative management, ranking executives involved many people in formulating a new one: personnel, control, marketing executives, and others—in fact, everyone but the managers who were to receive the bonuses. Top management is now dismayed that the new plan is as unsatisfactory as the old and is bitter that participation failed to work.

Another clue is the focus of company meetings. Some are devoted to intensifying the competition between units. Others lean heavily to exhortation and inspiration. Contrast these orientations with meetings in which people are apprised of problems and plan to cope with them.

2. GROUP ACTION

Every objectives and appraisal program should include group goal setting, group definition of both individual and group tasks, group appraisal of its accomplishments, group appraisal of each individual member's contribution to the group effort (without basing compensation on that appraisal), and shared compensation based on the relative success with which group goals are achieved. Objectives should include long-term as well as short-term goals.

The rationale is simple. Every managerial job is an interdependent task. Managers have responsibilities to each other as well as to their superiors. The reason for having an organization is to achieve more together than each could alone. Why, then, emphasize and reward individual performance alone, based on static job descriptions? That can only orient people to both incorrect and self-centered goals.

Therefore, where people are in complementary relationships, whether they report to the same superior or not, both horizontal and vertical goal formulation should be formalized, with regular, frequent opportunity for review of problems and progress. They should help each other define and describe their respective jobs, enhancing control and integration at the point of action.

In my judgment, for example, a group of managers (sales, promotion, advertising) reporting to a vice president of marketing should formulate their collective goals, and define ways both of helping each other and of assessing each others' effectiveness in the common task. The group assessment of each manager's work should be a means of providing each with constructive feedback, not for determining pay. However, in addition to his salary, each should receive, as part of whatever additional compensation is offered, a return based on the group effort.

The group's discussion among itself and with its superior should include examination of organizational and environmental obstacles to goal achievement, and particularly of what organizational and leadership supports are required to attain objectives. One important reason for this is that often people think there are barriers where none would exist if they initiated action. ("You mean the president really wants us to get together and solve this problem?")

Another reason is that frequently when higher management sets goals, it is unaware of significant barriers to achievement, leaving managers cynical. For example, if there is no comprehensive orientation and support program to help new employees adapt, then pressure on lower level managers to employ disadvantaged minority group members and to reduce their turnover can only be experienced by those managers as hollow mockery.

3. APPRAISAL OF APPRAISERS

Every management by objectives and appraisal program should include regular appraisals of the manager by his subordinates, and be reviewed by the manager's superior. Every manager should be specifically compensated for how well he develops people, based on such appraisals. The very phrase "reporting to" reflects the fact that although a manager has a responsibility, his superior also has a responsibility for what he does and how he does it.

In fact, both common sense and research indicate that the single most significant influence outside himself on how a manager does his job is his superior. If that is the case, then the key environmental factor in task accomplishment and managerial growth is the relationship between the manager and his superior.

Therefore, objectives should include not only the individual manager's personal and occupational goals, but also the corporate goals he and his superior share in common. They should together appraise their relationship vis-à-vis both the manager's individual goals and their joint objectives, review what they have done together, and discuss its implications for their next joint steps.

A manager rarely is in a position to judge his superior's overall performance, but he can appraise him on the basis of how well the superior has helped him to do his job, how well he is helping him to increase his proficiency and visibility, what problems the supervisor poses for him, and what kinds of support he himself can use. Such feedback serves several purposes.

Most important, it offers the superior some guidance on his own managerial performance. In addition, and particularly when the manager is protected by higher level review of his appraisal, it provides the supervisor with direct feedback on his own behavior. This is much more constructive than behind-his-back complaint and vituperative terminal interviews, in which cases he has no opportunity either to defend himself or correct his behavior. Every professional counselor has had recently fired executive clients who did not know why they had been discharged for being poor superiors when, according to their information, their subordinates thought so much of them. In his own self-interest, every manager should want appraisal by his subordinates.

The Basic Consideration

When the three organizational conditions we have just seen do in fact exist, then it is appropriate to think of starting management by objectives with a consideration of each man's personal objectives; if the underlying attitude in the organization toward him is that he is but an object, there is certainly no point in starting with the man. Nor is there any point in trying to establish his confidence in his superiors when he is not protected from their rivalry with him, or when they are playing him off against his peers. Anyone who expressed his fears and innermost wishes under these circumstances would be a damned fool.

For reasons I have already indicated, it should be entirely legitimate in every business for these concerns to be the basis for individual objectives-setting. This is because the fundamental managerial consideration necessarily must be focused on the question: "How do we meet both individual and organizational purposes?" If a major intention of management by objectives is to enlist the self-motivated commitment of the individual, then that commitment must derive from the individual's powerful wishes to support the organization's goals; otherwise, the commitment will be merely incidental to his personal wishes.

Having said that, the real difficulty begins. How can any superior know what a subordinate's personal goals and wishes are if the subordinate himself—as most of us are—is not clear about them? How ethical is it for a superior to pry into a man's personal life? How can he keep himself from forming a negative judgment about a man who, he knows, is losing interest in his work, or is not altogether identified with the company? How can he keep that knowledge from interfering with judgments he might otherwise make, and opportunities he might otherwise offer? How often are the personal goals, particularly in middle age, temporary fantasies that are better not discussed? Can a superior who is untrained in psychology handle such information constructively? Will he perhaps do more harm than good?

These are critically important questions. They deserve careful thought. My answers should be taken as no more than beginning steps.

EGO CONCEPTS

Living is a process of constant adaptation. A man's personal goals, wishes, and aspirations are continuously evolving, and being continuously modified by his experiences. That is one reason why it is so difficult for an individual to specify concrete personal objectives.

Nevertheless, each of us has a built-in road map, a picture of himself at his future best. Psychologists speak of this as an *ego ideal,* which is comprised of a man's values, the expectations parents and others have held out for him, his competences and skills, and his favorite ways of behaving. A man's ego ideal is essentially the way he thinks he ought to be. Much of a person's ego ideal is unconscious, which is another reason why it is not clear to him.

Subordinate's self-examination: Although a man cannot usually spell out his ego ideal, he can talk about those experiences that have been highly gratifying, even exhilarating, to him. He can specify those rare peak experiences that made him feel very good about himself. When he has an opportunity to talk about what he has found especially gratifying and also what he thinks would be gratifying to him, he is touching on central elements of his ego ideal.

Given the opportunity to talk about such experiences and wishes on successive occasions, he can begin to spell out for himself the central thrust of his life. Reviewing all of the occupational choices he has made and the reasons for making them, he can begin to see the common threads in those choices and therefore the momentum of his personality. As these become clearer to him, he is in a better position to weigh alternatives against the mainstream of his personality.

For example, a man who has successively chosen occupational alternatives in which he was individually competitive, and whose most exhilarating experiences have come from defeating an opponent or single-handedly vanquishing a problem, would be unlikely to find a staff position exhilarating, no matter what it paid or what it was called. His ideal for himself is that of a vanquishing, competitive man.

The important concept here is that it is not necessary that a man spell out concrete goals at any one point; rather, it is helpful to him and his organization if he is able to examine and review aloud on a continuing basis his thoughts and feelings about himself in relation to his work. Such a process makes it legitimate for him to bring his own feelings to consciousness and talk about them in the business context as the basis for his relationship to the organization.

By listening, and helping him to spell out how and what he feels, the superior does not *do* anything to the man, and therefore by that self-appraisal process cannot hurt him. The information serves both the man and his superior as a criterion for examining the relationship of the man's feelings and his, however dimly perceived, personal goals to organizational goals. Even if some of his wishes and aspirations are mere fantasy and impossible to gratify, if it is legitimate to talk about them without being laughed at, he can compare them with the realities of his life and make more reasonable choices.

Even in the safest organizational atmosphere, for reasons already mentioned, it will not be easy for managers to talk about their goals. The best-intentioned supervisor is likely to be something less than a highly skilled interviewer. These two facts suggest that any effort to ascertain a subordinate's personal goals is futile; but I think not.

The important point is not the specificity of the statement that any man can make, but the nature of a superior-subordinate relationship that makes it safe to explore such feelings and gives first consideration to the man. In such a context, both subordinate and superior may come closer to evolving a man-organization fit than they might otherwise.

Superior's introspection: A man-organization relationship requires the superior to do some introspection, too. Suppose he has prided himself on bringing along a bright young man who, he now learns, is thinking of moving into a different field. How can he keep from being angry and disappointed? How can he cope with the conflict he now has when it is time to make recommendations for advancement or a raise?

The superior cannot keep from being angry and disappointed. Such feelings are natural in that circumstance. He can express his feelings of disappointment to his protégé without being critical of the latter. But, if he continues to feel angry, then he needs to ask himself why another man's assertion of independence irritates him so. The issues of advancement and raises should continue to be based on the same realistic premises as they would have been before.

Of course, it now becomes appropriate to consider with the man whether—in view of his feelings—he wants to take on the burden of added responsibility and can reasonably discharge it. If he thinks he does, and can, he is likely to pursue the new responsibility with added determination. With his occupational choice conflict no longer hidden, and with fewer feelings of guilt about it, his commitment to his chosen alternative is likely to be more intense.

And if he has earned a raise, he should get it. To withhold it is to punish him, which puts the relationship back on a reward-punishment basis.

The question of how ethical it is to conduct such discussions as part of a business situation hinges on both the climate of the organization and on the sense of personal responsibility of each executive. Where the organization ethos is one of building trust and keeping confidences, there is no reason why executives cannot be as ethical as lawyers or physicians.

If the individual executive cannot be trusted in his relationships with his subordinates, then he cannot have their respect or confidence in any case, and the ordinary MBO appraisal process simply serves as a management pressure device. If the organization ethos is one of rapacious internal competition, backbiting, and distrust, there is little point in talking about self-motivation, human needs, or commitment.

Conclusion

Management by objectives and performance appraisal processes, as typically practiced, are inherently self-defeating over the long run because
they are based on a reward-punishment psychology that serves to intensify
the pressure on the individual while really giving him a very limited choice
of objectives. Such processes can be improved by examining the psychological assumptions underlying them, by extending them to include group
appraisal and appraisal of superiors by subordinates, and by considering
the personal goals of the individual first. These practices require a high
level of ethical standards and personal responsibility in the organization.

Such appraisal processes would diminish the feeling on the part of the
superior that appraisal is a hostile, destructive act. While he and his
subordinates would still have to judge the latter's individual performance,
this judgment would occur in a context of continuing consideration for
personal needs and reappraisal of organizational and environmental
realities.

Not having to be continuously on the defensive and aware of the organization's genuine interest in having him meet his personal goals as well
as the organization's goals, a manager would be freer to evaluate himself
against what has to be done. Since he would have many additional frames
of reference in both horizontal and vertical goal setting, he would need
no longer to see himself under appraisal (attack, judgment) as an isolated
individual against the system. Furthermore, he would have multiple modes
for contributing his own ideas and a varied method for exerting influence
upward and horizontally.

In these contexts, too, he could raise questions and concerns about qualitative aspects of performance. Then he, his colleagues, and his superiors
could together act to cope with such issues without the barrier of having
to consider only statistics. Thus a continuing process of interchange would
counteract the problem of the static job description and provide multiple
avenues for feedback on performance and joint action.

In such an organizational climate, work relationships would then become
dynamic networks for both personal and organizational achievements. No
incidental gain from such arrangements is that problems would more
likely be solved spontaneously at the lowest possible levels, and free
superiors simultaneously from the burden of the passed buck and the onus
of being the purveyors of hostility.

5. Qualitative Insights from Quantitative Methods

Robert H. Hayes

In this overview of the uses that management is making of qualitative methods, the author contends that this increased insight and expanded understanding of management processes, rather than the analytical techniques themselves, constitute the really important contribution of the quantitative approach to management science.

What does top management need to know about quantitative methods? The traditional response to this question is not particularly encouraging. At best, one gathers that quantitative analysis (under the name of *operations research, management science,* or whatever) has been able to develop a handful of tools that are sometimes useful in attacking certain types of management problems. This traditional view fails to see that there is a special *qualitative* difference between these methods and the other kinds of tools that managers use in problem solving. Because it fails to see this difference, the traditional view seriously understates the ultimate impact these methods are going to have.

I believe that the greatest impact of the quantitative approach will *not* be in the area of problem *solving*, although it will have growing usefulness there. Its greatest impact will be on problem *formulation: the way managers think about their problems*—how they size them up, bring new insights to bear on them, relate them to other problems, communicate with other people about them, and gather information for analyzing them. In this sense, the results that "quantitative people" have produced are beginning to contribute in a really significant way to the *art* of management.

Consider what the real impact of the computer has been. A few years ago, the computer was thought of as just a "very fast bookkeeper" really not much different from any other piece of expensive equipment. But management is beginning to recognize that the computer has the potential to exert a fundamental influence on business organization, communications, and control, and that its original view of these machines was almost painfully naive. It is unwise to underestimate the final, total effect that computerization or any other analytical, quantitative technology will have.

I want to examine in some detail three areas of vital interest to top managers in which quantitative techniques are contributing dramatic new insights—namely, management control, information evaluation, and executive motivation. Before doing so, however, I want to spell out by examples what I mean by the "transfer of insight" from one discipline to another via quantitative analysis—because this, in my opinion, is the key to understanding the broad significance, for the business world, of what the quantitative people are doing today.

Transfer of Insight

Many people are aware that quantitative methods can be immediately useful in improving our communication, even about traditional problems. For example, one executive has described a meeting of his company's planning board as follows:

"We argued for 45 minutes about what we should do right now and what it would cost to postpone a decision, but it wasn't until we put a decision tree on the board that people began to realize that we had all been talking about different problems!"

It is also well known that quantitative methods are useful in dealing with problems of unusual scale. To help management come to grips with problems that are so large and complicated that many people must work on them simultaneously, quantitative people have developed entirely new structures for describing and talking about them. PERT networks and decision trees, for example, are two ingenious frameworks for thinking and talking about certain types of large, complex problems and for gathering information needed to resolve them. Such structures represent valuable progress, but they are by no means the end of the story.

On a higher and more conceptual level, quantitative analysis is facilitating communication where it never existed before. When a problem has been stated quantitatively, one can often see that it is structurally similar to other problems (perhaps problems in completely different areas) which on the surface appear to be quite different. And once a common structure has been identified, insights and predictions can be transferred from one situation to another, and the quantitative approach can actually increase communication. Let us look at a couple of examples.

INVENTORY AND ELECTRICAL CIRCUITS

Suppose a company produces an item for which the demand is constant over time. It costs money to set up a production run, and it also costs money to carry items in inventory. Relatively, long production runs (large "lot sizes") decrease the first cost but increase the second. Now what is the appropriate compromise between the two types of expenses? In other words, what is the most economical lot size?

It has been found, analytically, that minimizing total costs leads to a square-root formula,

$$Q=\sqrt{CD},$$

where Q is the optimal lot size, C is a cost ratio that describes the internal system, and D is the demand rate. One insight this formula gives us is that a change in the demand rate for a given item does not ordinarily have a *proportionate* impact on either the lot size or the company's inventory of the item. For example, if the demand rate doubles, then the average inventory should increase by only about 40%.

What is more interesting for my purposes, however, is the fact that variants of this same formula crop up in a variety of seemingly unrelated contexts. The names of the variables are different, but the structure of the problem is similar. For example, the formula for finding the optimal time *between* production runs (that is, between economic lot sizes) is given by

$$T=Q/D=\sqrt{C/D},$$

which is similar to the formula for finding the time between swings of a pendulum:

$$T=2\pi\sqrt{C/D},$$

where C represents the length of the pendulum (a *system parameter*, so-called), and D the acceleration due to gravity. Electrical engineers have arrived at the same basic formula in analyzing certain simple types of electrical networks, using C to represent an appropriate system parameter and D to represent the force of an external voltage.

After quantitative formulation revealed the basic similarity between the lot-size problems and those associated with certain types of electrical networks, new lines of communication opened up. People began to ask if they could apply engineering knowledge about the behavior of electrical networks in which, say, the *voltage* is changing, to the problem of maintaining stability in an inventory control system in which the *demand level* is changing. They have found that to some extent this *is* possible. I shall discuss this particular transfer of information more thoroughly later.

ALLOCATION AND DISTRIBUTION

A production manager who is trying to allocate scarce resources (for example, manpower and machine capacity to product lines, or products to various markets) in an efficient fashion faces much the same problem as the advertising executive who must allocate limited funds to presentations in different media. The investor who must allocate limited funds to different capital projects faces this same problem in a different guise. Although this similarity tends to be concealed by different jargons, different units of measure, and so on, it shows up clearly when the problems are formulated quantitatively. Moreover, quantitative analysis has provided radically new and powerful solution techniques for this basic, common problem, under the imposing name "mathematical programming."

As an added bonus, an analysis of the logic behind these solution techniques shows that the problem of establishing appropriate prices for intra-company transfers is also similar in structure to the problem of efficiently allocating scarce resources—really just another way of looking at this same basic problem. Economists since Adam Smith, of course, have been claiming that a price system established by the supply-demand interaction in a free market provides the most efficient way for allocating goods to consumers. Hence this analytical thinking has established a common interest—and a *line of communication*—between the economists, on the one hand, and the production manager, the advertising executive, the investor, and the interdivisional manager of a corporation on the other. Any of these men can now begin to weigh the usefulness that the others' insights may have for him.

INSIGHT IS CONTAGIOUS

Once such techniques as mathematical programming have taken hold in one area, the useful effects and results in other areas can outrun all original expectations—even within a single company. Consider the following case:

□ A few years ago a large wood-products company faced a logistics problem which its personnel couldn't seem to handle adequately by traditional methods. The problem was this: given the locations and volumes of its logging operations, the locations and capacities of its lumber processing plants, and the costs of transporting logs between different locations, how could its plants be supplied most efficiently? The problem was complicated by the fact that each type of log had a different degree of suitability for each of the company's final products. Moreover, each of its mills produced more than one of these products.

The company decided to innovate, and began using a mathematical programming model to guide its log-allocation decisions.

Once the model had proved its effectiveness, the next step was to hook it into the demand side of the company's business. Given the current demands for its various final products, their prices, and the supply (and mix) of logs currently being provided by the logging operations, which products should each mill produce? The mathematical programming model was therefore extended to provide guidance in this more comprehensive type of allocation decision. As a by-product, it began providing information which improved the scheduling of the processing plants' day-to-day operations. Again, the model "proved out."

As executives gained a clearer view of the interrelationships between the processing and demand sides of their business, it occurred to them that perhaps more care should be taken in the supply side—that is, in deciding what kinds of trees at which locations should be harvested. They found that the kind of analytical thinking that linear programming had fostered in other areas was helpful here as well, and the model was accordingly expanded to integrate logging practices with the new downstream requirements. The company's whole activity, from forest to finished product, was improved as a result.

The model is now having its effects throughout the company. For example, it provides inputs into the company's cost accounting system, and hence is having an impact not only on product pricing and marketing decisions, but on internal-transfer pricing as well. It is also beginning to affect longer-term decisions about such things as land purchase, leasing, and plant construction.

In addition to increased efficiency, the use of mathematical programming in all these different areas meant that the personnel working in these areas had a new means of communication—almost a new language for communication. This communication was the key to the expansion of the original model; and this, in my opinion, is the vital point in the long run.

Three Areas

This transferability of insight between scientists, engineers, and managers is a very important phenomenon—not because these groups necessarily have a *lot* of problems in common, but because they now have a way of recognizing the ones that *are* common and they now share a language for talking and thinking about them. Furthermore, transfer of information between these groups has been accompanied by a slowly dawning recognition that the same transferability of insight is possible between different functional areas of management.

Why is it that this recognition is coming so slowly? Well, many in management feel that quantitative people are themselves poor communicators, and that they tend to get bogged down in their own techniques —they can't see the managerial forest because of all the decision trees. Quantitative people are likely to reply to such criticism by accusing nonquantitative people of carelessness and imprecision. This mutual hostility is just a fragment of the age-old antagonism between artists and engineers.

I must acknowledge that quantitative people have been partly responsible for this limited view of their contribution. Even though they have at times concerned themselves with major issues, by and large they have contented themselves with making small improvements in efficiency rather than investigating the larger conceptual issues that influence the way a top manager looks at his job.

For example, in "Practical Slants on Operations Research,"[1] Harvey M. Wagner suggests that 3%-10% is a typical range for the cost savings to be expected from a successful operations research study. Often the savings that quantitative people produce are of this nickel-and-dime kind, and such savings contrast strongly with the economic consequences of a merger or an acquisition, or a new-product decision. This state of affairs tends to diminish the real significance and validity of the quantitative approach in management's eyes.

Whatever the "rights" of this controversy are, it is time to drop these childish hostilities and look ahead to future developments.

ORGANIZATION STRUCTURE AND CONTROL

The area of management control is one of the best examples of a managerial preserve that is beginning to feel the impact of new insights from a seemingly unrelated discipline. Until fairly recently, much of the attention focused on the problems of management control was directed at its purely mechanical aspects—that is, at constructing information-flow systems and report systems that would provide the right man at the right level with the right information. As these problems were brought under some control, highly significant *second-level* problems began to emerge:

☐ Organizational and motivational problems associated with using these systems.

☐ Disruptive effects caused by the time lag between the moment that an event occurs and the time that it is sensed, transmitted, and finally acted on.

☐ Difficulties in predicting and protecting against a whole gallery of "unforeseen repercussions"—combinations of circumstances, in other words, which would cause the control system to malfunction.

Electrical engineering analogies: For over three decades, however, electrical engineers have been working on the problem of accurately predicting and directing the responses of complicated operating and communications systems in uncertain environments. (In fact, the term "control system" is derived from engineering terminology.) A number of management theorists

1. HBR May-June 1963, p. 61.

noted the similarity between this problem and some of their own. Following this clue, they have explored the possibility of transferring insights and solutions from the engineering context to the managerial context. The man most closely associated with this investigation is Jay W. Forrester of the Massachusetts Institute of Technology, an electrical engineer who assimilated the administrative point of view during his experience as head of the Whirlwind Computer development at M.I.T., just after World War II, and of the SAGE Air Defense Computer System a decade later.

Forrester used the fundamental concept of "feedback" to link the fields of electronics and management. The concept of feedback is, of course, fundamental to the analysis and design of electrical networks, where it denotes that a portion of the output of the network returns to the network as one of its inputs. In management, a decision made at one point in time affects the environment in which later decisions will be made, and in this sense feedback is a natural management concept.

In terms of an organizational network, feedback occurs in two readily definable ways: (a) formally, through the preparation of reports and projections based on past experience, and (b) informally, through the human tendency to remember past successes and mistakes and to adjust present behavior accordingly.

Expanding the analogy, one can see that industrial systems—organizational, operational, and logistic—have counterparts of many of the other ingredients of electrical networks:

□ Flows of raw materials, finished goods, and information correspond to the flow of electricity.

□ Both types of systems have delay components. I have already mentioned the obvious production, transportation, data processing, and transmission delays that exist in an industrial system. The use of economical order quantities introduces another kind of delay, by introducing a time lag between the occurrence of a demand at one level of an organization and the recognition of that demand, through a replenishment order, at a higher level.

□ Both systems have elements that act to amplify or dampen the flows through them. In a management system this effect might be as informal as the human tendencies to "play it down" and "blow it all out of proportion," or as formal (and measurable) as scrap losses and inventory deteriorations.

Like many convenient analogies, this one can be pushed too far. Forrester and his disciples tend to accept it literally, and over the past decade they have reported a number of attempts to construct models of actual organizations from this point of view—apparently with mixed success. Here, however, I shall discuss it simply as a valuable source of insight into the often puzzling behavior of complex industrial-economic systems.

The electrical engineering analogy, first of all, is helpful in distinguishing between the total system and its parts. Engineers have long been aware that an electrical network formed by connecting several subnetworks is likely to have entirely different characteristics from any of its parts. To understand the entire network's performance and alter it in a desired direction, the engineer must look at it *in toto*—this, in fact, is the basic rationale of all systems analysis. The same is ordinarily true of industrial systems, even those that seem relatively uncomplicated. For example:

□ A three-part system that is composed of (a) a simple demand-forecasting procedure, combined with (b) a simple inventory-production scheduling rule that responds to demand orders filtering up through several levels of a distribution hierarchy, and (c) a simple cost-control system that governs and supervises the other two subsystems—even this relatively simple system may have highly unstable properties.

Quantitative formulation and analysis of such systems can often help to identify the sources of instability and offer clues for correcting it. In the absence of such an analytical framework, "tampering with the system" on a piecemeal basis can be disastrous.

This type of systems analysis can also assist control by showing where a company is working at cross-purposes with itself. The familiar economic lot size, despite its mathematical virtues and its history of successful uses, is a frequent villain here. Although using such lot sizes may smooth the operation within one department, it may cause disproportionate and undesirable fluctuations and inefficiencies in other departments. In fact, in the parlance of electrical engineers, economic lot sizes can act as amplifiers, and thus substitute an erratic series of large shocks for a smooth series of small ones. In many cases this is an effect that is compounded with each additional level of a company's distribution system.

General systems analogies: Systems analysis can contribute a good deal to control by dispelling misleading illusion. For example, in his article, "Industrial Dynamics: A Major Breakthrough for Decision Makers,"[2] Forrester described a very reasonable-looking production-distribution complex in which a level demand pattern (with small random fluctuations about the average) resulted in a *highly cyclical* production pattern! The illusion of such a "seasonal" production cycle might very well affect every level of the organization, including the highest policy levels. A merger or acquisition might be consummated, for example, that is unjustifiable on economic grounds but seems necessary as a "counter-cyclical measure."

The behavior of the national economy provides examples of similar phenomena. Of necessity, economists have been forced to adopt the systems approach. Some of their experiments show that if a simple, realistic model of the economy is subjected to random shocks (a strike here, a drought

2. HBR July-August 1958, p. 37.

there, a police action over there), then the model responds by simulating a "business cycle." *Fortune*'s description of the "profit squeeze," for example, has a familiar ring to control engineers:

"In 1967 economic analysts stopped hailing the demise of the business cycle. . . . After five year-to-year increases in a row, the earnings of the 500 largest industrial corporations dipped 2.6 percent. What happened was that the year's moderate increase in sales—total revenues of the 500 advanced 8.9 percent—fell short of manufacturers' great expectations. In 1966, looking forward to boomy demand in 1967, manufacturers invested heavily in new capacity and in inventory accumulation. But a slowdown in sales began in the last quarter of 1966 and lasted through the third quarter of 1967. Burdened with excess inventories, manufacturers cut back on orders to their suppliers. . . .

"Unit labor costs went up too. So did interest costs, largely because companies had borrowed heavily at high rates to finance investment in plant and equipment. With these three kinds of costs going up, the total costs for the 500 rose by 9.7 percent. . . . A 9.7 percent rise in costs combined with an 8.9 percent rise in revenues led, by inescapable arithmetic, to a decline in profits."[3]

Good businessmen, of course, are not unaware of the conflicting currents at work in their businesses and the economy. They often use words such as "momentum," "overshoot," and "countervailing forces" to convey their qualitative awareness of the dynamic interplay of action and reaction. But a deeper understanding of this interplay, and possible means for controlling it, requires a more organized, quantitative approach.

Analysis can also be immediately helpful to companies that want to direct their progress and growth. Some corporations, for example, appear to thwart the best efforts of management to change their direction. A company may introduce new information and control systems, develop new sales procedures, define and implement new corporate policies, and so forth, but the same old problems may continue to plague it. A company of this kind resembles a bell, which will ring at the same frequency no matter how hard or how often it is struck. What is required here is a *systematic analysis and revision of the basic internal structure of the organization itself*. To get the frequency it wants, management may have to change the structure of the bell.

NEW INSIGHTS INTO INFORMATION

Everybody talks about information these days. Since the dawn of commerce, in fact, managers have been asking for more accurate, up-to-date, and relevant information. Today, however, the requests are somewhat more

3. June 15, 1968, p. 2.

sophisticated. The need now is for "better information *systems*" or "better information *processors*" (usually some form of computer). This attitude is certainly understandable; information is the glue that holds organizations together. Moreover, since the quality of communication in the modern corporation depends on the quality of information, to a very large degree this demand for better information is really a demand for a more accurate basis for communication.

As technology has responded to these needs, some thoughtful managers have realized that there is just as much danger in too much information as there is in too little. The real need is not just for information but for the *right type* of information. Since different types of information cost different amounts of money, the main problem is to balance the value of potential information against its cost. Otherwise, the natural tendency is to seek as much information as one can get for a given cost—a sure prescription for generating mountains of information of the cheapest and least useful kind.

But while businessmen have their own unique informational requirements, the need for pertinent information is common to all types of decision making, and other disciplines have long been grappling with such basic questions as: "What is information?" "How does one go about measuring and evaluating it?" "How can one predict the value of a system set up to provide information?" Within electrical engineering, in fact, a whole new area called information theory has grown up. What is taught at many graduate business schools as "statistical decision theory" could perhaps more properly be called "evaluation of information for management decision making." A consensus is now emerging from the various studies on information being carried on in engineering, statistics, and economics—a consensus that has surprising relevance to management thinking.

What is information? Information is now defined as anything that serves to affect the uncertainty associated with some quantity. This is not an operational definition, of course, until we define "uncertainty," but note the generality of this statement. Information, under this definition, could be obtained in a business context through preparing financial reports, sampling, doing research, seeking the advice of a consultant, or simply delaying a decision "until the situation clears a little." Note also that the definition says "affect," and not "reduce," uncertainty. Information can confuse as well as enlighten.

A precise and often convenient way to describe uncertainty is in terms of probabilities—that is, by assigning a weight to each possible value of a quantity to reflect its relative likelihood of occurring. Let us consider a simplified example:

□ A potential buyer of a certain company's common stock is interested

in its earnings per share during the current year. In light of his present
information, he feels that only three possible values are worth considering:
$2.00 per share, $2.50 per share, and $3.00 per share. He also feels that
the third value is twice as likely to occur as the first, and just as likely
as the second. "Normalizing" these relative assessments so that the total
of the probabilities is 1.0, he obtains this result:

Value	Probability
$2.00	.2
$2.50	.4
$3.00	.4
	――
	1.0

Increasing the number of possible outcomes would complicate the assessment problem a little, but the basic idea remains the same.

Tomorrow he may read that his company has just landed a government
subcontract and revise his probabilities as follows:

Value	Probability
$2.00	.1
$2.50	.5
$3.00	.4
	――
	1.0

The next day a labor spokesman voices a strike threat, and the probabilities
change again:

Value	Probability
$2.00	.3
$2.50	.4
$3.00	.3
	――
	1.0

The first piece of news made this potential buyer both more optimistic
and more certain, and the second made him less certain and a trifle more
pessimistic. Both pieces of news represent information in that they affect
the set of probabilities he assigns to the various outcomes.

Conversely, if neither bit of news affects the probabilities (possibly because he knows someone in the company who has informed him about
both events *before* he assesses our original set of probabilities), neither is
"information" under the present definition. Like many other reports, they
are merely words and numbers or, to use a particularly descriptive term
coined by electrical engineers, "noise."

What is its value? Theorists use a lot of formulas in measuring the
economic value of information, but the basic idea is still straightforward.
By changing the probabilities associated wth a certan event, new informa-

tion causes decisions to change. Hopefully these decisions will be better—that is, more profitable. And it is the increased profitability of the decision made on the basis of the new information, as distinguished from the decision that would have been made without it, that gives the information its value.

For example, suppose a company is thinking of bringing out a new product. The initial investment required is $1,000,000. For simplicity, assume that there are only two possible outcomes:

1. If the product is "successful," then the discounted present value of the cash flows resulting from the new product will be $1,200,000.

2. If it is not "successful," then this value will be only $800,000.

Assume that the probability of the favorable outcome is .7 (in other words, 70%). Then the probability of an unfavorable outcome is .3. Thus the company has a .7 chance of making $1,200,000 and a .3 chance of making $800,000 on its $1,000,000 investment. It therefore can *expect* to make, as a *weighted average*,

$$.7(\$1,200,000) + .3(\$800,000) - \$1,000,000 = \$80,000.$$

On the other hand, if it does *not* introduce the new product, it can expect to make nothing.

Now suppose a new market survey (call it Study I) indicates that the probability of the new product being successful is only .4 (or 40%). The chance of its being unsuccessful would therefore be .6, and the company could expect to *lose* money, since

$$.4(\$1,200,000) + .6(\$800,000) - \$1,000,000 = -\$40,000.$$

The company would probably reverse its decision to introduce the product, on the basis of the new information. Hence the value of this new market study is the expected "saving" to the company of $40,000.

This approach may sound simplistic, until one understands its corollary: *information that doesn't affect a decision is valueless.* To illustrate:

□ Several years ago I developed a new sales-forecasting procedure for a manufacturer of women's sportswear. I did a rather good job, I thought. The average error in my estimate of total season sales only three months into the season was about half that of the old forecasting procedure. I was certainly providing information, in the sense that I could guarantee considerably more certainty than the old procedure could; yet the information I was providing turned out to be almost valueless. It was having virtually no impact on the *really important* decisions—fabric commitments, marketing decisions, and initial producton decisions that had actually been made much earlier in the season. My new information was all after the fact.

□ Another good illustration of this approach involves one of the most "valuable" pieces of information of all time. This information was received by Nathan Rothschild in England via special family courier (some say by messenger pigeon) from the Continent on the morning of June 20, 1815. Realizing that it would be several hours before the same news would reach his countrymen, Rothschild hurried to the London stock exchange and proceeded to sell consols (British State Bonds). He was only 38 years old, but already the possessor of an awesome reputation for financial wizardry, and his action therefore attracted immediate suspicion. The rumor began to spread: "Napoleon has beaten Wellington. Rothschild has learned of it." A selling panic commenced and soon reached epic proportions. Then, just before the official news from Waterloo arrived, Rothschild's agents began buying back enormous quantities of consols at bargain prices.

Some say that Rothschild doubled his fortune on that day. The point is that only somebody in his position would have been been able to capitalize on it. To a poor man, the same information would have been valueless.

How can one predict its value? So far, I have shown how one can establish the value of a given piece of information, such as that provided by market research or a consultant's report. The next problem is to predict the value of information *before* it is received. This, of course, generalizes to the problem of trying to determine the value of an *information system*. The logic loses a bit of its directness here, but in rough terms it simply says that the decision maker should take into account, in advance, the likelihood that the information to be obtained *will change* a proposed decision by its impact on the probabilities involved, and that he should calculate its value if it *does* change the decision. This often represents an enormous computational task, but one entirely within the capabilities of a computer.

Let's return to an earlier example. Suppose the company, after obtaining the result of Study I, is debating whether or not the expenditure of an additional $15,000 for further market research (call it Study II) is warranted. Also, suppose this new study will:

  □ Either confirm that the previous study was correct, and that the new product has only a .4 chance of success.

  □ Or reject the results of the previous study and affirm the accuracy of the original assessment that the product has a .7 chance of success.

Finally, suppose the company management now feels that the first outcome is twice as likely to be obtained as the second.

From the previous discussion it should be clear that if Study II indicates that the previous decision (*not* to introduce the new product) is still the correct one, the new information will have been valueless (i.e., worth $0.00) to the company. On the other hand, if Study II refutes Study I (that is, if it indicates that the product's chance of success *is* .7, after all), the company should once again decide to introduce the product. If the company *does* introduce the product, then, as we have seen, it can expect to make $80,000 on it. This figure therefore represents the expected discounted value that this outcome of Study II would have. Now the question is: Should the company put up the additional $15,000 for Study II?

Since the respective probabilities of the two alternative outcomes are .333 and .667, the expected value that Study II has *before* it is undertaken is

.667($0.00)+.333($80,000)=$26,667.

Study II is therefore worth more to the company than it would cost (only $15,000). Hence $15,000 would appear to be a reasonable amount to pay for the additional information it would provide.

I could have made this example more realistic by including a variety of other possible outcomes from Study II, but the basic procedure would stay the same. That is, for each possible outcome, determine:

□ What the decision should be if that outcome were to occur.

□ The expected value of the new information under that new decision.

□ The expected value of the new information under the previous decision.

Multiplying each of these values by the probabilities we originally assigned to the various outcomes and summing provides a measure of the potential value of the new information.

Summarizing, then, from this qualitative framework:

1. Information is something that reduces uncertainty, usually at a cost.

2. Information only has value in the context of a specific situation.

3. The amount a decision maker should be willing to pay for information depends on the likelihood that it will change his decision.

These insights are perhaps little different from those that good, hard-headed "common sense" might have dictated. Yet, in the absence of this quantitative framework for evaluating the potential of new information, the decision whether to buy it is often governed more by fear of the unknown than by a rational assessment of the costs and benefits.

Management has much to gain from this area of quantitative analysis, especially in clearer thinking and more accurate communication about *risk*, for this is what is ultimately in question here. Broadly speaking, it is safer and wiser to weigh risk in the scales of probability than in the scales of personal intuition.

RISK AND MOTIVE

Many management theorists believe that if a group of rational people are each given the same information about a decision problem, they will arrive independently at about the same decision. Anybody who has sat on a committee knows that this is not necessarily so.

A variety of reasons are usually advanced to explain divergence of opinion, and these generally fall into either of two categories:

1. Different people usually have different amounts of information about, or experience with, any given situation.

2. Different people have different, and often directly conflicting, goals.

The first reason is both acceptable and correctable. If two people have basically different levels of understanding about a problem, they can generally discuss away their differences. A subtler aspect is that sometimes they have different perceptions of the *uncertainty* in a problem—a circumstance which is often fostered by reporting schemes which, in an effort to be concise, rely on single point estimates or predictions of uncertain quantities. This often lulls managers into a false sense of precision —particularly those high up the communication ladder.

The second reason, on the other hand, has a faintly sinister ring, carrying as it does dark hints of power struggles. Decision theorists suggest, however, that it may just as likely be due to the fact that different people have different psychological attitudes toward risk taking. Most of us know people who are highly conservative in the face of a risky decision; bankers and accountants are familiar stereotypes for this type of attitude. At the opposite end of the scale are the "plungers"; marketing people tend to fit this stereotype.

Corporate decisions are frequently made by a group of individuals whose risk attitudes fall everywhere in the spectrum between these two extremes, and it should not be surprising that they disagree. I have recently been doing some research on decision processes associated with acquisitions and divestitures, where this phenomenon shows up quite clearly. This phenomenon also frequently lies at the root of friction between the headquarters of a diversified corporation and a recently acquired subsidiary. For example, one often hears such comments as these: "He doesn't understand. He's not a little company any more; he's a little part of a big company!"

Ralph O. Swalm has described actual situations where not only do different individuals within a company have different risk attitudes, but also each one tends to use the same risk attitude in making corporate decisions as in making personal decisions—and this virtually guarantees a variety of opinions.

Pinpointing the *source* of disagreement sometimes helps resolve it, but not always. What should be done if it doesn't? How should one go about reconciling disagreement? One way, of course, is to centralize all decision making in one person. But then, which person? Rather than choose one individual to reflect the "corporate" attitude toward risk, shouldn't a company's top management attempt instead to *define* in advance what that attitude will be? There is some evidence that this is already being done informally—for example, in such statements of corporate goals as "maximum growth consistent with prudent risk."

Finally, how does one go about evaluating individual decision-making capabilities? And how do we motivate individuals to have risk attitudes that are more consistent with the corporate one? Empirical evidence indicates that most individuals are more risk-averse than the companies they work for. Although stock options are one common device for encouraging individuals to accept more risky projects, most other reward structures within a corporation—primarily the promotion system—tend to do just the opposite.

Here management seems to have blundered its way into a conceptual framework that asks more questions than it answers. I don't think this is really true, of course; what the concept of risk aversion has accomplished really, is to bring into sharper focus a number of fundamental issues that already existed, to facilitate communication about them, and possibly to suggest avenues for further research by more traditional management theorists.

Final Word

The crucial point is that these questions have been raised, and their answers are currently being pursued, by *quantitative* people. The focus of these questions is communication, taken in its broadest sense: between different parts of an organization (the "systems approach" to organizational design), between an organization and its environment (the valuation of information) and between individuals participating in a decision process (the analysis of risk aversion). Because of their backgrounds in exact disciplines, and because the quantitative approach tends to focus on the basic *structure* of a problem rather than its situational uniqueness, they tend to think about these problems in precise terms and use precise techniques in analyzing them. The result, in many cases, is not just a new management tool but a new conceptual framework for management, a new way of thinking.

6. Better Decisions with Preference Theory

John S. Hammond III

Decision-making techniques can now be tailored to risk-taking attitudes. Thus preference theory, the means to this end, has great potential value for the decision maker who wishes to improve the consistency of his decisions. It is also of great importance to the top management group that wants decision makers down the line to have better common understanding of a desired corporate attitude toward risk taking.

What is your company's attitude toward taking risk? Is it clearly expressed to your managers? How do they incorporate this risk-taking attitude in their decision making?

If your company is like most, its risk-taking attitude is neither clearly understood nor adequately communicated. And in the absence of a clearly stated policy, it is unlikely that decisions made by managers at various levels will adequately reflect the desired corporate attitude. Even in those situations where the company's risk-taking policy is more clearly stated, the degree to which it is properly incorporated in decision making is usually far from the ideal.

In this article I will show that it is possible to make a precise statement about a person's attitude toward risk in the form of a utility or preference curve, and then to make direct use of the curve to incorporate this attitude in many important types of business decisions involving uncertainty. The terms "utility theory" and "preference theory" can be used synonymously to describe our subject matter. While the former is used more frequently in the literature, it is also used to describe another subject in economics; hence the term "preference theory" will be used here.

Decisions and Risks

Most formal analyses of business decisions involving uncertainty assume that every individual or every company has (or ought to have) the same attitude toward risk. The underlying assumption is that a decision maker will want to choose that course of action which has the highest expected value of profit. (The expected value or mathematical expectation is the weighted average of the possible results anticipated from a particular course of action, where the weights are the probabilities.) In other words, the analysis usually assumes that decision makers will want to "play the averages" on all deals, regardless of the potential negative consequences that might result. But in fact, as every experienced executive knows, very few businessmen take this attitude toward risk when they make important decisions.

You can convince yourself of this by answering the simple question: What is the maximum amount that you would be willing to commit your company to pay for a 50-50 chance at winning $500,000 or losing $100,000? If you are the sort who plays the averages, your answer is $200,000 (i.e., .50 × $500,000 − .50 × $100,000), the expected value of the venture. But if you are like most people, your answer is less than $200,000, and perhaps considerably less, reflecting quite properly your attitude toward risk.

What is lacking in practice, then, is a formal scheme for tailoring the decision-making technique to the risk-taking attitude of the decision maker. I will attempt to fill that void by showing how a decision maker's risk-taking attitude can be blended into a decision-tree analysis.

This article also should add new dimensions to earlier HBR articles on decision making under uncertainty. It extends the methodology described in John F. Magee's decision-tree articles[1] to allow explicit consideration of risk-taking attitudes in a decision-tree analysis. Its point of view contrasts with that expressed in Ralph O. Swalm's HBR article on utility theory,[2] which employs that approach to *explain* or *describe* behavior rather than (as I prefer) to *guide* behavior, enabling the decision maker to make better choices. More specifically, in this article:

1. I will review the kind of decision-tree analysis which is designed to maximize the mathematical expectation of profit in order to point out its shortcomings. To do this concretely, I will focus on a simplified case about an oil wildcatter. The case contains all the elements needed to illustrate the important points without undue complication. It will serve as our example throughout the article.

2. Next I will show how to determine a decision maker's preference curve (a graph summarizing his risk-taking attitude) and how to incorporate the results in a decision-tree analysis.

3. I will then discuss a few topics designed to improve the decision

1. "Decision Trees for Decision Making," HBR July-August 1964, p. 126; and "How to Use Decision Trees in Capital Investment," HBR September-October, 1964, p. 79.

2. "Utility Theory—Insights Into Risk Taking," HBR November-December 1966, p. 123.

maker's ability to determine his preference curve and to interpret the results of an analysis based on its use.

4. Finally, I will turn to another use of this approach—as a vehicle for communication among managers.

This article requires little previous knowledge on the part of the reader and no sophisticated mathematics. However, the approach does require the reader to examine, honestly and in depth, his own attitudes toward risk taking.

Before proceeding, let me point out that I am not the originator of the methodology which I am about to describe. F. P. Ramsey[3] and John Von Neumann[4] deserve credit for its origin; Leonard J. Savage,[5] Robert O. Schlaifer,[6] and many others deserve credit for its development.

Case of Petro Enterprises

Our case for discussion concerns Petro Enterprises, a fledgling organization founded to wildcat in the Texas oil fields. Petro has a nontransferable short-term option to drill on a certain plot of land. The option is the only business deal in which the firm is involved now or that it expects to consider between now and December 31, the time drilling would be completed if the option were exercised. Two recent dry holes elsewhere have reduced Petro's net liquid assets to $130,000, and William Snyder, president and principal stockholder, must decide whether Petro should exercise its option or allow it to expire. It will expire in two weeks if drilling is not commenced by then. Snyder has three possible choices:

1. Drill immediately.

2. Pay to have a seismic test run in the next few days, and then, depending on the result of the test, decide whether or not to drill.

3. Let the option expire.

Having described Snyder's possible choices, let me say something about their potential economic consequences. To conserve capital and maintain flexibility, Petro subcontracts all drilling and seismic tests; also, it immediately sells the rights to any oil discovered, instead of developing the oil fields itself. It can have the seismic test performed on short notice at overtime rates for a fixed fee of $30,000, and the well can be drilled for a

3. See *The Foundations of Mathematics and Other Logical Essays*, edited by R. B. Braithwaite (London, Routledge and Kegan Paul, Ltd., 1931).

4. *Theory of Games and Economic Behavior*, written with Oskar Morgenstern (Princeton, New Jersey, Princeton University Press, 1947).

5. *Foundations of Statistics* (New York, John Wiley and Sons, Inc., 1954).

6. *Introduction to Statistics for Business Decisions* (New York, McGraw-Hill Book Company, Inc., 1961) and *Analysis of Decisions Under Uncertainty* (New York, McGraw-Hill Book Company, Inc., 1967); for a more formal presentation. see R. Duncan Luce and Howard Raiffa, *Games and Decisions* (New York, John Wiley and Sons, Inc., 1957).

Exhibit I. Snyder's decision problem

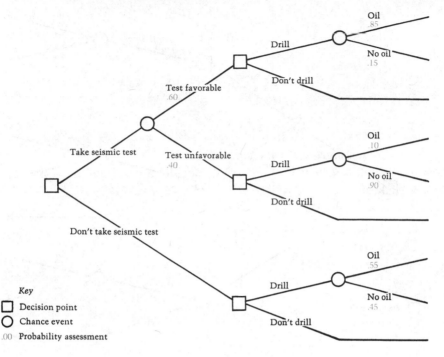

fixed fee of $100,000. A large oil company has promised that if Petro drills and discovers oil, it will purchase all of Petro's rights for a flat $400,000.

To complete the description, it is necessary to know the probabilities assigned to the various contingencies. The company's geologist has examined the geology in the region and states that there is a .55 probability that if a well is sunk, oil will be discovered. Data on the reliability of the seismic test indicate that if the test result is favorable, the probability of finding oil will increase to .85; but if the test result is unfavorable, it will fall to .10. The geologist has computed that there is a .60 probability the result will be favorable if a test is made. (There is a simple, but important, logical interrelationship between these probabilities, but I will not discuss it here; it is explained elsewhere.[7])

This decision problem involving uncertainty can be structured in the form of the decision tree shown in *Exhibit I*. The tree shows the probabilities, based on the judgment of the company geologist, for the various events; see the figures in gray on the event forks.

Expected Value Analysis

How would Snyder's problem be analyzed assuming that he is interested in "playing the averages" and maximizing profit—or, more precisely, that

7. Schlaifer, *Analysis of Decisions Under Uncertainty*, op. cit., Chapter 9.

Exhibit II. The decision diagram with cash flows

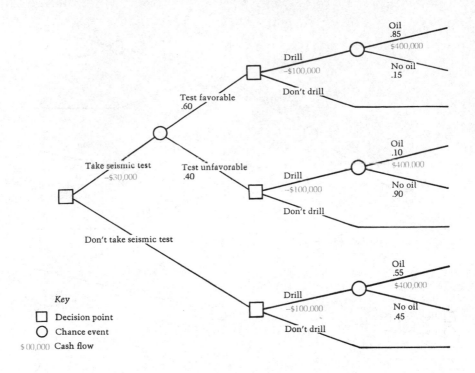

Key

☐ Decision point
◯ Chance event
$ 00,000 Cash flow

he wishes to maximize the mathematical expectation of his asset position (which is equivalent in this case to maximizing the mathematical expectation of profit)? These essential steps would be followed:

1. Determine the asset positions Petro Enterprises would have if it arrived at each of the nine end positions on the decision tree in *Exhibit I*.

2. Determine Petro's best strategy by working backward through the tree; that is, at each fork which represents a chance event (called an "event fork") compute the expected value, and at each fork which represents a choice of action (an "act fork") choose that act which has the highest expected value.

COMPUTING ASSET POSITIONS

Now let us turn to the numbers. Having diagrammed the decision problem, we can put the cash flow associated with each act and event on the diagram as is shown in gray in *Exhibit II*. For example, taking the seismic test costs $30,000, so an outflow of this amount is indicated by writing "—$30,000" by "Take seismic test." Similarly, the presence of oil results in an inflow of $400,000, so this figure appears by "Oil."

The nine end positions of the tree represent the terminals of nine possible sequences of acts and events. Corresponding to each is an asset position for Petro Enterprises. These asset positions can be computed by summing the

Exhibit III. Complete decision diagram showing Petro Enterprises' assets at each end position

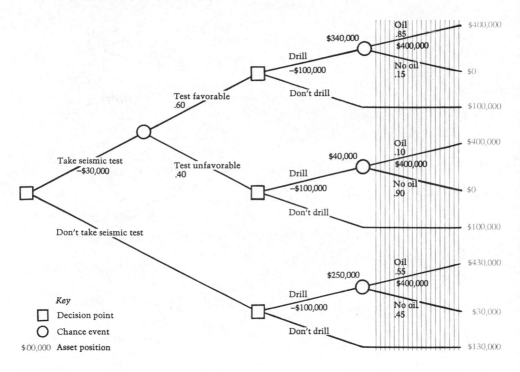

Key

☐ Decision point

○ Chance event

$00,000 Asset position

various cash flows from the origin of the diagram to each end position and adding the total to the firm's current asset position of $130,000. The results of these calculations are shown in gray at the nine end positions in *Exhibit III*. For instance, the uppermost of the nine end positions shows an asset position of $400,000. This is the sum of the receipts for the oil and the current asset position, minus the costs of taking the seismic test and drilling.

The economic quantity which the decision maker uses to describe the result of a particular path on his decision tree is called his *criterion*. In this case Snyder has chosen a criterion of net liquid assets, since his liquid asset position determines his ability to consider future deals. Other businessmen in other situations might well select earnings, net cash flow, or some other criterion. Obviously, the use of different criteria can lead to different decisions in some situations.

EXPECTATIONS AND CHOICES

The terminal forks in *Exhibit III* are event forks representing uncertainty about the results of drilling. At each terminal fork we proceed by computing the expected value of the firm's asset position, which is simply the weighted average of the numbers at the end positions emanating from the

Exhibit IV. First reduction of the decision diagram

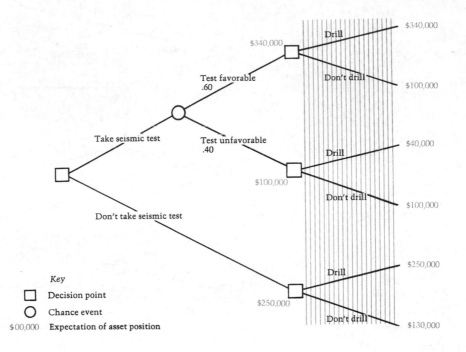

Key

□ Decision point

○ Chance event

$00,000 Expectation of asset position

fork. Taking the topmost terminal fork again for illustration, the expected value is $340,000 (i.e., .85 × $400,000 + .15 × $0).

An analysis based on mathematical expectation assumes that Snyder would accept a $340,000 sure asset position in exchange for a .85 chance of assets of $400,000 plus a .15 chance of $0 in assets, and vice versa. In other words, the asset position and the chance are equivalent. Later I shall discuss the realism of this assumption, but for the moment we will go along with it because it allows us to replace the event fork by its mathematical expectation. As a matter of fact, since each terminal event fork is assumed to be equivalent to its mathematical expectation, we can discard the terminal set of forks and replace them by their mathematical expectations. We are left with the reduced diagram shown in *Exhibit IV.*

Now the terminal forks are act forks where Snyder's choice is between drilling and not drilling. If he is maximizing mathematical expectation, his choice is easy. He simply chooses the act with the highest expected value. Following a favorable seismic test result, for example, the choice is between drilling, with a mathematical expectation of $340,000, and not drilling, with a mathematical expectation of $100,000. Obviously, Snyder should decide to drill. Hence if he were to arrive at the position of the diagram following a favorable seismic test result, we know he would

Exhibit V. *Further reductions of the decision diagram*

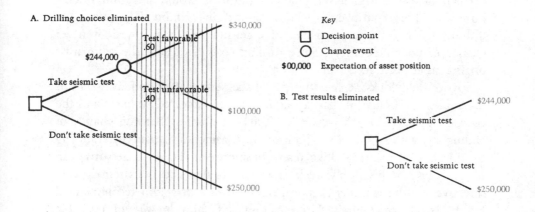

A. Drilling choices eliminated

Take seismic test

$244,000

Test favorable
.60
$340,000

Test unfavorable
.40
$100,000

Don't take seismic test

$250,000

Key

Decision point

Chance event

$00,000 Expectation of asset position

B. Test results eliminated

Take seismic test
$244,000

Don't take seismic test
$250,000

choose to drill and thus would look forward to an asset position whose expected value is $340,000. It follows that the fork is equivalent to an expected value of $340,000, so we put $340,000 at the base of the act fork. Once the results of similar choices have been placed at the base of each of the terminal act forks in *Exhibit IV*, we can replace each act fork by its equivalent mathematical expectation, as shown in *Exhibit V-A*.

Now we are faced with the reduction of the event fork representing the result of the test. The procedure is the same as with any event fork; we take the mathematical expectation of the numbers at the end positions—in this case, $244,000 (i.e., .60 × $340,000 + .40 × $100,000).

After replacing the event fork by the expected value of its end positions, we are left with the single act fork in *Exhibit V-B*. The resultant act choice is easy; since $250,000 is greater than $244,000, Synder should not have his firm take the seismic test. Instead, he should drill immediately.

Actually it is not necessary to redraw the tree after each reduction, as was done for illustrative purposes in *Exhibits IV* and *V*. We can simply write the appropriate mathematical expectation at the base of each event or act fork and then cross out the branch or branches not chosen.

DOES IT MAKE SENSE?

Let us now speculate on how Snyder might react to these results. Surely he is pleased that the expected value of his asset position following immediate drilling is $250,000—much higher than doing nothing and staying with a sure asset position of $130,000. Also, he would be very pleased if he struck oil and ended up with $430,000 in assets. However, he is quite disturbed by the fact that there is a .45 chance that he will end up with only $30,000 in assets, which for practical purposes would put him out of business. (This contingency is summarized in *Exhibit III*, where the drilling action following omission of a seismic test is followed by a .45 chance of no oil discovery. Since drilling costs $100,000, the company's original asset position is reduced by that amount.)

Snyder then looks at the strategy "Take seismic test and drill only if favorable." Although it has a slightly lower expected value than the chosen option ($244,000 versus $250,000), he notes that the chance of ending up with a low asset position is considerably reduced, from .45 to .09 (i.e., .60 × .15). Like many businessmen, he is conservative. In fact, because of his firm's weak financial position, he is extremely conservative, and he is rather skeptical of the course of action recommended by this mode of analysis. His intuition tells him he *should* take the seismic test, but this decision analysis tells him he is wrong.

Snyder, like many businessmen, is caught in a dilemma. Because uncertainty is a major factor in his decision, he is aware of the need to recognize it explicitly in his analysis; and he has, quite properly, structured his analysis with a tree. He feels he has correctly assessed the economic consequences of various contingencies. He also feels that the probabilities used in his analysis reflect his best judgment of the chances that the events will actually occur. Yet his intuition seems to be telling him that the conclusion of the analysis just isn't for *him*.

QUESTIONABLE ALTERNATIVES

Later, I will show how preference theory can help Snyder out of his dilemma. It is worth noting first, however, that Synder is not alone in his doubts about using a mode of analysis designed to maximize mathematical expectation. Many businessmen find that such an approach does such a poor job of reflecting their attitude toward risk that they resort to other analytical approaches. Unfortunately, their alternatives are equally questionable in many situations.

For example, many people flatly refuse to consider uncertainty explicitly in their analyses. Instead they make padded or "conservative" estimates of the unknown quantities that will affect the success or failure of the venture being analyzed. They then pretend that the world will be like their estimates and, in essence, make their decision under assumed certainty. This sweeps uncertainty, an important dimension of the problem, under the rug and, in most cases, is clearly an unsatisfactory approach.

An extreme example of this behavior is "worst case" analysis. To be "conservative," some companies will not market a new product unless it can be demonstrated that it will be profitable under the worst foreseeable combination of circumstances: highest production costs, highest distribution costs, greatest competition, lowest demand in each of the next few years, and so forth. They do a profitability calculation, assuming that all costs and revenues have their worst possible values. Then if the resultant calculation shows a profit, they go ahead; if not, the venture is dropped.

Closer examination often shows that the chance of all variables simultaneously taking on their worst values is extremely small—perhaps a thousand to one or even a million to one! As a result only riskless (and often low-yield) ventures are accepted, whereas ventures that have a small chance of unprofitability, but a high chance of great profitability, are dropped. For a small and acceptable amount of additional risk, much greater profitability would result; but the padded estimate approach will never show this. Only with explicit recognition of uncertainty and of one's attitude toward risk can the right combination of risk and return be found.

Other businessmen recognize the need to consider uncertainty in their analyses, but they take account of their conservatism by increasing the probabilities of those events that can lead to unfavorable consequences. For example, in a decision-tree analysis of a new product venture, the probabilities assigned to unfavorable costs, unfavorable levels of competition, unfavorable demand levels, and so forth, will be arbitrarily increased. The resultant probability does not represent the decision maker's best judgment on the chance that the event will occur; it is distorted by his attitude toward risk. Unless the decision maker in such a case has some magically consistent way of adjusting his probabilities, this "distorted" approach is also unsatisfactory, for there is no assurance that the resultant analysis properly reflects the degree of conservatism desired by the decision maker.

Another approach some companies use to take risk into account starts with the decision-tree structure. However, instead of using the analytical technique just described, the analysts determine the probability distribution of outcomes associated with various complete descriptions of action, called "strategies," described on the tree. Using Snyder's oil drilling problem as an example, you can see that the strategy "Don't take the seismic test—drill immediately" has a .55 chance of making $300,000 and a .45 chance of losing $100,000. This is compared with the strategy "Take seismic test—if it is favorable, drill, and if not, don't drill" which has a probability of .40 of losing $30,000, a probability of .09 (i.e., .60 × .15) of losing $130,000 and a probability of .51 (i.e., .60 × .85) of making $270,000, and with other possible strategies.

The distribution of outcomes associated with the strategies are then compared and, according to some criterion, a choice is made. For example, it may be decided that the second strategy is preferable because there is a much smaller chance of losing a large sum of money. Or the first strategy may be preferable because there is less chance of losing money and the amount to be gained is larger.

The Snyder case is extremely simplified; for each strategy there are only a few possible outcomes. In more realistic cases the number of strategies to be compared usually becomes extremely large, as does the number of possible outcomes. In these cases decisions are sometimes made on the basis of comparison of the expected value and variance of the various distributions of profit, of the expected value and coefficient of variation (the coefficient of variation is the square root of the variance divided by the expected value), or of the probability distributions of those outcomes corresponding to a loss, or other criteria.

Major difficulties arise because of the very large number of alternatives to be compared in most situations. Other difficulties come when there are alternatives with conflicting characteristics. For example, using the first of the criteria just mentioned, one would like to choose the strategy with the largest expected value and the smallest variance.

However, very seldom does one find an alternative that simultaneously has both characteristics. Therefore some companies decide on a maximum acceptable variance and then select that course of action with the highest expected value. The danger in doing this is that an alternative with a much higher expected value and a variance only slightly above the limit may be passed up—an alternative that on reflection may be preferable to others. As a matter of fact, it is even possible to find two alternatives with the same expected value and the same variance that have different intuitive attractiveness to the decision maker.

This catalog of ways that businessmen deal with risk is by no means exhaustive. The main point is this: although there are clearly times when some of the described techniques will work satisfactorily, there are many situations, especially ones involving complicated decisions, where the methods are likely to take improper account of the decision maker's risk-taking attitude.

Fresh Approach

Now let us consider an approach that does *not* require the business decision maker to play the long-run averages if he does not want to. This approach begins with an examination of his basic attitude.

DEFINING RISK ATTITUDE

If the decision maker is not a player of long-run averages, we must replace the event forks on his decision tree by numbers *other* than mathematical expectations. The new numbers must simultaneously take three things into account: probabilities, economic consequences, and an attitude toward risk taking that is different from playing the long-run averages. For example:

Let us go back to *Exhibit III*, where the top terminal event fork has a mathematical expectation of $340,000. This is the minimum sure asset position which a player of long-run averages would be willing to accept in place of the gamble represented by the fork. If he were more conservative, however, the fork would be "worth" less than $340,000 to him. The exact amount can only be decided by the decision maker, since it is his attitude toward risk that we wish to reflect in the analysis.

Just what do I mean by "worth," and how is it determined? Let us tackle both questions together. Suppose we ask Snyder the following questions regarding the event fork under discussion:

"Imagine you have committed your firm to drill on land where you believe there is a .85 chance of striking oil. If oil is struck, your firm's asset position will increase to a sure $400,000; whereas if you get a dry hole, you will be left with nothing (zero assets).

"Imagine further that a wealthy investor is interested in paying you cash for the rights to any oil which may be discovered, before either of you learn the results of the drilling. In other words, he'll take over the risk of the drilling and the rewards, too, if there are any. You'll be free of the risk and keep the amount he pays you for your rights. If he offers to buy your rights for an amount that will increase your assets to $150,000, will you sell out?"

Snyder's reply is an emphatic *no!* Thus he has told us that, as far as he is concerned, $150,000 in hand is less valuable than a .85 chance of assets of $400,000 and a .15 chance of nothing. If he is offered assets of only $150,000, in other words, he would rather take his chances with drilling.

Next we ask Snyder if he will sell out for $250,000 of assets, and his answer is *yes*. We now know that he prefers a sure $250,000 to running the risk of proceeding with drilling—in spite of the fact that the venture has an expected value equivalent to $340,000 of assets.

We now ask a third question: "What if there is only one potential bidder and his maximum offer is equivalent to only $225,000 in assets to you? Will you still sell out?" Snyder thinks a bit and answers *yes*.

Snyder's answers to our three questions tell us that the gamble represented by the event fork is "worth" somewhere between $150,000 and $225,000 in sure assets to him, where the word "worth" is used in a special sense. It means the rock bottom asset position that Snyder would accept in exchange for the risky outcome of drilling. In other words, there should be some amount which, if offered to him, would make him indifferent as to whether he should go ahead with the venture or sell out. If he were offered just a few dollars more, he would sell out; if he were offered just a few dollars less, he would prefer to take the risk of drilling.

We refer to this amount or "worth" as Snyder's *certainty equivalent* for the event fork. This certainty equivalent is a precise measure of his attitude toward risk in this particular situation. It should be obvious that the lower his certainty equivalent, the more conservative he is, and vice versa.

By asking Snyder just a few more questions, similar to the ones already asked, we should be able to zero in quickly on his certainty equivalent. Once he understands the concept being applied here, we should be able to ask for his certainty equivalent in a single question, rather than in a series of questions.

PRACTICAL APPLICATION

Thus, to take the decision maker's attitude toward risk into account, we must find for each event fork a certain (sure) amount that is equivalent in the decision maker's mind to running the risk represented by the event fork. This certain amount, his certainty equivalent for the event fork, is measured in units of the decision maker's criterion and can be used to replace the event fork in a decision diagram. So far we have used mathematical expectations as certainty equivalents.

One way in which the analyst can obtain the decision maker's certainty equivalents for event forks is to ask the decision maker to supply them fork by fork as the analyst works backwards through the tree. While this is relatively easy in decision problems as simple as the Petro Enterprises example, it would be out of the question in more realistic problems. There are two reasons for this: (1) In more realistic problems the number of event forks is so large that the process would become hopelessly time consuming; (2) event forks with many branches would likely be encountered, and it is difficult to think sensibly about certainty equivalents for such complicated uncertainties.

Using Preference Curves

The answers to the problems just mentioned lie in the use of a preference curve. This curve is a complete summary of the decision maker's attitude toward risk over the range required to solve a particular business problem. The curve can be used to determine the certainty equivalents for the event forks in a problem (including those forks with many branches) in a straightforward, mechanical way. In fact, we will see that it is possible

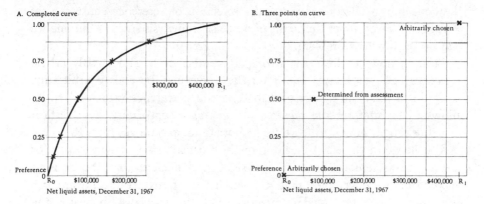

Exhibit VI. *Snyder's preference curve*

A. Completed curve

1.00
0.75
$300,000 $400,000 R_1
0.50
0.25
Preference
0
R_0 $100,000 $200,000
Net liquid assets, December 31, 1967

B. Three points on curve

1.00
Arbitrarily chosen
0.75
0.50
Determined from assessment
0.25
Preference Arbitrarily chosen
0
R_0 $100,000 $200,000 $300,000 $400,000 R_1
Net liquid assets, December 31, 1967

to use preference values, derived from the decision maker's preference curve, as "proxies" for certainty equivalents in an analysis using decision trees. Fortunately, the decision maker's preference curve can be determined by finding his certainty equivalents for just a few very simple two-branch gambles.

Let us now examine the characteristics of preference curves and the means of obtaining them. Snyder's preference curve (*Exhibit VI-A*) will serve as an example.

SALIENT CHARACTERISTICS

The horizontal axis displays the consequences of the decisions, measured in units of the decision maker's criterion on a certain date. In Snyder's case the units are net liquid assets on December 31. For other decision makers in other situations they might be earnings or net cash flow for the period ending on a particular date or something else.

One of the most important things to notice about the horizontal axis is the range that it covers. Since the curve is to be used to analyze his drilling decision problem, it must (and does) cover the range of consequences possible in the problem, $0 to $430,000. More generally, a *preference curve must accurately reflect the decision maker's attitude toward risk over a range of consequences encompassing at least the worst and best results that can arise in a given problem.* Of course, it is all right (and occasionally advantageous) to measure the attitude over a range *greater* than that needed, but it is not all right to cover a shorter range. (The need to make sure that the diagram is complete before choosing the range will be discussed later.)

The end points of the range have special status, which is signified by calling them the *reference consequences*. The symbol R_0 has been assigned to represent the lower reference consequence, and R_1 represents the upper reference consequence. In Snyder's case, R_0 must be less than or equal to $0, and R_1 must be greater than or equal to $430,000. Provided they encompass all consequences, the selection of reference consequences should in no way affect the result of a decision analysis such as the one we will do on Snyder's problem.

Turning now to the vertical axis, as readers of Swalm's HBR article (cited earlier) know, two points on the curve may be chosen arbitrarily. Assigning a preference value of 0 to R_0 and a preference value of 1 to R_1 allows us to interpret the preference index as a probability. The vertical axis thus ranges from 0 to 1, while the horizontal axis ranges from R_0 to R_1.

Knowledge of the exact meaning of the vertical axis is not necessary for use of the preference curve in analysis. It is sufficient that the decision maker simply understands that it is an index of his attitude toward risk and knows how it is used in practice. For the specialist, however, the following technical note may be useful:

A preference $P(C)$ assigned to consequence C means that the decision maker is indifferent between having an amount C for certain or having a chance $P(C)$ of achieving R_1 and a chance $1 - P(C)$ of achieving R_0. Thus in *Exhibit* VI-A, for example, Snyder has indicated that he is indifferent between achieving an asset position of $100,000 for certain or having a .60 chance of getting $430,000 and a .40 chance of ending up with nothing, since the curve passes through the point ($100,000, 0.6).

OBTAINING THE CURVE

The process of obtaining the decision maker's preference curve, called "assessment," consists of two stages: (1) the assessment of a "preliminary" curve, and then (2) the verification and correction of that curve (that is, checking its behavioral implications to see if it truly reflects the decision maker's risk-taking attitude).

It is not the purpose of this article to present an exhaustive discussion of ways to assess preference curves; there are many ways, and each has advantages and disadvantages. The method to be described has been selected because it is very easily understandable (though the reader should be warned that in practice it often results in irregular-shaped preliminary curves that require much correction in the process of verification). This method consists of obtaining points on the decision maker's curve by asking for his certainty equivalents for a series of simple 50-50 gambles, and then drawing a smooth curve through the points. Let us focus on the details by imagining that we are obtaining Snyder's curve.

To begin, suppose that Snyder, like most businessmen, has never heard of a certainty equivalent. Since it plays a pivotal role in what follows, an essential first step is to make sure he understands exactly what we mean by the term. Once the concept is understood, we can proceed to get his preliminary curve.

Assessing the preliminary curve: Since we have already assigned preference values of 0 and 1 to the two reference consequences, we have two points on Snyder's curve. To obtain the third, we ask for Snyder's certainty equivalent for a 50-50 chance of assets of $0 or $430,000. Let us suppose that Snyder thinks carefully about the question and finally answers $72,000. Since this is the first certainty equivalent we have obtained, we will call it CE_1.

Snyder's conservatism is already quite apparent. If he were an "averages player," his response would have been the mathematical expectation of the gamble: $215,000 (i.e., $.50 \times \$430,000 + .50 \times \$0$). But since he is conservative, his response is $72,000. We call the difference between the mathematical expectation for a gamble and a decision maker's certainty equivalent the *risk premium*; in this case the risk premium, $143,000, is substantial.

To obtain the preference corresponding to $72,000, we make use of the following principle: the preference of a gamble is the mathematical expectation of preferences corresponding to the consequences of the gamble. Thus:

Preference of $CE_1 = .50 \times$ preference of $0 + .50 \times$ preference of $430,000 = .50 \times 0 + .50 \times 1 = .50$.

We now have three points on Snyder's preference curve: the two arbitrarily chosen points and a third which we have just inferred from his answer to our question. Let us plot these as shown in *Exhibit VI-B.*

We obtain another point by asking him a similar question involving the third point on the curve and one of the reference consequences, such as "What certain asset position in dollars would make you indifferent between a 50-50 chance at asset positions of $72,000 or $430,000?"

Suppose he replies that his certainty equivalent is $163,000. Then, using the same principle, we can determine the preference corresponding to $163,000 as follows:

Preference of $CE_2 = .50 \times$ preference of $72,000 + .50 \times$ preference of $430,000 = .50 \times .50 + .50 \times 1 = .75$.

We might ask a similar question about a 50-50 chance at asset positions of $0 or $72,000. Suppose Snyder's reply is $28,000, which can be denoted as CE_3. His preference for $28,000 is .25 (i.e., $.50 \times 0 + .50 \times .50$).

We would continue in this manner until we obtained a sufficient number of points through which we could draw a smooth curve (*Exhibit VI-A*).

SUMMARY OF PROCEDURE

By now the pattern must be clear, so let me tie it together:

1. We first selected reference consequences R_1 and R_0 encompassing the

best and worst consequences that could arise in the decision problem. We arbitrarily assigned a preference value of 1 to R_1 and of 0 to R_0 and plotted them as the first two points on our preference curve.

2. Next we asked the decision maker a series of questions about his certainty equivalents for 50-50 gambles involving various consequences in the range between R_1 and R_0. We started by asking for his certainty equivalent for a 50-50 chance at the extreme case, $430,000 or $0 (i.e., the two reference consequences, R_0 and R_1). We determined that the preference corresponding to this certainty equivalent was .50 and plotted this point on the graph. Then we obtained the certainty equivalents for two more gambles, CE_2, having a preference of .75, and CE_3, having a preference of .25, and plotted these points on our graph.

3. We started with only one pair of points on our curve, R_0 and R_1, and assessed CE_1. Next, we used the two new pairs of points generated by the assessment of CE_1 (i.e., R_1 and CE_1, and R_0 and CE_1) to assess CE_2 and CE_3. Now, CE_2 and CE_3 gave us *five* new pairs of points (R_1 and CE_2, R_1 and CE_3, R_0 and CE_2, R_0 and CE_3, and CE_2 and CE_3) which we could have used to assess five more certainty equivalents; and these in turn would have generated a large number of possibilities for more assessments. This "boot-strapping" process would end quickly, however, for soon we would have enough points through which to draw a smooth curve, as is done in *Exhibit* VI-A.

VERIFICATION OF CURVE

Before using the preference curve, it is imperative to make consistency checks to see that it correctly reflects the decision maker's attitude. If it is to be useful, it must correctly represent his attitude toward risk for *all* gambles in the range between the reference consequences. If it does not do this, inconsistencies exist. Inconsistencies are best illustrated by example, so let us return to Snyder.

Using his preference curve (*Exhibit* VI-A), we would determine his certainty equivalent for a 50-50 chance at assets of $100,000 or $350,000. First we compute the preference of the gamble:

.50 × preference for $100,000 + .50 × preference for $350,000 = .50 × .60 + .50 × .95 = .775.

We then read the certainty equivalent corresponding to .775 from the preference curve; it is $180,000.

Now suppose we ask Snyder to assess his certainty equivalent for the same gamble, and his reply is $210,000. Then clearly the attitude toward risk implied by his preference curve is inconsistent with that expressed by the assessment just described. Something has to give; if the problem is due to improper smoothing of the curve, the solution is easy. If not, either part of the preference curve must be reassessed or the new assessment does not truly reflect Snyder's attitude.

As a general rule, such checks for inconsistency should be made after the first plot of a preference curve is done; and, if necessary, changes and additional checks should be made until the decision maker is confident that the curve is a correct reflection of his attitude toward risk. Only then is it appropriate to make some of the practical uses of the curve that will be described in a later section of this article. (At a subsequent point we will also look at other suggestions for making consistency checks.)

Some argue that the inconsistencies which often result in the assessment of preference curves are a reason for avoiding their use. On the contrary, the fact that the decision makers are inconsistent in their attitudes toward risk is one of the strongest reasons for the use of preference theory. The process of assessment points up these inconsistencies and permits their removal—*before* they can adversely affect a decision.

BENEFITS ACHIEVED

In principle, the assessment procedure is extremely easy; but, in practice, especially the first few times it is tried, it is extremely difficult. Strangely enough, the reason for the difficulty is the stark simplicity of the process. And the simplicity is, in turn, the source of the power of the technique. By isolating attitude toward risk from the other aspects of a complex decision problem and eliciting the attitude by simple questions, we force the decision maker to be far more explicit about his attitude than he has ever been. Formerly he could take refuge in the complexity of a decision; attitude toward risk was muddled in with the risk itself and all the other complexities. The painful soul searching required to answer the question, "*Exactly* how big a risk taker am I?" was avoided. Now, however, the attitude is forced out in the open.

A common misconception (or perhaps it is an escape) is that the certainty equivalents can be treated as "estimates." Because the decision maker has never been faced with such questions, he thinks it is impossible to answer them exactly. But he can and he must; he makes difficult and precise quantitative decisions all the time on his job, and he can learn to make the decisions described here, too. A certainty equivalent of "about $75,000" is as inappropriate as writing a check for "about $100"!

If one wishes to make rational decisions consistent with his attitude toward risk, one must make the attitude precise. These "small" decisions are the stuff of which the larger decision under analysis is made; if they are made vaguely or carelessly, the quality of the larger decision will be affected. Even if one were not planning to make explicit use of the resultant preference curve in a formal analysis (as we are about to do here), one's intuitive decision-making powers would be enhanced by the better self-awareness that results from this process.

Analysis with Preferences

To get the certainty equivalent of an event fork in a decision diagram, we use the following procedure, based on a principle of preference theory:

1. *Convert the consequences of the gamble to their corresponding preferences.*

2. *Compute the mathematical expectation of these preferences.* The resultant number is the preference for the event fork.

3. *Go to the preference curve and find the criterion value corresponding to the preference of the fork.* This value is the certainty equivalent of the gamble.

The procedure can be illustrated with the event fork in the upper right corner of *Exhibit VII:*

1. From the preference curve in *Exhibit VI-A* we know that the preference of $400,000 is .98, and the preference of $0 is 0.

2. The mathematical expectation of these preferences is .83 (i.e., .98 × .85 + 0 × .15).

3. Returning to the preference curve, we see that the certainty equivalent of the fork is $215,000, considerably less than the mathematical expectation of $340,000 computed earlier. We can use this certainty equivalent to continue the analysis by moving back to the drilling act fork; since $215,000 is greater than $100,000, the act chosen would be to drill.

We could complete the analysis in this manner, but it can be done more simply. After obtaining the preferences of the event forks, it is unnecessary to convert to certainty equivalents before making the act choices. Instead, the same results can be obtained if the act choices are made to maximize preference.

Thus, use of the preference curve with decision trees requires only a simple modification of the procedures described earlier for maximizing mathematical expectations. The basic principle is this: *if the decision maker wishes to make the best decision consistent with his attiude toward risk, he must choose that course of action which has the highest preference.* To implement the principle, the following procedure should be followed:

1. *Convert all of the end positions of the decision diagram into preferences,* as highlighted in gray in *Exhibit VII.* For example, at the uppermost end position, the preference of $400,000 is .98 (taken from the preference curve in *Exhibit VI-A*).

Exhibit VII. *Analysis using preferences*

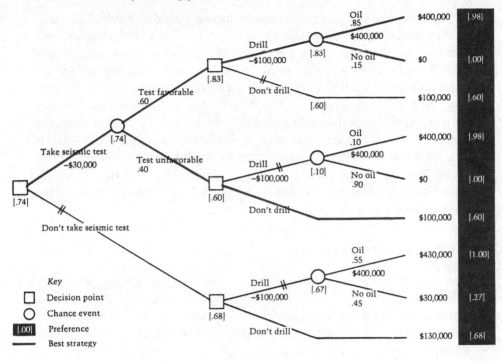

2. *To find the decision maker's preference for an event fork, take the mathematical expectation of the preference values at the end position of the fork.* In other words, instead of multiplying the dollar values by probabilities, as in a decision-tree analysis using expected value, multiply the preferences by the probabilities. Thus at each event fork take a weighted average of the preferences, where the weights are the probabilities. For example, at the uppermost event fork representing "Oil-No oil," the preference is .83 (i.e., .85 × .98 + .15 × 0). Write the preference in brackets at the base of the fork, as in *Exhibit VII.*

3. *At each act fork, choose that act with the highest preference.* For example, at the uppermost decision fork in *Exhibit VII*, the choice is between "Drill" with a preference of .83 and "Don't drill" with a preference of .60, so the choice is to drill. Write the preference of the act chosen, .83, in brackets at the base of the fork and cross off the act not chosen (as shown by the double bar in *Exhibit VII*).

4. *Continue backwards through the tree, repeating steps 2 and 3 until the base of the tree is reached.* For instance, the preference of the decision to take the seismic test is .74 (i.e., .60 × .83 + .40 × .60), while the preference of the decision not to take the test is .68.

The analysis using preference theory therefore indicates that Snyder's best strategy is to take the test and, if it gives a favorable result, drill; if an unfavorable result, don't drill.

How does the foregoing conclusion compare with that reached by maximizing mathematical expectations? As might be expected, the two answers are sharply different; the mathematical expectation approach tells Snyder to drill immediately and thus to run a 45% chance of ending up with an asset position of $30,000. The preference theory approach, which takes into account Snyder's conservatism, tells him to take the seismic test first and drill only if it is favorable, with a mere 9% chance at a low asset position (in this case, $0). The seismic test, then, is a form of "insurance policy" which is a good buy for a man as conservative as Snyder but not worth its price to an "averages player." Thus we have a clear example of the old saying that "one man's meat is another man's poison"; preference theory allows each to have his meat.

ADDED INTERPRETATIONS

You may wonder if any interpretation can be given to the preference value assigned to the best strategy (in Snyder's case, .74). As has been pointed out elsewhere, a preference value is not an index of desirability in any absolute sense; we cannot say that a strategy with a value of .74, for example, is twice as attractive as a strategy with a value of .37, any more than we can say that 74°F is twice as hot as 37°F.

Yet certain interpretations can be made which are occasionally useful in the decision-making process.

Worth of option: If the decision maker will read from his preference curve the criterion value corresponding to the preference of his best strategy, he will know his certainty equivalent for the entire decision tree. In other words, he will be indifferent between receiving the certainty equivalent amount for sure and taking a chance at following the best strategy. In Snyder's case, the certainty equivalent corresponding to his best strategy is found by locating on *Exhibit VI-A* the asset position corresponding to .74 on his preference curve. That position is $160,000, which means that Snyder is indifferent between a sure $160,000 in assets and going ahead with the best strategy.

We could go a step further and use this result to get an implicit minimum selling price for the option, if it were transferable. We know that Petro's current asset position is $130,000; this implies that Synder should be willing to consider any offer for his option to drill that is greater than $30,000 (i.e., $160,000 − $130,000).

NEED FOR COMPLETE DIAGRAM

In the extremely simple case we have been studying, the only business deal under consideration concerns the option. Our diagram correctly summarizes the possible acts and uncertainties necessary to deal with the problem; that is, everything that might possibly affect net liquid assets on December 31.

What if things were more complicated? For example, suppose there were several other deals under consideration (e.g., the purchase of other options) and perhaps other uncertainties (e.g., a pending lawsuit regarding rights to oil in another pool) that might be resolved before the completion of drilling on the land under option? Each of these uncertainties and deals has potential impact on the value of Snyder's criterion on December 31. How would these complications change our analysis?

The temptation is to treat each as a separate problem. In fact, the potential asset positions and risks associated with one package of deals may be sharply different from those of another combination. For example, exercising some risky option *by itself* may seem worthwhile, and the same might hold true of another option *by itself*. But the two options *together* may entail a considerable risk of very negative consequences, an exposure the company may not wish to take.

Therefore, it is necessary in theory to include in the diagram all decisions and uncertainties that can have a significant effect on the decision maker's criterion in the time period under analysis. Preference theory applied with a decision-tree analysis will then result in that combination of decisions which is most consistent with the company's (or decision maker's) attitude toward risk.

While a complete diagram is necessary theoretically, in most situations it is impossible to be so comprehensive without unduly complicating the analysis. The tree would become hopelessly large. Thus, as is the case in many quantitative analyses, real art and skill are required to capture just enough detail for the analysis to be useful.

An impression may have been created that every time a new decision is faced a new preference curve must be assessed. This is not necessarily so. Suppose, for example, we have assessed a curve that applies to net liquid assets on June 1, and we use it to make a group of decisions that will affect assets on that date. Then, a few weeks later we find ourselves faced with an important and unanticipated new decision, which will also affect assets on that date. Suppose the reference consequences on the old curve were $R_0 = -\$500,000$ and $R_1 = \$2,000,000$. Then, if the results of the earlier decisions *and* the new decision together will fall within this range, and there have been no essential changes in the decision maker's attitude toward risk, the earlier preference curve can be used. On the other hand, if the reference consequences no longer encompass the best and worst consequences, a new curve must of course be assessed.

The main point is this: it is often advantageous to place the reference consequences a bit further apart than necessary to encompass the consequences of a particular decision problem. Any unanticipated new

Exhibit VIII. Three commonly observed types of preference curves

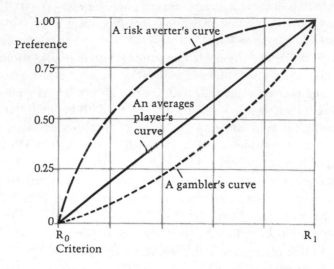

decision can then be analyzed without having to obtain a new curve. The reference consequences should not be too broadly spaced, however, for then the values of real interest will be such a small portion of the curve that they cannot be assessed or read with the accuracy needed to analyze the problem.

Commonly Observed Curves

Although a preference curve is a highly subjective expression of a decision maker's attitude, certain types of curves are observed frequently enough to warrant being classified. Awareness of these various types will help the businessman to verify his own curve, as well as understand the significance of other persons' curves. Three curves corresponding to three different risk-taking attitudes are illustrated in *Exhibit VIII*. Let me comment on them briefly:

1. *Risk averter*—The conservative man's curve is characterized by the fact that it is concave as viewed from below. This is equivalent to saying that the decision maker has a positive risk premium for all gambles in the range covered by the curve. (Recall that the risk premium is defined as the mathematical expectation of the gamble less the certainty equivalent of the gamble.) Curves showing varying degrees of risk aversion are the type most commonly observed in practice; most of us are conservative to a degree. The executive who is in this class will want to be sure that his curve is concave at all points as viewed from below.

2. *Averages player*—This person's curve is the straight line in *Exhibit VIII*. The risk premiums are 0 for all gambles in the range covered, which

means that he wishes to play the long-run averages. A linear preference curve (or a preference curve that is for all practical purposes linear) is frequently observed when a man makes a decision whose consequences are small compared to the total asset position of the company, as is frequently the case in large corporations.

The person with a linear preference curve is the person for whom analysis by mathematical expectation was designed. For this reason, he has no need at all to use a preference curve in his analysis.

If a decision maker faces a decision whose consequences are small compared to the total asset position, the assessment of a preference curve may possibly be avoided. If he feels that his certainty equivalent for every gamble in the range covered by the decision is (for practical purposes) equal to its mathematical expectation, then he can proceed directly to an expected value analysis.

3. *Gambler*—This man is the rarest of the three types. He has a preference curve that is convex when viewed from below and is characterized by a negative risk premium for all gambles. He is, in effect, willing to pay a premium above the mathematical expectation for the "thrill" of gambling or for other reasons.

Sometimes preference curves are observed that are composites of the types just described. For example, a curve might show risk aversion in its upper region and gambling inclinations in its lower region, resulting in a curve shaped like an "S."

DECREASING RISK AVERSION

Referring to Snyder's curve (*Exhibit VI-A*), we can easily see that he is a risk averter. However, his curve is a very special type of risk averter's curve —yet one often observed in practice. We say that it displays *decreasing risk aversion*, by which we mean that the decision maker becomes less conservative as his asset position increases.

To see that this is so, compare the risk premium for several 50-50 gambles where the consequences differ by $100,000. For example, consider the following 50-50 gambles, which I will call Gamble A and Gamble B:

□ Gamble A's consequences are $0 and $100,000. The expected value is therefore $50,000. To find the certainty equivalent, compute the preference of the gamble, in this case .30 (i.e., .50 × 0 + .50 × .60). Then read the certainty equivalent corresponding to .30 from the curve—$35,000. The risk premium is thus $15,000 (i.e., $50,000 − $35,000).

□ Gamble B's consequences are $300,000 and $400,000. The risk premium, computed in the same manner as for Gamble A, is $5,000 (i.e., $350,000 − $345,000). This is considerably less than the $15,000 risk pre-

Exhibit IX. Preference curve illustrating the zero illusion

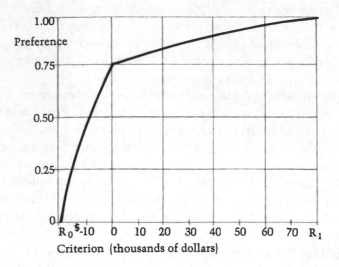

mium of Gamble A. It is easy to show that for Snyder the risk premiums for 50-50 gambles decline as the size of the asset position increases, provided that the difference in consequences remains constant, in this case $100,000.

What is the explanation of decreasing risk aversion? Many people tend to get braver as their criterion increases in value or, conversely, more conservative as it shrinks. People who feel they are decreasingly risk-averse should, as a part of the verification of their curve, check to see if their preference curve bears out the notion. The phenomenon of decreasing risk aversion is one reason that Snyder expressed the consequences of his decision in terms of assets rather than incremental cash flows.

THE ZERO ILLUSION

Another frequently observed phenomenon is the so-called zero illusion, illustrated in *Exhibit IX* (and also found in several of the curves in Swalm's article). As shown here, the zero illusion consists of a rather sharp break in the slope of the preference curve over zero on the horizontal scale. This means that the decision maker reacts very aversely to his asset position going negative. (Instead of asset position, it could be cash flow, earnings, or other criterion.)

While this phenomenon is perfectly understandable and in no sense wrong or irrational, many people whose preference curves initially display the zero illusion decide later to modify them when the behavioral implications of the sharp break in the curve are pointed out. A person can check his curve for the zero illusion by seeing if his risk aversion takes a sudden jump for gambles having both positive and negative consequences near zero (e.g., a 50-50 chance at assets of $5,000 or a net liability of $5,000), as compared with gambles near zero involving only negative consequences (e.g., a 50-50 chance of a liability of $1 or of $10,001) or only positive consequences (like a 50-50 chance of $1 or $10,001). Behaviorally, this means extreme conservatism around zero and much smaller conservatism for positions that are slightly positive or negative. Few people say they wish to adhere to such a preference curve once this implication has been pointed out.

Company vs. Individual

A person's attitude toward risk clearly depends on whose money he is taking chances with. Obviously his attitude will be much different when he is making a decision regarding personal finances than when he is making a decision on behalf of a company of which he is not an owner. This implies that he will have a different preference curve for each of the two types of decisions. While top executives may well be concerned about the implications of this for decision making, there is a subtler difference that is of greater importance. There is reason for them to worry that the curve the individual manager uses for making decisions on behalf of the company is not the curve that top management would like him to use.

In the majority of cases, the individual's preference curve reflects considerably more conservatism than the company would consider desirable. The curves that Swalm obtained are prime examples; he concluded that "our managers are surely not the takers of risk so often alluded to in the classical defense of the capitalistic system."

Why is this so?

CONTRADICTORY CONTROLS

I strongly suspect the trouble lies in the control systems we have set up to reward and punish our managers. These systems are generally hard on the managers if they have short-run failures, or at least the managers think the systems work that way. Moreover, the added reward to the manager for a huge financial success is perceived to be a relatively small increment to the reward for simply "doing a good job." A very important reason for this bias is that control systems highlight a financial loss but fail to show the potential lost profit on ventures that the manager has avoided. As a result, he plays it safe, avoiding opportunities which have even minutely small probabilities of significant failures. And chances for big successes are usually passed up, too, since they are usually accompanied by chances for significant failures.

The company's preference curve, on the other hand, is usually much less risk-averse than the individual's, since the company sees things in the aggregate. It is involved in many ventures and can afford to absorb a few failures because such a strategy has a good chance of producing a number of big successes. In the aggregate its position is improved by taking bigger risks.

If individual managers are behaving contrary to corporate desires, what can be done? One approach is to build control systems that reward managers for taking risks consistent with corporate objectives. These systems must avoid the tendency for short-term second guessing and must allow for the greater number of failures that will accompany the taking of bigger risks. Top management cannot expect managers down the line to take greater risks if it continues to treat an occasional loss as a "crisis" and fails to give adequate rewards for brilliant successes.

BETTER COMMUNICATION

A second approach, which complements the first, is to see if the desired attitude toward risk taking can be communicated better to decision makers in the company. Has management written an explicit statement on this attitude? (Chances are that it has not.) If so, does the statement spell out clearly what kinds of risks executives should take and what kinds they should avoid? (Chances are that it is rather vague on this count.) If such a management statement does not exist, how is the risk-taking posture of the company defined? Is there an implicit company position? Or does top management simply leave things up to the decision maker? In the latter case, there are probably as many different "company positions" as there are decision makers.

I believe that the preference curve may be the best way of communicating a desired attitude toward risk. Its superiority arises from the fact that it tells *exactly* which risks to take and which to avoid. Used in conjunction with a decision-tree analysis, it correctly incorporates the company's risk-taking posture with the decision maker's determination of potential courses of action for analysis, structuring of the problem, assessment of probabilities, and determination of economic consequences.

In most cases of poor communication of corporate risk-taking attitude, the trouble is probably more fundamental than lack of an adequate means of precise communication. It is probable that the corporate officers themselves do not have a precise idea of what their position is. Happily, preference theory is an aid in solving this more fundamental problem too. The process of assessment should promote dialogue among officers that will enable them to define the corporate position precisely. This position can then be communicated to the rest of the company.

It is clear, however, that the preference curve will not be a good vehicle of communication if the desired audience is not accustomed to thinking explicitly about uncertainty in making business decisions. The necessity for adequate preparation is obvious, and so is the need for a well-thought-out program for the gradual introduction of the probabilistic approach to decision making over a period ranging from months to several years.

Important Distinction

Earlier I mentioned that without the use of preference theory, some decision makers tend to "distort" their probability assessments by increasing the probability assigned to events with particularly unattractive consequences. This is undesirable because it confuses the decision maker's judgments about probabilities with his attitude toward risk.

With the use of preference theory in decision-tree analysis it is not only possible but *necessary* to separate the two or there will be danger of double counting. It is absolutely essential that the decision maker think only about the chances of occurrence of an event when he is assessing a probability, paying no attention whatever to the desirability or undesirability of the consequences which might result if the event occurred. Similarly, in assessing a preference curve, it is absolutely essential that the decision maker think only about what his attitudes would be should he ever face a gamble of the sort for which he is being asked to assess a certainty equivalent. He should pay absolutely no attention to the chances that he will ever face such a gamble.

LIMITATIONS ON USE

It should be noted that while there are many important classes of business decision problems to which preference theory applies, there are other classes to which it does *not*. It applies to most problems of a short-term nature; but it does not apply to longer term problems where there are uncertain receipts and expenditures significantly separated in time, and where the date of resolution of the uncertainty is very important to the decision maker. If the date when he learns the outcome of the uncertainties is important to the decision maker, the necessary adjustments for time differences in receipts and expenditures cannot be made simply by discounting. Unfortunately, many capital budgeting problems fall into this class because some alternatives allow the decision maker to obtain strategic information sooner than others do.

Research is being done that aims at extending preference theory to cover such problems, but so far the theoretical results have been too complex for practical application.

Summing Up

In this article we have considered the use of preference theory to improve business decisions. I have shown that preference theory is needed in decision-tree analysis because present practice does not properly reflect attitudes toward risk in some situations. The ways of assessing a preference curve and incorporating it in decision-tree analysis can be mastered by a manager who does not have special mathematical skills (although such a mastery does take time, concentration, and practice).

In addition to the value of preference theory as a direct aid in a businessman's own decision making, this discussion has made it apparent that the theory can help a businessman gain insights into the thinking of other decision makers. The preference curves of decision makers can be classified as risk-averse, linear, and risk-prone; the risk-averse curve seems to be by far the most common of these classes. Decreasing risk aversion and the so-called zero illusion are also commonly observed phenomena. Preference theory can also be valuable to top management in communicating a desired attitude toward risk taking to all decision makers in the organization.

It therefore appears that preference theory is a powerful tool in the manager's arsenal. It forces a precise definition of attitude toward risk and then permits explicit consideration of this attitude in decision making. It permits the separation of two important subjective inputs to a business decision problem; namely, judgments about probabilities of events and attitudes toward risk. No longer need these two elements be confused, as they have so often been in the past.

Part II

Planning and Strategy

Preface

Whether it is a "mom-and-pop" grocery anticipating next week's demand for bologna, a multibillion-dollar conglomerate determined to meet growing competition in the Common Market, or a social welfare agency anticipating economic trends in its service area, every organization finds planning and formulation of strategy necessary. It is obvious that a manager must plan his action before he takes it (and then observe the results). But it is not obvious to many how planning—particularly corporate planning—has changed in the last two decades or so as a result of changing economic, societal, and market forces.

Time was when almost every business concentrated on a single product or a group of related products or services. Planning was essentially a matter of making sure that the products moved out of the factory, that the demand for them was present (sometimes created, if not already present), and that the demand was met at a profit. Long-term strategy often was confined to such questions as whether to extend the market territory west of the Mississippi or whether to expand the product line to more fully meet the needs of customers. Usually, the objectives of the organization were more or less fixed; its management carried on the planning process, most often informally, to make sure that those objectives were being met.

Then came World War II. The dislocations it caused in operational and in managerial terms, coupled with the economic boom that followed it, made the old way of conducting business hopelessly inadequate and obsolete. New markets opened up, first in the United States, then elsewhere; competition stiffened as new rivals sprang up and the imaginary limits of spheres of activity vanished; and the surging stock market set a premium on performance translated into earnings per share. The informal, single-minded planning process had to adjust accordingly. As Frank Gilmore wrote in his contribution to this section, the managers of business organizations "recognized that—

. . . concern for short-term problems would have to shift to plans for capitalizing on long-term opportunities;

. . . sizing up the situation as a basis for a new course of action would have to give way to reappraising existing strategy in the light of the changing environment;

. . . sporadic diagnosis would have to be replaced by constant surveillance;
. . . concern for immediate profits and for adaptability to meet changes in
current conditions needed to shift to focusing on long-range ROI, growth,
flexibility, and stability.

In the most progressive corporations—in the most progressive large nonbusiness organizations too—planning departments were established. As top
executives increasingly became aware of the value of this function, planners
gained access to their offices. By 1970 a leader in the upgrading of this function,
George A. Steiner, was able to write in the Harvard Business Review, "As recently as 1965, [the corporate planner] was viewed in many corporations as,
at best, a fad and, at worst, a necessary overhead. . . . This view . . . is disappearing and is not prevalent at all in the advanced larger companies."

A principal task for the planner became scanning the external environment.
Increasing government regulation and surveillance of business, the more demanding and more strident voice of consumers, the accelerating pace of technology, the increasing interdependence of national economies—these factors
and many more added greater complexity and difficulty to the task of strategic
planning. The pricing of a product made by a German subsidiary, for example,
might depend to an extent on the valuation in inventory of its components, and
that value would hinge in part on the fluctuating worth of the Deutschmark
against the dollar.

In different ways, the three articles in this section reflect the enlarged scope
of planning and strategy formulation. Myles Mace's contribution stresses the
active role which the top officer of the organization must play in the process
on a continuous basis. The second article demonstrates the importance of
including both "reach" and "realism"—that is, what might be as well as what
should be—in the planning activity. Finally, Frank Gilmore outlines a procedure for developing strategy in smaller organizations, where resources are
limited and where busy executives often tend to focus on tomorrow's imperatives at the expense of problems and opportunities on the horizon.

7. The President and Corporate Planning

Myles L. Mace

What is effective planning? Here a person who has both participated in the exercise in a large corporation and studied it as a scholar and teacher outlines the steps to be taken to ensure that corporate objectives are defined, communicated, adhered to, reviewed, and redefined. The most essential ingredient in the process is the active involvement of the chief executive; he cannot delegate to subordinates his role as the leader.

Throughout the early 1960's, many top executives were concerned about the need for more formalized corporate planning in their respective organizations. Some chief operating executives searched for the "best system" and the "best methods" with the hope that the installation of another company's successful approach would achieve more effective results in their own corporate planning function. This situation is somewhat similar to that of the early 1950's, when many company executives were searching for the best system to provide for the growth and development of key personnel.

As in the 1950's, preoccupation with the forms, procedures, and techniques of a best system produces lip service to an important management function, but accomplishes little toward achievement of real, honest-to-goodness plans for the future direction of corporations. To mechanically adopt the methods and procedures which appear to be useful in the ABC Corporation does not assure fulfillment of the planning function in the XYZ Corporation. Such thinking is analogous to believing that the adoption of a "suggestion system" automatically builds employee morale.

Administrative Focus

Effective corporate planning does not consist simply of a system. Rather, it is an administrative process and a critically important job which should concern the management of every corporation. Forms and procedures may be employed as convenient and useful tools. But the success of corporate planning is not measured by the writing of procedures, the addition of a new box on the organization chart, or the production of an impressive-looking book entitled "Corporate Goals and Plans—Confidential."

Some executives have indicated that corporate planning is required only in large and diverse enterprises and that managements of small and medium sized companies need not be concerned. Planning as an essential business function is as important to the small company as it is to the large. Indeed, individual planning is important for each person who has aspirations for success in a business organization.

In 1961 and 1962, George G. Montgomery, Jr., now a vice president of White Weld Company in New York, and I made a research study of the problems involved in the acquisition of one company by another.[1] A segment of that study was concerned with planning for growth through acquisition. With this background, which has been augmented by continued interest and experience, especially with regard to the planning function, I shall undertake to deal in this article with what seem to be some of the most important and practical steps involved in the attainment of effective and useful corporate planning.

PRESIDENT'S INVOLVEMENT

Probably the single most important problem in corporate planning derives from the belief of some chief operating executives that corporate planning is not a function with which they should be directly concerned. They regard planning as something to be delegated, which subordinates can do without responsible participation by chief executives. They think the end result of effective planning is the compilation of a "Plans" book. Such volumes get distributed to key executives, who scan the contents briefly, file them away, breathe a sigh of relief, and observe, "Thank goodness that is done—now let's get back to work."

George Montgomery and I found in the course of the acquisition research mentioned above that effective corporate planning is not possible without the personal involvement and leadership of the chief operating executive. Subsequent study confirmed this conclusion. Involvement and leadership mean spending the time and energy to manage the function—to see that something concrete is done. They mean personally putting into action what is too often abrogated by general words and phrases. In specific terms, there are two fundamental functions which absolutely demand the chief executive's active involvement:

(1) *Leadership in the tough and laborious process of realistically evalu-*

1. *Management Problems of Corporate Acquisitions* (Boston, Division of Research, Harvard Business School, 1962).

ating existing product lines, markets, trends, and competitive positions in the future.

(2) *Leadership in the establishment of corporate objectives.*

After examining each of these critically important leadership functions, I shall discuss the basic elements of a planning program.

Realistic Evaluation

Among many corporate executives, the concept of planning is believed necessary only to find new areas of product opportunity. Planning programs organized to achieve this limited scope completely overlook the possibility of augmenting or strengthening existing product lines or product divisions.

Analysis of the history of sales, margins, and profits by product or product line discloses significant trends which are frequently unnoticed in the course of the day-to-day management of companies. For example:

A five-year history was compiled of the products which comprised 80% of a company's sales. It became clear that some product margins had steadily declined, others had remained stable, and the increase in total company sales and profits was attributable to a few high gross-margin items. The company's success had camouflaged what was happening to products which once had been substantial contributors to profits.

This relatively simple analysis led to further study of market prospects for the less profitable items. It was concluded that an inability to raise market prices or reduce costs required the addition of new, higher margin products if the sales and profits of the corporation were to be maintained or grow in the future.

Some chief operating executives find it difficult to recognize that product lines which have produced generous profits over many years are in jeopardy. Competitive facts of life encroach on markets, but a sentimental attachment to the past leads to a euphoric attitude about the future. Reluctance to face up to the situation is characterized by such statements as, "We have been through tough times before and we can do it again," or, "This business has been mighty good to us in the past and we are going to stick with it," or, "Sooner or later the competitor's prices have got to come back in line, and when that happens, we will be on our way again."

Admittedly it is painful to accept the unpleasant fact that uncontrollable outside competitive forces have depleted long-standing markets and margins. But a chief operating executive who procrastinates in adopting an action-planning program to adjust to changing conditions jeopardizes profits and, in some cases, the company's solvency. For example:

In a situation where competitors had moved in and taken over a certain company's once very profitable market, the chief operating executive of the company recognized the fact that the market was completely gone. However, sentimentally aware of the score of key people whose careers were identified only with that market, he refused to make the hard decision to reduce sharply or eliminate outright the jobs of the people working on the lost cause. The last several years have been characterized by increasing annual deficits, and the inevitable decision remains to be made.

When chief operating executives do not, as an integral part of their planning role, recognize realistically the status of their existing operations and fulfill the leadership role by adapting to changing conditions, they jeopardize current profits as well as the capacity of the organization to prosper in the future.

Corporate Objectives

In some companies a distinction is made between corporate objectives and corporate goals. Here I regard objectives and goals as synonymous, because corporate planning consists of creating the goals and defining in detail the corporate plans to achieve those goals.

I have found that the phrase "creation of corporate objectives" is regarded by some chief operating executives as rather meaningless, academic language—they think creating objectives is something professors talk about, and that such goals have little real value in the management of a business enterprise. Discounting the value of defining corporate objectives probably arises in part from the many published statements which describe the goals in broad general terms—such as increased sales, increased profits, a broader base of operations, a better environment for the growth of personnel, and so forth. Such expressions of objectives are, indeed, neither meaningful nor useful.

DIRECTION NEEDED

In some companies I have found no explicit or implicit concepts of corporate goals. One consequence of this lack of direction is that product and division managers more often than not create their own goals, and the result is a hodgepodge of unrelated, unintegrated, and expensive internal research and product development programs. Consider this example:

In one company, the division managers were urged by the chief operating executive to "do something about increasing sales and broadening the base of operations." Each of four division managers embarked on independent and uncoordinated product development projects. Later, capital appropriations and operating budgets were approved by headquarters management, and after a four-year period and a loss of $3 million, the four division managers were engaged in liquidating their respective abortive ventures.

A product development program with carefully defined goals certainly is no guarantee that the product produced and marketed will be successful. But a product development program with goals certainly is financially more economical and less wasteful of management talent at the division level.

Discussions with chief executives about the concept of creating corporate goals indicate that many think there is something mysterious about the process. There is concern about the method or approach to be used in outlining corporate objectives. How does one go about deciding the mission of an organization? Do statements of goals spring full blown from the minds of presidents? Should we hire consultants to tell us what our objectives should be? Or perhaps hire an economist who can forecast the most promising markets of the future? How do we know what business conditions will be like two years or five years from now? How can we plan effectively when our business is so fast moving that the creation of long-range goals means anticipating what we will do next week?

THINKING REQUIRED

Some companies neglect corporate planning because the process intrinsically requires thinking about the future and the future is always uncertain. Anticipating all the factors which affect a company's sales and profits means dealing intellectually with mercurial and intangible elements. This is especially difficult for the action-minded, decision-oriented executive who enjoys and derives great satisfaction from "doing things." Also, and this is one of the most common reasons for deferring thinking about the future, day-to-day crises need decisions right now, and there are usually enough crises to occupy most or all of each business day.

One president stated that "the tyranny of the moment prevents me from paying attention to the important future of the company." Another president said:

"Thinking seems to have lost respectability in some companies. If a vice president is caught sitting at his desk without papers, people, or telephone calls and, in response to a query by the president as to what he is doing, says 'thinking,' the typical reaction of the president is likely to be, 'Thinking! If you are going to think, think on your own time.'"

But despite the obstacles, real and imagined, to corporate planning, many chief executives regard the function as one of their principal duties and are actively engaged in planning the future paths of their organizations.

SIMPLE PROCESS

Yet the process of corporate planning is relatively simple and straightforward. Much of the mystery of planning comes from the many general admonitions provided by students of management who describe planning as a composite of abstract elements made up of strategy, tactics, purpose, specifications, alternatives, and so on. Chief executives who are doing effective planning jobs describe the process in more practical and meaningful terms. From conversations with them, I shall summarize and illustrate briefly the five basic elements of a planning program, including the creation of corporate goals.

Analyzing the Present

Planning for the future starts with an intimate and realistic understanding of existing products, divisions, markets, margins, profits, return on investment, cash flow, availability of capital, research and development abilities, and skills and capacities of personnel. These significant aspects of operations can be looked at in an orderly manner, and there is nothing mysterious about an analysis of the company's strength and weakness in each of these areas. Basic to consideration of a mission for the company in the future is a clear recognition of how well the organization is doing today.

Analysis of present operations can be done effectively by reviewing the past few years' performance as part of the evaluation of the current year's operating and capital budget forecasts. In some cases, top managements ask division or functional managers to submit the proposed annual budgets together with budgets for the next three to five years. The headquarters review of the short-term forecast is thus combined with the long-term forecast, which otherwise would be a separate, second step. This method of reviewing and evaluating both forecasts simultaneously has the apparent advantage of economy of management time and effort.

However, many top executives find that the discussion invariably focuses on the short-term prospect because of its imminence, and that the long-term problems are deferred or given only brief attention. Current operating problems should be distinguished from the longer-term goals and plans. The purposes of evaluating short-term forecasts and long-term projections—both extremely important—are so different that two separate presentations and evaluations need to be made. Short-term budgets require headquarters modification and approval for financial commitments, whereas long-term forecasts are not subject to authority to spend or commit.

Predicting the Future

Forecasts for each of the next three to five years, based on current operations and existing plans for improving operations, are an important element of a sound planning program. If the company continues to do what it is doing and planning to do today, what will be its future sales, profit, market position, and so on?

Many different approaches produce useful forecasts. These vary from elementary dollar results to more detailed and complex breakdowns of business functions. In one company, which is organized on the basis of decentralized, autonomous divisions for which profit and loss are measurable, each of the seven division managers is asked to submit five-year plans based on an eight-point outline. (A detailed breakdown of this type of outline is given in the Appendix for the reader who would like a more concrete picture of such a forecast.)

In another company, as an illustration, division managers are asked to supply the following information for a three-year forecast:

- Sales by product line.
- Gross profits by product line.
- Personnel requirements.
- Capital expenditure needs.

Normally, the data prepared by division or functional managers is submitted in writing two or three weeks in advance of a review date so that the president and other headquarters executives can thoroughly examine the forecasts prior to the meeting.

Reviewing the Forecasts

Here again, practices vary among the companies I have observed. In one, for example, eight divisional managers meet for two days at headquarters, and each manager is allowed two hours to make a presentation of his present operations and his plans for the future. The president and key headquarters executives listen to each presentation and typically ask general, unchallenging questions. It is an essentially meaningless exercise for all concerned.

In contrast, in a certain company where the president regards corporate planning as his most important job, full-day reviews are made of each division manager's report on his goals and his plans to achieve those goals for each of the next three years. Here the president and key headquarters executives study the written portions of the presentation prior to the meeting and are well armed with perceptive and challenging questions about the validity of their managers' forecasts. Several years' experience with this approach has resulted in increasingly effective, realistic forecasts by the division managers and complete recognition by executives in the company that, while the president is the leader in planning, all key personnel have a share in making the planning function real and meaningful.

Critical evaluation of forecasts prepared by division or functional managers is also required to prevent subordinates from regarding the process of preparing forecasts as an exercise and not an integral part of responsible planning. For example:

□ In some companies managers supply financial forecasts by product line by mechanically projecting 5% increases in sales and profits for each year. Such an approach observes the amenities of corporate procedures but, if unchallenged by top executives, adds little effectiveness to statements of what can be expected in the future.

□ In other companies managers purposely overstate their expectations with the hope of manifesting to headquarters executives what fine performances can be expected in the future.

□ Still other managers employ the strategy of understating forecasts for the purpose of establishing financial goals relatively easy to achieve. Thus approbation will come from headquarters if the forecasts are subsequently exceeded. Hopefully, this will be expressed in higher salaries and bonuses.

Careful and thoughtful review, therefore, is required to validate the reasonableness of managers' forecasts and to provide a realistic composite picture of the future achievement of the entire enterprise.

Critical evaluation by top executives of division or functional managers' longer-range goals and plans has another important advantage. A discussion by able, experienced, and interested executives about the operations of a division inevitably results in the disclosure of some new opportunity not thought of previously. The interplay of active minds dedicated to greater growth and success stimulates new avenues of thought which can be enormously helpful to the division and to the company.

When all of the division or functional managers' goals and plans have been reviewed, a composite report representing the totals for the entire company should be prepared. Some companies accept the forecasts of divisions as presented, and the total becomes the program. In others, the chief executive and his key subordinates review again all the separate programs and adjust the division figures according to their previous experience with the respective division managers. History indicates that some managers are unreformed optimists and others are perpetual pessimists. If discussion during the review does not result in adjustment, the chief executive must make appropriate increases or decreases in order to arrive at a realistic overall forecast.

Evaluating the Program

When all managers' forecasts have been reviewed critically and adjusted to represent more appropriately the judgment of the company's top executives, the total program can be evaluated for the purpose of (1) accepting the forecasted performance as reasonable, or (2) deciding that the stated program does not comprise a suitable growth rate for the company.

DOMINANT CONSIDERATIONS

A significant and controlling determinant in arriving at a conclusion as to the adequacy of proposed division or functional plans is the attitude, personal desire, and aspiration of the chief operating executive. It is frequently assumed that every chief executive aspires to head a growing and increasingly profitable enterprise—that by taking into account the interests of stockholders, employees, customers, and the communities within which the company operates, he will make thoughtful decisions to grow, prosper, and fulfill social and public responsibilities. While this is generally true, some chief executives are motivated by other primary considerations which dominate many major policy decisions. For example:

In a western consumer products company the president and his key subordinates recognized that their major strengths were in the research, development, and manufacturing of potentially profitable new products, but the company's marketing organization had proved to be ineffective in establishing distribution to thousands of outlets in the United States. Several unsuccessful attempts were made to strengthen the marketing group.

Meanwhile, a competitor with a superb marketing staff continued to increase its share of the market. The president of the competing company, in planning the future growth of his enterprise, perceived that continued growth in sales and profits would be possible only with more effective product research, development, and manufacturing facilities. Dissatisfied with the time which would be required to build a stronger development and manufacturing group, he explored the alternative of acquiring another company with the necessary strengths to complement his organization.

A study of possible acquisitions resulted in the identification of the western company described above, and the two presidents initiated negotiations to merge the two companies. Continued discussions disclosed that the fit was even better than originally conceived—stock prices and dividend policies were substantially alike, terms of exchange were agreed on, antitrust laws were not an obstacle— and a plan for the integration of the two organizational structures was evolved which met the desires and aspirations of both groups.

The one snag was: Who would be the chief operating executive of the merged enterprises? It was clear that joining the two companies would substantially benefit the stockholders, the employees, and the communities where the companies had operations. Negotiations continued intensively for several weeks, but were terminated when it was apparent that both presidents wanted to be the chief operating executive of the merged companies. Neither was willing to take the second position, although many possible divisions of authority and responsibility were considered and rejected in turn. The personal desire of each president to retain the position as chief executive prevented the merger, and the two companies continued to operate competitively.

I have found similar examples of dominant personal considerations in other situations, but the real reasons for termination of merger discussions are rarely publicized. The usual explanation is that differences on price or differences on major policies have led both parties to conclude that each company should remain independent and autonomous.

HIDDEN MOTIVES

In other cases, the chief operating executives disguise their personal desires and goals for their companies. They profess the conviction that their companies should adjust to changed conditions in their respective industries, that new areas of activity should be searched for and entered. But personal, and usually unexpressed, reasons control the decisions not to take the risks involved in moving into promising market opportunities.

At a research seminar conducted at the University of California, Los Angeles, to discuss long-range planning, one of the participants, Rex Land, described his experience with a company which tried to hide its basic objectives, but eventually was found out. Land said:

"I know of a company, very closely held, the executives of which (after a great deal of probing action) finally admitted they were primarily interested in maintaining the prestige of other members of the family. The top executive was not going to take certain risks that would jeopardize his income or that of four or five members of his family. His could have been a growing and healthy company if it had brought in and held executives, but he could not keep people for very long. It took people five years to realize what the real objectives of this company were."[2]

In another company, the president made a review of a five-year forecast of sales and profits based on the continuation of status quo operations. It seemed possible with existing products, he reasoned, to maintain the same flat curve of sales and profits achieved over the last several years. He concluded, therefore, that the company's plan would be to maintain this level of performance and not to try to grow in size or profitability. In a lengthy discussion of his plan and planning process, he conceded that he felt personally comfortable heading the organization at its present size. "If I grow and take on more people, I am not too sure I could do it. And even if I could, I am not willing to pay the price of the extra effort required."

2. Reported in *Managerial Long-Range Planning*, edited by George A. Steiner (New York, McGraw-Hill Book Company, 1963), p. 38.

Other chief operating executives, after reviewing forecasts of gradually declining sales and profits based on present operations and plans, resignedly accept the anticipated results because of personal fears of risking substantial sums of development or capital expenditure money. Consider this example:

The president of a large family corporation in the East regarded his role as that of a conservator. Several members of the family held corporate executive titles, and the value of the company constituted the principal of the family trust created for them by their deceased father, who had founded the company.

Technological changes in the industry resulted in a gradual erosion of the company's sales and profits which, for years, had enjoyed the dominant position in a segment of the industrial instruments business. None of the company's top executives could foresee anything except continued declines in sales, profit, and market position unless the company risked an estimated $3 million investment in product development.

The policy dilemma of whether to risk $3 million of what was regarded as the assets of the family trust or whether to accept the forecasted future of further declines was resolved by the president when he chose to "ride out this temporary decline trend." The company president has continued to reject the alternative risk, and the company sales and profits have continued to deteriorate.

While these foregoing examples illustrate the importance and influence of attitudes, personal desire, and aspirations of chief operating executives, indeed they are not at all typical of the majority of companies.

Usually presidents are found to be searching for ways to increase the size and profitability of their respective corporations. And if the forecasted performance of existing operations fails to produce expectations of profitable growth, plans are initiated to build on the business of the present. In my studies the more common president is one who is rarely satisfied with nominal growth rates, who stretches the forecasts of divisional or functional managers, and who establishes new and challenging standards of performance for the organization to achieve. Such presidents regard lack of growth as stagnation, an attribute they abhor.

When chief operating executives review and evaluate the forecasted performance for three to five years and conclude that the financial figures are reasonable and plans for their realization feasible, the composite documents constitute the corporate plan for the stated period of years ahead. Sometimes these "working papers" are regarded as "company goals and plans." In other cases the significant elements of them are formalized into "corporate goals," and the various segments of the corporate plans for achievement are spelled out in great detail. The mission and the plan for achievement are thus clearly defined.

However, when the chief operating executives conclude that the anticipated results are not adequate, it becomes imperative to think through and construct a new or modified set of goals and a new plan to fulfill these desired objectives.

Creating the Goals

In my discussions with presidents who are concerned about the anticipated lack of growth in their companies, the query recurs, "Just how do I go about creating a new set of corporate goals?"

While I have found several successful approaches in the many companies studied, my major conclusions will be discouraging to those who are looking for a quick and easy method. There is no mechanical or expert "instant answer method." Rather, defining corporate goals—and modifying those goals as the future becomes the present—is a long, time-consuming, and continuous process. Each president in each company must regard the construction and adjustment of goals as an important, absolute, and—in a sense—unique requirement of his job.

There are, however, several ways of defining company goals that may suggest a modus operandi to those concerned with this requirement.

REORGANIZE WORK HABITS

With the background and essential information resulting from (1) a realistic analysis of existing operations, including opportunities for growth, (2) adjusted forecasts by division or functional managers of their anticipated performance, and (3) an evaluation of the three-, four-, and five-year forecasts, the chief operating executive can embark on the difficult process of creating a structure of corporate goals.

The process is particularly difficult for some chief executives because accepting corporate planning as an important function means not engaging in parts of the satisfying activities which have kept them completely occupied in the past. Planning takes time, and time becomes available for busy men largely through modification of their work habits. The president of a large eastern company stated recently, "The creation and manning of three new group vice presidential positions to cover nine domestic divisions and our international subsidiaries ought to enable me to give more attention to our corporate goals."

Another said, "In the past I did not take the time as skipper of this corporate ship to plot our course. The absence of direction created a vacuum into which rushed improvisation. The resulting chaos and hodge-podge forced me to recognize that I must take the time to think through where we want to go."

ENLIST KEY PEOPLE

While the main responsibility for defining corporate goals rests on the chief executives, they can enlist the minds and imaginations of other key people in their organizations. To do this, some chief operating executives ask the top eight or ten executives to join them in a three- or four-day retreat to help them start thinking through together what the corporate goals should be. Preferably, such a meeting should be held away from "headquarters" to avoid the diversions of telephones, problems, and decisions. Such "think" or "skull" sessions are found to be most effective when tentative drafts of ideas are prepared prior to the meeting to serve as the focus of discussion. Such preliminary drafts can, but need not, delimit the considerations, since thoughtful and imaginative executives usually extrapolate quickly. One president observes that these sessions should also provide for a break of an hour or two in the afternoon for exercise; otherwise everyone gets to thinking in circles.

Some company presidents look for more from such skull sessions than can be reasonably expected. The thinking and planning process, as indictated earlier, is a long, continuing, and tough process. It is long because answers are not easily come by; continuing because the corporate goals are subject to change, adapting to new conditions; and tough because the process of thinking about the future means dealing with intangibles and assumptions. If an organization is formalizing its planning program for the first time, the most that can be expected from such a meeting is the beginning of an understanding of the magnitude of the problems and the start of the process of formulating possible elements of a statement of goals.

Some presidents assign the job of defining corporate goals to a task force made up of three or four key members of the organization. Others ask an experienced line or staff executive to study the problems and recommend a statement of mission for the company. But, irrespective of the approach used, I find that no real and meaningful goals are outlined without the direct involvement of the chief operating executive. Without his active leadership in the function, resulting concepts are usually interesting but irrelevant products of an academic exercise. With his leadership, it is possible to analyze, to think through alternatives, and to arrive at a practical, workable, and useful outline of the mission of the enterprise.

Other presidents employ management consultants to advise on what the goals of their corporation should be. Responsible consultants, unbiased and unprejudiced by the way things have been done, can bring to the task the benefit of outside objectivity. Most organizations include undisclosed sacred cows which executives of the company have learned not to molest. Sometimes the unmolested sacred cow is the reason for lack of interest in growth, and the consultant feels a responsibility to report his conclusions objectively. Many times suggestions by consultants on sacrosanct subjects have opened them up for re-examination and, sometimes, even change. New points of view injected by consultants often stimulate corporate top management to audit anew many policies, practices, and other matters which have continued unchallenged over the years. Here is an example:

In one company in the East a substantial part of its sales and profits over the last 20-year period had been derived from one product line in the electronics industry. More recently, competitive Japanese products had entered the United States and pre-empted a large portion of the market. The eastern company sought protection through increased tariffs and intercountry agreements on the amounts to be imported, but neither approach stemmed the increasing market share taken over by the Japanese products. The company management was slow in recognizing the business facts of life and continued to maintain a large and expensive manufacturing facility and a high-salaried marketing group.

A consultant was employed to analyze the company's operations and to recommend a program of remedial action. A few months after he began his analysis of the company, he asked the president and the executive committee, "Why do you stay in that part of the electronics industry when you have been losing money steadily for three years and there are no prospects you can ever make profits there again?"

The directness of the question on a clearly vulnerable point jarred the executives into facing up to a decision not previously even discussed—liquidation of the unprofitable product line with no potential for improvement.

In addition to a hard-nosed look at sacrosanct subjects, the consultant (with wider experience in different companies and industries than corporate executives whose careers may have been limited to one company, one industry, or one geographical area) can often bring to the task new insights. In one company, the president and nine out of ten of the other top executives had devoted their entire careers to the same company. Their understanding of business was limited to a single industry with its small tangential and related activities. Here the consultant—knowing that the world of business is larger than the manufacture and sale of umbrellas, or file cabinets, or maple furniture—was able to suggest possibilities for a broadened base of operations.

No consultants are known, however, who have instantaneous, magic answers as to what goals a particular company might adopt. Surprisingly, some presidents think, "There must be someone, somewhere, who can tell us quickly what we ought to do." Here again, no such consulting sources can be found. The responsible consultant will take the time—and this does take time—to analyze objectively a company's existing operations before he is prepared to recommend programs of action and goals.

ADOPT A STATEMENT

The form and detail of the actual statements which define company goals vary from very simple to elaborate verbal descriptions. In one company, for example, the corporate goals were briefly stated:

1. To increase the return on investment from 4% to 6% by next year.

2. To increase earnings from $3 per share this year to $5 per share in two years.

Another company's objectives are stated in a more detailed way:

1. To raise after-tax earnings from $12 million to $18 million within two years without diluting the equity.

2. To change the proportion of the company's military business from 65% to 40% in two years. (In another company a goal was expressed "to raise the percentage of military business from 40% to 65%.")

3. To liquidate in an orderly manner Division A and those parts of Division B which are unprofitable as soon as possible.

4. To search for and acquire one or more companies in the United States with sales of at least $10 million in the XYZ industry.

5. To establish in the Common Market at least three bases of operations, either by acquisition or by starting our own operations, within two years.

DESIGN A PLAN

The creation of a statement of reasonable goals, in turn, leads to the need for a plan to realize those goals. Here, again, the plan may be a written description or exist only in the minds of top executives, and it may be relatively simple or exceedingly detailed and complex. Many companies of substantial size write descriptions of their goals and an over-all company plan to arrive at those goals, and support these with a marketing plan, a technical plan, a manufacturing plan, a personnel plan, and a financial plan which includes a cash-flow plan.

Planning Staff

The importance of involvement by the chief operating executive has been stressed throughout this article to underline my conviction of the need for his participation. But clearly much of the data collection, procedures for the collection of data, and analysis can and should be done by subordinates in the organization or by a corporate planning office. The need for a separate planning staff is determined largely by the capacities, interests, and time of line and staff executives available. Sometimes the vice president of finance is given the responsibility of heading the planning function because the number aspects constitute a common language of plans.

I find, however, that the most effective way of accomplishing corporate planning is to create a new staff group—reporting to the president—free from the diversion of day-to-day crises and charged with the responsibility of assisting the president. The assistance includes, among other things, helping the chief operating executive "to crystallize goals in the leadership and direction of the company."

FUNCTIONS AND QUALIFICATIONS

The functions of a planning group vary, but the vital ones are included in the following statement adopted by a large western company:

1. To assure that divisions and subsidiaries prepare annual and five-year plans for growth.

2. To assist divisions and subsidiaries in the preparation of annual and five-year projections.

3. To identify areas of product opportunity for divisions and subsidiaries, and for corporate investment.

4. To perform market research as requested by divisions and subsidiaries.

5. To coordinate and monitor the preparation of a written, company-wide, five-year plan.

6. To analyze the economic future of existing operations and to recommend programs of growth or divestment.

7. To make analyses of business, economic, and political conditions bearing on existing or prospective areas of operations.

8. To be responsible for all negotiations with possible companies to be acquired.

During the past few years, many company managements have come to recognize the need for more formalized planning activities. This often leads to the creation of new units, ranging in size from one man to a dozen or more. Frequently, the personnel assigned to the function are transferred from existing line or staff activities. In some cases, these people perform admirable jobs. In a New York chemical company, for example, when the need for intensive planning was recognized, a statement was drafted of the ideal personal qualifications and experience for the job. Here are the important elements of that statement:

☐ Technical knowledge of organic and inorganic chemistry.

☐ Ability to manage people.

☐ Ability to inculcate division managers and headquarters staff officers with the importance of planning as an essential part of their jobs.

☐ Analytical capacity.

☐ Knowledge of financial data, including ability to analyze balance sheets, profit and loss statements, cash-flow forecasts, and operating and capital budgets.

☐ Imagination—ability to perceive new applications for corporate competence.

A review of personnel employed within the company disclosed that the manager of the research and development laboratory possessed most of the desired qualities, and he was moved to the new post, "Director of Product Development and Corporate Planning."

JOB REQUIREMENTS

Often, however, chief operating executives do not think through the job requirements of the important role to be performed by the head of planning. Consequently, they assign somebody who just happens to be available. In some companies, retired, about-to-retire, pseudo-retired, or quasi-retired executives are asked to take on this function during their remaining years with the company. The rationale is: "Joe has been with the company for 40 years, and he knows it inside and out. The planning responsibility will keep him busy for three or four years, and, besides, we need a younger man in his important operational job." When the planning group is regarded so lightly that it becomes a dumping ground for the aging or less competent, it is likely to achieve nothing of consequence. Planning today is a critically important function in management, and it requires the best talent, not the infirm of mind or body.

The need for additional personnel is dictated by the magnitude of the corporate tasks and the availability of staff help in the organization. For example:

☐ In one company, the director of budgets had had extensive experience in another company with financial operating forecasts and cash flows, and their analyses. He was able and interested in serving the needs of the director of plans, and it was not necessary to assign a financial analyst to the plans office.

☐ In another company, the market research department, part of the marketing group, regarded assignments from the plans department as an important part of its responsibilities and was equipped to handle them.

Many companies have assigned only a few personnel to the planning task initially and added others only when the job requirements indicated need for additional help.

Planners' Problems

Two critical problems which are sometimes encountered by the director of plans call for special attention and close monitoring by the chief executive to assure the success of the corporate planning function. Let's look at what can be done about each one.

INCULCATING AWARENESS

One difficult problem of a director of plans is to inculcate line managers of divisions, subsidiaries, or other company operations with an awareness of the importance of planning as a vital part of *their* jobs. In some situations, long-range planning means nothing more to a division manager than going through the needless task of preparing an annual operating budget, getting it done, sending it to the vice president of finance, and forgetting about it until the next year.

In one eastern company with five years' experience with formalized corporate planning, the vice president for plans summarized his concepts of what remained to be done on this problem in future planning meetings:

1. *Create an awareness in division managers of the need for planning beyond the next 12 months into the following two years and beyond.* This can be done by directing the questions and discussion away from the current year whenever possible and talking about objectives for the following two years.

2. *Assess how well the divisions have integrated all the elements of planning in their programs (including timing) to make sure that programs have been thought through.* The use of a checklist in this connection may be helpful, of which the key elements should be:

☐ Analysis (e.g., product line breakdowns).
☐ Potentials—available skills, and available and needed resources.
☐ Problems—deficiencies evident.
☐ Establishment of best alternatives—suggested economic goals.
☐ Coordination-implementation-timing—the results expected, both financial and nonfinancial.

3. *Create a means of implementing* continued *planning so that the divisions will complete any unfinished plan or revise any inadequate parts of it during the coming year.* As the discussion progresses, it is wise to examine areas in which planning is not complete and ask that a timetable and action plan be set up for putting together the missing elements after the meeting. Such a plan can be worked up between the division and the director of plans. In this instance, it is necessary to cover (a) the need for planning responsibility to be centered in a capable individual, and (b) the

importance that management attaches to this function—which might require additional expenditure.

4. *Determine what standards for measurement, if any, the divisions have in setting goals.* For example, have the divisions set some over-all goal to strive for in sales, profits, investment, and return, as a measuring stick of their own performance? Do they feel that the goals are adequate? What restrictions are holding them back from enlarging these goals?

5. *Determine whether the divisions have compared the amount of technical effort (either at the division level or at the company's headquarters laboratory) on their long-range projects with the profit potential in these projects.* In addition, it is important to determine whether they have considered the degree to which they should be investing profits from existing business in technical effort for potential future rewards. (Similar consideration can be given to marketing's planning for future sales by strengthening or adding to the market organization.)

6. *Get across to the divisions that they should be striving to add more projects to their existing base than they or the corporation can absorb in terms of research and development and capital facilities, so that the most desirable projects can be selected from a wide list.*

7. *Assess the reasonableness of the goals, so as to come up with a consolidated, long-term corporate goal, adjusted to take into account undue optimism or pessimism in the divisions.* The plans should be weighed against past ability to get the job done, how tight a timetable is possible, and how capable the organization is, or can rapidly become, to accomplish the task.

8. *Determine the degree to which the headquarters staff, including marketing, planning, research laboratory, market research, manufacturing, can help implement the divisions' programs.*

9. *Make sure a program is established to see that the advice given by the headquarters staff is followed up.*

10. *Identify the ways in which the divisions can work together in projects requiring complementary skills.*

UNPLANNED PLANS

Another critical—and frustrating—problem of directors of corporate planing evolves from the actions of the chief operating executive who accepts and approves a carefully worked out set of corporate goals and plans for achievement and then, by his arbitrary decisions, moves the company into activities neither related nor contemplated. Indeed, the most carefully thought-out corporate goals and plans must yield to the emergence of some new and previously unthought-of opportunity. Any planning program must be flexible. But, on fundamental plan principles, deviation from agreed-upon programs ought to be restudied before commitments are made. Consider:

In a company where a substantial part of its total investment was subject to the risks of operations abroad, the chief operating executive stated that the ratio of domestic to foreign investment should be increased and that no new money should be exposed to risks from abroad. Shortly after the corporation goals were discussed and adopted by the executive committee, the president learned of a possible acquision in Italy. He flew to Rome and, within a relatively short time, negotiated and arranged for the purchase of a company. The foreign investment commitment increased by several million dollars, and the stated ratio goals became meaningless standards for the organization.

Concluding Note

Corporate planning is an inseparable part of the job of all chief operating executives; the futures of their companies depend upon the corporate courses prescribed by them. The only constant in the management of business organizations is change. The leadership in adapting corporate operations to the changing business world must come from the chief executives. Unless company presidents who have heretofore shunned the role give hard and fast attention to the future of their enterprises by personal involvement in planning, only the most fortuitous circumstances will enable their companies to avoid declines in sales, profits, and market positions.

I. *Product-Line and Customer-Class Planning*

A. Reports on major long-term, high-priority product-line or customer-class programs. Each such report should be a 15-30 minute summary giving the highlights of the technical marketing and production aspects of the program with a general timetable and financial projections. These reports should cover the two or three most important programs aimed at any one of these:

1. Markedly expanding the division's participation in present product lines.

2. Expanding present customer classes.

3. Entering a new product area.

B. A report on the compilation of information needed to do an effective job of long-range planning. Such information might include:

1. Lists of appropriate product lines in which the division is now making products and product lines which might be considered for the division in the future.

2. Lists of appropriate customer classes now being served by the division and new ones that might feasibly be served by it in the future.

3. Market data on:

    a. Size of market—past, present, future.

    b. Rate of growth of market.

    c. Our sales to the market, if any.

    d. Rate of growth of our sales, if any.

4. Financial data to cover these questions:

    a. In each product line and customer class in which we now participate, what is our *net* profit, investment, and return on investment?

    b. To the extent that it is possible to say, what are our competitors' profits in the same fields?

    c. In new areas, what level of profitability can be expected?

5. Analyses of:

    a. Resources (technical, marketing, production) available and re-
quired to expand our position.

    b. Competitive situation.

II. *Marketing Planning*

Obviously the previous section has included much of marketing planning,
but more general subjects should be discussed under this heading. Possible
examples are—

    A. Marketing organization planning, including possible changes in:

    1. Assignment of responsibilities by product line vs. customer class
vs. geographical areas.

    2. Greater use of product managers, market managers, or specialists.

    B. Increase or decrease in the use of dealers or distributors to sell the
division's products.

    C. Possibility of distributing products manufactured by others.

    D. Statement of pricing policy and pricing practices and discussion of
possible changes.

    E. Salesmen's compensation plan—evaluation, expense control, incen-
tives.

III. *Technical Planning*

Insofar as possible give a breakdown of this year's actual and next year's
estimated expenses of the division's technical program, both in division
laboratories and at central research, by the classes of work listed below.
Cite the principal projects now being worked on and being considered for
the future.

    A. Long-range offensive research—work requiring more than one year
to complete that will be aimed at creating new or improved products for
markets in which the division either does not participate or has such a
small share as to be negligible.

    B. Long-range defensive research—work requiring more than one year
to complete that will be aimed at maintaining or expanding the division's
business in its present markets.

    C. Offensive development work—work requiring more than a few days,
but usually less than a year, to complete that will be aimed at developing
products for markets in which the division either does not participate or
has a very small position.

    D. Defensive development work.

    E. Production service—short-range work aimed at troubleshooting in
plant, routine formulation changes, routine process improvements, and the
like.

F. Customer service—work required to help the customer use the division's products.

G. Quality control—inspection of incoming raw materials, in-process materials, and finished goods.

IV. *Production Planning*

A. What major new facilities are being considered?

B. What, if any, possibilities are there for major improvements in processing efficiency, and what plans are being made to investigate them?

C. Report on status of program to obtain data on the capacity of each plant, preferably by major departments, covering:

1. What percent of capacity is now being utilized.

2. What further capacity will be required.

3. What steps must be taken to provide more capacity where needed or to utilize excess capacity where available.

V. *Export Planning*

A. Summary of past export sales by product line.

B. Plans, if any, for expanding these sales or adding new product lines.

VI. *Acquisition Suggestions*

A. In which geographical areas, product lines, and/or customer classes does the division think that acquisition of allied businesses should be considered as a route toward future growth?

B. What specific companies, if any, might be desirable acquisitions?

VII. *Manpower Planning*

A. Projection of manpower requirements in the next three years for:

1. Key salaried employees.

2. Other salaried employees.

3. Production (manufacturing) labor.

B. In forecasting manpower requirements consider the present number in the group modified by:

1. Turnover (including anticipated requirements).

2. Needs anticipated for future growth of organization.

[An expanded outline must be prepared to assist the divisions in estimating manpower requirements, and mailed to division heads in advance.]

C. Brief summary of recruiting and training program.

VIII. *Financial Statements*

    A. Last two years actual; next three years projected.
    B. Sales by product line.
    C. Gross profit by product line.
    D. Sales, administrative, and general expense.
    E. Profit.
    F. Investment—working and fixed.
    G. Return on investment.
[Sample forms must be provided for these items.]

8. Balance "Creativity" and "Practicality" in Formal Planning

John K. Shank, Edward G. Niblock,
and William T. Sandalls, Jr.

This article contends that to be effective every formal long-range planning sys-tem must achieve a compromise between "creativity" and "practicality"—goals for planning that are often in conflict. The authors also argue that the problem of maintaining a satisfactory balance can be directly addressed by varying the design features of the planning/budgeting interface. After specifying the set of design features, they go on to show how six companies have used various combinations of them to achieve an appropriate degree of creativity that is consistent with practicality.

Every company engaged in long-range planning would like its efforts to attain two fundamental but often conflicting goals. On the one hand, management wants the planning function to reflect pragmatic judgments based on what is possible. On the other hand, it wants planning to reflect forward-looking, assertive, and creative thinking.

The primary way of enhancing "realism" is to give the planning func-tion a clear action orientation. Generally, this is done by relating long-range planning closely with short-term budgetary control. And this is where the difficulty lies. While close linkage between planning and budgeting puts the stress on the desired action, it also promotes a focus that can be disastrous to mind-stretching "reach."

We are making the assumption, of course, that for the formal planning system to operate effectively it must achieve a balanced compromise between realism and reach. In this article, we shall argue that these dual objectives need not be mutually exclusive. In fact, our purpose is to illus-trate that the long-range planning system can be structured to achieve both an action orientation and a focus on mind stretching. Our discussion will proceed in two steps.

In the first stage, it is important for long-range planners to begin think-ing about the realism-reach trade-off as a problem they can do something about. That "something" involves varying those aspects of the long-range planning system which relate to its interface with the short-range budgeting process. In this regard, we shall summarize the general features of the planning system which relate to plan-budget linkage, illustrating both the "tight" and "loose" form of each "linkage device."

Then, in the second step, we shall illustrate some of the most interesting devices actually being used. These reflect the experiences of six companies which we selected because they (a) are successful in terms of compound earnings growth and (b) have long-range planning systems with both action-oriented and mind-stretching characteristics.

In short, we believe that management can control the focus a planning system will exhibit with respect to the realism versus reach problem. It may not always be possible to achieve a totally satisfactory trade-off, but we shall describe the mechanisms being used by a sample of successful companies to achieve what for each of them is a satisfactory compromise.

Plan-Budget Design

On close examination, it quickly becomes apparent that the different aspects of plans and budgets can be linked in three distinct ways:

1. *Content linkage* relates to the correspondence between the data presented in the plan document and that presented in the budget.

2. *Organizational linkage* focuses on the relationship between the units responsible for planning and budgeting.

3. *Timing linkage* concerns the sequencing of the annual planning and budgeting cycles.

Within each of these categories, there are several specific features of the planning system that can be manipulated to influence the extent of plan-budget linkage. Let us take a closer look at each of these linkage devices.

FINANCIAL FEATURES

One important feature of content linkage is the amount of detail in the financial statements included in the plan document. The tightest linkage would be to include statements with the same level of detail as in the monthly reporting package which compares budgeted with actual results. The loosest linkage would be not to include financial statements at all.

Another design feature related to the financial content is the level of rounding in the plan document. Although it may not seem particularly significant at first blush, there is evidence that rounding to a much higher level in the plan than in the budget (e.g., millions of dollars in the plan versus thousands in the budget) can foster a kind of mental distinction between plan and budget numbers which reduces the tendency to view the plan as solely a long-range budget. This can in turn facilitate a much more creative planning effort by making it clear that the managers do not have to commit themselves (in a budgetary sense) to delivering the planned financial results.

Still another important content feature is the conformity between plan and budget numbers for those years which are common to both documents. If the numbers differ, planning may face a credibility gap. Many companies, however, feel that allowing such differences is critical to maintaining the aggressive forward thrust of the planning effort.

For example, one conglomerate includes in the first year of its five-year plan the earnings from acquisitions that are projected to be closed during the next twelve months but which are not yet finalized. The company does not include these earnings in the budgeted results for the next year which line managers are asked to commit themselves to deliver.

Several other companies show differences between planned and budgeted profit for the next year because the two documents are prepared at different times. The one prepared later in the year would reflect the latest thinking and this might differ from projections made earlier in the year.

Situations like these may or may not be desirable, but they certainly reflect loose content linkage. If numerical differences are permitted, one way of moving back toward tightness is to require that some kind of formal reconciliation of them be included in the plan. Many companies which permit differences require such reconciliation.

Related to plan-budget conformity for years common to both documents is the issue of the uniformity of the numbers for any given year as they appear in succeeding annual plan documents. If the planned figures for any one future period change significantly each time a plan is put together, the perceived realism of the planning effort can suffer.

Our evidence suggests, however, that rarely do companies require the numbers for a given year to be "cast in concrete" the very first time that year appears in a plan document. This degree of linkage is probably unrealistically tight.

As we shall illustrate later, a few companies do require formal explanations in the plan for any changes in the projections related to a given future year. This clearly reflects a tighter linkage form of this planning-system variable than would otherwise be reflected by complete freedom to change future years' projections at each iteration of the planning cycle. At least a few companies feel that some tightness at this point is desirable.

A final important design feature is the structure of the content of the plan. In most companies, the budget is structured in terms of the organizational units which will be responsible for carrying it out. Such an approach is a fundamental part of what is often referred to as "responsibility accounting."

Given this situation, it is possible to restructure the plan to focus on programs rather than on the organizational units. The total expenditures for a given year are the same in either case, but there is nevertheless a distinctly looser impact on the way in which the plan document is interpreted.

ORGANIZATIONAL RELATIONSHIPS

The major design feature in this category is the relationship between the organizational units responsible for the long-range planning and those responsible for the budgetary-control processes. The loosest form is to lodge planning and budgeting in separate organizational channels reporting to different top-level executives. The tightest form is to have the two functions combined in one department.

Even in those situations in which planning and budgeting are separated in terms of formal organizational relationships, there is wide latitude in the extent to which the controller is formally involved in the long-range planning effort. Naturally, the loosest linkage situation is to have scant involvement on the part of the controller. However, because of his expertise in analyzing and communicating financially oriented data, it is probably neither possible nor desirable to exclude him completely from the formal planning effort.

Between this extreme of separate planning and budgeting channels and the complete integration of these functions lies a very broad middle ground which can be probed to achieve an appropriate level of involvement for any given company. Among the relevant questions to ask in this regard are the following:

□ Does the controller provide staff support for the preparation of the financial data in the plan document?

□ Does the controller review the plan document before it is finalized?

□ Does the controller have any direct or indirect responsibility for approving the plan?

□ Does the controller have any direct or indirect responsibility for monitoring planned financial results against actual results?

The more questions of this kind that can be answered *yes*, the tighter the plan-budget linkage, even though the functions may officially be separate.

TIMING CONSIDERATIONS

The most important design feature here is concerned with the sequencing of the annual planning and budgeting cycles. If the two cycles are carried out sequentially, which one is done first? How much time elapses between the completion of the first cycle and the beginning of the one which follows it? If the two cycles are undertaken concurrently, what is the relationship between initiation dates, completion dates, and approval dates?

The loosest timing linkage is to have the planning cycle done before the budgeting cycle and to have several months elapse between the two. One major food products manufacturer, for example, completes the annual planning cycle in February and does not begin the budgeting phase until November. Situations like this are least inhibiting to the achievement of "reach" in the planning effort.

The tightest form of the design feature related to sequencing would be to complete the budgeting cycle first and to have the planning cycle follow it with minimal elapsed time in between. Since the budgeting cycle almost always concludes in the last quarter of the fiscal year, it is rare to find a company in which the planning cycle comes last. There are, however, many companies that undertake the two cycles concurrently.

In general, the more the budget process precedes the plan preparation—in terms of initiation, completion, and approval dates—the tighter the linkage, since the budgeting focus will tend to dominate the joint planning-budgeting effort.

One final timing-related design feature is the time horizon for the long-range planning effort. Usually, the shorter this span, the closer the relationship between the budget and the planning process and thus the tighter the plan-budget linkage. Conversely, the longer the time frame, the easier it becomes to clearly distinguish the process from budgeting and thus the looser the plan-budget linkage.

Nowhere in the whole range of system-design features is the trade-off between realism and reach more clearly defined than in the choice of a planning horizon. The longer the time frame, the wider the range of factors which can be varied and thus the broader the range of strategies which can be considered in moving the company toward its long-range objectives.

At the same time, a longer time span increases the uncertainty regarding environmental assumptions, corporate strengths, and the financial parameters which shape the strategy formulation and evaluation process. At some point, uncertainty overcomes the gain in flexibility.

What constitutes an appropriate time horizon certainly varies from industry to industry. It is probably easier, for example, for most public utilities to do fifteen-year planning than it is for defense-aerospace companies to do five-year planning. Within the reasonable range for any given industry, however, the longer the time considerations, the looser the plan-budget linkage. Furthermore, in our opinion, a planning horizon of three or four years reflects a heavy emphasis on realism at the expense of reach, regardless of the industry.

Linkage Examples

In the preceding section of this article, we concentrated on a general framework for considering the plan-budget problem. Now, we shall turn our attention to some of the interesting devices actually being used by the six manufacturing companies that we selected as a small but representative sample of those which have (a) participated in formal planning studies, (b) earned the reputation for having both action-oriented and creative planning systems, and (c) been highly successful in terms of compound EPS growth. Since we believe it unlikely that their records of sustained performance could have been achieved without the help of good planning, it should be revealing to examine in some detail how these companies cope with the linkage problem.

The six companies we observed were Cincinnati Milacron, General Mills, Quaker Oats, Raytheon, Toro, and Warnaco. In them, we encountered such a large number of different linkage devices that we concluded the variety of specific links is limited only by the imagination of the personnel. We shall use the same categories as in the preceding section in reviewing the most interesting linkage practices in these sample companies.

But, first, a note of caution. It is not our intent to propose *the* right answer to the linkage problem, but only to identify some of the more important factors to be considered in determining *a* right answer for a given company at a specific point in time.

CONTENT-RELATED APPROACHES

One of the most innovative attempts to use structure as a mechanism to overcome the creativity-practicality problem is the distinct separation between group and division planning at Warnaco. Each division manager prepares a three-year plan, while each group vice president plans five years out.

Warnaco's objective here is to encourage the group vice presidents to think in more general and longer range terms. They then carry this framework with them to meetings with their division managers. This encourages them to do more creative planning.

It is important to note that the formats of these two plans are much different, with the divisional plans being done in much greater detail than the group plans. This serves to focus the group manager's attention on the strategy of the group itself rather than on the specific details of the divisions' operating programs.

A mechanism we mentioned earlier to overcome the problem of loose linkage is the comparison of a plan with its predecessor from a year earlier. Consider, for example, this situation taken from the planning records of a large paper manufacturer. Here are this company's profit projections for 1971 as shown in—

Five-year plan done in 1966	$60 million
Five-year plan done in 1967	$50 million
Five-year plan done in 1969	$36 million
1971 budget prepared in 1970	$16 million

At the very least, a plan-to-plan comparison would have called the company's attention to the increasing lack of realism the further the projections extended into the future. The threat of having to formally justify this ever-receding bonanza might have served as a sobering influence to the planners.

It is also possible to use plan-to-plan comparisons to overcome the problems of overly conservative forecasting. Thus, if the paper company's profit projections had demonstrated an ascending pattern, the happy surprise of realizing more profits than expected might also have been accompanied by the undesirable development of capacity shortages and missed market opportunities. In such a case, a plan-to-plan comparison could serve as an impetus for more expansive projections.

Of the six companies we visited, only General Mills requires the reporting and justification of significant changes from the preceding year's plan. At General Mills, management feels that this checking device is sufficiently useful in preventing blue-sky fantasizing to justify its risk in terms of discouraging open-ended mind stretching.

A third content-related mechanism worth noting is the relationship between the plan and budget formats. As we noted earlier, if the two documents differ in form and style, it is more difficult to directly transpose the plan to the budget. Both Toro and Raytheon approach a program format for planning and a functional format for budgeting, but they also retain the program and project breakout in the budget as well as the functional allocation. In the other companies we sampled, this split is less distinct since the divisions are largely organized by program area or product line. We view this loosening device as a very significant one that has potential applicability in many companies.

Finally, all six of the sample companies vary the level of detail between the plan and the budget. It is interesting to note, however, that the absolute level of details in the plan also varies significantly among the six companies. Cincinnati Milacron shows only very highly aggregated summary data, whereas Raytheon's plans approach the same level of detail as its budgets. The other four companies fall in between these extreme approaches.

ORGANIZATION COORDINATION

At the corporate level, it is important to understand who is coordinating the planning and who is coordinating the budgeting. The basic question here is whether the company wants to split the two processes. The splitting of this coordination function has the effect of loosening the linkage between planning and budgeting. Both Toro and Cincinnati Milacron provide excellent examples of this.

At Toro, planning is coordinated by the Corporate Planner and budgeting by the Controller. No formal attempt is made to ensure that these two functions proceed in a similar fashion. Cincinnati Milacron handles this in much the same way that Toro does.

At General Mills, the end result is the same but the mechanisms are much more complex, with coordination being handled by groups instead of individuals.

Different handling at the division level can also affect the linking process. The basic split here is between strategy formulation and the quantified explication of that strategy. While in almost all instances both are coordinated by the division manager, the degree of delegation of the quantification phase can vary significantly.

It is noteworthy that there is very little divergence in the way quantification of plan results is handled by the six sample companies. All of them largely delegate this phase to the divisional controller. This has a loosening effect by focusing the division manager's attention on policy rather than on detailed profit and loss information.

Although it is not a "device" in the usual sense, a company's informal communication process can function in a way that tightens the linkage between planning and budgeting. A great deal of informal information transfer across the corporate/divisional interface increases top management's cognizance of what is in the plan and how it relates to the budget. The presence of informal channels of communication may make top management appear to have an omniscient awareness of these issues, even if this is actually not the case.

At Cincinnati Milacron, where the planning and budgeting systems are very closely linked, one division manager stated that he really felt strongly committed to delivering the performance projected in his five-year plan. At Quaker Oats and Toro, where there are loose linkage systems, two division managers reported similar feelings of commitment. It is difficult for us to assess what precise influence the informal communication processes in the foregoing companies had in forging the personal commitments of these three division managers to delivering the planned results. However, the counter-intuitive coincidence of loose systems and strong commitments at least offers circumstantial evidence that this influence does exist and should not be overlooked.

TIME HORIZONS

A separation in time between the end of the planning cycle and the beginning of the budgeting cycle, as we noted earlier, has the effect of loosening the linkage between the two processes. When the time to worry about next year's performance commitment is still several months away, it is easier to be expansive about the future. In addition, since forecast conditions are always changing, the more time that elapses subsequent to submission of the plan, the easier it is to justify a revision in the budget.

Of the six sample companies, only Raytheon pursues its planning and budgeting cycles concurrently. Cincinnati Milacron has a six-month separation between the end of planning and the beginning of budgeting. General Mills, Quaker Oats, Toro, and Warnaco all have at least a two- to three-month separation.

In general, as the number of years in the budget is extended, or the number of years in the plan contracted, the similarity between the plan and the budget increases. Different time horizons for the two processes tend to emphasize the different purposes of each. Five of the six companies we sampled have either a four- or five-year planning range and a one- or two-year budget span. The exception is Warnaco, which we noted previously.

Appropriate Equilibrium

Individual linkage devices impact on the planning system by facilitating an overall planning effort which is either more creative or action oriented. As is evident from the preceding discussion, some devices serve to promote a stronger action orientation in planning while others encourage more creativity.

Since a single planning system will utilize several devices which may have opposing effects on the plan-budget balance, an "algebraic" sum of the devices is needed to determine where the planning system is located on the linkage continuum. This plays a pivotal role in achieving an appropriate equilibrium between divergent requirements for both creative and action-oriented planning.

Whether or not a particular planning balance is appropriate for a given company hinges on the corporate setting. Thus, if the underlying essence of planning is to improve a company's ability to cope with changes, it follows that, as the changes are realized, the need for specific forms of planning will also change. In other words, a dynamic corporate setting may call for heavy emphasis on creativity at one point in time and heavy emphasis on practicality at another. The implication is that, as a company's needs change, devices must be added or subtracted in order to adjust the balance between these planning objectives.

The concept of a dynamic corporate setting seems particularly relevant to the four of the six sample companies which are now diversifying extensively beyond the boundaries of their traditional industries. Consider:

☐ The Toro Company has changed from a manufacturer of lawn

mowers and snow blowers to a broad-based participant in the environmental beautification market.

□ General Mills's Fashion Division, which was established only recently, already contributes significantly to the company's sales and earnings and competes in markets dramatically different from those served by Cheerios and other ready-to-eat cereals.

□ Quaker Oats, in one recent fiscal year, derived 25% of its sales from nongrocery product sources, including 12% from Fisher-Price Toys. The company has since further diversified in nongrocery areas through acquisition of Louis Marx & Co. Toys and the Needlecraft Corporation of America.

□ Cincinnati Milacron, the largest manufacturer of machine tools in the world, is seeking points of entry into the minicomputer and semiconductor markets.

A dynamic corporate setting, however, is not necessarily dependent on the diversification activity of a company. For example:

□ Cincinnati Milacron, with 80% of its sales in the machine tool industry, contends with market cycles which brought machine tool sales volume in one recent year down 50% to 60% below the peak reached two years earlier.

□ The Raytheon Equipment Division, a defense contractor, faces rapid turnover in eletronics technology—a contract bidding process that sometimes makes a ticket in the Irish Sweepstakes look like a sure bet—and concomitant uncertainties and headaches in dealing with mercurial government customers.

□ Warnaco, competing with 30,000 other companies in the apparel industry, finds that although total sales volume is relatively stable, individual markets are highly volatile as fashions come and go in quick succession.

Whether the result of extensive diversification programs or corporate response to the challenges of traditional markets, all six companies are in a state of perpetual change.

Given this state of flux, it is significant to note that the planning systems in five of the companies have recently been changed, are in the process of being changed, or will be changed in the near future (the exception is Raytheon Equipment). To illustrate:

□ At Toro, David M. Lilly, Chairman and Chief Executive Officer, recently projected the development of looser linkage between the planning and budgeting systems.

□ At General Mills, one recent year's planning instructions announced a procedure to highlight where that year's plan deviated from the previous year's plan; the same instructions reemphasized a year-old procedure which required "new" businesses to be differentiated from "present" businesses.

☐ At Quaker Oats, the corporate planner foresees the emergence of tighter linkage as the company becomes acclimated to its new divisionalized structure.

☐ At Cincinnati Milacron, a new planning system is in operation; this system is very loosely linked to budgeting and shifts the burden of planning from the division managers to the group managers.

☐ At Warnaco, as we noted earlier, a systems modification has been implemented; this requires group vice presidents to plan five years into the future and their subordinate division managers three years ahead.

In seeking a comprehensive explanation of the planning system changes just described, we find particularly pertinent the observation that management control systems must be consistent with top management's objectives in order to be truly effective. If the same can be said of formal planning systems, then it follows that a change in an effective planning system is usually triggered by a change in top management's objectives.

The implication here is that whether or not a given change improves a planning system may be beside the point. To paraphrase Marshall McLuhan, the planning system and the changes made in it may be "the medium that is the message"—i.e., the message from top management.

CRITERION OF CONSISTENCY

In this section of the article, we shall examine more closely two of the planning system changes previously mentioned to see what inferences about top management's objectives we can draw from them.

Since 1971, Cincinnati Milacron has been pulling out of a severe recession that afflicted the entire machine tool industry. Operating management's ordeal during the past two years has been something akin to a day-to-day struggle. As the company has begun to emerge from this traumatic experience, top management has installed a new planning system to allow maximum opportunity for broad-level mind stretching. Furthermore, the burden of planning has been shifted upward to a level of management where there exists the opportunity and authority to implement a diversification program.

The message of Cincinnati Milacron's two planning-system changes appears to be rather straightforward: top management wants aggressive diversification planning.

In his memorandum covering General Mills's 1971 planning instructions, James P. MacFarland, Chairman and Chief Executive Officer, indicated the need for a more aggressive capital investment program in the years ahead to achieve the company's sales and earnings objectives. He also referred to progress in the control of capital use and to a change in the planning procedures which would allow top management to focus easily on the changes made subsequent to the previous planning cycle. His general instructions described this procedural change in more detail and reiterated a year-old procedure which separated the planning for new businesses from that for current businesses.

In our judgment, it is a fair guess that it will be a tougher task to revise estimates upward in order to justify additional capital for a current business than to submit new estimates in order to justify seed capital for a new business. The message of the announcement of both a new procedure and reemphasis on an old one appears to be that the encouragement of heavier investments is intended for new and not for current businesses.

(This message, incidentally, is clearly reflected in the chairman's and president's letter to General Mills's stockholders and employees in the 1971 Annual Report.)

The procedure at General Mills of separating current and new businesses is particularly noteworthy in that it creates an opportunity to differentiate the planning perspectives, and to apply different standards of expectation to each type of business. In this manner, top management can encourage a division manager to be creative in planning for his new businesses and action oriented in planning for his current businesses.

Future-oriented businesses will be best suited for loosely linked planning/budgeting systems. As the potential of a business begins to be realized, tighter linkage will be desirable in order to transform promises into results. At that point, a balance between creative planning and action-oriented planning would be especially appropriate. Later, as the business exhausts its growth potential and evolves into a "cash generator," even tighter linkage will be desirable to accommodate the corporation's capital needs for the next generation of new businesses.

In short, recognition of divergent corporate objectives for both the mature and the future-oriented business is manifested in different degrees of linkage in their respective planning/budgeting systems. As evident at Quaker Oats, for example, a divisionalized company can find itself at several points—up and down—on the linkage continuum at the same time. In evaluating whether or not any point on the continuum is "right" or "wrong," the sole criterion must be its consistency with corporate objectives.

Conclusion

To be effective, every formal long-range planning system must achieve a workable compromise between creativity and practicality—twin goals that are often in conflict. This problem of maintaining a satisfactory balance between "reach" and "realism" can be directly addressed by varying those design features of planning which relate to its interface with budgeting. However, in order to put in perspective the importance of loosening the plan/budget linkage, it is important to consider the role of informal communications and the personalities of management.

At the corporate/division interface, companies that have a great deal of informal communication transfer are likely to be constantly aware of what was written in the plan and how that relates to the budget. This has the effect of very tightly linking the plan and the budget, even in structurally loose systems, unless management makes a conscious effort to demonstrate that this is not wanted. Even if this intent is demonstrated at the corporate level, there still may be tight linkage built in at the division level because of the division manager's personality.

Generally speaking, the divisional planning and budgeting are either both done by the division manager himself or at least coordinated by him. As he coordinates the preparation of the budget, he often feels—either consciously or subconsciously—an obligation to justify the value of the plan by reflecting much of it in the budget which represents his short-term game plan for the division.

Briefly, loosening devices have much broader applications than to just those companies which have structurally tight linkage systems. In fact, some of them may be needed in any action-oriented planning system.

We believe that managers should consider these devices as variables they can and should manipulate in the interest of more effective planning. Viewed in this context, the linkage continuum can be considered as a powerful interpreter of the top-management objectives implicit in the planning system.

Although at first this may seem to be counter-intuitive, we believe that it is not the planning system which generates corporate objectives but rather the corporate objectives which dictate the appropriate planning system. We are neither proposing that there is a "correct" form for any of these design features, nor that it is always possible to structure a planning system so that "realistic creativity" is ensured.

We do believe, however, that "realistic reach" in planning is not just an illusory phenomenon which exists independent of management's actions. Rather, it is well within management's control to influence the focus of the efforts by changing the structure of the planning system. That, we feel, is all any manager can ask.

9. Formulating Strategy in Smaller Companies

Frank F. Gilmore

While many sophisticated concepts of formulating corporate strategy are being studied with interest by large corporations, they hold little promise for medium-sized and smaller companies—at least, in the foreseeable future. For the latter, strategic planning is still more of an art than a science. A conference table approach to strategy, based on executive judgment and intuition, is outlined in this article. The author describes six major steps in the process and lists the types of questions the chief executive should ask his management team to consider.

Corporate planning, aimed at strategy formulation for the company, has now become so generally accepted that many executives are having second thoughts about their approaches. Indeed, the top management group of one major corporation has concluded that, since each of its members has at one time or another been in charge of his company's corporate planning department, there is little need to go through the formal planning cycle that characterized its approach for the past decade. Inasmuch as all of them think like planners, they feel that they have outgrown their initial planning approach and are groping for something better.

In other large companies, consideration is being given to possible ways in which management science and the computer may be applied to the strategy formulation problem. A suggestion offered by Russell L. Ackoff in the form of an adaptive approach appears to hold promise as a frame of reference within which such improvements may be developed over time.[1]

But for the medium-sized or small company that does not have planning departments, operations research groups, or large-scale computing capacity, and that simply cannot afford to engage in planning research, a more modest approach must be sought. This does not mean that the managers of such companies can afford to neglect their planning responsibilities. Today's widespread adoption of strategic planning will not permit such a course. What is needed is a simple, practical approach that is within the

1. *Concept of Corporate Planning* (New York, Wiley-Interscience, 1970).

reach of these smaller companies. I shall try to meet that need in this article.

Evolution of Approach

Prior to the middle 1950's, the major task of the chief executive was viewed as that of adapting the company to changing conditions. This traditional approach developed during the period between World Wars I and II, when unpredictable and violent fluctuations meant adaptation or failure.

In this traditional top management approach, determination of objectives presupposed a size-up of the situation of the company as a whole. The objectives could then provide direction and unity of purpose for the development of a program of action covering the various activities of the company.

Size-ups were made in various ways, depending on the background of the management involved, the organization of the company, and the position of the company in terms of its growth and its place in its industry. Any one of several approaches could serve the purpose. Size-ups were most commonly conducted along departmental lines because most companies were more or less centralized then and were therefore organized by major functions, such as marketing, production, and finance. For this reason, the functional size-up approach will be examined more closely.

Exhibit I shows this traditional approach. It indicates the process required to reach a diagnosis of the company's prospects and problems:

1. An analysis was made of the total picture. Its components were analyses of the competitive situation and of the various functions. (Some executives found it useful to look at the competitive situation first, and then analyze the financial and operating picture. They felt that a size-up of these two areas often provided measuring sticks or raised pertinent questions that served to sharpen the analysis of other functional areas. Moreover, many analysts found it helpful to defer the size-up of the executive organization to the last because of the light that was shed on management performance by the examination of the functional areas.)

2. Under each topic in the breakdown, significant findings were noted and classified, and an effort was made to reach a conclusion on each major topic.

3. The separate conclusions were then combined, and an attempt was made to arrive, inductively, at the overall diagnosis. Particular attention was paid to interrelationships that might be significant for the company as a whole.

This painstaking, sizing-up, inductive process became the basis for

Exhibit I. Example of traditional approach to strategy formulation

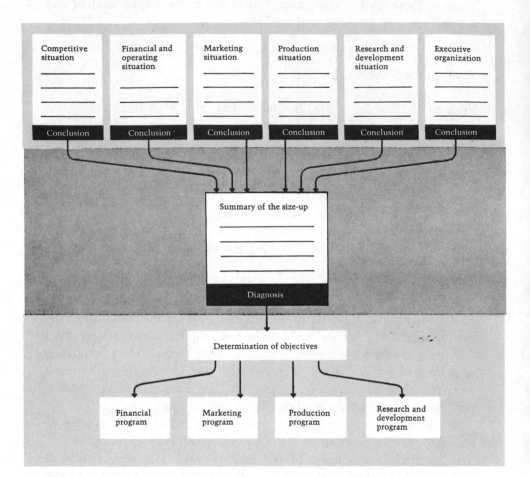

determining objectives for the future. The chief executive then faced the task of deciding on a course of action and, in the light of the objectives, choosing between alternative ways of solving the problem diagnosed in the size-up.

This approach was actually incomplete, since the process remained open-ended, as shown in Part A of *Exhibit II*. There was a definite tendency for top management to size up the situation, starting at the very base; formulate objectives and programs of action; organize to carry out the plans; and exercise executive control; but then drift along until serious problems made it necessary to size up the situation again.

FORMALIZING THE ANALYSIS

During the 1950's, it became increasingly clear that a new approach to policy formulation was urgently needed. It was recognized that—

Exhibit II. *Formulating strategy*

A. Traditional open-loop process

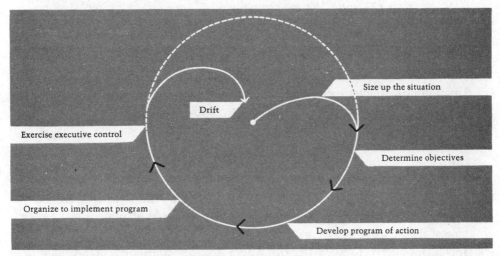

B. Modern closed-loop process

. . . concern for short-term problems would have to shift to plans for capitalizing on long-term opportunities;

. . . sizing up the situation as a basis for a new course of action would have to give way to reappraising existing strategy in the light of the changing environment;

. . . sporadic diagnosis would have to be replaced by constant surveillance;

. . . concern for immediate profits and for adaptability to meet changes in current conditions needed to shift to focusing on long-range ROI, growth, flexibility, and stability.

In other words, occasional preoccupation with such questions as "Where are we?" and "Where are we going?" needed to be replaced by frequent consideration of such questions as "Are we making satisfactory progress with respect to plan?" and "Are our plans still valid?"

Not surprisingly, therefore, since the 1950's there has been a significant shift to formal, long-range, strategic planning. The most significant distinguishing characteristic of this approach has been that executives are now managing in accordance with a constantly updated strategic plan. Instead of just sizing up the situation at a given point of time, they schedule reappraisals of current strategy. The effect of this change is a shift from an open-loop, short-range approach to a closed-loop, long-range approach, illustrated in Part B of *Exhibit II*.

As this conceptual scheme shows, the size-up of the situation can be thought of as a spring-board; and as long as reappraisal of present strategy closes the loop, the system continues to cycle. Feedback and regular surveillance serve to keep the company's strategy constantly before management. Thus, after the first cycle, reappraisal of current strategy takes the place of the size-up of the situation. Such reappraisal examines the same areas, but analysis is focused on the possible consequences of continuing the current strategy, given trends and developments in the external environment, and existing internal operating conditions and results.

Accompanying the change from sporadic size-up to frequent, and in many cases regular, reappraisal, there has been a shift in emphasis from size-up to formulation. In keeping with Peter F. Drucker's advice in the early 1950's, management attention has been focused more on the discovery of opportunities than on the solution of problems.[2] As a result, more emphasis has been placed on the evaluation of alternative courses of action and on maximization of performance.

In the formulation of strategy, management may, in time, have the assistance of tools and techniques from management science. But before significant progress along these lines can be made (as I shall discuss in the next section), there must be a better understanding of the structure of the problem itself.

STRUCTURE OF RELATIONSHIPS

One approach to structuring the problem of strategy formulation is summarized in *Exhibit III*. In this model, which was developed during a Cornell research project, the relationship between the company and its competitive environment is expressed by the strategy of the enterprise, which has three basic components:

2. *The Practice of Management* (New York, Harper & Brothers, 1954).

Exhibit III. Model of new approach

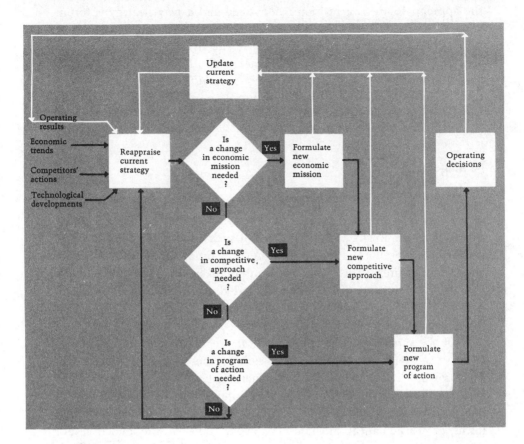

1. *Economic mission*—This is concerned with the kind of business the company should be in, and what its performance objectives should be.

2. *Competitive approach*—This is concerned with finding the product-market-sales approach that will accomplish the economic mission, and with deriving pertinent goals in the various areas of the business.

3. *Program of action*—This involves a search for efficient means of implementing the competitive approach.

In summary form, the process works as follows: Current strategy is reappraised from time to time in the light of internal operating results, economic trends, competitors' actions, and technological developments. When opportunities or threats have been disclosed, management proceeds to ask questions designed to indicate when and in what respect strategy should be changed. If a new economic mission is called for, the planners proceed to formulate a revised approach. This, in turn, calls for revision of the competitive approach and of the program of action. If the economic mission is considered sound, the competitive approach is questioned. If the competitive approach seems appropriate, the process continues until the appropriate area for revision is identified and a new strategy is formulated.

Of course, it might be concluded that the overall current strategy is sound. Then no revision would take place, and another reappraisal would be made at a later date. The white lines in *Exhibit III* indicate the feedback of operating results (part of the control process) and the updating of current strategy as a result of formulation.

Management Science?

At first thought, it would appear that management science would offer several possible approaches to strategy formulation. However, the few approaches that might prove useful are in such an early stage of development that they hold little promise at this time. While a number of operations research (OR) approaches are useful in decision making at the operations level, most of these are of limited use in strategy formulation because of the large number of variables involved. For example, consider mathematical programming and simulation:

□ Of the various forms of mathematical programming, the best known is linear programming, which is applicable to those situations where relationships are linear and there is no uncertainty (or it may be assumed away). Under these conditions, linear programming results in optimization, but the limitations may be too restrictive for strategy formulation. Other forms of mathematical programming avoid some of the difficulties of linear programming, but computation becomes considerably more difficult and often necessitates trial-and-error approaches.

□ Simulation may be useful in strategy situations that do not fall within the limitations of linear programming. For example, such nonlinear relationships as those due to economies of scale may be easily incorporated, and probabilistic data reflecting the presence of uncertainty may be used. But whereas mathematical programming requires only that data be provided for an already established model, simulation requires that the model itself be constructed. This is a formidable task, involving many assumptions as to the interaction of the various components within the company and of the company with its environment. A simulation model thus requires a great deal of time and effort to construct and test, and is extremely difficult to validate. And, even if these tasks are successfully completed, there is little assurance that the same model will continue to be valid.

Other OR approaches are not relevant to the overall decision, but are applicable to parts of the strategy decision process. Among these are capital budgeting, inventory theory, scheduling theory, and so forth. They are useful as components in strategy formulation, but they cannot handle all the major aspects of the problem.

Thus, OR is only appropriate for the solution of well-defined problems where the relevant relationships can be specified and the objectives have been decided on. Under such conditions, calculations are dominant, and mathematics is often almost a substitute for judgment.

Actually, "systems analysis"—or the "systems approach," as it is often called—may offer more promise in strategy formulation than OR. Systems analysis has been defined as an approach to solving complex problems of choice under uncertainty by systematic examination of the costs, effectiveness, and risks of various alternatives. It is appropriate for use in poorly structured problems, where the relationships are not clear and where decisions must be made among alternative objectives. It became a major instrument in governmental decision making during the 1960's, and is attracting increasing attention in business as a useful way of analyzing top management planning problems.

All in all, however, the potentials of management science for strategic purposes seem limited to use in large companies that possess considerable technical resources for their development and use. For the foreseeable future, managements in medium-sized and small companies will have to use the generalizing, inductive, empirical method which has evolved out of the old, size-up approach. And this approach remains more an art than a science.

Simple, Practical Method

I shall describe now a simple, practical planning method that can be employed by top executives in medium-sized and small companies. Several influences have shaped the sequence of steps to be suggested. John Dewey's concepts of how people think provide a useful rationale for the approach as a whole: the process of strategy formulation may be viewed as a form of reflective thinking, where one progresses step by step from recognition of the problem to solution.[3] The experience of management, teachers, and consultants during the past half century has also had a strong impact: the older, size-up approach has contributed to early steps in the sequence, while recent developments in strategy formulation have helped shape later steps. Finally, the need for top management to advocate its proposals, when formulated, to the board of directors has influenced the scheme to be described.

The process of strategy formulation may be carried out in six progressive steps. I shall describe them in detail and illustrate them with notes made at a series of top management meetings in a small company that was applying this approach. The company, a manufacturer of insulated wire and cable, will be identified as "IWAC Co."

3. *How We Think* (Boston, D. C. Heath & Co., 1933).

1. RECORD CURRENT STRATEGY

The recording of current strategy is an important foundation for subsequent steps. In a company that is managing according to a well-defined
strategy, it will be easy for the manager to record his plans. Typically today,
the strategy of large corporations is a matter of record. But many medium-
sized and small companies operate informally with a loosely defined
strategy. In these cases, the task of recording current strategy becomes more
difficult. Nevertheless, it is usually possible to infer from trends and
executive behavior what strategy is impicit in the company's operations. If
efforts to record current strategy fail, one can fall back on the size-up
approach for the first step.

In recording current strategy, it is important to clarify top management's
criteria as to the kind of company it wants to operate. These criteria will
be expressed in terms of values held by the top management group. Also,
what kind of company does top management think it *should* operate?
Criteria for this answer will be expressed in terms of management's concept
of social responsibility.

Such criteria will be important in later steps, when the core of the
strategy problem is discovered, and alternative strategies are formulated
and evaluated. To illustrate, in the case of IWAC Co., the top management group described the strategy that had characterized its operations
for some years as follows:

"The company develops, manufactures, and sells standard telephone
wire and cable to independent telephone companies. It is attempting to
diversify into such products as electronic connectors, printed electronic
circuits, heavy-duty lighting cords, and retractile cords. The company
markets all its products through distributors."

2. IDENTIFY PROBLEMS

The current strategy must be reappraised to determine whether problems
exist. A strategy problem is one which may have a significant influence
on the future success of the enterprise as a whole.

Management must first look at the company's environment. In order
to estimate the consequences of continuing the current strategy, it needs
to study external trends and developments and to make assumptions about
the economic outlook, the shape of future technology, and competitors'
actions. In short, it needs to establish premises about the environment
on which analysis of company operations can be based. In effect, it asks,
"Given the environmental outlook, is our strategy still valid? Are any
opportunities or threats disclosed by this outlook?"

Then management must examine the operating situation of the company as disclosed by financial results and progress made under the current strategy in the various areas of operations. As with the old, size-up approach, a useful next step is to analyze the financial and operating picture. Meaningful reappraisal of current strategy is facilitated by a careful analysis of financial and operating trends, since, as noted earlier, useful measuring sticks for appraising other aspects of the company's operations can be derived from the financial phase of the analysis.

Executives can then proceed to reappraise the marketing, production, and research and development policies, and the management organization of the company. In particular, they must be on the alert for significant weaknesses or unutilized strengths. Throughout this part of the analysis they ask, "Is the company making satisfactory progress according to plan?"

Cutting through symptoms: Strategy problems may take the form of threats or opportunities in the environment; failure to meet plans; signs of organizational strife; adverse trends with respect to share of market, competitive advantage, or financial results or condition; or other indications of loss of health or vigor. These problems are likely to be symptoms of a more deep-seated difficulty. To illustrate in terms of a real-life situation, let us turn back to the IWAC case.

When the top executives began analyzing the problems, risks, and opportunities of the company, they were surprised by the shape of the picture that began to emerge. I shall mention just some of the highlights of the findings management considered:

"Changes in industry structure are intensifying competition. The number of independent telephone companies is declining largely because of acquisitions by General Telephone. Vertical integration into wire and cable insulation is taking place among both suppliers and end users. Some of the larger wire and cable companies are owned by major suppliers of wire and insulation material.

"In the last five years, the number of companies making plastic-insulated telephone wires and cables has increased from 5 to 13. A slump in wire demand, along with falling copper prices early in the current year, led to price cutting in the industry. With the economy experiencing a recession, the wire and cable industry is faced with overcapacity.

"Our competitors are moving toward direct selling; of 25 competing companies, 20 have sales offices, 10 have warehouses, and 13 have no distributors at all. General Cable attributes its great success to the establishment of sales offices and stock distribution centers. Yet our company continues to leave its sales effort largely in the hands of exclusive distributors. Indeed, our company is unique in its nonaggressive, competitive approach in sales.

"In addition to the increase in competition as a result of changes in industry structure and the trend toward direct selling, other competitive pressures are becoming evident. Competitors are underselling us in connection with broadcast wires and cord sets because of our insistence on excessively high quality.

"Despite the fact that competition is growing more intense, the company's immediate position is sound. Our sales have declined less this year (12%) than has been true for the insulated wire and cable industry as a whole (15%). Return on stockholders' investment, while sporadic, has been generally favorable. The company is financially liquid and has a reasonable long-term debt/equity ratio.

"Some moves have been made to offset the impact of increased competition. First, a new works manager has been brought into the company, and already he has achieved significant operating economies. Inventory investment has been reduced 30%, and purchasing costs have declined significantly.

"A promising outlook exists for some of the company's special products. The company holds patents on commercial applications of heavy-duty lighting cords, a recent addition to the product line. There are few competitors in this field, but the company is limiting its opportunity by selling the systems through one exclusive distributor.

"The product line is being broadened through the addition of color-sheathed cords, oilproof cords, large flexible cables, and secondary power cables. But the market potential of these new products is not known by the company. Prospects in the power cable field look attractive, with only a few manufacturers currently competing. But the company is moving very slowly in this area.

"Although some changes have been made in the executive organization, among them the appointment of the new works manager, several long-term employees are still entrenched in established ways of doing business which will have to be changed in light of competitive trends. Particularly notable are broadly held values about the desirability of extremely high-quality products and the feeling that the present method of selling through distributors can be changed only at great cost."

3. DISCOVER THE CORE ELEMENTS

If the reappraisal discloses that major problems exist, it is necessary to discover their core. The basic difficulty may take many forms. For example, the current strategy may require greater competence and/or resources than the company possesses; the strategy may fail to exploit adequately the company's distinctive competence; the company may lack sufficient competitive advantage, or it may fail to exploit opportunities and/or meet threats in the environment; or the strategy may not be internally consistent. Diagnosis with respect to the company's performance against plan and prognosis as to the future consequences of continuing the current strategy are both involved in this step. To return to IWAC:

Management concluded that a shift in strategy was needed. It saw that IWAC could not continue on its traditional course and keep growing profitably. Two major considerations were involved. "First, the company can no longer concentrate on *standard* wire and cable products," it was reported. "All signs point to a loss of market share in this area. There appear to be better opportunities in *specialized* wire and cable products, where the company possesses distinctive competence. Second, the current policy of selling through distributors no longer appears appropriate. It is neither consistent with industry practice nor compatible with specialization."

4. FORMULATE ALTERNATIVES

Once the core of the strategy problem has been discovered, management can formulate alternative ways of solving the problem. It is characteristic of modern planning approaches that one must try to conceive of all alternatives that might offer some possibility of providing a solution. Then consideration must be given in a preliminary way to limitations imposed by the company's competence and resources. Also, management's values and sense of social responsibility will set some boundaries.

But this is more the time for imagination and innovation than for logic. More rigorous evaluation can come in the next step. In the IWAC case, the thinking of executives was summarized as follows:

"The company has three alternative strategies it might follow. First, it could merge with a supplier or end user of insulated wire and cable. Second, it could specialize in insulated wire and cable products that require strict quality specifications and technological expertise, and at the same time improve its marketing effectiveness by distributing its products directly through its own sales force. Third, it could become an aggressive marketer of a relatively full line of insulated wires and cables with an extensive direct-sales organization.

"The first alternative is a distinct possibility. Current trends toward vertical integration in the industry make the company a possible investment opportunity for an end user or supplier. The company's research capabilities, manufacturing know-how, and capacity to produce telephone wire and cable might make it an attractive acquisition for a company such as General Telephone.

"The second alternative would require a closer relationship with our customers. In particular, a technical sales force would be needed that could work directly with customers in determining the end user's needs, product quality, technical characteristics of the product, and new systems applications.

"The third alternative would emphasize an aggressive competitive approach embracing a full line of products and extensive marketing organization, not unlike that used by General Cable. The company would become a manufacturer of a wide line of insulated wires and cables, utilizing its technological know-how to develop new products. Increased marketing expenditures would be required in advertising and in the development of a sizable sales organization, establishment of warehouses, maintenance of inventories in the field, and development of sales branch offices."

5. EVALUATE ALTERNATIVES

In this step, management looks at the bearing of the various vital factors on the choice of a strategy. The alternatives must be compared in terms of:

□ Relative effectiveness in solving the strategic problem.

□ The degree to which each matches the company's competence and resources.

□ Their relative competitive advantage.

□ The extent to which they satisfy management's preferences and sense of social responsibility.

□ Their relative ability to minimize the creation of new problems.

In strategy problems, more than in other types of problems, executives would like to be able to optimize with respect to *several* relevant factors. Therefore, trade-offs are necessary, for optimization with respect to one factor will be at the expense of another. This is a characteristic of business strategy problems which, along with the premium placed on discovering the core elements, makes them the most difficult challenges facing management. Probably the best one can hope to do at this time is to choose that alternative which, in his judgment, offers the best blend of advantages. If the reasoning of the IWAC executives were to be reconstructed, it might run as follows:

"All three alternatives would meet the strategic challenge presented by the increasing competition in the industry. The merger route might involve the risk of lengthy and costly litigation under antitrust laws. Merger would also raise a question as to how much basic research the company as a 'captive shop' would be encouraged to do. It would probably limit the scope of technological problems considered by the laboratory. This alternative would meet the threat of the declining market in telephone wires and cables more effectively than the other two alternatives, but would provide less of an outlet for management's innovativeness or entrepreneurship.

"The success of the second alternative, the specialization approach, would depend largely on the company's ability to continue as an innovator. It would capitalize on the organization's capabilities in solving customers' needs. To be successful under this approach, the company would have to carve out a special niche in the insulated wire and cable market. This approach could constitute a good match between the company's capabilities and resources and the opportunities in the industry. But considerable expenditure would be needed for the development of the technically expert sales force that would be required.

"The third alternative, an aggressive marketing approach involving a full line of products and a greatly enlarged marketing organization, would tax the innovative capabilities of the laboratory and would set the company into direct competition with larger companies, such as General Cable. Compared with the other two alternatives, this would require the largest additional investment. The risk involved in this alternative would center on financial problems, with the possibility of overextension with respect to long-term debt or loss of control through sale of common stock to outsiders.

"We conclude that the second alternative is superior to the third, but the choice between merger and specialization is less apparent. The merger alternative might be rejected largely on the basis of management's implied emphasis on quality, innovation, and entrepreneurship."

6. CHOOSE THE NEW STRATEGY

In this last step, management identifies those factors which are of overriding importance. These are the factors on which the decision turns. In a strategy problem, where there may appear to be five or six relevant factors of significance, one or two of them may seem pivotal, and the relative standing of the alternatives with respect to these factors provides the basis for the final choice. Here is what happened in the IWAC case:

Management concluded that the best strategy was the second of the three possibilities considered—specializing in insulated wire and cable products which required high-quality specifications, and marketing its products directly through its own sales force. This meant eliminating products that did not utilize the company's distinctive competence in insulation, such as printed circuits and electronic connectors, and ceasing at the earliest practical moment to rely on distributors. Under this strategy, the company would undertake aggressive development and marketing of power cable and heavy-duty lighting cords.

Exhibit IV. Questions to use in formulating strategy

1. Record current strategy:
   a. What is the current strategy?
   b. What kind of business does management want to operate (considering such management values as desired return on investment, growth rate, share of market, stability, flexibility, character of the business, and climate)?
   c. What kind of business does management feel it ought to operate (considering management's concepts of social responsibility and obligations to stockholders, employees, community, competitors, customers, suppliers, government, and the like)?

2. Identify problems with the current strategy:
   a. Are trends discernible in the environment that may become threats and/or missed opportunities if the current strategy is continued?
   b. Is the company having difficulty implementing the current strategy?
   c. Is the attempt to carry out the current strategy disclosing significant weaknesses and/or unutilized strengths in the company?
   d. Are there other concerns with respect to the validity of the current strategy?
   e. Is the current strategy no longer valid?

3. Discover the core of the strategy problem:
   a. Does the current strategy require greater competence and/or resources than the company possesses?
   b. Does it fail to exploit adequately the company's distinctive competence?
   c. Does it lack sufficient competitive advantage?
   d. Will it fail to exploit opportunities and/or meet threats in the environment, now or in the future?

   e. Are the various elements of the strategy internally inconsistent?
   f. Are there other considerations with respect to the core of the strategy problem?
   g. What, then, is the real core of the strategy problem?

4. Formulate alternative new strategies:
   a. What possible alternatives exist for solving the strategy problem?
   b. To what extent do the company's competence and resources limit the number of alternatives that should be considered?
   c. To what extent do management's preferences limit the alternatives?
   d. To what extent does management's sense of social responsibility limit the alternatives?
   e. What strategic alternatives are acceptable?

5. Evaluate alternative new strategies:
   a. Which alternative *best* solves the strategy problem?
   b. Which alternative offers the *best* match with the company's competence and resources?
   c. Which alternative offers the *greatest* competitive advantage?
   d. Which alternative *best* satisfies management's preferences?
   e. Which alternative *best* meets management's sense of social responsibility?
   f. Which alternative *minimizes* the creation of new problems?

6. Choose a new strategy:
   a. What is the *relative significance* of each of the preceding considerations?
   b. What should the new strategy be?

Conclusion

The approach described in this article is most valuable for medium-sized and small companies. Top executives of these companies, working at the conference table, can approach strategy formulation as a joint effort. In such group problem solving, one of the principal tools contributing to effective leadership by the president is a carefully prepared outline for guiding the discussion. The six-step approach I have described can be the starting point for such an outline. *Exhibit IV* exemplifies the kinds of questions that might be asked. The president, as chairman of the meeting, can phrase the questions in terms of the situation under discussion, note pertinent additional questions at appropriate points, and thus guide the meeting. Each of the six main tasks becomes a milepost to be passed in the progress toward a solution.

The chairman can advance group thinking by offering interpretative summaries, and, using transitional statements, he can lead the group from one major step to the next. The constant challenge for him is to maintain that balance between freedom and control which makes for progress and yet does not act to stifle creative thinking.

Since 1960 the job of top executives has undergone substantial change. Corporate strategy has become their dominant concern. But strategy is not yet a science even in large corporations, despite recent developments in management science and computers. And for the medium-sized or small company which cannot afford OR, planning departments, or large-scale computer capacity, the task is likely to remain an art during the foreseeable future. In such circumstances, strategy should be formulated by the top management team at the conference table. Judgment, experience, intuition, and well-guided discussions are the key to success, not staff work and mathematical models.

Part III

Marketing

Preface

Marketing is often called a function of management, but it is more than that. For many companies it is practically synonymous with corporate strategy, and for most it is at least the keystone in the strategic arch. In this section, therefore, marketing is discussed in fairly broad management terms. Marketing goals are seen not as the goals of a department or division in the organization but as corporate-wide goals. Sales executives are seen not as experts in salesmanship but as company planners and policy makers. Marketing and sales techniques are seen not as tools of specialists but as methods that many managers should know about.

In "Marketing Myopia," one of the most influential articles ever published in HBR, the focus is on the way businessmen think of their companies' roles and missions. Conceiving an organization's mission as selling particular products or services, rather than meeting certain customer needs, is a form of tunnel vision that has got many businesses into serious trouble. "Marketing Planning for Industrial Products," based on a study of 50 industrial marketers, analyzes the three principal causes of problems in putting marketing planning concepts into practice in industrial companies. "Get the Most Out of Your Sales Force," also based on a survey, offers guidelines to executives who want to tailor hiring and managing practices to the job the company is trying to do. "Manage the Customer, Not Just the Sales Force" is an application of the "Marketing Myopia" concept to the activities of sales managers in particular. "Demarketing—Yes, Demarketing" discusses a need that a growing number of companies are becoming aware of—how to relate to customers during times of shortages, excess demand, or unwanted demand. "Grass Roots Market Research" focuses on the opportunities for field sales forces to do research tasks traditionally reserved to centralized market research departments.

10. Marketing Myopia

Theodore Levitt

Today's growth product is tomorrow's buggy whip—and often management does not seem to realize it. A company must learn to think of itself not as producing goods and services but as buying, creating, and satisfying customers. This approach should permeate every nook and cranny of the organization; if it doesn't, no amount of efficiency in operations can compensate for the lack. Marketing myopia is not easy to overcome, but unless it is, an organization cannot achieve greatness. This is the lesson learned by many companies in many industries, including the most glamorous "growth" industries.

Every major industry was once a growth industry. But some that are now riding a wave of growth enthusiasm are very much in the shadow of decline. Others which are thought of as seasoned growth industries have actually stopped growing. In every case the reason growth is threatened, slowed, or stopped is *not* because the market is saturated. It is because there has been a failure of management.

Fateful Purposes

The failure is at the top. The executives responsible for it, in the last analysis, are those who deal with broad aims and policies. Thus:

□ The railroads did not stop growing because the need for passenger and freight transportation declined. That grew. The railroads are in trouble today not because the need was filled by others (cars, trucks, airplanes, even telephones), but because it was *not* filled by the railroads themselves. They let others take customers away from them because they assumed themselves to be in the railroad business rather than in the transportation business. The reason they defined their industry wrong was because they were railroad-oriented instead of transportation-oriented; they were product-oriented instead of customer-oriented.

◻ Hollywood barely escaped being totally ravished by television. Actually, all the established film companies went through drastic reorganizations. Some simply disappeared. All of them got into trouble not because of TV's inroads but because of their own myopia. As with the railroads, Hollywood defined its business incorrectly. It thought it was in the movie business when it was actually in the entertainment business. "Movies" implied a specific, limited product. This produced a fatuous contentment which from the beginning led producers to view TV as a threat. Hollywood scorned and rejected TV when it should have welcomed it as an opportunity—an opportunity to expand the entertainment business.

Today TV is a bigger business than the old narrowly defined movie business ever was. Had Hollywood been customer-oriented (providing entertainment), rather than product-oriented (making movies), would it have gone through the fiscal purgatory that it did? I doubt it. What ultimately saved Hollywood and accounted for its recent resurgence was the wave of new young writers, producers, and directors whose previous successes in television had decimated the old movie companies and toppled the big movie moguls.

There are other less obvious examples of industries that have been and are now endangering their futures by improperly defining their purposes. I shall discuss some in detail later and analyze the kind of policies that lead to trouble. Right now it may help to show what a thoroughly customer-oriented management *can* do to keep a growth industry growing, even after the obvious opportunities have been exhausted; and here there are two examples that have been around for a long time. They are nylon and glass—specifically, E. I. Du Pont de Nemours & Company and Corning Glass Works:

Both companies have great technical competence. Their product orientation is unquestioned. But this alone does not explain their success. After all, who was more pridefully product-oriented and product-conscious than the erstwhile New England textile companies that have been so thoroughly massacred? The Du Ponts and the Cornings have succeeded not primarily because of their product or research orientation but because they have been thoroughly customer-oriented also. It is constant watchfulness for opportunities to apply their technical know-how to the creation of customer-satisfying uses which accounts for their prodigious output of successful new products. Without a very sophisticated eye on the customer, most of their new products might have been wrong, their sales methods useless.

Aluminum has also continued to be a growth industry, thanks to the efforts of two wartime-created companies which deliberately set about creating new customer-satisfying uses. Without Kaiser Aluminum &

Chemical Corporation and Reynolds Metals Company, the total demand for aluminum today would be vastly less than it is.

Some may argue that it is foolish to set the railroads off against aluminum or the movies off against glass. Are not aluminum and glass naturally so versatile that the industries are bound to have more growth opportunities than the railroads and movies? This view commits precisely the error I have been talking about. It defines an industry, or a product, or a cluster of know-how so narrowly as to guarantee its premature senescence. When we mention "railroads," we should make sure we mean "transportation." As transporters, the railroads still have a good chance for very considerable growth. They are not limited to the railroad business as such (though in my opinion rail transportation is potentially a much stronger transportation medium than is generally believed).

What the railroads lack is not opportunity, but some of the same managerial imaginativeness and audacity that made them great. Even an amateur like Jacques Barzun saw what is lacking when he said:

"I grieve to see the most advanced physical and social organization of the last century go down in shabby disgrace for lack of the same comprehensive imagination that built it up. [What is lacking is] the will of the companies to survive and to satisfy the public by inventiveness and skill."[1]

Shadow of Obsolescence

It is impossible to mention a single major industry that did not at one time qualify for the magic appellation of "growth industry." In each case its assumed strength lay in the apparently unchallenged superiority of its product. There appeared to be no effective substitute for it. It was itself a runaway substitute for the product it so triumphantly replaced. Yet one after another of these celebrated industries has come under a shadow. Let us look briefly at a few more of them, this time taking examples that have so far received a little less attention:

□ *Dry cleaning*—This was once a growth industry with lavish prospects. In an age of wool garments, imagine being finally able to get them safely and easily clean. The boom was on.

Yet here we are only a few decades after the boom started and the industry is in trouble. Where has the competition come from? From a

---

1. Jacques Barzun, "Trains and the Mind of Man," *Holiday*, February 1960, p. 21.

better way of cleaning? No. It has come from synthetic fibers and chemical additives that have cut the need for dry cleaning. But this is only the beginning. Lurking in the wings and ready to make chemical dry cleaning totally obsolescent is that powerful magician, ultrasonics.

□ *Electric utilities*—This is another one of those supposedly "no-sub-stitute" products that has been enthroned on a pedestal of invincible growth. When the incandescent lamp came along, kerosene lights were finished. Later the water wheel and the steam engine were cut to ribbons by the flexibility, reliability, simplicity, and just plain easy availability of electric motors. The prosperity of electric utilities continues to wax extrava-gant as the home is converted into a museum of electric gadgetry. How can anybody miss by investing in utilities, with no competition, nothing but growth ahead?

But a second look is not quite so comforting. A score of nonutility com-panies are well advanced toward developing a powerful chemical fuel cell which could sit in some hidden closet of every home silently ticking off electric power. The electric lines that vulgarize so many neighborhoods will be eliminated. So will the endless demolition of streets and service interruptions during storms. Also on the horizon is solar energy, again pioneered by nonutility companies.

Who says that the utilities have no competition? They may be natural monopolies now, but tomorrow they may be natural deaths. To avoid this prospect, they too will have to develop fuel cells, solar energy, and other power sources. To survive, they themselves will have to plot the obsoles-cence of what now produces their livelihood.

□ *Grocery stores*—Many people find it hard to realize that there ever was a thriving establishment known as the "corner grocery store." The supermarket has taken over with a powerful effectiveness. Yet the big food chains of the 1930's narrowly escaped being completely wiped out by the aggressive expansion of independent supermarkets. The first genuine super-market was opened in 1930, in Jamaica, Long Island. By 1933 supermarkets were thriving in California, Ohio, Pennsylvania, and elsewhere. Yet the established chains pompously ignored them. When they chose to notice them, it was with such derisive descriptions as "cheapy," "horse-and-buggy," "cracker-barrel storekeeping," and "unethical opportunists."

The executive of one big chain announced at the time that he found it "hard to believe that people will drive for miles to shop for foods and sacrifice the personal service chains have perfected and to which Mrs. Consumer is accustomed." As late as 1936, the National Wholesale Gro-cers convention and the New Jersey Retail Grocers Association said there was nothing to fear. They said that the supers' narrow appeal to the price buyer limited the size of their market. They had to draw from miles around. When imitators came, there would be wholesale liquidations as volume fell. The current high sales of the supers was said to be partly due to their novelty. Basically people wanted convenient neighborhood grocers. If the neighborhood stores "cooperate with their suppliers, pay attention to their costs, and improve their service," they would be able to weather the competition until it blew over.

It never blew over. The chains discovered that survival required going into the supermarket business. This meant the wholesale destruction of their huge investments in corner store sites and in established distribution and merchandising methods. The companies with "the courage of their convictions" resolutely stuck to the corner store philosophy. They kept their pride but lost their shirts.

SELF-DECEIVING CYCLE

But memories are short. For example, it is hard for people who today confidently hail the twin messiahs of electronics and chemicals to see how things could possibly go wrong with these galloping industries. They probably also cannot see how a reasonably sensible businessman could have been as myopic as the famous Boston millionaire who unintentionally sentenced his heirs to poverty by stipulating that his entire estate be forever invested exclusively in electric streetcar securities. His posthumous declaration, "There will always be a big demand for efficient urban transportation," is no consolation to his heirs who sustain life by pumping gasoline at automobile filling stations.

Yet, in a casual survey I recently took among a group of intelligent business executives, nearly half agreed that it would be hard to hurt their heirs by tying their estates forever to the electronics industry. When I then confronted them with the Boston streetcar example, they chorused unanimously, "That's different!" But is it? Is not the basic situation identical?

In truth, *there is no such thing* as a growth industry, I believe. There are only companies organized and operated to create and capitalize on growth opportunities. Industries that assume themselves to be riding some automatic growth escalator invariably descend into stagnation. The history of every dead and dying "growth" industry shows a self-deceiving cycle of bountiful expansion and undetected decay. There are four conditions which usually guarantee this cycle:

1. The belief that growth is assured by an expanding and more affluent population.

2. The belief that there is no competitive substitute for the industry's major product.

3. Too much faith in mass production and in the advantages of rapidly declining unit costs as output rises.

4. Preoccupation with a product that lends itself to carefully controlled scientific experimentation, improvement, and manufacturing cost reduction.

I should like now to begin examining each of these conditions in some detail. To build my case as boldly as possible, I shall illustrate the points with reference to three industries—petroleum, automobiles, and electronics —particularly petroleum, because it spans more years and more vicissitudes. Not only do these three have excellent reputations with the general public and also enjoy the confidence of sophisticated investors, but their managements have become known for progressive thinking in areas like financial control, product research, and management training. If obsolescence can cripple even these industries, it can happen anywhere.

Population Myth

The belief that profits are assured by an expanding and more affluent population is dear to the heart of every industry. It takes the edge off the apprehensions everybody understandably feels about the future. If consumers are multiplying and also buying more of your product or service, you can face the future with considerably more comfort than if the market is shrinking. An expanding market keeps the manufacturer from having to think very hard or imaginatively. If thinking is an intellectual response to a problem, then the absence of a problem leads to the absence of thinking. If your product has an automatically expanding market, then you will not give much thought to how to expand it.

One of the most interesting examples of this is provided by the petroleum industry. Probably our oldest growth industry, it has an enviable record. While there are some current apprehensions about its growth rate, the industry itself tends to be optimistic. But I believe it can be demonstrated that it is undergoing a fundamental yet typical change. It is not only ceasing to be a growth industry, but may actually be a declining one, relative to other business. Although there is widespread unawareness of it, I believe that within a fairly short time the oil industry may find itself in much the same position of retrospective glory that the railroads are now in. Despite its pioneering work in developing and applying the present-value method of investment evaluation, in employee relations, and in working with backward countries, the petroleum business is a distressing example of how complacency and wrongheadedness can stubbornly convert opportunity into near disaster.

One of the characteristics of this and other industries that have believed very strongly in the beneficial consequences of an expanding population, while at the same time being industries with a generic product for which there has appeared to be no competitive substitute, is that the individual companies have sought to outdo their competitors by improving on what they are already doing. This makes sense, of course, if one assumes that sales are tied to the country's population strings, because the customer can compare products only on a feature-by-feature basis. I believe it is significant, for example, that not since John D. Rockefeller sent free kerosene lamps to China has the oil industry done anything really outstanding to create a demand for its product. Not even in product improvement has it showered itself with eminence. The greatest single improvement, namely, the development of tetraethyl lead, came from outside the industry, specifically from General Motors and Du Pont. The big contributions made by the industry itself are confined to the technology of oil exploration, production, and refining.

ASKING FOR TROUBLE

In other words, the industry's efforts have focused on improving the *efficiency* of getting and making its product, not really on improving the generic product or its marketing. Moreover, its chief product has continuously been defined in the narrowest possible terms, namely, gasoline, not energy, fuel, or transportation. This attitude has helped assure that:

□ Major improvements in gasoline quality tend not to originate in the oil industry. Also, the development of superior alternative fuels comes from outside the oil industry, as will be shown later.

□ Major innovations in automobile fuel marketing are originated by small new oil companies that are not primarily preoccupied with production or refining. These are the companies that have been responsible for the rapidly expanding multipump gasoline stations, with their successful emphasis on large and clean layouts, rapid and efficient driveway service, and quality gasoline at low prices.

Thus, the oil industry is asking for trouble from outsiders. Sooner or later, in this land of hungry inventors and entrepreneurs, a threat is sure to come. The possibilities of this will become more apparent when we turn to the next dangerous belief of many managements. For the sake of continuity, because this second belief is tied closely to the first, I shall continue with the same example.

Idea of Indispensability

The petroleum industry is pretty much persuaded that there is no competitive substitute for its major product, gasoline—or if there is, that it will continue to be a derivative of crude oil, such as diesel fuel or kerosene jet fuel.

There is a lot of automatic wishful thinking in this assumption. The trouble is that most refining companies own huge amounts of crude oil reserves. These have value only if there is a market for products into which oil can be converted—hence the tenacious belief in the continuing competitive superiority of automobile fuels made from crude oil.

This idea persists despite all historic evidence against it. The evidence not only shows that oil has never been a superior product for any purpose for very long, but it also shows that the oil industry has never really been a growth industry. It has been a succession of different businesses that have gone through the usual historic cycles of growth, maturity, and decay. Its over-all survival is owed to a series of miraculous escapes from total obsolescence, of last-minute and unexpected reprieves from total disaster reminiscent of the Perils of Pauline.

PERILS OF PETROLEUM

I shall sketch in only the main episodes:

□ First, crude oil was largely a patent medicine. But even before that fad ran out, demand was greatly expanded by the use of oil in kerosene lamps. The prospect of lighting the world's lamps gave rise to an extravagant promise of growth. The prospects were similar to those the industry now holds for gasoline in other parts of the world. It can hardly wait for the underdeveloped nations to get a car in every garage.

In the days of the kerosene lamp, the oil companies competed with each other and against gaslight by trying to improve the illuminating characteristics of kerosene. Then suddenly the impossible happened. Edison invented a light which was totally nondependent on crude oil. Had it not been for the growing use of kerosene in space heaters, the incandescent lamp would have completely finished oil as a growth industry at that time. Oil would have been good for little else than axle grease.

□ Then disaster and reprieve struck again. Two great innovations occurred, neither originating in the oil industry. The successful development of coal-burning domestic central-heating systems made the space heater obsolescent. While the industry reeled, along came its most magnificent boost yet—the internal combustion engine, also invented by outsiders. Then when the prodigious expansion for gasoline finally began to level off in the 1920's, along came the miraculous escape of a central oil heater. Once again, the escape was provided by an outsider's invention and development. And when that market weakened, wartime demand for aviation fuel came to the rescue. After the war the expansion of civilian aviation, the dieselization of railroads, and the explosive demand for cars and trucks kept the recently been proclaimed—ran into severe competition from natural gas. While the oil companies themselves owned the gas that now competed with their oil, the industry did not originate the natural gas revolution, nor has it to this day greatly profited from its gas ownership. The gas revolution was made by newly formed transmission companies that marketed the product with an aggressive ardor. They started a magnificent new industry, first against the advice and then against the resistance of the oil companies.

By all the logic of the situation, the oil companies themselves should have made the gas revolution. They not only owned the gas; they also were the only people experienced in handling, scrubbing, and using it, the only people experienced in pipeline technology and transmission, and they understood heating problems. But, partly because they knew that natural gas would compete with their own sale of heating oil, the oil companies pooh-poohed the potentials of gas.

The revolution was finally started by oil pipeline executives who, unable to persuade their own companies to go into gas, quit and organized the spectacularly successful gas transmission companies. Even after their success became painfully evident to the oil companies, the latter did not go into gas transmission. The multibillion dollar business which should have been theirs went to others. As in the past, the industry was blinded by its narrow preoccupation with a specific product and the value of its reserves. It paid little or no attention to its customers' basic needs and preferences.

□ The postwar years have not witnessed any change. Immediately after World War II the oil industry was greatly encouraged about its future by the rapid expansion of demand for its traditional line of products. In 1950 most companies projected annual rates of domestic expansion of around 6% through at least 1975. Though the ratio of crude oil reserves to demand in the Free World was about 20 to 1, with 10 to 1 being usually considered a reasonable working ratio in the United States, booming demand sent oil men searching for more without sufficient regard to what the future really promised. In 1952 they "hit" in the Middle East; the ratio skyrocketed to 42 to 1. If gross additions to reserves continue at the average rate of the past five years (37 billion barrels annually), then by 1970 the reserve ratio will be up to 45 to 1. This abundance of oil has weakened crude and product prices all over the world.

UNCERTAIN FUTURE

Management cannot find much consolation today in the rapidly expanding petrochemical industry, another oil-using idea that did not originate in the leading firms. The total United States production of petrochemicals is equivalent to about 2% (by volume) of the demand for all petroleum products. Although the petrochemical industry is now expected to grow by about 10% per year, this will not offset other drains on the growth of crude oil consumption. Furthermore, while petrochemical products are many and growing, it is well to remember that there are nonpetroleum sources of the basic raw material, such as coal. Besides, a lot of plastics can be produced with relatively little oil. A 50,000-barrel-per-day oil refinery is now considered the absolute minimum size for efficiency. But a 5,000-barrel-per-day chemical plant is a giant operation.

Oil has never been a continuously strong growth industry. It has grown by fits and starts, always miraculously saved by innovations and developments not of its own making. The reason it has not grown in a smooth progression is that each time it thought it had a superior product safe from the possibility of competitive substitutes, the product turned out to be inferior and notoriously subject to obsolescence. Until now, gasoline (for motor fuel, anyhow) has escaped this fate. But, as we shall see later, it too may be on its last legs.

The point of all this is that there is no guarantee against product obsolescence. If a company's own research does not make it obsolete, another's will. Unless an industry is especially lucky, as oil has been until now, it can easily go down in a sea of red figures—just as the railroads have, as the buggy whip manufacturers have, as the corner grocery chains have, as most of the big movie companies have, and indeed as many other industries have.

The best way for a firm to be lucky is to make its own luck. That requires knowing what makes a business successful. One of the greatest enemies of this knowledge is mass production.

Production Pressures

Mass-production industries are impelled by a great drive to produce all they can. The prospect of steeply declining unit costs as output rises is more than most companies can usually resist. The profit possibilities look spectacular. All effort focuses on production. The result is that marketing gets neglected.

John Kenneth Galbraith contends that just the opposite occurs.[2] Output is so prodigious that all effort concentrates on trying to get rid of it. He says this accounts for singing commercials, desecration of the countryside with advertising signs, and other wasteful and vulgar practices. Galbraith has a finger on something real, but he misses the strategic point. Mass production does indeed generate great pressure to "move" the product. But what usually gets emphasized is selling, not marketing. Marketing, being a more sophisticated and complex process, gets ignored.

2. *The Affluent Society* (Boston, Houghton Mifflin Company, 1958), pp. 152-160.

The difference between marketing and selling is more than semantic. Selling focuses on the needs of the seller, marketing on the needs of the buyer. Selling is preoccupied with the seller's need to convert his product into cash; marketing with the idea of satisfying the needs of the customer by means of the product and the whole cluster of things associated with creating, delivering, and finally consuming it.

In some industries the enticements of full mass production have been so powerful that for many years top management in effect has told the sales departments, "You get rid of it; we'll worry about profits." By contrast, a truly marketing-minded firm tries to create value-satisfying goods and services that consumers will want to buy. What it offers for sale includes not only the generic product or service, but also how it is made available to the customer, in what form, when, under what conditions, and at what terms of trade. Most important, what it offers for sale is determined not by the seller but by the buyer. The seller takes his cues from the buyer in such a way that the product becomes a consequence of the marketing effort, not vice versa.

LAG IN DETROIT

This may sound like an elementary rule of business, but that does not keep it from being violated wholesale. It is certainly more violated than honored. Take the automobile industry:

Here mass production is most famous, most honored, and has the greatest impact on the entire society. The industry has hitched its fortune to the relentless requirements of the annual model change, a policy that makes customer orientation an especially urgent necessity. Consequently the auto companies annually spend millions of dollars on consumer research. But the fact that the new compact cars are selling so well indicates that Detroit's vast researches have for a long time failed to reveal what the customer really wanted. Detroit was not persuaded that he wanted anything different from what he had been getting until it lost millions of customers to other small car manufacturers.

How could this unbelievable lag behind consumer wants have been perpetuated so long? Why did not research reveal consumer preferences before consumers' buying decisions themselves revealed the facts? Is that not what consumer research is for—to find out before the fact what is going to happen? The answer is that Detroit never really researched the customer's wants. It only researched his preferences between the kinds of things which it had already decided to offer him. For Detroit is mainly product-oriented, not customer-oriented. To the extent that the customer is recognized as having needs that the manufacturer should try to satisfy, Detroit usually acts as if the job can be done entirely by product changes.

Occasionally attention gets paid to financing, too, but that is done more in order to sell than to enable the customer to buy.

As for taking care of other customer needs, there is not enough being done to write about. The areas of the greatest unsatisfied needs are ignored, or at best get stepchild attention. These are at the point of sale and on the matter of automotive repair and maintenance. Detroit views these problem areas as being of secondary importance. That is underscored by the fact that the retailing and servicing ends of this industry are neither owned and operated nor controlled by the manufacturers. Once the car is produced, things are pretty much in the dealer's inadequate hands. Illustrative of Detroit's arm's-length attitude is the fact that, while servicing holds enormous sales-stimulating, profit-building opportunities, only 57 of Chevrolet's 7,000 dealers provide night maintenance service.

Motorists repeatedly express their dissatisfaction with servicing and their apprehensions about buying cars under the present selling setup. The anxieties and problems they encounter during the auto buying and maintenance processes are probably more intense and widespread today than 30 years ago. Yet the automobile companies do not *seem* to listen to or take their cues from the anguished consumer. If they do listen, it must be through the filter of their own preoccupation with production. The marketing effort is still viewed as a necessary consequence of the product, not vice versa, as it should be. That is the legacy of mass production, with its parochial view that profit resides essentially in low-cost full production.

WHAT FORD PUT FIRST

The profit lure of mass production obviously has a place in the plans and strategy of business management, but it must always *follow* hard thinking about the customer. This is one of the most important lessons that we can learn from the contradictory behavior of Henry Ford. In a sense Ford was both the most brilliant and the most senseless marketer in American history. He was senseless because he refused to give the customer anything but a black car. He was brilliant because he fashioned a production system designed to fit market needs. We habitually celebrate him for the wrong reason, his production genius. His real genius was marketing. We think he was able to cut his selling price and therefore sell millions of $500 cars because his invention of the assembly line had reduced the costs. Actually he invented the assembly line because he had concluded that at $500 he could sell millions of cars. Mass production was the *result* not the cause of his low prices.

Ford repeatedly emphasized this point, but a nation of production-oriented business managers refuses to hear the great lesson he taught. Here is his operating philosophy as he expressed it succinctly:

Our policy is to reduce the price, extend the operations, and improve the article. You will notice that the reduction of price comes first. We have never considered any costs as fixed. Therefore we first reduce the price to the point where we believe more sales will result. Then we go ahead and try to make the prices. We do not bother about the costs. The new price forces the costs down. The more usual way is to take the costs and then determine the price, and although that method may be scientific in the narrow sense; it is not scientific in the broad sense, because what earthly use is it to know the cost if it tells you that you cannot manufacture at a price at which the article can be sold? But more to the point is the fact that, although one may calculate what a cost is, and of course all of our costs are carefully calculated, no one knows what a cost ought to be. One of the ways of discovering . . . is to name a price so low as to force everybody in the place to the highest point of efficiency. The low price makes everybody dig for profits. We make more discoveries concerning manufacturing and selling under this forced method than by any method of leisurely investigation.[3]

PRODUCT PROVINCIALISM

The tantalizing profit possibilities of low unit production costs may be the most seriously self-deceiving attitude that can afflict a company, particularly a "growth" company where an apparently assured expansion of demand already tends to undermine a proper concern for the importance of marketing and the customer.

The usual result of this narrow preoccupation with so-called concrete matters is that instead of growing, the industry declines. It usually means that the product fails to adapt to the constantly changing patterns of consumer needs and tastes, to new and modified marketing institutions and practices, or to product developments in competing or complementary industries. The industry has its eyes so firmly on its own specific product that it does not see how it is being made obsolete.

The classical example of this is the buggy whip industry. No amount of product improvement could stave off its death sentence. But had the industry defined itself as being in the transportation business rather than the buggy whip business, it might have survived. It would have done what survival always entails, that is, changing. Even if it had only defined its business as providing a stimulant or catalyst to an energy source, it might have survived by becoming a manufacturer of, say, fanbelts or air cleaners.

What may some day be a still more classical example is, again, the oil industry. Having let others steal marvelous opportunities from it (e.g., natural gas, as already mentioned, missile fuels, and jet engine lubricants), one would expect it to have taken steps never to let that happen again.

3. Henry Ford, *My Life and Work* (New York, Doubleday, Page & Company, 1923), pp. 146-147.

But this is not the case. We are now getting extraordinary new developments in fuel systems specifically designed to power automobiles. Not
only are these developments concentrated in firms outside the petroleum
industry, but petroleum is almost systematically ignoring them, securely
content in its wedded bliss to oil. It is the story of the kerosene lamp versus
the incandescent lamp all over again. Oil is trying to improve hydrocarbon
fuels rather than to develop *any* fuels best suited to the needs of their
users, whether or not made in different ways and with different raw materials from oil.

Here are some of the things which nonpetroleum companies are working
on:

☐ Over a dozen such firms now have advanced working models of energy
systems which, when perfected, will replace the internal combustion engine
and eliminate the demand for gasoline. The superior merit of each of these
systems is their elimination of frequent, time-consuming, and irritating
refueling stops. Most of these systems are fuel cells designed to create
electrical energy directly from chemicals without combustion. Most of
them use chemicals that are not derived from oil, generally hydrogen and
oxygen.

☐ Several other companies have advanced models of electric storage
batteries designed to power automobiles. One of these is an aircraft producer that is working jointly with several electric utility companies. The
latter hope to use off-peak generating capacity to supply overnight plug-in
battery regeneration. Another company, also using the battery approach,
is a medium-size electronics firm with extensive small-battery experience
that it developed in connection with its work on hearing aids. It is collaborating with an automobile manufacturer. Recent improvements arising
from the need for high-powered miniature power storage plants in rockets
have put us within reach of a relatively small battery capable of withstand-
ing great overloads or surges of power. Germanium diode applications and
batteries using sintered-plate and nickel-cadmium techniques promise to
make a revolution in our energy sources.

☐ Solar energy conversion systems are also getting increasing attention.
One usually cautious Detroit auto executive recently ventured that solar-
powered cars might be common by 1980.

As for the oil companies, they are more or less "watching developments,"
as one research director put it to me. A few are doing a bit of research on
fuel cells, but almost always confined to developing cells powered by hydrocarbon chemicals. None of them are enthusiastically researching fuel cells,
batteries, or solar power plants. None of them are spending a fraction as
much on research in these profoundly important areas as they are on the
usual run-of-the-mill things like reducing combustion chamber deposit in
gasoline engines. One major integrated petroleum company recently took a

tentative look at the fuel cell and concluded that although "the companies actively working on it indicate a belief in ultimate success . . . the timing and magnitude of its impact are too remote to warrant recognition in our forecasts."

One might, of course, ask: Why should the oil companies do anything different? Would not chemical fuel cells, batteries, or solar energy kill the present product lines? The answer is that they would indeed, and that is precisely the reason for the oil firms having to develop these power units before their competitors, so they will not be companies without an industry.

Management might be more likely to do what is needed for its own preservation if it thought of itself as being in the energy business. But even that would not be enough if it persists in imprisoning itself in the narrow grip of its tight product orientation. It has to think of itself as taking care of customer needs, not finding, refining, or even selling oil. Once it genuinely thinks of its business as taking care of people's transportation needs, nothing can stop it from creating its own extravagantly profitable growth.

"CREATIVE DESTRUCTION"

Since words are cheap and deeds are dear, it may be appropriate to indicate what this kind of thinking involves and leads to. Let us start at the beginning—the customer. It can be shown that motorists strongly dislike the bother, delay, and experience of buying gasoline. People actually do not buy gasoline. They cannot see it, taste it, feel it, appreciate it, or really test it. What they buy is the right to continue driving their cars. The gas station is like a tax collector to whom people are compelled to pay a periodic toll as the price of using their cars. This makes the gas station a basically unpopular institution. It can never be made popular or pleasant, only less unpopular, less unpleasant.

To reduce its unpopularity completely means eliminating it. Nobody likes a tax collector, not even a pleasantly cheerful one. Nobody likes to interrupt a trip to buy a phantom product, not even from a handsome Adonis or a seductive Venus. Hence, companies that are working on exotic fuel substitutes which will eliminate the need for frequent refueling are heading directly into the outstretched arms of the irritated motorist. They are riding a wave of inevitability, not because they are creating something which is technologically superior or more sophisticated, but because they are satisfying a powerful customer need. They are also eliminating noxious odors and air pollution.

Once the petroleum companies recognize the customer-satisfying logic of what another power system can do, they will see that they have no

food chains had a choice about going into the supermarket business, or the vacuum tube companies had a choice about making semiconductors. For their own good the oil firms will have to destroy their own highly profitable assets. No amount of wishful thinking can save them from the necessity of engaging in this form of "creative destruction."

I phrase the need as strongly as this because I think management must make quite an effort to break itself loose from conventional ways. It is all too easy in this day and age for a company or industry to let its sense of purpose become dominated by the economies of full production and to develop a dangerously lopsided product orientation. In short, if management lets itself drift, it invariably drifts in the direction of thinking of itself as producing goods and services, not customer satisfactions. While it probably will not descend to the depths of telling its salesmen, "You get rid of it; we'll worry about profits," it can, without knowing it, be practicing precisely that formula for withering decay. The historic fate of one growth industry after another has been its suicidal product provincialism.

Dangers of R & D

Another big danger to a firm's continued growth arises when top management is wholly transfixed by the profit possibilities of technical research and development. To illustrate I shall turn first to a new industry—electronics—and then return once more to the oil companies. By comparing a fresh example with a familiar one, I hope to emphasize the prevalence and insidiousness of a hazardous way of thinking.

MARKETING SHORTCHANGED

In the case of electronics, the greatest danger which faces the glamorous new companies in this field is not that they do not pay enough attention to research and development, but that they pay *too much* attention to it. And the fact that the fastest growing electronics firms owe their eminence to their heavy emphasis on technical research is completely beside the point. They have vaulted to affluence on a sudden crest of unusually strong general receptiveness to new technical ideas. Also, their success has been shaped in the virtually guaranteed market of military subsidies and by military orders that in many cases actually preceded the existence of facilities to make the products. Their expansion has, in other words, been almost totally devoid of marketing effort.

Thus, they are growing up under conditions that come dangerously close to creating the illusion that a superior product will sell itself. Having created a successful company by making a superior product, it is not surprising that management continues to be oriented toward the product rather than the people who consume it. It develops the philosophy that continued growth is a matter of continued product innovation and improvement.

A number of other factors tend to strengthen and sustain this belief:

1. Because electronic products are highly complex and sophisticated, managements become top-heavy with engineers and scientists. This creates a selective bias in favor of research and production at the expense of marketing. The organization tends to view itself as making things rather than satisfying customer needs. Marketing gets treated as a residual activity, "something else" that must be done once the vital job of product creation and production is completed.

2. To this bias in favor of product research, development, and production is added the bias in favor of dealing with controllable variables. Engineers and scientists are at home in the world of concrete things like machines, test tubes, production lines, and even balance sheets. The abstractions to which they feel kindly are those which are testable or manipulatable in the laboratory, or, if not testable, then functional, such as Euclid's axioms. In short, the managements of the new glamour-growth companies tend to favor those business activities which lend themselves to careful study, experimentation, and control—the hard, practical realities of the lab, the shop, the books.

What gets shortchanged are the realities of the *market*. Consumers are unpredictable, varied, fickle, stupid, shortsighted, stubborn, and generally bothersome. This is not what the engineer-managers say, but deep down in their consciousness it is what they believe. And this accounts for their concentrating on what they know and what they can control, namely, product research, engineering, and production. The emphasis on production becomes particularly attractive when the product can be made at declining unit costs. There is no more inviting way of making money than by running the plant full blast.

Today the top-heavy science-engineering-production orientation of so many electronics companies works reasonably well because they are pushing into new frontiers in which the armed services have pioneered virtually assured markets. The companies are in the felicitous position of having to fill, not find markets; of not having to discover what the customer needs and wants, but of having the customer voluntarily come forward with specific new product demands. If a team of consultants had been assigned specifically to design a business situation calculated to prevent the emergence and development of a customer-oriented marketing viewpoint, it could not have produced anything better than the conditions just described.

STEPCHILD TREATMENT

The oil industry is a stunning example of how science, technology, and mass production can divert an entire group of companies from their main task. To the extent the consumer is studied at all (which is not much), the focus is forever on getting information which is designed to help the oil companies improve what they are now doing. They try to discover more convincing advertising themes, more effective sales promotional drives, what the market shares of the various companies are, what people like or dislike about service station dealers and oil companies, and so forth. Nobody seems as interested in probing deeply into the basic human needs that the industry might be trying to satisfy as in probing into the basic properties of the raw material that the companies work with in trying to deliver customer satisfactions.

Basic questions about customers and markets seldom get asked. The latter occupy a stepchild status. They are recognized as existing, as having to be taken care of, but not worth very much real thought or dedicated attention. Nobody gets as excited about the customers in his own backyard as about the oil in the Sahara Desert. Nothing illustrates better the neglect of marketing than its treatment in the industry press:

The centennial issue of the *American Petroleum Institute Quarterly*, published in 1959 to celebrate the discovery of oil in Titusville, Pennsylvania, contained 21 feature articles proclaiming the industry's greatness. Only one of these talked about its achievements in marketing, and that was only a pictorial record of how service station architecture has changed. The issue also contained a special section on "New Horizons," which was devoted to showing the magnificent role oil would play in America's future. Every reference was ebulliently optimistic, never implying once that oil might have some hard competition. Even the reference to atomic energy was a cheerful catalogue of how oil would help make atomic energy a success. There was not a single apprehension that the oil industry's affluence might be threatened or a suggestion that one "new horizon" might include new and better ways of serving oil's present customers.

But the most revealing example of the stepchild treatment that marketing gets was still another special series of short articles on "The Revolutionary Potential of Electronics." Under that heading this list of articles appeared in the table of contents:

"In the Search for Oil"
"In Production Operations"
"In Refinery Processes"
"In Pipeline Operations"

Significantly, every one of the industry's major functional areas is listed, *except* marketing. Why? Either it is believed that electronics holds no revolutionary potential for petroleum marketing (which is palpably wrong), or the editors forgot to discuss marketing (which is more likely, and illustrates its stepchild status).

The order in which the four functional areas are listed also betrays the alienation of the oil industry from the consumer. The industry is implicitly defined as beginning with the search for oil and ending with its distribution from the refinery. But the truth is, it seems to me, that the industry begins with the needs of the customer for its products. From that primal position its definition moves steadily backstream to areas of progressively lesser importance, until it finally comes to rest at the "search for oil."

BEGINNING AND END

The view that an industry is a customer-satisfying process, not a goods-producing process, is vital for all businessmen to understand. An industry begins with the customer and his needs, not with a patent, a raw material, or a selling skill. Given the customer's needs, the industry develops backwards, first concerning itself with the physical *delivery* of customer satisfactions. Then it moves back further to *creating* the things by which these satisfactions are in part achieved. How these materials are created is a matter of indifference to the customer, hence the particular form of manufacturing, processing, or what-have-you cannot be considered as a vital aspect of the industry. Finally, the industry moves back still further to *finding* the raw materials necessary for making its products.

The irony of some industries oriented toward technical research and development is that the scientists who occupy the high executive positions are totally unscientific when it comes to defining their companies' over-all needs and purposes. They violate the first two rules of the scientific method —being aware of and defining their companies' problems, and then developing testable hypotheses about solving them. They are scientific only about the convenient things, such as laboratory and product experiments. The reason that the customer (and the satisfaction of his deepest needs) is not considered as being "the problem" is not because there is any certain belief that no such problem exists, but because an organizational lifetime has conditioned management to look in the opposite direction. Marketing is a stepchild.

I do not mean that selling is ignored. Far from it. But selling, again, is not marketing. As already pointed out, selling concerns itself with the tricks and techniques of getting people to exchange their cash for your product. It is not concerned with the values that the exchange is all about. And it does not, as marketing invariably does, view the entire business process as consisting of a tightly integrated effort to discover, create, arouse, and satisfy customer needs. The customer is somebody "out there" who, with proper cunning, can be separated from his loose change.

Actually, not even selling gets much attention in some technologically minded firms. Because there is a virtually guaranteed market for the abundant flow of their new products, they do not actually know what a real market is. It is as if they lived in a planned economy, moving their products routinely from factory to retail outlet. Their successful concentration on products tends to convince them of the soundness of what they have been doing, and they fail to see the gathering clouds over the market.

Conclusion

Less than 75 years ago American railroads enjoyed a fierce loyalty among astute Wall Streeters. European monarchs invested in them heavily. Eternal wealth was thought to be the benediction for anybody who could scrape a few thousand dollars together to put into rail stocks. No other form of transportation could compete with the railroads in speed, flexibility, durability, economy, and growth potentials. As Jacques Barzun put it, "By the turn of the century it was an institution, an image of man, a tradition, a code of honor, a source of poetry, a nursery of boyhood desires, a sublimest of toys, and the most solemn machine—next to the funeral hearse—that marks the epochs in man's life."[4]

Even after the advent of automobiles, trucks, and airplanes, the railroad tycoons remained imperturbably self-confident. If you had told them 60 years ago that in 30 years they would be flat on their backs, broke, and pleading for government subsidies, they would have thought you totally demented. Such a future was simply not considered possible. It was not even a discussable subject, or an askable question, or a matter which any sane person would consider worth speculating about. The very thought was insane. Yet a lot of insane notions now have matter-of-fact acceptance —for example, the idea of 100-ton tubes of metal moving smoothly through the air 20,000 feet above the earth, loaded with 100 sane and solid citizens casually drinking martinis—and they have dealt cruel blows to the railroads.

What specifically must other companies do to avoid this fate? What does customer orientation involve? These questions have in part been answered by the preceding examples and analysis. It would take another article to show in detail what is required for specific industries. In any case, it should be obvious that building an effective customer-oriented company involves far more than good intentions or promotional tricks; it involves profound matters of human organization and leadership. For the present, let me merely suggest what appear to be some general requirements.

VISCERAL FEEL OF GREATNESS

Obviously the company has to do what survival demands. It has to adapt to the requirements of the market, and it has to do it sooner rather than later. But mere survival is a so-so aspiration. Anybody can survive in some

4. Op. cit., p. 20.

way or other, even the skid-row bum. The trick is to survive gallantly, to feel the surging impulse of commercial mastery, not just to experience the sweet smell of success, but to have the visceral feel of entrepreneurial greatness.

No organization can achieve greatness without a vigorous leader who is driven onward by his own pulsating *will to succeed*. He has to have a vision of grandeur, a vision that can produce eager followers in vast numbers. In business, the followers are the customers. To produce these customers, the entire corporation must be viewed as a customer-creating and customer-satisfying organism. Management must think of itself not as producing products but as providing customer-creating value satisfactions. It must push this idea (and everything it means and requires) into every nook and cranny of the organization. It has to do this continuously and with the kind of flair that excites and stimulates the people in it. Otherwise, the company will be merely a series of pigeonholed parts, with no consolidating sense of purpose or direction.

In short, the organization must learn to think of itself not as producing goods or services but as *buying customers*, as doing the things that will make people *want* to do business with it. And the chief executive himself has the inescapable responsibility for creating this environment, this viewpoint, this attitude, this aspiration. He himself must set the company's style, its direction, and its goals. This means he has to know precisely where he himself wants to go, and to make sure the whole organization is enthusiastically aware of where that is. This is a first requisite of leadership, for *unless he knows where he is going, any road will take him there.*

If any road is okay, the chief executive might as well pack his attaché case and go fishing. If an organization does not know or care where it is going, it does not need to advertise that fact with a ceremonial figurehead. Everybody will notice it soon enough.

11. Marketing Planning for Industrial Products

B. Charles Ames

Why should the marketing concepts that work so well in consumer goods companies be so difficult to apply successfully in the industrial products field? Is it fair to blame the marketing function when planning results fall short of expectations? What lessons can be learned from the experience of the industry leaders who can point to concrete results from their marketing planning activities? Drawing on a study of the planning practices and results of 50 industrial companies, the author answers these questions and discusses the three principal causes of problems in putting marketing planning concepts into practice.

Corporate life would be a lot easier if management could forget or wish away the whole idea of formal marketing planning. For no one yet has been able to figure out how to get marketing plans into written form without a lot of hard work. But, if anything, this process is likely to become a more important management tool in the future as companies continue their scramble to add new products and markets to their base.

Consumer goods companies have relied increasingly on a formal marketing planning approach to focus and coordinate product strategies, and to map the tactics for sales and profit growth. Going through this discipline helps avoid the dumbbell mistakes that are bound to occur when one tries to ad lib his way to the marketplace with a complex product line.

Not surprisingly, many industrial goods companies have tried to follow suit. If marketing planning can sell more products to housewives, it ought to sell more tractors, more chemicals, or more electronic components to industrial customers. So reasoning, makers of industrial goods have set up sophisticated planning systems designed to gear their business more closely to the requirements of the marketplace.

Yet many—and perhaps even most—of these companies have found that this approach, which works so well for consumer goods makers, somehow loses its magic in the industrial marketing context. Too often, their top executives are sadly disappointed in the results of costly and time-consuming planning efforts. The comment of one vice president is typical:

"We knock ourselves out every year with a major time commitment and massive paper flow to put a plan for the business together that is heavily based on marketing input. But we can't really point to any substantive benefits that are directly traceable to all the extra effort. As I see it, our marketing group has not done the planning job it should. If it had, we'd have a lot stronger edge in the marketplace. At this point I am not sure whether it is something important that we ought to do better or whether it is just a fad that we ought to get rid of."

Why should his reaction be the rule rather than the exception? Why should the concepts that work so well in consumer goods companies be so difficult to apply successfully in the industrial field? Is it really fair to blame the marketing function when planning results fall short of expectations? Most important, what lessons can be learned from the experience of those few industrial companies which can honestly point to concrete results from their marketing planning activities?

These are the questions that a project team from McKinsey & Company set out to answer through a study of the planning practices and their effectiveness in 50 industrial companies. The names of these companies cannot be disclosed, but since they are all large, multidivision businesses listed in *Fortune's* "500," they can be presumed to have all the necessary skills and sophistication to do an effective planning job. In carrying out this project, the team worked directly with general managers and marketing executives of each of the participating companies to get a comprehensive picture of where marketing planning fits into the management process, what approaches are being followed, which are working, and which are not.

Practitioners' Pitfalls

Ignorance of planning theory or mechanics is not the cause of the disappointments so many companies are experiencing. Most of the executives we talked to—in both line and staff positions—were well aware that effective planning (a) depends on market and economic facts, (b) focuses on points of leverage, and (c) results in operating programs, not just budgets. Few executives appeared to be at all mystified by formal planning concepts. These concepts have of course received their share of emphasis in business literature and the academic world in past years, and apparently most executives have learned their lessons well.

Yet major problems crop up when companies set about putting these concepts into practice. Our study findings strongly suggest that these problems fall into three categories:

□ Failure to fit the concept to the industrial context.

□ Overemphasis on the system at the expense of content.

☐ Nonrecognition of alternative strategies.

Let us examine each of the problem categories a bit more closely before moving on to see what vital steps have been taken by those participating companies which have successfully applied marketing planning in the industrial context.

FAILURE TO FIT CONCEPT

To a large extent, the disappointing results encountered by industrial companies reflect their failure to realize that the concept of marketing planning cannot be borrowed intact from consumer goods companies and applied successfully to their particular situation. Large industrial companies have two distinguishing characteristics that set them apart and dictate the need for a different planning approach.

The first is the multiplicity of markets and channels in which they operate, each requiring a discrete marketing strategy. A consumer goods company typically markets its several brands through one or two channels, but a multiproduct industrial manufacturer is likely to sell in a wide range of different markets through a variety of channels. For example, one electrical equipment company which participated in our study sold one of its major product lines in 30 distinct markets through several different channels. The company had been trying to cover this complex network of markets and channels with a single marketing plan; what was actually needed was 30 separate marketing plans.

Juggling a large number of markets and channels is not the only feat an industrial marketing department must perform. The second distinguishing characteristic is that the marketing department must also plan around the constraints imposed by other functions, since marketing simply does not control the factors that make or break performance in the marketplace. In the industrial world, marketing success depends largely on the activities of other functions, such as engineering, manufacturing, and technical service. This means, in turn, that changes in marketing strategy are likely to be based on product design, cost, or service innovations. Contrast this with a consumer goods company, where advertising, promotion, and merchandising are generally the core elements of the marketing plan.

Since the success of marketing plans is dependent on activities in other functional areas and on the share of total company resources each product/market business receives, it is unrealistic to expect product managers, market managers, or even the head of marketing to handle the job without the full participation of corporate and operating managers throughout the process.

Thus the role of the marketing planner in an industrial company is significantly different from that of his counterpart in consumer goods.

Rather than developing self-contained marketing plans, he analyzes and interprets market requirements so that top and operating management can decide how best to respond.

Obvious as this point might seem, it is frequently overlooked in industrial companies. Having embraced formal marketing planning as a sophisticated way of running the business, many executives try to implement the concept by turning the entire job over to marketing. After a couple of years of frustration, they are ready to write off marketing planning as a monumental waste of time. The real cause of their disappointment lies not in the concept, however, but in the way it has been applied.

For example, one major chemical company added a group of six industry planning managers to its marketing organization. Once on board, each was given a marketing planning format to follow and was told to develop a written plan for achieving a stronger and more profitable position in his assigned markets. All six men, eager to earn their spurs, embarked on a massive fact-gathering and writing effort. After several months, hundreds of pages of plans and supporting documentation had been written, but no one in top management was much impressed. The president put it this way:

"I'm being generous when I say the end products are only slightly better than useless. Admittedly, we have some better market facts now, but the plans are based on a lot of ideas for product and market development that just aren't in line with my idea of the direction this business should take. On top of that, they've left out a lot of technical and capital considerations that really count. I've concluded that our industry managers are simply too far out of the mainstream of the business to do an intelligent job of planning for us."

Not surprisingly, the industry managers felt that they too had good cause for complaint. As one of them put it:

"The first month of effort was worthwhile. We were putting a fact base together that is essential for intelligent planning. But after that we were flying blind. We never had any idea from top management on the kind of business the company wanted or didn't want, the minimal return it expected, or the kind of support it would be willing to throw into various markets. Worse still, we had no cooperation from the development group or the plants, where decisions are made that really control the business. The planning we did was bound to be a bust."

Unfortunately, this kind of situation has occurred in a great many otherwise well-managed companies. And instead of building marketing planning solidly into the management process, far too much of it is carried on as a parallel activity that gets plenty of lip service but little real attention from the decision makers.

OVEREMPHASIS ON SYSTEM

During the past several years, makers of industrial goods have put more and more effort into committing plans to writing for their various product/ market businesses. Many companies have developed comprehensive planning systems that lay out formats and procedures in great detail. Although some of this structure is unquestionably necessary, we saw a number of cases where the system was so detailed and so highly structured that it acted as a hindrance rather than a help to the planning process. In effect, the system serves as the end product rather than the means to an end.

Of all the problems described to us, this one drew the most vehement reactions from executives. They recognize that good planning is hard work and cannot be done without a certain amount of pencil pushing. But they bitterly resent demands for excessive writing that serves no practical business purpose. A product manager for an electronic equipment manufacturer voiced this complaint:

"As part of my planning responsibility, I have to follow a format prescribed by the corporate planning group that calls for a point-by-point discussion of history and a laundry list of problems and opportunities. I'm 'gigged' if I don't cover every point in the format, and there's no way to do it in less than 10 pages of text. That takes a lot of time—mostly wasted time. All the product managers are sore about it. Much of what we have to write is a rehash of the same old things year after year. In effect, we're being discouraged from concentrating on the aspects of the business that are really critical. What they want to see, apparently, is a nice, neat set of plans that all look alike. It just doesn't make sense."

The study team encountered a great number of similar situations and comments. As a rule, someone or some group had designed an overstructured and overdetailed planning system that was out of phase with the realities of the business. Typically, the resulting paper work chewed up great blocks of precious time without producing anything more than a codification of what would have been done anyway.

NONRECOGNITION OF ALTERNATIVES

In company after company, when we compared the plans that were developed for a particular product or market over several years, we were surprised to see how many planners had tunnel vision in thinking about how the business should be run. In fact, so many plans were based on nothing more than straight-line extrapolation of the past and on repetition of prior programs that they seemed hardly worth the paper they were written on.

This tendency to base current plans on past programs was forced into the open in one company when each planner was asked by top management to outline alternative strategies for developing his assigned market area and to summarize the commitments (e.g., financial, manpower, facilities) required and the payoff expected (sales, profits, ROI). The request drew a complete blank. The planners were so locked into their accustomed way of thinking about their markets that they could not conceive of a different approach that made any commercial sense at all.

Insufficient or less-than-candid analysis is a prime cause of unimaginative planning. Many planners either misjudge or fail to understand the underlying economics of the business or the changes going on in the marketplace (e.g., competitive moves, shifts in usage or demand patterns) that call for alternative strategies. Many planners also appear reluctant to face up to unpleasant truths about their competitive situation—such as high price, low product quality, or poor service—that place the company in an untenable marketing position. Without a thorough, candid appraisal of the business climate, the need for fresh ways of running the business goes unrecognized. Thus, instead of getting a choice among alternatives, top management has to content itself with a single recommendation which usually calls for the continuation of stale or imitative strategies.

Imaginative Insights

Considering that the whole purpose of formal planning is to conceive more imaginative ways of developing the business, the record so far is pretty dismal. Yet the experience of the handful of participating companies which have successfully applied marketing planning in the industrial context provides some encouragement and some useful insights. Without exception, these companies have taken the necessary steps to avoid the pitfalls just described. And they are now concentrating on developing marketing-oriented plans for their businesses that are part and parcel of the management process of each company. Our study indicates that they have reached this level of sophistication primarily because of three factors:

□ Better definition and direction from the top.
□ Development of fact-founded product/market strategies.
□ Superior programming for strategy implementation.

The balance of this article will consider each of these vital factors and how they can lead to better ways of doing things and to improved results when applied in the industrial marketing context.

BETTER DEFINITION AND DIRECTION

The marketing planning done in leader companies produces results because it is carried out with full recognition of the multiplicity of products, markets, and channels, and the need for a technical, rather than a sales or merchandising, orientation. As one president in our survey commented:

"It took me three years to realize that our marketing people couldn't come up with the kind of plans I wanted for our products and markets unless I worked closely with them. They have always been able to develop a picture of where our markets are heading, identify the opportunities that exist, and interpret what we have to do to build the business. But so many considerations and options require a general management perspective that marketing can't be expected to come up with recommendations that make sense from my point of view. Unless I set the basic direction for our business, specify who is to plan what, see to it that engineering and manufacturing really work with marketing to provide what is needed, and then challenge and contribute any ideas I can on how our business can be developed, the whole planning effort is nothing more than a paper-work exercise."

Let us look at this comment more closely, for it underscores the four ways in which top management must participate in marketing planning to make it pay off.

1. *Specify corporate objectives:* Throughout our study, inadequate direction from the top was a common complaint from planners. "If only top management would tell me what they want!" I am sure we heard a hundred variations on this theme. A few of these men no doubt would like top management to spell everything out for them in detail, and they are using its failure to do so as an excuse for their own inability to do the planning job.

Nevertheless, top management guidelines that spell out the rules of the game are unquestionably a necessity for anyone who holds a marketing planning responsibility. At a minimum, these guidelines should include definite long-range growth targets or a statement of corporate objectives that expresses in specific terms how fast top management wants the business to grow, what products and markets should be emphasized, what kinds of businesses should be avoided, and what profit returns are acceptable. These guidelines do not have to be expressed with precision, and they are certainly not immutable. But without some definition like this, product/ market planners will be working in a vacuum, and they will almost inevitably come up with marketing plans that are out of phase with top management's interests and objectives.

2. *Determine organization arrangements:* It is an important step in any company to determine organization arrangements, but it is particularly vital in a large-scale industrial complex with its numerous product/market

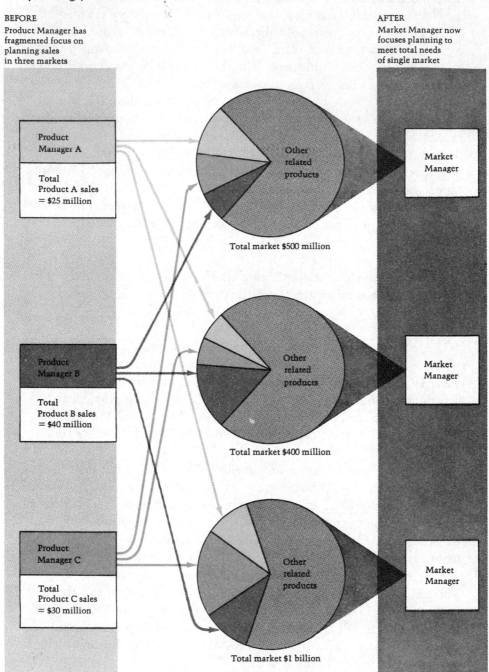

Exhibit I. Organization shift to provide capital goods company with better planning focus

BEFORE
Product Manager has fragmented focus on planning sales in three markets

Product Manager A

Total Product A sales = $25 million

Product Manager B

Total Product B sales = $40 million

Product Manager C

Total Product C sales = $30 million

Other related products

Total market $500 million

Other related products

Total market $400 million

Other related products

Total market $1 billion

AFTER
Market Manager now focuses planning to meet total needs of single market

Market Manager

Market Manager

Market Manager

businesses. Since marketing planning requirements vary so widely from business to business, there is no one organization that is valid for all companies. Nor is the same organization necessarily valid for all time. Leader companies understand the importance of appraising and reappraising organization arrangements to make sure that the planners have the right focus and that their roles are clearly understood by everyone in the organization.

For example, the marketing organization in a capital goods company had traditionally been structured around products—that is, the product managers were responsible for planning the growth and profits of each of their major product lines (see left column in *Exhibit I*). Obliged to sell to three distinct markets, each product manager was spread so thin that he could not do a thorough job of planning for any one of them. Also, since his focus was on his product lines, he was blinded to the broader needs of the individual markets.

Management soon recognized that this traditional organization arrangement greatly restricted the company's ability to plan for development of the total market. Therefore, to provide the market orientation it wanted, the company restructured its organization around the market managers, who were responsible for identifying and planning to meet all the needs of their assigned markets (see right column in *Exhibit I*).

This example is not meant to suggest that market managers will do a better job of planning for a company than product managers. But it does demonstrate how important it is for top management to think through the planning objectives and requirements for each business, and then to design an organization structure that will provide the right focus.

3. *Provide interfunctional coordination:* Even the most carefully conceived marketing organization structure will fail unless the marketing planners (a) work effectively with the other functions that influence the performance of a business in the marketplace, and (b) command the respect of their functional counterparts. And all concerned must have a clear understanding of how they are expected to work together. This is especially important in industrial companies, for without interfunctional coordination the planners do not stand a chance.

A manufacturer in the building products field set up a product planning group in its marketing organization to spearhead the marketing planning for each product area. During the first two years of the group's existence, the plans developed fell far short of everyone's expectations, and there was much friction between the planning group and other functions.

One of the product planning managers put his finger on the problem when he pointed out the many functions other than marketing and sales he had to work with to do a good planning job. Much of the difficulty he encountered, he said, stemmed from misunderstanding on the part of many functional managers about how the marketing planning job was to be done. Even the product planning managers themselves, he added, were unsure about their responsibilities.

Recognizing the need to put the product planning group on a more sound footing for dealing with other functions, the marketing vice president took three steps. He decided first to replace four of the five product planning managers, who were basically sales-oriented, with men who had stronger technical backgrounds and better grasp of the business as a whole. He then eliminated the position of group product planning managers— putting the product planning managers on an organization par with their major contacts in other functional areas. Since they had a broader understanding of the business, they were able to communicate more effectively. Even more important, as a result of the reorganization, they now reported directly to the head of marketing and, therefore, were in close touch with top management thinking.

Finally, the marketing head persuaded the president of the company to hold a meeting with the executives of all major functions to explain what the product planning managers were trying to accomplish and how the different functions should work with them. At this meeting, the president made it clear that he was looking to the product planning managers to develop plans geared to the characteristics and requirements of the marketplace:

"We are going to bank everything on their interpretation of where the market is heading and what we must do internally to respond to market needs. I expect all functions to cooperate with our marketing planners and follow their lead completely. If we don't operate along these lines, all of our talk about being a market-oriented company is just a lot of hot air."

This no-nonsense statement on the role of marketing cleared away any misconceptions blocking effective interaction between the product planning managers and other functions.

4. *Contribute to marketing plans:* If top management truly wants to find ways of improving profits and growth, it must actively participate in the development of marketing plans by challenging their underlying assumptions and by contributing alternative ideas on strategy and programs. To be sure, most top executives try to do this; but the way they do it often stifles rather than encourages new ideas. They must take pains to avoid any atmosphere of an inquisition and, instead, must stimulate open exchange of ideas and opinions.

In such an environment one idea leads to another, and the management team soon finds itself exploring new and imaginative ways of developing the business. An interfunctional give-and-take discussion like this led a heavy machinery manufacturer to adopt a new market strategy that gave its parts operation a chance for survival. Consider:

In this company, as in many others, parts sales had traditionally been a major source of profits. Now management was concerned because "parts pirates" (local parts producers) were cutting sharply into their business. Asked to develop a marketing strategy that would reverse the trend, the parts manager first came up with a plan that called for adding three salesmen and cutting prices on a large number of parts to be more competitive. As he acknowledged, his plan was essentially no more than a holding action.

During the planning review session in which all functions took part, the company president encouraged everyone to take an entrepreneurial look at the parts business and to try to think of ways to preserve or even enlarge it. Predictably, fresh ideas were hard to come by in a business that had been run the same way for years. But eventually three embryonic ideas emerged that were considered worthwhile: (1) Build a service organization and sell contracts for maintenance service instead of just parts; (2) decentralize the parts business and set up local parts and repair shops to compete head to head with local competitors; and (3) start to buy and sell parts for other manufacturers' equipment in order to spread overhead costs.

The parts manager was naturally somewhat reluctant to do any of these things, since they would revolutionize his end of the business. But with top management backing and encouragement, he did the required analytical work and came back with alternative strategies, based on the first two ideas, that offered a much more attractive outlook.

Of course, to think that this process always leads to a more viable product/market strategy would be a foolhardy assumption. It is not always possible to overcome the scarcity of fresh ideas characteristic of a business run the same way for years. Moreover, alternative strategies are not always available. But the more successful companies insist that their planners seek out alternative strategies and avoid getting locked into a self-defeating "business as usual" pattern of thinking.

This kind of give-and-take among marketing, top management, and other functions is really the heart of the planning process. For it is during these discussions that marketing presents the requirements of the marketplace and the other functions discuss feasible ways of responding to them. With all the opportunities and constraints out in the open, top manage-

Exhibit II. *Forces likely to affect industrial company's market position and outlook*

A. Identifying points of leverage

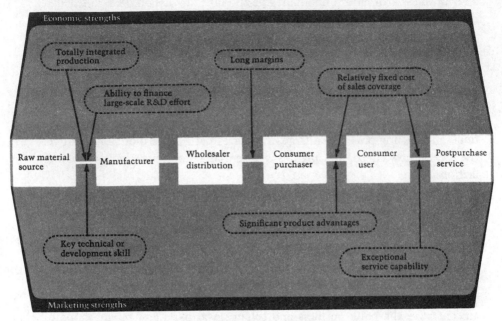

B. Identifying points of vulnerability

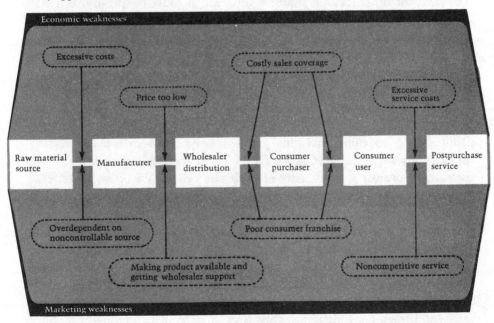

then in a position to make commitments on the timing and costs of the alternative actions that underlie the marketing plan. Leader company executives insist this is the best vehicle for triggering fresh ideas and ensuring interfunctional coordination.

FACT-FOUNDED STRATEGIES

The marketing planning done by leader companies is aimed at the development of strategies for each product/market business realistically tied to market and economic facts. Once developed, these strategies point the way for each present business, serve as underpinning for overall corporate long-range planning, and provide direction for programming key activities and projects in all functional areas.

Strategy development is an art few companies have mastered. Those that have this expertise stress the need for comprehensive knowledge of the economics of the business and the trends of the market. More specifically, this means that planners need to know the economics of their competitors as well as of their own businesses—that is, where value is added, how costs behave with changes in volume, where assets are committed, and so on. To complete their understanding, planners must also know how the market is structured and what forces are likely to affect the company's market position and outlook.

With this understanding, planners can recognize points of leverage where the company can exercise an advantage, as well as points where the company might be vulnerable to competitive thrusts. *Exhibit II* illustrates what some of these points of leverage or vulnerability might be in a typical industrial operation.

One outstanding company built a marketing strategy for its major product line on just this sort of understanding. The planners in this company, which I shall call Company A, recognized that they were operating in a slow-growth business, offering a commodity product for which demand was highly inelastic. They therefore concluded that (a) it would not make sense to sacrifice short-term profits to build a larger share position, since the value of a share point would not increase enough to pay off such an investment, and (b) although price is an important consideration in market share, it would not influence total demand.

This market analysis brought a further important trend to light: Company A was losing market position to the strong second-place factor in the industry, Company B. As no other important shifts in market share had occurred, Company A concluded that its marketing strategy should be aimed first and foremost at reversing its losses to Company B.

Next, the planners at Company A compared their own profit structure with that of Company B to find the weaknesses and strengths of the

Exhibit III. Comparative analysis of two competitive companies

[Dollar figures in millions]

Economic indicators	Companies A	Companies B	Conclusions
Current dollar sales	$403	$146	A's sales volume is roughly twice B's
Breakeven point	$217	$121	B's breakeven point is lower, but B is operating much closer to breakeven than A
Contribution margin rate (sales dollars less variable costs)	48%	45%	Contribution margin rates are about the same
Contribution loss from 5 percentage point drop in unit margin	$20	$7.3	However, because of differences in dollar volume, Company A stands to lose far more marginal income than B by lowering unit margin
Volume gain to offset 5 percentage point drop in unit margin	$46.5	$18.2	Thus, the volume needed to offset a 5 percentage point drop in unit margin would be much greater for Company A
Equivalent share point gain	7.0 pts.	2.8 pts.	

two companies. Their analysis produced the information shown in *Exhibit III.* (Admittedly, obtaining information of this sort about competitors is unquestionably tough. No one is going to hand it to you, and it is not likely to be available in published material. But bits of data on competitor sales and capacity levels can be pieced together from annual reports, newspaper articles, and trade and government publications. By combining such data with one's own experience, conservative assumptions can be made about competitor costs and efficiency to complete the picture.)

By the time the planners in Company A had completed this comparative analysis, they were in a position to predict what Company B's strategy was likely to be. This is what they thought Company B would do, assuming that B knew its own market and economic position:

□ Cut prices on the products competitive with Company A's highest volume products to upset price stability and to force Company A to retaliate or give up volume.

□ Add new industrial distributors by giving larger discounts, and go after Company A's distributors in prime markets.

□ Emphasize development of lower-cost products, thereby gaining more flexibility to compete on a price basis.

Starting from these assumptions, the planners in Company A proceeded to develop a counter-strategy. These were its key points:

□ Avoid going for volume on a price basis or by adding to unit costs.

□ Hold a firm price line with distributors—even at the risk of losing share in the most price-sensitive markets.

□ Build the marketing program around the changes in costs which are nonvariable with volume—e.g., upgrading and enlarging the sales force, strengthening distributor programs, and improving the physical distribution and warehousing network.

A superficial review of the situation would undoubtedly have led the planners to come up with quite a different strategy. For, in view of the high contribution rate and apparent profit leverage on volume, the most obvious strategy would have been to cut price to counteract any aggressive pricing actions of Company B. Instead, Company A planners decided to avoid price concessions or any actions that would raise unit costs. They recommended concentrating on marketing programs where costs could be amortized over their much larger unit volume and on other programs that would reduce their cost base. Management agreed, reasoning that this strategy would enable the company to lead from strength rather than play into the hands of its major competitor.

The details of Company A's strategy may be open to dispute. In themselves, however, they are not important. The purpose of the example is to show how a penetrating analysis of market and economic facts can provide a reasoned basis for strategy development. This is the process by which sophisticated planners are gaining significant advantages over their competitors, and it is easy to see the three reasons why:

1. Planners can help focus management attention on actions that really count in the marketplace and make sure that these are based on facts and judgment, not hunch or opinion.

2. They can adopt an aggressive posture instead of having to rely on retaliation or defensive maneuvers.

3. They can minimize the impact of surprise competitive moves by developing alternative contingency plans.

SUPERIOR PROGRAMMING

Everybody goes through the motions of programming, but leader companies follow three ground rules that enable them to do a superior job of strategy implementation.

First, management will approve no major program or project that is not inextricably linked to a product/market strategy. This approach may sound a little stuffy, but it makes eminently good sense, for there is really no way to evaluate a program's usefulness without the background of a product/market strategy. Moreover, the linkage keeps the functional areas of a business working together for a common purpose and prevents them from being sidetracked on functionally interesting activities that lack commercial relevance.

Second, management makes some sort of organization provision for follow-through on major programs, particularly those that cut across functional lines. In some cases, they have enlarged the role of their product managers. In others, they have set up a task force with responsibility for following a program through to completion.

Take, for example, the case of an industrial controls producer we surveyed. When it became clear that the company's product line had slipped behind competitors', the management team saw that holding market position would require a complete redesign of the product line, both to improve performance characteristics and to take out cost.

Even though the bulk of the actual work had to be done by engineering and manufacturing, the president pulled the responsible product manager out of the marketing department, placed him directly under his wing, and made him fully accountable for coordinating and pushing the program through to completion. As the president told us:

"This program can make or break us in the marketplace. It's so vital to us I'd watch over it myself if I could let some other things slip. Since I can't, I want someone to do it for me, and the product manager is the logical one to do it. I know I'm stretching his role somewhat in giving him this assignment, and I know some noses are going to be out of joint in engineering and manufacturing, but the job is too important not to have a full-time program manager."

This is one way of shepherding a crucial program. As discussed, there are others; but the objective is always to ensure interfunctional coordination for all major programs and to break through any obstacles to successful completion.

Third, leader companies see to it that the detailed steps involved in major programs are mapped out in such a way that performance can be measured against these individual steps. For some time, of course, companies in the aerospace, military electronics, construction, and other industries have been using network scheduling techniques (e.g., PERT, RAMPS) to control large and complex projects. Now, however, a few industrial goods makers are applying similar techniques to ensure interfunctional coordination on a wide variety of programs that affect market performance, since they permit management to flag potential problem areas and initiate corrective action before the program slips or gets off track.

In one company, the program for introducing a new line of flow meters was broken down into 25 steps over an 18-month span. The first step was a kick-off meeting between R&D, engineering, manufacturing, and marketing to define performance and cost requirements. Subsequent steps tracked the new product idea through development, manufacture, and market launching. Each week management received a report showing whether scheduled steps had been completed and, if not, where the bottleneck was. This feedback made it much easier to trace problems to their source for corrective action. Said the president: "The program is too important to us to rely for control on typical accounting reports. They simply tell us after the fact whether we won or lost. They're no help when it comes to making sure the program doesn't collapse."

It would be absurd to structure every program in so much detail. But detailed planning is essential for effective control over major programs that involve many functions and require tight scheduling and careful adherence in order to achieve profit and market objectives.

In Summary

Formal marketing planning can undoubtedly make a real contribution to the performance of any industrial company, just as it has in consumer goods companies. But if marketing planning is to have real impact on the industrial side, it will have to be adapted much more closely to the particular requirements of the business. This demands much less emphasis on the system—that is, format, sophisticated techniques, and lengthy writing assignments. Instead, the whole focus must be on achieving substantive improvements in thinking and actions through tough-minded analysis, continual interchange between marketing and technical executives, and more top management inputs. This is the only approach that can really lead to better ways of doing things and to improved results, thus making the formal marketing planning process something more than a costly facade.

12. Get the Most Out of Your Sales Force

Derek A. Newton

Sales management practice is like Topsy—it just grew. Each sales executive tends to work out his own style of managing from the assortment of principles he inherits from his predecessor, the customs of the industry in which he is operating, his own ideas, the expressed preferences of his corporate superiors, and so on. There has been a signal lack of method in this vital and challenging area of management. The research results presented in this article represent a considerably more scientific approach to the problem. By querying a large sample of companies on their practices and then matching the responses with indicators of high success, the author has derived a useful set of management guidelines for each of the major kinds of selling activity he has considered.

The typical sales executive does a lot of wondering about his sales force, not only about what they are doing "out there," but about his own management practices. Is he deploying his men correctly? How good are the selection and training procedures? Are controls sufficient? Is he paying his men too little or too much? His goals are good performance and low turnover on the selling staff; in order to achieve them he must find the right men and get the most out of them, and obtain their loyalty so that he can keep them. How can he best do this?

Advice for the sales executive in that dilemma has had to be pretty vague up to now. I have completed a research project, however, which sheds considerable light on the problem of improving performance and reducing turnover in the sales force. This study was designed to answer four specific questions:

1. How does the selling task to be performed differ for each of the main kinds of selling that are done today; and do these differences call for differences in management approach?

2. What management practices increase performance for each kind of selling?

The study reports the responses of 1,029 sales executives to a questionnaire designed to probe management practices and to measure performance and turnover. Of the 1,029 respondents, 75% identified themselves as working at the level of general sales manager or higher. The sample comprised many kinds of manufacturing, wholesaling, and service businesses.

Four Kinds of Selling

In one sense, the very variety of companies represented in this sample constitutes a stumbling block. A specialized sample, on the other hand, would probably lead only to specialized conclusions. As it happens, pretests of the questionnaire indicated that one can effectively isolate four basic styles of selling that cut across industry boundaries to a large degree, and I shall present the results in this article in the context of these four basic styles:

1. Trade selling.
2. Missionary selling.
3. Technical selling.
4. New-business selling.

Each sales executive queried was asked to specify the primary responsibility of his force—whether it was trade, missionary, technical, or new-business selling. The responses showed that the breakdown of the total sample was fairly even among these four categories.

But before I discuss each of these four kinds of selling in detail, I shall explain the indexes that were used to measure performance and turnover, and present eight findings that apply to the entire sample, regardless of classification.

MEASUREMENTS

The questionnaire gathered data for a two-year period. From these data, several quantitative measurements were derived for each of the responding organizations.

Turnover rate: This quantity is the number of salesmen who quit or were discharged from a company divided by the average size of the company's sales force during the two-year period. (This is the same formula as that used by the Bureau of Labor Statistics.) While this formula has some disadvantages, it has the signal advantages of being simple, easily understood, and widely used.

Performance index: This quantity is the rate of growth of sales divided by the rate of growth of sales force. It represents the increase in sales volume per salesman over the two-year period—if you will, the increase in per-man productivity.

The reader may wonder why I did not measure performance directly, by change in sales volume. The reason for this ought to be obvious: factors other than sales force performance bear on changes in sales volume—industry growth rates, mergers and acquisitions, market conditions, management efficiency and marketing efficiency, and so on—and these factors are largely beyond the control of the sales force executive. The executive *does* control the rate of growth of his sales force, however, and I have therefore used this rate as the divisor in the index to counteract the effects of "outside" influences on changes in sales volume. This index reflects the quality of management practices more accurately than mere change in sales volume.

This performance index has its advantages and limitations. For example, while it does reward companies that increase sales faster than they increase manpower, it has the effect of penalizing the company that must temporarily deploy many salesmen to achieve an increase in market coverage. Still, the responses to the questionnaire show that the sales executive judges his own performance along a dimension parallel to this index; that is, the index was high for those companies whose executives thought that their forces were performing well, and the index was low for those companies that thought their forces were performing poorly.

Compensation rates: Compensation rates were tabulated for each company within each of the four sales classifications for the average-, highest-, and lowest-paid salesman. By comparing these data with performance and turnover rates for each company, it was possible to determine how much a salesman working on a given kind of sales force ought to be paid. Conversely, it indicated how high a level of performance and how low a rate of turnover the sales executive ought to expect for paying his men a given amount. The questionnaire also elicited information on methods of compensation—the mixture of straight salary, commission, and bonus that produces the best results in each kind of selling task.

Span of control: This quantity is the average number of salesmen on a force divided by the average number of field supervisors. As we shall see, high performance and low turnover correlate with different spans of control for each of the four sales classifications.

Opportunity rate: The percentage of men transferred out and promoted from the sales force measures advancement opportunity. The specific findings indicate that the sales executive should be careful to see that this rate of opportunity is neither too high nor too low, and the data collected suggest the optimal range for each sales classification.

Earnings opportunity ratio (EOR): This is the ratio of the compensation of the highest-paid salesman on a sales force to that of the average-paid salesman. Extremely high or low ratios correlate with high turnover. For a reason I shall explain later, the executive ought to keep an eye on this quantity as well.

Eight Major Findings

The digested data from the study exhibit eight strong conclusions that apply to all the sales force classifications alike.

1. *The turnover rate of a sales force does not directly influence its performance index.*

High performance, in other words, is just as likely to be accompanied by high turnover as by low; and the same is true for low performance.

2. *A turnover rate of 10% or more is excessively costly in all classifications, and should be avoided if possible.*

The extra costs associated with turnover, such as interruption of customers' ordering routines, and its less tangible costs, such as the disruption of customer-salesman rapport, are obvious evils. But the executive ought to look beyond these obvious considerations to a much more important one: according to the data, the factor discriminating most strongly between sales forces that are expensive to operate and those that are economical is the level of hiring activity. Hence low turnover is likely to mean a low-cost sales force, and the executive who wants a low-cost force should therefore devote a good deal of his attention to his hiring practices.

3. *The turnover rate is directly influenced by the opportunity rate.*

Sales forces which exhibit opportunity rates in excess of 6% are likely to be plagued by high turnover. I think this fact is explained easily enough: an opportunity rate of 6% or more suggests that the company is using the sales force as a convenient training ground for future marketing managers and supervisory sales personnel, and many applicants will be drawn to such sales forces by the prospect of advancement rather than by the appeal of sales work per se. But selling per se is their main function; and when management becomes aware of any lack of commitment to sales work on the part of its salesmen, it is likely to pass them over, thus inducing them to quit in disgust. In some cases, no doubt, management simply fires them.

4. *Turnover is also directly influenced by compensation level.*

Sales forces that have low average pay scales exhibit high turnover. It is not equally true, on the other hand, that high pay means low turnover. Paying one's best salesman overgenerously is ineffective in reducing turnover (of course, there may be other, valid reasons for tolerating a high EOR). The data show that an EOR greater than 2.0 in any sales force tends to drive up costs without reducing turnover.

5. *The compensation level, however, does not directly influence the performance index, although the method of compensation does.*

Once the executive has satisfied himself that his force's compensation level is on a par with the competition's, he ought to check carefully to see that the balance of fixed salary, commission, and bonus is "right" for the psychological temper of his crew. We shall look into the various payment mixes which are appropriate to each of the sales force classifications later in the article.

6. *The performance index is directly influenced by the character and effectiveness of the reporting system used to control the force.*

The universal characteristic of the high-performance force is that its management *insists* on receiving the frequent and regular reports that are critical to controlling sales force behavior. Because different kinds of reporting are critical to different kinds of forces, and because insistence on excessive reporting boosts the turnover rate rapidly, the sales executive must be extremely careful to identify the truly critical and necessary reports and play down or eliminate all others. The study identifies the specific reports that are critical for success in trade and technical selling; for the rest, the executive must use his own good judgment.

These six results are augmented by some discoveries about two other key quantities investigated by the questionnaire.

7. *Average chronological age differs among the four sales force classifications, but for each classification there is an optimal average age.*

For example, a "younger" force typically has high turnover, but also has abundant energy. Hence it may perform highly where energy is a major requisite. On the other hand, an "older" force has more maturity and stability, and is likely to perform best where these characteristics are most useful.

8. *Job content is a critical factor affecting performance and turnover.*

The kind of challenge in a particular selling job and the actual work which the salesman is called on to do determine the kind of man the executive ought to hire. This is primary. Once he has the kind of men that he wants, he must then *match his management practice to the men in their jobs*.

Let's take a careful look, now, at each of the four basic kinds of selling jobs that I studied and see (a) what kinds of men are required for each, and (b) how the executive ought to handle his men once he has them.

Trade Selling

The primary responsibility of the trade sales force is to build up the volume of a company's sales to its customers by providing them with *promotional assistance*. This generally amounts to improving the company's distribution channels, or, where the customer is himself a manufacturer, helping him to become a more effective seller. The trade sales force therefore "sells *through*," rather than "sells *to*," its customers.

Trade selling is a feature of many industries, but it predominates in food, textiles, apparel, and wholesaling. Products sold in this way tend to be well established; hence a company's selling effort, as such, is often less important than its advertising and promotion efforts. Much of this kind of selling is low-key, and the trade salesman is not as highly pressured from above as are his cousins in new-business sales, for example; but his job can easily become dull and repetitious if he has to do too much shelf-stocking or too much order-taking. The good trade salesman must be helpful and persuasive, and must thoroughly understand how the customer runs his business. Aggressiveness is less important than maturity, and technical competence is often less important than "wearing well" with customers.

Managers of high-performance forces appear to recognize many of the requirements and limitations of this kind of sales activity. For example, the high-performance groups in trade selling are older. *Exhibit I* compares the average ages of salesmen in the four classifications, and shows the average age of the highest- and lowest-performance quintiles in each. Maturity is quite evident in the highest-performance quintile in trade selling, as it is in the highest-performance quintile in new-business sales.

While maturity may be desirable here, seniority is not necessarily so. The study data exhibit no such useful correlation between seniority and turnover, for example. Turnover is largely a phenomenon of the first few years on the job; in other words, the longer a man has been with a company, the less likely he is to quit or be discharged. But turnover is also a function of chronological age: the younger the force, the higher the turnover. Age and job turnover are in fact so strongly interrelated that observations about the impact of seniority on turnover are pointless.

Exhibit I. The impact of average age on performance

Age of salesmen	Trade force performance by quintile			Missionary force performance by quintile		
	Highest	Average	Lowest	Highest	Average	Lowest
Less than 30 years old	18.8%*	19.7%	23.7%	22.2%	17.8%	13.1%
30-39 years old	32.4	35.0	39.6	31.9	34.4	37.9
40 years old or older	48.8	45.3	36.7	45.9	47.8	49.0

*Read: salesmen under 30 years of age account for 18.8% of the sales force personnel of firms within the highest-performance quintile, and so on.

The kind of comparison made in *Exhibit I*, when applied to other data from the study, provides a number of useful findings. In sketching out the guidelines presented in this article, my general method of analysis has been to find out what is "standard operating procedure" (i.e., average age of existing sales forces, average compensation, standard methods of pay, and so forth) and then to judge what variations in standard procedure conduce to a sales force showing performance in the highest quintile and turnover in the lowest quintile.

GUIDELINES

Obviously, the trade sales executive should do what he can to improve performance. Also, although turnover does not directly influence performance, it is expensive when it is excessive, and he should do what he can to hold it down. Note that the following recommendations do not involve any trading-off between performance goals and turnover goals; that is, the executive can apply them all without being forced to choose between improving performance and reducing turnover.

To begin with, the executive ought to give considerable thought to job content. Any action he can take to reduce drudgery or the salesman's lurking feeling that he is nothing but a pawn in a giant chess game will improve performance and reduce turnover. Therefore, the executive should:

□ Transfer salesmen among territories as infrequently as possible—except, of course, at their own request.

□ Design the sales-call pattern so that the salesman feels he is making important sales-related calls and not merely putting in appearances for

	Technical force performance by quintile			New-business force performance by quintile			Total-sample average
Highest	Average	Lowest	Highest	Average	Lowest	
18.1%	17.8%	13.9%	18.5%	22.1%	22.4%	19.2%
39.4	37.2	39.4	32.7	34.8	39.9	35.6
42.5	45.0	46.7	48.8	43.1	37.7	45.2

the sake of the company's image. On the average, the salesman should be given three to five chances a day to actually make a sale. Requiring more than five calls a day, even on regular accounts, is associated with high turnover.

□ Avoid asking the salesman to peddle "easy-to-buy" products—it makes him feel like a deliveryman. If a product line requires no persistence to sell it, then it may well not require a salesman at all.

The source of employees has more influence on turnover than the methods used to select applicants. Whereas the number of interviews, tests administered, and so forth do not appear to be associated with performance or turnover, companies that place heavy reliance on employment agencies and advertisements exhibit higher-than-average rates of turnover as well as disproportionately high sales force costs.

Compared with the industry grapevine and company initiative, for example, these methods of procuring applicants tend to be highly impersonal. Hiring applicants "off the street," so to speak, invites turnover trouble—which suggests that executives ought to know more than they do about their salesmen *before* they hire them.

So far as the composition of the sales force is concerned, as I have said, the balance tips in favor of the older salesman. Therefore, the executive should:

□ Use company contacts to seek out and hire salesmen in their forties or late thirties, and avoid placing heavy reliance on advertisements and employment agencies for recruitment.

The *amount* a salesman is paid appears to be an important factor in turnover, and the *method* by which he is paid appears to be an important factor in performance. The desirability of having the trade salesman view himself and his job as important to the company's marketing efforts and the influence of the size of a man's paycheck on his perception of himself indicate that generosity is called for in making compensation decisions about the trade sales force. Therefore, the executive should:

□ Make sure that, unless industry pay scales dictate otherwise, his lowest-paid salesman earns about $8,000 a year, his average salesman about $13,000, and his highest-paid salesman between $20,000 and $26,000.[1]

Quite surprisingly, the study data bearing on optimal methods of payment show that paying a low ratio of salary to commission works best. The practice of the high-performance, low-turnover forces suggests that the executive should:

□ Pay only about 60% of the average salesman's compensation in the form of fixed salary. (For every other sales force classification this proportion is 80%. That 60% works best here may surprise those executives who believe that, of the four classifications of salesmen, the salesman on the trade force has the least direct influence on sales volume. I was not prepared for this result myself. After all, trade sales volume is very heavily influenced by "outside" factors like promotion and advertising efforts; and it seems to follow that the trade salesman ought to receive a high proportion of his pay in fixed form. But consider the salesman's point of view. If he knows that a larger proportion of his pay is variable, this helps to offset his natural perception that his efforts are unimportant in comparison with his company's promotion and advertising; this increases his job satisfaction and thus improves his performance. Also, if he has the impression that he himself can really influence sales volume, he is less likely to get discouraged and quit. Thus a high proportion of variable pay tends to depress turnover as well.)

Close personal supervision, particularly for experienced salesmen, does little to improve performance and may—as a source of job dissatisfaction— encourage high turnover. Also, many salesmen appear to perceive quotas and paper work as childish or unnecessary. The study data support the conclusion that use of quotas merely boosts turnover and reduces performance. On the other hand, using an intelligent system of reporting to control the critical functions of the sales job improves performance and substitutes for close personal supervision. The data indicate that the executive should:

1. Dollar figures, here and elsewhere in the article, reflect what was reported at the time of the study; hence represent 1967 values.

□ Maintain a ratio of salesmen to field supervisors of around 12 to 1, depending on the proportion of inexperienced men in his sales force. (With a high proportion of experienced men, I would increase this span of control to 16 to 1.)

□ Avoid the use of personal sales quotas for salesmen.

□ Avoid requesting reports from salesmen except for those reports critical to controlling sales force behavior. (In these latter instances, the executive should *insist* on receiving them. For example, the *customer inventory report* is critical in trade sales.)

The company's training programs also significantly affect performance. Hence the executive should:

□ Compare in-house training effects with those of the successful competition. (In my study, high-performing forces use: less initial training and less classroom training, probably because they seek out better-qualified applicants; more on-the-job training for new men, to make sure of a smooth launching; and less on-the-job training for experienced men, a condition which probably reflects more acute management reporting controls.)

A company that uses the salesman's job as a training ground for marketing management careers may be inviting a turnover problem, as I have already stated. Therefore, the executive should:

□ Refrain from viewing the sales force assignment as a form of purgatory necessary for further advancement in the company. (Specifically, the executive should strive to keep the opportunity rate below 4%, perhaps partly by broadening the supervisory span of control and partly by reducing the number of management levels so as to make the sales organization as "horizontal" as possible.)

The general thrust of these recommendations for trade force management is twofold:

□ The executive must make the salesman perceive himself as an important element in his company's marketing strategy. To some extent, current trade force practice follows these recommendations. Trade sales executives, compared to executives in the other three classifications, emphasize commission compensation, and tend to design territories for equal earnings opportunities; they play down close personal supervision and opportunities for promotion, and avoid recruiting members of the sales force from agencies.

□ On the other hand, the executive must avoid some current trade force management practice which tends to defeat the goals as they have been stated here (and which, as a matter of fact, accounts for much of the lack of correlation between high performance and low turnover in the sample).

This practice—emphasizing use of personal sales quotas, maximizing the number of selling calls per day, and selling the easiest-to-buy items in the line—tends to undercut the importance of the total compensation that the salesman receives.

Following all these recommendations may pose problems for certain sales executives. To begin with, it is not always possible to have salesmen perceive themselves as important elements in the marketing strategy. In many companies, particularly the large, mass-distribution organizations, the salesman just is not very important, and no amount of telling him that he *is* important will offset his observation that advertising and promotion move the merchandise and he merely keeps the shelves stocked. If a company just needs someone to call on the dealers, if marketing management personnel need trade sales experience as training, and if the *real* sales activity must be restricted to a few executive salesmen who call on key customers—well, there may be no justification for making the changes necessary to attract and keep high-caliber trade salesmen.

In other companies, particularly the smaller ones for which the cost of operating the sales force is a significant percentage of the sales dollar, it may be difficult to invest the necessary money in salesman compensation to attract and keep high-caliber salesmen. High costs, however, appear to be more closely associated with high hiring levels than with high compensation levels. Here the small-company executive should pay very serious attention to his applicants.

Missionary Selling

The primary responsibility of the missionary force is to increase its company's sales volume by providing its direct customers with *personal selling assistance*. It performs this function by persuading its indirect customers to purchase company products through these direct customers—distribution channels, wholesalers, and so forth. The familiar "medical detail man," who calls on doctors as the representative of a pharmaceutical house, is a typical example of the missionary.

Like trade selling, missionary selling is low-key, but it differs in its primary objective; the missionary force "sells *for*" its direct customers, whereas the trade force "sells *through*" them. Responses to the questionnaire indicate that this type of selling is common in many industry categories —especially so in foods, chemicals, transportation and warehousing, wholesaling, and the utilities.

Good coverage of the market and the ability to make a succinct, yet persuasive, presentation of product benefits is vitally important in missionary

Exhibit II. Average performance index by frequency of transfer and by number of calls to produce an order from a new customer

	Number of companies	Average performance index
Frequency of transfer		
Never	33	102.9
Seldom	105	108.2
Occasionally	54	109.3
Calls required		
One	12	110.3
Two or three	57	108.0
Four or five	56	109.2
Six to ten	27	99.6
Eleven or more	17	105.8

sales. One missionary executive refers to his salesmen as "animated direct mail." This term is perhaps a bit harsh. Nevertheless, the missionary salesman tends to be more a communicator and persuader than a problem-solver.

This observation is supported by the relationships between the performance index and (a) the number of calls the missionary makes, (b) the number of calls he must make to produce a sale, and (c) the frequency of territorial transfer. First, the more calls the missionary is required to make, the higher his performance is likely to be. Second, as *Exhibit II* shows, the performance index rises as the number of calls required to make a sale declines. This implies that frequent call-backs are less likely to be productive in missionary selling than fresh calls, underscoring the fact that close customer-salesman relationships are relatively unimportant in this classification. Third, *Exhibit II* shows that the performance index also rises as the number of territorial transfers increases. This indicates that occasional transfers may have a mildly salutary effect on both the customers and the salesmen.

Clearly the situation here is quite different from the trade selling situation, and clearly it calls for a different kind of man.

A BASIC DILEMMA

The good missionary salesman, then, is energetic and articulate. He need not be a good "closer," because his primary audience does not buy directly from him. His personality is very important, but the cultivation of long-term customer relationships is less important than it is for the trade sales force. The major drawback in this kind of selling is that the salesman is not challenged intellectually and lacks the opportunity to develop personally satisfying relationships with his customers.

The successful missionary sales force sidesteps these drawbacks by hiring young men with the physical stamina to make a lot of calls and then making them "run like Yellow Dog Dingo," to use Kipling's phrase. (Note the age spreads for this classification in *Exhibit I*.) Little premium is placed on applicants' previous sales experience. Because of their relative youth and inexperience, their compensation package includes a high proportion of fixed salary, and the general level of pay tends to be low. Because the job may not be basically difficult and because the influence of supervision on performance may be hard to detect, the *amounts* of training and supervision are kept at minimum levels, commensurate with getting the job done.

High performance results from keeping the salesman busy; low turnover results from hiring an older sales force. The low-turnover force is relatively well paid; the high-performance sales force is not. The missionary sales executive is thus forced to choose between an older, more stable, higher-paid, relatively low-performing sales force and a younger, more volatile, lower-paid, but relatively high-performing sales force. This dilemma is reflected in the guidelines for missionary sales management that I have drawn from the study.

GUIDELINES

The missionary sales executive can afford to pay less attention to making the salesman's job activities satisfying, since the impact of this factor on turnover is low. On the other hand, he needs to devote *more* attention to making his men's call routines as efficient as possible, since the impact of this factor on performance is high. Therefore, he should:

◻ Deploy salesmen to maximize sales volume at minimum sales force cost.

As I have said, the young sales force outperforms the older, and the need for a high degree of selling skill is not so important, since much of the closing activity is left to resellers. Therefore, the executive should:

◻ Seek out and hire inexperienced men in their twenties or early thirties.

◻ Avoid judging an applicant by his previous sales experience.

◻ As in trade selling, avoid relying on agencies and advertisements for applicants.

Compensation higher than the industry average does little to improve performance, but it does reduce turnover. In addition, a high proportion of fixed earnings is a positive factor in controlling operating costs. Therefore, the executive should:

◻ Make sure that, unless industry pay scales dictate otherwise, his lowest-paid salesman earns about $8,000, his average salesman between $11,000 and $12,000, and his highest-paid salesman between $17,000 and $18,000.

◻ Use a compensation method whereby at least 80% of the average salesman's earnings comes to him in the form of salary.

To improve sales-call efficiency, the executive can encourage his supervisors to plan more thoroughly to achieve maximum volume at minimum cost. Since the span of control appears to influence performance very little and has a mixed influence on turnover, the average span exhibited by the highest-performance quintile is a good guide. Thus he should:

◻ Maintain a ratio of salesmen to supervisors of about 10 to 1.

Although high advancement opportunity may induce costly turnover problems without necessarily improving performance, the executive must permit enough advancement opportunity to attract the energetic young man. The forces in the highest-performance quintile seem to have achieved this balance, and the executive might well be guided by their practice. Accordingly, he should:

◻ Keep the opportunity rate below 6%.

Current practice in the missionary sector agrees with many of these guidelines. It emphasizes cold-calling, many calls per day, and many accounts per man; and it plays down call-back and the importance of high compensation. Current practice diverges from these guidelines by emphasizing maturity and previous sales experience as an applicant-selection criterion, and pays excessive attention to close personal supervision. The missionary sales executive can readily check his own practices against these criteria.

Implementing these recommendations poses problems for many companies, particularly the smaller ones that assign a dual role to the sales force. Although missionary selling may be the sales force's primary responsibility, trade, technical, or new-business selling is often an important secondary role, and certain sales management practices better suited to these latter roles conflict with my recommendations for missionary sales management. One possible alternative is to split the sales force, but this action is either impractical or uneconomical for many companies.

If important secondary selling activities require a different kind of selling from the "animated direct mail" function suggested by the data on the missionary sales force, a company may downgrade the total selling capabilities of its current sales force by following these recommendations too closely. If, on the other hand, a careful review of the job content reveals that the sales-force function can be performed by younger, less-experienced, and lower-paid personnel making more calls per day, the increase in per-man productivity may offset the added costs caused by the higher rate of turnover that these procedures will induce.

Technical Selling

The primary responsibility of the technical sales force is to increase the company's volume of sales to its existing customers by providing them with technical advice and assistance. The industral-products salesman who sells to the customer's purchasing agents is a good example of this type. Unlike the trade or missionary salesman, the technical salesman sells directly *to* the user or buyer. The technical sales force is well represented in chemicals, machinery, and the heavy-equipment categories.

In this area, the ability to identify, analyze, and solve customers' problems is vitally important, and in this sense technical selling is very much like professional consulting. As in consulting, both technical competence and personality are important qualities in the salesman—he must be able to penetrate deeply into customers' problems and persuasively present his products' benefits as the partial or complete solution to them. Too much aggressiveness, on the one hand, can undermine this delicate relationship; too little, on the other, will result in lost sales opportunities.

The executive who manages a successful technical sales force provides his men with a good deal of support, especially by emphasizing training and retraining activities and encouraging a close, continuing rapport between salesman and supervisor. The executive selects his men primarily for their ability to achieve technical competence, and then provides them with the assistance they need to master this difficult kind of selling job.

The high-performance sales force is relatively young. This reflects the need for recent education; indeed, the proportion of college graduates is higher in this classification than in any of the others. Pay scales must therefore be high enough to attract the intelligent, educated, and personable young men who are suited for this kind of work.

In the high-performance force, close personal supervision is supplemented by the judicious use of salesmen's reports. The critical report here is the *competitive* or *market information report*. This is just as important to high performance here as the customer inventory report is to high trade sales performance.

GUIDELINES

The technical sales executive faces the same dilemma as the missionary sales executive: the younger force outperforms the older one, but the younger one exhibits excessive—and hence costly—turnover. In advancing the following recommendations, I am not disregarding this conflict but, rather, am making the assumption that high performance accompanied by a mild degree of turnover is more desirable than low performance accompanied by vitrification of the sales force.

The executive should control those aspects of the work—cold-calling, most notably—that are likely to jar the nerves of the man who has the basic talents and qualities to succeed in technical sales; otherwise, turnover will rise. He must also key his deployment decisions to building up customer-salesman relations, or performance will suffer. These relations are particularly critical in technical sales, where the salesman is frequently responsible for coordinating or supplying customer services, solving customers' problems, and negotiating contracts and the like. Therefore, the executive should:

□ Design sales territories so as to optimize the customer's satisfaction with the sales-call pattern.

□ Avoid requiring excessive cold-call activity, unless the salesman receives very generous compensation for it.

□ Transfer salesmen among territories as infrequently as possible (except, of course, at their own request).

When he makes a hiring decision, the executive should place more emphasis on what a man will bring to his job, as opposed to what he will be able to get out of it for himself. Whatever else, the technical salesman is not in business for himself—he is in business for his company.

In addition, the possession of a college degree, while not associated with high performance, *is* associated with low turnover; this suggests that technical selling provides more satisfaction to the educationally higher-qualified man than any other kind of selling. Therefore, the executive should:

□ Base hiring decisions more on an applicant's technical knowledge than on his desire to make money.

□ Seek out and hire college graduates in their late twenties and early thirties. (For this classification, employment agencies and advertisements are fair sources of applicants.)

For the technical sales force, training can play an important part in improving performance and reducing turnover. In addition, the data shown in *Exhibit III* indicate that the executive who faces major turnover problems might well consider the possibility of lengthening the period of initial training with a view to preparing the trainee more adequately before sending him out to face the company's customers. Therefore, the executive should:

□ Make sure trainees are adequately prepared to handle the selling and technical aspects of the job before assigning them to their territories.

□ Rely heavily on brief, but regular, retraining sessions to achieve the major training objectives.

Unlike the trade sales executive, who should be generous with salesman's

Exhibit III. *Length of initial training period in technical sales forces by turn-over quintiles*

Turnover quintile	Average length of period (in days)	Average turnover rate
Very low	125	1.0%
Low	95	4.2
Average	97	7.5
High	62	11.7
Very high	65	24.3

pay, and the missionary sales executive, who can afford to be niggardly, the technical sales executive should ordinarily pay approximately the going industry rate. Because the competition for good technical salesmen is severe, the executive should recognize that he is likely to have to pay a premium for certain of his strategic deployment and selection decisions. Once again, a sensible pay scale appears to be the one suggested by the average of the companies in the highest-performance quintile, and the proportion of variable pay suggested by the average of the companies in the lowest-turnover quintile. Therefore, the executive should:

□ Make sure that, unless industry pay scales dictate otherwise, his lowest-paid salesman earns about $9,000, his average salesman between $12,000 and $13,000, and his highest-paid salesman earns between $20,000 and $26,000.

□ Adjust pay scales upward to compensate for either excessive cold-call activity or a college degree.

The incentive offered by commission and bonus payment may not be as important to the good technical salesman; the executive can follow the practice suggested by the high-performance sales forces here:

□ Pay about 80% of the average salesman's earnings in the form of fixed salary.

Close contact between salesman and supervisor supplements training and provides closer liaison between the home office and the marketplace. A good reporting system conduces to this close contact. The practice of companies in the highest-performance quintile suggests that the sales executive should:

□ Maintain a ratio of salesmen to field supervisors of about 7 to 1.

□ Place heavy emphasis on developing and improving the salesmen's reporting system, with special attention to the market information report.

Once again, a high rate of advancement opportunity, while not necessarily improving performance, contributes to excessive-turnover problems. On the other hand, this kind of environment may be necessary—within reasonable limits—to attract the younger salesmen necessary for achieving high levels of sales force performance. In keeping with practices associated with high-performance technical groups, then, the executive should:

 □ Strive to keep the opportunity rate below 6%.

Implementing these recommendations demonstrates to the salesman that his *problem-solving skills are important*. He sees that his supervisor does not insist that he run around drumming up new business; that his job has been organized around the opportunity to provide important services to his customers; that he has been selected for his potential to become technically competent, and that he receives continuous training; that the company is investing above-average amounts in his fixed earnings; that it provides him with management assistance and guidance; and that he is given a fair chance of promotion.

The general thrust of these recommendations is that performance is maximized and turnover minimized when the executive makes the salesman perceive himself as performing an important consulting function for his customers on behalf of his company. Current practice is congruent with most of these recommendations. It emphasizes hiring college graduates, bringing in new salesmen through in-company transfers, training and continuously retraining them (especially in product knowledge), and paying a high proportion of compensation as fixed salary. It plays down cold-calling and calling at random. Other current practices are self-defeating —for example, building a force with a high average age and discounting the importance of the supervisor-salesman relationship.

It is interesting to note that technical sales forces as a whole exhibit a closer association between actual practice and desirable practice than the other three sales force classifications. This phenomenon is perhaps due to the wider recognition—among industrial marketers in particular—that selling has become a professional activity. In many instances, the new generation of products requires a professional to articulate their benefits. More important, new attitudes on the part of an increasingly sophisticated generation of purchasers demand a professional who can go beyond the articulation of product benefits and help the customer identify and solve a whole set of problems in which his product may play only a small part.

Using this concept of technical selling may pose problems for certain sales executives. A line may not need—or be able to support—this kind of salesman, especially if it is approaching the "commodity stage" because of customer familiarity and low margins. If it is important to a company that someone merely *calls on* users to keep them reordering, a shift to trade sales tactics may be in order.

Small organizations in which the cost of operating the sales force is a significant percentage of the sales dollar may find it difficult to invest the necessary money in training and supervision. Nevertheless, the increasing competition for both sales and salesmen makes it mandatory for even the small company to field a sales force well equipped to handle the challenges of the new technology.

New-Business Selling

This kind of selling has been variously called "canvassing," "bird-dogging," and "cold-calling." The primary responsibility of the new-business sales force is to obtain new accounts for its company, and the ability to convert a total stranger into a customer is the critical skill.

The great difficulty in this kind of selling is that the cold-calling it requires keeps the turnover rate high. The good new-business salesman is the rare bird dog who can balance the all-too-frequent exhilaration of "closing the tough one" and the equally frequent deflation that comes with the polite—or sometimes brutal—rejection.

The younger forces perform poorly and the older forces perform well, as the reader can clearly see from the percentages shown in *Exhibit I*. This bears out the conclusion that emotional maturity contributes to success in this area of selling. Younger men frequently find this activity impossibly difficult and burdensome, and tend to quit early in the game. Hence we find that the very young forces not only perform poorly, but are afflicted with excessive turnover.

The study data show that management practices are less important to successful sales operation than finding the right kind of man to begin with —the kind of man, as one executive phrased it, who has "the tough skin and the killer instinct of a shark."

The successful salesman also tends to be rather more independent of supervisory control than salesmen in the other classifications. To some extent, this must be adventitious: this classification showed much the highest rate of sales growth of the forces for the two-year period covered by the questionnaire—and the higher this growth rate, the less attention a company is likely to pay to providing training for its salesmen, presumably because the need for training is less obvious. Partly for this reason, therefore, there are no observable relationships between any training factors and the performance index.

GUIDELINES

The study makes it clear that applicant sources and selection methods are not correlated with performance levels, although they are correlated with turnover rate. This suggests that although executives have found ways to reduce failure (i.e., quick turnover) through their selection processes, they have not yet found ways to predict success (i.e., high performance). So far as the composition of the force is concerned, the balance turns in favor of the older man. Thus the executives should:

◻ Seek out and hire salesmen in their forties and late thirties who enjoy cold-calling and have demonstrated their proficiency at it. (Company initiative is most important here.)

To some extent, the executive can regulate cold-calling where it is troublesome. One method is to restructure working patterns so that each man has enough regular business from established customers to take the sting out of the cold-call routine. The study data indicate that he should:

◻ Schedule a salesman for no more than two cold calls a day unless the man is a proven "new-business specialist."

Younger sales forces really need adequate preparation for the cold-calling associated with new-business selling, and it appears worthwhile to spend considerable time and effort to improve initial and on-the-job phases of training. Therefore, the executive should:

◻ Make sure that trainees are adequately prepared to cope with the vicissitudes of cold-calling before assigning them to their territories.

◻ Rely heavily on on-the-job training for both new and experienced sales personnel.

The executive can be tempted toward generosity in making compensation decisions about the *average* for the new-business sales force, but be restrained in his attitude toward the *highest-paid* salesman. Also, a review of job content and fringe benefits appears worthwhile. The practices of companies in the lowest-turnover quintile suggest sensible guidelines here. The executive should:

◻ Make sure that, unless industry pay scales dictate otherwise, his lowest-paid salesman earns about $8,000, his average salesman between $12,000 and $13,000, and his highest-paid salesman earns between $19,000 and $24,000. (*Exhibit IV* summarizes the optimal earnings levels for holding turnover down in the four sales classifications.)

◻ Adjust pay scales upward to compensate for excessive cold-call activity.

◻ After a thorough examination, consider adding new, or making increases in established, fringe benefits.

The optimal proportion of fixed salary to total earnings is just as surprising in this classification as it is in trade sales. The data indicate that it is much higher than I had expected—around 80% for the average new-business salesman.

Exhibit IV. Optimal levels of salesmen's earnings for controlling turnover

Sales force classification	Lowest-paid salesman	Average salesman	Highest-paid salesman
Trade	$8,000	$13,000	$20,000-26,000
Missionary	8,000	11,000-12,000	17,000-18,000
Technical	9,000	12,000-13,000	20,000-26,000
New-business	8,000	12,000-13,000	19,000-24,000

Many executives would reason that the new-business salesman exerts more direct influence on sales volume than any other kind of salesman, and therefore one ought to spur him on by increasing the proportion of commission and incentive in his total paycheck. But, here again, it is the salesman's point of view that is important. The cold-calling that the new-business salesman must do creates considerable tension for him in his job. Knowing that a large part of his earnings are fixed relieves him of a measure of financial uncertainty and allows him to concentrate better on the vital aspect of his work. Achieving victory in the cold call is difficult enough, it seems, without the salesman feeling that he is playing roulette with his take-home pay as well. Thus the executive should:

□ Pay 80% of the average salesman's earnings in fixed form.

Since the data on new-business sales force supervision and control exhibit very little correlation with data on performance and turnover, the executive is well advised to follow the pattern of the companies in the highest-performance quintile. He should:

□ Maintain a ratio of salesmen to field supervisors of around 10 to 1.

□ Avoid the use of personal sales quotas for salesmen (these are particularly irritating to the older salesmen); improve the reporting system instead.

□ Strive to keep the opportunity rate between 2% and 6%.

Implementing these recommendations would indicate to the salesman that he is a *valued and supported company employee,* not merely a bird dog. Salesmen are continually told this fact, but implementation convinces them: the salesman sees the company investing training time and money in him to ensure his success on the job; he sees the company compensating him in executive fashion; he sees himself protected insofar as possible from the tensions associated with cold-call activity; he feels responsible for his own performance, and is not pressed by an arbitrary quota; and he perceives his job as an important end in itself, not as a proving ground for a better one.

The broad concept here is that to achieve maximum performance and minimum turnover, the executive must hire men temperamentally compatible with cold-calling and then provide them with support and encouragement. In two ways, current practice reflects the trend of these recommendations: *one*, it emphasizes suitable methods of compensation; and *two*, it steers away from employee referrals as a source of applicants.

In a number of other ways, however, current practice is self-defeating. It encourages excessive cold-calling, use of advertisements to attract applicants, hiring on the basis of the applicant's drive to make money, and hiring young men. It also discourages significant training efforts, and plays down the importance of adequate levels of compensation. The executive should check his own practices against this list of trouble spots.

It is interesting to note that current practices in new-business selling diverge more from the study's recommendations than do those of any of the other three classifications. This may be because the new-business sales executive has usually been promoted from the ranks. He is likely to say, "I was a successful salesman, and the job was easy for *me*." But the job is not an easy one for the average salesman, as the high average turnover rate for this classification indicates.

Giving their salesmen more support may be difficult for some sales executives. Marketing strategy may dictate a great deal of cold-call activity, period. Unless he discovers better methods of selecting salesmen, the executive may have to resign himself to high turnover or pay very high salaries to attract and keep high-caliber people.

Conclusion

To some extent, every sales organization is a hybrid of the four main kinds of sales force, and the executive who wants to take practical advantage of the findings of this study may have to balance his practices to suit the mix of roles he must administrate. If, by chance, he is supervising a selling effort that uses both technical and new-business tactics, he will have to juggle the proportions of younger, better-educated, and highly talented men and older, aggressive, hard-shelled men on his force. As both the pretests of the survey and the survey itself show, however, it is usually easy to identify the main role of any given force easily.

It may be more difficult for the executive to identify the exact goals he wishes to pursue. As we have seen, maximizing performance and minimizing turnover are not always compatible goals; in the prescription for managing the missionary force, for example, the two goals come into direct collision. Each company, or each sales executive, must decide what turnover level is tolerable; once this has been established, the executive can concentrate on specific methods to improve performance.

The study yielded a good many results that could not be included here —for instance, data and conclusions relating to field superintendents, their development, their compensation, and so forth. Also, I could not document the methods of statistical manipulation and interpretation that were used to wash the effects of interacting variables out of the data. I could not even include full statistical evidence for any of the conclusions presented. Still, the working executive will perhaps find these conclusions challenging and thought-provoking, and they may help him make his practices more effective.

Appendix to Chapter 12

Study Sample

The survey population comprised companies and corporate divisions that employed 10 or more salesmen. It excluded companies that were primarily engaged in retail selling ("behind the counter") and delivery selling (route selling, for example). It also excluded companies whose businesses were primarily banking, insurance, and real estate. Retailing and delivery forces were excluded because companies engaged in these kinds of selling do not ordinarily compete for the kind of salesmen one ordinarily associates with "outside" selling. Banking, insurance, and real estate companies were excluded because their methods of measuring sales performance and turnover are not easily compared with those of the rest of industry.

Companies that employed fewer than 10 salesmen were not included, because pretests of the questionnaire indicated that such companies are likely to use only limited, *ad hoc* supervisory procedures in their sales force management.

13. Manage the Customer, Not Just the Sales Force

Benson P. Shapiro

The subject of sales management has many parts, each of them very important. One of the tasks of the sales manager is to see these parts in perspective and to understand their relationships. If, as so often happens, one activity or group of activities is magnified out of proportion, the overall goals of management are bound to suffer. This article discusses the four key areas of sales management: defining the role of personal selling, deploying the sales force, managing the accounts, and understanding the selling costs.

Recently I investigated the sales management problems of an apparel company that I will refer to by the fictitious name of Fitwell. At that time, the Fitwell Company had 50 salespeople and sales of $40 million in the medium to medium-high priced dress lines. The salespeople were paid on a variable commission rate, receiving 7% on dresses with a high gross margin for Fitwell and down to 5% on dresses with the lowest gross margin. The salespeople called on retail stores, paid their own out-of-pocket expenses, and averaged about $46,000 each in gross compensation per year.

A few years ago Fitwell introduced a higher priced dress line to keep pace with the market and to improve its margins. The line did not sell well despite its apparently fashion-right design, relatively heavy advertising, and extra high commissions (9%). The top executives who had developed the concept of the line were personally chagrined by the results.

The immediate reaction of Fitwell's sales managers was to push harder. The annual sales meeting included speeches by the chairman of the board, the president, the marketing vice president, and the national sales manager on the importance of the new line to the company and to the salespeople. The sales managers urged their regional managers to motivate their salespeople to "push the line." Contests were developed (e.g., a trip to Europe for the salesperson with the largest percentage of sales in the higher priced line and an automobile for the person with the largest total dollar volume). The more the sales managers "motivated," the more they frustrated themselves. Sales did not improve, and increasingly "powerful" speeches were met with frequent yawns.

The Fitwell Company's determination to motivate its salespeople to "push the line" is typical of the misplaced emphasis that occurs all through the business world. Too often top management thinks that motivation is the key to getting its people to follow a particular policy. However, management would be better off reevaluating its policy rather than focusing on motivating its employees, since often the problem is that top management has failed to develop an appropriate policy to begin with.

Let me hasten to say that the emphasis on managing the sales force is understandable. Since most sales managers—even national sales managers and sales vice presidents—were once active salespeople themselves, they naturally regard the sales force from the point of view of a salesperson. They ask, "How can we get more cooperation and more selling from the sales force?" But they do not ask, "How can we generate greater sales and profits?"

Sales managers sometimes forget that sales and profits are generated by the customer and that their objective is the management of the customer through the sales program, which is in turn implemented by the sales force. Their misplaced emphasis is serious because when they face problems like decreasing sales or market share, they change the means of managing the sales force but not its purpose.

Typically, sales managers change the compensation scheme, the most visible and talked about part of sales force management and the one which can be altered most rapidly. After monkeying around with compensation, sales managers usually focus on recruiting and selecting ("If we had more highly motivated salespeople to begin with, we wouldn't need such a clever compensation scheme"). So they have a brief romance with various testing and interviewing fads. Then they try training ("The salespeople don't know what we want or how to sell"). And finally they experiment with other motivational approaches like contests.

Although all of the foregoing are important, they should not be the only, or even the primary, consideration of sales managers. Sales management should be divided into two equally important parts: (1) formulating the sales policy and (2) implementing that policy. The first includes the detailed specification of the objectives, and the second, the accomplishment of the specified objectives.

Since the ultimate purpose of sales management is to generate loyal customers and high sales at reasonable costs, let us examine the four key questions that must be considered in formulating a customer-oriented sales program:

1. What is the general role that personal selling will play in the company's marketing strategy?

2. How will the salespeople be assigned or deployed to various customers and prospects, products, territories, and selling tasks?

3. How will each account and prospective account be managed?

4. What will the program cost, and will that cost be justified?

Role of Personal Selling

From management's point of view, the customer is served not only by the company's personal representatives but also by its total marketing strategy, including product policy, pricing decisions, distribution channels, and communications methods. Personal selling and advertising are the two primary methods of communication.

One of the major marketing decisions facing all companies, and particularly those marketing consumer goods, is that of personal selling "push" versus advertising "pull." The choice largely depends on the way in which consumers make up their minds, the influence different communications approaches have on them, and the relative cost of the different approaches.

On the one hand, advertising is inexpensive in terms of cost per person reached, but its impact is relatively low. In addition, the message is standardized, at least for each advertisement, and the flow of communication is totally one way. On the other hand, personal selling is expensive, but its impact is high. In addition, the message can be tailored to the individual customer, and the flow of communication is in both directions.

Often, companies forget that there are two intermediate points on the scale between media advertising and personal selling: *direct mail advertising,* which can be more targeted than media advertising but is still a one-way communication flow, and *telephone selling,* which is more expensive than direct mail but has greater impact, more flexibility, and is a two-way flow. Telephone selling is cheaper than face-to-face selling but has less impact. With the increasing cost of the face-to-face sales call, telephone selling has received new impetus. It eliminates travel time and expense.

Because of its expense, personal selling should be used only in situations in which (a) the high impact, flexibility, and two-way communication flow are needed, and (b) the high cost is justified. Personal selling can be most effectively used when it is carefully coordinated with other communications tools and other parts of the marketing strategy.

For example, a company may choose to deemphasize its personal selling effort and pass on the savings to the customer as a price cut. At the retail level, this has been part of the strategy of the discount store. Cash-and-carry wholesalers have also chosen this route.

Then again, some companies may choose to take over the role of their distribution channels and in the process to emphasize personal selling.

Most consumer goods manufacturers have relatively small sales forces that call on wholesalers and retailers, who then sell the product to the consumer. Two major exceptions to this pattern are Avon Products and Fuller Brush, which employ large sales forces to sell their products directly to the consumer. To these companies, the personal selling effort is a basic part of their marketing strategy.

The customer is best served when the sales force is assigned only those tasks which it can perform more effectively and efficiently than other parts of the marketing strategy. Careful delineation of the role of personal selling in the marketing mix will help to prevent unfortunate situations in which sales managers attempt to motivate their salespeople to do things which are not in the interest of the company, the salesperson, or the customer.

Deploying the Sales Force

In assigning salespeople to territories, to accounts and prospective accounts, and to products, management should be aware that there are two parts to effective deployment: developing a policy and getting the salespeople to follow that policy. As we noted earlier, management sometimes emphasizes implementation of a particular policy without considering that it might have been incorrect to begin with. Let us return to the Fitwell Company as an example of such a management error. Fitwell's mistake was at the policy level, in the deployment of the selling effort across accounts and prospects:

When sales of Fitwell's higher priced dress line failed to increase in spite of the product's known appeal, the sales management team decided to step back and take a fresh look at the entire selling effort. It soon became clear that the problem was one of deployment, not motivation.

The individual salesperson knew he or she could make more money by selling the traditional lower priced lines to existing customers than by prospecting for new accounts for the new line. To prospect effectively, the salesperson would have had to learn about a new product line, a new type of customer, and a new sales approach. Also, to the better salespeople who made in excess of $60,000 per year, the contests were irrelevant. They also knew that they were impervious to management displeasure as long as they were selling in the vicinity of $1,000,000 worth of merchandise per year.

It soon became obvious that these salespeople should never have been assigned to the new line. And once the problem was identified as one of deployment, the sales managers could cope with it. No longer did they harangue the sales force. Instead, they went about developing an additional new sales force that was recruited, selected, and trained to call on the new type of outlet. Field sales managers were given the responsibility of opening accounts that could use a sizable volume of the line.

In the end, everyone at Fitwell was satisfied. But everyone would also have been better off had the problem been carefully analyzed in the first place. If management had approached the situation properly, it would have seen that the choice was between having a new line with new retailers served by a new sales force or having no new line.

Deployment of the sales force across products, geography, and tasks (e. g., opening new accounts, selling, serving existing accounts) can be approached in the same analytical way (a) by striking a balance between policy development and policy implementation, and (b) by focusing on the generation and maintenance of profitable accounts.

Managing the Account

The development and maintenance of account relationships are especially important in business selling (e.g., one company selling to another) because in almost all instances the selling process is continuous—a supplier sells the same type of merchandise to a buyer over and over again. Since the market for most products is finite, each seller must constantly face the same buyers. This is less true for the consumer market, where there are many more buying units and where the repeat buying process is infrequent for many products, such as houses, television sets, and so forth.

ORGANIZATIONAL INTERACTION

An account must be defined in terms of both the organization and the individuals within it. Selling to an organization is much more complex than selling to an individual for two reasons: an organization is made up of different individuals with different needs, and those individuals interact with one another in complex ways. Consider the different explicit needs of the various participants in a purchase decision.

When a company buys a large piece of equipment, the manufacturing managers want an efficient machine that will require little repair and is technically advanced, the treasurer's department is interested in the financing terms, and the purchasing department is primarily interested in the total cost of the manufacturing system (e.g., raw materials, depreciation, installation) and the outright cost of the machine.

Consider also that the selling company must take into account the various participants' needs as well as their importance and power in the company. Every participant has both organizational needs, based on his or her position and professional interests, and personal needs. Buying decisions, because they involve authority and responsibility, represent a primary focus for the satisfaction of personal needs in the organizational setting.

Thus the young treasurer, say, might be trying to consolidate his newly won power by showing how well he can do the job. Then again, the manufacturing people might be smarting over a recent rebuff by the engineering people and therefore seeking revenge.

The astute company, sales manager, and salesperson should of course work hard to find out any information such as that just mentioned. Knowing the buying company's dynamics is part of what selling and account management are all about.

THE SELLING PROCESS

The actual sale consists of five sequential steps: opening the relationship, qualifying the prospect, presenting the message, closing the sale, and servicing the account.

The *opening* has the dual purpose of determining the right person in the organization to approach initially and of generating enough interest so that it is possible to obtain the information necessary for the qualification. The end result of a good opening should be an appointment with an appropriate and enthusiastic person.

The *qualification* is the process by which a salesperson determines whether or not the prospect is worth the effort of a sales presentation. Although scholars tend to gloss over the qualifying process, salespeople and sales managers constantly discuss it.

The *presentation* is the core of the selling process and requires astute management by the salesperson. It is the "pitch" (i.e., the actual attempt at persuasion). The presentation sooner or later culminates in an attempt to close the sale.

The *closing* is obtaining the final agreement to purchase. This is the Achilles' heel of many a would-be-successful salesperson.

After the sale comes the *service* aspect. Often the salesperson will be reselling supplies, materials, parts, and so on. This service part of the sale is frequently the opening to new sales.

Multilevel selling: Traditionally, the salesperson has sold to a purchasing agent in the industrial area or to a store buyer in the consumer goods field. Since it was a one-on-one relationship, the sales manager could structure his policies and programs on that basis. But the situation is changing, and the policies used to manage the sales force must now reflect these changes.

One important change is the introduction of multilevel selling—the process by which several authority levels are called on. The salesperson calling on a retailer, say, may attempt to contact both the buyer and the merchandise manager so that when the buyer seeks approval of the sales proposal, the merchandise manager is presold or at least receptive. Thus multilevel selling is in a sense a product of system selling because the chief buying influence (a) is at a higher organizational level than are the traditional buyers and (b) is responsible for the total system instead of just the individual components.

For example, consider the case of a manufacturing company for which one person purchases the raw materials and another buys the machinery. If the selling company wants to sell a system involving both raw materials and machinery, it is almost required to move upward in the purchasing organization to reach the chief buying influence in charge of both.

Team selling: The one-on-one selling process is further broken down by the introduction of team selling, a process in which several people from the selling company call on the buying organization. Thus, in a team approach, each level of the selling company calls on his or her counterpart in the prospective buying organization.

One reason for team selling is business etiquette (e.g., it is more appropriate for the national sales manager to call on the general merchandise manager than to climb beyond his or her own level or to descend beneath it). It also demonstrates appropriate interest on the part of the selling company's management. Still another reason is that this method allows for an exchange of power. The two top managers can make arrangements (e.g., private branding, special products) that their subordinates cannot.

Team selling is not limited to different hierarchical levels in the buying and selling organizations. Often it involves people in different functional areas in both companies. Members of different functional areas in the buying organization have specific needs and viewpoints that can best be met and understood by their functional equivalents in the selling organization.

For example, if the treasurer of the buying organization is concerned about financing arrangements, then the treasurer of the selling company is probably better suited to deal with that executive than is the salesperson, whose primary job is to deal with manufacturing and purchasing personnel.

There are three important considerations to keep in mind about team selling:

1. It is not always appropriate. Sometimes the sale is simple, repetitive, or small. The team approach is most suitable for the selling of heavy capital equipment or long-term supply relationships, either formal contracts or informal commitments. These involve enough dollars and enough different functions in the buying organization to justify team selling's high expenditure of time.

2. It is complex and difficult to manage. Actually, it is possible for the sales team to spend more time getting coordinated than selling. Or worse, it can spend too little time getting coordinated and end up presenting contradictory impressions to the buying influences.

3. It is in a sense an extension of the marketing concept that stresses the

importance of having all parts of the selling company directed toward satisfying customer needs. Here, all relevant functional units become involved in the actual selling process.

Although team selling usually involves relatively high-level personnel and is used primarily to "open" an account, it can also involve lower level personnel and be used to provide continuing maintenance selling. A soft drink bottler, for example, may primarily use a route delivery person for selling but may supplement his efforts with an in-store display and merchandising expert. In other situations, inside sales liaison people, expediters, or shipping personnel may join the sales team in keeping accounts satisfied.

THE PYRRHIC SALE

The truly astute management is not interested in just making sales; it wants to build account relationships. These, of course, must result in sales sooner or later. The trade-off between immediate sales and long-term account relationships is part of the phenomenon that I call the Pyrrhic sale —one that immediately benefits the company but jeopardizes its future relationship with the account.

In business selling the customer is in the position of repeatedly being able to purchase the product. Thus this situation requires careful account management by the salesperson, who must be willing to forgo a sale that is not in the best long-term interest of the account and therefore of his relationship with it.

For example, the apparel salesperson who is willing to tell a customer that some items in his line do not sell well at retail in spite of their apparent appeal is helping his customer and himself over the long run. Or picture the response to the pump salesperson who says, "Yes, we offer the best pumps for your needs in applications a, b, and c, but unfortunately our pumps are not as good in application d as those offered by our competitors." The Pyrrhic sale, in contrast, occurs when the salesperson "forces" a marginal sale but risks losing the account.

THE SALESPERSON'S ROLE

Account relationships depend on more than just the salesperson's prudence in not pushing for orders. The salesperson can perform functions for the customer that make him or her valuable to the customer's organization. Two most important roles, merchandiser and ombudsman, are at the crux of the salesperson's account maintenance function.

As merchandiser, it is the salesperson's job to present those items in his product line which are most appropriate to the customer. In complex industrial situations, the salesperson is often responsible for designing the product to fit the customer's specific needs. In the apparel and furniture industries, the salesperson helps the buyer choose items which will sell best in his store.

As ombudsman, the salesperson is the customer's representative to the selling company in handling problems such as damaged merchandise, late or early shipments, credit arrangements, and the like. Obviously, the more effective the salesperson is in dealing with his own company, the more effective he can be in helping his customers.

THE COMPANY'S ROLE

The salesperson's function should not be the only important aspect of the company's account management procedures and policies. Many successful marketers develop special programs to help their customers. Some wholesalers, for example, offer site selection advice and store layout assistance to their retailers. Many companies provide their distributors with sales training assistance. Other companies help their dealers manage inventories.

Delivery and credit are two other important account management techniques. Fast delivery or emergency backup of spare parts inventories can cut down on the dealer's and user's inventory carrying costs. Special credit arrangements can help customers with their businesses. One important credit arrangement is "dating"—that is, extended credit provided in highly seasonal industries like toys that encourages the dealer to accept early delivery.

Some of these programs may be companywide, while others may be directed toward special categories of distributors or particular accounts. However, it is important to bear in mind that, according to the Robinson-Patman Act, all customers who compete with each other must be treated equitably.

As I indicated earlier, the nonselling parts of the company have an important role to play in account management. The rude receptionist and the truculent delivery man have probably lost as many accounts as the insensitive salesperson.

THE SALES MANAGER'S ROLE

All too often sales managers are more responsive to competitors than to customers in developing account management programs. Their attitude seems to be at best "we'll do it if they do it" but more often "it's a nice idea, but it costs money." They overlook the competitive benefits of being first with an innovative approach to customer satisfaction. They do not spend enough time thinking about the needs of the customer, because they are too busy motivating their salespeople.

Sales managers must make careful trade-offs between the costs of account management programs and the benefits to their customers. The ideal programs, of course, provide large benefits for small costs. Analytical, creative, and flexible sales managers can undoubtedly find a large number of approaches that meet this criterion.

The account management area is central to the difference between managing a sales program and a sales force. The real emphasis of the sales manager should be on customer management. The sales force should act as a conduit of communication, not as a barrier between the sales manager and the customer.

Understanding Selling Costs

In pursuing their ultimate objective of profitable account relationships, sales managers must look carefully at the cost of the sales force and the benefits received from it. Some of the concepts that we noted earlier in considering the role of personal selling in the marketing strategy are useful in deciding how much to spend on a sales force. The two primary determinants are the complexity of the selling task and the profit to be derived from the work done by one salesperson. The more complex the selling task, the more reason to have a talented sales force. The higher the profit created by a single salesperson, the greater the company's ability to pay for a "high-powered" sales force.

When the selling task is complex, the salesperson may actually be called on to "design the product" for the customer, as noted earlier. In tailoring the equipment to a particular customer's needs, the salesperson is developing a "product policy" for the smallest market segment—one buyer. To accomplish this difficult task, the salesperson operates in a customer-oriented, client-centered, problem-solving mode. He or she must transmit a great deal of complex intellectual information while providing reassurance in answer to psychological needs.

At the other extreme is the salesperson with the simple product whose function is to "go out and sell it." The mode is typically either persuasion or merely making the product available (e.g., the milkman). Little information needs to be transmitted. Often the task is merely to be "likeable," or at least not "unlikeable," and to actually deliver the products. Selling of this type demands only a low-powered sales force.

The high-powered sales force is expensive. The salesperson must be carefully selected. Often he or she has had substantial training prior to joining the company (e.g., the graduate engineer who sells complex equipment). Specialized training after joining the company is standard procedure. The only way to attract such an intelligent, trained, and trainable individual is to compensate well.

Exhibit I. *The nature of the selling effort*

		Intricacy of sales task			
		Simple	Moderately simple	Moderately complex	Complex
Aspects of the task	Mode	persuasion or delivery			problem solving
	Importance of information transmittal	low			high
	Needs served	personal and physical			intellectual and psychological
	Where prevalent	consumer and retail			industrial and commercial
Profit impact		low			high
Management of the sales force	Training	less			more
	Compensation	low			high
	Independence	low			high
	Number of customers	high			low
Typical examples	Consumer selling	milk	clothing	real estate insurance	stocks and bonds
	Industrial and commercial selling	simple industrial supplies		industrial equipment	high-volume OEM components
				fashion at wholesale	large private-label sales

Usually, such a salesperson thrives on independence. A "programmed pitch" does not work. Geographical territories are often large, but the number of customers per salesperson is small. Because each customer requires individualized service, the salesperson cannot cover many customers.

Other parts of the marketing mix also affect the nature of the selling effort. The more the company relies on sales service, the more it needs highly skilled salespeople. Conversely, if the company relies on its established reputation, innovative products, meticulous delivery, low price, or other attractions, the importance of the selling effort and the money available to pay for it are reduced. *Exhibit I* illustrates in diagrammatic fashion much of the preceding discussion on the nature of the selling task.

VARIABLE VS. FIXED COSTS

The total amount is only one important aspect of costs; often the relationship of cost to volume is equally important. Media advertising costs are fixed; they do not vary with the unit sales volume. But sales costs may be either fixed or variable.

Sales overhead costs, such as the salaries of sales managers, are usually fixed. Sometimes, however, they include a bonus portion that varies with unit or dollar sales volume. Order processing costs are usually semivariable with the costs going up in a partially stepwise manner.

The major costs of the sales force itself may be either fixed or variable. A commission sales force, whether independent representatives or company salespeople, is a variable cost except for fixed salary guarantees, fringe benefits, and expenses. A salaried sales force is primarily a fixed cost. Usually, however, as sales volume per salesperson increases, there is a tendency to increase salaries.

The cost for a particular company of a straight-salaried sales force is directly related to the number of calls made. Clearly, if the number of calls a salesperson can make in a given period of time is relatively fixed, the total number of calls which the sales force can make in a given period of time must depend on the number of salespeople. The number, in turn, is the key to the cost of the sales force.

Theoretically, expenses are a fixed cost. In practice, however, most companies are more liberal with expense money in times of high sales than in times of low sales. One could argue that this is contrary to the way it should be. When business is dismal, perhaps all possible action should be taken to increase expense money. Such reasoning is usually not followed, however, because the emphasis on cost control increases in poor times, especially among publicly held companies.

Sales promotion occupies an important point on the continuum between personal selling and media advertising. Some forms of promotion (like certain contests, presentation aids, and sales or distributor meetings) are fixed costs. However, price-off deals, special packages, certain other contests, and most types of promotions are purely variable costs.

Each type of cost has its own advantage. Variable costs are more conservative since they protect the company in times of poor sales (i.e., costs automatically decrease as volume does). Thus they lessen the effect of poor sales on profits. They also help those companies with a small share of the market.

On the one hand, whereas the largest competitor in a market can spread the fixed costs over the largest volume, yielding a low communication cost per unit sold, the smaller competitor does not have that advantage. If he spends as much per unit, his fixed costs of advertising or personal selling will be much smaller, but his program probably will not have as much impact. If the smaller competitor has as large a program, his costs per unit, and thus his percentage of sales spent on advertising or a salaried sales force, will be much higher, and his profits, all other things about equal, will be much lower.

On the other hand, competition on the basis of variable costs (like sales promotions) gives the smaller competitor a better chance. He can spend as much per unit as the larger competitor spends, yet enjoy equal impact.

Fixed costs have their advantages too. They offer great upside opportunity. As sales grow, costs increase more slowly and profits more rapidly. And as we just noted, fixed costs also provide the large competitor with an advantage over the smaller one.

Regardless of the situation, it is important for sales and marketing managers first to understand the relationship between costs and sales volume and then to build a program which provides the cost structure they desire.

Concluding Note

The customer ultimately determines the success (or failure) of a company's marketing approach. Every aspect of marketing, including the personal selling effort, must focus on the customer.

The sales force is important. It must be carefully managed. But in the final analysis, it is only a conduit to the customer. The object is customer satisfaction and sales. A disproportionate emphasis on the means must lead to a lack of attention to the objective. The prescription: manage the customer, not just the sales force.

14. Demarketing—Yes, Demarketing

Philip Kotler and Sidney J. Levy

The way marketers try to cope with excess demand or unwanted demand may affect the company's long-run objectives just as much as do marketing policies for normal times. What kinds of situations lead companies to cut back on their marketing efforts? How do methods of de-emphasis differ depending on the type of problem? This instructive and sometimes amusing analysis answers these and other questions that have never before been raised in HBR. It also suggests new directions for the study of marketing.

The popular conception of marketing is that it deals with the problem of furthering or expanding demand. Whether one takes the traditional view that marketing is finding customers for existing products, or the more recent view that it is developing new products for unmet consumer wants, it is seen as the technology of bringing about increases in company sales and profits. The marketer is a professional builder of sales volume who makes deft use of product, price, place, and promotion variables.

This is a narrow concept of marketing and the potential applications of marketing technology. It is a concept that arose in a period of goods over-supply. It also reflects a widespread tendency to define marketing in terms of what marketers ought to do rather than to analyze what they actually do under various circumstances. Much marketing literature approaches marketing with exhortations: define your objectives, know your market, meet consumer needs, and so on—all underlaid with the implied promise that then you will sell more. As a result, marketing has been too closely identified with the problem of buyer markets.

But suppose that an economy were suddenly plunged into a state of widespread product shortages. What would be the role of marketing management then? Would it evolve into a minor business function? Would it disappear altogether? Or would it continue to perform critical functions for the company?

Most production, financial, and marketing men who are asked this question opine that marketing's role would be greatly reduced in a scarcity economy. They see marketing as a "fair weather" profession, one that seems to be important chiefly in periods of excess supply. In this respect marketing differs from manufacturing, accounting, and other business functions that are critical in all stages of the economy.

But this is an untenable position. True, if marketers are narrowly seen as responsible primarily for finding customers or increasing demand, then they would seem superfluous when demand becomes unmanageably great. However, in practice *excess demand* is as much a marketing problem as excess supply. A company faces a host of difficult customer-mix and marketing-mix decisions in periods of excess demand. It has to find ways of reducing total demand or certain classes of demand to the level of supply without damaging long-run customer relations.

Our name for this kind of activity is "creative demarketing." More formally, we define demarketing as *that aspect of marketing that deals with discouraging customers in general or a certain class of customers in particular on either a temporary or permanent basis*. The tasks of coping with shrinking demand or deliberately discouraging segments of the market call for the use of all the major marketing tools. As such, marketing thinking is just as relevant to the problem of reducing demand as it is to the problem of increasing demand.

Once this view is appreciated, the true character of marketing's mission becomes clearer. Marketing is the business function concerned with controlling the level and composition of demand facing the company. Its short-run task is to adjust the demand to a level and composition that the company can, or wishes to, handle. Its long-run task is to adjust the demand to a level and composition that meets the company's long-run objectives.

In this article we will describe three different types of demarketing:

1. *General* demarketing, which is required when a company wants to shrink the level of total demand.

2. *Selective* demarketing, which is required when a company wants to discourage the demand coming from certain customer classes.

3. *Ostensible* demarketing, which involves the appearance of trying to discourage demand as a device for actually increasing it.

(A fourth type, *unintentional* demarketing, is also important but does not need to be considered here. So many abortive efforts to increase demand, resulting actually in driving customers away, have been reported in recent years that the dreary tale does not need to be told again.)

General Demarketing

At times excess demand can characterize a whole economy, and at other times, only a limited number of firms. Even in the absence of a general scarcity economy, there are always individual sellers who are facing excess demand for one or more of their products. While most other companies may be looking for customers, these sellers face the need to discourage customers, at least temporarily. Their marketing stance may become one of indifference or of arrogance. In a responsible organization, however, attempts are made to act in a framework that respects the marketing concept, i.e., the long-run aim of developing satisfied customers.

It is possible to distinguish at least three different situations that may give rise to general demarketing by a company. Let us consider each situation briefly.

TEMPORARY SHORTAGES

Many companies have the periodic fortune—or misfortune—of finding particular products in excess demand. Management underestimated demand, overestimated production, or did both. The following cases illustrate:

□ Eastman Kodak introduced its Instamatic camera in the early 1960's and found itself facing runaway demand. A few years passed before Kodak achieved enough capacity to handle demand.

□ Wilkinson Sword introduced its new stainless steel blade in the early 1960's and was besieged for supplies by regular and new dealers, not all of whom could be satisfied.

□ Anheuser-Busch underestimated the rate of growth in demand for its popular Budweiser beer and found itself in the late 1960's having to ration supplies to its better dealers and markets while it was making a crash effort to expand its plants.

□ Savings and loan associations in 1970-1971 faced an oversupply of savings relative to their ability to invest the funds and sought means to discourage the savings customers. They were willing to encourage small accounts, but refused large depositors.

These cases reflect temporary shortages of products that are corrected as the company manages to bring about sufficient plant expansion. In the interim, management must carry out two distinct tasks. The first is that of demand containment, i.e., curbing the growth of total demand. The second is that of product allocation, i.e., deciding which dealers and customers will receive the available product.

Steps to encourage deconsuming: Demand containment is the attempt to stabilize or reduce demand so that the product shortage is not further aggravated. This is largely accomplished by using the classic marketing instruments in reverse. To bring about deconsuming, management can:

□ Curtail advertising expenditures for the product, modifying the content of the messages.

□ Reduce sales promotion expenditures, investing less in trade exhibits, point-of-purchase displays, catalog space, and so on.

□ Cut back salesmen's selling time on the product and their entertainment budgets, asking them to concentrate on other products, spend more time in service and intelligence work, and learn to say *no* in a way that customers find acceptable.

□ Increase the price and other conditions of sale to the advantage of the marketing company. (This may include eliminating freight allowances, trade discounts, and so on.)

□ Add to the time and expense necessary for the buyer to procure the product or service—what might be called his "effort and psychological costs"—as a means of discouraging demand.

□ Reduce product quality or content, either to encourage deconsuming or to make more of the product available and thus demarket at a slower rate.

□ Curtail the number of distribution outlets, using the product shortage as an opportunity to eliminate undesirable dealers and/or customers.

Marketing management does not usually take these steps in isolation, but rather as part of a demarketing mix. It should make judicious estimates of the elasticity and cross-elasticities of the different instruments, i.e., their impact on demand when employed with varying intensity, both individually and in combination. Otherwise, the demarketing program may overinhibit demand, and the company may find itself facing a shortage of customers.

Alternatives in allocation: While these demarketing steps are being undertaken, marketing management should also develop a sound plan of product allocation. It must decide how, to whom, and in what quantities to allocate existing supply. There are four plausible solutions to this problem:

1. Management can allocate the product on a *first-come, first-serve* basis. This is a standard method regarded as fair by almost everyone except new customers. Dealers and customers get their stock in the order of their ordering.

2. Management can allocate the product on a *proportional demand* basis. This means determining that the company can satisfy x% of total demand and then supplying each customer with x% of its original order level. This is also held to be a fair solution.

3. A company can allocate supply on a *favored customer* basis. It determines its most valuable customers and satisfies their demand levels completely; the remaining customers may receive some fraction of their original order levels, with the rest being back-ordered. This is held to be a discriminatory solution, even if an understandable one.

4. A company can allocate products on a *highest bid* basis. The supply goes to those customers who offer the highest premium for early delivery. While many people consider this an exploitative strategy, economists typically argue that it makes the most sense since the product flows to those who presumably need it most.

Policies for allocating supply should be made by top management with marketing executives playing a central role in advising what impact the alternatives would have on long-run customer relations. If it assumes that the shortage is temporary, management should estimate customer feeling toward the company in the post-shortage period when the demand-supply balance is reestablished. Each general solution involves some amount and distribution of customer disappointment. If the company seeks to maximize its long-run, rather than short-run profits, it should choose solutions that minimize the total disappointment of customers during the period in question.

CHRONIC OVERPOPULARITY

There are some real, although perhaps rare, situations where an organization is faced with chronic overpopularity, and it wishes for one reason or another to bring demand down to a permanently lower level. Two situations can be distinguished:

In the first, the product's present popularity may be seen as posing a serious threat to the long-run "quality" of the product. For example, the island of Bali in the South Pacific has long been a tourist's dream. In recent years, it has attracted a larger number of tourists than can be handled comfortably with its facilities. The island is in danger of becoming overcrowded and spoiled. If tourism goes unchecked, Bali faces the same fate as Hawaii, which has lost its pristine appeal because of teeming crowds and soaring prices.

The authorities in Bali are aware of this danger and are considering measures to reduce demand. Their demarketing strategy is to reduce the island's attractiveness to middle-income tourists while maintaining or increasing its appeal to high-income tourists. They prefer fewer higher-spending tourists to a larger number of lower-spending tourists (in contrast to the savings and loan example cited earlier). To accomplish this, they will build luxury hotels and restaurants, place their advertising in media reaching the rich, and build a distinct image of catering to the affluent class.

Also because of fear that the area's natural beauty will be spoiled by congestion, officials in the state of Oregon are demarketing to prospective settlers. But the state does promote tourist trade; the governor encourages people to visit so long as they do not stay.

In the second situation, overpopularity is a problem because management does not want the strain of handling all of the demand. For example, there is an exceptionally fine restaurant in London that can seat only 30 persons. Word-of-mouth advertising has been so good that the restaurant is fully booked for months in advance. Nevertheless, tourists without reservations crowd around in the hope of cancellations. They add noise and detract from the intended atmosphere of leisurely dining.

The two men who run the restaurant enjoyed their role as managers of a small, intimate restaurant noted for its fine cuisine. For this reason, they decided on demarketing. They added a doorman who discouraged people from waiting for cancellations and from phoning about the availability of reservations. They also raised the prices. They were able to do all this without creating increased demand as a result of scarce resources—the reverse phenomenon to be described later in our discussion of ostensible demarketing.

PRODUCT ELIMINATION

Deft demarketing is called for when a company would like to elimate a product or service that some loyal customers still require or desire, e.g., a superseded model. Demand at any point in time can be considered as temporarily excessive in relation to the level at which the company prefers to see demand. So as not to create customer ill will, the company's task is not only to reduce production and inventory as soon as possible but also to reduce demand.

Among the demarketing strategies available are: informing the customer as to why the product is being dropped, offering partial or full compensation to important customers who are hurt by the disappearance of the product, and maintaining a minimal stock of the product to satisfy the hard-core customers. These strategies are warranted where the same customers purchase other items from the company and their goodwill must be maintained.

Selective Demarketing

Often an organization does not wish to contain or reduce the level of total demand but rather the demand coming from specific segments of the market. These segments or customer classes may be considered relatively unprofitable in themselves or undesirable in terms of their impact on other segments of demand. The company is not free to refuse sales outright, either as a matter of law or of public opinion. So it searches for other means to discourage demand from the unwanted customers. To illustrate:

☐ A luxury hotel catering to middle-aged, conservative people has recently attracted rich hippies who come wearing long hair and odd clothes, and who sit on the lobby floor making a good deal of noise. This has turned off the hotel's main clientele, and the management must rapidly take steps to discourage further reservations by hippies.

□ An automobile manufacturer of a luxury car purchased mainly by affluent whites as a status symbol has discovered that an increasing number of sales are going to newly rich members of the black community. As a result, affluent whites are switching to another well-known luxury automobile. The automobile manufacturer has to decide whether to let the market take its natural course, attempt to market to both groups, or to demarket to the new customer class.

□ A small appliance manufacturer wants to keep one of its popular brands in selective distribution, but it receives continuous pressure from marginal channels that want to carry the product. Not wanting to put his product through these channels, the manufacturer faces the problem of depriving them without alienating them.

The common problem faced by management in such cases is that the main clientele is threatened by the emergence of a new clientele. The organization does not find it possible to maintain both clienteles simultaneously. Gresham's Law seems to operate: the "cheaper" segment appears to drive the "dearer" segment from circulation. For one reason or another, the organization expects a higher risk and/or lower return (whether financial or psychological) from the new clientele. The alternative is to demarket selectively to the new clientele.

METHODS AND IMPLICATIONS

How is this done? When a company markets to one segment of the public, it may discourage other prospects who are unresponsive to, or alienated by, the appeals employed. For instance, advertising which plays up the joys of conventional home life demarkets the product to singles. In this sense, demarketing is the negative of marketing.

Selective demarketing refers to (a) the deliberate choice of segments that are to be avoided and (b) the specific means chosen to ward off the undesired customers. Management decreases the benefit/cost ratio which the wanted segment receives from patronage.

In examples like those cited, the marketer is typically not free to charge a discriminatory price to the undesirable segment. The demarketing mix has to be built out of other elements. Activities like these may be pursued:

□ The company discourages hope for product availability. The hotel fears it will be out of rooms, or the automobile company indicates that the customer must wait a long time for delivery.

□ The salesmen do not make calls on small organizations.

□ The company provides poor service to the undesirable segment. The undesirable customers receive poorer hotel rooms, slower service, insolent treatment—all suggesting that their business is not welcome.

□ The company makes it harder for the undesirable segment to find product channels or information. Auto companies are careful to locate dealerships away from changing neighborhoods, and hotels are selective about where they advertise and who receives their information.

To describe these steps is not to approve them. They are cited as familiar examples of what companies may do to discourage demand from certain classes of customers. The steps may raise thorny issues in social ethics. On the one hand, it seems understandable that an organization should have the right to choose or protect its major clientele, especially if its long-run profits are at stake. On the other hand, it is unjust to discriminate against buyers who have long hair, black skin, lower status, or small orders. The injustice seems especially intolerable if the discriminated buyers are left without equivalent alternatives. In that case demarketing becomes entwined with the social, legal, and political problems relating to unacceptable forms of discriminatory demarketing.

Ostensible Demarketing

Sometimes an establishment goes through the motions of demarketing in the hope of achieving the opposite effect. By creating the appearance of not wanting more customers, it hopes to make the product even more desirable to people. The marketer works on the principle that people want what may be hard to get and may even masochistically "enjoy" being neglected by the seller. Consider the following possibilities:

□ An artist operates a small gallery in which hang some of his own and other artists' paintings. He works in the back room and seems to resent the intrusion of would-be buyers. A buyer has to wait for the artist to emerge from the back room, and even then is treated brusquely. But the sales are good; many persons enjoy being mistreated and buying on the artist's terms.

□ An antique dealer keeps his store in relative disarray with very good objets d'art buried in dust-laden clusters of junk. Patrons often comment that he would attract more customers by cleaning up his store, eliminating the junk, and thus achieving better presentation. But they may be mistaken. The owner feels he attracts more customers this way, reasoning that people love a bargain and dream of discovering a Rembrandt buried among the ancient cracking canvasses of third-rate painters.

□ A department store arranges very carefully a stock of new blouses on a counter to make sure all sizes are represented. Then, a few minutes before the first customers arrive, the sales personnel pull the blouses out of their boxes and mix them about in chaotic fashion, ostensibly making the goods less attractive. But the customers spot the blouses and are attracted in large crowds to the counter in search of a bargain.

□ The managers of a rock concert advertise it on the radio in a discouraging way, saying the crowds will be too large, and that seats are practically sold out. The hidden intention is to increase the number of attendees by attracting those who hate to feel left out.

Questions for Study

Marketers have dealt with the problem of increasing demand for so long that they have overlooked a host of situations where the problem is to reduce demand or cope with inability to meet it. Whether the task is to reduce the level of total demand without alienating loyal customers, to discourage the demand coming from certain segments of the market that are either unprofitable or possess the potential of injuring loyal buyers, or to appear to want less demand for the sake of actually increasing it, the need is for creative demarketing.

It is easy to assume that demarketing is only marketing in reverse—product, price, place, and promotion policies can also be used to *discourage* demand. Yet the optimal demarketing mix is not obvious. First, there is the danger of overreducing short-run demand, which can be more serious than increasing it too much. Second, there is the danger of doing irreparable harm to long-run demand through indelicate handling of current customers.

This means that there is a need for careful research into the phenomenon of demarketing. Some important issues are:

1. When do companies face demarketing situations? What are the major types of situations and how extensive are they?

2. What demarketing policies and instruments are commonly used by these companies? How do companies reduce total demand and selective demand? How do they allocate scarce products?

3. What are optimal marketing policies for different demarketing situations?

4. What role is played by marketing management in advising or deciding on appropriate demarketing policies? Does top management recognize that specialized marketing skill is as essential in demarketing situations as in marketing situations?

5. What are the public policy issues and needs with respect to company demarketing practices, especially discriminatory demarketing?

Research into these questions should help clarify the important and neglected phenomenon of demarketing. Of equal importance, it should help establish a more objective and realistic conception of marketing. Marketing's task is not blindly to engineer increases in demand; that view came about because marketing developed during a period of economic growth and surpluses, and it is too casually related to "hard sell" tactics and pervasive advertising. Rather, marketing functions to regulate the level and shape of demand so that it conforms to the organization's current supply situation and to its long-run objectives.

When this view is accepted, it is not necessary to contrast marketing and demarketing. We have used the term "demarketing" to dramatize semantically a neglected phenomenon, but this would not be necessary if all marketing situations were recognized. Marketing inevitably has a role to play in the face of excess demand: the challenge is to demarket thoughtfully and skillfully.

15. Grass Roots Market Research

Louis W. Stern and J. L. Heskett

Every sales territory in which a company operates is different. This is why the centralized marketing research organization operates at a disadvantage. It is not necessary that field sales forces usurp the traditional long-range planning role of centralized marketing research groups, only that the local sales people perform certain research tasks for themselves. Grass roots intelligence enables branch managers to acquire the flexibility needed to capitalize on sudden market shifts and to adjust rapidly to new challenges and trends in their territories.

The basic intent of this article is to demonstrate that market research tasks which are traditionally the responsibility of centralized marketing research departments can be performed better by the field sales force in certain cases. We have observed that a real need for a "grass roots" market research approach exists because:

□ Centralized research groups in corporations which operate in geographically dispersed areas are separated by space, time, and attitude from actual day-to-day operations of the field sales personnel.

□ Branch sales managers are at a serious disadvantage in trying to adjust to local competitive changes, which often occur at a faster rate than top-level corporate marketing intelligence would indicate or support.

□ Headquarters' insistence that branch managers rely on corporate policy directives, which originate from centralized research findings and top-management decisions, often encumbers the sales force in successfully meeting on-the-spot market changes.

□ In creating a centralized research group for planning long-range marketing efforts, top management neglects the possibilities for enlightened short-range sales action based on organized research carried out by qualified sales personnel in the field.

□ The intelligence made available to branch managers—as a by-product of their selling activities—can permit them to make on-the-spot decisions to stay abreast of sudden market shifts and to capitalize on or adjust to the changing competitive situation in their territories.

In this presentation we will look at some of the shortcomings in centralized marketing research, and discuss the various steps involved in initiating, implementing, and controlling a grass roots program. Our position will be supported by an authentic, but disguised, case example drawn from the dairy industry. Along the way, we will describe the strategic and tactical benefits to be derived from—as well as the potential problems in—such a system. Finally, we will point out the criteria for deciding whether to adopt a grass roots market research approach that, in turn, will enable corporations with far-flung operations to develop superior local marketing intelligence and managerial relationships with top-level decision-makers.

Centralized Shortcomings

Out of centralized corporate marketing research activities can arise one or more of these organizational shortcomings: (1) closed-circuit thinking; (2) proliferation of excessive, oftentimes unused data; (3) shortsighted directives.

Closed-circuit thinking on the part of central-staff marketing researchers is characterized by a distrust of all information inputs except the primary data that are collected by the researchers themselves. At the same time, the findings of the organization's research may have longer and longer range application and less and less meaning for day-to-day marketing efforts. As closed-circuit thinking develops, the rest of the company's organization becomes divorced from the input effort and, consequently, finds the output of decreasing practical value. Martineau has observed: "Too many research people have spun themselves a web of self-communication, a perfect system of mutual feedback whereby they have insulated themselves from the needs . . . of the business community."[1]

In addition, corporate marketing research departments have consistently prevailed on line marketing personnel for an excessive amount of data, often on a nonselective basis. Once fed into the system, much of this information may never be heard of again as it overwhelms its collectors with sheer volume.

Lastly, headquarters directives based on centralized research findings often suggest a sales strategy without any accompanying rationale for applying the strategy in future situations. Although the sales directives may be based on an effective field data collection effort involving sales personnel and first-rate analysis by a corporate staff, their rationale often becomes obscured as they move through lengthy channels from the bottom to the top and then back to the bottom of the organization.

1. See "Martineau Hits 'Sterility' in Market Research," *Advertising Age*, May 25, 1964, p. 64.

Program Characteristics

In contrast with centralized corporate *marketing* research, grass roots *market* research has these major characteristics: (1) collection of data accomplished by the lowest sales echelon or first-line sales management, (2) involvement of field marketing personnel not only in data collection but also in analysis and follow-up in the form of positive sales action, and (3) primary emphasis on market, rather than marketing, research. All of these must be present if a grass roots market research program is to be successfully implemented.

The fact that data are collected by field sales personnel does not necessarily distinguish grass roots market research from existing practice. The most common example of the use of field sales personnel for data collection is provided by the "sales force composite" method of preparing sales forecasts. However, when field sales effort is extended to the analysis and interpretation of data preliminary to taking action based on it, this constitutes a departure from current practice in all but a handful of companies. In those rare instances, top management and corporate market research groups supply only occasional policy guidance. In short, data collection for transmission to top management is a natural by-product, not an end objective, of true grass roots market research.

The primary emphasis of this type of research is on a continuing examination of local market situations as the basis for determining immediate sales strategy. This activity is centered on the identification of trade customers most likely to change sources of supply, and the design of both offensive and defensive strategies to improve company sales performance, based on an evaluation of local research and sales results. While data might be collected for top-level marketing research purposes as well, grass roots market research normally is not aimed at or concerned with the broader, longer-range questions of marketing policy.

SPLIT NEEDS

Rapidly changing market structures and vast differences among market areas are commonplace in certain industries and serve to emphasize critical factors which favor a split in research labor. Although these facts of marketing life offer evidence of the need for better on-the-spot local marketing decisions, the distance—in terms of time, space, and attitude—between the centralized corporate research staff and marketing line personnel represents a barrier to the flow of information on which those decisions can be based. The psychological distance between the branch manager and top-level corporate management may be so great as to restrict the flow of strategic communications between them except where company policy dictates.

In addition, corporate staff researchers traditionally become so deeply involved in marketing research efforts with long-term importance that investigations of individual short-term market situations have been neglected and perpetually orphaned. Clearly, some division of research labor is warranted.

MARKET CHANGES

Aggregate data often conceal the comparatively rapid competitive shifts which typify many local markets. Closer examinations of individual markets on a continuing basis are required to point out these shifts. For example, the analysis of a large metropolitan market undertaken for the producer and national distributor of a convenience food item disclosed that within the space of seven years the market situation would shift from one which was currently dominated by manufacturer-owned operations marketing their products by means of wholesale and retail stores and house-to-house distribution to one dominated by retail chains owning "captive" plants.

While the amount of time over which market shifts occur may be relatively lengthy from the point of view of local sales management, longer-term shifts typically are the result of a number of specific shorter-term decisions. Many of these decisions can be predicted in advance and affected by local sales action. Where such longer-term trends are identified by top management, the selling force can be an effective means not only of implementing policies to counteract or reinforce a trend, but also of maintaining up-to-date information about further shifts in structure, particularly those involving important current or potential customers.

TERRITORIAL DIFFERENCES

The days of the nationwide decision, if they ever existed, are gone for most marketing executives. Structural differences in seemingly related markets may alter the number and type of competing producers, the types of channels used for distribution and the popularity of each, and customer buying habits.

These factors are important in the distribution of home appliances, for which illustrative figures are shown in *Exhibit I*. In the home appliances industry problems of local distributor relationships also create distinctive market structures in different parts of the country. Together all of these forces, and perhaps others, explain why the importance of a given market for two nationally competing brands may vary widely.

For example, as shown in the exhibit, 31% of Brand A's sales were made

Exhibit I. *Proportion of selected brands of home appliances sold in major market areas*

	Market region				
Brands	Northeast	North Central	South	West	Total
A	32%	25%	31%	12%	100%
B	28	26	21	25	100
C	40	29	5	26	100
D	33	24	31	12	100
E	30	43	24	3	100
F	25	25	24	26	100
All other	27	29	26	18	100
Total	29%	29%	23%	19%	100%

SOURCE: "Myth of the National Market," based on data prepared by Audits & Surveys, Inc., *Dun's Review and Modern Industry*, May 1964, p. 40.

in the South in sharp contrast both to Brand C, which realized only 5% of its sales there, and the industry, which sold 23% of its goods in that region. This would suggest that, where nonstandard approaches to marketing problems are desirable, decisions ought to be based on research and follow-up action carried out by field managers most familiar with local problems.

DISTANCE DIMENSIONS

Three dimensions of distance—the temporal, spatial, and attitudinal—create a problem which exists between staff and line personnel, particularly in a decentralized organization with widespread markets. The importance of the distance problem is suggested by one sales training specialist who asserted, "Sales executives say that failure to communicate—upward and downward . . . is one of the ten greatest mistakes first-line sales managers make."

The time and space problems can be overcome with improved communications methods and a reporting routine. Attitudinal gaps are more difficult to bridge, as suggested by complaints voiced by one-half of a surveyed group of top company officers about their field sales managers. The managers were labeled as "often ineffective" in the vital areas of coordination, follow-through, problem diagnosis, and decision making. Attitudinal gaps can be lessened best by the development of a mutual respect on the part of communicants, coupled with a convenient method of organizing, analyzing, and reporting information.

A development which increases the need for improved two-way information flow in the marketing organization is the growing concentration of corporate sales efforts among a smaller number of important customers. Top management demonstrates a growing interest in these key accounts as the risks attendant on the loss of any one such account grow. To this extent, the company's local sales managers should be called on to develop a greater amount of information on a continuing basis about key-account activities. A grass roots market research program can assist in accomplishing the needed control for key-account management and a generally improved system of information feedback and marketing control.

Within a regional or local sales organization, psychological barriers may exist between sales representatives and the branch manager, restricting the flow of vital information at its very source. This may be the case to a greater extent in the future if companies utilize the findings of recent research which indicate strongly that the determinants for success in sales management are greatly different from those for success in selling. Growing differences between the psychological makeup of branch managers and that of their sales representatives will require organized communications programs—the sort of programs which usually die a natural death when conducted on a voluntary basis—as a counteracting force.

Locally oriented market research has not been totally neglected. Where its importance is recognized, however, too often it is carried out by marketing research staff members from the headquarters organization. Typically, it requires a close observation of individual customer and competitor actions. Completely aside from the fact that specially assigned research personnel generally have greater difficulty and incur more expense obtaining accurate information than do permanently assigned sales personnel, the expenditure of effort on this type of research often precludes research work of longer-range significance at the headquarters level. Sales personnel have a comparative advantage in gathering local data.

Favoring Trends

Grass roots market research can be implemented relatively easily today, thanks to a number of trends observed in recent years. Among the trends are (1) involvement of the sales organization in various managerial activities; (2) decentralization of marketing decision making through the vehicles of brand and product management concepts; (3) improved qualifications of field sales personnel; (4) ready-made programs for the collection of sales control information.

SALES FORCE INVOLVEMENT

From time to time, companies have announced various programs designed to involve sales personnel and branch managers to a greater extent in various corporate activities. Information collection is perhaps the most common of these, ranging from product, price, and service comparisons with competitors to estimates of the amount of sales expected for a given period as part of the corporate sales forecasting process. A General Electric market-ing consultant described one such extensive information collection process thus:

"Once we pulled together a complete picture of a competitor's distribu-tion from reports turned in by 120 salesmen even up to and including its warehousing in the most strategic locations. It put us in a better position to plan and implement our own distribution needs. We have a planned program of sending questionnaires to our salesmen requesting information for a competitive analysis and we get a great deal of valuable information from them.

"We get research into how our competitors are marketing their products, how many salesmen they have, and how their products compare as to service, function, and quality. "

However, involvement extends beyond mere information collection. Many marketing organizations, including those of General Electric and Du Pont, have instituted product development systems which utilize sales-men in the first phases of the work. Sylvania Electric's Photolamp Division several years ago decided to go to its salesmen for more advice and partici-pation in marketing strategy.

In many companies, regional sales management is being called on to assume some responsibility for such activities as packaging, test marketing, product planning, product evaluation, and individual promotions.

DECENTRALIZED DECISION MAKING

The emergence of brand and product management has been, in part, a result of the emphasis on the marketing concept. Typically, the tasks of the brand manager have been to assume both line and staff authority for a given product or group of products and coordinate production with advertising, research, and personal selling. This has resulted in some decentralization of responsibility and authority, and a shortening of com-munication channels from the field to a high-level managerial control center. Further, the decentralization of marketing decision making has pro-vided the opportunity for a variety of research efforts geared to meet the particular needs of different markets.

Widespread developments in customer purchasing policies have influ-enced qualifications required for effective and intelligent sales representa-tion and sales management. Such developments include not only the broadening of buying influences, many of which are hidden, but the relent-less pressure on price, streamlining of procurement procedures, entrench-ment of value analysis in purchasing programs, proliferation of purchasing committees, predetermined minimum inventories, computerized reorder systems, interminable demands for special services, centralized purchasing in large companies, and the systematizing of reciprocal buying procedures. As the analysts conducting one study concluded:

"These complex forces interact in the industrial marketplace and create new problems for the sales executive.

"He must re-evaluate the role of personal selling in his over-all marketing machine. He must continually weigh its contribution against that of advertising and promotion . . . decide whether to hire a new man or boost the ad budget.

"He may have to seek a different caliber of salesman, train him differently, pay him differently. Inevitably, he has got to send into the field a more knowledgeable and better equipped man."

Since field sales representatives already are prevailed on for a wide range of information by their organization managers, sales personnel of the type needed should prove to be made-to-order for the tasks facing them under a grass roots market research program.

Although grass roots market research consists of much more than just information collection, the vehicle necessary for this phase of the research —the sales control form—currently exists in many companies.

A Case Example

Despite the fact that this example has been disguised, the situation presented in the following pages is similar to that which actually existed.

A corporate staff group for a fluid milk processor was called on to design and implement a grass roots market research program.[2] We will trace the steps involved in the grass roots approach, which covered the program's initiation, implementation, and control.

PROGRAM INITIATION

Initiated by top management, the effort was delegated to the corporate staff, which had, through its previous work, obtained a broad overview of the structural operations of the marketplace and, therefore, had gained the background necessary to isolate key variables for intensive study at the grass roots level.

Step 1: Analysis. The initial task of the staff marketing research group

2. In accomplishing the adaptation of the example, the authors are grateful to Professors Daniel I. Padberg and Elmer F. Baumer, Department of Agricultural Economics, The Ohio State University; the following publication was particularly useful: *Structural Changes in the California Fluid Milk Industry* by Daniel I. Padberg and D. A. Clarke, Jr., Bulletin 802, California Agricultural Experimental Station, June 1964.

was to undertake an analysis of important industry trends and indicators. In the marketing of fluid milk, a major consideration was a study of demand-supply relations, with special reference to such factors as consumption patterns and excess production capacity. As a result of its analysis, the staff group found that the amount of fluid milk consumed per person was likely to remain quite stable and would not change quickly over the next ten years.

On the other hand, widespread adoption of high-temperature, short-time pasteurizing techniques had permitted shifts from batch processing to continuous flow operations, and therefore the production levels required for the profitable operation of fluid milk processing plants had increased significantly during recent years. These developments led to a further concentration of production in the hands of fewer processors and growing excess capacity.

The adoption of paper containers had brought about further technological changes. A monthly volume of about 250,000 gallons was normally sufficient to gain essentially all apparent scale economies for a glass operation, while such scale economies for a paper operation extended beyond 600,000 gallons per month. A paper container operation therefore created a considerable advantage for large-scale operations. Combining the information available on demand-supply relations, it was possible for the staff group to predict a situation of rather severe supply-demand disequilibrium in the industry.

The following factors were found to have important influence on the marketing programs of competitors in any given geographically defined market area: (1) concentration of wholesale selling and retail buying power, (2) private label movements, (3) acquisition or divestment of captive plants, (4) changes in market outreach, and (5) changes in distribution technology.

Among the findings the staff group uncovered in studying these factors were:

1. The concentration of grocery buying among relatively few centers of power strongly affected wholesale purchases. In eight selected urban areas in the Northeastern section of the United States, over 75% of total retail food sales were controlled by corporate and cooperative chain organizations. In addition, 40% of fluid milk sales were made by food stores, a fact which underlined the importance of keeping abreast of competitive activity in this sector.

2. Because of the desire of chains to enter into private label arrangements, large processors were virtually compelled to pursue private label sales in order to avoid production and distribution problems. In some instances, chains had given fluid milk processors the alternative of packing a private label brand or losing a large and important store account.

3. In some cases, chains actually became fluid milk processors, primarily

through the acquisition of plants of marginal companies. Conversely, other grocery chains owning fluid milk processing plants had divested themselves of the local plants for various reasons. Still others had been persuaded to forgo unprofitable milk processing operations when offered an attractive private label program from an independent processor.

4. Expansion of areas served by any one milk processor could be expected to increase at a fairly modest rate, particularly because of the development of major highways and better insulated transportation equipment. The likelihood of invasion from companies not serving any one particular area had increased. Actually, the growth of market outreach capabilities had facilitated dumping in some instances.

5. Because the adoption of self-service in retail food outlets had revolutionized distribution technology, shelf or case space had become an important determinant in the success or failure of specific brands. Many consumers showed indifference to brands of milk when the price was equated. Therefore, the processor had to strongly differentiate his brand from others or gain additional case space for his brand, or do both.

An analysis of these five factors enabled the marketing research group to appraise the relative growth of marketing and manufacturing institutions and activities in the fluid milk industry. However, because these factors were dynamic in nature and varied among geographically defined markets, the need for market research on a continuing basis was established.

Step 2: Assessment. At this point in designing the program, it was necessary to determine thresholds for changes in trade relationships. Once known or estimated, these thresholds could serve as guidelines for field sales managers (or plant managers) in deciding whether or not a shift in any one of the industry's local market structures was about to take place.

Specifically, it was essential that a field sales manager or plant manager have some prior knowledge of when and whether a retail food chain would add private brands. Through empirical evidence, developed by research analysis, it was determined that any grocery chain group that supplied as few as five large retail stores (stores with total sales approximately $15,000 per week or more) had a strong probability of being capable of managing a private label milk program. With such information, and with constant surveillance of his market area, the sales manager could present his private label program at the most opportune time.

Among a variety of estimated thresholds developed was one relating to the activities of small companies. It was known that a monthly volume of 600,000 gallons was necessary in order to utilize satisfactorily the equipment needed for a paper container operation. Therefore, it was established that when the sales of an organization selling milk in such containers fell below 500,000 gallons, its actions should be watched closely for signs of market withdrawal or "demoralizing" price or concessional activities. Desperation moves by a marginal company could positively or negatively affect the sales of all the plants in the market area.

In addition to, and in conjunction with, the determination of thresholds, it was necessary for the marketing research group, in cooperation with top-level executives, to develop rules of thumb on which field sales managers could base their decisions, if and when a threshold was reached. With regard to the two instances cited above, rules of thumb were established indicating the basic guidelines of private label programs to be offered, and the actions to be taken in exploiting the weakness of a marginal competitor.

It was known that several fluid milk processors had entered into unprofitable private label arrangements. In their zeal to make the sale, these companies had made concessions which had proved extremely costly, such as providing case service when the margin of profit would not pay for this service. On the other hand, large fluid milk processors had to be extremely cautious in their handling of competition vis-à-vis marginal companies. Their actions could be construed by the federal government as attempts to monopolize or restrain trade in a market area.

Step 3: Determination of Methods. After thresholds and rules of thumb were established by the corporate research group through top management, it was then appropriate to develop well-defined procedures to facilitate the collection of the right data at the grass roots level. For example, an essential piece of information to be obtained in each field sales manager's territory —defined as the area serviced by the home-delivery routes under his control —was an estimate of the market shares of retail grocery chains.

To obtain market shares of grocery chains, the sales manager was first advised to outline his territory on a map which distinguished counties within the territory. He could then arrive at an estimate of total food store sales by consulting *Sales Management's Annual Survey of Buying Power*, which provides county-by-county food store sales data.

Secondly, he was urged to obtain from newspapers, food brokers, or any similar source, estimates of the number of stores in each chain group— both corporate and cooperative—in his territory and the volume of sales for each group. In most instances these estimates were reliable enough for approximation purposes.

For the third step, the sales manager was asked to compare his territory with those outlined by the newspapers and brokers. If the territories differed, he was to adjust the estimates to reflect the differences by adding or subtracting the sales volume of stores falling within or outside his territory.

The sales manager was next counseled in using a set of estimating procedures, which not only provided information relating to a particular store's sales volume but could also be used as checks against each other. The following are illustrative of the types of guidelines generated by the corporate research staff:

◻ Multiply the square footage of store selling space by a factor of $2 to $12. The factor used varies with the aggressiveness of the store and can often be approximated by knowing the performance of the chain in the area, as shown by the newspaper's or brokers' data. The resulting figure gives an estimate of total store sales per week.

◻ Determine the number of full-time employees, and estimate the total number of man-hours per week for these employees. Multiply the number of man-hours by a factor of $12 to $25 to obtain an estimate of total sales per week.

◻ Obtain from suppliers estimates of weekly sales of certain staple items, and divide these by their percentage of total store sales to obtain an estimate of total sales per week for the store.

◻ Multiply the number of active checkout lanes (in use at least one day of the week) by $3,500 to $5,000. This will provide another estimate of weekly sales.

◻ Harvest the trade grapevine. Others may be attempting to make similar estimates.

When estimates of all chains' sales in the territory had been made, each was divided by the total food store sales figure obtained from *Sales Management* to arrive at an estimate of market share for each group. The residual—the difference between all chains' sales and total sales in food stores—served as a good approximation of the sales volume of unaffiliated independent food stores.

In addition to other well-defined procedures, the staff marketing research group also had the responsibility of isolating certain key regional estimators, such as the percent to be applied against store sales to determine the sales for any one product category. In the case example, fluid milk sales within grocery stores were estimated to be between 2% and 3% of total store sales. These estimates were sometimes achieved through a study of analyses made by trade publications. In other instances they were arrived at directly by asking the appropriate store buyers.

Step 4: Design of Data-Collection Form. The final step in the initiation of a grass roots market research program was the design of data-collection form which would facilitate analysis. The work sheets were relatively uncomplicated, which permitted speedy classification and tabulation of data. Field sales managers had little time to devote to additional paper work; their efforts were better spent in cultivating markets than in preparing long, complicated, and tedious forms for recording purposes.

Several work sheets were designed for use by field sales managers in determining the status of the fluid milk market in their territories. Primarily, these work sheets, shown in *Exhibit II*, concentrated on an analysis of sales to and by grocery chains, because these chains represented the key accounts for the company. The work sheets related, both directly and indirectly, to the analysis of industry trends and indicators mentioned previously.

PROGRAM IMPLEMENTATION

If it was to launch such a program in its field sales territories, top management had to take steps to provide a rationale, along with encouragement and incentives, in order to convince the field personnel that their efforts would be rewarded. One means for providing a rationale was through the use of a game technique. During a periodic meeting at corporate headquarters, sales managers were collectively introduced to the concept of grass roots market research. This was accomplished by an orientation session in which they completed a series of work sheets based upon hypothetical data given them. They were then asked to suggest courses of action which they might take when faced with the market conditions indicated in their reports. Not only did such a game provide a training experience, but it was useful in showing front-line managers the value of collecting data on a continuing basis.

Top management also provided an incentive system that furnished rewards relating to the fulfillment of research tasks. Copies of the data-collection work sheets or forms were required to be sent to corporate headquarters. This permitted headquarters to review field operations and to question the information appearing on the forms. It also provided top management with an over-all perspective, through a comparison of all field sales managers' reports. Rewards, in the form of bonuses, were paid if and when a manager capitalized on the information collected.

PROGRAM CONTROL

The work sheets designated in this situation also served as simple "feedback" mechanisms, because they facilitated the logging of essential data regarding the competitive elements in the company's sales territories. Through the program, it became possible for a branch manager to perceive basic changes in the market strategies and tactics of milk processors and grocery chains, provided he reviewed and revised his work sheets at least once every quarter. By maintaining the work sheets he was able to note, for example, the potential rewards of various private-label arrangements. As the market structures were altered, he was prepared to exploit the alternatives.

But what is most important is that information on which the branch

Exhibit II. Company X—forms used by branch managers to determine market status

Work Sheet A: Food store structure

Food stores	(1) Number of stores in Company X's market area	(2) Total dollar sales per week*	(3) Average dollar sales per store — (2) ÷ (1)†	(4) Market share — (2) ÷ grand total of sales	PRIVATE LABEL ARRANGEMENTS‡ Supplier	Products supplied	Delivery arrangements	Wholesale prices and discount policies	Other information
Corporate chains with captive plants									
1. Chain A	6	$186,000	$31,000	10.2%					
2. Chain B	8	276,800	34,600	15.2					
3. Chain C	14	308,000	22,000	16.9					
Etc.									
Subtotal	35	$890,500		48.8%					
Corporate chains without captive plants									
1. Chain D	6	$144,000	$24,000	7.9%	Company R gal.;½gal.	Store-Door		1-1000 gal.: 60¢/gal.; 35¢/½gal.	
2. Chain E	2	79,000	39,500	4.3					
3. Chain F	2	37,000	18,500	2.0	Company S	½gal.	Dock	1-1000 gal.: 34¢/½gal.	
Etc.									
Subtotal	14	$302,400		16.6%					
Cooperative chains									
1. Chain G	10	$85,000	$8,500	4.6%	Company S	½gal.	Dock	1-1000 gal.: 34¢/½gal.	
2. Chain H	8	105,000	13,200	5.8	Company T	½gal.;qts.	Dock	1-750 gal.: 35¢/½gal.	
3. Chain I	8	88,000	11,000	4.8	Company X	½gal.	Store-Door	1-750 gal.: 34¢/½gal.	
4. Chain J	2	54,800	27,400	3.0					
Etc.									
Subtotal	34	$360,500		19.7%					
Independents §	137	273,400		14.9%					
Grand total		$1,826,800		100%					

* Based on estimates obtained from local sources.
† Obviously, this figure suffers from the weaknesses of any average.
‡ Some of this information may have to be obtained through an intelligence system.
§ Independents' sales = grand total minus sum of all chain sales.

Work Sheet B: Private label sales

Corporate and cooperative grocery chains without captive plants	Company X (1) Estimated percentage of total fluid milk sales represented by label*	Company X (2) Number of gallons sold per week†	Company R (1) Estimated percentage of total fluid milk sales represented by label*	Company R (2) Number of gallons sold per week†	Company S (1) Estimated percentage of total fluid milk sales represented by label*	Company S (2) Number of gallons sold per week†	Company T (1) Estimated percentage of total fluid milk sales represented by label*	Company T (2) Number of gallons sold per week†	Total private label sales per week within chains (in gallons) — sum of (2) figures
1. Chain D	—	—	75%	3,240	—	—	—	—	3,240
2. Chain E	—	—	—	—	60%	1,422	—	—	1,422
3. Chain F	—	—	—	—	—	—	—	—	
4. Chain G	—	—	—	—	60%	1,530	—	—	1,530
5. Chain H	—	—	—	—	—	—	70%	2,218	2,218
6. Chain I	50%	1,320	—	—	—	—	—	—	1,320
7. Chain J	—	—	—	—	—	—	—	—	
Etc.									
Total		1,320		5,240		2,952		3,418	
Grand total									13,430

* By observing stores within a chain, an estimate of the percentage of shelf space allotted to private labels can be made.
† The total dollar sales column in Work Sheet A is relevant for this work sheet.

Exhibit II (continued)

Work Sheet C: Processors' food store sales

Captive plants*	(1) Total sales in Company X's territory per week	(2) Fluid milk sales — (1) × 3%	(3) Estimated percentage of captive plant sales out of total†	(4) Estimated captive plant milk sales in dollars — (2) × (3)	(5) Average retail price per gallon‡	(6) Total number of gallons sold per week — (4) ÷ (5)	Market share
1. Chain A	$186,000	5,580	80%	$4,464	$0.853	5,230	5.6%
2. Chain B	276,800	8,304	75	6,228	0.861	7,230	7.8
3. Chain C	308,000	9,240	85	7,854	0.848	9,270	9.9
Etc.							

Independent processors	(1) Grocery routes competitive with Company X in territory§	(2) Average fluid milk sales per route per week (in dollars)	(3) Average wholesale price per gallon‡	(4) Number of gallons sold per route per week	(5) Total number of gallons sold per week — (1) × (4)	
1. Company X	10	$770	$0.713	1,078	10,780	11.6%
2. Company R	8	1,825	0.695	2,627	21,020	22.5
3. Company S	9	800	0.702	1,141	10,270	11.0
4. Company T	13	1,090	0.695	1,564	20,340	21.8
Etc.						
Grand total					93,140	100%

* Fluid milk processing plants that are owned by food store chains.
† This estimate can be made either by observing shelf space allocations or asking store managers (or buyers) to estimate this percentage.
‡ Weighted average price for all sizes of containers.
§ In making this estimate, sales managers can draw on information secured by their salesmen in informal conversations with competitors' salesmen.

Work Sheet D: Processors' home delivery sales

Processors	(1) Home delivery routes competitive with Company X in territory*	(2) Average fluid milk sales per route per week (in dollars)	(3) Average retail price per gallon†	(4) Number of gallons sold per route per week — (2) ÷ (3)	(5) Total number of gallons sold per week — (1) × (4)	Market share of home delivery
1. Company X	42	550	$0.9425	580	24,360	21.9%
2. Company R	66	500	0.9425	530	34,980	31.4
3. Company S	30	590	0.9425	630	18,900	17.0
4. Company T	52	600	0.9425	635	33,020	29.7
Grand total	190				111,260	100%

* In making this estimate, sales managers can draw on information secured by their salesmen in informal conversations with competitors' salesmen.
† Weighted average price for all sizes of containers.

Work Sheet E: Combined food store and home delivery sales

Processors — independent and captive	(1) Total number of gallons sold per week — food stores*	(2) Total number of gallons sold per week — home delivery†	(3) Combined total — (1) + (2)‡	Market share combined total
1. Company X	10,780	24,360	35,140	17.1%
2. Company R	21,020	34,980	56,000	27.4
3. Company S	10,270	18,900	29,170	14.2
4. Company T	20,340	33,020	53,360	26.1
5. Chain A	5,230	—	5,230	2.6
6. Chain B	7,230	—	7,230	3.5
7. Chain C	9,270	—	9,270	4.5
Etc.				
Grand total	93,140	111,260	204,400	100%

* Data can be obtained from Work Sheet C.
† Data can be obtained from Work Sheet D.
‡ The combined total is useful in isolating marginal companies.

NOTE: Differences between individual items and total, if any, represent unspecified amounts for "Etc."

manager could base his day-to-day decisions became available at the local level through the work sheet system. Such a system provided an inexpensive means of collecting, tabulating, and analyzing essential data. After the first attempt at completing the work sheets, it was estimated that each field sales manager would need to spend no more time to keep them up-to-date than three man-days once every three months.

In order to be certain that the program was operating as originally conceived, top management authorized periodic checks by the corporate marketing research department to determine the accuracy of the grass roots information and also the extent of its usage by the local sales organizations. In addition, annual surveys were made by the corporate staff to define the extent of the program's cost.

Program Benefits

A grass roots market research program, if properly implemented and controlled, can be expected to facilitate two-way communications among field sales representatives, their branch managers, and centralized top management, and to establish a precedent for special field sales information collection efforts. Because the basic emphasis in such a program is on consultative management, it can also be expected to improve the morale of sales and first-line managerial personnel by giving them more important roles in determining local marketing tactics.

Other than these rather explicit benefits, such a program should: (1) grant management at several levels a "license" to act; (2) provide additional measurements of sales and managerial performance; (3) furnish aids for long-range planning; and (4) maintain "instant" information for use in emergency-decision situations.

License to act—Any research program that invests responsibility for information collection and analysis in the first-line sales manager must provide him with the authority to act within well-defined limits. While this is implicit in every grant of authority, too often the area of decision making is nebulous, and authority is left to be tested on a somewhat "cut-and-try" basis by the manager. Because of the magnitude of the decisions that can be based on market research conducted in a grass roots program, some definition of limits on authority and cues for managerial action should be instituted during the implementation of the program.

In the dairy industry example discussed previously, top management was able to reappraise the extent of the local manager's authority in making decisions based on experience gained through the program. It revised rules of thumb, established at the initiation of the program, in the light of market shifts. The program provided management with the information to determine when flexibility of action on the local level was necessary and when adherence to policies or operating plans should be relaxed or strengthened. Rather than being viewed in the negative sense of a limitation on authority, such rules of thumb were and should be regarded positively as licenses for action.

Additional measurements—Share-of-market trends along with key-account data generated by a grass roots market research program can provide measures of marketing performance in a given territory. In addition, managerial performance can be judged by a periodic top-management evaluation of information collection and analyses performed by field sales managers. Top management can determine whether or not a particular branch manager has a firm understanding of the competitive situation in his area by gauging the caliber of his analyses.

Under a program of this type, top management has an opportunity to judge actual front-line management decisions in the context of the available information on which the decisions are based. No longer is it necessary to carry out performance reviews in the vacuum of uncollected or disorganized information. Greater latitude in decision authority should accrue to the manager who effectively comprehends his role in the system and acts shrewdly in the light of market developments.

Long-range planning aids—If conducted on a continuing basis, a grass roots market research program provides periodic measures of the importance of various types of customers in a market area, the share of market being realized by the company conducting the program, and information regarding the economic stability of various types of competitors. By being able to trace past, and forecast future, market shifts of some significance, as outlined by the field sales managers, corporate planners can build more realistic long-range projections, or suggest ways of meeting competitive crises before they spread to other marketing territories.

Provision for crises—When a marketing crisis occurs, there is typically little time to collect information. A branch manager must act on past information, current incomplete impressions of the problem, and his own intuition. Even where necessary information on which to base an intelligent crisis decision exists somewhere in the company, first-line sales managers typically are unaware of its existence, unable to specify the type of information needed, or reluctant to involve others in the crisis. A grass roots market research program provides a continuing source of information immediately available to sales managers, and the availability of the information on a continuing basis may allow them to anticipate and alleviate crises before they occur.

As a case in point, the program in the dairy industry example was eventually extended to encourage the cross communication of information among local managers, especially among those in adjacent territories where there existed a similarity of competitive conditions prior to market invasion of one of the territories by a distant competitor. Where this happened, the sales manager in the invaded territory was encouraged to pass along information relative to the nature of the invasion to the sales manager in the territory not yet affected.

Potential Pitfalls

Although the benefits which can be realized from insights into competition and consultative management heavily favor the grass roots approach, this is not the whole story. There are some potential pitfalls inherent in such a market research program. Most important among these potential problems are (1) data availability, (2) individual bias, (3) union opposition, (4) time and cost, (5) morale, (6) local autonomy, and (7) duplication of research effort.

Data availability—The basic obstacle to the collection of data, in most cases, is the inability or the unwillingness of the source to provide the desired information. When the effectiveness of personal relations must be relied on in this phase of a research effort, success may hang by a thin thread. However, to the extent that most information-collection efforts under a grass roots program consist of direct observations and estimations by highly qualified sales representatives, this obstacle can be greatly minimized.

For example, head counts of store personnel, observations of store traffic, estimates of production rates and component material needs, counts of retail store checkout lanes, and the like, can generally be carried out with no personal contact or prearranged agreement. Measurement rules of thumb provided by the corporate research staff should free information-collection procedures from total dependency on personal relations.

Individual bias—All research efforts are accompanied by bias. It is perhaps especially prevalent when the research is conducted by those whose skills lie elsewhere. In a local research program bias in information collection and analysis can be introduced by both the sales representative and his branch manager.

There is the danger, too, that managerial analyses, performed in the territorial or local sales office, might be flavored to justify a given decision already reached by the branch manager involved. In the short run it is possible that bias of this type might arise. However, control induced by a

Exhibit III. Cost of grass roots program for milk processor

Cost center	Amount
START-UP COSTS	
Corporate executives' time (10 man-days)	$1,500
Corporate researchers' time (25 man-days)	1,875
Local sales managers' time (3 man-days for each of 15 managers)	3,375
Travel	2,500
Total start-up costs	$9,250
CONTINUING PROGRAM COSTS PER YEAR	
Corporate executives' time (15 man-days)	$ 2,250
Corporate researchers' time (12 man-days)	900
Local sales managers' time (9 man-days for 15 managers)	10,125
Local sales representatives' time (5 man-days for each of 150 representatives)	15,750
Travel (for field control purposes)	3,000
Total continuing costs	$32,025

decision review process and periodic appraisal by corporate staff and line personnel should alleviate managerial bias over the long run.

Union opposition—In specialized selling situations a sales force may be unionized. This is particularly true for the company that employs driver-salesmen in the distribution of its goods. In these cases the assignment of information collection in addition to current tasks may be a subject for contract negotiation.

Time and cost—The time and cost required for a grass roots market research program depend largely on the nature of customer operations, competitive pressures, personnel capabilities, and a number of other factors. The approach designed for the fluid milk processor, discussed earlier, was estimated to cost the amounts shown in *Exhibit III*.

The estimated annual cost of about $32,000 for the program was somewhat inflated and, therefore, conservative. The milk processing company for which the estimates were generated had an extensive sales force. The information collection duties of the field men were handled, for the most part, during the performance of their regular duties, and could be accomplished during waiting periods at customers' places of business. Further, the importance of each of a number of key customers to this company was such that either gaining or forestalling the loss of one key account in one sales territory as a result of the program could have defrayed the total annual costs of the program for the entire company.

Loss of morale—A tendency for sales personnel to regard a grass roots program as either imposing additional paper work with little attendant value or allowing additional top management "spying" from above may be typical at the outset. Whether or not this attitude continues largely depends on the way the program is presented initially by top management to the field sales managers, and later by the managers to their sales personnel. Successful application of program-generated information and analyses is the best solvent for this type of problem.

Unbalancing "prerogatives"—Objection to implementing a grass roots market research program has centered around the sometimes unvoiced concern that, once given the opportunity to base certain decisions on research performed locally, a sales manager will assume additional decision-making freedoms not previously granted him. A company in which this is a prevalent practice is not likely to be in a position to implement a grass roots research program; the degree of centralization with which it operates would neither allow it nor make it advisable.

On the other hand, a major asset of decentralized management is the encouragement of lower- and middle-management personnel to take on greater responsibility and authority. To the extent this freedom is increased under the grass roots program, the opportunity for management development at lower organization levels is broadened.

Duplication of effort—Research efforts carried out by local sales staffs can overlap. This is especially probable where product-specialist sales representatives are employed, several of whom call on the same customers. It may involve little waste, however, where products sold by specialists have distinctly different market structures, with only occasional institutional duplication. At times, this duplication of effort can provide the basis for a top-management check on the relative quality of the research and analysis carried on by two or more sales representatives or territorial offices.

Program Criteria

So far in this article, we have discussed the potential profits and pitfalls inherent in employing grass roots market research. But how can top management decide whether to institute such a program? The following specific items should be examined: (1) market shifts, (2) existence of key accounts, (3) strong corporate staff, (4) decentralized control, (5) "bottoms-up" receptivity, and (6) capability of sales personnel in the field.

Market shifts—Consumer goods, particularly those bought on a convenience basis, are distributed through constantly shifting channels. Market patterns shift to a lesser extent for other consumer and industrial products.

A volatile market structure bears observation of the type which can be provided through a grass roots market research program.

Existence of key accounts—Corporations competing for business in an industry characterized by a limited number of large customers depend to a great extent on their success with those key accounts. A limited number of large customers can be observed closely enough through grass roots research to predict their economic health in the future. To the extent that drastic structural shifts in markets are the result of economic upheaval among important participants, this is a vital aspect of the program.

Strong corporate staff—Just as most successfully decentralized organizations have capable top-level managerial talent, so a grass roots market research program requires initiation and continuing guidance from a strong corporate marketing research organization. Responsibilities which encompass, for example, the recommendation and revision of guidelines for estimation to be followed by field sales managers, comparison and interpretation of system-wide research reports, and measurement of the profit performance of the grass roots program on a periodic basis, all require a corporate staff able not only to carry out its research mission effectively but to supervise and communicate with line marketing personnel who are also engaged in research activity.

Decentralized control—Organizations accustomed to a management philosophy which places emphasis on decentralization will have a head start in initiating a market research program of the type described in this article. Decentralization of other activities can set the precedent for the delegation necessary to accomplish research at the local or territorial level.

"Bottoms-up" receptivity—A grass roots market research effort doubly challenges management's receptivity to "bottoms-up" management. It is likely that both line-management personnel and corporate research staff members are not accustomed to the challenge. Whether the latter are capable of meeting the challenge will largely determine the success of the program.

Capability of sales personnel—This grass roots approach depends not only on individual abilities, but also on whether or not the local sales personnel are in a position to observe customer operations as a regular part of their sales efforts. The latter factor requires a type of call that is regularly made to the customer's place of business, whether it be a warehouse, wholesale, or retail facility. It goes without saying that a strategically positioned sales representative who is not otherwise capable of collecting the simple information needed under the program may not be of much value to the sales organization.

Conclusion

The prime value of the grass roots market research concept is its inherent recognition that each and every sales territory in which a company operates is different. This provides a mechanism whereby field personnel can capitalize on individual market shifts.

The processing and analysis of information by field sales personnel should enable both local and top management to develop strategies and tactics superior to those being used by competitors.

The program can furnish a formal means of facilitating communication among headquarters personnel, field managers, and salesmen. Feedback of important competitive information from salesmen to supervisors is assured. It can also provide both top and local management with licenses to act, particularly because current information is generated on a continuing basis for use in meeting rapid market changes. Once established, a grass roots program can furnish a lead-in, background, and/or precedent for special data-collection efforts, in addition to evidence on which to base long-range plans.

Aside from strategic and tactical benefits, the program can supply a means for evaluating, stimulating, and training management personnel. The decisions made or the strategies suggested by branch managers on the basis of an analysis of the data collected can be carefully scrutinized by those in a position to develop sales managers for positions of greater responsibility.

Although there are some potential pitfalls inherent in a grass roots research program, the benefits gained through competitive insights and consultative management far outweigh those problems. Although the program may require additional effort and forbearance on the part of line and staff personnel alike, this exercise in itself may bear fruit, even if no information outputs of great value are generated. For, when the chips are down in the commercial marketplace, the individual sales manager with the most local marketing intelligence *and* the most effective managerial relationships with corporate headquarters does have significant means to achieve his objectives.

Part IV

Finance

Preface

"*The chief value of money lies in the fact that one lives in a world in which it is overestimated.*"—H. L. MENCKEN

To many others besides the irreverent Mencken, money is indeed overestimated. But to a corporate executive weighing the possibilities of financing his company's operations over the next two years, or substituting long-term debt for short-term debt, the value of money as power cannot be overestimated.

Like almost everything else in corporate life, finance has taken on great complexity in recent years. As everyone knows, there are two ways of obtaining capital for use in a business: from earnings it generates and by tapping outside sources. A table bearing the heading "Sources and Uses of Funds," which commonly details the disposition of dollars generated internally as well as any raised outside the company, is now a common sight in the corporate annual report. Retained earnings, once an internal source of funds every financial officer took for granted, have received much greater attention in the last two decades. Indeed, management of cash flows has become a high art, as corporate treasurers try to make every spare dollar work for the company—gathering interest, at least, if not being used directly to advance the business. Money markets have greatly expanded or have even been created (such as the bank certificate of deposit) as financial institutions rushed to meet the market need.

The question of how to tap the savings of others—corporate, governmental, or personal savings—is even more complicated. A host of considerations, both inside and outside the company, throw their weight into the decision. Obviously, a utility with a slow growth rate, a high dividend on its common stock, and an incessant need for money to underwrite construction will have a different financing problem from a fast-growing life insurance company with a steady cash inflow from premium payments and a record of low, if any, cash dividends. The former may well sell debentures to institutional investors, while the latter may prefer to shop for bank loans.

But a company cannot undertake financing in a vacuum; external considerations must be factored into the analysis. The most common consideration, of course, is the cost of money. Linked to it are its general availability in banks and other financial institutions and the health of the bond and equity markets.

As the issues and problems surrounding finance have grown in difficulty and complexity, the sophistication and resourcefulness of managers have grown to meet them. One important factor in that growth has been the ingenuity and research of practitioners and academics like those represented in this section. One of them, John G. McLean, was first an academic (professor at the Harvard Business School), then a corporate executive (chief executive officer of Continental Oil Company when he died in 1974).

His article outlines the use of the discounted cash flow technique—which places a time value on money—in weighing capital investment choices at Continental. Few companies employed the method as a matter of course when McLean and his associates introduced it in 1955; now it is used routinely everywhere.

Another, equally influential article was written by Gordon Donaldson as a result of his perception that standard rules of thumb for gauging debt capacity (such as industry norms) were grossly inadequate. For them he substituted a determination of the individual circumstances and needs of the company and analysis of its cash flows. Donaldson's work contributed to a more extensive and more imaginative use of long-term debt in financing. The third article in this section, by William Sihler, provides a helpful rationale for putting the financing questions into perspective.

16. Framework for Financial Decisions

William W. Sihler

This article is for the financial executive who would like to take advantage of the work of scholars and theorists but who has no time to absorb the literature himself. Distilling many leading contributions of financial theorists as he proceeds, the author begins with the question of how much debt a company should have. He examines two basic approaches to that question and their implications for policy makers. Then he takes up the matter of dividend policy, describing the relationships emphasized in theory, practical considerations that complicate the situation, and the significance of all these for deciding on a policy. Next he shows how the cost of capital is determined, following with a discussion of the minimum rate of return to use in evaluating proposed investment projects. Throughout the article, financial theory is seen as a very useful tool for businessmen if employed selectively and translated into terms that are pertinent and comprehensible.

The past few years have seen an extraordinary proliferation in ideas and theories about the two sides of the corporate financial management coin: capital structure and capital asset management. One can find at least one article on these subjects together with rebuttals and rejoinders to past articles in the current issue of any academically oriented financial management journal. Unfortunately, these essays, while making a contribution to theoretical frameworks, are frequently incomprehensible to the corporate financial executive. Even those articles that tend to confirm the assumptions under which he has operated all along are more comforting than they are practical; implementation of the insights is more difficult than explaining them to the general manager.

If we are to transform some of the leading ideas and theories into a usable form for management, we must first consider its needs and problems and look at what the scholars and theorists offer as answers.

The major financial issues confronting management are:
□ Which investments should be accepted?

Exhibit I. Asset-capital structure relationships

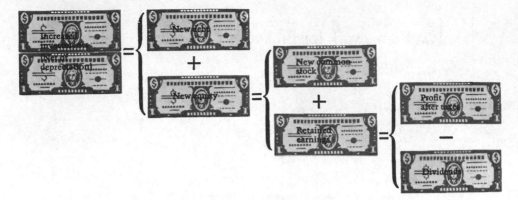

□ How much debt should the company have?

□ What portion of the equity should be financed by retention of earnings? What should be the dividend policy?

I believe it helps to consider these questions separately and sequentially: First, management should tentatively decide on the investment levels it wishes and prepare an estimate of cash flow and earnings over a planning period. Then the impact of debt/equity alternatives can be appraised, given the estimate of funds needed and available. At this point can come the question of whether to pay out dividends at a sufficiently high level so that new stock is required to provide the necessary equity base.

Finally, these three preliminary investment decisions should be reconsidered in order to look at their overall impact. Do they make sense together? Should the level of investment be altered? Does the debt/equity policy appear consistent with the dividend decision? Is it consistent with the investment plans?

This approach reflects the realities of life to the financial manager: *assets* must equal *liabilities* plus *equity*. Hence increases or decreases in net working capital and net fixed assets (investments) must be matched by increases or decreases in the capital structure—the debt, common stock, and retained earnings accounts. When the retained earnings account is traced to its source in profits less dividends, the entire arena for financial policy decisions can be shown as diagrammed in *Exhibit I*.

Alternative decision patterns are available, such as relating dividends directly to investment requirements. In practice, however, these other combinations are generally inferior and substantially more confusing than the one I have sketched and will elaborate. Much of the ink spilled and tempers lost in arguments on financial policy appear to be the result of inconsistent or needlessly complex structuring of the trade-offs that must be made.

Having suggested a framework for analysis, I will review some of the more relevant thinking on these various points and bring together a number of the most useful ideas so that the manager can easily apply them to the financial policy of his company.

The Debt/Equity Decision

The debt/equity issue—that is, how much debt a company should carry in its capital structure—has been attacked in two ways. The more pragmatic approach[1] puts its emphasis on the following factors (sometimes known by the acronym FRICT): flexibility, risk, income, control, and timing.

In smaller companies, control may be more important, but, in any case, it is a straightforward problem to analyze and so I will not treat it here. Similarly, the timing problem is fairly straightforward, once the capitalization strategy has been settled. The other three items, more vital to the strategic decision, will be discussed in this section.

VITAL FACTORS

Let us begin with the question of *income*. It is easy to see that adding debt to the capital structure, in the vast majority of instances, increases earnings per share more than does raising the same amount of money from common stock. Once interest is paid, all additional income goes to the existing shareholders, and it does not have to be shared with new-comers. *Exhibit II* shows a typical example.

One exception occurs when the price/earnings ratio is in the "super-growth" range. In this instance, the earnings yield (earnings per share divided by price) is less than the after-tax interest cost. Even in this case, however, as earnings rise, the additional shares will result in slower growth than would be the case if debt were added. Hence, assuming super-growth, after a short period debt wins out as the more attractive approach from an earnings standpoint. *Exhibit III* shows an example of this case comparable with the one illustrated in *Exhibit II*.

Given the favorable impact of leverage (as the effect of debt is called) on income for the common shareholder, there are obviously compensating factors that restrain companies in their use of borrowing. Two important ones are risk and flexibility:

□ *Risk* can be associated with events that have happened in the past

1. This analytical method is perhaps most fully developed by Pearson Hunt, Charles Williams, and Gordon Donaldson in their book, *Basic Business Finance*, 3rd edition (Homewood, Illinois, Richard D. Irwin, Inc., 1966).

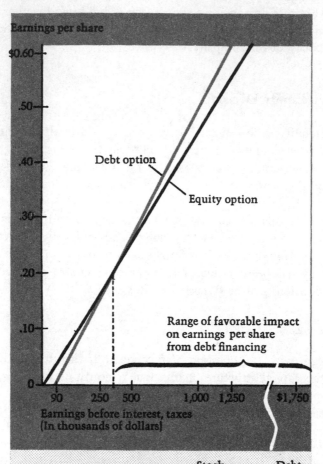

Exhibit II. *Impact of new financing on earnings per share ($1,000,000 new financing required)*

Earnings per share

Debt option

Equity option

Range of favorable impact on earnings per share from debt financing

Earnings before interest, taxes
(In thousands of dollars)

	Stock alternative	Debt alternative
Anticipated earnings before interest, taxes	$1,000,000	$1,000,000
Less: interest on $1,000,000 new debt at 9%	---	90,000
Earnings before taxes	$1,000,000	$910,000
Less: taxes at 55%	550,000	500,500
Earnings after taxes	$450,000	$409,500
New shares to finance ($1,000,000 at $5 net per share)	200,000	---
Old shares outstanding	1,000,000	1,000,000
Total shares outstanding	1,200,000	1,000,000
Earnings per share	$0.375	$0.41

Exhibit III. Impact of new financing on earnings per share in the high price/ earnings case ($1,000,000 new financing required)

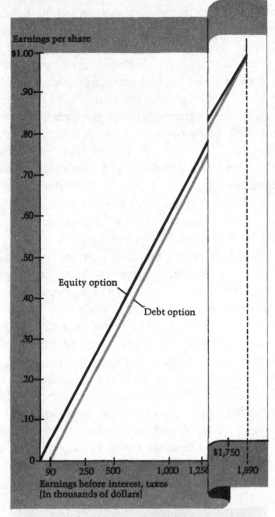

	Stock alternative	Debt alternative
Anticipated earnings	$1,000,000	$1,000,000
Less: interest on $1,000,000 new debt	---	90,000
Earnings before taxes	$1,000,000	$910,000
Less: taxes	550,000	500,500
Earnings after taxes	$450,000	$409,500
New shares to finance ($1,000,000 at post-dilution p/e ratio of 46.5)	50,000	---
Old shares outstanding	1,000,000	1,000,000
Total shares outstanding	1,050,000	1,000,000
Earnings per share	$0.43	$0.41

and that could happen again in the future. Because there are historic data, management can assess the probability and impact of these events. For example, it is not unreasonable for management to expect a recession from time to time. But the recession's timing and magnitude cannot be estimated precisely. Nor is it possible to be absolutely accurate in forecasting the impact of a specified recession on the company's cash flows. Nevertheless, because of historical knowledge and experience with recessions and cash-flow problems, both the recession and the company's cash-flow response do fall into foreseeable categories of risk.

Most companies limit their debt to a level that can be easily serviced in risky circumstances. For example, one automotive parts producer simulated its operations in order to test its probable cash-flow patterns under a variety of adverse business conditions. It found that it could safely manage these risky circumstances with a debt/capitalization ratio of 40% in all but the most severe, sustained depression.

□ *Flexibility* can be defined as the ability to borrow during periods of unexpected adversity—after "things that go bump in the night" have occurred. These are the "unexpected" unknowns, events whose likelihood or even magnitude are not easily assessible since they have not happened before. The automotive parts company mentioned in the last paragraph also explored how the company's finances would be affected if some of its plans were upset or failed. Such conditions as price cuts, product obsolescence, international difficulties, and loss of investment returns were investigated. It was found that several possible reverses would each require about $30 million, although others would be much less costly.

Management was thus faced with a question of how much borrowing capacity should be preserved to allow for these dangers. How much under the 40% debt/capitalization ratio should it go in order to protect itself against the unexpected?

DECISION RULES

Over the years a number of rules of thumb have been developed to assist management in making decisions about the capital structure. The rules are often stated in such forms as "Don't lose your bond rating," "Don't lose a double-A rating," "Borrow as much as you can get," or "Don't borrow more than the industry average." Gordon Donaldson, in his excellent study, *Corporate Debt Capacity*, enumerates and critically evaluates many of these traditional guidelines.[2] He doubts the usefulness of them all.

As a more operative alternative, he suggests that management should explore its firm's cash flows under various risky and adverse conditions, as did the management of the automotive parts company in the example

2. Boston, Division of Research, Harvard Business School, 1961; see also Donaldson's article, p. 326.

described earlier. The data thus generated suggest the maximum debt the company should have if it is to survive a period of business crisis without serious embarrassment. Of course the full extent of the potential crisis and its impact must be estimated by management on the basis of the specific nature of the company. Industry averages or other external points of reference should be used, but with care.

Management must also decide how severe a crisis it is willing to prepare for. This task is accomplished by weighing the likelihood of the situation against the impacts of the action which must be taken to allow for it. The cost of preparing for *all* eventualities is obviously prohibitively high— even an investment in government bonds is not without some risks. The cost of capital structure "insurance" for *many* possible disasters, however, is worthwhile. In the case of the automotive parts management, a 30% debt/capitalization ratio left the company with a minimum of $30 million for major adversities. Management decided that the company could afford to hold this amount as a debt reserve, but that it could not afford to hold $60 million or $90 million in the extremely unlikely event that several "bumps in the night" happened simultaneously.

IMPACT ON VALUE

A second approach to the debt/equity question identifies the impact of additional debt on the price/earnings ratio. As stated by Franco Modigliani and Merton H. Miller, in a taxless and economically "perfect" world the total market value of a company's debt plus equity should not change as debt is substituted for equity.[3] Although expected earnings per share will increase as debt is substituted for equity (or additional financing is done with debt rather than equity), this effect is exactly offset by a markdown in the company's price/earnings ratio. The markdown occurs because the additional debt exposes the common shareholders to an extra financial risk.

In the Modigliani and Miller position, the impact of these changes would be exactly offsetting. For example, if a company were to raise debt to repurchase shares, the value of the asset position of the shareholders before repurchase (stock only) and after (stock and cash) would be exactly the same. The total value of the company's securities would also be constant.

A less extreme point of view, often thought of as a more traditional approach, grants that debt levels can have an impact on the price/earnings ratio. For very low levels of debt, the added risk may be perceived as small relative to the risk that would be involved if the individual tried to lever

3. See "The Cost of Capital, Corporation Finance, and the Theory of Investment," *American Economic Review*, June 1958, p. 261.

his own portfolio in a similar way. Hence low levels of debt may be ignored by the market and have no negative impact on the price/earnings ratio. In fact, it has even been suggested that some companies do not have enough debt, that the assumption of debt would in these cases be a signal of more aggressive investment and financial policies, and that the result would be a favorable impact on the price/earnings ratio.

As more debt is added, however, it does become noticeable. The price/earnings ratio may indeed begin to fall. But as long as the ratio does not fall as fast as extra earnings are added by leveraging the company, the ultimate market price will still be more favorable than if equity were used to raise additional sums. With increasing amounts of debt, the price/earnings ratio may at some point fall faster than the earnings rise, clearly indicating that an excessive amount of debt has been put on the books.

According to the traditional approach, the ideal capital structure is the one in which an additional dollar of debt adds no additional net value to the total market value of the company's securities. An additional dollar of debt would drive the price/earnings ratio down sufficiently so that the value of the equity would fall by a dollar despite the additional earnings generated from the debt funds.

But it is by no means easy to determine the precise response of the price/earnings ratio to the debt/equity ratio. It certainly varies by industry, and it no doubt varies within industries by company. In addition, the relationship probably varies over time, as is witnessed by the comment of a man who attended a conference of institutional investors shortly after Penn Central filed for protection from its creditors. "I have never seen," he remarked, "such a Victorian interest in the balance sheet or so many younger men paying attention to their elders." It is up to the corporate financial officers to determine this relationship and project its likely future. Their judgments are aided by keeping in touch with the company's professional advisers in the financial markets.

Among practicing financial executives, the traditional view has by far the widest support. It is not the purpose here to review the pros and cons and the many pages of evidence that have been adduced in support of the extreme or infinite number of intermediate positions.

DEFINING THE LIMITS

Although the FRICT factors approach and the valuation approach to capital structure are not formally related, they together form a pair of constraints which define a company's debt capacity. First, it is unlikely that a management would care to leverage the company's financial structure to such a point that it would be in frequent danger of financial failure, even if the price/earnings ratio were not depressed. But because the price/earnings ratio *would* be depressed, there is a second constraint. With great exposure to risk, the company's market value would begin to shrink. The high leverage from debt would create added potential earnings for the equity owners, but this advantage would be more than offset by a reduction in the price/earnings ratio.

Thus, management should decide on debt capacity only after appraising all aspects of the situation to ensure that the capital structure is not having an adverse impact on any of them. To illustrate:

The management of a major integrated foods company recently decided that entering potential markets would require large capital investments. These investments, totaling well over $100 million, far exceeded the internal funds which the company expected to generate during the period. Management was reluctant to dilute equity unnecessarily by issuing common stock to raise funds. Hence it studied the company's ability to service additional debt under a variety of conditions and concluded that it was extremely unlikely a cash-flow problem would arise.

At the same time, management was very uncertain about the impact of an additional $100 million of debt on the firm's price/earnings ratio. Debt of this magnitude would place the company's debt-to-capitalization ratio substantially in excess of the ratio common in its industry. To help secure an answer to the debt problem, company managers interviewed executives of financial institutions and investment bankers to determine their opinions and get their predictions of the public's reaction to the additional debt.

Management was pleased to find that there probably would be no diminution of the price/earnings ratio if it borrowed within the range contemplated. Concluding that the increase of debt would not exceed the bounds tolerated by the marketplace, it undertook an aggressive debt program to finance the capital expenditures.

Dividend Policy

Given decisions on the investment requirements and on the debt/equity structure of the company, the dividend question becomes simpler than is often suggested in financial literature. It has been common to mix the analysis of the dividend decision with either the debt or the investment question (or both). Such trade-offs are possible, but I do not recommend them because they blur the essential nature of the dividend problem.

For the sake of clarity, let's begin with an oversimplification. With the "givens" of investment and capital structure, management can choose either to (a) pay higher dividends at the expense of lower growth in earnings per share or (b) restrain its dividend policy in favor of higher earnings per share.

Exhibit IV. Shareholder responses to company policies

	Company policy	
Shareholder policy	a. Low dividends, no new stock	b. High dividends, new stock
1. Maintain position	No action needed	Purchase shares pro rata (as many as required to make the owner's position equivalent to that in 1a)
2. Reduce position	Sell shares (as many as required to make the owner's position equivalent to that in 2b)	Do not purchase new shares – ownership percentage falls

This proposition can be easily verified by referring to the relationships diagramed in *Exhibit I*. With investments fixed and with the appropriate debt/equity relationship established, the dividend question becomes one that involves *only* the equity account. If sufficient sums are paid out in the form of dividends so that *retained earnings* are smaller than *new equity required*, then these funds must be replaced by new equity raised from the capital market. Because the new shareholders will participate in the existing earnings as well as in the future earnings of the company, high dividends today serve to spread the total earnings, including growth, over a larger number of shares. Hence per-share growth is slowed. Therefore the choice is higher dividends today or higher earnings per share tomorrow.

COMPLICATING FACTORS

From a stockholder's point of view, the comparison just suggested may capture the essence of the problem. However, it is not actually a comparison of like alternatives because it makes different assumptions about the shareholder's actions. In the case of the low-dividend policy described, the shareholder is presumed to retain his proportionate equity position by virtue of the fact that no new shares are sold. In the high-dividend policy instance, however, the shareholder's position is presumably diluted because he fails to purchase additional shares. *Exhibit IV* shows the possible combinations of corporate and shareholder policies and consistent stockholder actions. The truly comparable alternatives are a and b opposite policies 1 and 2.

In early 1968, the General Public Utilities Corporation found occasion to make an explicit investigation of the impact on its shareholders of a high- versus a low-payout policy. A careful calculation of the differences showed that, *assuming a constant price/earnings ratio under either corporate policy,* the before-tax impact on the shareholder following consistent decision rules (the actions under a and b opposite 1 and 2 in *Exhibit IV*) would be the same under either corporate policy. That is, the shareholder's before-tax position, if he followed action 1a, was the same as for action

1b; and actions 2a and 2b also led to the same before-tax positions. However, the introduction of tax considerations did change this result. For example:

□ A shareholder who wished to reduce his position (shareholder policy 2 in *Exhibit IV*) had a greater after-tax benefit under a low-dividend policy than under a high-dividend policy. Under the low-dividend policy, his increase in wealth was subject primarily to capital gains taxes, whereas under the high-dividend policy it was subject to regular income taxation.

□ A similar differential was present for the shareholder who wished to maintain a position. In the high-dividend case, payments to the shareholder were subject to income taxes in the course of their round trip from the company to the owner and then back to the company again. A company policy of high retentions obviously reduced the tax impact by postponing taxes until the shares were sold and a capital gains tax was imposed.

The major critical assumption underlying this comparison, the big "if" of the analysis, is that the price/earnings ratio will remain constant under the high- and low-dividend options. The validity of this assumption is by no means certain. It is also far from certain that the stockholder can always make the responses (indicated in *Exhibit IV*) which are needed to maintain or reduce his position.

The realities creating these uncertainties will be described briefly.

Industry practices: Certain dividend patterns have become widely accepted in various industries. The utility industry, for instance, is characterized by the retention of a relatively small percentage of earnings. At the other extreme, the high-technology industries tend to pay little, if any, cash to their shareholders. A company which deviates greatly from the central tendency of its industry may get little credit and much harm from its deviation unless it has an unusual story to support its claim to special consideration.

Shareholder composition: An industry and a company may develop a special shareholder following partly because of industry dividend and growth practices. The "widows and orphans" in the utility stocks, the businessmen's risks on the fringes of the seasoned industrials, and the wild-eyed speculators investing in companies with potential but no established record of success are all security market stereotypes with a reasonable grounding in fact. Since one dividend policy may have attracted one group, a major change will perhaps require a substantial restructuring of the shareholders. For a time, at least, this may result in a disorderly market for a company's shares, as shown by depressed prices and price/earnings ratios.

Shareholder misconceptions: The analysis made in the General Public Utilities situation is neither straightforward to explain nor easy to follow. The shareholder must be convinced, for example, that the sale of some of his holdings is precisely the same in principle as a higher dividend policy. But this is not an easy point to make even to a sophisticated analyst, let alone to an average shareholder in whom the "do not touch capital" rule is deeply ingrained. One company of considerable size, for example, has paid stock dividends because members of the founding families liked to give the dividends away to charity, although they would not consider touching the shares which their grandfathers had left them.

Legal distinctions: The capital-income distinction is not merely a figment of the nonfinancial imagination. There is also a legal distinction between capital and income, and it becomes a critical factor for a trustee who must manage an estate for the present benefit of those with a life interest in the income and yet protect the capital or the ultimate beneficiaries. In some states, even stock dividends are troublesome because they count as principal rather than income. Selling off "capital" for the benefit of income beneficiaries is even more generally prohibited or hedged with legal complexities.

Institutional problems: The bookkeeping of receipt of cash dividends is relatively straightforward for income and tax accounting purposes. The complexities that occasional stock dividends create for individual tax returns are severe, but nothing compared to the problems they create for trustees who must prepare income tax returns for their clients. Furthermore, even for large shareholders, the problems of creating the equivalent of a cash dividend through a sale of stock would normally involve partial shares and rounding. For smaller shareholders, the equivalency would probably be virtually impossible to create. Thus, it is not easy to equate a liquidation of shares with the receipt of cash dividends, as indicated opposite shareholder policy 2 in *Exhibit IV*.

The General Public Utilities Corporation found that various factors like these weighed heavily against its proposed conversion from cash dividends to quarterly stock dividends. According to the case material, shareholder response was strongly opposed to the plan. The opposition was partly the "uninformed" variety, coming from shareholders who simply had not understood the nature of the plan. Perhaps more significant was the institutional response; institutional managers opposed the plan because of the paperwork the stock dividends would involve. General Public Utilities' management concluded that as much as 12% of the company's outstanding stock, representing two years of average trading, might change hands if the plan for low payouts and stock dividends were adopted.

Despite the conceptual inconsistency of the alternative, the basic decision management must make is one that its shareholders will interpret as a payout-growth choice. It must be made in light of the circumstances of the particular opportunities and environment. For instance, if the opportunities for growth are not attractive, if more cash is being generated than can be invested, or if the investor has a high propensity for "income today," then it is wise for management to pay liberal dividends even at the expense of raising additional equity. It can be argued, in terms of the U.S. financial scene at least, that many utilities display one or more of these characteristics. Their equity holders do not expect substantial growth; they are investing more for a current yield with some growth prospects rather than for major growth opportunities.

Companies with greater growth prospects, such as those in electronics and data processing, are quite justified, according to this concept, in retaining most or all of the funds generated internally. Their shareholders would perhaps interpret an increase in the payout as a sign of lack of internal investment opportunities and hence of possible declining growth rather than as an indication of a strong market position.

Cost of Capital

The remaining financial policy variable, which until this point has been assumed to have been fixed, is the capital investment program. It is now appropriate to review how the size of this budget is determined and to consider how the projects to be included in it are selected.

Basically the microeconomic approach to the investment decision is straightforward. It argues that the cost of a scarce resource rises as a greater quantity of that resource is demanded. Capital costs increase as the volume of financing rises in response to an increase in the investments undertaken. Also, as more investments are made, the return on the additional investment is presumed to fall. Thus investments are made and money raised until the point is reached at which the cost of the funds on the marginal financing equals the returns promised from the marginal investment. This is shown graphically in Part A of *Exhibit* V.

Wise decisions on the debt and dividend parameters, as indicated earlier, should put the company in the position of having a "minimum cost of capital" for each level of financing. Note that this position is reached without involvement in mechanical and mathematical manipulations (although these could be developed to supplement the strategy).

But how should management calculate capital costs? Many techniques

Exhibit V. Determination of optional financial policy

A. Microeconomic concept

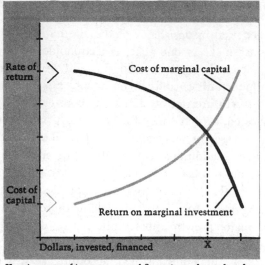

X = Amount of investment and financing to be undertaken

B. Managerial concept

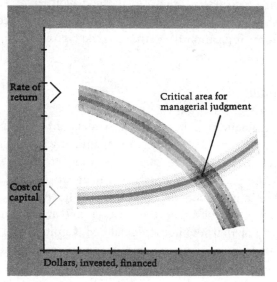

Key

 Anticipated project returns, with uncertainty reflecting imperfect calculations of returns, questions of risk, and similar problems

Capital costs representing the best capital structure and dividend policies for each volume and best set of investment projects, with uncertainty due to problems in measuring capital costs, weights, and the interaction between investment and capital costs in current use obviously provide unreasonable answers, and a better method should be found. Authorities continue to debate how capital costs should be measured, although they generally agree that the process involves a weighting both by the shareholders and by the suppliers of fixed obligation funds of the returns expected. Hence an approach is required to determine both the costs to be assigned and the weights to be used. Let us examine these problems in turn.

ESTIMATING COSTS

The cost of *fixed obligations* is generally considered to be the coupon rate on debt and the dividend rate on straight preferred stock that would be demanded by the *current* market (temporary market aberrations aside).

Some companies may wish to use the embedded cost of existing obligations—that is, the cost of debt as it appears on the books. This should not result in major problems provided the proportion of debt in the capital structure is small. However, use of an embedded cost by a utility could result in serious erosion of the equity position as debt is rolled over into higher cost instruments. A debt-heavy nonutility that used this approach would be overinvesting in low-return projects.

Equity costs are more hotly debated; their dividend yield, the earnings yield, or one of these in some combination with an estimate of growth all have been advanced at various times. It is far easier (and no less appropriate) for the manager to estimate what total rate of return (in a combination of dividends and growth) the stockholder expects to receive on his investment that will justify holding on to his stock.

This estimate can be greatly simplified by categorizing companies in different "return groups" according to whether their equities have the characteristics of bonds, high-cash income with some risk, moderate risk, or high-risk situations. By thus reducing the "universe" to four, five, or perhaps a few more return categories, it is relatively easy to assign a company to its appropriate spot. The loss of accuracy—which is more often than not a spurious accuracy in many measuring methods—is more than compensated for by the fact that a sensible analysis, easily understood and utilized by management, can be quickly made and defended.

The cost of *convertible issues* is the most difficult cost to determine. (Also, to the best of my knowledge, no satisfactory treatment of this subject is available.) One possibility is to finance continually with convertibles so that as one issue is converted, another issue is put out. In this case, the coupon rate might be used. If, however, the company's use of convertibles is more of a one-shot transaction, designed to "issue common stock today at tomorrow's prices," then it is clear that a cost approximating the cost of common equity ought to be adopted for the security.

Whenever a cost of capital is being calculated, it is necessary to put the debt and equity on the same tax basis, computing both either before or after taxes.

A variety of weights have been suggested as appropriate for the cost-averaging calculation. These suggestions include book value of the capitalization, its market value, and the "target" capitalization (at either book or market) for which the company is aiming over the long run.

If the company has a target capital structure (as the preceding debt/equity discussion presumes that it will have), then the book value of the capital structure will eventually approach the target structure. Thus, the target structure is more appropriate to use than the book structure.

From another point of view, the microeconomist is concerned with the cost *on the margin* for new money—the cost of the funds raised today as opposed to the cost of those raised previously. Given a target capital structure, it is obvious that this marginal cost must be an average of some sort unless the company plans to use equity funds only. The presence of a planned proportion of debt means that some debt will be raised from time to time to match the retained earnings, but it would be blatantly inappropriate to specify the company's capital cost as the debt coupon in the year that debt is the primary financing vehicle. Thus the company's *marginal funds*, which are being raised at *current market value*, will be raised in proportion to the amounts called for in the target structure.

I suggest that the most defensible weights to use in averaging various costs are those of the company's long-run target capital structure.

To illustrate the technique just described, let us use the hypothetical example of a chemical company which has decided to change its capital structure from 25% debt to 30% debt:

Management concludes that this change will neither harm the company's ability to borrow at the prevailing interest rate (say, 8%) nor increase the rate of return that the stockholders demand. Management believes that although the company has some high-risk (and high-return) operations, it should not be classified as truly speculative because it does have a sufficiently stable and profitable product base.

Yet earnings have fluctuated significantly in the past, and the dividends have been cut occasionally despite the directors' efforts never to establish a quarterly rate that cannot be maintained. In the bull market of 1965, the company traded at a price/earnings ratio of 30. Since then its ratio once

Exhibit VI. Capital cost calculation

	Debt (D)	Equity (E)	Weighted average target cost (D+E)
(A) Cost after 50% tax	4.0%	13.5%	—
(B) Proportion in target capital structure	30.0	70.0	—
(C) Weighting calculation (A × B)	1.2	9.4	10.6%

dropped to 10, when the market fell, although earnings remained strong at that time. Earnings have since suffered, but the price has held, so that the price/earnings ratio is back to 15.

After some thought, management concludes that the investor in the company is probably expecting the type of return he might get from a fairly mature organization, but one riskier than AT&T. It concludes that in the long run, and ignoring exceptionally high or low stock market levels, the investor is probably expecting a return of between 12% and 15%. A compromise of 13.5% is reached.

Management then calculates the new capital cost as shown in *Exhibit VI*. This cost may not be precisely the "true" cost in the platonic sense of the "true form." However, if prepared by an experienced management, it is probably as close to the mark as can reasonably be expected, given the inherent judgments made and the use of the figure as a rough screen for capital investments.

Capital Investments

The particular techniques for analyzing capital investments will not be treated in detail here. Over the years, these measures have developed from the simple payback (which remains an excellent measure in many circumstances) through more elaborate return-on-investment calculations and into the realm of discounted cash flows. One school of thought argues that the "net present value" method is the most correct conceptually and the least likely to result in confusing decisions.[4] Another approach admits the conceptual validity of the "net present value" calculation, but prefers an "internal rate of return" or "investors' yield" discounting technique because it is believed that management normally thinks in terms of rates of

4. Harold Bierman, Jr., and Seymour Smidt, *The Capital Budgeting Decision*, 2nd edition (New York, The Macmillan Company, 1966).

return, not net-present-value dollars.[5] Other refinements include discounting the depreciation flows at one rate and the remainder of the proceeds at another as a way of adjusting for risk.[6]

The remainder of this article will be concerned with the more philosophical question of whether the *minimum* demanded rate of return should be set equal to the company's cost of capital. A strict interpretation of microeconomics, supported by considerable literature, suggests that the capital cost should be the cutoff rate. I shall argue that it should *not* be.

MISPLACED EMPHASIS

Consider the supply of funds to the corporation. Investors, and particularly equity investors and others who do not have secured rights to income and assets, put their money into a diverse "basket of assets." The components of the basket have a variety of different earnings and different risk characteristics. The investor, in essence, buys a preselected portfolio, one structured for him by corporate management. In fact, the theoretical support for diversification and conglomeration is that such investment portfolios offer a higher return for a lower risk than do investments made by individuals in undiversified corporations.

It is likely that some of a corporation's investments have a lower risk and a lower return than the *average* risk and return characteristics of the entire portfolio. Other assets will have high-return and risk characteristics. The investor sets his overall or average return expectation on the basis of the combined performance of these various investments. His expectation is then used (with the expectations of other investors) as the basis for the company's cost of capital figure.

If management adopts the investors' average criterion as the company's minimum rate, it precludes investments in the lower risk, lower return projects. The company will tend to put all funds into higher risk, higher return opportunities. If this policy is followed over any length of time, its result will be ironic—a substantial shift in the nature of the company's assets and a change in its "portfolio" toward a higher risk and higher return character.

This action may induce investors, in turn, to compensate for the higher risk by demanding yet a higher average rate on their investment in the company's securities. If so, and if management then responds by further raising the hurdle rates set for acceptable investments, the company is again advanced to an even riskier state. The average cost of capital is thus

5. A. J. Merritt and Allen Sykes, *The Finance and Analysis of Capital Projects* (London, Longmans, 1963).

6. Pearson Hunt, *Financial Analysis in Capital Budgeting* (Boston, Division of Research, Harvard Business School, 1964).

ratcheted up, and value may be destroyed. Consider a situation like the following:

An integrated company in the energy business has operations ranging from wildcat petroleum exploration to refining of petroleum for its own use and for sale on the open market, to pipeline operation and retail market facilities. According to the company's calculations, its capital cost falls substantially above the returns offered by the less profitable but less risky portions of the venture, such as the retail units and the pipelines. On the other hand, it is clear that exclusion of additional investments in these areas would have the ultimate effect of liquidating such operations and of concentrating the company in areas such as wildcatting. Thus, slavish use of the cost of capital as a cutoff is clearly inappropriate for management.

REALISTIC APPROACH

Rather than regard the cost-return intersection as a point (a presumption of basic microeconomic thought illustrated in Part A of *Exhibit* V), it is more realistic and useful for management to think of it as an area or band of rather fuzzy boundaries (as Part B shows). There are several basic reasons for this imprecision:

1. The imperfections in the measurement of capital costs and of returns on projects blur the precision that is often presumed to be present in both types of calculations.

2. The interaction of investment decisions, financing decisions, and capital costs cannot be clearly defined except in unusual circumstances. Thus, for each level of investment, the capital structure and dividend policies appropriate for the company may change. These changes may frequently be imperceptible and recognizable only at major turning points. To allow for these uncertainties requires an *area* of choice.

3. The projects themselves differ with respect to risk. The effects of these differences are difficult to estimate. However, one way to explain the problem is to recognize that a project may return more or less on a risk-adjusted basis (that is, when the anticipated returns are weighted according to the amount of risk involved) than it will on the basis of the most likely outcome.

The intersection of these two broad bands of costs and returns roughly delineates the area where maximum managerial judgment is required—on both the financing policy and the investment policy sides of the equation. It is relatively easy to identify unquestionably good projects and unquestionably unattractive ones. Similarly, obviously good and poor capitalization policies do not require much talent to identify. Judgment is required when the decisions are no longer so obvious—that is, when the imprecision of the numbers, of the circumstances, or of both is present to confound the inflexible guidelines and thwart the rules of thumb.

The scheme suggested in Part B of *Exhibit* V does not provide any easy answer to problems falling in the critical area; rather, it is intended to warn the unwary of the area's existence and to suggest how its boundaries may be located. Then the best talents of the corporation can be focused on problems in the area, and management can be spared the routine task of settling the more obvious and less demanding questions.

SHARE REPURCHASE

Although the subject is tangential, it is appropriate at this point to comment briefly on the question of share repurchase. Many analysts have treated this common question as an investment decision, as though repurchase of a company's stock falls in the same category as buying another office machine or a lathe. This treatment confuses the investment decision with the capital structure decision; it is in the latter category that share repurchase most logically should be placed.

Adjustments to the capital structure are called for when funds are needed for attractive investment, when funds are generated in quantities larger than required for investment opportunities, or when the nature of the company's risk changes so that more or less debt should be undertaken. Thus the generation of excess funds indicates that excess capital is available to the company and that the organization can lower its capital costs (moving backward, or to the left, down the cost curve in Part A of *Exhibit* V) by decapitalizing. Whether this is done by reducing debt or equity, or some mixture of the two, depends on a determination of the appropriate capitalization for the company. The important thing is to keep the investment question separate and not mix it with the question of retiring equity by repurchasing stockholders' shares. The proper question now is only how best to lower capital costs—by retiring debt, buying back stock, increasing dividends, or using some combination of these steps.

It is not necessary to wait for fund needs or surpluses to arise before addressing the capital structure issue. In fact, capital structure should always be kept under evaluation. It is prefectly in order for management to consider continuously whether it should readjust the company's capital structure by borrowing and retiring stock or by issuing stock to retire debt.

Conclusion

It does not require an elaborate mathematical justification to show that the debt/equity and dividend polices affect the investment portfolio through their impact on the capital cost. Investment decisions, in turn, influence the capital cost and other areas of financial policy because of their impact on the return received from the company's assets and the risks taken in order to get that return.

Ideally, it would be desirable to settle simultaneously the problems raised in the three financial areas reviewed in this article. But the magnitude and complexity of the problems make this impossible in all but the simplest cases.

A more productive approach is the one outlined—that executives analyze the parts of the problem sequentially and then recheck their preliminary decisions in order to correct any early steps which may require adjustments as a result of later actions. I believe it is best to work on the decisions in the order discussed in this article. That means taking these steps:

1. Assume projected capital requirements of the company.

2. Tentatively settle the debt/equity question.

3. Make the dividend-growth analysis within the framework of the debt/equity choice.

4. Investigate the impact of steps 2 and 3 on capital costs and the impact of the capital costs on the investment volume.

The last step should determine whether the total result is reasonable in light of the company's situation and its posture in the financial market. If it is not, executives can change their original assumptions and go through the four steps again.

While this approach adds no new dimensions to the theory of financial management, it does enable management to profit from some of the excellent work done by theorists. This approach makes the issues clearer to executives. It enables them to decide more readily what they should do and to move in accordance with a sound, consistent plan of action.

17 How to Evaluate New Capital Investments

John G. McLean

Dissatisfied with the yardsticks it had been using to evaluate capital investment opportunities, Continental Oil Company determined to find a better way to measure one investment against another and extrapolate the potential returns which projects might earn on its investments. Continental settled on the method of discounting cash flows to present value. The author, who helped install this approach, describes how this major oil company employs it.

In evaluating new investment projects, why are return-on-investment figures preferable to years-to-pay-out figures? Of various possible methods for calculating return on investment, why is the discounted-cash-flow procedure likely to yield the best results? What techniques and assumptions will help executives who want to make practical use of the discounted-cash-flow method?

Obviously, I cannot answer these questions satisfactorily for all companies. I shall attempt only to describe some of the answers developed by the Continental Oil Company. Faced with a need for better methods of evaluating investment proposals, management decided in 1955 to adopt the discounted-cash-flow method. The procedures adopted, the reasons for choosing them, and the results obtained during the first three years may serve as a useful "case example" for other companies to study.

Of course, the techniques that I shall describe were not invented by Continental. They have been used for centuries in the field of finance and banking and have been fully described in many textbooks and articles in the field of industrial management and business economics.

Management Concern

Prior to 1955, we had relied heavily—as many oil companies do—on years-to-pay-out figures as the primary means of judging the desirability of investments and as a yardstick for measuring one investment opportunity against another. We had also made use of return-on-investment figures computed in a variety of different ways, which I shall describe later.

In the latter part of 1954 our financial group, consisting of the controller, the financial vice president, and myself, undertook a comprehensive review of the techniques we were then using in making capital investment decisions. We were concerned about this matter because of the large amounts of new money we found it necessary to channel back into the oil business each year. Characteristically, oil companies have a very high rate of capital turnover because they operate assets which deplete at high rates, and large amounts of new funds must be reinvested each year if earnings are to be maintained and increased.

The capital expenditures of Continental Oil, for example, normally run in the neighborhood of $100 million per year, or about $385,000 each working day—roughly twice our net income, which is about $50 million per year. To the best of my knowledge, there are few, if any, other major industries with such a high ratio of capital expenditures to current net income.

In the oil business, therefore, the making of capital investment decisions assumes considerably more significance as a part of top management's job than is usually the case. In our own situation it was apparent that the management judgment exercised in directing the flow of new funds into our business had a very significant bearing upon current and future earnings per share and a profound influence on the long-term growth and development of our company. We decided, therefore, that we should make a maximum effort to develop the best possible yardstick for comparing one investment opportunity against another and for evaluating the returns that particular projects would earn on the stockholder's dollar.

New Techniques

As a background for outlining the new techniques which our financial group recommended as a result of its study and which were later implemented throughout the company, let me first outline the steps which are normally involved in the appraisal of new capital investments:

1. Estimate the volume of sales, prices, costs of materials, operating expenses, transportation costs, capital investment requirements, strength and nature of competition, rates of obsolescence or depletion, and other economic and business factors.

2. Summarize basic estimates of annual income, life of project, and capital investment in convenient form for appraisal purposes. (Commonly used yardsticks include years to pay out and return on investment.)

3. Exercise managerial judgment in determining whether or not:

(a) The anticipated return is large enough to warrant the business risks involved;

(b) The investment opportunity is attractive in view of the various alternative opportunities for capital spending;

(c) The timing of the investment is right relative to anticipated developments in the near future.

The discounted-cash-flow techniques which we introduced in 1955 had to do only with Step 2; that is, with the way we did our arithmetic in adding up the basic estimates of annual incomes, life of project, and capital investments to arrive at payout and return on investment.

It was clearly recognized that there was nothing in the discounted-cash-flow method which would make it any easier to estimate the items listed in Step 1 or which would improve the accuracy of those estimates. It was likewise recognized that there was nothing in the discounted-cash-flow techniques which would relieve management at any level of the responsibility for exercising judgment on the various matters listed under Step 3. We were concerned fundamentally, at this time, with improving the mechanics of our capital investment analyses in order that management might render better judgments on the three points under Step 3.

PAYOUT VS. RETURN

Our first recommendation was that we use the return-on-investment figures as the primary yardstick for evaluating new capital investments and pay much less attention to years-to-pay-out figures than had been our custom in the past.

Our reason for de-emphasizing payout figures was simply that they do not provide an adequate means of discriminating among new investment opportunities. They merely indicate how long it will take to recover the original capital outlay and do not tell us anything about the earning power of an investment. There is, of course, no point in making investments which just give us our money back. The true worth of an investment depends on how much income it will generate *after* the original outlay has been recovered, and there is no way that can be determined from a payout figure. Generally speaking, payout figures are reliable measures of the relative worth of alternative investments only when the income-producing life of all projects under consideration is about the same—which is far from the case in our particular situation.

To illustrate how misleading payout figures can be, I have prepared an example consisting of three different projects, each involving an investment of $125,000 (see *Exhibit I*:

The annual income generated by the investments begins at $25,000 and

Exhibit I. Differences in rates of return when payout periods are equal

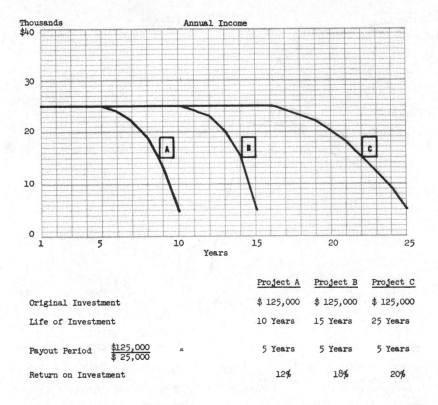

		Project A	Project B	Project C
Original Investment		$ 125,000	$ 125,000	$ 125,000
Life of Investment		10 Years	15 Years	25 Years
Payout Period	$\frac{\$125,000}{\$\ 25,000}$ =	5 Years	5 Years	5 Years
Return on Investment		12%	18%	20%

then declines in later years in each case as shown on the graph. Since the annual incomes are identical in the early years, each project has the same payout period; namely, five years. By this standard of measurement, therefore, the projects would be equal from an investment standpoint. But actually the returns on investment range from 12% per year for Project A, which has the shortest life, to 20% per year for Project B, which has the longest life.

At first glance, you might be inclined to say that this is all pretty simple —all you have to do is look at both the payout period and the total estimated life to reach a correct decision. And it *is* relatively easy if the payout periods are all the same, as they are in this example, or even if the payout periods are different but the total economic lives are the same.

Unfortunately, however, we are usually looking at projects where there is a difference in both the payout period and the project life. Under such circumstances, it becomes very difficult to appraise the relative worth of two or more projects on the basis of payout periods alone. For example, consider the three projects shown in *Exhibit II*:

The payout periods here range from 8 years in the case of Project A, which has a high initial income and a short life, to 11.5 years in the case of

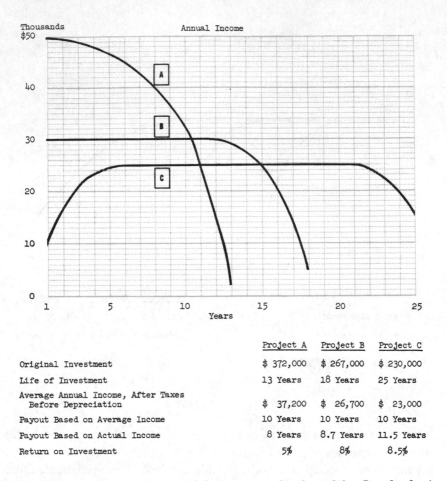

	Project A	Project B	Project C
Original Investment	$ 372,000	$ 267,000	$ 230,000
Life of Investment	13 Years	18 Years	25 Years
Average Annual Income, After Taxes Before Depreciation	$ 37,200	$ 26,700	$ 23,000
Payout Based on Average Income	10 Years	10 Years	10 Years
Payout Based on Actual Income	8 Years	8.7 Years	11.5 Years
Return on Investment	5%	8%	8.5%

Project C, which has a low initial income and a long life. On the basis of payout periods, therefore, Project A would appear to be the best of the three. Actually, however, the true rates of return on investment range from 5% for Project A to 8.5% for Project C. The order of desirability indicated by payout periods is thus exactly the reverse of that indicated by return-on-investment figures.

It was for these reasons that our financial group recommended that in the future we make use of return-on-investment figures as our primary guide in evaluating new projects rather than the payout figures which had customarily been our main guide in the past.

ALTERNATIVE CALCULATION

Our second recommendation had to do with the procedures used in calculating the return-on-investment figures. There are at least three general ways to make the calculation:

1. In the first method, the return is calculated on the *original investment*; that is, the average annual income from a project is divided by the total original capital outlay. This is the procedure we had been using in our producing, refining, petrochemical, and pipeline departments.

2. In the second method, the return is calculated on the *average investment*. In other words, the average annual income is divided by half the original investment or by whatever figure represents the mid-point between the original cost and the salvage or residual land value in the investment. This is the procedure which was used in our marketing department for calculating returns on new service station investments.

3. The third procedure—the *discounted-cash-flow* technique—bases the calculation on the investment actually outstanding from time to time over the life of the project. This was the procedure used in our financial department in computing the cost of funds obtained from various sources or in estimating the yields we might obtain by investing reserve working capital in various types of government or commercial securities.

These three methods will produce very different results, and the figures obtained by one method may be as much as twice as great as those obtained by another—i.e., a project that showed a return of 10% under the procedures used in our refining department could show as much as 20% under the procedures used by our marketing department, and might show 15% or 18% under those used by our financial department.

It was clear, therefore, that we must settle on one of these three methods and use it uniformly throughout all departments of the company. Otherwise, we would be measuring some investments with long yardsticks, others with short yardsticks, and we would never be sure exactly what we were doing.

RELATIVE ADVANTAGES

Our selection of discounted cash flow was based on three primary considerations:

□ It gives the true rate of return offered by a new project. Both of the other methods merely give an approximation of the return. The original-investment method usually understates the return, while the average-investment method usually overstates the return. By contrast, the discounted-cash-flow method is a compromise and usually gives figures lying in between those that would be obtained by the other two methods.

□ It gives figures which are meaningful in relation to those used throughout the financial world in quoting interest rates on borrowed funds, yields on bonds, and for various other purposes. It thus permits direct comparison of the projected returns on investments with the cost of borrowing money —which is not possible with the other procedures.

Exhibit III. Comparison of return-on-investment calculations

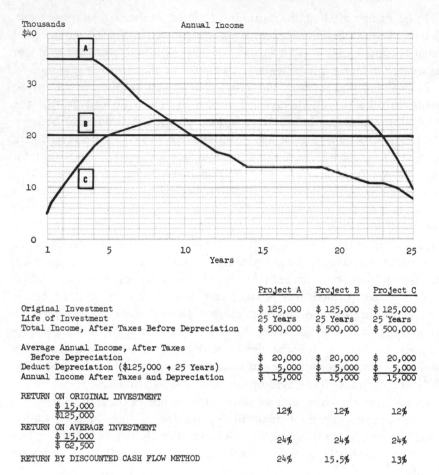

	Project A	Project B	Project C
Original Investment	$ 125,000	$ 125,000	$ 125,000
Life of Investment	25 Years	25 Years	25 Years
Total Income, After Taxes Before Depreciation	$ 500,000	$ 500,000	$ 500,000
Average Annual Income, After Taxes			
Before Depreciation	$ 20,000	$ 20,000	$ 20,000
Deduct Depreciation ($125,000 ÷ 25 Years)	$ 5,000	$ 5,000	$ 5,000
Annual Income After Taxes and Depreciation	$ 15,000	$ 15,000	$ 15,000
RETURN ON ORIGINAL INVESTMENT			
$ 15,000 / $125,000	12%	12%	12%
RETURN ON AVERAGE INVESTMENT			
$ 15,000 / $ 62,500	24%	24%	24%
RETURN BY DISCOUNTED CASH FLOW METHOD	24%	15.5%	13%

☐ It makes allowance for *differences in the time* at which investments generate their income. That is, it discriminates among investments that have (a) a low initial income which gradually increases, (b) a high initial income which gradually declines, and (c) a uniform income throughout their lives.

The last point was particularly important to us, because the investment projects which we normally have before us frequently have widely divergent income patterns. Refining projects usually have a relatively uniform annual income, because they must be operated at 75% to 100% of capacity from the time they go on stream in order to keep unit costs at reasonable levels. On the other hand, producing wells yield a high initial income, which declines as the oil reservoir is depleted; while new service station investments have a still different pattern in that they frequently increase their income as they gain market acceptance and build up their volume of business.

As an illustration of the usefulness of the discounted-cash-flow method in discriminating among investments with different income patterns, consider the three examples presented in *Exhibit III*:

These three projects all require the same original outlay, have the same economic life, and generate exactly the same total income after taxes and depreciation. The return on the original investment would be 12%, and the return on average investment 24% in each case. By these standards, therefore, the projects would appear to be of equal merit. Actually, however, Project A is by far the best of the three because it generates a larger share of its total income in the early years of its life. The investor thus has his money in hand sooner and available for investment in other income-producing projects. This highly important difference is clearly reflected in the discounted-cash-flow figures, which show 24% for Project A, 15.5% for Project B, and 13% for Project C.

Simple Application

To facilitate the adoption of the new system on a company-wide basis, we recommended a very simple application. Assumptions were made at many points in order to reduce the complexity of the calculations involved. In most instances, we found the range of possible error introduced by these simplifying assumptions to be negligible relative to that involved in the basic estimates of income, costs, and economic life of a project. As a further means of facilitating the computations, we prepared a number of special arrangements of the discount tables.

UNIFORM INCOME

The procedures that we developed for investments with a uniform annual income are illustrated in *Exhibit IV*.

The payout period is computed in the usual manner by dividing the cash flow after taxes into the original investment. Then, since the life of the project is estimated at 15 years, the payout period is carried into the 15-year line of a cumulative discount table, and the column in which a matching number is found indicates the discounted-cash-flow rate of return. The numbers in this table are simply sums of the discount factors for the time periods and rates indicated. Thus, $4.675 is the present worth of $1.00 received annually for 15 years, discounted at a 20% rate.

It is apparent, therefore, that the discounted-cash-flow procedure involves nothing more than finding the discount rate which will make the present worth of the anticipated stream of cash income from the project equal to the original outlay. In this case, the anticipated cash flow of $20,000 per annum for 15 years has a present worth equal to the original outlay—

Exhibit IV. *Application of discounted-cash-flow method in a situation with uniform income*

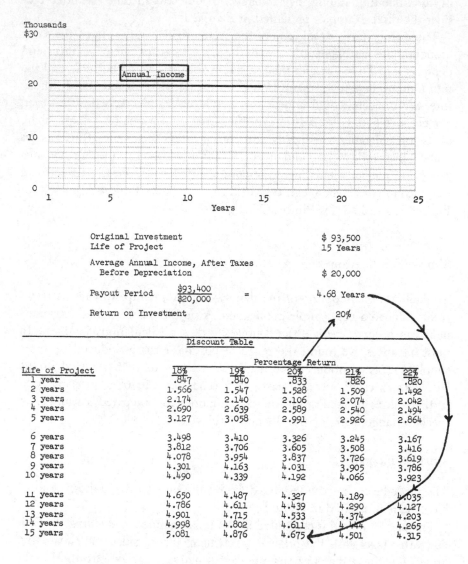

| Original Investment | $ 93,500 |
| Life of Project | 15 Years |

| Average Annual Income, After Taxes Before Depreciation | $ 20,000 |

Payout Period $\dfrac{\$93,400}{\$20,000}$ = 4.68 Years

Return on Investment   20%

<u>Discount Table</u>

| Life of Project | Percentage Return | | | | |
	18%	19%	20%	21%	22%
1 year	.847	.840	.833	.826	.820
2 years	1.566	1.547	1.528	1.509	1.492
3 years	2.174	2.140	2.106	2.074	2.042
4 years	2.690	2.639	2.589	2.540	2.494
5 years	3.127	3.058	2.991	2.926	2.864
6 years	3.498	3.410	3.326	3.245	3.167
7 years	3.812	3.706	3.605	3.508	3.416
8 years	4.078	3.954	3.837	3.726	3.619
9 years	4.301	4.163	4.031	3.905	3.786
10 years	4.490	4.339	4.192	4.066	3.923
11 years	4.650	4.487	4.327	4.189	4.035
12 years	4.786	4.611	4.439	4.290	4.127
13 years	4.901	4.715	4.533	4.374	4.203
14 years	4.998	4.802	4.611	4.444	4.265
15 years	5.081	4.876	4.675	4.501	4.315

$93,400—when discounted at 20%. Alternatively, it can be said that the discounted-cash-flow procedure simply computes the rate of return on the balance of the investment actually outstanding from time to time over the life of the project, as illustrated in *Exhibit V*.

The cash flow of $20,000 per annum, continuing over 15 years, is shown in Column 1. Some part of this must be set aside to return the original outlay over the 15-year period, as shown in Column 2. The remainder, tabulated in Column 3, represents the true earnings.

On this basis, the balance of the original capital outlay outstanding (not yet returned to the investor) at the beginning of each year is shown in

Exhibit V. Return calculated by discounted-cash-flow method

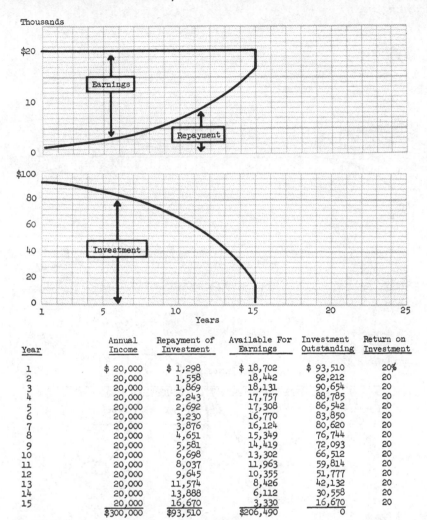

Year	Annual Income	Repayment of Investment	Available For Earnings	Investment Outstanding	Return on Investment
1	$ 20,000	$ 1,298	$ 18,702	$ 93,510	20%
2	20,000	1,558	18,442	92,212	20
3	20,000	1,869	18,131	90,654	20
4	20,000	2,243	17,757	88,785	20
5	20,000	2,692	17,308	86,542	20
6	20,000	3,230	16,770	83,850	20
7	20,000	3,876	16,124	80,620	20
8	20,000	4,651	15,349	76,744	20
9	20,000	5,581	14,419	72,093	20
10	20,000	6,698	13,302	66,512	20
11	20,000	8,037	11,963	59,814	20
12	20,000	9,645	10,355	51,777	20
13	20,000	11,574	8,426	42,132	20
14	20,000	13,888	6,112	30,558	20
15	20,000	16,670	3,330	16,670	20
	$300,000	$93,510	$206,490	0	

Column 4. The ratio of the earnings to this outstanding investment is 20% year by year throughout the life of the project, as shown in Column 5. The graph at the top of the form shows the declining balance of the investment and the division of the annual cash flow between repayment of principal and earnings.

It will immediately be recognized that the mechanism of the discounted-cash-flow procedure here is precisely the same as that involved in a household mortgage where one makes annual cash payments to the bank of a fixed amount to cover interest and payments on the principal. This is the reason for my earlier statement; i.e., that the discounted-cash-flow procedure gives rates of return directly comparable to the interest rates generally quoted for all financial purposes. It is worth noting that in this particular case the conventional procedure of computing a return on the original

Exhibit VI. *Application of discounted-cash-flow method in a situation with increasing income*

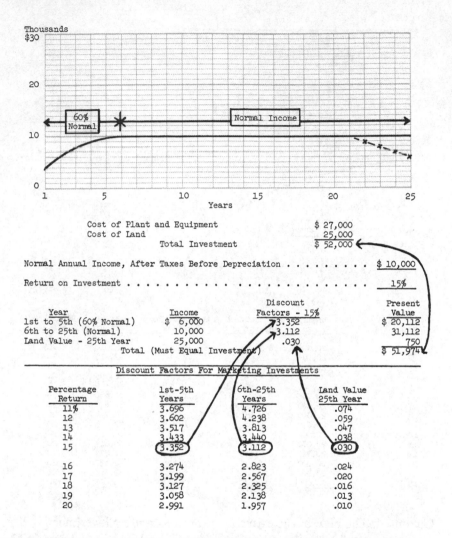

Cost of Plant and Equipment	$ 27,000
Cost of Land	25,000
Total Investment	$ 52,000

Normal Annual Income, After Taxes Before Depreciation . . . . $ 10,000

Return on Investment 15%

Year	Income	Discount Factors - 15%	Present Value
1st to 5th (60% Normal)	$ 6,000	3.352	$ 20,112
6th to 25th (Normal)	10,000	3.112	31,112
Land Value - 25th Year	25,000	.030	750
Total (Must Equal Investment)			$ 51,974

Discount Factors For Marketing Investments

Percentage Return	1st-5th Years	6th-25th Years	Land Value 25th Year
11%	3.696	4.726	.074
12	3.602	4.238	.059
13	3.517	3.813	.047
14	3.433	3.440	.038
15	3.352	3.112	.030
16	3.274	2.823	.024
17	3.199	2.567	.020
18	3.127	2.325	.016
19	3.058	2.138	.013
20	2.991	1.957	.010

investment would have given a figure of 15%. Had the calculation been based on the average investment, a figure of 30% would have been obtained (assuming straight-line depreciation in both cases and zero salvage value).

INCREASING INCOME

Our application of the discounted-cash-flow procedure in a situation with increasing income—e.g., investment in new service stations—is illustrated in *Exhibit VI*. In this case, we assume a build-up of income during the first 5 years, a 20-year period of relatively stable income, and a 5-year period of declining income at the end of the station's life (assumptions now undergoing modification in the light of recent statistical studies of volume performance).

To simplify the calculations and to avoid discounting the income on a year-by-year basis, however, we break the calculations into three parts. We assume that the income in the first to the fifth years is roughly comparable to a uniform series of payments of 60% of the normal level. We also ignore the decline in income at the end of the life, since it would have little effect on the results, and assume that the normal level of income will continue for the sixth to twenty-fifth years. And, finally, we assume that the land would, or could, be sold at the end of the twenty-fifth year at its original cost.

We have thus been able to make use of a special, and much simplified, discount table like the one shown at the bottom of *Exhibit VI*. The first column contains the sum of the discount factors for the first five years, and the second column shows the sum of the factors for the sixth to twenty-fifth years. The last column shows the present worth of $1.00 received 25 years from now. These factors may then be applied directly to the three segments of the anticipated cash flow from the project in the manner shown. The calculation proceeds by trial and error until a series of factors, and a corresponding discount rate, are found which will make the present value of the future cash flow equal to the original outlay.

DECLINING INCOME

Our application of the discounted-cash-flow procedure in a situation of declining income is shown in *Exhibit VII*. In this case—e.g., an investment in producing wells with a gradually depleting oil reservoir—we have found, again, that the cash flow can usually be divided into three pieces, with a uniform annual income assumed for each. The first year must be treated separately, since the cash flow is usually high as a result of the tax credits for intangible drilling costs. We then select a middle and end period of varying lengths, depending on the characteristics of the particular well, and simply assume an average annual income throughout each period.

These assumptions make it possible to use a simplified arrangement of the discount tables. The first line contains the discount factors for the first year alone, while the remainder of the table consists of cumulative factors beginning in the second year.

The factors for the first year and the middle period may then be read directly from the table, and the factor for the end period is obtained by deduction, as shown. The calculation proceeds by trial and error until discount factors are found which will make the present value of the cash flow equal to the original outlay—in this case 22%.

Exhibit VII. *Application of discounted-cash-flow method in a situation with declining income*

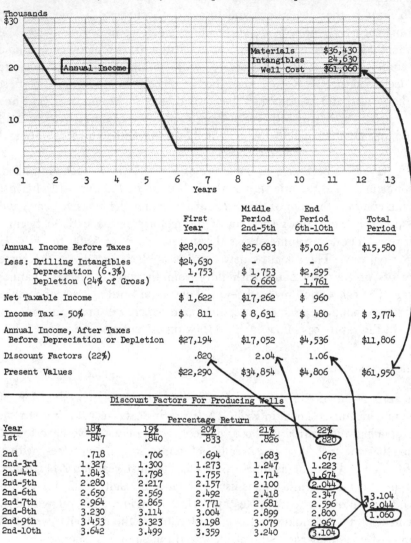

Annual Income, After Taxes, Before Depreciation and Depletion

	First Year	Middle Period 2nd-5th	End Period 6th-10th	Total Period
Annual Income Before Taxes	$28,005	$25,683	$5,016	$15,580
Less: Drilling Intangibles	$24,630	-	-	
Depreciation (6.3%)	1,753	$ 1,753	$2,295	
Depletion (24% of Gross)	-	6,668	1,761	
Net Taxable Income	$ 1,622	$17,262	$ 960	
Income Tax - 50%	$ 811	$ 8,631	$ 480	$ 3,774
Annual Income, After Taxes Before Depreciation or Depletion	$27,194	$17,052	$4,536	$11,806
Discount Factors (22%)	.820	2.04	1.06	
Present Values	$22,290	$34,854	$4,806	$61,950

Materials $36,430
Intangibles   24,630
Well Cost $61,060

Discount Factors For Producing Wells

Year	\multicolumn{5}{c}{Percentage Return}				
	18%	19%	20%	21%	22%
1st	.847	.840	.833	.826	.820
2nd	.718	.706	.694	.683	.672
2nd-3rd	1.327	1.300	1.273	1.247	1.223
2nd-4th	1.843	1.798	1.755	1.714	1.674
2nd-5th	2.280	2.217	2.157	2.100	2.044
2nd-6th	2.650	2.569	2.492	2.418	2.347
2nd-7th	2.964	2.865	2.771	2.681	2.596
2nd-8th	3.230	3.114	3.004	2.899	2.800
2nd-9th	3.453	3.323	3.198	3.079	2.967
2nd-10th	3.642	3.499	3.359	3.240	3.104

3.104
2.044
1.060

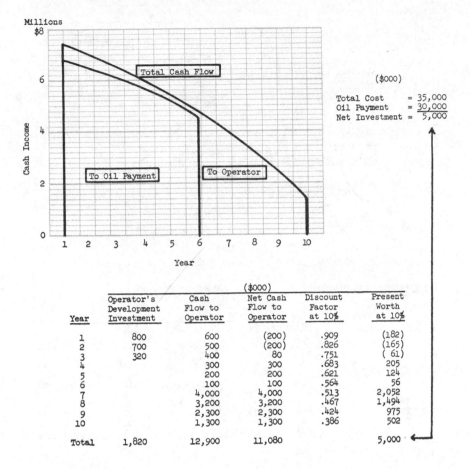

	Operator's Development	Cash Flow to	Net Cash Flow to	Discount Factor	Present Worth
Year	Investment	Operator	Operator	at 10%	at 10%
1	800	600	(200)	.909	(182)
2	700	500	(200)	.826	(165)
3	320	400	80	.751	(61)
4		300	300	.683	205
5		200	200	.621	124
6		100	100	.564	56
7		4,000	4,000	.513	2,052
8		3,200	3,200	.467	1,494
9		2,300	2,300	.424	975
10		1,300	1,300	.386	502
Total	1,820	12,900	11,080		5,000

($000)

Total Cost = 35,000
Oil Payment = 30,000
Net Investment = 5,000

IRREGULAR CASH FLOW

Somewhat more complicated applications of the discounted-cash-flow procedure occur whenever the cash flow is more irregular. To illustrate, here are two special situations:

A. *Oil Payment Deals.* Exhibit VIII shows the application when the problem is to analyze the profitability of acquiring a producing property under an oil payment arrangement.

The total cost of the property is $35 million, of which $30 million is supplied by an investor purchasing an oil payment. The terms of sale provide that he shall receive a specified percentage of the oil produced until he has recovered his principal and interest at 6%. The remaining $5 million is supplied by the new operator, who purchases the working and remaining interest and who agrees to do certain additional development drilling as shown in Column 1.

Exhibit IX. *Application of discounted-cash-flow method in a situation with irregular cash flow (B)*

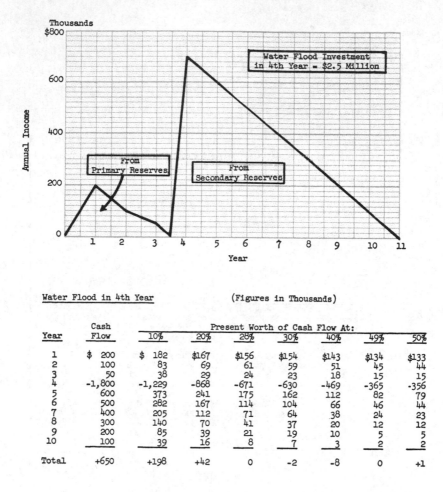

Water Flood in 4th Year		(Figures in Thousands)						
	Cash	Present Worth of Cash Flow At:						
Year	Flow	10%	20%	28%	30%	40%	49%	50%
1	$ 200	$ 182	$167	$156	$154	$143	$134	$133
2	100	83	69	61	59	51	45	44
3	50	38	29	24	23	18	15	15
4	-1,800	-1,229	-868	-671	-630	-469	-365	-356
5	600	373	241	175	162	112	82	79
6	500	282	167	114	104	66	46	44
7	400	205	112	71	64	38	24	23
8	300	140	70	41	37	20	12	12
9	200	85	39	21	19	10	5	5
10	100	39	16	8	7	3	2	2
Total	+650	+198	+42	0	-2	-8	0	+1

The cash flow from the properties after expenses accruing to the operator is shown in Column 2. Column 3 shows the operator's net cash flow after deduction of the development expenses in Column 1. It is negative in the first two years, and remains small until the oil payment obligation is liquidated. Thereafter, it increases sharply and ultimately amounts to more than twice the original investment of $5 million. The discounted-cash-flow method recognizes that most of this income does not become available until late in the life of the project, and the resulting return on investment is 10% per annum. (If the same total income had been received in equal annual installments, the return would have been 15%.)

In situations of this kind, it is difficult to see how the analysis could be handled without resorting to the discounted-cash-flow approach. The conventional methods of calculating rates of return would give wholly misleading results.

B. *Water Flood Project. Exhibit IX* contains a second application of the discounted-cash-flow approach to situations in which the income generated by an investment is irregular. Normally, the free flow of oil from a reservoir (primary recovery) diminishes with the passage of time. In some cases, however, secondary recovery measures, such as injection of water into the reservoir, may result in a substantial increase in the total amount of oil produced.

The problem is to determine the profitability of acquiring a small producing property. The primary reserves have been nearly exhausted, and an investment of $2.5 million will be needed at the appropriate time for a water flood to accomplish recovery of the secondary reserves. No immediate payment will be made to the selling party, but he will receive a 12½% royalty on all oil produced from the property, whether from primary or secondary reserves.

The calculations in *Exhibit IX* are made under the assumption that the water flood investment will be made in the fourth year. During the first three years all the primary reserves will be recovered, and income in the fourth to the tenth years will be attributable solely to the water flood project.

As shown by the table, the discounted-cash-flow analysis gives *two solutions* to this problem. At both 28% and 49%, the net present worth of the cash flow is zero; i.e., the present worth of the cash income is equal to the present worth of the $2.5 million investment. The correct solution is 28%, because the net present worth is declining as we move from the lower to the higher discount rates. The reverse is true at the 49% level.

In general, two solutions may arise whenever the net cash flow switches from positive to negative at some stage in the life of the project, possibly as a result of additional capital outlays required at that time, as in the case of secondary recovery projects. It is important, therefore, to recognize the possibility of two solutions and not to settle for the first one found. A false solution can easily be identified by noting the direction of change in the present worths as higher discount rates are introduced in the trial-and-error calculations.

BENCH MARKS

As a final step in applying the discounted-cash-flow procedure to our business, it was necessary to develop some bench marks that could be used in appraising the figures resulting from the calculations.

As a starting point, we recommended that approximately 10% after taxes be regarded as the minimum amount we should seek to earn on investments involving a minimum of risk, such as those in new service stations and other marketing facilities. We further recommended that the minimum acceptable level of returns should be increased as the risks involved in the investment projects increased. Accordingly, we set substantially higher standards for investments in manufacturing, petrochemical, and exploration and production ventures.

We arrived at these bench-mark figures by considering:

□ Our long-term borrowing costs.

□ The returns which Continental and other oil companies have customarily earned on their borrowed and invested capital (substantially more than 10%).

□ The returns which must be earned to make our business attractive to equity investors.

□ The returns which must be earned to satisfy our present shareholders that the earnings retained in the business each year are put to good use.

In this latter connection, it may be noted that whenever we retain earnings instead of paying them out as dividends, we in effect force our stockholders to make a new investment in the Continental Oil Company. And clearly, we have little justification for doing that unless we can arrange to earn as much on the funds as the stockholders could earn by investing in comparable securities elsewhere.

Conclusion

The discounted-cash-flow method rests on the time-honored maxim that "money begets money." Funds on hand today can be invested in profitable projects and thereby yield additional funds to the investing company. Funds to be received at some future date cannot be profitably invested until that time, and so have no earning power in the interim. For this reason, a business concern must place a *time value* on its money—a dollar in hand today is much more valuable than one to be received in the distant future. The discounted-cash-flow method simply applies this general concept to the analysis of new capital investments.

The procedures which I have been describing in regard to the discounted-cash-flow method of analyzing new capital investments were adopted by Continental's top management in the fall of 1955 and were implemented throughout the company. Our subsequent experience in using the discounted-cash-flow approach may be summarized as follows:

□ We have found it to be a very powerful management tool. It is an extremely effective device for analyzing routine investments with fairly regular patterns of cash flow, and also for analyzing very complicated problems like those involved in mergers, acquisitions of producing properties under oil payment arrangements, and other ventures that require a series of capital outlays over a period of many years and generate highly irregular cash flows.

□ We have also found that the discounted-cash-flow techniques are far easier to introduce and apply than is commonly supposed. We had anticipated considerable difficulty in gaining acceptance of the new methods and in teaching people throughout the organization to use them; however, this turned out to be a very minor problem. Once the new methods were properly explained, they were quickly adopted throughout our operating and field organizations, and the mechanics of the calculations presented no problems of any importance.

□ There is one major theoretical and practical problem in using the discounted-cash-flow procedure for which we have not yet found a fully satisfactory solution. This problem is that of developing a return-on-investment figure for whole departments or groups of departments which may be computed year by year and compared with the returns calculated under the discounted-cash-flow procedures at the time individual investment projects were undertaken. Clearly, division of the cash income or the net income after taxes and depreciation by either the cost investment or the depreciated investment for the department as a whole will not produce statistics comparable to the discounted-cash-flow figures.

On the whole, our experience with the discounted-cash-flow techniques has been very satisfactory. To my mind, these techniques represent part of the oncoming improvements in the field of finance and accounting. Just as new technological discoveries continually bring us new opportunities in the fields of exploration, production, manufacturing, transportation, and marketing, so too there are occasionally new techniques in finance and accounting that offer opportunities to improve operations. The discounted-cash-flow method of investment analysis falls in that category.

18. New Framework for Corporate Debt Policy

Gordon Donaldson

How much debt is proper or prudent to take on? Conventional methods for evaluating debt capacity—such as analyzing what comparable companies are doing—can be misleading, claims an authority on the subject. In this landmark HBR article, he uses as his principal criterion the degree of risk which management thinks it can assume in deciding its investment priorities, risk being described as the chances of running short of cash. The question then becomes the extent to which the risks would be increased as the result of incurring a certain amount of debt, a question that is resolved by a test of cash adequacy.

◻ Why are many common rules of thumb for evaluating a company's debt capacity misleading and even dangerous?

◻ Why is outside experience and advice of limited value as a guide to top management's thinking about capacity?

◻ What approach will enable management to make an independent and realistic appraisal of risk on the basis of data with which it is already familiar and in terms of judgments to which it has long been accustomed?

The problem of deciding whether it is wise and proper for a business corporation to finance long-term capital needs through debt, and, if so, how far it is safe to go, is one which most boards of directors have wrestled with at one time or another. For many companies the debt-capacity decision is of critical importance because of its potential impact on margins of profitability and on solvency. For *all* companies, however large and financially sound they may be, the decision is one to be approached with great care. Yet, in spite of its importance, the subject of corporate debt policy has received surprisingly little attention in the literature of business management. One might infer from this either that business has already developed a reliable means of resolving the question or that progress toward a more adequate solution has been slow.

In my opinion, the latter inference is closer to the truth. The debt-equity choice is still a relatively crude art as practiced by a great many corporate borrowers. It follows that there is a real opportunity for useful refinement in the decision-making process. However, there is little evidence, at present, of serious dissatisfaction with conventional decision rules on the part of those responsible for making this decision. In recent years I have been engaged in sampling executive opinions on debt policy, and I have found little indication of the same kind of ferment as is going on with regard to capital budgeting decisions.

The primary purpose of this article, therefore, is to stimulate dissatisfaction with present-day conventions regarding debt capacity and to suggest the direction in which the opportunity for improvement lies. I intend to show that the widely used rules of thumb which evaluate debt capacity in terms of some percentage of balance sheet values or in terms of income statement ratios can be seriously misleading and even dangerous to corporate solvency. I also intend to develop the argument that debt policy in general and debt capacity in particular cannot be prescribed for the individual company by outsiders or by generalized standards; rather, they can and should be determined by management in terms of individual corporate circumstances and objectives and on the basis of the observed behavior of patterns of cash flows.

The question of corporate debt capacity may be looked at from several points of view—e.g., the management of the business concerned, its shareholders or potential shareholders, and, of course, the lender of the debt capital. Because each of these groups may, quite properly, have a different concept of the wise and proper limit on debt, let me clarify the point of view taken in this article. I intend to discuss the subject from the standpoint of the management of the borrowing corporation, assuming that the board of directors which will make the final decision has the customary mandate from the stockholders to act on all matters concerning the safety and profitability of their investment. For the reader who ordinarily looks at this problem as a lender, potential stockholder, or investment adviser, the analysis described in this article may appear at first sight to have limited application. Hopefully, however, the underlying concepts will be recognized as valid regardless of how one looks at the problem, and they may suggest directions for improvement in the external as well as the internal analysis of the risk of debt.

Nature of the Risks

In order to set a background for discussing possible improvements, I will first describe briefly certain aspects of conventional practice concerning decision rules on long-term debt. These observations were recorded as a part of a research study which sampled practice and opinion in a group of relatively large and mature manufacturing corporations.[1] The nature

1. The complete findings have been published in book form; see Gordon Donaldson, *Corporate Debt Capacity* (Boston, Division of Research, Harvard Business School, 1961).

of this sample must be kept in mind when interpreting the practices described.

The nature of the incentive to borrow as an alternative to financing through a new issue of stock is common knowledge. Debt capital in the amounts normally approved by established financial institutions is a comparatively cheap source of funds. Whether it is considered the cheapest source depends on whether retained earnings are regarded as "cost free" or not. In any case, for most companies it is easy to demonstrate that, assuming normal profitability, the combination of moderate interest rates and high levels of corporate income tax enable debt capital to produce significantly better earnings per share than would a comparable amount of capital provided by an issue of either common or preferred stock. In fact, the advantage is so obvious that few companies bother to make the calculation when considering these alternatives.

Under these circumstances it is apparent that there must be a powerful deterrent which keeps businesses from utilizing this source to the limits of availability. The primary deterrent is, of course, the risks which are inevitably associated with long-term debt servicing. While it is something of an oversimplification to say that the debt decision is a balancing of higher prospective income to the shareholders against greater chance of loss, it is certainly true that this is the heart of the problem.

When the word "risk" is applied to debt, it may refer to a variety of potential penalties; the precise meaning is not always clear when this subject is discussed. To most people, however, risk—so far as debt is concerned—is the chance of running out of cash. This risk is inevitably increased by a legal contract requiring the business to pay fixed sums of cash at predetermined dates in the future regardless of the financial condition at that time. There are, of course, a great many needs for cash—dividends, capital expenditures, research projects, and so on—with respect to which cash balances may prove inadequate at some future point.

The ultimate hazard of running out of cash, however, and the one which lurks in the background of every debt decision, is the situation where cash is so reduced that legal contracts are defaulted, bankruptcy occurs, and normal operations cease. Since no private enterprise has a guaranteed cash inflow, there must always be *some* risk, however remote, that this event could occur. Consequently, any addition to mandatory cash outflows resulting from new debt or any other act or event must increase that risk.

I have chosen to use the term "cash inadequacy" to refer to a whole family of problems involving the inability to make cash payments for any purpose important to the long-term financial health of the business; "cash insolvency" is the extreme case of cash inadequacy. It should be emphasized that although debt necessarily increases the chances of cash inadequacy, this risk exists whether the company has any debt or not, so that the debt-equity choice is not between some risk and no risk, but between more and less.

Conventional Approaches

Observation of present-day business practice suggests that businessmen commonly draw their concepts of debt capacity from one or more of several sources. Thus, they sometimes—

1. *Seek the counsel of institutional lenders or financial intermediaries (such as investment bankers)*—Most corporate borrowers negotiate long-term debt contracts at infrequent intervals, while the lender and the investment banker are constantly involved in loan decisions and so, presumably, have a great deal more experience and better judgment. Further, it is apparent that unless the lender is satisfied on the question of risk, there will be no loan. Finally, banks and insurance companies have a well-established reputation for being conservative, and conservative borrowers will take comfort from the fact that if the lender errs, it will likely be on the safe side.

2. *See what comparable companies are doing in this area of financial management*—Every business has an idea of those other companies in or out of the industry which are most like themselves so far as factors affecting risk are concerned. Since this is an aspect of corporate policy which is public information, it is natural that the debt-equity ratios of competitors will be carefully considered, and, lacking more objective guides, there will be a tendency to follow the mode and reject the extremes. This approach has an added practical appeal; group norms are important in the capital market's appraisal of a company's financial strength. If a company is out of line, it may be penalized—even though the deviation from the average may be perfectly appropriate for this company.

3. *Follow the practices of the past*—There is a very natural tendency to respect the corporation's financial traditions, and this is often apparent with regard to debt policy. Many businesses take considerable pride in "a clean balance sheet," an *Aa* rating, or a history of borrowing at the prime rate. It would border on sacrilege to propose a departure which would jeopardize these cherished symbols of financial achievement and respecta-

bility! The fact that these standards have apparently preserved corporate solvency in the past is a powerful argument for continuing them, particularly if the implications of a change cannot be precisely defined.

4. *Refer to that very elusive authority called "general practice," "industry practice," "common knowledge," or, less respectfully, "financial folklore"* —Remarkable as it seems in view of the great diversity among companies classified as industrials, there is widespread acceptance of the belief that an appropriate limit to the long-term borrowing of industrial companies is 30% of capitalization (or, alternatively, one third). The origin of, or rationale for, this particular decision rule has been obscured by the passage of time, but there is no doubt that it has become a widely honored rule of thumb in the decisions of both borrowers and lenders.

FALLACY OF DOUBLE STANDARD

Without denying the practical significance of some of the considerations which have led businessmen to follow these guides in formulating debt policy, it must be recognized that there are serious limitations inherent in using them (separately or as a group) as the *only* guides to appropriate debt capacity.

First, consider the practice of accepting advice from the lender. As the lender views the individual loan contract, it is one of a large number of investments which make up a constantly changing portfolio. When negotiated it is only one of a stream of loan proposals which must be acted on promptly and appraised in terms of the limited information to which generalized standards are applied. The nature of the risk to the lender is necessarily influenced by the fact that this loan is only a small fraction of the total sum invested and that intelligent diversification goes a long way to softening the impact of individual default. Further, even when default occurs, all may not be lost; in time the loan may be "worked out" through reorganization or liquidation.

All this is small comfort to the borrower. The individual loan which goes sour—if it happens to be *his* loan—is a catastrophe. There are few businessmen who can take a lighthearted attitude toward the prospect of default on a legal contract with the associated threat of bankruptcy. To most, this is viewed as the end of the road. Also, it is important to recognize that while the lender need only be concerned about servicing his own (high priority) claims, the borrower must also consider the needs which go unsatisfied during the period prior to the time of actual default when debt servicing drains off precious cash reserves.

This is not to imply that the lender is insensitive to individual losses and their effect on the business concerned; but it does mean that risk to the lender is not the same thing as risk to the borrower, and, consequently, the standards of one are not necessarily appropriate for the other. The lender's standards can at times be too liberal—as well as too conservative—from the borrower's point of view. Some will argue that, as a practical matter, the borrower must accept the debt-capacity standards of the lender, else there will be no contract. However, this implies that there is no bargaining over the upper limit of the amount that will be supplied, no differences among lenders, and/or no shopping around by borrowers. While all institutional lenders do have absolute limits on the risks they will take (even at a premium interest rate), there is often some room for negotiation if the borrower is so disposed. Under some circumstances there may be valid reasons for probing the upper limits of the lender's willingness to lend.

LESSONS OF EXPERIENCE

The second source of guidance mentioned is the observed practices of comparable businesses. This, too, has its obvious limitations. Even assuming strict comparability—which is hard to establish—there is no proof that the companies concerned have arrived at their current debt proportions in a deliberate and rational manner. In view of the wide variations in debt policy within any industry group, there can be little real meaning in an industry average. And what happens if every member of the group looks to the other for guidance? The most that can be said for this approach to debt policy is that the company concerned can avoid the appearance of being atypical in the investment market so far as its capital structure is concerned. But, as in most areas of business, there is a *range* of acceptable behavior, and the skill of management comes in identifying and taking advantage of the limits to which it can go without raising too many eyebrows.

Even a company's own direct experience with debt financing has its limitations as a guide to debt capacity. At best, the evidence that a particular debt policy has not been a cause of financial embarrassment in the past may only prove that the policy was on the conservative side. However, if assurance of adequate conservatism is the primary goal, the only really satisfactory policy is a no-debt policy.

For companies with some debt the experience of past periods of business recession is only partial evidence of the protection a particular policy affords. In most industries, the period of the past 20 years has produced a maximum of four or five periods of decline in sales and earnings. This limited recession experience with the behavior of cash flows—the critical consideration where debt servicing is involved—can be misleading since cash flows are affected by a variety of factors and the actual experience in any single recession is a somewhat unique combination of events which may not recur in the future. Thus, the so-called test of experience cannot be taken at face value.

INESCAPABLE RESPONSIBILITY

In summing up a criticism of the sources from which management commonly derives its debt-capacity standard, there are two aspects which must be emphasized. Both of these relate to the practice of relying on the judgment of others in a situation where management alone is best able to appraise the full implications of the problem. The points I have in mind are as follows:

1. In assessing the risks of running out of cash because of excessive fixed cash obligations, the special circumstances of the individual firm are the primary data that the analyst has to work with. Management has obvious advantages over outsiders in using this data because it has free and full access to it, the time and incentive to examine it thoroughly, and a personal stake in making sensible judgments about what it observes. Even the judgments of predecessors in office are judgments made on information which is inadequate when compared to what management now has in its possession—if only because the predecessor's information is now 10 or 20 years old. (Subsequently, we will consider how management may approach an independent appraisal of risk for the individual business.)

2. The measurement of risk is only one dimension of the debt-capacity decision. In a free enterprise society, the assumption of risk is a voluntary activity, and no one can properly define the level of risk which another should be willing to bear. The decision to limit debt to 10%, 30% or any other percentage of the capital structure reflects (or should reflect) both the magnitude of the risk involved in servicing that amount of debt *and* the willingness of those who bear this risk—the owners or their duly authorized representatives—to accept the hazards involved.

In the last analysis, this is a subjective decision which management alone can make. Indeed, it may be said that a corporation has defined its debt policy long before a particular financing decision comes to a vote; it has done this in its choice of the men who are to make the decision. The ensuing decisions involving financial risk will reflect their basic attitudes— whether they see a situation as an opportunity to be exploited or a threat to be minimized.

A most interesting and fundamental question comes up here—one that underlies the whole relationship between management and the shareholder; namely, does management determine the attitude toward risk bearing which the stockholders must then adopt, or vice versa? This is part of the broader question of whether management should choose those financial policies which it prefers and attract a like-minded stockholder group (taking the "if they don't like it, they can sell out" approach) or by some means or other determine the attitudes and objectives of its present stockholder group and attempt to translate these into the appropriate action.

I do not propose to pass judgment on this difficult problem in the context of this article. The fact is, by taking one approach or the other—or some blend—management *does* make these decisions. With respect to risk bearing, however, one point is clear: responsible management should not be dealing with the problem in terms of purely personal risk preferences. I suspect that many top executives have not given this aspect the attention it deserves.

REASONS FOR CURRENT PRACTICE

Having considered the case for a debt policy which is internally rather than externally generated, we may well ask why so many companies, in deciding how far to go in using O.P.M. (other people's money), lean so heavily on O.P.A. (other people's advice). The answer appears to be threefold:

1. A misunderstanding of the nature of the problem and, in particular, a failure to separate the subjective from the objective elements.

2. The inherent complexity of the objective side—the measurement of risk.

3. The serious inadequacy of conventional debt-capacity decision rules as a framework for independent appraisal.

It is obvious that if a business does not have a useful way of assessing the general magnitude of the risks of too much debt in terms of its individual company and industry circumstances, then it will do one of two things. Either it will fall back on generalized (external) concepts of risk for "comparable" companies, or it will make the decision on purely subjective grounds—on how the management "feels" about debt. Thus, in practice, an internally generated debt-capacity decision is often based almost entirely on the management's general attitude toward this kind of problem without regard for how much risk is actually involved and what the potential rewards and penalties from risk bearing happen to be in the specific situation. The most obvious examples are to be found in companies at the extremes of debt policy that follow such rules as "no debt under any circumstances" or "borrow the maximum available." (We must be careful, however, not to assume that if a company has one or another of these policies, it is acting irrationally or emotionally.)

One of the subjects about which we know very little at present is how individual and group attitudes toward risk bearing are formed in practice. It is apparent, however, that there are important differences in this respect among members of any given management team and even for an individual executive with regard to different dimensions of risk within the business. The risk of excessive debt often appears to have a special significance; a man who is a "plunger" on sales policy or research might also be an arch-conservative with regard to debt. The risk of default on debt is more directly associated with financial ruin, regardless of the fundamental cause of failure, simply because it is generally the last act in a chain of events which follows from a deteriorating cash position.

There are other bits of evidence which are possible explanations for a Jekyll-and-Hyde behavior on risk bearing in business:

☐ Debt policy is always decided at the very top of the executive structure whereas other policies on sales or production involving other dimensions of risk are shaped to some degree at all executive levels. The seniority of the typical board of directors doubtless has some bearing on the comparative conservatism of financial policy, including debt policy.

☐ There is also some truth in the generalization that financial officers tend to be more conservative than other executives at the same level in other phases of the business, and to the extent that they influence debt policy they may tend to prefer to minimize risk per se, regardless of the potential rewards from risk bearing.

WHAT IS A SENSIBLE APPROACH?

The foregoing is, however, only speculation in an area where real research is necessary. The point of importance here is that, whatever the reason may be, it is illogical to base an internal decision on debt policy on attitudes toward risk *alone*, just as it is illogical to believe that corporate debt policy can be properly formulated without taking these individual attitudes into account.

For the purposes of a sensible approach to corporate debt policy we need not expect management to have a logical explanation for its feelings toward debt, even though this might be theoretically desirable. It is sufficient that managers know how they feel and are able to react to specific risk alternatives. The problem has been that in many cases they have not known in any objective sense what it was that they were reacting to; they have not had a meaningful measure of the specific risk of running out of cash (with or without any given amount of long-term debt).

It is therefore in the formulation of an approach to the measurement of risk in the individual corporation that the hope for an independent appraisal of debt capacity lies.

Inadequacy of Current Rules

Unfortunately, the conventional form for expressing debt-capacity rules is of little or no help in providing the kind of formulation I am urging. Debt capacity is most commonly expressed in terms of the balance sheet relationship between long-term debt and the total of all long-term sources, viz., as some per cent of capitalization. A variation of this ratio is often found in debt contracts which limit new long-term borrowing to some percentage of net tangible assets.

The alternative form in which to express the limits of long-term borrowing is in terms of income statement data. This is the *earnings coverage ratio*—the ratio of net income available for debt servicing to the total amount of annual interest plus sinking fund charges. Under such a rule, no new long-term debt would be contemplated unless the net income available for debt servicing is equal to or in excess of some multiple of the debt servicing charges—say, three to one—so that the company can survive a period of decline in sales and earnings and still have enough earnings to cover the fixed charges of debt. As we will see shortly, this ratio is more meaningful for internal formation of policy but also has its limitations.

Now, let us go on to examine each type of expression more closely.

CAPITALIZATION STANDARD

Consider a company which wishes to formulate its own debt standard as a per cent of capitalization. It is apparent that in order to do so the standard must be expressed in terms of data which can be related to the magnitude of the risk in such a way that changes in the ratio can be translated into changes in the risk of cash inadequacy, and vice versa. But how many executives concerned with this problem today have any real idea of how much the risk of cash inadequacy is increased when the long-term debt of their company is increased from 10% to 20% or from 20% to 30% of capitalization? Not very many, if my sample of management information in this area has any validity. This is not surprising, however, since the balance sheet data on which the standard is based provide little direct evidence on the question of cash adequacy and may, in fact, be highly unreliable and misleading.

While we do not need to go into a full discussion here of the inadequacies of relating the principal amount of long-term debt to historical asset values as a way of looking at the chances of running out of cash, we should keep in mind the more obvious weaknesses:

1. There is a wide variation in the relation between the principal of the debt and the annual obligation for cash payments under the debt contract. In industrial companies the principal of the debt may be repaid serially over the life of the debt contract, which may vary from 10 years or less to 30 years or more. Thus, the annual cash outflow associated with $10 million on the balance sheet may, for example, vary from $500,000 (interest only at 5%) to $833,000 (interest plus principal repayable over 30 years) to $1,500,000 (interest plus principal repayable over 10 years).

2. As loans are repaid by partial annual payments, as is customary under industrial term loans, the principal amount declines and the per-cent-of-capitalization ratio improves, but the annual cash drain for repayment *remains the same* until maturity is reached.

3. There may be substantial changes in asset values, particularly in connection with inventory valuation and depreciation policies, and as a consequence, changes in the per-cent-of-capitalization ratio which have no bearing on the capacity to meet fixed cash drains.

4. Certain off-the-balance-sheet factors have an important bearing on cash flows which the conventional ratio takes no cognizance of. One factor of this sort which has been receiving publicity in recent years is the payments under leasing arrangements. (While various authorities have been urging that lease payments be given formal recognition as a liability on balance sheets and in debt-capacity calculations, there is no general agreement as to how this should be done. For one thing, there is no obvious answer as to what the capitalization rate should be in order to translate lease payments into balance sheet values. In my opinion this debate is bound to be an artificial and frustrating experience—and unnecessary for the internal analyst—since, as will be discussed later, it is much more meaningful to deal with leases, as with debt, in terms of the dollars of annual cash outflow rather than in terms of principal amounts. Thus, a footnoting of the annual payments under the lease is entirely adequate.)

EARNINGS-COVERAGE STANDARD

The earnings-coverage standard affords, on the surface at least, a better prospect of measuring risk in the individual company in terms of the factors which bear directly on cash adequacy. By relating the total annual cash outflow under all long-term debt contracts to the net earnings available for servicing the debt, it is intended to assure that earnings will be adequate to meet charges at all times. This approach implies that the greater the prospective fluctuation in earnings, the higher is the required ratio (or the larger the "cushion" between normal earnings and debt-servicing charges).

This standard also has limitations as a basis for internal determination of debt capacity:

1. The net earnings figure found in the income statement and derived under normal accounting procedures is *not* the same thing as net cash inflow—an assumption which is implicit in the earnings-coverage standard. Even when adjustments are made for the noncash items on the income statement (depreciation charges), as is commonly done in the more sophisticated applications, this equivalence cannot safely be assumed. The

time when it may be roughly true is the time when we are least concerned about the hazards of debt, i.e., when sales are approximately the same from period to period. It is in times of rapid change (including recessions) that we are most concerned about debt burden, and then there *are* likely to be sharp differences between net income and net cash flow.

2. The question of what the *proper* ratio is between earnings and debt servicing is problematical. In a given case should the ratio be two to one or twenty to one? If we exclude externally derived standards or rules of thumb and insist that a company generate its own ratio in terms of its own circumstances, how does it go about doing it? Perhaps the best that could be done would be to work backward from the data of past recessions, which would indicate the low points of net earnings, toward a ratio between this experience and some measure of "normal" earnings with the intention of assuring a one-to-one relationship between net earnings and debt servicing at all times. However, if this is the way it is to be done, the estimate of minimum net earnings would itself provide the measure of debt capacity, and it would be unnecessary to translate it into a ratio. Further, as already noted, there are hazards in a literal translation of past history as a guide for the future. And what of the case where the company has experienced net losses in the past? Does this mean that it has no long-term debt capacity? If a net loss is possible, *no* ratio between normal net earnings and debt servicing, however large, will assure the desired equality in future recessions.

The earnings-coverage standard does not appear to be widely used by industrial corporate borrowers as a basis for formulating debt policy. Where it is used, it appears either to derive from the advice of institutional lenders or investment bankers or merely to reflect the borrower's attitude toward risk bearing. Its use does not seem to indicate an attempt to measure individual risk by some objective means.

A More Useful Approach

Granted the apparent inadequacies of conventional debt-capacity decision rules for purposes of internal debt policy, is there a practical alternative? I believe there is, but it must be recognized immediately that it rests on data which are substantially more complex than what the conventional rules require, and involve a considerably larger expenditure of time and effort to obtain and interpret. However, in view of the unquestioned importance of the debt-equity decision to the future of individual businesses, and in view of the fact that, as will be shown later, the data have a usefulness which goes well beyond the debt-capacity decision, there is reason to give this alternative serious consideration.

The basic questions in the appraisal of the magnitude of risk associated with long-term debt can be stated with deceptive simplicity: What are the chances of the business running out of cash in the foreseeable future? How are these chances changed by the addition of X thousands of dollars o⸳ annual interest and sinking fund payments? First, it is necessary to specify whether our concern is with "running out of cash" in an absolute sense (cash insolvency) or merely with the risk of cash inadequacy, i.e., running out of cash for certain purposes considered essential to management (for example, a minimum dividend on common stock). We can consider both of these possibilities, but let us focus for the moment on the ultimate hazard, the one commonly associated with excessive debt—the chance of complete depletion of cash reserves resulting in default on the bond contract and bankruptcy.

There are, of course, a variety of possible circumstances under which a company might have its cash reserves drained off. However, considering the problem from the point of view of mature, normally profitable, and reasonably well-managed companies, it is fair to say that the primary concern with debt is with what might happen during a general or industry recession when sales and profits are depressed by factors beyond the immediate control of management. Thus, when the experienced business executive wishes to instill the proper respect for the hazards of too much debt in the minds of aggressive young men eager for leverage, he will recount harrowing tales of disaster and near-disaster in the early 1930's.

REFOCUSING ON PROBLEM

The data we seek are information on the behavior of cash flows during the recession periods. An internal analysis of risk must therefore concern itself not with balance sheet or income statement ratios but directly with the factors which make for changes in cash inflow and outflow. Further, since we are dealing with the common denominator of all transactions, analysis must inevitably take into account *all* major influences on cash flow behavior. In short, the problem is a company-wide problem. All decisions involving cash should be included, and where cash solvency is at stake, there can be no meaningful boundaries on risk except those imposed by the corporate entity itself.

Therefore, it is somewhat artificial to think in terms of "the cash available for debt servicing," as the earnings-coverage standard does, as if it were an identifiable hoard when a number of needs equally as urgent are competing for a limited cash reserve. Consequently, the problem to which this article was originally addressed—determining the capacity to bear the incremental fixed charges of long-term debt—is in reality a much more general one: viz., the problem of *determining the capacity to bear incremental fixed cash outflows for any purpose whatever.*

ASSESSING KEY FACTORS

The analysis which is proposed in this article as a way of resolving this problem can only be briefly summarized here. It includes:

1. *Identification*—At the outset, it is important to identify the primary factors which produce major changes in cash flow with particular reference to contractions in cash flow. The most significant factor will be sales volume; many of the other factors will be related in greater or lesser degree to sales. However, to cite the example of another major factor, cash expenditures for raw materials, the relationship to sales volume in a down-swing is not at all an automatic one since it also depends on:

◻ The volume of finished-goods inventory on hand at the onset of the recession.

◻ The working relationship between finished goods on hand, work scheduled into production, and raw-materials ordering.

◻ The level of raw-materials inventory.

◻ The responses of management at all levels to the observed change in sales.

For most factors affecting cash flow there will be a degree of interdependence and also a range of independent variation, both of which must be identified for the purpose of the analysis.

2. *Extent of refinement desired*—Obviously the list of factors affecting cash flow which are to be given separate consideration could be lengthy depending on the degree of refinement desired; and the longer the list, the greater the complexity of the analysis. It is therefore essential to form a judgment in advance as to how far refinement in the analysis can or should be carried in view of the objectives of the analysis. It is possible for this cash flow analysis to range all the way from simple and relatively crude approximations to the other extreme of involved mathematical and statistical formulas and even to the programming of recession cash flows on a computer.

In their simplest form, cash flows can be considered in terms of accounting approximations derived from balance sheet and income statement data. Thus, for example, sales revenues might be adjusted for changes in accounts receivable to derive current cash inflow, and cost of goods sold could be converted into expenditures for goods actually produced by adjusting for changes in inventory levels. However, the hazard of simplification is that important changes may be obscured by combining factors that at one time may "net each other out" and at some other time may reinforce each other. For instance, changes in dollar sales are produced by changes in product mix, physical volume, and price.

Here is where the internal analyst has a major advantage. Experience tells him what factors should be given separate treatment, and he has access to the data behind the financial statements so he can carry refinement as far as he wishes. Ideally, the analysis should be in terms of cash and not accrual accounting information; that is, it should be in terms of cash receipts (not dollar sales) and cash expenditures for raw materials received (not an accounting allocation for raw materials according to the number of units sold).

3. *Analysis of behavior*—Given a list of all major factors affecting cash flow, the next step is to observe their *individual* behavior over time and in particular during recessions. The objection raised earlier to using historical evidence as a guide to debt capacity was that, as usually employed, it is an observation of the *net* effect of change in all these factors on particular occasions—an effect which can be seriously misleading. But if management takes the individual behavior of these factors into account, the problem is minimized to a point where it can be disregarded.

Past experience in a company with an established position in its industry commonly leads its management to the sensible conclusion that, while it is theoretically possible for the physical volume of sales, for example, to contract to zero in a recession period, in practice there are reasons why this is highly unlikely to occur. These reasons relate to fundamental and enduring forces in the economy, the industry, the competitive position of the firm, consumer buying habits, and so on. Thus, past experience will suggest a range of recession behavior which describes the outside limits of what recession can be expected to do in the future. These limits I wish to refer to as the *maximum favorable limit* and the *maximum adverse limit* (referring to the effect on cash flows and the cash position). By combining the evidence contained in historical records and the judgment of management directly involved in the making of this history, we can describe these limits of expected behavior for all factors affecting cash flow. It will be part of our analysis to do so, taking careful account of interdependent variation for reasons given earlier.

4. *Expected range of recession behavior*—On the basis of such informed observation it may be concluded, for example, that the recession contraction in physical volume of sales is not expected to be less than 5% nor more than 25% of the sales of the period immediately preceding the recession. These are the maximum favorable and maximum adverse limits of sales for the company in question. It may also be concluded that the recession is not expected to last less than one year nor more than three years and that no more than 40% of the contraction will be concentrated in the first year of the recession. Naturally, our interest focuses on the maximum *adverse* limit, since we are attempting to assess the chances of running out of cash. By setting such boundaries on the adverse recession behavior of a major factor influencing cash flows we are beginning to set similar boundaries on the recession behavior of the cash flows themselves.

At this point a question presents itself which has major implications for the subsequent character of the analysis: Is it possible to say anything meaningful about the behavior of sales volume or any other factor *within* the limits that have just been described?

Probability Analysis

It is possible that there may be some historical evidence in the company on the comparative chances or probabilities of occurrence of sales contractions of, say 5%-11%, 12%-18%, 19%-25% (or any other breakdown of the range), but the statistical data are likely to be sketchy. It is perhaps more likely that management might, on the basis of experience, make some judgments such as, for example, that the contraction is most likely— say, five chances out of ten—to fall in the 12%-18% range; that the chances of its falling in the 5%-11% range are three chances out of ten; and that the chances of falling in the 19%-25% range are two chances out of ten.

If this kind of information can be generated for all factors affecting cash flow, then it is possible to come up with a range of estimates of the cash flow in future recession periods based on all possible combinations of the several factors, and for each estimate a numerical measure of its probability of occurrence. The whole set collectively will describe all anticipated possibilities. By totaling the separate probabilities of those combinations of events exhausting the initial cash balance, we can describe in quantitative terms the over-all chances of cash insolvency. Ideally we want to know that the chances of cash insolvency, as described by this process of analysis of cash flows are, say, one in twenty or one in fifty.

PROBLEMS TO SURMOUNT

However, in order to get such a precise measure of the risk of cash insolvency, we need estimates of probability that are within the expected range of behavior and not just the limits of behavior. There are important practical problems that stand in the way of obtaining this type of information and conducting this type of analysis:

☐ Although the analysis suggested above appears relatively simple, in practice it could be quite complex, requiring the guidance of someone experienced in probability theory as well as in financial analysis to steer the study of cash flows around potential pitfalls. The problems center mainly on (1) accurately describing the patterns of adjustment over time, and (2) assessing the varying degrees of interdependence among the variables. These difficulties are not insurmountable, however, since statisticians have resolved similar ones in the case of other types of business problems.

☐ Past recession periods may not have provided enough experience with respect to the behavior of sales, collections, inventory levels, and so forth, on which to base firm estimates of probabilities over the entire range of possible behavior. Some companies have had only two or three recessions in the past 20 years, and even then sometimes statistics are lacking (although presumably management will have some impressions about the events). But *some* experience with varying recession circumstances is essential even to make a guess. Speaking generally, this limitation on a comprehensive appraisal of the risk magnitude is far more serious than the one of technical competence mentioned first.

□ Top management will not base critical decisions, such as debt policy, on data which it does not understand and/or in which it does not have confidence. This, I believe, is the primary obstacle which stands in the way of widespread use of a comprehensive cash flow analysis as a basis for risk measurement and the determination of debt capacity at the present time. Because the method is complex (particularly in contrast to the customary rules of thumb) and because the judgments on probabilities and other aspects of the analysis may appear—and may in fact be—tenuous, management may well be unwilling to use the results, particularly when corporate solvency is at stake.

However, when all this is said, the fact remains that much of present-day practice is seriously inadequate, and there is an urgent need for a more meaningful approach to the problem, particularly so far as the borrower is concerned. Thus, there is a strong incentive to explore the opportunities for partial or approximate measures of the risk of cash insolvency within the general framework suggested by the comprehensive analysis. One such approach is that to be described. Its aim is to produce an indicator of risk magnitude which can be derived from more conventional and less complex data in which management has confidence.

ANALYSIS OF ADVERSE LIMITS

The new approach focuses on the expected *limits* of recession behavior and in particular on the maximum adverse limit. It is based on the assumption that while management may be unable to assess with confidence the probabilities within the range, it usually has strong opinions as to the expected limits and would be prepared to base decisions upon such expectations. Thus, to return to the example of the sales contraction, management may be unwilling to assign the "betting odds" to the three intervals between a 5% and a 25% contraction, but it probably does have strong feelings that 25% is the "absolute" limit of adversity within the foreseeable future. This feeling is based not merely on past statistics but on an expert appraisal of all the facts surrounding the customer's buying habits and circumstances, the competitive situation, and so on.

Following this procedure leads to a set of estimates of the maximum adverse limit of recession behavior covering each factor affecting cash flow, and it is a comparatively simple matter then to come up with an estimate of the maximum adverse behavior in any future recession of net cash flow itself—in terms of the minimum dollars of net inflow (or maximum dollars of net outflow), period by period. Making similar judgments as to the maximum adverse conditions immediately preceding the recession —including prerecession cash balances—it is next possible to determine whether, under such maximum assumptions, the company would become insolvent and, if so, how soon and by how much.

This calculation in itself will give management some "feel" for the nearness or remoteness of the event of cash insolvency. It may demonstrate, as I have done in the case of certain companies, that even under these maximum adverse assumptions the company still has a positive cash balance. If this is so, the amount of this minimum balance is an objective judgment of the total amount of incremental fixed cash charges which the company could assume without *any* threat of insolvency. Making some assumptions about the nature and the terms of the debt contract, this figure could be converted into the principal amount of additional debt which could be assumed with the expectation of complete safety.

Suppose, on the other hand, that the maximum adverse assumptions produce a negative cash balance, indicating the possibility of insolvency under certain adverse conditions. This does not mean that the long-term debt is excluded (except for those managements for whom any action which creates or increases the risk of insolvency, no matter how small it may be, is intolerable). The more likely response will be that, provided the chances are "sufficiently remote," the company is fully prepared to run the risk.

Thus, we are back to the problem of assessing the magnitude of the risk and the extent to which it would be increased by any given amount of debt. As a means of gaining a more precise impression of the chances of insolvency at the adverse end of the range of recession behavior, without going through the formal process of assigning probability values, I suggest that a second adverse limit be defined for each of the factors affecting cash flow. This will be called the *most probable adverse limit*. It reflects management's judgment as to the limit of *normal* recession behavior, as opposed to the maximum adverse limit, which includes all possibilities, however remote.

MODES AND RANGES

A visual representation of these two adverse limits of behavior is shown in *Exhibit I*. Assuming experience and expected behavior are somewhat

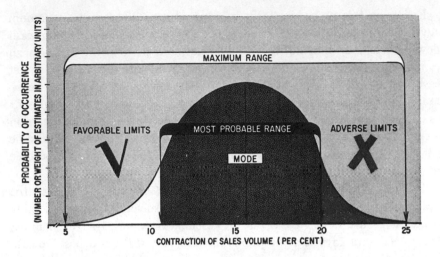

normally distributed about a mode (i.e., the value of most frequent occurrence), there will be:

1. A range of values clustered around this point, where most of past experience has been concentrated and where "bets" as to what the future is likely to bring will also be concentrated.

2. Extremes at either end of the range representing events that have a relatively small chance of happening.

It will be seen that the most probable limit cuts off the extreme "tail" of the frequency distribution in a somewhat imprecise and yet meaningful way. In setting the limits of expected sales contractions, for example, management would be saying that while sales *could*, in its judgment, contract as much as 25%, a contraction is *not likely* to exceed, say, 20%. This 20% is then the most probable adverse limit. While my terms may be new to businessmen, the distinction described is one which is commonly made and one on which judgments as to risk are often based.

From the data on the most probable adverse limits of the various factors affecting cash flow, the most probable adverse limit of recession *net* cash flows would be calculated and, from this, the most probable minimum recession cash *balance*. This last figure reflects management's best judgment as to the adverse limit of what is "likely to happen" as opposed to what "could happen" to net cash flows.

GUIDELINES FOR POLICY

At this point it should be noted that, when considering cash flows from the point of view of solvency, the list of possible expenditures would be stripped down to those which are absolutely essential for continuity of corporate existence and for the generation of current income. (We will presently bring into consideration other less mandatory expenditures such as dividends and capital expenditures.) Thinking in these terms, suppose the recession cash flow analysis indicates that under the maximum adverse assumptions the minimum cash balance would be negative, say, a deficit of $1,500,000. Suppose further that under the most probable adverse assumptions the minimum recession cash balance is a surplus of $3,000,000. How are these estimates to be interpreted as a guide to corporate debt capacity?

First, it is obvious in this example that management's expectations about the factors governing cash flow include the possibility that the company could become insolvent without any additional debt. However, this possibility is considered to have a relatively remote chance of occurrence since when the analysis is restricted to the most probable limit of recession behavior, the company is left with a positive minimum cash balance. The amount of this balance is a rough measure of the *total amount of additional fixed cash outflows (e.g., debt charges) which could be incurred without creating the threat of insolvency* in the event of normal recession conditions. Thus:

If the likely limit of the recession is expected to be two years, the company could stand additional debt servicing of $1,500,000 per year of recession. This sum can be readily converted into an equivalent principal amount. Assuming a 20-year term loan repayable in equal annual installments and bearing 5% interest, an additional debt of approximately $15,000,000 could be considered safe under ordinary recession conditions.

Let me emphasize that the cash balance would not be taken as a guide to debt capacity unless management were prepared to live with some chance of insolvency—a chance which would obviously be increased by the new debt. If management were not so inclined, it would reject debt or alternatively adopt a debt limit somewhere between zero and $15,000,000. In any case, management would not increase debt *beyond* $15,000,000 unless it were prepared to accept the chance of insolvency within the most probable range of recession experience. Because of the way the most probable limit has been defined, the chances of insolvency would be expected to increase rapidly and substantially if debt were to exceed $15,000,000 by any significant amount.

There is, of course, nothing sacred about the $15,000,000 limit set by management's judgment on the limits of normal recession experience. There is no reason why some managements would not increase debt capital substantially above this figure, assuming the funds were available. Such a step depends entirely on the willingness to bear the financial risks and on the potential rewards for such risk bearing. The foregoing type of analysis does, however, perform the essential function of alerting management to the range of debt beyond which risks may be expected to increase substantially.

PRACTICAL ADVANTAGES

It is now apparent that the analytical approach proposed here produces a criterion stated in terms of *the number of dollars of debt servicing* that are acceptable within management's concepts of risk bearing at a given point in time. The criterion is derived entirely from within and is completely independent of external judgments or rules of thumb. While it is admittedly crude and approximate when compared with the theoretical ideal of risk management, I believe it to be meaningful and useful in practice and, in this as in other respects, superior to the conventional forms for expressing debt limits.

It must be added, however, that because the recommended analysis is partial and approximate, those who adopt it must use it as they use current decision rules. That is, they must use it as a general guide and not as a precision instrument. For most managements this will be entirely adequate.

Better Decision Making

One of the real advantages of this approach to debt capacity is that it raises—and answers—a much broader question. As previously indicated, the analysis is actually concerned with the capacity to assume additional fixed cash outflows of any kind, and whatever capacity is demonstrated is not confined to debt servicing. Thus, if it is concluded from the example just given that the company in question can stand an additional outflow in recessions totaling $3,000,000, the first decision to be made by management is *how to use this capacity*.

There are a variety of ways in which the capacity may be used: to cover payments under a lease contract, to maintain a continuous research program, to stabilize employment, to pay a regular dividend in good times and bad, and so on. These are all competing uses for whatever capacity exists. With the information that the cash flow analysis provides, management now can begin to assign priorities and have some idea of how far it can hope to go in realizing its objectives. If debt servicing is given top priority, then the data have been a means of defining debt capacity.

It is because the proposed analysis has much broader significance than the question of debt (important as that question may be) that I believe the expenditure of time, effort, and money required to generate the data needed is well justified for the individual corporation. The analysis provides information which lies at the base of a whole range of financial and other decisions and has continuing significance. Moreover, most corporate treasurers have the staff and the basic data to undertake a careful and detailed study of the behavior of factors affecting cash flow.

TESTING FOR CASH ADEQUACY

Up to this point the analysis of cash flows has been discussed in terms of cash solvency. As indicated earlier, this means that attention is confined to outflows which are vital to survival. It was also indicated, however, that the risk of insolvency was part of a broader family of risks, described as the risk of cash inadequacy. In discussing the question of solvency with management we often find that while there are certain expenditures which *could* be slashed to zero in an emergency, there is a reluctance to take action which would put management in a position of having to do so. These are expenditures which must be treated as mandatory for policy reasons, because management believes that to interrupt them would be detrimental to the long-term interest of the corporation. Among the best examples of such expenditures are certain minimum payments for research, for capital assets, and for preferred and common dividends.

This situation can readily be incorporated into the type of analysis outlined earlier. I refer to the method for doing this as the *test for cash adequacy* as opposed to the test for cash solvency. As soon as management has defined the "irreducible minimum" for these expenditures under recession conditions, they are merely added to the outflows of the previous analysis; then the figure generated for the maximum adverse or most probable adverse recession cash balance is the balance which remains over and above such payments. To return to the example previously used:

The effect would be to wipe out all or some portion of the most probable minimum balance ($3,000,000) or to add to the maximum adverse deficit ($1,500,000). Thus, if the irreducible minimum is considered to be two years of common dividends at $500,000 a year plus $1,000,000 of minimum capital expenditures, the result would be to cut the most probable balance back to $1,000,000. The capacity to assume additional fixed cash outflows is thereby substantially reduced. Obviously management in this case is giving priority to the dividend and capital expenditures over debt leverage —or over any other use for the funds on hand.

One of the benefits of such an analysis is to make management's priorities explicit, to recognize their competing character, and to make possible a re-evaluation of their relative importance to the company.

Making separate tests for cash solvency and cash adequacy serves another important purpose. Most discussions of the hazards of debt imply that the danger is the risk of insolvency, and this danger is usually treated with proper respect. However, our analysis may demonstrate that within the range of management's expectations there is little or no risk of insolvency but a substantial risk of cash inadequacy, particularly if large amounts of long-term debt are added. If, in the past, management has been setting limits on debt in terms of an assumed risk of insolvency and now finds that the only significant risk is that of inability to meet certain minimum dividend payments and the like, it may well be disposed to assume a greater magnitude of risk and take on more debt. A management which would reject the risk of insolvency if it exceeded a chance of one in fifty might be prepared to accept a risk of abandoning cash dividends for a year or two if the chance did not exceed, say, one in twenty.

In short, once management knows the *kind* of risk it is taking, it may begin to draw distinctions between one form of contingency and another and not operate on the general assumption that the only concern is that of possible insolvency. Better information is thus a prerequisite for better decisions.

REAPPRAISING PRESENT RULES

Assuming management can, by the means described, come up with an independent appraisal of its long-term debt capacity, what does this imply for existing decision rules obtained from external sources or inherited from the past? Does it mean that they will be ignored completely? The answer is likely to be no. Debt policy cannot be made in a vacuum. It must take account of the lenders' willingness to lend and also of the reactions of equity investors who make judgments on the risks inherent in the corporation.

One of the first results of the analysis, therefore, is to reappraise existing debt-capacity decision rules. To illustrate:

Suppose a company has been assuming, as many do, that it can safely incur long-term debt up to a maximum of 30% of capitalization. This rule can be translated into its equivalent of dollars of annual debt-servicing charges and directly compared with the results of the recession cash flow analysis. In view of the fact that the rule probably has been derived from external sources, it is likely that the annual debt servicing which it permits either exceeds or falls short of the amount of cash flow indicated by the internal analysis.

In view of the approximate nature of the analysis, however, this is not likely to cause a change in debt policy unless the amount of the variation is substantial. It is also possible, of course, that the existing decision rule and the cash flow analysis will produce the same result—in which case the existing rule will appear verified. But this cannot be known in advance of the analysis, and in any case the data have been converted into a form which is much more meaningful for the purposes involved.

Such a comparison gives a measure of management's attitude toward the risk that is implicit in the existing decision rule (although management probably had no clear idea of what the risk magnitude was at the time the rule was established).

The results of the cash flow analysis can also be compared with the lender's concept of debt capacity—if different from that of the corporation. While lenders are often reluctant to make statements on the outside limits of what they will lend, they will, from time to time, give indications of what they consider an appropriate capital structure for a given industry and company. If the borrower's appraisal of his capacity exceeds that of the lender, he may well decide to push the latter to the limit of his willingness to lend. Without good cash flow data, many borrowers appear reluctant to argue their case aggressively, probably because of uncertainty as to where the safe limit lies.

The results can also be related to other aspects of the debt-capacity question, such as the requirements for an A bond rating or the risk expectations of equity investors which appear to be implicit in some price-earnings ratio (assuming this can be determined). Once again, the comparison is between whatever unused debt capacity is indicated by the internal analysis and the standards imposed by external considerations with the aim of probing the acceptable and useful upper limits of long-term debt.

I have carried out this type of analysis for a sample of companies in different industries and made comparisons with existing debt-capacity standards of both the corporations themselves and their lending institutions. The data strongly indicate that there are, in fact, major inconsistencies between managements' explicit expectations regarding recession cash flows and the expectations which are implicit in accepted ratios of debt capacity. The evidence is by no means adequate to make any safe or meaningful generalization about the over-all character of industrial debt policy. Nevertheless, among the large and mature corporations which are the basis of the study the evidence seems to suggest:

□ Either the risks of debt have been significantly overrated by a substantial number of firms;

□ Or some managements tend to be unusually conservative toward this aspect of corporate risk.

Future Trends

The trend of economic events in the past few decades suggests that there is both a need and an opportunity for a more refined approach to the debt-equity choice in corporate structures. As the specter of the depression of the 1930's has faded into the past and confidence in our capacity to avoid a repetition of extreme economic stagnation has grown, a new generation of corporate executives has shown increasing willingness to use long-term debt financing as a source of funds for consolidation and expansion.

So long as long-term debt is avoided or kept to minor proportions, crude decision rules providing wide margins of safety are quite adequate. As the proportions of debt increase, however, the need for a sharper pencil and a more careful analysis grows. This need is further reinforced by the increase in other kinds of fixed cash commitments such as lease payments and the noncontractual but none-the-less-vital steady flows required for research, dividends, and the like. Greater stability in the economy over an extended period is likely to encourage a variety of rigidities in cash outflows, and simple rules of thumb are inadequate to cope with the problems these present.

Along with the increasing need for improved analysis has come a greater capacity to carry out this analysis. This improvement derives both from better data and from improved techniques of processing and analyzing data. Financial executives today have access to far more data on cash flows and the factors behind cash flows than they did 20 years ago—far more, in fact, than many are actually putting to use. They also have access to more sophisticated approaches to the analysis of complex data and to machines which can reduce it to manageable proportions. As time goes on and financial management becomes increasingly familiar with these tools of analysis and more aware of the opportunities they afford, the current reluctance to adopt a more complex analytical framework is bound to diminish.

But there is one hitch. However sophisticated the financial officer may be in the newer techniques, there is little merit in serving up a diet of financial data to the board of directors, as a basis for the financial decision, which is too rich for their current digestive capacity. It is for this reason that I have not attempted in this article to convert the reader to a full-scale internal analysis of risk and its components. Rather, I have taken on the more modest objective of alerting top management to four key points bearing on the debt-capacity decision:

1. While external sources of advice can and should be consulted as an aid to decision making, the question of debt capacity is essentially an internal one to be settled by management with reference to its individual circumstances and individual preferences.

2. Current rules of thumb regarding debt capacity are seriously inadequate as a framework for this decision.

3. The answer lies in a knowledge of the behavior of cash flows and in having a useful measure of the capacity to assume incremental fixed cash outflows.

4. Management needs approaches that will enable it to approximate its

debt capacity within the context of data with which it is already familiar and in terms of judgments to which it has long been accustomed. The approach described in this article meets these criteria.

By accepting and acting on these points, management would take an important step forward toward debt-equity decisions in which borrowers and lenders alike could have greater confidence.

Part V
The Individual
and the Organization

Preface

For centuries social philosophers have been investigating the proper relationship between individuals and societies or organizations; the balance between order and chaos. Early thinkers, such as Hobbes, Rousseau, and Machiavelli, in varying ways thought that the intractable nature of man had to be subjugated to the wishes of the whole in order for there to be peace and security. The aims of the individual and those of the collective were thought to be incompatible.

For many years business leaders thought the same about workers in organizations. It was assumed that if left to themselves, workers would come to work late, not produce to highest capacity, in fact, would do little unless supervised. Accordingly, workers were given rules to work by and treated as if order and productivity were inimical to them.

Then, in 1924, experiments conducted at Western Electric's Hawthorne plant, outside of Chicago, proved that workers can be more productive—work for the ends of the organization—if their human needs are satisfied. With this discovery the authoritarian age came to a jolting stop. The idea that satisfying human needs can lead to higher productivity opened a whole new branch of inquiry for social scientists. What is the best way to integrate the goals of organizations and individuals?

This central inquiry raises many attendant questions:

☐ What are the human needs that require satisfying?
☐ What motivates people at work?
☐ Is there one best way to fit individuals to the tasks that need performing to ensure high productivity?
☐ Is satisfying human needs at work a legitimate end in itself, despite productivity?

Currently, organizational theorists disagree on exactly what the most important questions are; whether emphasis should be placed on fitting tasks to individuals, finding the proper motivators, or designing management systems that will enable individuals to express their will in an organized way. The differences between theorists, however, are not in the main as important to the development of productive relationships between individuals and organizations as the similarities are. Underlying most current thought on individuals and or-

ganizations is the central assumption that organizations need to distinguish between individuals and recognize their universal need to express competence. The aims of organizations and individuals are not necessarily incompatible.

In "Improving the Quality of Work Life," Richard E. Walton discusses eight human aspirations that need attending to at work, and remarks that although measuring the productivity that results if these areas are covered is difficult, organizations still need to accommodate diversity among individuals. In his authoritative article, "One More Time: How Do You Motivate Employees?" Frederick Herzberg asserts that regardless of how organizations shift tasks, fit tasks to individuals and individuals to tasks, the individuals will not be motivated unless their jobs entail some elements that allow them to grow and expand their competence. In "Beyond Theory Y," John J. Morse and Jay W. Lorsch would add that an effective organization must also be designed so that its tasks fit its people, not some universal theory. In describing another area where the individual is important in organizations, Paul R. Lawrence maintains in "How to Deal with Resistance to Change" that organizational problems occur when changes in social relationships are made at the same time technological innovations are introduced.

19 Improving the Quality of Work Life

Richard E. Walton

The "quality of work life" is no longer simply an issue of compensations and benefit programs; more and more it involves the human factors at work. It concerns what people require from their work environment so that their needs as people not just as workers are met. In this short article, the author lists eight conceptual categories that the "quality of work life" encompasses and then discusses how productivity is affected by the satisfaction of human needs. Accepting that this is often hard to measure, he claims that regardless of that difficulty, organizations need to accommodate the differences between individuals.

Many employee groups are finding serious deficiencies in the quality of their work lives. Restless and alienated blue-collar and office workers want to alter the content of their jobs to give them challenge and more satisfying contact with others. Engineers and scientists are increasingly concerned about technical obsolescence. Even corporate managers have made the news by dropping out of the career "rat race" to redress the imbalance between work and other aspects of their lives.

The term "quality of work life" has come to mean far more than the needs satisfied by the 40-hour week, workmen's compensation laws, and job guarantees through collective bargaining—even more than equal employment opportunity and job enrichment schemes. The term also includes other human needs and aspirations; here are eight conceptual categories that it encompasses:

1. *Adequate and fair compensation*—Does pay received meet socially determined standards of sufficiency or the recipient's subjective standard? Does pay received for certain work bear an appropriate relationship to pay received for other work?

2. *Safe and healthy environment*—That employees should not be exposed to physical conditions or work arrangements that are unduly hazardous or unhealthy is widely accepted. In the future, when health will be less the issue than comfort, more stringent standards than today's will possibly be imposed. These may include minimizing odors, noise, or visual annoyances.

3. *Development of human capacities*—To varying degrees work has become fractionated, deskilled, and tightly controlled; planning the work is often separated from implementing it. So jobs differ in how much they enable the worker to use and develop his skills and knowledge, which affects his involvement, self-esteem, and the challenge obtained from the work itself.

4. *Growth and security*—Attention needs to be given to (a) the extent to which the worker's assignments contribute to maintaining and expanding his capabilities, rather than leading to his obsolescence; (b) the degree to which expanded or newly acquired knowledge and skills can be utilized in future work assignments; and (c) the availability of opportunities to advance in organizational or career terms which peers, family members, or associates recognize.

5. *Social integration*—Whether the employee achieves personal identity and self-esteem is influenced by such attributes in the climate of his workplace as these: freedom from prejudice, a sense of community, interpersonal openness, and the absence of stratification in the organization and the existence of upward mobility.

6. *Constitutionalism*—What rights does the worker have and how can he (or she) protect these rights? Wide variations exist in the extent to which the organizational culture respects personal privacy, tolerates dissent, adheres to high standards of equity in distributing rewards, and provides for due process in all work-related matters.

7. *The total life space*—A person's work should have a balanced role in his life. This role encompasses schedules, career demands, and travel requirements that take a limited portion of the person's leisure and family time, as well as advancement and promotion that do not require repeated geographical moves.

8. *Social relevance*—Organizations acting in a socially irresponsible manner cause increasing numbers of their employees to depreciate the value of their work and careers. For example, does the worker perceive the organization to be socially responsible in its products, waste disposal, marketing techniques, employment practices, and participation in political campaigns?

Effect on Productivity

Will gains in quality of work life result in gains in the organization's ability to perform its tasks? The answer is not simple.

If an organization fails to meet minimum employee expectations on each point, deep dissatisfaction will hamper effectiveness. Satisfaction of an expectation often causes a thirst for more; minimum standards tend to move upward. Sometimes the movement is gradual—as rising levels of education and economic security influence expectations. Sometimes expectations increase dramatically, as events and the mass media raise public consciousness of these workplace issues.

When we go beyond the idea of some minimum conditions below which acute dissatisfactions impair functioning, these eight criteria have quite different implications for productivity.

On the one hand, it is usually possible to redesign work in ways that simultaneously increase the opportunity to use and develop human skills and improve productivity. For example, a self-managing work team with flexible roles, access to relevant information, and responsibility for some planning can increase the organization's ability to solve problems like production bottlenecks, high rates of defective productivity, and poor utilization of equipment.

On the other hand, the rigorous guarantee of human rights, embraced in the term "constitutionalism," often involves a trade-off with strict task efficiency. Provisions for due process—the right of appeal to an impartial authority and protective rules of evidence—introduce constraints on managerial action.

Similarly, managing the creation of goods and distribution of services can be greatly complicated by open dissent within management that focuses on sensitive areas, such as the safety of the company's products, the truthfulness of its ads, the nature of its endeavors to influence governmental bodies, and the morality of its foreign operations. So, if employees' rights of due process and dissent in the workplace win more recognition it must be because we believe in these rights, even if they reduce productivity.

Accommodating for Diversity

Regardless of how we approach the issue of the quality of work life, we must acknowledge the diversity of human preferences—diversity relating to culture, social class, family rearing, education, and personality. There is a growing heterogeneity in life styles in America. Different definitions of a high-quality work life accompany differences in subcultures and life styles. And the young person with a college degree who elects to work as an auto mechanic, a taxi driver, or a mail carrier is saying something significant about his or her preferred pattern of work life.

Of two employees equally skilled in their jobs, one may prefer to be autonomous and the other to be supervised closely. One may prefer to be closely integrated into a team and the other relatively unencumbered by work relations. How can we accommodate differing preferences like these?

We can tailor work assignments to fit individual preferences. We can organize work differently from one unit to another, allowing employees to select the pattern they prefer. Or we can encourage each organization to develop a unique and internally consistent pattern of work life and provide persons on the job market with enough information to choose organizations that are good fits for them. This procedure may give persons a free and informed choice that takes into account some subtler aspects of the quality of work life.

20. One More Time: How Do You Motivate Employees?

Frederick Herzberg

KITA—*the externally imposed attempt by management to "install a generator" in the employee—has been demonstrated to be a total failure, the author says. The absence of such "hygiene" factors as good supervisor-employee relations and liberal fringe benefits can make a worker unhappy, but their presence will not make him want to work harder. Essentially meaningless changes in the tasks that workers are assigned to do have not accomplished the desired objective either. The only way to motivate the employee is to give him challenging work in which he can assume responsibility.*

How many articles, books, speeches, and workshops have pleaded plaintively, "How do I get an employee to do what I want him to do?"

The psychology of motivation is tremendously complex, and what has been unraveled with any degree of assurance is small indeed. But the dismal ratio of knowledge to speculation has not dampened the enthusiasm for new forms of snake oil that are constantly coming on the market, many of them with academic testimonials. Doubtless this article will have no depressing impact on the market for snake oil, but since the ideas expressed in it have been tested in many corporations and other organizations, it will help—I hope—to redress the imbalance in the aforementioned ratio.

"Motivating" with KITA

In lectures to industry on the problem, I have found that the audiences are anxious for quick and practical answers, so I will begin with a straightforward, practical formula for moving people.

What is the simplest, surest, and most direct way of getting someone to do something? Ask him? But if he responds that he does not want to do it,

AUTHOR'S NOTE: I should like to acknowledge the contributions that Robert Ford of the American Telephone and Telegraph Company has made to the ideas expressed in this article, and in particular to the successful application of these ideas in improving work performance and the job satisfaction of employees.

then that calls for a psychological consultation to determine the reason for his obstinacy. Tell him? His response shows that he does not understand you, and now an expert in communication methods has to be brought in to show you how to get through to him. Give him a monetary incentive? I do not need to remind the reader of the complexity and difficulty involved in setting up and administering an incentive system. Show him? This means a costly training program. We need a simple way.

Every audience contains the "direct action" manager who shouts, "Kick him!" And this type of manager is right. The surest and least circumlocuted way of getting someone to do something is to kick him in the pants—give him what might be called the KITA.

There are various forms of KITA, and here are some of them:

□ *Negative Physical KITA.* This is a literal application of the term and was frequently used in the past. It has, however, three major drawbacks: (1) it is inelegant; (2) it contradicts the precious image of benevolence that most organizations cherish; and (3) since it is a physical attack, it directly stimulates the autonomic nervous system, and this often results in negative feedback—the employee may just kick you in return. These factors give rise to certain taboos against negative physical KITA.

The psychologist has come to the rescue of those who are no longer permitted to use negative physical KITA. He has uncovered infinite sources of psychological vulnerabilities and the appropriate methods to play tunes on them. "He took my rug away"; "I wonder what he meant by that"; "The boss is always going around me"—these symptomatic expressions of ego sores that have been rubbed raw are the result of application of:

□ *Negative Psychological KITA.* This has several advantages over negative physical KITA. First, the cruelty is not visible; the bleeding is internal and comes much later. Second, since it affects the higher cortical centers of the brain with its inhibitory powers, it reduces the possibility of physical backlash. Third, since the number of psychological pains that a person can feel is almost infinite, the direction and site possibilities of the KITA are increased many times. Fourth, the person administering the kick can manage to be above it all and let the system accomplish the dirty work. Fifth, those who practice it receive some ego satisfaction (one-upmanship), whereas they would find drawing blood abhorrent. Finally, if the employee does complain, he can always be accused of being paranoid, since there is no tangible evidence of an actual attack.

Now, what does negative KITA accomplish? If I kick you in the rear (physically or psychologically), who is motivated? *I* am motivated; *you* move! Negative KITA does not lead to motivation, but to movement. So:

□ *Positive KITA.* Let us consider motivation. If I say to you, "Do this for me or the company, and in return I will give you a reward, an incentive, more status, a promotion, all the quid pro quos that exist in the industrial organization," am I motivating you? The overwhelming opinion I receive from management people is, "Yes, this is motivation."

I have a year-old Schnauzer. When it was a small puppy and I wanted it to move, I kicked it in the rear and it moved. Now that I have finished its obedience training, I hold up a dog biscuit when I want the Schnauzer to move. In this instance, who is motivated—I or the dog? The dog wants the biscuit, but it is I who want it to move. Again, I am the one who is motivated, and the dog is the one who moves. In this instance all I did was apply KITA frontally; I exerted a pull instead of a push. When industry wishes to use such positive KITAs, it has available an incredible number and variety of dog biscuits (jelly beans for humans) to wave in front of the employee to get him to jump.

Why is it that managerial audiences are quick to see that negative KITA is *not* motivation, while they are almost unanimous in their judgment that positive KITA *is* motivation? It is because negative KITA is rape, and positive KITA is seduction. But it is infinitely worse to be seduced than to be raped; the latter is an unfortunate occurrence, while the former signifies that you were a party to your own downfall. This is why positive KITA is so popular: it is a tradition; it is in the American way. The organization does not have to kick you; you kick yourself.

MYTHS ABOUT MOTIVATION

Why is KITA not motivation? If I kick my dog (from the front or the back), he will move. And when I want him to move again, what must I do? I must kick him again. Similarly, I can charge a man's battery, and then recharge it, and recharge it again. But it is only when he has his own generator that we can talk about motivation. He then needs no outside stimulation. He *wants* to do it.

With this in mind, we can review some positive KITA personnel practices that were developed as attempts to instill "motivation":

1. *Reducing time spent at work*—This represents a marvelous way of motivating people to work—getting them off the job! We have reduced (formally and informally) the time spent on the job over the last 50 or 60 years until we are finally on the way to the "6½-day weekend." An interesting variant of this approach is the development of off-hour recreation programs. The philosophy here seems to be that those who play together, work together. The fact is that motivated people seek more hours of work, not fewer.

2. *Spiraling wages*—Have these motivated people? Yes, to seek the next

wage increase. Some medievalists still can be heard to say that a good depression will get employees moving. They feel that if rising wages don't or won't do the job, perhaps reducing them will.

3. *Fringe benefits*—Industry has outdone the most welfare-minded of welfare states in dispensing cradle-to-the-grave succor. One company I know of had an informal "fringe benefit of the month club" going for a while. The cost of fringe benefits in this country has reached approximately 25% of the wage dollar, and we still cry for motivation.

People spend less time working for more money and more security than ever before, and the trend cannot be reversed. These benefits are no longer rewards; they are rights. A 6-day week is inhuman, a 10-hour day is exploitation, extended medical coverage is a basic decency, and stock options are the salvation of American initiative. Unless the ante is continuously raised, the psychological reaction of employees is that the company is turning back the clock.

When industry began to realize that both the economic nerve and the lazy nerve of their employees had insatiable appetites, it started to listen to the behavioral scientists who, more out of a humanist tradition than from scientific study, criticized management for not knowing how to deal with people. The next KITA easily followed.

4. *Human relations training*—Over 30 years of teaching and, in many instances, of practicing psychological approaches to handling people have resulted in costly human relations programs and, in the end, the same question: How do you motivate workers? Here, too, escalations have taken place. Thirty years ago it was necessary to request, "Please don't spit on the floor." Today the same admonition requires three "please"s before the employee feels that his superior has demonstrated the psychologically proper attitudes toward him.

The failure of human relations training to produce motivation led to the conclusion that the supervisor or manager himself was not psychologically true to himself in his practice of interpersonal decency. So an advanced form of human relations KITA, sensitivity training, was unfolded.

5. *Sensitivity training*—Do you really, really understand yourself? Do you really, really, really trust the other man? Do you really, really, really, really cooperate? The failure of sensitivity training is now being explained, by those who have become opportunistic exploiters of the technique, as a failure to really (five times) conduct proper sensitivity training courses.

With the realization that there are only temporary gains from comfort and economic and interpersonal KITA, personnel managers concluded that the fault lay not in what they were doing, but in the employee's failure to appreciate what they were doing. This opened up the field of communications, a whole new area of "scientifically" sanctioned KITA.

6. *Communications*—The professor of communications was invited to join the faculty of management training programs and help in making

employees understand what management was doing for them. House organs, briefing sessions, supervisory instruction on the importance of communication, and all sorts of propaganda have proliferated until today there is even an International Council of Industrial Editors. But no motivation resulted, and the obvious thought occurred that perhaps management was not hearing what the employees were saying. That led to the next KITA.

7. *Two-way communication*—Management ordered morale surveys, suggestion plans, and group participation programs. Then both employees and management were communicating and listening to each other more than ever, but without much improvement in motivation.

The behavioral scientists began to take another look at their conceptions and their data, and they took human relations one step further. A glimmer of truth was beginning to show through in the writings of the so-called higher-order-need psychologists. People, so they said, want to actualize themselves. Unfortunately, the "actualizing" psychologists got mixed up with human relations psychologists, and a new KITA emerged.

8. *Job participation*—Though it may not have been the theoretical intention, job participation often became a "give them the big picture" approach. For example, if a man is tightening 10,000 nuts a day on an assembly line with a torque wrench, tell him he is building a Chevrolet. Another approach had the goal of giving the employee a *feeling* that he is determining, in some measure, what he does on his job. The goal was to provide a *sense* of achievement rather than a substantive achievement in his task. Real achievement, of course, requires a task that makes it possible.

But still there was no motivation. This led to the inevitable conclusion that the employees must be sick, and therefore to the next KITA.

9. *Employee counseling*—The inital use of this form of KITA in a systematic fashion can be credited to the Hawthorne experiment of the Western Electric Company during the early 1930's. At that time, it was found that the employees harbored irrational feelings that were interfering with the rational operation of the factory. Counseling in this instance was a means of letting the employees unburden themselves by talking to someone about their problems. Although the counseling techniques were primitive, the program was large indeed.

The counseling approach suffered as a result of experiences during World War II, when the programs themselves were found to be interfering with the operation of the organizations; the counselors had forgotten their role of benevolent listeners and were attempting to do something about the problems that they heard about. Psychological counseling, however, has managed to survive the negative impact of World War II experiences and today is beginning to flourish with renewed sophistication. But, alas, many of these programs, like all the others, do not seem to have lessened the pressure of demands to find out how to motivate workers.

Since KITA results only in short-term movement, it is safe to predict that the cost of these programs will increase steadily and new varieties will be developed as old positive KITAs reach their satiation points.

Hygiene vs. Motivators

Let me rephrase the perennial question this way: How do you install a generator in an employee? A brief review of my motivation-hygiene theory of job attitudes is required before theoretical and practical suggestions can be offered. The theory was first drawn from an examination of events in the lives of engineers and accountants. At least 16 other investigations, using a wide variety of populations (including some in the Communist countries), have since been completed, making the original research one of the most replicated studies in the field of job attitudes.

The findings of these studies, along with corroboration from many other investigations using different procedures, suggest that the factors involved in producing job satisfaction (and motivation) are separate and distinct from the factors that lead to job dissatisfaction. Since separate factors need to be considered, depending on whether job satisfaction or job dissatisfaction is being examined, it follows that these two feelings are not opposites of each other. The opposite of job satisfaction is not job dissatisfaction but, rather, *no* job satisfaction; and, similarly, the opposite of job dissatisfaction is not job satisfaction, but *no* job dissatisfaction.

Stating the concept presents a problem in semantics, for we normally think of satisfaction and dissatisfaction as opposites—i.e., what is not satisfying must be dissatisfying, and vice versa. But when it comes to understanding the behavior of people in their jobs, more than a play on words is involved.

Two different needs of man are involved here. One set of needs can be thought of as stemming from his animal nature—the built-in drive to avoid pain from the environment, plus all the learned drives which become conditioned to the basic biological needs. For example, hunger, a basic biological drive, makes it necessary to earn money, and then money becomes a specific drive. The other set of needs relates to that unique human characteristic, the ability to achieve and, through achievement, to experience psychological growth. The stimuli for the growth needs are tasks that induce growth; in the industrial setting, they are the *job content*. Contrariwise, the stimuli inducing pain-avoidance behavior are found in the *job environment*.

The growth or *motivator* factors that are intrinsic to the job are: achievement, recognition for achievement, the work itself, responsibility, and growth or advancement. The dissatisfaction-avoidance or *hygiene* (KITA) factors that are extrinsic to the job include: company policy and ad-

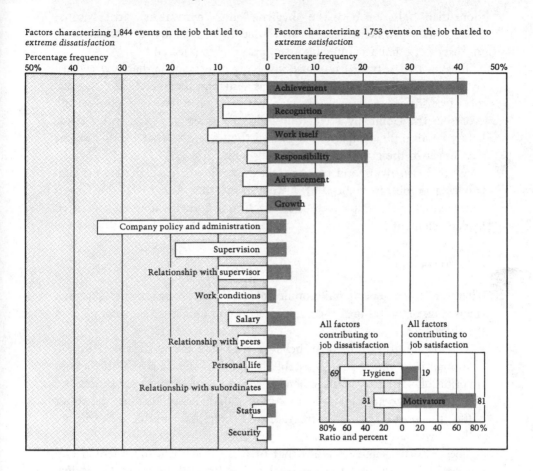

Factors characterizing 1,844 events on the job that led to *extreme dissatisfaction*

Percentage frequency

Factors characterizing 1,753 events on the job that led to *extreme satisfaction*

Percentage frequency

ministration, supervision, interpersonal relationships, working conditions, salary, status, and security.

A composite of the factors that are involved in causing job satisfaction and job dissatisfaction, drawn from samples of 1,685 employees, is shown in *Exhibit I.* The results indicate that motivators were the primary cause of satisfaction, and hygiene factors the primary cause of unhappiness on the job. The employees, studied in 12 different investigations, included lower-level supervisors, professional women, agricultural administrators, men about to retire from management positions, hospital maintenance personnel, manufacturing supervisors, nurses, food handlers, military officers, engineers, scientists, housekeepers, teachers, technicians, female assemblers, accountants, Finnish foremen, and Hungarian engineers.

They were asked what job events had occurred in their work that had led to extreme satisfaction or extreme dissatisfaction on their part. Their responses are broken down in the exhibit into percentages of total "positive" job events and of total "negative" job events. (The figures total more than 100% on both the "hygiene" and "motivators" sides because often at least two factors can be attributed to a single event; advancement, for instance, often accompanies assumption of responsibility.)

To illustrate, a typical response involving achievement that had a negative effect for the employee was, "I was unhappy because I didn't do the job successfully." A typical response in the small number of positive job events in the Company Policy and Administration grouping was, "I was happy because the company reorganized the section so that I didn't report any longer to the guy I didn't get along with."

As the lower right-hand part of the exhibit shows, of all the factors contributing to job satisfaction, 81% were motivators. And of all the factors contributing to the employees' dissatisfaction over their work, 69% involved hygiene elements.

ETERNAL TRIANGLE

There are three general philosophies of personnel management. The first is based on organizational theory, the second on industrial engineering, and the third on behavioral science.

The organizational theorist believes that human needs are either so irrational or so varied and adjustable to specific situations that the major function of personnel management is to be as pragmatic as the occasion demands. If jobs are organized in a proper manner, he reasons, the result will be the most efficient job structure, and the most favorable job attitudes will follow as a matter of course.

The industrial engineer holds that man is mechanistically oriented and economically motivated and his needs are best met by attuning the individual to the most efficient work process. The goal of personnel management therefore should be to concoct the most appropriate incentive system and to design the specific working conditions in a way that facilitates the most efficient use of the human machine. By structuring jobs in a manner that leads to the most efficient operation, the engineer believes that he can obtain the optimal organizaion of work and the proper work attitudes.

The behavioral scientist focuses on group sentiments, attitudes of individual employees, and the organization's social and psychological climate. According to his persuasion, he emphasizes one or more of the various hygiene and motivator needs. His approach to personnel management generally emphasizes some form of human relations education, in the hope of instilling healthy employee attitudes and an organizational climate which he considers to be felicitous to human values. He believes that proper attitudes will lead to efficient job and organizational structure.

There is always a lively debate as to the overall effectiveness of the approaches of the organizational theorist and the industrial engineer. Manifestly they have achieved much. But the nagging question for the behavioral

Exhibit II. 'Triangle' of philosophies of personnel management

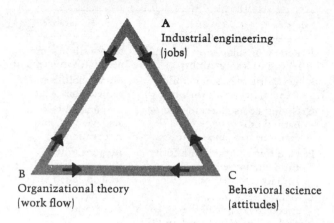

A
Industrial engineering
(jobs)

B
Organizational theory
(work flow)

C
Behavioral science
(attitudes)

scientist has been: What is the cost in human problems that eventually causes more expense to the organization—for instance, turnover, absenteeism, errors, violation of safety rules, strikes, restriction of output, higher wages, and greater fringe benefits? On the other hand, the behavioral scientist is hard put to document much manifest improvement in personnel management, using his approach.

The three philosophies can be depicted as a triangle, as is done in *Exhibit II*, with each persuasion claiming the apex angle. The motivation-hygiene theory claims the same angle as industrial engineering, but for opposite goals. Rather than rationalizing the work to increase efficiency, the theory suggests that work be *enriched* to bring about effective utilization of personnel. Such a systematic attempt to motivate employees by manipulating the motivator factors is just beginning.

The term *job enrichment* describes this embryonic movement. An older term, job enlargement, should be avoided because it is associated with past failures stemming from a misunderstanding of the problem. Job enrichment provides the opportunity for the employee's psychological growth, while job enlargement merely makes a job structurally bigger. Since scientific job enrichment is very new, this article only suggests the principles and practical steps that have recently emerged from several successful experiments in industry.

JOB LOADING

In attempting to enrich an employee's job, management often succeeds in reducing the man's personal contribution, rather than giving him an opportunity for growth in his accustomed job. Such an endeavor, which I shall call horizontal job loading (as opposed to vertical loading, or providing motivator factors), has been the problem of earlier job enlargement programs. This activity merely enlarges the meaninglessness of the job. Some examples of this approach, and their effects, are:

Exhibit III. *Principles of vertical job loading*

Principle	Motivators involved
A. Removing some controls while retaining accountability	Responsibility and personal achievement
B. Increasing the accountability of individuals for own work	Responsibility and recognition
C. Giving a person a complete natural unit of work (module, division, area, and so on)	Responsibility, achievement, and recognition
D. Granting additional authority to an employee in his activity; job freedom	Responsibility, achievement, and recognition
E. Making periodic reports directly available to the worker himself rather than to the supervisor	Internal recognition
F. Introducing new and more difficult tasks not previously handled	Growth and learning
G. Assigning individuals specific or specialized tasks, enabling them to become experts	Responsibility, growth, and advancement

□ Challenging the employee by increasing the amount of production expected of him. If he tightens 10,000 bolts a day, see if he can tighten 20,000 bolts a day. The arithmetic involved shows that multiplying zero by zero still equals zero.

□ Adding another meaningless task to the existing one, usually some routine clerical activity. The arithmetic here is adding zero to zero.

□ Rotating the assignments of a number of jobs that need to be enriched. This means washing dishes for a while, then washing silverware. The arithmetic is substituting one zero for another zero.

□ Removing the most difficult parts of the assignment in order to free the worker to accomplish more of the less challenging assignments. This traditional industrial engineering approach amounts to subtraction in the hope of accomplishing addition.

These are common forms of horizontal loading that frequently come up in preliminary brain storming sessions on job enrichment. The principles of vertical loading have not all been worked out as yet, and they remain rather general, but I have furnished seven useful starting points for consideration in *Exhibit III*.

A SUCCESSFUL APPLICATION

An example from a highly successful job enrichment experiment can illustrate the distinction between horizontal and vertical loading of a job.

Exhibit IV. *Shareholder service index in company experiment*

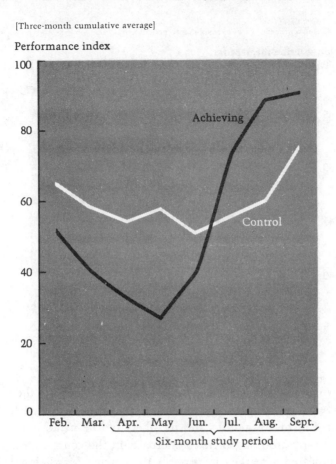

[Three-month cumulative average]

Performance index

Six-month study period

The subjects of this study were the stockholder correspondents employed by a very large corporation. Seemingly, the task required of these carefully selected and highly trained correspondents was quite complex and challenging. But almost all indexes of performance and job attitudes were low, and exit interviewing confirmed that the challenge of the job existed merely as words.

A job enrichment project was initiated in the form of an experiment with one group, designated as an achieving unit, having its job enriched by the principles described in *Exhibit III*. A control group continued to do its job in the traditional way. (There were also two "uncommitted" groups of correspondents formed to measure the so-called Hawthorne Effect—that is, to gauge whether productivity and attitudes toward the job changed artificially merely because employees sensed that the company was paying more attention to them in doing something different or novel. The results for these groups were substantially the same as for the control group, and for the sake of simplicity I do not deal with them in this summary.) No changes in hygiene were introduced for either group other than those that would have been made anyway, such as normal pay increases.

Exhibit V. Changes in attitudes toward tasks in company experiment

[Changes in mean scores over six-month period]

Job reaction mean score

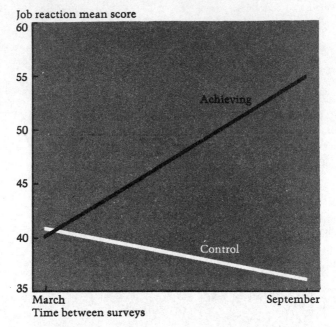

The changes for the achieving unit were introduced in the first two months, averaging one per week of the seven motivators listed in *Exhibit III*. At the end of six months the members of the achieving unit were found to be outperforming their counterparts in the control group, and in addition indicated a marked increase in their liking for their jobs. Other results showed that the achieving group had lower absenteeism and, subsequently, a much higher rate of promotion.

Exhibit IV illustrates the changes in performance, measured in February and March, before the study period began, and at the end of each month of the study period. The shareholder service index represents quality of letters, including accuracy of information, and speed of response to stockholders' letters of inquiry. The index of a current month was averaged into the average of the two prior months, which means that improvement was harder to obtain if the indexes of the previous months were low. The "achievers" were performing less well before the six-month period started, and their performance service index continued to decline after the introduction of the motivators, evidently because of uncertainty over their newly granted responsibilities. In the third month, however, performance im-

Exhibit VI. Enlargement vs. enrichment of correspondents' tasks in company experiment

Horizontal loading suggestions (rejected)	Vertical loading suggestions (adopted)	Principle
Firm quotas could be set for letters to be answered each day, using a rate which would be hard to reach.	Subject matter experts were appointed within each unit for other members of the unit to consult with before seeking supervisory help. (The supervisor had been answering all specialized and difficult questions.)	G
The women could type the letters themselves, as well as compose them, or take on any other clerical functions.	Correspondents signed their own names on letters. (The supervisor had been signing all letters.)	B
All difficult or complex inquiries could be channeled to a few women so that the remainder could achieve high rates of output. These jobs could be exchanged from time to time.	The work of the more experienced correspondents was proofread less frequently by supervisors and was done at the correspondents' desks, dropping verification from 100% to 10%. (Previously, all correspondents' letters had been checked by the supervisor.)	A
The women could be rotated through units handling different customers, and then sent back to their own units.	Production was discussed, but only in terms such as "a full day's work is expected." As time went on, this was no longer mentioned. (Before, the group had been constantly reminded of the number of letters that needed to be answered.)	D
	Outgoing mail went directly to the mailroom without going over supervisors' desks. (The letters had always been routed through the supervisors.)	A
	Correspondents were encouraged to answer letters in a more personalized way. (Reliance on the form-letter approach had been standard practice.)	C
	Each correspondent was held personally responsible for the quality and accuracy of letters. (This responsibility had been the province of the supervisor and the verifier.)	B, E

proved, and soon the members of this group had reached a high level of accomplishment.

Exhibit V shows the two groups' attitudes toward their job, measured at the end of March, just before the first motivator was introduced, and again at the end of September. The correspondents were asked 16 questions, all involving motivation. A typical one was, "As you see it, how many opportunities do you feel that you have in your job for making worthwhile contributions?" The answers were scaled from 1 to 5, with 80 as the maximum possible score. The achievers became much more positive about their job, while the attitude of the control unit remained about the same (the drop is not statistically significant).

How was the job of these correspondents restructured? *Exhibit VI* lists the suggestions made that were deemed to be horizontal loading, and the actual vertical loading changes that were incorporated in the job of the achieving unit. The capital letters under "Principle" after "Vertical loading" refer to the corresponding letters in *Exhibit III*. The reader will note that rejected forms of horizontal loading correspond closely to my list of common manifestations of the phenomenon.

Steps to Job Enrichment

Now that the motivator idea has been described in practice, here are the steps that managers should take in instituting the principle with their employees:

1. Select those jobs in which (a) the investment in industrial engineering does not make changes too costly, (b) attitudes are poor, (c) hygiene is becoming very costly, and (d) motivation will make a difference in performance.

2. Approach these jobs with the conviction that they can be changed. Years of tradition have led managers to believe that the content of the jobs is sacrosanct and the only scope of action that they have is in ways of stimulating people.

3. Brainstorm a list of changes that may enrich the jobs, without concern for their practicality.

4. Screen the list to eliminate suggestions that involve hygiene, rather than actual motivation.

5. Screen the list for generalities, such as "give them more responsibility," that are rarely followed in practice. This might seem obvious, but the motivator words have never left industry; the substance has just been rationalized and organized out. Words like "responsibility," "growth," "achievement," and "challenge," for example, have been elevated to the lyrics of the patriotic anthem for all organizations. It is the old problem typified by the pledge of allegiance to the flag being more important than contributions to the country—of following the form, rather than the substance.

6. Screen the list to eliminate any *horizontal* loading suggestions.

7. Avoid direct participation by the employees whose jobs are to be enriched. Ideas they have expressed previously certainly constitute a valuable source for recommended changes, but their direct involvement contaminates the process with human relations *hygiene* and, more specifically, gives them only a *sense* of making a contribution. The job is to be changed, and it is the content that will produce the motivation, not attitudes about being involved or the challenge inherent in setting up a job. That process will be over shortly, and it is what the employees will be doing from then on that will determine their motivation. A sense of participation will result only in short-term movement.

8. In the initial attempts at job enrichment, set up a controlled experiment. At least two equivalent groups should be chosen, one an experimental unit in which the motivators are systematically introduced over a period of time, and the other one a control group in which no changes are made. For both groups, hygiene should be allowed to follow its natural course for

the duration of the experiment. Pre- and post-installation tests of perform-ance and job attitudes are necessary to evaluate the effectiveness of the job enrichment program. The attitude test must be limited to motivator items in order to divorce the employee's view of the job he is given from all the surrounding hygiene feelings that he might have.

9. Be prepared for a drop in performance in the experimental group the first few weeks. The changeover to a new job may lead to a temporary reduction in efficiency.

10. Expect your first-line supervisors to experience some anxiety and hostility over the changes you are making. The anxiety comes from their fear that the changes will result in poorer performance for their unit. Hostility will arise when the employees start assuming what the supervisors regard as their own responsibility for performance. The supervisor without checking duties to perform may then be left with little to do.

After a successful experiment, however, the supervisor usually discovers the supervisory and managerial functions he has neglected, or which were never his because all his time was given over to checking the work of his subordinates. For example, in the R&D division of one large chemical company I know of, the supervisors of the laboratory assistants were theo-retically responsible for their training and evaluation. These functions, however, had come to be performed in a routine, unsubstantial fashion. After the job enrichment program, during which the supervisors were not merely passive observers of the assistants' performance, the supervisors actually were devoting their time to reviewing performance and adminis-tering thorough training.

What has been called an employee-centered style of supervision will come about not through education of supervisors, but by changing the jobs that they do.

Concluding Note

Job enrichment will not be a one-time proposition, but a continuous management function. The initial changes, however, should last for a very long period of time. There are a number of reasons for this:

◻ The changes should bring the job up to the level of challenge com-mensurate with the skill that was hired.

◻ Those who have still more ability eventually will be able to demon-strate it better and win promotion to higher-level jobs.

◻ The very nature of motivators, as opposed to hygiene factors, is that they have a much longer-term effect on employees' attitudes. Perhaps the job will have to be enriched again, but this will not occur as frequently as the need for hygiene.

Not all jobs can be enriched, nor do all jobs need to be enriched. If only a small percentage of the time and money that is now devoted to hygiene, however, were given to job enrichment efforts, the return in human satisfaction and economic gain would be one of the largest dividends that industry and society have ever reaped through their efforts at better personnel management.

The argument for job enrichment can be summed up quite simply: If you have someone on a job, use him. If you can't use him on the job, get rid of him, either via automation or by selecting someone with lesser ability. If you can't use him and you can't get rid of him, you will have a motivation problem.

21. Beyond Theory Y

John J. Morse and Jay W. Lorsch

The concept of participative management, as symbolized by Douglas McGregor's "Theory Y," was an important insight into improving organizational effectiveness. But, many managers assume that Theory Y is the only correct approach. In this article, the authors go "beyond Theory Y" to propose that the most productive organization is one that fits the needs of its task and people in any particular situation. In some cases, this may well mean a more directive approach. Even more significant, the proper "fit" among task, organization, and people seems to develop strong "competence motivation" in individuals, regardless of the organizational style.

During the past few decades, managers have been bombarded with two competing approaches to the problems of human administration and organization. The first, usually called the classical school of organization, emphasizes the need for well-established lines of authority, clearly defined jobs, and authority equal to responsibility. The second, often called the participative approach, focuses on the desirability of involving organization members in decision making so that they will be more highly motivated.

Douglas McGregor, through his well-known "Theory X and Theory Y," drew a distinction between the assumptions about human motivation which underlie these two approaches, to this effect:

□ Theory X assumes that people dislike work and must be coerced, controlled, and directed toward organizational goals. Furthermore, most people prefer to be treated this way, so they can avoid responsibility.

□ Theory Y—the integration of goals—emphasizes the average person's intrinsic interest in his work, his desire to be self-directing and to seek responsibility, and his capacity to be creative in solving business problems.

It is McGregor's conclusion, of course, that the latter approach to organization is the more desirable one for managers to follow.[1]

1. Douglas McGregor, *The Human Side of Enterprise* (New York, McGraw-Hill Book Company, Inc., 1960), pp. 34-35 and 47-48.

McGregor's position causes confusion for the managers who try to choose between these two conflicting approaches. The classical organizational approach that McGregor associated with Theory X does work well in some situations, although, as McGregor himself pointed out, there are also some situations where it does not work effectively. At the same time, the approach based on Theory Y, while it has produced good results in some situations, does not always do so. That is, each approach is effective in some cases but not in others. Why is this? How can managers resolve the confusion?

A New Approach

Work by a number of students of management and organization may help to answer such questions.[2] These studies indicate that there is not one best organizational approach; rather, the best approach depends on the nature of the work to be done. Enterprises with highly predictable tasks perform better with organizations characterized by the highly formalized procedures and management hierarchies of the classical approach. With highly uncertain tasks that require more extensive problem solving, on the other hand, organizations that are less formalized and emphasize self-control and member participation in decision making are more effective. In essence, according to these newer studies, managers must design and develop organizations so that the organizational characteristics *fit* the nature of the task to be done.

While the conclusions of this newer approach will make sense to most experienced managers and can alleviate much of the confusion about which approach to choose, there are still two important questions unanswered:

1. How does the more formalized and controlling organization affect the motivation of organization members? (McGregor's most telling criticism of the classical approach was that it did not unleash the potential in an enterprise's human resources.)

2. Equally important, does a less formalized organization always provide a high level of motivation for its members? (This is the implication many managers have drawn from McGregor's work.)

We have recently been involved in a study that provides surprising answers to these questions and, when taken together with other recent

---

2. See for example Paul R. Lawrence and Jay W. Lorsch, *Organization and Environment* (Boston, Division of Research, Harvard Business School, 1967); Joan Woodward, *Industrial Organization: Theory & Practice* (New York, Oxford University Press, Inc., 1965); Tom Burns and G. M. Stalker, *The Management of Innovation* (London, Tavistock Publications, 1961); Harold J. Leavitt, "Unhuman Organizations," HBR July-August 1962, p. 90.

Exhibit I. Study design in "fit" of organizational characteristics

Characteristics	Company I (predictable manufacturing task)	Company II (unpredictable R&D task)
Effective performer	Akron containers plant	Stockton research lab
Less effective performer	Hartford containers plant	Carmel research lab

work, suggests a new set of basic assumptions which move beyond Theory Y into what we call "Contingency Theory: the fit between task, organization, and people." These theoretical assumptions emphasize that the appropriate pattern of organization is *contingent* on the nature of the work to be done and on the particular needs of the people involved. We should emphasize that we have labeled these assumptions as a step beyond Theory Y because of McGregor's own recognition that the Theory Y assumptions would probably be supplanted by new knowledge within a short time.

The Study Design

Our study was conducted in four organizational units. Two of these performed the relatively certain task of manufacturing standardized containers on high-speed, automated production lines. The other two performed the relatively uncertain work of research and development in communications technology. Each pair of units performing the same kind of task were in the same large company, and each pair had previously been evaluated by that company's management as containing one highly effective unit and a less effective one. The study design is summarized in *Exhibit I*.

The objective was to explore more fully how the fit between organization and task was related to successful performance. That is, does a good fit between organizational characteristics and task requirements increase the motivation of individuals and hence produce more effective individual and organizational performance?

An especially useful approach to answering this question is to recognize that an individual has a strong need to master the world around him, including the task that he faces as a member of a work organization.[3] The accumulated feelings of satisfaction that come from successfully mastering one's environment can be called a "sense of competence." We saw this sense of competence in performing a particular task as helpful in understanding how a fit between task and organizational characteristics could motivate people toward successful performance.

3. See Robert W. White, "Ego and Reality in Psychoanalytic Theory," *Psychological Issues*, Vol. III, No. 3 (New York, International Universities Press, 1963).

ORGANIZATIONAL DIMENSIONS

Because the four study sites had already been evaluated by the respective corporate managers as high and low performers of tasks, we expected that such differences in performance would be a preliminary clue to differences in the "fit" of the organizational characteristics to the job to be done. But, first, we had to define what kinds of organizational characteristics would determine how appropriate the organization was to the particular task.

We grouped these organizational characteristics into two sets of factors:

1. Formal characteristics, which could be used to judge the fit between the kind of task being worked on and the formal practices of the organization.

2. Climate characteristics, or the subjective perceptions and orientations that had developed among the individuals about their organizational setting. (These too must fit the task to be performed if the organization is to be effective.)

We measured these attributes through questionnaires and interviews with about 40 managers in each unit to determine the appropriateness of the organization to the kind of task being performed. We also measured the feelings of competence of the people in the organizations so that we could link the appropriateness of the organizational attributes with a sense of competence.

Major Findings

The principal findings of the survey are best highlighted by contrasting the highly successful Akron plant and the high-performing Stockton laboratory. Because each performed very different tasks (the former a relatively certain manufacturing task and the latter a relatively uncertain research task), we expected, as brought out earlier, that there would have to be major differences between them in organizational characteristics if they were to perform effectively. And this is what we did find. But we also found that each of these effective units had a better fit with its particular task than did its less effective counterpart.

While our major purpose in this article is to explore how the fit between task and organizational characteristics is related to motivation, we first want to explore more fully the organizational characteristics of these units, so the reader will better understand what we mean by a fit between task and organization and how it can lead to more effective behavior. To do this, we shall place the major emphasis on the contrast between the high-

Characteristics	Akron	Stockton
1. Pattern of formal relationships and duties as signified by organization charts and job manuals	Highly structured, precisely defined	Low degree of structure, less well defined
2. Pattern of formal rules, procedures, control, and measurement systems	Pervasive, specific, uniform, comprehensive	Minimal, loose, flexible
3. Time dimensions incorporated in formal practices	Short-term	Long-term
4. Goal dimensions incorporated in formal practices	Manufacturing	Scientific

performing units (the Akron plant and Stockton laboratory), but we shall also compare each of these with its less effective mate (the Hartford plant and Carmel laboratory respectively).

FORMAL CHARACTERISTICS

Beginning with differences in formal characteristics, we found that both the Akron and Stockton organizations fit their respective tasks much better than did their less successful counterparts. In the predictable manufacturing task environment, Akron had a pattern of formal relationships and duties that was highly structured and precisely defined. Stockton, with its unpredictable research task, had a low degree of structure and much less precision of definition (see *Exhibit II*).

Akron's pattern of formal rules, procedures, and control systems was so specific and comprehensive that it prompted one manager to remark:

"We've got rules here for everything from how much powder to use in cleaning the toilet bowls to how to cart a dead body out of the plant."

In contrast, Stockton's formal rules were so minimal, loose, and flexible that one scientist, when asked whether he felt the rules ought to be tightened, said:

"If a man puts a nut on a screw all day long, you may need more rules and a job definition for him. But we're not novices here. We're professionals and not the kind who need close supervision. People around here *do* produce, and produce under relaxed conditions. Why tamper with success?"

These differences in formal organizational characteristics were well suited to the differences in tasks of the two organizations. Thus:

◻ Akron's highly structured formal practices fit its predictable task because behavior had to be rigidly defined and controlled around the automated, high-speed production line. There was really only one way to accomplish the plant's very routine and programmable job; managers defined it precisely and insisted (through the plant's formal practices) that each man do what was expected of him.

On the other hand, Stockton's highly unstructured formal practices made just as much sense because the required activities in the laboratory simply could not be rigidly defined in advance. With such an unpredictable, fast-changing task as communications technology research, there were numerous approaches to getting the job done well. As a consequence, Stockton managers used a less structured pattern of formal practices that left the scientists in the lab free to respond to the changing task situation.

□ Akron's formal practices were very much geared to *short-term* and *manufacturing* concerns as its task demanded. For example, formal production reports and operating review sessions were daily occurrences, consistent with the fact that the through-put time for their products was typically only a few hours.

By contrast, Stockton's formal practices were geared to *long-term* and *scientific* concerns, as its task demanded. Formal reports and reviews were made only quarterly, reflecting the fact that research often does not come to fruition for three to five years.

At the two less effective sites (i.e., the Hartford plant and the Carmel laboratory), the formal organizational characteristics did not fit their respective tasks nearly as well. For example, Hartford's formal practices were much less structured and controlling than were Akron's, while Carmel's were more restraining and restricting than were Stockton's. A scientist in Carmel commented:

"There's something here that keeps you from being scientific. It's hard to put your finger on, but I guess I'd call it 'Mickey Mouse.' There are rules and things here that get in your way regarding doing your job as a researcher."

CLIMATE CHARACTERISTICS

As with formal practices, the climate in both high-performing Akron and Stockton suited the respective tasks much better than did the climates at the less successful Hartford and Carmel sites.

Perception of structure: The people in the Akron plant perceived a great deal of structure, with their behavior tightly controlled and defined. One manager in the plant said:

"We can't let the lines run unattended. We lose money whenever they do. So we make sure each man knows his job, knows when he can take a break, knows how to handle a change in shifts, etc. It's all spelled out clearly for him the day he comes to work here."

In contrast, the scientists in the Stockton laboratory perceived very little structure, with their behavior only minimally controlled. Such perceptions encouraged the individualistic and creative behavior that the uncertain, rapidly changing research task needed. Scientists in the less successful Carmel laboratory perceived much more structure in their organization and voiced the feeling that this was "getting in their way" and making it difficult to do effective research.

Distribution of influence: The Akron plant and the Stockton laboratory also differed substantially in how influence was distributed and on the character of superior-subordinate and colleague relations. Akron personnel felt that they had much less influence over decisions in their plant than Stockton's scientists did in their laboratory. The task at Akron had already been clearly defined and that definition had, in a sense, been incorporated into the automated production flow itself. Therefore, there was less need for individuals to have a say in decisions concerning the work process.

Moreover, in Akron, influence was perceived to be concentrated in the upper levels of the formal structure (a hierarchical or "top-heavy" distribution), while in Stockton influence was perceived to be more evenly spread out among more levels of the formal structure (an egalitarian distribution).

Akron's members perceived themselves to have a low degree of freedom vis-à-vis superiors both in choosing the jobs they work on and in handling these jobs on their own. They also described the type of supervision in the plant as being relatively directive. Stockton's scientists, on the other hand, felt that they had a great deal of freedom vis-à-vis their superiors both in choosing the tasks and projects, and in handling them in the way that they wanted to. They described supervision in the laboratory as being very participatory.

It is interesting to note that the less successful Carmel laboratory had more of its decisions made at the top. Because of this, there was a definite feeling by the scientists that their particular expertise was not being effectively used in choosing projects.

Relations with others: The people at Akron perceived a great deal of similarity among themselves in background, prior work experiences, and approaches for tackling job-related problems. They also perceived the degree of coordination of effort among colleagues to be very high. Because Akron's task was so precisely defined and the behavior of its members so rigidly controlled around the automated lines, it is easy to see that this pattern also made sense.

By contrast, Stockton's scientists perceived not only a great many differences among themselves, especially in education and background, but also that the coordination of effort among colleagues was relatively low. This was appropriate for a laboratory in which a great variety of disciplines and skills were present and individual projects were important to solve technological problems.

Time orientation: As we would expect, Akron's individuals were highly oriented toward a relatively short time span and manufacturing goals. They responded to quick feedback concerning the quality and service that the plant was providing. This was essential, given the nature of their task.

Stockton's researchers were highly oriented toward a longer time span and scientific goals. These orientations meant that they were willing to wait for long-term feedback from a research project that might take years to complete. A scientist in Stockton said:

"We're not the kind of people here who need a pat on the back every day. We can wait for months if necessary before we get feedback from colleagues and the profession. I've been working on one project now for three months and I'm still not sure where it's going to take me. I can live with that, though."

This is precisely the kind of behavior and attitude that spells success on this kind of task.

Managerial style: Finally, the individuals in both Akron and Stockton perceived their chief executive to have a "managerial style" that expressed more of a concern for the task than for people or relationships, but this seemed to fit both tasks.

In Akron, the technology of the task was so dominant that top managerial behavior which was not focused primarily on the task might have reduced the effectiveness of performance. On the other hand, although Stockton's research task called for more individualistic problem-solving behavior, that sort of behavior could have become segmented and uncoordinated, unless the top executive in the lab focused the group's attention on the overall research task. Given the individualistic bent of the scientists, this was an important force in achieving unity of effort.

All these differences in climate characteristics in the two high performers are summarized in *Exhibit III.*

As with formal attributes, the less effective Hartford and Carmel sites had organization climates that showed a perceptibly lower degree of fit with their respective tasks. For example, the Hartford plant had an egalitarian distribution of influence, perceptions of a low degree of structure,

Exhibit III. Differences in "climate" characteristics in high-performing organizations

Characteristics	Akron	Stockton
1. Structural orientation	Perceptions of tightly controlled behavior and a high degree of structure	Perceptions of a low degree of structure
2. Distribution of influence	Perceptions of low total influence, concentrated at upper levels in the organization	Perceptions of high total influence, more evenly spread out among all levels
3. Character of superior-subordinate relations	Low freedom vis-à-vis superiors to choose and handle jobs, directive type of supervision	High freedom vis-à-vis superiors to choose and handle projects, participatory type of supervision
4. Character of colleague relations	Perceptions of many similarities among colleagues, high degree of coordination of colleague effort	Perceptions of many differences among colleagues, relatively low degree of coordination of colleague effort
5. Time orientation	Short-term	Long-term
6. Goal orientation	Manufacturing	Scientific
7. Top executive's "managerial style"	More concerned with task than people	More concerned with task than people

and a more participatory type of supervision. The Carmel laboratory had a somewhat top-heavy distribution of influence, perceptions of high structure, and a more directive type of supervision.

Competence Motivation

Because of the difference in organizational characteristics at Akron and Stockton, the two sites were strikingly different places in which to work. But these organizations had two very important things in common. First, each organization fit very well the requirements of its task. Second, although the behavior in the two organizations was different, the result in both cases was effective task performance.

Since, as we indicated earlier, our primary concern in this study was to link the fit between organization and task with individual motivation to perform effectively, we devised a two-part test to measure the sense of competence motivation of the individuals at both sites. Thus:

The *first* part asked a participant to write creative and imaginative stories in response to six ambiguous pictures.

The *second* asked him to write a creative and imaginative story about what he would be doing, thinking, and feeling "tomorrow" on his job. This is called a "projective" test because it is assumed that the respondent projects into his stories his own attitudes, thoughts, feelings, needs, and wants, all of which can be measured from the stories.

The results indicated that the individuals in Akron and Stockton showed significantly more feelings of competence than did their counterparts in

Exhibit IV. Basic contingent relationships

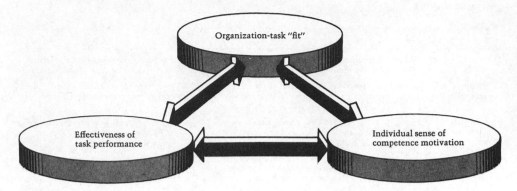

the lower-fit Hartford and Carmel organizations. [Differences between the two container plants are significant at .001 and between the research laboratories at .01 (one-tailed probability).] We found that the organization-task fit is simultaneously linked to and interdependent with both individual motivation and effective unit performance. (This interdependency is illustrated in *Exhibit IV.*)

Putting the conclusions in this form raises the question of cause and effect. Does effective unit performance result from the task-organization fit or from higher motivation, or perhaps from both? Does higher sense of competence motivation result from effective unit performance or from fit?

Our answer to these questions is that we do not think there are any single cause-and-effect relationships, but that these factors are mutually interrelated. This has important implications for management theory and practice.

Contingency Theory

Returning to McGregor's Theory X and Theory Y assumptions, we can now question the validity of some of his conclusions. While Theory Y might help to explain the findings in the two laboratories, we clearly need something other than Theory X or Y assumptions to explain the findings in the plants.

For example, the managers at Akron worked in a formalized organization setting with relatively little participation in decision making, and yet they were highly motivated. According to Theory X, people would work hard in such a setting only because they were coerced to do so. According to Theory Y, they should have been involved in decision making and been self-directed to feel so motivated. Nothing in our data indicates that either set of assumptions was valid at Akron.

Conversely, the managers at Hartford, the low-performing plant, were in a less formalized organization with more particpation in decision making, and yet they were not as highly motivated as the Akron managers. The Theory Y assumptions would suggest that they should have been more motivated.

A way out of such paradoxes is to state a new set of assumptions, the Contingency Theory, that seems to explain the findings at all four sites:

1. Human beings bring varying patterns of needs and motives into the work organization, but one central need is to achieve a sense of competence.

2. The sense of competence motive, while it exists in all human beings, may be fulfilled in different ways by different people depending on how this need interacts with the strengths of the individuals' other needs—such as those for power, independence, structure, achievement, and affiliation.

3. Competence motivation is most likely to be fulfilled when there is a fit between task and organization.

4. Sense of competence continues to motivate even when a competence goal is achieved; once one goal is reached, a new, higher one is set.

While the central thrust of these points is clear from the preceding discussion of the study, some elaboration can be made. First, the idea that different people have different needs is well understood by psychologists. However, all too often, managers assume that all people have similar needs. Lest we be accused of the same error, we are saying only that all people have a need to feel competent; in this *one* way they are similar. But in many other dimensions of personality, individuals differ, and these differences will determine how a particular person achieves a sense of competence.

Thus, for example, the people in the Akron plant seemed to be very different from those in the Stockton laboratory in their underlying attitudes toward uncertainty, authority, and relationships with their peers. And because they had different need patterns along these dimensions, both groups were highly motivated by achieving competence from quite different activities and settings.

While there is a need to further investigate how people who work in different settings differ in their psychological makeup, one important implication of the Contingency Theory is that we must not only seek a fit between organization and task, but also between task and people and between people and organization.

A further point which requires elaboration is that one's sense of competence never really comes to rest. Rather, the real satisfaction of this need is in the successful performance itself, with no diminishing of the motivation as one goal is reached. Since feelings of competence are thus reinforced by successful performance, they can be a more consistent and reliable motivator than salary and benefits.

IMPLICATIONS FOR MANAGERS

The major managerial implication of the Contingency Theory seems to rest in the task-organization-people fit. Although this interrelationship is complex, the best possibility for managerial action probably is in tailoring the organization to fit the task and the people. If such a fit is achieved, both effective unit performance and a higher sense of competence motivation seem to result.

Managers can start this process by considering how certain the task is, how frequently feedback about task performance is available, and what goals are implicit in the task. The answers to these questions will guide their decisions about the design of the management hierarchy, the specificity of job assignments, and the utilization of rewards and control procedures. Selective use of training programs and a general emphasis on appropriate management styles will move them toward a task-organization fit.

The problem of achieving a fit among task, organization, and people is something we know less about. As we have already suggested, we need further investigation of what personality characteristics fit various tasks and organizations. Even with our limited knowledge, however, there are indications that people will gradually gravitate into organizations that fit their particular personalities. Managers can help this process by becoming more aware of what psychological needs seem to best fit the tasks available and the organizational setting, and by trying to shape personnel selection criteria to take account of these needs.

In arguing for an approach which emphasizes the fit among task, organization, and people, we are putting to rest the question of which organizational approach—the classical or the participative—is best. In its place we are raising a new question: What organizational approach is most appropriate given the task and the people involved?

For many enterprises, given the new needs of younger employees for more autonomy, and the rapid rates of social and technological change, it may well be that the more participative approach is the most appropriate. But there will still be many situations in which the more controlled and formalized organization is desirable. Such an organization need not be coercive or punitive. If it makes sense to the individuals involved, given their needs and their jobs, they will find it rewarding and motivating.

Concluding Note

The reader will recognize that the complexity we have described is not of our own making. The basic deficiency with earlier approaches is that they did not recognize the variability in tasks and people which produces this complexity. The strength of the contingency approach we have outlined is that it begins to provide a way of thinking about this complexity, rather than ignoring it. While our knowledge in this area is still growing, we are certain that any adequate theory of motivation and organization will have to take account of the contingent relationship between task, organization, and people.

22. How to Deal with Resistance to Change

Paul R. Lawrence

Many executives think that to overcome resistance to technological change in organizations, some form of participative management is necessary. Often real causes of resistance are overlooked, however, if simple management devices are assumed to be the answer. The author of this article asserts that what people resist is not technical innovation in their work but change in their social relationships in the organizations. If managers would concern themselves with this problem and encourage their staffs to respect the knowledge of workers and to give up their own preoccupations with technical change, they could help create common purpose and understanding in work situations where there often is anxiety and logrolling. The author's retrospective commentary, written fifteen years after the original publication date, emphasizes that though there are limits to the approach he advocated, the difficulties associated with co-ordinating groups are becoming more acute. The problem of resistance is still very alive and deserving of inquiry by management.

One of the most baffling and recalcitrant of the problems which business executives face is employee resistance to change. Such resistance may take a number of forms—persistent reduction in output, increase in the number of "quits" and requests for transfer, chronic quarrels, sullen hostility, wildcat or slowdown strikes, and, of course, the expression of a lot of pseudological reasons why the change will not work. Even the more petty forms of this resistance can be troublesome.

All too often when executives encounter resistance to change, they "explain" it by quoting the cliché that "people resist change" and never look further. Yet changes must continually occur in industry. This applies with particular force to the all-important "little" changes that constantly take place—changes in work methods, in routine office procedures, in the location of a machine or a desk, in personnel assignments and job titles.

No one of these changes makes the headlines, but in total they account for much of our increase in productivity. They are not the spectacular once-in-a-lifetime technological revolutions that involve mass layoffs or the obsolescence of traditional skills, but they are vital to business progress.

Does it follow, therefore, that business management is forever saddled with the onerous job of "forcing" change down the throats of resistant people? My answer is *no*. It is the thesis of this article that people do *not* resist technical change as such and that most of the resistance which does occur is unnecessary. I shall discuss these points, among others:

1. A solution which has become increasingly popular for dealing with resistance to change is to get the people involved to "participate" in making the change. But as a practical matter "participation" as a device is not a good way for management to think about the problem. In fact, it may lead to trouble.

2. The key to the problem is to understand the true nature of resistance. Actually, what employees resist is usually not technical change but social change—the change in their human relationships that generally accompanies technical change.

3. Resistance is usually created because of certain blind spots and attitudes which staff specialists have as a result of their preoccupation with the technical aspects of new ideas.

4. Management can take concrete steps to deal constructively with these staff attitudes. The steps include emphasizing new standards of performance for staff specialists and encouraging them to think in different ways, as well as making use of the fact that signs of resistance can serve as a practical warning signal in directing and timing technological changes.

5. Top executives can also make their own efforts more effective at meetings of staff and operating groups where change is being discussed. They can do this by shifting their attention from the facts of schedules, technical details, work assignments, and so forth, to what the discussion of these items indicates in regard to developing resistance and receptiveness to change.

Let us begin by taking a look at some research into the nature of resistance to change. There are two studies in particular that I should like to discuss. They highlight contrasting ways of interpreting resistance to change and of coping with it in day-to-day administration.

Is Participation Enough?

The first study was conducted by Lester Coch and John R. P. French, Jr. in a clothing factory.[1] It deserves special comment because, it seems to me, it is the most systematic study of the phenomenon of resistance to change that has been made in a factory setting. To describe it briefly:

The two researchers worked with four different groups of factory opera-

1. See Lester Coch and John R. P. French, Jr., "Overcoming Resistance to Change," *Human Relations*, Vol. 1, No. 4, 1948, p. 512.

tors who were being paid on a modified piece-rate basis. For each of these four groups a minor change in the work procedure was installed by a different method, and the results were carefully recorded to see what, if any, problems of resistance occurred. The four experimental groups were roughly matched with respect to efficiency ratings and degree of cohesiveness; in each group the proposed change modified the established work procedure to about the same degree.

The work change was introduced to the first group by what the researchers called a "no-participation" method. This small group of operators was called into a room where some staff people told the members that there was a need for a minor methods change in their work procedures. The staff people then explained the change to the operators in detail, and gave them the reasons for the change. The operators were then sent back to the job with instructions to work in accordance with the new method.

The second group of operators was introduced to the work change by a "participation-through-representation" method—a variation of the approach used with the third and fourth groups which turned out to be of little significance.

The third and fourth groups of operators were both introduced to the work change on a "total-participation" basis. All the operators in these groups met with the staff men concerned. The staff men dramatically demonstrated the need for cost reduction. A general agreement was reached that some savings could be effected. The groups then discussed how existing work methods could be improved and unnecessary operations eliminated. When the new work methods were agreed on, all the operators were trained in the new methods, and all were observed by the time-study men for purposes of establishing a new piece rate on the job.

RESEARCH FINDINGS

The researchers reported a marked contrast between the results achieved by the different methods of introducing this change:

□ *No-participation group*—The most striking difference was between Group #1, the no-participation group, and Groups #3 and #4, the total-participation groups. The output of Group #1 dropped immediately to about two thirds of its previous output rate. The output rate stayed at about this level throughout the period of 30 days after the change was introduced. The researchers further reported:

"Resistance developed almost immediately after the change occurred. Marked expressions of aggression against management occurred, such as conflict with the methods engineer, . . . hostility toward the supervisor, deliberate restriction of production, and lack of cooperation with the supervisor. There were 17% quits in the first 40 days. Grievances were filed about piece rates; but when the rate was checked, it was found to be a little 'loose.'"

□ *Total-participation groups*—In contrast with this record, Groups #3 and #4 showed a smaller initial drop in output and a very rapid recovery not only to the previous production rate but to a rate that exceeded the previous rate. In these groups there were no signs of hostility toward the staff people or toward the supervisors, and there were no quits during the experimental period.

APPRAISAL OF RESULTS

Without going into all the researchers' decisions based on these experiments, it can be fairly stated that they concluded that resistance to methods changes could be overcome by *getting the people involved in the change to participate in making it.*

This was a very useful study, but the results are likely to leave the manager of a factory still bothered by the question, "Where do we go from here?" The trouble centers around that word "participation." It is not a new word. It is seen often in management journals, heard often in management discussions. In fact, the idea that it is a good thing to get employee participation in making changes has become almost axiomatic in management circles.

But participation is not something that can be conjured up or created artificially. You obviously cannot buy it as you would buy a typewriter. You cannot hire industrial engineers and accountants and other staff people who have the ability "to get participation" built into them. It is doubtful how helpful it would be to call in a group of supervisors and staff men and exhort them, "Get in there and start participation."

Participation is a feeling on the part of people, not just the mechanical act of being called in to take part in discussions. Common sense would suggest that people are more likely to respond to the way they are customarily treated—say, as people whose opinions are respected because they themselves are respected for their own worth—rather than by the stratagem of being called to a meeting or being asked some carefully calculated questions. In fact, many supervisors and staff men have had some unhappy experiences with executives who have read about participation and have picked it up as a new psychological gimmick for getting other people to think they "want" to do as they are told—as a sure way to put the sugar coating on a bitter pill.

So there is still the problem of how to get this thing called participation. And, as a matter of fact, the question remains whether participation was the determining factor in the Coch and French experiment or whether there was something of deeper significance underlying it.

Resistance to What?

Now let us take a look at a second series of research findings about resistance to change. . . . While making some research observations in a
factory manufacturing electronic products, a colleague and I had an opportunity to observe a number of incidents that for us threw new light on
this matter of resistance to change. One incident was particularly illuminating:

▢ We were observing the work of one of the industrial engineers and
a production operator who had been assigned to work with the engineer
on assembling and testing an experimental product that the engineer was
developing. The engineer and the operator were in almost constant daily
contact in their work. It was a common occurrence for the engineer to
suggest an idea for some modification in a part of the new product; he
would then discuss his idea with the operator and ask her to try out the
change to see how it worked. It was also a common occurrence for the
operator to get an idea as she assembled parts and to pass this idea on to
the engineer, who would then consider it and, on occasion, ask the operator
to try out the idea and see if it proved useful.

A typical exchange between these two people might run somewhat as
follows:

Engineer: "I got to thinking last night about that difficulty we've been
having on assembling the x part in the last few days. It occurred to me
that we might get around that trouble if we washed the part in a cleaning
solution just prior to assembling it."

Operator: "Well, that sounds to me like it's worth trying."

Engineer: "I'll get you some of the right kind of cleaning solution, and
why don't you try doing that with about 50 parts and keep track of what
happens."

Operator: "Sure, I'll keep track of it and let you know how it works."

With this episode in mind, let us take a look at a second episode involving the same production operator. One day we noticed another
engineer approaching the production operator. We knew that this particular engineer had had no previous contact with the production operator.
He had been asked to take a look at one specific problem on the new
product because of his special technical qualifications. He had decided
to make a change in one of the parts of the product to eliminate the
problem, and he had prepared some of these parts using his new method.
Here is what happened:

▢ He walked up to the production operator with the new parts in his
hand and indicated to her by a gesture that he wanted her to try assembling
some units using his new part. The operator picked up one of the parts and

proceeded to assemble it. We noticed that she did not handle the part with her usual care. After she had assembled the product, she tested it and it failed to pass inspection. She turned to the new engineer and, with a triumphant air, said, "It doesn't work."

The new engineer indicated that she should try another part. She did so, and again it did not work. She then proceeded to assemble units using all of the new parts that were available. She handled each of them in an unusually rough manner. None of them worked. Again she turned to the engineer and said that the new parts did not work.

The engineer left, and later the operator, with evident satisfaction, commented to the original industrial engineer that the new engineer's idea was just no good.

SOCIAL CHANGE

What can we learn from these episodes? To begin, it will be useful for our purposes to think of change as having both a technical and a social aspect. The *technical* aspect of the change is the making of a measurable modification in the physical routines of the job. The *social* aspect of the change refers to the way those affected by it think it will alter their established relationships in the organization.

We can clarify this distinction by referring to the two foregoing episodes. In both of them, the technical aspects of the changes introduced were virtually identical: the operator was asked to use a slightly changed part in assembling the finished product. By contrast, the social aspects of the changes were quite different.

In the first episode, the interaction between the industrial engineer and the operator tended to sustain the give-and-take kind of relationship that these two people were accustomed to. The operator was used to being treated as a person with some valuable skills and knowledge and some sense of responsibility about her work; when the engineer approached her with his idea, she felt she was being dealt with in the usual way. But, in the second episode, the new engineer was introducing not only a technical change but also a change in the operator's customary way of relating herself to others in the organization. By his brusque manner and by his lack of any explanation, he led the operator to fear that her usual work relationships were being changed. And she just did not like the new way she was being treated.

The results of these two episodes were quite different also. In the first episode there were no symptoms of resistance to change, a very good chance that the experimental change would determine fairly whether a cleaning solution would improve product quality, and a willingness on the part of the operator to accept future changes when the industrial engineer

Exhibit I. Two contrasting patterns of human behavior

| | Change | | |
	Technical aspect	Social aspect	Results
Episode 1	Clean part prior to assembly	Sustaining the customary work relationship of operator	1. No resistance 2. Useful technical result 3. Readiness for more change
Episode 2	Use new part in assembly	Threatening the customary work relationship of operator	1. Signs of resistance 2. No useful technical result 3. Lack of readiness for more change

suggested them. In the second episode, however, there were signs of resistance to change (the operator's careless handling of parts and her satisfaction in their failure to work), failure to prove whether the modified part was an improvement or not, and indications that the operator would resist any further changes by the engineer. We might summarize the two contrasting patterns of human behavior in the two episodes in graphic form; see *Exhibit I.*

It is apparent from these two patterns that the variable which determines the result is the *social* aspect of the change. In other words, the operator did not resist the technical change as such but rather the accompanying change in her human relationships.

CONFIRMATION

This conclusion is based on more than one case. Many other cases in our research project substantiate it. Furthermore, we can find confirmation in the research experience of Coch and French, even though they came out with a different interpretation.

Coch and French tell us in their report that the procedure used with Group #1, i.e., the no-participation group, was the usual one in the factory for introducing work changes. And yet they also tell us something about the customary treatment of the operators in their work life. For example, the company's labor relations policies are progressive, the company and the supervisors place a high value on fair and open dealings with the employees, and the employees are encouraged to take up their problems and grievances with management. Also, the operators are accustomed to measuring the success and failure of themselves as operators against the company's standard output figures.

Now compare these *customary* work relationships with the way the

Group #1 operators were treated when they were introduced to this particular work change. There is quite a difference. When the management called them into the room for indoctrination, they were treated as if they had no useful knowledge of their own jobs. In effect, they were told that they were not the skilled and efficient operators they had thought they were, that they were doing the job inefficiently, and that some "outsider" (the staff expert) would now tell them how to do it right. How could they construe this experience *except* as a threatening change in their usual working relationship? It is the story of the second episode in our research case all over again. The results were also the same, with signs of resistance, persistently low output, and so on.

Now consider experimental Groups #3 and #4, i.e., the total-participation groups. Coch and French referred to management's approach in their case as a "new" method of introducing change; but, from the point of view of the *operators* it must not have seemed new at all. It was simply a continuation of the way they were ordinarily dealt with in the course of their regular work. And what happened? The results—reception to change, technical improvement, better performance—were much like those reported in the first episode between the operator and the industrial engineer.

So the research data of Coch and French tend to confirm the conclusion that the nature and size of the technical aspect of the change does not determine the presence or absence of resistance nearly so much as does the social aspect of the change.

Roots of Trouble

The significance of these research findings, from management's point of view, is that executives and staff experts need not expertness in using the devices of participation but a real understanding, in depth and detail, of the specific social arrangements that will be sustained or threatened by the change or by the way in which it is introduced.

These observations check with everyday management experience in industry. When we stop to think about it, we know that many changes occur in our factories without a bit of resistance. We know that people who are working closely with one another continually swap ideas about short cuts and minor changes in procedure that are adopted so easily and naturally that we seldom notice them or even think of them as change. The point is that because these people work so closely with one another, they intuitively understand and take account of the existing social arrangements for work and so feel no threat to themselves in such everyday changes.

By contrast, management actions leading to what we commonly label "change" are usually initiated outside the small work group by staff people. These are the changes that we notice and the ones that most frequently bring on symptoms of resistance. By the very nature of their work, most of our staff specialists in industry do not have the intimate contact with operating groups that allows them to acquire an intuitive understanding of the complex social arrangements which their ideas may affect. Neither do our staff specialists always have the day-to-day dealings with operating people that lead them to develop a natural respect for the knowledge and skill of these people. As a result, all too often the men behave in a way that threatens and disrupts the established social relationships. And the tragedy is that so many of these upsets are inadvertent and unnecessary.

Yet industry must have its specialists—not only many kinds of engineering specialists (product, process, maintenance, quality, and safety engineers) but also cost accountants, production schedulers, purchasing agents, and personnel men. Must top management therefore reconcile itself to continual resistance to change, or can it take constructive action to meet the problem?

I believe that our research in various factory situations indicates why resistance to change occurs and what management can do about it. Let us take the "why" factors first.

SELF-PREOCCUPATION

All too frequently we see staff specialists who bring to their work certain blind spots that get them into trouble when they initiate change with operating people. One such blind spot is "self-preoccupation." The staff man gets so engrossed in the technology of the change he is interested in promoting that he becomes wholly oblivious to different kinds of things that may be bothering people. Here are two examples:

□ In one situation the staff people introduced, with the best of intentions, a technological change which inadvertently deprived a number of skilled operators of much of the satisfaction that they were finding in their work. Among other things, the change meant that, whereas formerly the output of each operator had been placed beside his work position where it could be viewed and appreciated by him and by others, it was now being carried away immediately from the work position. The workmen did not like this.

The sad part of it was that there was no compelling cost or technical reason why the output could not be placed beside the work position as it had been formerly. But the staff people who had introduced the change were so literal-minded about their ideas that when they heard complaints on the changes from the operators, they could not comprehend what the trouble was. Instead, they began repeating all the logical arguments why the change made sense from a cost standpoint. The final result here was a chronic restriction of output and persistent hostility on the part of the operators.

☐ An industrial engineer undertook to introduce some methods changes in one department with the notion firmly in mind that this assignment presented him with an opportunity to "prove" to higher management the value of his function. He became so preoccupied with his personal desire to make a name for his particular techniques that he failed to pay any at· tention to some fairly obvious and practical considerations which the operating people were calling to his attention but which did not show up in his time-study techniques. As could be expected, resistance quickly developed to all his ideas, and the only "name" that he finally won for his techniques was a black one.

Obviously, in both of these situations the staff specialists involved did not take into account the social aspects of the change they were introducing. For different reasons they got so preoccupied with the technical aspects of the change that they literally could not see or understand what all the fuss was about.

We may sometimes wish that the validity of the technical aspects of the change were the sole determinant of its acceptability. But the fact remains that the social aspect is what determines the presence or absence of resistance. Just as ignoring this fact is the sure way to trouble, so taking advantage of it can lead to positive results. We must not forget that these same social arrangements which at times seem so bothersome are essential for the performance of work. Without a network of established social relationships a factory would be populated with a collection of people who had no idea of how to work with one another in an organized fashion. By working *with* this network instead of *against* it, management's staff representatives can give new technological ideas a better chance of acceptance.

KNOW-HOW OF OPERATORS OVERLOOKED

Another blind spot of many staff specialists is to the strengths as well as to the weaknesses of firsthand production experience. They do not recognize that the production foreman and the production operator are in their own way specialists themselves—specialists in actual experience with production problems. This point should be obvious, but it is amazing how many staff specialists fail to appreciate the fact that even though they themselves may have a superior knowledge of the technology of the production process involved, the foreman or the operators may have a more practical understanding of how to get daily production out of a group of men and machines.

The experience of the operating people frequently equips them to be of real help to staff specialists on at least two counts: (1) The operating people are often able to spot practical production difficulties in the ideas of the specialists—and iron out those difficulties before it is too late; (2) the operating people are often able to take advantage of their intimate acquaintance with the existing social arrangements for getting work done. If given a chance, they can use this kind of knowledge to help detect those parts of the change that will have undesirable social consequences. The staff experts can then go to work on ways to avoid the trouble area without materially affecting the technical worth of the change.

Further, some staff specialists have yet to learn the truth that, even after the plans for a change have been carefully made, it takes *time* to put the change successfully into production use. Time is necessary even though there may be no resistance to the change itself. The operators must develop the skill needed to use new methods and new equipment efficiently; there are always bugs to be taken out of a new method or piece of equipment even with the best of engineering. When a staff man begins to lose his patience with the amount of time that these steps take, the people he is working with will begin to feel that he is pushing them; *this* amounts to a change in their customary work relationships, and resistance will start building up where there was none before.

The situation is aggravated if the staff man mistakenly accuses the operators of resisting the idea of the change, for there are few things that irritate people more than to be blamed for resisting change when actually they are doing their best to learn a difficult new procedure.

Management Action

Many of the problems of resistance to change arise around certain kinds of *attitudes* that staff men are liable to develop about their jobs and their own ideas for introducing change. Fortunately, management can influence these attitudes and thus deal with the problems at their source.

BROADENING STAFF INTERESTS

It is fairly common for a staff man to work so hard on one of his ideas for change that he comes to identify himself with it. This is fine for the organization when he is working on the idea by himself or with his immediate colleagues; the idea becomes "his baby," and the company benefits from his complete devotion to his work.

But when he goes to some group of operating people to introduce a change, his very identification with his ideas tends to make him unreceptive to any suggestions for modification. He just does not feel like letting anyone else tamper with his pet ideas. It is easy to see, of course, how this attitude is interpreted by the operating people as a lack of respect for their suggestions.

This problem of the staff man's extreme identification with his work is one which, to some extent, can only be cured by time. But here are four suggestions for speeding up the process:

1. The manager can often, with wise timing, encourage the staff man's interest in a different project that is just starting.

2. The manager can also, by his "coaching" as well as by example, prod the staff man to develop a healthier respect for the contributions he can receive from operating people; success in this area would, of course, virtually solve the problem.

3. It also helps if the staff man can be guided to recognize that the satisfaction he derives from being productive and creative is the same satisfaction he denies the operating people by his behavior toward them. Experience shows that staff people can sometimes be stimulated by the thought of finding satisfaction in sharing with others in the organization the pleasures of being creative.

4. Sometimes, too, the staff man can be led to see that winning acceptance of his ideas through better understanding and handling of human beings is just as challenging and rewarding as giving birth to an idea.

USING UNDERSTANDABLE TERMS

One of the problems that must be overcome arises from the fact that the typical staff man is likely to have the attitude that the reasons why he is recommending any given change may be so complicated and specialized that it is impossible to explain them to operating people. It may be true that the operating people would find it next to impossible to understand some of the staff man's analytical techniques, but this does not keep them from coming to the conclusion that the staff specialist is trying to razzle-dazzle them with tricky figures and formulas—insulting their intelligence —if he does not strive to his utmost to translate his ideas into terms understandable to them. The following case illustrates the importance of this point:

□ A staff specialist was temporarily successful in "selling" a change based on a complicated mathematical formula to a foreman who really did not understand it. The whole thing backfired, however, when the foreman tried to sell it to his operating people. They asked him a couple of sharp questions that he could not answer. His embarrassment about this led him to resent and resist the change so much that eventually the whole proposition fell through. This was unfortunate in terms not only of human relations but also of technological progress in the plant.

There are some very good reasons, both technical and social, why the staff man should be interested in working with the operating people until his recommendations make "sense." (This does not mean that the operating people need to understand the recommendations in quite the same way or ir the same detail that the staff man does, but that they should be able to visualize the recommendations in terms of their job experiences.) Failure of the staff man to provide an adequate explanation is likely to mean that a job the operators had formerly performed with understanding and satisfaction will now be performed without understanding and with less satisfaction.

This loss of satisfaction not only concerns the individual involved but also is significant from the standpoint of the company which is trying to get maximum productivity from the operating people. A person who does not have a feeling of comprehension of what he is doing is denied the opportunity to exercise that uniquely human ability—the ability to use informed and intelligent judgment on what he does. If the staff man leaves the operating people with a sense of confusion, they will also be left unhappy and less productive.

Top line and staff executives responsible for the operation should make it a point, therefore, to know how the staff man goes about installing a change. They can do this by asking discerning questions when he reports to them, listening closely to reports of employee reaction, and, if they have the opportunity, actually watching the staff man at work. At times they may have to take such drastic action as insisting that the time of installation of a proposed change be postponed until the operators are ready for it. But, for the most part, straightforward discussions with the staff man in terms of what they think of his approach should help him, over a period of time, to learn what is expected of him in his relationships with operating personnel.

NEW LOOK AT RESISTANCE

Another attitude that gets staff men into trouble is the *expectation* that all the people involved will resist the change. It is curious but true that the staff man who goes into his job with the conviction that people are going to resist any idea he presents with blind stubbornness is likely to find them responding just the way he thinks they will. The process is clear: whenever he treats the people who are supposed to buy his ideas as if they were bullheaded, he changes the way they are used to being treated; and they *will* be bullheaded in resisting *that* change!

I think that the staff man—and management in general—will do better to look at it this way: When resistance *does* appear, it should not be thought of as something to be *overcome*. Instead, it can best be thought of as a useful red flag—a signal that something is going wrong. To use a rough analogy, signs of resistance in a social organization are useful in the same way that pain is useful to the body as a signal that some bodily functions are getting out of adjustment.

The resistance, like the pain, does not tell what is wrong but only that something *is* wrong. And it makes no more sense to try to overcome such resistance than it does to take a pain killer without diagnosing the bodily ailment. Therefore, when resistance appears, it is time to listen carefully to find out what the trouble is. What is needed is not a long harangue on the logic of the new recommendations but a careful exploration of the difficulty.

It may happen that the problem is some technical imperfection in the change that can be readily corrected. More than likely, it will turn out that the change is threatening and upsetting some of the established social arrangements for doing work. Whether the trouble is easy or difficult to correct, management will at least know what it is dealing with.

NEW JOB DEFINITION

Finally, some staff specialists get themselves in trouble because they assume they have the answer in the thought that people will accept a change when they have participated in making it. For example:

□ In one plant we visited, an engineer confided to us (obviously because we, as researchers on human relations, were interested in psychological gimmicks!) that he was going to put across a proposed production layout change of his by inserting in it a rather obvious error, which others could then suggest should be corrected. We attended the meeting where this stunt was performed, and superficially it worked. Somebody caught the error, proposed that it be corrected, and our engineer immediately "bought" the suggestion as a very worthwhile one and made the change. The group then seemed to "buy" his entire layout proposal.

It looked like an effective technique—oh, so easy—until later, when we became better acquainted with the people in the plant. Then we found out that many of the engineer's colleagues considered him a phony and did not trust him. The resistance they put up to his ideas was very subtle, yet even more real and difficult for management to deal with.

Participation will never work so long as it is treated as a device to get somebody else to do what you want him to. Real participation is based on respect. And respect is not acquired by just trying; it is acquired when the staff man faces the reality that he needs the contributions of the operating people.

If the staff man defines his job as not just generating ideas but also getting those ideas into practical operation, he will recognize his real dependence on the contributions of the operating people. He will ask them for ideas and suggestions, not in a backhanded way to get compliance, but in a straightforward way to get some good ideas and avoid some unnecessary mistakes. By this process he will be treating the operating people in such a way that his own behavior will not be perceived as a threat to their customary work relationships. It will be possible to discuss, and accept or reject, the ideas on their own merit.

The staff specialist who looks at the process of introducing change and at resistance to change in the manner outlined in the preceding pages may not be hailed as a genius, but he can be counted on in installing a steady flow of technical changes that will cut costs and improve quality without upsetting the organization.

Role of the Administrator

Now what about the way the top executive goes about his *own* job as it involves the introduction of change and problems of resistance?

One of the most important things he can do, of course, is to deal with staff people in much the same way that he wants them to deal with the operators. He must realize that staff people resist social change, too. (This means, among other things, that he should not prescribe particular rules to them on the basis of this article!)

But most important, I think, is the way the administrator conceives of his job in coordinating the work of the different staff and line groups involved in a change. Does he think of his duties *primarily* as checking up, delegating and following through, applying pressure when performance fails to measure up? Or does he think of them *primarily* as facilitating communication and understanding between people with different points of view—for example, between a staff engineering group and a production group who do not see eye to eye on a change they are both involved in? An analysis of management's actual experience—or, at least, that part of it which has been covered by our research—points to the latter as the more effective concept of administration.

I do not mean that the executive should spend his time with the different people concerned discussing the human problems of change as such. He *should* discuss schedules, technical details, work assignments, and so forth. But he should also be watching closely for the messages that are passing back and forth as people discuss these topics. He will find that people—himself as well as others—are always implicitly asking and making answers to questions like: "How will he accept criticism?" "How much can I afford to tell him?" "Does he really get my point?" "Is he playing games?" The answers to such questions determine the degree of candor and the amount of understanding between the people involved.

When the administrator concerns himself with these problems and acts to facilitate understanding, there will be less logrolling and more sense of common purpose, fewer words and better understanding, less anxiety and more acceptance of criticism, less griping and more attention to specific problems—in short, better performance in putting new ideas for technological change into effect.

Appendix to Chapter 22

Retrospective Commentary

In the years since this article was published, we have seen a great deal of change in industry, but the human aspects of the topic do not seem very different. The human problems associated with change remain much the same even though our understanding of them and our methods for dealing with them have advanced.

The first of the two major themes of the article is that resistance to change does not arise because of technical factors per se but because of social and human considerations. This statement still seems to be true. There is, however, an implication in the article that the social and human costs of change, if recognized, can largely be avoided by thoughtful management effort. Today I am less sanguine about this.

It is true that these costs can be greatly reduced by conscious attention. Managements that have tried have made much progress. Here are some examples of what has been done:

□ Fewer people are now pushed out of the back doors of industry—embittered and "burned out" before their time.

□ Fewer major strikes are the result of head-on clashes over new technology and its effects on jobs.

□ Progress is being made in putting the needs of people into the design of new technological systems.

□ Relevant inputs of ideas and opinions of people from all ranks are being solicited and used *before* (not after) plans for change are frozen.

□ At the same time that well-established work groups are disrupted by technical imperatives, special efforts are made to help newly formed work groups evolve meaningful team relations quickly.

□ Time and care have been taken to counsel individuals whose careers have to some degree been disrupted by change.

All of these ways of reducing the human costs of change have worked for the companies that have seriously applied them. Still, I am more aware than in 1954 of the limits of such approaches. They do not always enable management to prevent situations from developing in which some individuals win while others lose. The values lost as skills become obsolete cannot always be replaced. The company's earnings may go up but the percentage payouts from even an enlarged "pie" have to be recalculated, and then the relative rewards shift. In these situations enlightened problem solving will not completely displace old-fashioned bargaining, and better communication will only clarify the hard-core realities.

The second theme of the article deals with ways of improving the relations between groups in an organization—particularly when a staff group is initiating change in the work of an operating or line group. The gap that exists in outlook and orientation between specialized groups in industry has increased, even as the number of such groups has continued to escalate. These larger gaps have in turn created ever more difficult problems of securing effective communication and problem solving between groups. Coordinating the groups is probably the number one problem of our modern corporations. So this second theme is hardly out-of-date.

Today, however, there is both more knowledge available about the problem than there was in 1954 and more sophisticated skill and attention being given to it. And there is increasing understanding of and respect for the necessity for differences between groups. There is less striving for consistency for its own sake. More managerial effort is being applied, in person and through impersonal systems, to bridge the gaps in understanding. While the conflicts between specialized groups are probably as intense now as ever, they are more frequently seen as task-related—that is, natural outgrowths of different jobs, skills, and approaches—rather than as redundant and related only to personality differences.

The major criticism that has been brought to my attention about the article is that it has damaged the useful concept of participation. Perhaps this is true. But the view of participation as a technique for securing compliance with a predetermined change was a widespread and seductive one in 1954—and it is not dead yet. Subsequent research has not altered the general conclusion that participation, to be of value, must be based on a search for ideas that are seen as truly relevant to the change under consideration. The shallow notion of participation, therefore, still needs to be debunked.

As a final thought, I now realize that the article implied that workers resist change while managers foster and implement change. Many of the changes of the intervening period, such as the computer revolution, have exposed the inadequacy of this assumption. It is difficult to find any managers today who do not at times feel greatly distressed because of changes, with their own resistance level running fairly high. We are all, at times, resistors as well as instigators of change. We are all involved on both sides of the process of adjusting to change.

In light of this, let me reemphasize the point that resistance to change is by itself neither good nor bad. Resistance may be soundly based or not. It is always, however, an important signal calling for further inquiry by management.

Part VI

Interpersonal Relations

Preface

In 1916 Henri Fayol, the French industrialist, listed the principles of management that he most frequently applied as a manager. The list included, among others, authority, discipline, remuneration, and unity of command and direction. The closest he came to stressing interpersonal relations as an area of importance was when he discussed esprit de corps. He thought that part of the manager's job is to make a unified and harmonious work force; one of the ways to do this, he said, is simply to avoid memo writing and to indulge in direct communication. The latter takes less time and usually cuts out the misunderstandings and bitterness that memos can create.

Since his time, managers have found that dealing with people successfully, avoiding bitterness and misunderstandings, has become more involved than merely choosing verbal over written communication. People problems seem to head the list as the most difficult, perplexing, and crucial that managers have to face.

Just what does "interpersonal relations" include? Just what is the problem that everyone finds so difficult? According to current research, effective organizations are ones that are free of or at least not hampered by tight, restrictive, nonsupportive emotional atmospheres. They are ones where a certain amount of risk taking, honesty, and trust predominate. Regardless of how desirable "openness" is, however, most people seem to have difficulty interacting in an assertive, nondefensive way. And to compound their difficulties, if the current writers in the field are correct, most people are not trained to investigate their feelings, and are taught that the expression of feelings is a sign of immaturity.

But in the real world it is obviously not helpful, for example, for managers to be openly angry with their subordinates, for subordinates to be openly rivalrous, or for women and blacks to show the hostility they feel toward a white-male-dominated culture. Why then is there so much encouragement for people to express their feelings? As with many things the clue to dealing with interpersonal problems and personal feelings that are destructive is to find a way to let the constructive ones dominate. This takes learning, and learning in an open and trusting atmosphere. It takes naming the devil, facing the problems squarely, and trying to recognize where one's own emotional weaknesses add to destructive barriers.

The message of the articles in this section is that if honesty and trust exist, people can relate to each other better, and organizations will benefit. The key to the issue is that in every organization each person has a different position title, personnel number, and place of work. But what they have in common is that they are all human beings. Their relations with each other, therefore, are going to be first of all personal, and only secondarily functional.

Fernando Bartolomé, in his article "Executives as Human Beings," asserts that by gaining awareness of their feelings and expressing them openly, managers can find life more rewarding at home and on the job. In "Interpersonal Barriers to Decision Making," Chris Argyris shows what the personal tensions are that can intrude upon effective decision making and gives some suggestions as to what can be done to overcome these problems. The final article in this section, "What It's Like to Be a Black Manager," by Edward W. Jones, Jr., shows how organizations not only need to realize that blacks are different from whites because for the most part they are unfamiliar with the ethic of white business, but also must recognize that bigotry exists and acts upon blacks in insidious and hurtful ways. Equal opportunity is more than putting a black man in a white man's job; it is ferreting out the bigotry and removing it.

23. Executives as Human Beings

Fernando Bartolomé

Like most men, business executives have difficulty in showing tenderness toward the persons they love and in acknowledging any need for others. "It's difficult for me to express dependence," one businessman told the author of this article. "Feelings of dependence are identified with weakness or 'untoughness,' and our culture doesn't accept these things in men." The author's revealing interviews of 40 mid-career corporate officers and their wives throw light on the effects of masculine reticence and aloofness on their home life. He shows how cultural values (including the notion that the toughest men are the most successful), fear of losing others' respect, and the work environment inhibit men from openly expressing warmth or love toward others. Being able to deal with one's emotions is important to an executive who is in constant contact with people, the author says, and it is essential to becoming a more alive human being.

Since man's only possession is his life, or rather his living, man's most fundamental question is, "How will I do my living?" So the search for a meaningful way of being alive should be a central aspect of man's life.

Man should be free from stereotypes, self-imposed or otherwise, and rigid role definitions that limit his existence. The American business executive is, in my opinion, a man caught in a stereotype. He is limited by a role definition obliging him to be super-masculine, super-tough, super-self-sufficient, and super-strong. It allows him very little freedom to be that mixture of strength and weakness, independence, and dependence, toughness and tenderness which a human being is.

When one thinks of the executive's situation, several questions come to mind:

□ How does he relate to himself, to others, and to the world?

□ Does he conceive of different ways of living his life, different ways of relating to himself, to others, and to the world?

□ Does he want to live his life differently? Is he tired of being the strong and reliable one, the one who is always on top of things?

The executive, I suspect, has great difficulty conceiving of alternative life styles in realistic terms. But only when he understands and is "tuned in" to these alternatives can he be in a position to choose his own life style.

Not long ago I conducted a study dealing with these questions. At great length I interviewed 40 younger executives and their wives. The executives' average age was 37 and they had been married an average of 13 years. Nearly half (19) were employed by large or medium-sized companies, 5 by small companies; 7 were entrepreneurs, and 9 were managers of organizations other than business.

I tried to learn how the executive relates to himself, to others, and to the world; and I tried to understand why he lives the way he does. In this article I shall discuss what I learned and say what I think it means in terms of alternatives open to the executive.

In the study I tried to discover to what extent executives acknowledge to themselves their own feelings of dependence and tenderness and reveal those feelings at home. And I tried to establish connections between their behavior or "styles" at the office and at home. In general, I tried to discover the factors that influenced the degree to which these executives acknowledged to themselves their own feelings and disclosed or expressed them at home.

Under the label "feelings of dependence" I grouped a complex set of feelings. All of them relate to the experiencing of a temporary or permanent inability or insufficient capacity to cope alone with a situation or event, and the feeling (conscious or unconscious) of a need for outside help to deal with the phenomenon. When somebody fills that need—with love, money, cooperation, sympathy, companionship, or whatever—the one in need experiences a feeling of dependence on that person.

By "feelings of tenderness" I mean feelings of caring for, being moved by, loving, taking care of, or being involved with another human being. In other words, I mean all those emotions aroused when a person allows himself to be deeply touched by another person and, being touched, feels warmth toward the other.

Relevance to Executives

A human being should have the courage and the skill to become aware of his feelings, to keep trying to learn how to deal with them, and to become free to choose how and when to express them. It would be good for the executive to increase this awareness, to develop those skills, and to gain that freedom.

Will this sensitivity and this skill improve his performance on the job? The executive's personal growth will improve his functioning in any area of human relations. Moreover, many organizational problems arise from people's inability to cope openly with emotions aroused in performance of their jobs. So, as the executive develops his capacity in private life to relate to his feelings and deal with them constructively, the greater is his capacity to deal with them in performing his executive functions.

If, however, the cultural environment is very rigid in its established behavioral patterns and highly resistant to change, not much individual self-exploration will take place. There are signs that the rigid cultural environment in the United States is breaking down. (More on this later.)

At any rate, the home milieu, because of its small size and private nature, is more flexible than the work milieu. So it is a more suitable place for a man to start exploring himself and trying new behavioral styles.

The failure of methods to improve the executive's performance in the area of relating to others at work is partly due to the erroneous assumption that we should focus our attention on his tasks and behavioral demands at work. In other words, try to improve the executive, not the man. This false dichotomy, executive/man, is the basis for many mistakes. When we do not directly address the man, we fail; and everything that we provide "the executive" so he can manage people better is a gimmick and will not last.

Therefore, I have chosen to relate to the executive as a man and to care about his growth as a human being. This growth will have a positive effect when the person is engaged in his managerial functions.

Expression of Feeling

In the interviews I conducted, nearly all the men (36) described themselves as seldom experiencing feelings of dependence. While unable to confirm it, I believe they experienced these feelings more often than they acknowledged to themselves. Also, the great majority (32) admitted great reluctance to reveal to their wives their feelings of dependence when they experienced them.

"It's difficult for me to express dependence," said one executive. "Feelings of dependence are identified with weakness or 'untoughness' and our culture doesn't accept these things in men."

With respect to feelings of tenderness, the executives (with one or two exceptions) acknowledged having them often. Nevertheless, they recognized some difficulty in expressing them and great difficulty in full experiencing and sharing of these feelings.

Most of the men acknowledged that their expressions of tenderness were usually limited to members of their families, especially young children. And even displays of tenderness to their children, particularly boys, were inhibited by fear of "smothering" them or making them too dependent on their parents. "Doing things is more important than people," said one executive during an interview. "I want my children to learn to ski well. In skiing one only needs man and hill; nobody else is needed."

With few exceptions, the women I interviewed shared their husbands' reticence in expressing feelings and desire to encourage children's independence. The wife of the executive I just quoted said, "I'm trying to make my children stand on their own feet. I wouldn't express openly my affection for them because I don't want to smother them. I'm quite cold."

During the course of many hours of interviewing and many purely social occasions, I observed little physical contact between couples and their children, although the parents seemed to love them a lot.

To my surprise, I heard very few complaints on the part of husband or wife about the other's inability to express tenderness, even in those cases where I perceived displays of affection to be rather meager and not very rich in form.

Expression of tenderness to outsiders, including friends—especially a man's display of affection or even regard for a male friend—was very difficult for the men. One of them said, "I consider myself a sentimentalist and I think I am quite able to express my feelings. But the other day my wife described a friend of mine to some people as being my best friend and I felt embarrassed when I heard her say it."

On thinking about what these men and women had told me, I emerged with some ideas about the factors that seem to influence their expression of feelings of dependence and tenderness. They are cultural beliefs, fear of repercussions, and job characteristics. I shall discuss each in turn in the sections that follow.

Cultural Beliefs

All the persons I interviewed mentioned that the Anglo-Saxon culture discourages open and rich expression of emotion—any kind of emotion. Only the four couples of Irish extraction described themselves as experiencing less difficulty in expressing their feelings.

The men interviewed considered character traits such as strength, self-reliance, and "keeping a stiff upper lip" as both masculine and conducive to success. The picture of an executive one gets from one couple's remarks was typical.

Wife: My husband is very self-reliant, secure, self-sufficient. He never expresses his needs.

Husband: At work one gets accustomed not to express dependence and one does the same at home. As a matter of fact, at work I never think in terms of asking for help or expressing my needs but rather in terms of making good use of the available human resources. When I get home, I don't want to talk about any big problem; I just want to rest.

In contrast, the executives considered such characteristics as dependency, a need to be cared for, enjoyment of passive things, and tenderness as unmasculine and leading to failure—except for persons such as artists and "people of that kind." One gets a flavor of this point of view from what one executive said:

"I group my friends in two ways, those who have made it and don't complain and those who haven't made it. And only the latter spend time talking to their wives about their problems and how bad their boss is and all that. The ones who concentrate more on communicating with their wives and families are those who have realized that they aren't going to make it and therefore they have changed their focus of attention.

"The top executive really enjoys himself; he has the company plane and a lot of staff and has it easy. The ones who get the ulcers are those who are trying to get up there."

In some cases the men seemed to agree fully with the cultural beliefs and were intent on inculcating them and developing those culturally desirable characteristics in their children. In other cases, however, I saw indications that these men and women were becoming aware of the relative value of those cultural norms, and I got the impression that they had started to explore the worth of different value systems.

But even in those cases where the process of reevaluation had started on an intellectual level, the executives still appeared to be willing to conform to societal values even if they opposed them. Their conformity influenced what feelings they revealed to their wives and to others.

The values of strength and self-reliance remained unquestioned, while the values of toughness and controlled expressiveness were starting to be reconsidered. Often I heard these couples criticize the excessive competitiveness of the American elementary and high school systems, while at the same time they indicated they valued highly the development of the child's strength by facing life without returning to ask for shelter. They wanted to make their children more sensitive but also strong and with equally big needs for high achievement.

With respect to themselves, they were quite conscious of the difficulty of abiding by the values they had adopted. But at the same time they seemed unable to move in another direction. An example of what I mean is their relationship with friends. Their restraint is typified by one executive's remark: "A very good friend of mine, a school roommate, came to visit and grabbed and hugged me. I felt very uncomfortable and awkward."

Many of the men acknowledged that they felt more affection, and with more intensity, than they were able to show, and they would like to express affection more fully. Yet none of them manifested any intention of exploring ways of establishing new and more open forms of relating to their friends and expressing their feelings to them.

Some of the executives believed strongly that, in the conduct of life, you must be either dependent or independent, expressive or restrained in expression. As one of them put it:

"You can't express dependence when you feel it, because it's a kind of absolute. If you are loyal 90% of the time and disloyal 10%, would you be considered to be loyal? Well, the same happens with dependence: you are either dependent or independent; you can't be both."

They were educated to believe that you cannot develop "contradictory" traits at the same time—you cannot, for example, develop both artistic self-expression and manly self-restraint. This sounds very logical. Furthermore, this dichotomic educational philosophy attaches judgmental labels to character traits, considering some to be "good" and some to be "bad."

So it is no surprise that, having been educated in a system filled with either/or choices and having learned that in developing a character trait you have to do it at the expense of something else, most of these executives believe in the impossibility of being two things at once and having "conflicting" characteristics. Therefore they try to eliminate the "bad" tendencies in themselves—if they admit to them at all—and encourage their children to do the same.

Effects of Fear

Carl R. Rogers describes how "as experiences occur in the life of the individual they are either (a) symbolized, perceived, and organized into some relation to the self, (b) ignored, because there is no perceived relationship to the self-structure, (c) denied symbolization, or given a distorted symbolization, because the experience is inconsistent with the structure of the self."[1]

The desire to avoid or ignore experience which the person unconsciously perceives as damaging to his concept of himself appeared to be quite strong in the group of men I interviewed. They had difficulty in admitting or even thinking about the possibility that "opposing" feelings or characteristics could exist within them at the same time.

1. *Client-Centered Therapy* (Boston, Houghton Mifflin, 1951), p. 503.

The "either/or" value system made it hard to accept as belonging to them those "bad" character traits that the culture condemns. According to Rogers' theory, when the organism encounters information about an experience that threatens the organism's need to view itself as consistent, it automatically sets up defense mechanisms to repress or distort the disturbing information.

Such a reaction could also be construed as a result of a person's natural inclination to adapt to the environment in order to avoid being hurt by it. One executive expressed this reaction in saying, "I know I'm inhibited, but when one has felt dependent many times in his life and has been rebuffed, he finally learns and becomes independent for reasons of security."

This statement implies that the process is conscious, but it actually seldom is. The person fears to acknowledge even to himself the existence of culturally defined negative characteristics that if recognized could trigger punitive action from his social environment.

PERSONAL RELATIONSHIPS

Fear of injury in personal relationships appeared to be a significant factor in inhibiting the executives from fuller and more open expression of their feelings.

Most important was the fear of rejection—that is, if you let your defenses down and let somebody know the depth of your needs, he will not only fail to satisfy your needs but will also lose respect for you. As a consequence, you learn to "play it cool," as evidenced by this executive's remark: "You act out certain games or rituals to provoke the desired reaction in the other and have your needs satisfied without having to ask for anything."

The fear of rejection is closely related to the man's belief that it is his manliness that makes him attractive to his wife and motivates her to give him what he needs. The traits which the culture calls masculine are toughness, strength, self-sufficiency, and ability to succeed. Therefore, a man avoids expressing his needs, disclosing his dependence, or showing tenderness lest his wife think him a weakling and be "turned off" by him.

When a man thinks this way, it becomes easy for him to rationalize his reluctance to "open up" in any way to his wife. "I try to solve my problems by myself before asking for help," one executive asserted. "Anyway, what's the use of troubling my wife about my job problems when there's nothing she can do about them?"

When the husband expresses dependency, he is for the moment giving up any pretension of superiority or ability to control and determine the relationship. The husband who is engaged in a power struggle with his wife perceives such a temporary abdication as very risky. Here are the comments of one couple.

Husband: If I express tenderness to my wife or let her get away with it in front of my friends, they give me hell. Besides, if you express tenderness and don't get it back, that's also a problem. And it's also a problem because you're always trying to have some authority at home and there is often competition with the wife about who wears the pants, and you can't afford to show dependence or tenderness when these other things are going on.

Wife: We compete all the time, for our friends' affection, for the children's affection, for authority at home, for everything!

When such a power struggle is going on, a man's expression of dependence or tenderness to his wife is conditioned on her previous submission to him. She must already have abdicated her power some time ago.

Today women are reexamining the male-female relationship and trying to reclaim equal dignity and equal rights within the relationship. As they do, the issues of power and domination will become central; men, who have previously had the upper hand, will find themselves put increasingly on the defensive. In a defensive position men will tend to disclose less of their feelings of dependence and tenderness than they do now.

Eventually, new ground rules will be established, and, one hopes, women will be less constrained by a definition of what they should be and what their role in the marital relationship should be. In other words, they will gain for themselves the right and the freedom to become more fully themselves.

At the same time, men will be deprived of the unjust privileges that they have enjoyed until today at the expense of women. But they also will be liberated to some extent from the limitations that have been imposed on them by a narrow definition of the masculine role. This deprives them of their freedom to acknowledge their feelings to themselves and to enjoy and express them.

Harming the child: Still another inhibiting factor for the executives was fear of hurting others, particularly their children.

Most of the parents considered themselves free to express physically and in other ways their feelings of tenderness to their children. Only a few recognized having difficulty doing it. However, my impression was that they were far from free in this regard; they seemed quite restrained in showing affection to their children. Their children also seemed to need affection shown to them more openly and frequently and more physically than they were getting it.

The parents' rationale was, as I mentioned earlier, their fear of smothering them, making them overdependent and weak, or violating their right to be independent.

The fear of harming the child by giving him "too much" affection is a wrong interpretation of the basic educational principle of respecting the child as an individual. Giving him love provides him with the confidence and strength to accept his own limitations and the fact of interdependence with other human beings. Acceptance of dependence as well as achievement of self-sufficiency is essential to the development of the mature person.

Job Characteristics

Most of the executives seemed quite satisfied with their work, though they complained that their jobs left too little time for family and other activities. Some of them were indeed putting in a lot of hours.

The consequences can be inhibiting for both husband and wife, as illustrated by the candid remarks of one couple.

Husband: A lot of executives are seduced by their jobs. They become fanatical about their jobs because they like the work and because their companies reward their fanaticism. But as a result they have very little time to be at home and talk about their feelings. When they come back home, there are a thousand things to do or take care of before they have time for themselves.

Wife: When he goes away because of his job, I'm left alone and I have to take care of things. When he comes back, I resent him for abandoning me and it takes some time to unwind, to relax, and be able to feel and express tenderness.

Those who seemed to be most involved in their work described how it took not only most of their time, but also nearly all of their energy. So when they returned home, they felt "drained" and able to communicate very little with their wives and children.

The competitive atmosphere, the premium placed on success, and the great value given to self-reliance on the job obviously affect the way an executive feels about himself when he leaves the office for home. And his attitude toward his performance affects his ability, once at home, to "unwind," let his needs be known, and accept affection from his family. As one wife put it:

"When they don't achieve what they think they should, they don't like themselves. And when they don't like themselves, how can they let others know them, how can they believe that others love them?"

Restive Achievers

Most of the men I talked with seemed to have abandoned any romantic views they once had of their marriages. They had seen their marital relationships turn from being in love to loving each other. They had come to realize how marriages change, mature, and lose their original charm and intensity to become partnerships in living. The observation of one man reflected this pragmatic realization:

"It's much riskier to express tenderness and dependence when you're married because you can't interrupt the relationship. Therefore, if your needs are not satisfied or your tenderness is rejected—if the other person doesn't accept what you have to give, or doesn't fulfill your needs, or doesn't understand you and rejects you—there is very little you can do about it. You are rejected and yet you can't abandon the boat you share with the other person."

These men, being very competent and doing interesting work, I felt had learned to examine their jobs for rewards as important as those they received at home—for a sense of work accomplished, objectives achieved, and something built. In their jobs these men sought and often found their creativity, a limited transcendence, and sometimes a way of spending their lives without being aware of too much pain.

Why do they devote so much of their lives to their work and so little, comparatively speaking, to achieving awareness in living and experiencing their feelings? It seems to me there are two reasons:

1. While we train men to become "doers," to succeed in the world of action, we do not train them to explore the world of emotions. As the testimony of executives and their wives in this article has shown, feelings are to be controlled, channeled, repressed, or forced into acceptable molds. Not only are men told how they should express their feelings—big boys don't cry—they are also told what and how to feel.

In the world of business, feelings are considered a nuisance that must be coped with or a possible threat to the effective functioning of the organization. The research of Chris Argyris has amply demonstrated the practice in organizations of denial of feelings and the maneuvers of people in those organizations to avoid situations where emotions might come into play and to smooth over situations where deep emotions have been expressed.

The result is a vicious circle: the less we recognize our feelings and learn to relate to them, the less chance we have of developing skills to deal with them—our own and others'. And the less skillful we are, the more threatening feelings seem, and the more vehemently we deny them or avoid dealing with them.

Men's lack of skill in relating to their feelings exists not only in the business milieu but also in the home environment and in their personal relationships. If you are skeptical of this, stop and think for a minute about the means that you have available to express your tenderness or your needs or your joy to your wife, children, and close friends. Then reflect on your ability to express richly these feelings to people who are close to you.

2. One always falls frustratingly short of gaining complete satisfaction of

one's needs. In our personal relationships we often search, in vain, for somebody who will fulfill us completely, give us all we need.

On the other hand, at work we can complete something—reach our goal. (The goal being usually modest, achieving it may give us a sense of being let down—and perhaps we will feel the shadow of death that is present whenever anything ends.) For an instant we touched our work and it gave us a good feeling because we had created it.

So, men seem to learn to enjoy their achievements as they have learned to give up the search for "everything" in a relationship. Their more or less meaningful world of companionship and work is enough for them.

It should be kept in mind that executives are people with high achievement needs, and one of their characteristics is the desire to measure accurately and unambiguously the extent of their achievement. This is not difficult in the world of action, but indications of achievement in the unstable world of feelings and personal relationships are hard to perceive and measure.

It Begins at Home

As long as the individual perceives the culture as standing ready to condemn him if he acts or feels in a manner counter to its norms and expectations, it is unlikely that he will explore new forms of behavior. So in trying to modify behavior we have to be concerned not only with the "unfreezing" and rearranging of the individual's value system and the development of courage and skills to implement his new values, but also with the unfreezing of his environment.

The environment at home, it seems to me, is already ripe for change. The younger generation insists on the validity of the emotions and wants to become "together" (a great cliché expressing the idea of a better balance of action and feeling, reason and sentiment, objectivity and fantasy). The home is the best place today for a member of the older generation to try exploring the world of feeling actively.

The next time you return home from work and see your son, stop for a second and try to get in touch with what you feel at that moment on seeing him. The feeling may be intense or weak, positive or negative, familiar or unfamiliar, painful or joyful—or to your surprise, you may seem to feel very little. Take it easy and try to stay with your feeling and experience it as fully as you can. Keep exploring your feelings at home and start trying new behavior there.

The executive is *a man relating to the world*. When he walks into his place of work, he is still himself. He should remain true to himself not only by doing but also by opening up his feelings as he lives.

Tomorrow, when you walk into your office and meet those you work with, take a minute to establish contact with your feelings or lack of feelings toward them. Try to become aware of how alive (or how numb) you are. If you discover that you have strong positive or negative feelings toward the men and women you work with, then ask yourself the simple questions that follow:

▫ "What am I doing with these feelings?"

▫ "What do I want to do with them?"

▫ "How do they affect my living as a man and therefore as a man/executive?"

In suggesting this, I am not talking to you as an executive, a manager, or a businessman. I am talking to you as a man—a man who can become a fuller, more alive human being.

The development of an ability to get in touch with and deal with one's own feelings and those of others, and to express one's feelings as richly as one wishes, is functional for any man and essential to an executive who has constant contact with other individuals.

But being able to get more closely in contact with our own feelings and engaging more deeply in experiencing and expressing them is not something that we can make happen overnight. It requires the development of difficult skills—skills to contact our feelings without being overwhelmed or scared by them, skills to cope with the feelings once we get in touch with them, skills to express our feelings when we want to, and skills to experience and express those feelings richly and confidently.

I have no method to offer for proceeding down this road, but I have found some of the suggestions of the Gestalt therapists very helpful in the process of owning more of one's self. Try, for example, the exercises suggested by Frederick Perls, Ralph F. Hefferline, and Paul Goodman in *Gestalt Therapy* (New York, Dell, 1951).

The principal purpose of this article is not to offer solutions but to present the landscape of an exciting territory to explore: the land of our own feelings. I could try to incite you to explore this territory by saying that, when you know it better, you will have become a better administrator or a better father and husband. But nobody can guarantee you that.

All I can tell you is that in the process of getting more in touch with our own feelings, we become more fully ourselves and we live more fully the only thing we have, our own lives.

24. Interpersonal Barriers to Decision Making

Chris Argyris

Interpersonal relationships probably frustrate managers more than any other aspect of their lives at work. They recognize that how people affect each other affects how their organizations run. What they might not recognize is, however, that people problems do not stop at the executive level when important decisions have to be made. In fact, the author of this article claims, they are even more intractable in a high-level, risk environment. In a study of six companies, in which 265 decision-making meetings were observed, the author found that executive behavior often creates an atmosphere of distrust and inflexibility, even though the executives themselves think trust and innovation crucial to good decision making. To acquire competency in interpersonal relationships, the author suggests that executives try asking important feedback questions at a time when the risk is low, seeing their executive groups as potentially effective, and, finally, using devices, such as tapes and training laboratories, to learn more about their own behavior.

□ The actual behavior of top executives during decision-making meetings often does not jibe with their attitudes and prescriptions about effective executive action.

□ The gap that often exists between what executives say and how they behave helps create barriers to openness and trust, to the effective search for alternatives, to innovation, and to flexibility in the organization.

□ These barriers are more destructive in important decision-making meetings than in routine meetings, and they upset effective managers more than ineffective ones.

□ The barriers cannot be broken down simply by intellectual exercises. Rather, executives need feedback concerning their behavior and opportunities to develop self-awareness in action. To this end, certain kinds of questioning are valuable; playing back and analyzing tape recordings of meetings has proved to be a helpful step; and laboratory education programs are valuable.

These are a few of the major findings of a study of executive decision making in six representative companies. The findings have vital implications for management groups everywhere; for while some organizations are less subject to the weaknesses described than are others, *all* groups have them in some degree. In this article I shall discuss the findings in detail and examine the implications for executives up and down the line. (For information on the company sample and research methods used in the study, see Appendix.)

Words vs. Actions

According to top management, the effectiveness of decision-making activities depends on the degree of innovation, risk taking, flexibility, and trust in the executive system. (Risk taking is defined here as any act where the executive risks his self-esteem. This could be a moment, for example, when he goes against the group view; when he tells someone, especially the person with the highest power, something negative about his impact on the organization; or when he seeks to put millions of dollars in a new investment.)

Nearly 95% of the executives in our study emphasize that an organization is only as good as its top people. They constantly repeat the importance of their responsibility to help themselves and others to develop their abilities. Almost as often they report that the qualities just mentioned —motivation, risk taking, and so on—are key characteristics of any successful executive system. "People problems" head the list as the most difficult, perplexing, and crucial.

In short, the executives vote overwhelmingly for executive systems where the contributions of each executive can be maximized and where innovation, risk taking, flexibility, and trust reign supreme. Nevertheless, the *behavior* of these same executives tends to create decision-making processes that are *not* very effective. Their behavior can be fitted into two basic patterns:

Pattern A—thoughtful, rational, and mildly competitive. This is the behavior most frequently observed during the decision-making meetings. Executives following this pattern own up to their ideas in a style that emphasizes a serious concern for ideas. As they constantly battle for scarce resources and "sell" their views, their openness to others' ideas is relatively high, not because of a sincere interest in learning about the point of view of others, but so they can engage in a form of "one-upmanship"—that is, gain information about the others' points of view in order to politely discredit them.

Pattern B—competitive first, thoughtful and rational second. In this pattern, conformity to ideas replaces concern for ideas as the strongest

Exhibit I. *Management groups with Pattern A and Pattern B characteristics*

	PATTERN A				PATTERN B			
	GROUP 1 198		GROUP 2 143		GROUP 3 201		GROUP 4 131	
TOTAL NUMBER OF UNITS ANALYZED*								
UNITS CHARACTERIZED BY:	NUMBER	PERCENT	NUMBER	PERCENT	NUMBER	PERCENT	NUMBER	PERCENT
OWNING UP TO OWN IDEAS	145	74	105	74	156	78	102	78
CONCERN FOR OTHERS' IDEAS	122	62	89	62	52	26	56	43
CONFORMITY TO OTHERS' IDEAS	54	27	38	26	87	43	62	47
OPENNESS TO OTHERS' IDEAS	46	23	34	24	31	15	25	19
INDIVIDUALITY	4	2	12	8	30	15	8	6
ANTAGONISM TO OTHERS' IDEAS	18	9	4	3	32	16	5	4
UNWILLINGNESS TO HELP OTHERS OWN UP TO THEIR IDEAS	5	2	3	2	14	7	4	3

* A unit is an instance of a manager speaking on a topic. If during the course of speaking he changes to a new topic, another unit is created.

norm. Also, antagonism to ideas is higher—in many cases higher than openness to ideas. The relatively high antagonism scores usually indicate, in addition to high competitiveness, a high degree of conflict and pent-up feelings.

Exhibit I summarizes data for four illustrative groups of managers —two groups with Pattern A characteristics and two with Pattern B characteristics.

PRACTICAL CONSEQUENCES

In both patterns executives are rarely observed:
. . . taking risks or experimenting with new ideas or feelings;
. . . helping others to own up, be open, and take risks;
. . . using a style of behavior that supports the norm of individuality and trust as well as mistrust;
. . . expressing feelings, positive or negative.

These results should not be interpreted as implying that the executives do not have feelings. We know from the interviews that many of the executives have strong feelings indeed. However, the overwhelming majority (84%) feel that it is a sign of immaturity to express feelings openly *during decision-making meetings.* Nor should the results be interpreted to mean that the executives do not enjoy risk taking. The data permit us to conclude only that few risk-taking actions were *observed* during the meetings. (Also, we have to keep in mind that the executives were always observed in groups; it may be that their behavior in groups varies significantly from their behavior as individuals.)

Before I attempt to give my views about the reasons for the discrepancy between executives' words and actions, I should like to point out that these results are not unique to business organizations. I have obtained similar behavior patterns from leaders in education, research, the ministry, trade unions, and government. Indeed, one of the fascinating questions for me is why so many different people in so many different kinds of organizations tend to manifest similar problems.

Why the Discrepancy?

The more I observe such problems in different organizations possessing different technologies and varying greatly in size, the more I become impressed with the importance of the role played by the values or assumptions top people hold on the nature of effective human relationships and the best ways to run an organization.

BASIC VALUES

In the studies so far I have isolated three basic values that seem to be very important:

1. *The significant human relationships are the ones which have to do with achieving the organization's objective.* My studies of over 265 different types and sizes of meetings indicate that executives almost always tend to focus their behavior on "getting the job done." In literally thousands of units of behavior, almost none are observed where the men spend some time in analyzing and maintaining their group's effectiveness. This is true even though in many meetings the group's effectiveness "bogged down" and the objectives were not being reached because of interpersonal factors. When the executives are interviewed and asked why they did not spend some time in examining the group operations or processes, they reply that they were there to get a job done. They add: "If the group isn't effective, it is up to the leader to get it back on the track by directing it."

2. *Cognitive rationality is to be emphasized; feelings and emotions are to be played down.* This value influences executives to see cognitive, intellectual discussions as "relevant," "good," "work," and so on. Emotional and interpersonal discussions tend to be viewed as "irrelevant," "immature," "not work," and so on.

As a result, when emotions and interpersonal variables become blocks to group effectiveness, all the executives report feeling that they should *not* deal with them. For example, in the event of an emotional disagreement, they would tell the members to "get back to facts" or "keep personalities out of this."

3. *Human relationships are most effectively influenced through unilateral direction, coercion, and control, as well as by rewards and penalties that sanction all three values.* This third value of direction and control is implicit in the chain of command and also in the elaborate managerial controls that have been developed within organizations.

INFLUENCE ON OPERATIONS

The impact of these values can be considerable. For example, to the extent that individuals dedicate themselves to the value of intellectual rationality and "getting the job done," they will tend to be aware of and emphasize the intellectual aspects of issues in an organization and (consciously or unconsciously) to suppress the interpersonal and emotional aspects, especially those which do not seem relevant to achieving the task.

As the interpersonal and emotional aspects of behavior become suppressed, organizational norms that coerce individuals to hide their feelings or to disguise them and bring them up as technical, intellectual problems will tend to arise.

Under these conditions the individual may tend to find it very difficult to develop competence in dealing with feelings and interpersonal relationships. Also, in a world where the expression of feelings is not valued, individuals may build personal and organizational defenses to help them suppress their own feelings or inhibit others in such expression. Or they may refuse to consider ideas which, if explored, could expose suppressed feelings.

Such a defensive reaction in an organization could eventually inhibit creativity and innovation during decision making. The participants might learn to limit themselves to those ideas and values that were not threatening. They might also decrease their openness to new ideas and values. And as the degree of openness decreased, the capacity to experiment would also decrease, and fear of taking risks would increase. This would reduce the *probability* of experimentation, thus decreasing openness to new ideas still further and constricting risk taking even more than formerly. We would thereby have a closed circuit which could become an important cause of loss of vitality in an organization.

Some Consequences

Aside from the impact of values on vitality, what are some other consequences of the executive behavior patterns earlier described on top management decision making and on the effective functioning of the organization? For the sake of brevity, I shall include only examples of those consequences that were found to exist in one form or another in all organizations studied.

RESTRICTED COMMITMENT

One of the most frequent findings is that in major decisions that are introduced by the president, there tends to be less than open discussion of the issues, and the commitment of the officers tends to be less than complete (although they may assure the president to the contrary). For instance, consider what happened in one organization where a major administrative decision made during the period of the research was the establishment of several top management committees to explore basic long-range problems.

As is customary with major decisions, the president discussed it in advance at a meeting of the executive committee. He began the meeting by circulating, as a basis for discussion, a draft of the announcement of the committees. Most of the members' discussion was concerned with raising questions about the wording of the proposal:

"Is the word *action* too strong?"

"I recommend that we change 'steps can be taken' to 'recommendations can be made.' "

"We'd better change the word 'lead' to 'maintain.' "

As the discussion seemed to come to an end, one executive said he was worried that the announcement of the committees might be interpreted by the people below as an implication "that the executive committee believes the organization is in trouble. Let's get the idea in that all is well."

There was spontaneous agreement by all executives: "Hear, hear!"

A brief silence was broken by another executive who apparently was not satisfied with the concept of the committees. He raised a series of questions. The manner in which it was done was interesting. As he raised each issue, he kept assuring the president and the group that he was not against the concept. He just wanted to be certain that the executive committee was clear on what it was doing. For example, he assured them:

"I'm not clear. Just asking."

"I'm trying to get a better picture."

"I'm just trying to get clarification."

"Just so that we understand what the words mean."

The president nodded in agreement, but he seemed to become slightly impatient. He remarked that many of these problems would not arise if the members of these new committees took an overall company point of view. An executive commented (laughingly), "Oh, I'm for motherhood too!"

The proposal was tabled in order for the written statement to be revised and discussed further during the next meeting. It appeared that the proposal was the president's personal "baby," and the executive committee members would naturally go along with it. The most responsibility some felt was that they should raise questions so the president would be clear about *his* (not *their*) decision.

At the next meeting the decision-making process was the same as at the first. The president circulated copies of the revised proposal. During this session a smaller number of executives asked questions. Two pushed (with appropriate care) the notion that the duties of one of the committees were defined too broadly.

The president began to defend his proposal by citing an extremely long list of examples, indicating that in his mind "reasonable" people should find the duties clear. This comment and the long list of examples may have communicated to others a feeling that the president was becoming impatient. When he finished, there was a lengthy silence. The president then turned to one of the executives and asked directly, "Why are you worried about this?" The executive explained, then quickly added that as far as he could see the differences were not major ones and his point of view could be integrated with the president's by "changing some words."

The president agreed to the changes, looked up, and asked, "I take it now there is common agreement?" All executives replied "yes" or nodded their heads affirmatively.

As I listened, I had begun to wonder about the commitment of the executive committee members to the idea. In subsequent interviews I asked each about his view of the proposal. Half felt that it was a good proposal. The other half had reservations ranging from moderate to serious. However, being loyal members, they would certainly do their best to make it work, they said.

SUBORDINATE GAMESMANSHIP

I can best illustrate the second consequence by citing from a study of the effectiveness of product planning and program review activities in another of the organizations studied.

It was company policy that peers at any given level should make the decisions. Whenever they could not agree or whenever a decision went beyond their authority, the problem was supposed to be sent to the next higher level. The buck passing stopped at the highest level. A meeting with the president became a great event. Beforehand a group would "dry run" its presentation until all were satisfied that they could present their view effectively.

Few difficulties were observed when the meeting was held to present a recommendation agreed to by all at the lower levels. The difficulties arose when "negative" information had to be fed upward. For example, a major error in the program, a major delay, or a major disagreement among the members was likely to cause such trouble.

The dynamics of these meetings was very interesting. In one case the problem to present was a major delay in a development project. In the dry run the subordinates planned to begin the session with information that "updated" the president. The information was usually presented in such a way that slowly and carefully the president was alerted to the fact that a major problem was about to be announced. One could hear such key phrases as:

"We are a bit later than expected."

"We're not on plan."

"We have had greater difficulties than expected."

"It is now clear that no one should have promised what we did."

These phrases were usually followed by some reassuring statement such as:

"However, we're on top of this."

"Things are really looking better now."

"Although we are late, we have advanced the state of the art."

"If you give us another three months, we are certain that we can solve this problem."

To the observer's eyes, it is difficult to see how the president could deny the request. Apparently he felt the same way because he granted it. However, he took nearly 20 minutes to say that this shocked him; he was wondering if everyone was *really* doing everything they could; this was a serious program; this was not the way he wanted to see things run; he was sure they would agree with him; and he wanted their assurances that this would be the final delay.

A careful listening to the tape after the meeting brought out the fact that no subordinate gave such assurances. They simply kept saying that they were doing their best; they had poured a lot into this; or they had the best technical know-how working on it.

Another interesting observation is that most subordinates in this company, especially in presentations to the president, tended to go along with certain unwritten rules:

1. Before you give any bad news, give good news. Especially emphasize the capacity of the department to work hard and to rebound from a failure.

2. Play down the impact of a failure by emphasizing how close you came to achieving the target or how soon the target can be reached. If neither seems reasonable, emphasize how difficult it is to define such targets, and point out that because the state of the art is so primitive, the original commitment was not a wise one.

3. In a meeting with the president it is unfair to take advantage of another department that is in trouble, even if it is a "natural enemy." The sporting thing to do is say something nice about the other department and offer to help it in any way possible. (The offer is usually not made in concrete form, nor does the department in difficulty respond with the famous phrase, "What do you have in mind?")

The subordinates also were in agreement that too much time was spent in long presentations in order to make the president happy. The president, however, confided to the researcher that he did not enjoy listening to long and, at times, dry presentations (especially when he had seen most of the key data anyway). However, he felt that it was important to go through this because it might give the subordinates a greater sense of commitment to the problem!

LACK OF AWARENESS

One of our most common observations in company studies is that executives lack awareness of their own behavioral patterns as well as of the negative impact of their behavior on others. This is not to imply that they are completely unaware; each individual usually senses some aspects of a problem. However, we rarely find an individual or group of individuals who is aware of enough of the scope and depth of a problem so that the need for effective action can be fully understood.

For example, during the study of the decision-making processes of the president and the 9 vice presidents of a firm with nearly 3,000 employees, I concluded that the members unknowingly behaved in such a way as *not* to encourage risk taking, openness, expression of feelings, and cohesive, trusting relationships. But subsequent interviews with the 10 top executives showed that they held a completely different point of view from mine. They admitted that negative feelings were not expressed, but said the reason was that "we trust each other and respect each other." According to 6 of the men, individuality was high and conformity low; where conformity was agreed to be high, the reason given was the necessity of agreeing with the man who is boss. According to 8 of the men, "We help each other all the time." Issues loaded with conflict were not handled during meetings, it was reported, for these reasons:

◻ "We should not discuss emotional disagreements before the executive committee because when people are emotional, they are not rational."

◻ "We should not air our dirty linen in front of the people who may come in to make a presentation."

◻ "Why take up people's time with subjective debates?"

◻ "Most members are not acquainted with all the details. Under our

Exhibit II. Contradictory statements

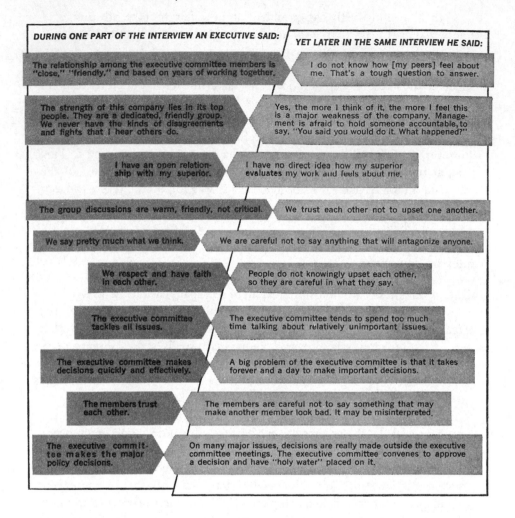

DURING ONE PART OF THE INTERVIEW AN EXECUTIVE SAID:	YET LATER IN THE SAME INTERVIEW HE SAID:
The relationship among the executive committee members is "close," "friendly," and based on years of working together.	I do not know how [my peers] feel about me. That's a tough question to answer.
The strength of this company lies in its top people. They are a dedicated, friendly group. We never have the kinds of disagreements and fights that I hear others do.	Yes, the more I think of it, the more I feel this is a major weakness of the company. Management is afraid to hold someone accountable, to say, "You said you would do it. What happened?"
I have an open relationship with my superior.	I have no direct idea how my superior evaluates my work and feels about me.
The group discussions are warm, friendly, not critical.	We trust each other not to upset one another.
We say pretty much what we think.	We are careful not to say anything that will antagonize anyone.
We respect and have faith in each other.	People do not knowingly upset each other, so they are careful in what they say.
The executive committee tackles all issues.	The executive committee tends to spend too much time talking about relatively unimportant issues.
The executive committee makes decisions quickly and effectively.	A big problem of the executive committee is that it takes forever and a day to make important decisions.
The members trust each other.	The members are careful not to say something that may make another member look bad. It may be misinterpreted.
The executive committee makes the major policy decisions.	On many major issues, decisions are really made outside the executive committee meetings. The executive committee convenes to approve a decision and have "holy water" placed on it.

system the person who presents the issues has really thought them through."

☐ "Pre-discussion of issues helps to prevent anyone from sandbagging the executive committee."

☐ "Rarely emotional; when it does happen, you can pardon it."

The executive committee climate or emotional tone was characterized by such words as:

☐ "Friendly."

☐ "Not critical of each other."

☐ "Not tense."

☐ "Frank and no tensions because we've known each other for years."

How was I to fit the executives' views with mine? I went back and listened to all the interviews again. As I analyzed the tapes, I began to realize that an interesting set of contradictions arose during many of the

CHARACTERISTIC RATED	NUMBER OF MANAGERS RATING THE COMMITTEE AS:		
	LOW	MODERATE	HIGH
OPENNESS TO UNCOMFORTABLE INFORMATION*	12	6	4
RISK TAKING	20	4	1
TRUST	14	9	2
CONFORMITY	0	2	23
ABILITY TO DEAL WITH CONFLICTS	19	6	0

* Three executives gave a "don't know" response.

interviews. In the early stages of the interviews the executives tended to say things that they contradicted later; *Exhibit II* contains examples of contradictions repeated by 6 or more of the 10 top executives.

What accounts for these contradictions? My explanation is that over time the executives had come to mirror, in their behavior, the values of their culture (e.g., be rational, nonemotional, diplomatically open, and so on). They had created a culture that reinforced their own leadership styles. If an executive wanted to behave differently, he probably ran the risk of being considered a deviant. In most of the cases the executives decided to forgo this risk, and they behaved like the majority. These men, in order to live with themselves, probably had to develop various defenses and blinders about their acquiescence to an executive culture that may not have been the one they personally preferred and valued.

Incidentally, in this group there were two men who had decided to take the other route. Both men were viewed by the others as "a bit rough at the edges" or "a little too aggressive."

To check the validity of some of the findings reported, we interviewed the top 25 executives below the executive committee. If our analysis was correct, we knew, then they should tend to report that the members of the executive committee were low in openness to uncomfortable information, risk taking, trust, and capacity to deal with conflicts openly, and high in conformity. The results were as predicted (see *Exhibit III*).

BLIND SPOTS

Another result found in all organizations studied is the tendency for executives to be unaware of the negative feelings that their subordinates have about them. This finding is not startling in view of the fact that the executive problem-solving processes do not tend to reward the upward communication of information about interpersonal issues that is emotionally laden and risky to communicate. To illustrate:

In one organization, all but one of the top executive committee members reported that their relationships with their subordinates were "relatively good to excellent." When asked how they judged their relationships, most of the executives responded with such statements as: "They do everything that I ask for willingly," and "We talk together frequently and openly."

The picture from the middle management men who were the immediate subordinates was different. Apparently, top management was unaware that:

—71% of the middle managers did not know where they stood with their superiors; they considered their relationships as ambiguous, and they were not aware of such important facts as how they were being evaluated.

—65% of the middle managers did not know what qualities led to success in their organizations.

—87% felt that conflicts were very seldom coped with; and that when they were, the attempts tended to be inadequate.

—65% thought that the most important unsolved problem of the organization was that the top management was unable to help them overcome the intergroup rivalries, lack of cooperation, and poor communications; 53% said that if they could alter one aspect of their superior's behavior, it would be to help him see the "dog eat dog" communication problems that existed in middle management.

—59% evaluated top management effectiveness as not too good or about average; and 62% reported that the development of a cohesive management team was the second most important unsolved problem.

—82% of the middle managers wished that the status of their function and job could be increased but doubted if they could communicate this openly to the top management.

Interestingly, in all the cases that I have observed where the president asked for a discussion of any problems that the top and middle management men present thought important, the problems mentioned above were never raised.

Rather, the most frequently mentioned problem (74% of the cases) was the overload problem. The executives and managers reported that they were overloaded and that the situation was getting worse. The president's usual reply was that he appreciated their predicament, but "that is life." The few times he asked if the men had any suggestions, he received such replies as "more help," "fewer meetings," "fewer reports," "delay of schedules," and so on. As we will see, few of these suggestions made sense, since the men were asking either for increases in costs or for a decrease in the very controls that the top management used to administer the organization.

DISTRUST AND ANTAGONISM

Another result of the behavior patterns earlier described is that management tends to keep promotions semisecret and most of the actual reasons for executive changes completely secret. Here is an example from an organization whose board we studied in some detail over a period of two years:

The executives complained of three practices of the board about which the board members were apparently unaware: (1) the constant alteration of organizational positions and charts, and keeping the most up-to-date versions semiconfidential; (2) shifting top executives without adequate discussion with all executives involved and without clearly communicating the real reasons for the move; and (3) developing new departments with product goals that overlapped and competed with the goals of already existing departments.

The board members admitted these practices but tended not to see them as being incompatible with the interests of the organization. For example, to take the first complaint, they defended their practice with such statements as: "If you tell them everything, all they do is worry, and we get a flood of rumors"; "The changes do not *really* affect them"; and, "It will only cut in on their busy schedule and interrupt their productivity."

The void of clear-cut information from the board was, however, filled in by the executives. Their explanations ranged from such statements as "They must be changing things because they are not happy with the way things are going" to "The unhappiness is so strong they do not tell us." Even the executives who profited from some of these moves reported some concern and bewilderment. For example, three reported instances where they had been promoted over some "old-timers." In all cases they were told to "soft-pedal the promotion aspect" until the old-timers were diplomatically informed. Unfortunately, it took months to inform the latter men, and in some cases it was never done.

There was another practice of the board that produced difficulties in the organization:

Department heads cited the board's increasing intervention into the detailed administration of a department when its profit picture looked shaky. This practice was, from these subordinates' view, in violation of the stated philosophy of decentralization.

When asked, board members tended to explain this practice by saying that it was done only when they had doubts about the department head's competence, and then it was always in the interests of efficiency. When they were alerted about a department that was not doing well, they believed that the best reaction was to tighten controls, "take a closer and more frequent look," and "make sure the department head is on top of things." They quickly added that they did not tell the man in question they were beginning to doubt his competence for fear of upsetting him. Thus, again we see how the values of de-emphasizing the expression of negative feelings and the emphasizing of controls influenced the board's behavior.

The department heads, on the other hand, reported different reactions. "Why are they bothered with details? Don't they trust me? If not, why don't they say so?" Such reactions tended to produce more conformity, antagonism, mistrust, and fear of experimenting.

Still another board practice was the "diplomatic" rejection of an executive's idea that was, in the eyes of the board, offbeat, a bit too wild, or not in keeping with the corporate mission. The reasons given by the board for not being open about the evaluation again reflected adherence to the pyramidal values. For example, a board member would say, "We do not want to embarrass them," or "If you really tell them, you might restrict creativity."

This practice tended to have precisely the impact that the superiors wished to *avoid*. The subordinates reacted by asking, "Why don't they give me an opportunity to really explain it?" or "What do they mean when they suggest that the 'timing is not right' or 'funds are not currently available'?"

PROCESSES DAMAGED

It is significant that defensive activities like those described are rarely observed during group meetings dealing with minor or relatively routine decisions. These activities become most noticeable when the decision is an important one in terms of dollars or in terms of the impact on the various departments in the organization. *The forces toward ineffectiveness operate most strongly during the important decision-making meetings.* The group and organizational defenses operate most frequently when they can do the most harm to decision-making effectiveness.

Another interesting finding is that the more effective and more committed executives tend to be upset about these facts, whereas the less effective, less committed people tend simply to lament them. They also tend to take on an "I told them so" attitude—one of resignation and noninvolvement in correcting the situation. In short, it is the better executives who are negatively affected.

What Can Be Done?

What can the executive do to change this situation?

I wish that I could answer this question as fully as I should like to. Unfortunately, I cannot. Nevertheless, there are some suggestions I can make.

BLIND ALLEYS

First, let me state what I believe will *not* work.

Learning about these problems by listening to lectures, reading about them, or exploring them through cases is not adequate; an article or book can pose some issues and get thinking started, but—in this area, at least—it cannot change behavior. Thus, in one study with 60 top executives:

Lectures were given and cases discussed on this subject for nearly a week. A test at the end of the week showed that the executives rated the lecturers very high, liked the cases, and accepted the diagnoses. Yet when they attempted to apply their new-found knowledge outside the learning situation, most were unable to do so. The major problem was that they had not learned how to make these new ideas come to life in their behavior.

As one executive stated, pointing to his head: "I know up here what I should do, but when it comes to a real meeting, I behave in the same old way. It sure is frustrating."

Learning about these problems through a detailed diagnosis of executives' behavior is also not enough. For example:

I studied a top management group for nearly four months through interviews and tape recordings of their decision-making meetings. Eventually, I fed back the analysis. The executives agreed with the diagnosis as well as with the statement by one executive that he found it depressing. Another executive, however, said he now felt that he had a clearer and more coherent picture of some of the causes of their problems, and he was going to change his behavior. I predicted that he would probably find that he would be unable to change his behavior—and even if he did change, his subordinates, peers, and superiors might resist dealing with him in the new way.

The executive asked, "How can you be so sure that we can't change?" I responded that I knew of no case where managers were able to alter successfully their behavior, their group dynamics, and so forth by simply realizing intellectually that such a change was necessary. The key to success was for them to be able to show these new strategies in their behavior. To my knowledge, behavior of this type, groups with these dynamics, and organizational cultures endowed with these characteristics were very difficult to change. What kind of thin-skinned individuals would they be, how brittle would their groups and their organizations be if they could be altered that easily?

Three of the executives decided that they were going to prove the prediction to be incorrect. They took my report and studied it carefully. In one case the executive asked his subordinates to do the same. Then they tried to alter their behavior. According to their own accounts, they were unable to do so. The only changes they reported were (1) a softening of the selling activities, (2) a reduction of their aggressive persuasion, and (3) a genuine increase in their asking for the subordinates' views.

My subsequent observations and interviews uncovered the fact that the first two changes were mistrusted by the subordinates, who had by now adapted to the old behavior of their superiors. They tended to play it carefully and to be guarded. This hesitation aggravated the executives, who felt that their subordinates were not responding to their new behavior with the enthusiasm that they (the superiors) had expected.

However, *the executives did not deal with this issue openly*. They kept working at trying to be rational, patient, and rewarding. The more irritated they became and the more they showed this irritation in their behavior, the more the subordinates felt that the superiors' "new" behavior was a gimmick.

Eventually, the process of influencing subordinates slowed down so much that the senior men returned to their more controlling styles. The irony was that in most cases the top executives interpreted the subordinates' behavior as proof that they needed to be needled and pushed, while the subordinates interpreted the top managers' behavior as proof that they did not trust their assistants and would never change.

The reason I doubt that these approaches will provide anything but temporary cures is that they do not go far enough. If changes are going to be made in the behavior of an executive, if trust is to be developed, if risk taking is to flourish, he must be placed in a different situation. He should be helped to (a) expose his leadership style so that he and others can take a look at its true impact; (b) deepen his awareness of himself and the dynamics of effective leadership; and (c) strive for these goals under conditions where he is in control of the amount, pace, and depth of learning.

These conditions for learning are difficult to achieve. Ideally, they require the help of a professional consultant. Also, it would be important to get away from the organization—its interruptions, pressures, and daily administrative tensions.

VALUE OF QUESTIONS

The executive can strive to be aware that he is probably programmed with a set of values which cause him to behave in ways that are not always helpful to others and which his subordinates will not discuss frankly even when they believe he is not being helpful. He can also strive to find time to uncover, through careful questioning, his impact on others. Once in a while a session that is focused on the "How am I doing?"

question can enlighten the executive and make his colleagues more flexible in dealing with him.

One simple question I have heard several presidents ask their vice presidents with success is: "Tell me what, if anything, I do that tends to prevent (or help) your being the kind of vice president you wish to be?" These presidents are careful to ask these questions during a time when they seem natural (e.g., performance review sessions), or they work hard ahead of time to create a climate so that such a discussion will not take the subordinate by surprise.

Some presidents feel uncomfortable in raising these questions, and others point out that the vice presidents are also uncomfortable. I can see how both would have such feelings. A chief executive officer may feel that he is showing weakness by asking his subordinates about his impact. The subordinate may or may not feel this way, but he may sense that his chief does, and that is enough to make him uncomfortable.

Yet in two companies I have studied where such questions were asked, superiors and subordinates soon learned that authority which gained strength by a lack of openness was weak and brittle, whereas authority resting on open feedback from below was truly strong and viable.

WORKING WITH THE GROUP

Another step that an executive can take is to vow not to accept group ineffectiveness as part of life. Often I have heard people say, "Groups are no damned good; strong leadership is what is necessary." I agree that many groups are ineffective. I doubt, however, if either of the two leadership patterns described earlier will help the situation. As we have seen, both patterns tend to make the executive group increasingly less effective.

If my data are valid, the search process in executive decision making has become so complicated that group participation is essential. No one man seems to be able to have all the knowledge necessary to make an effective decision. If individual contributions are necessary in group meetings, it is important that a climate be created that does not discourage innovation, risk taking, and honest leveling between managers in their conversations with one another. The value of a group is to maximize individual contributions.

Interestingly, the chief executive officers in these studies are rarely observed making policy decisions in the classic sense, viz., critical selections from several alternatives and determination of future directions to be taken. This does not mean that they shy away from taking responsibility. Quite the contrary. Many report that they enjoy making decisions by themselves. Their big frustration comes from realizing that most of the major decisions they face are extremely complex and require the coordinated, honest inputs of many different executives. They are impatient at the slowness of meetings, the increasingly quantitative nature of the inputs, and, in many cases, their ignorance of what the staff groups did to the decision inputs long before they received them.

The more management deals with complexity by the use of computers and quantitative approaches, the more it will be forced to work with inputs of many different people, and the more important will be the group dynamics of decision-making meetings. If anyone doubts this, let him observe the dry runs subordinates go through to get a presentation ready for the top. He will observe, I believe, that much data are included and excluded by subordinates on the basis of what they believe those at the top can hear.

In short, *one of the main tasks of the chief executive is to build and maintain an effective decision-making network*. I doubt that he has much choice *except* to spend time in exploring how well his group functions.

Such explorations could occur during the regular workday. For example:

In one organization the president began by periodically asking members of his top group, immediately after a decision was made, to think back during the meeting and describe when they felt that the group was not being as effective as they wished. How could these conditions be altered?

As trust and openness increased, the members began to level with each other as to when they were inhibited, irritated, suppressed, confused, and withholding information. The president tried to be as encouraging as he could, and he especially rewarded people who truly leveled. Soon the executives began to think of mechanisms they could build into their group functioning so they would be alerted to these group problems and correct them early. As one man said, "We have not eliminated all our problems, but we are building a competence in our group to deal with them effectively if and when they arise."

UTILIZING FEEDBACK

Another useful exercise is for the superior and his group members to tape-record a decision-making meeting, especially one which is expected to be difficult. At a later date, the group members can gather and listen to the tape. I believe it is safe to say that simply listening to the tape is an education in itself. If one can draw from skilled company or outside help, then useful analyses can be made of group or individual behavior.

Recently, I experimented with this procedure with an "inside" board of directors of a company. The directors met once a month and listened to tape recordings of their monthly board meetings. With my help they analyzed their behavior, trying to find how they could improve their individual and group effectiveness. Listening to tapes became a very involving experience for them. They spent nearly four hours in the first meeting discussing less than ten minutes of the tape.

"Binds" Created. One of the major gains of these sessions was that the board members became aware of the "binds" they were creating for each other and of the impact they each had on the group's functioning. Thus:

Executive A was frequently heard antagonizing Executive B by saying something that B perceived as "needling." For example, A might seem to be questioning B's competence. "Look here," he would say, "anyone who can do simple arithmetic should realize that. . . ."

Executive B responded by fighting. B's way of fighting back was to utilize his extremely high capacity to verbalize and intellectualize. B's favorite tactic was to show A where he missed five important points and where his logic was faulty.

Executive A became increasingly upset as the "barrage of logic" found its mark. He tended to counteract by (a) remaining silent but manifesting a sense of being flustered and becoming red-faced; and/or (b) insisting that his logic *was* sound even though he did not express it in "highfalutin language" as did B.

Executive B pushed harder (presumably to make A admit he was wrong) by continuing his "barrage of logic" or implying that A could not see his errors because he was upset.

Executive A would respond to this by insisting that he was not upset. "The point you are making is so simple, why, anyone can see it. Why should I be upset?"

Executive B responded by pushing harder and doing more intellectualizing. When Executive A eventually reached his breaking point, he too began to shout and fight.

At this point, Executives C, D, and E could be observed withdrawing until A and B wore each other out.

Progress Achieved. As a result of the meetings, the executives reported in interviews, board members experienced fewer binds, less hostility, less frustration, and more constructive work. One member wondered if the group had lost some of its "zip," but the others disagreed. Here is an excerpt from the transcript of one discussion on this point:

EXECUTIVE A: My feeling is, as I have said, that we have just opened this thing up, and I for one feel that we have benefited a great deal from it. I think I have improved; maybe I am merely reflecting the fact that you [Executive B] have improved. But at least I think there has been improvement in our relationship. I also see signs of not as good a relationship in other places as there might be.

I think on the whole we are much better off today than we were a year ago.

I think there is a whole lot less friction today than there was a year ago, but there's still enough of it.

Now we have a much clearer organization setup; if we were to sit down here and name the people, we would probably all name exactly the same people. I don't think there is much question about who should be included and who should not be included; we've got a pretty clean organization.

EXECUTIVE B: You're talking now about asking the consultant about going on with this week's session?

EXECUTIVE A: It would be very nice to have the consultant if he can do it; then we should see how we can do it without him, but it'd be better with him.

EXECUTIVE B: But that's the step, as I understand it, that should be taken at this stage. Is that right?

EXECUTIVE A: Well, I would certainly favor doing something; I don't know what. I'm not making a specific recommendation; I just don't like to let go of it.

EXECUTIVE C: What do you think?

EXECUTIVE D: I'm not as optimistic as A. I wonder if anybody here agrees with me that maybe we haven't made as much progress as we think. I've personally enjoyed these experiences, and I'd like to see them continued.

EXECUTIVE A: Would you like to venture to say why I think we have made progress and why I might be fooled?

EXECUTIVE D: Well, I think maybe you are in the worst position to evaluate progress because if the worst possible thing that can happen is for people to no longer fight and struggle, but to say, "yes, sir," you might call that progress. That might be the worst thing that could happen, and I sort of sense some degree of resignation—I don't think it's progress. I don't know. I might be all alone in this. What do you think?

EXECUTIVE C: On one level it is progress. Whether it is institutional progress and whether it produces commensurate institutional benefits is a debatable question. It may in fact do so. I think it's very clear that there is in our meetings and in individual contact less heat, less overt friction, petulance, tension, than certainly was consistently the case. Do you agree?

EXECUTIVE D: Yes, I think so.

EXECUTIVE C: It has made us a great deal more aware of the extent and nature of the friction and clearly has made all of us intent on fighting less. There's some benefit to it; but there are some drawbacks.

EXECUTIVE A: Well, if you and D are right, I would say for that reason we need more of the program.

LABORATORY TRAINING

Another possibility is for the executive to attend a program designed to help increase competence in this area, such as laboratory education and its various offshoots ("T-groups," the "managerial grid," "conflict management labs," and so on). These learning experiences are available at various university and National Training Laboratory executive programs. They can also be tailor-made for the individual organization.

I believe outside programs offer the better way of becoming acquainted with this type of learning. Bear in mind, though, that since typically only one or two executives attend from the same organization, the biggest pay-off is for the individual. The inside program provides greater possibilities for payoff to the organization.

At the same time, however, it should also be kept in mind that in-house programs *can* be dangerous to the organization. I would recommend that a thorough study be made ahead of time to ascertain whether or not a laboratory educational experience would be helpful to company executives individually and to the organization.

OPEN DISCUSSION

I have never observed a group whose members wanted it to decay. I have never studied a group or an organization that was decaying where there were not some members who were aware that decay was occurring. Accordingly, one key to group and organizational effectiveness is to get this knowledge out into the open and to discuss it thoroughly. The human "motors" of the group and the organization have to be checked periodically, just as does the motor of an automobile. Without proper maintenance, all will fail.

Appendix to Chapter 24

Nature of the Study

□ The six companies studied include: (1) an electronics firm with 40,000 employees, (2) a manufacturer and marketer of a new innovative product with 4,000 employees, (3) a large research and development company with 3,000 employees, (4) a small research and development organization with 150 employees, (5) a consulting-research firm with 400 employees, and (6) a producer of heavy equipment with 4,000 employees.

□ The main focus of the investigation reported here was on the behavior of 165 top executives in these companies. The executives were board members, executive committee members, upper-level managers, and (in a few cases) middle-level managers.

□ Approximately 265 decision-making meetings were studied and nearly 10,000 units of behavior analyzed. The topics of the meetings ranged widely, covering investment decisions, new products, manufacturing problems, marketing strategies, new pricing policies, administrative changes, and personnel issues. An observer took notes during all but 10 of the meetings; for research purposes, these 10 were analyzed "blind" from tapes (i.e., without ever meeting the executives). All other meetings were taped also, but analyzed at a later time.

□ The major device for analyzing the tapes was a new system of categories for scoring decision-making meetings.* Briefly, the executives' behavior was scored according to how often they—

... owned up to and accepted responsibility for their ideas or feelings;
... opened up to receive others' ideas or feelings;
... experimented and took risks with ideas or feelings;
... helped others to own up, be open, and take risks;
... did not own up; were not open; did not take risks; and did not help others in any of these activities.

□ A second scoring system was developed to produce a quantitative index of the *norms* of the executive culture. There were both positive and negative norms. The positive norms were:

* For a detailed discussion of the system of categories and other aspects of methodology, see my book, *Organization and Innovation* (Homewood, Illinois, Richard D. Irwin, Inc., 1965).

1. *Individuality*, especially rewarding behavior that focused on and valued the uniqueness of each individual's ideas and feelings.
2. *Concern* for others' ideas and feelings.
3. *Trust* in others' ideas and feelings.

The negative norms were:

1. *Conformity* to others' ideas and feelings.
2. *Antagonism* toward these ideas and feelings.
3. *Mistrust* of these ideas and feelings.

□ In addition to our observations of the men at work, at least one semi-structured interview was conducted with each executive. All of these interviews were likewise taped, and the typewritten protocols served as the basis for further analysis.

25. What It's Like to Be a Black Manager

Edward W. Jones, Jr.

This author contends that most companies fail to recognize the crucial difference between recruiting blacks with executive potential and providing the much-needed organizational support to help them realize this potential. He cites his own experience in a large company to illustrate the type of lonely struggle that faces a black man in the absence of such support. Then he draws some lessons from this experience that should help management to overcome the subtle ramifications of racial differences within organizations.

When I was graduated from a predominantly black college, I was offered a job in one of the largest corporations in America. On reporting for work, I received a motivational speech from the personnel officer and acknowledged that I agreed with his opinion: the job was going to be challenging in its own right; however, the added burden of prejudice could make it unbearable. In a tone of bravado I said, "I promise you that I won't quit; you'll have to fire me."

At the time, I did not know how important that promise would become. For I was about to begin the most trying experience of my life—the rise to middle management in a white corporation. During those years, I found myself examining my actions, strategies, and emotional stabilty. I found myself trying desperately to separate fact from mental fiction. I found myself enveloped in almost unbearable emotional stress and internal conflict, trying to hold the job as a constant and evaluate my personal shortcomings with respect to it. At times I would look at myself in a mirror and wonder whether I had lost my mental balance. Somehow I always managed to answer positively, if not resolutely.

I think that my experiences should prove helpful to companies that are wrestling with the problem of how to move black employees from the entry level into positions of greater responsibility. I say this because the manner in which many companies are approaching the problem indicates to me that a number of well-intentioned efforts are doomed to failure.

Failure is likely because most companies merely substitute blacks in positions formerly filled by whites and then, acting as if the corporate environment is not color-sensitive, consider their obligation over. In short, U.S. business has failed to recognize the embryonic black manager's increased chances of failure due to the potentially negative impact of racially based prejudgments. Gaining acceptance in the organization, which the embryonic white manager takes for granted, can be a serious problem for his black counterpart.

The Job Offer

My story begins when I happened to bump into a recruiter who was talking to a friend of mine. On gathering that I was a college senior, the recruiter asked whether I had considered his company as an employer. I responded, "Are you kidding me—you don't have any black managers, do you?" He replied, "No, but that's why I'm here."

I did well in a subsequent interview procedure, and received an invitation for a company tour. Still skeptical, I accepted, feeling that I had nothing to lose. During a lunch discussion concerning the contemplated job and its requirements, I experienced my first reminder that I was black. After a strained silence, one of the executives at our table looked at me, smiled, and said, "Why is it that everyone likes Roy Campanella, but so many people dislike Jackie Robinson?"

I knew that this man was trying to be pleasant; yet I felt nothing but disgust at what seemed a ridiculous deterioration in the level of conversation. Here was the beginning of the games that I expected but dreaded playing. The question was demeaning and an insult to my intelligence. It was merely a rephrasing of the familiar patronizing comment, "One of my best friends is a negro." Most blacks recognize this type of statement as a thinly veiled attempt to hide bias. After all, if a person is unbiased, why does he make such a point of trying to prove it?

In the fragment of time between the question and my response, the tension within me grew. Were these people serious about a job offer? If so, what did they expect from me? I had no desire to be the corporate black in a glass office, but I did not wish to be abrasive or ungracious if the company was sincere about its desire to have an integrated organization.

There was no way to resolve these kinds of questions at that moment, so I gathered up my courage and replied, "Roy Campanella is a great baseball player. But off the field he is not an overwhelming intellectual challenge to anyone. Jackie Robinson is great both on and off the baseball field. He is very intelligent and therefore more of a threat than Roy Campanella. In fact, I'm sure that if he wanted to, he could outperform you in your job."

There was a stunned silence around the table, and from that point on until I arrived back at the employment office, I was sure that I had ended any chances of receiving a job offer.

I was wrong. I subsequently received an outstanding salary offer from the recruiter. But I had no intention of being this company's showcase black and asked seriously, "Why do you want me to work for you? Because of my ability or because you need a black?" I was reassured that ability was the "only" criterion, and one month later, after much introspection, I accepted the offer.

Initial Exposure

I entered the first formal training phase, in which I was the only black trainee in a department of over 8,000 employees. During this period, my tension increased as I was repeatedly called on to be the in-house expert on anything pertaining to civil rights. I was proud to be black and had many opinions about civil rights, but I did not feel qualified to give "the" black opinion. I developed the feeling that I was considered a black first and an individual second by many of the people I came into contact with. This feeling was exacerbated by the curious executive visitors to the training class who had to be introduced to everyone except me. Everyone knew my name, and I constantly had the feeling of being on stage.

The next phase of training was intended to prepare trainees for supervisory responsibilities. The tension of the trainee group had risen somewhat because of the loss of several trainees and the increased challenges facing us. In my own case, an increasing fear of failure began to impact on the other tensions that I felt from being "a speck of pepper in a sea of salt." The result of these tensions was that I began behaving with an air of bravado. I wasn't outwardly concerned or afraid, but I was inwardly terrified. This phase of training was also completed satisfactorily, at least in an official sense.

At the conclusion of the training, I received a "yes, but" type of appraisal. For example: "Mr. Jones doesn't take notes and seems to have trouble using the reference material, but he seems to be able to recall the material." This is the type of appraisal that says you've done satisfactorily, yet leaves a negative or dubious impression. I questioned the subjective inputs but dropped the matter without any vehement objections.

Prior to embarking on my first management assignment, I resolved to learn from this appraisal and to use more tact and talk less. These resolutions were re-emphasized by my adviser, who was an executive with responsibility for giving me counsel and acting as a sounding board. He also suggested that I relax my handshake and speak more softly.

On the Job

A warm welcome awaited me in the office where I was to complete my first assignment as a supervisor. I looked forward to going to work because I felt that subjectivity in appraisals would now be replaced by objectivity. Here was a situation in which I would either meet or fail to meet clearly defined numerical objectives.

There were no serious problems for three weeks, and I started to relax and just worry about the job. But then I had a conflict in my schedule. An urgent matter had to be taken care of in the office at the same time that I had an appointment elsewhere. I wrote a note to a supervisor who worked for another manager, asking him if he would be kind enough to follow up on the matter in the office for me.

I chose that particular supervisor because he had given me an embarrassingly warm welcome to the office and insisted that I "just ask" if there was anything at all that he could do to help me. I relied on the impersonality of the note because he was out on a coffee break and I had to leave immediately. The note was short and tactfully worded, and ended by giving my advance "thanks" for the requested help. Moreover, the office norms encouraged supervisory cooperation, so the fact that we worked under different managers did not seem to be a problem.

When I returned to the office, the manager I worked for called me in. He was visibly irritated. I sat down and he said, "Ed, you're rocking the boat." He stated that the supervisor I had asked for help had complained directly to the area manager that I was ordering him around and said he wasn't about to take any nonsense from a "new kid" in the office.

In a very calm voice, I explained what I had done and why I had done it. I then asked my manager, "What did I do wrong?" He looked at me and said, "I don't know, but whatever it is, cut it out. Stop rocking the boat." When I asked why the note wasn't produced to verify my statements, he said that it "wasn't available."

I left my manager's office totally perplexed. How could I correct my behavior if I didn't know what was wrong with it? I resolved that I had no choice except to be totally self-reliant, since one thing was obvious: what I had taken at face value as friendliness was potentially a fatal trap.

The feelings aroused in this incident were indicative of those I was to maintain for some time. While I felt a need for closeness, the only option open to me was self-reliance. I felt that my manager should support and defend me, but it was obvious that he was not willing to take such a stance. Worst of all, however, was my feeling of disappointment and the ensuing confusion due to my lack of guidance. I felt that if my manager was not willing to protect and defend me, he had an increased responsibility to give me guidance on how to avoid future explosions of a similar nature.

For some months I worked in that office without any additional explosions, although I was continually admonished not to "rock the boat." During a luncheon with the area manager one day, I remember, he said, "Ed, I've never seen a guy try so hard. If we tell you to tie your tie to the right, you sure try to do it. But why can't you be like Joe [another trainee the area manager supervised]? He doesn't seem to be having any problems."

THE APPRAISAL INCIDENT

I directed my energies and frustrations into my work, and my supervisory section improved in every measured area of performance until it led the unit. At the end of my first six months on the job, I was slated to go on active duty to fulfill my military requirements as a lieutenant in the Army. Shortly before I left, my manager stated, "Ed, you've done a tremendous job. You write your own appraisal." I wrote the appraisal, but was told to rewrite it because "it's not good enough." I rewrote the appraisal four times before he was satisfied that I was not being too modest. As I indicated earlier, I had resolved to be as unabrasive as possible, and, even though I had met or exceeded all my objectives, I was trying not to be pompous in critiquing my own performance.

Finally, on my next to last day on the job, my manager said, "Ed, this is a fine appraisal. I don't have time to get it typed before you go, but I'll submit this appraisal just as you have written it." With that, I went into the service, feeling that, finally, I had solved my problems.

Six months later, I took several days' leave from the Army to spend Christmas in the city with my family. On the afternoon of the day before Christmas, I decided to visit the personnel executive who had originally given me encouragement. So, wearing my officer's uniform, I stopped by his office.

After exchanging greetings and making small talk, I asked him if he had seen my appraisal. He answered, "yes," but when his face failed to reflect the look of satisfaction that I expected, I asked him if I could see it. The appraisal had been changed from the one that I had originally written to another "yes, but" appraisal. The numerical results said that I had met or exceeded all objectives, but under the section entitled "Development Program" the following paragraph had been inserted:

"Mr. Jones's biggest problem has been overcoming his own impulsiveness. He has on occasion, early in his tour, jumped too fast with the result that he has incurred some resentment. In these cases his objectives have been good, but his method has ruffled feathers."

I asked the personnel executive to interpret my overall rating. He answered, "Well, we can run the business with people with that rating." I then asked him to explain the various ratings possible, and it became clear that I had received the lowest acceptable rating that wouldn't require the company to fire me. I could not see how this could be, since I had exceeded all my objectives. I explained how I had written my own appraisal and that this appraisal had been rewritten. The personnel officer could not offer an explanation; he recommended that I speak to my old area manager, who had had the responsibility to review and approve my appraisal, and ask him why I had been treated in that manner.

A BLEAK CHRISTMAS

I tried to sort things out on my way to see my former area manager. My head was spinning, and I was disgusted. The appraisal was not just unfair —it was overtly dishonest. I thought of standing up in righteous indignation and appealing to higher authority in the company, but I had always resisted calling attention to my blackness by asking for special concessions and wanted to avoid creating a conflict situation if at all possible. While the 15-minute walk in the cold air calmed my anger, I still hadn't decided what I was going to do when I arrived at the area manager's office.

I walked into a scene that is typical of Christmas Eve in an office. People were everywhere, and discarded gift wrappings filled the wastebaskets. The area manager still had on the red Santa Claus suit. I looked around at the scene of merriment and decided that this was a poor time to "rock the boat."

The area manager greeted me warmly, exclaimed how great I looked, and offered to buy me a drink on his way home. I accepted, and with a feeling of disgust and disappointment, toasted to a Merry Christmas. I knew then that this situation was hopeless and there was little to be gained by raising a stink while we were alone. I had been naïve, and there was no way to prove that the appraisal had been changed.

I was a very lonely fellow that Christmas Eve. My feelings of a lack of closeness, support, and protection were renewed and amplified. It became obvious that no matter how much I achieved, how hard I worked, or how many personal adjustments I made, this system was trying to reject me.

I didn't know which way to turn, whom to trust, or who would be willing to listen. The personnel executive had told me to expect prejudice, but when he saw that I was being treated unfairly, he sent me off on my own.

"What do they expect?" I thought. "They know that I am bound to run into prejudice; yet no one lifts a finger when I am treated unfairly. Do they expect a person to be stupid enough to come right out and say, 'Get out, blackie; we don't want your type here'? This surely wouldn't happen—

such overt behavior would endanger the offending person's career."

After the Christmas Eve incident, I went off to finish the remaining time in the Army. During that period, I tossed my work problems around in my mind, trying to find the right approach. The only answer I came up with was to stand fast, do my best, ask for no special favors, and refuse to quit voluntarily.

New Challenges

When I returned to the company, I was assigned as a supervisor in another area for five or six weeks, to do the same work as I had been doing prior to my departure for the military service. At the end of this uneventful refamiliarization period, I was reassigned as a manager in an area that had poor performance and was recognized as being one of the most difficult in the company. The fact that I would be responsible for one of three "manager units" in the area was exciting, and I looked forward to this new challenge.

I walked into my new area manager's office with a smile and an extended hand, anxious to start off on the right foot and do a good job. After shaking hands, my new boss invited me to sit down while he told me about the job. He began by saying, "I hope you don't, but I am pretty sure you are going to fall flat on your face. When you do, my job is to kick you in the butt so hard that they'll have to take us both to the hospital."

I was shocked and angry. In the first place, my pride as a man said you don't have to take that kind of talk from anyone. I fought the temptation to say something like, "If you even raise your foot, you may well go to the hospital to have it put in a cast."

As I held back the anger, he continued, "I don't know anything about your previous performance, and I don't intend to try to find out. I'm going to evaluate you strictly on your performance for me."

The red lights went on in my mind. This guy was making too much of an issue about his lack of knowledge concerning my previous performance. Whom was he trying to kid? He had heard rumors and read my personnel records. I was starting off with two strikes against me. I looked at him and said, "I'll do my best."

MORE APPRAISAL TROUBLES

The area's results failed to improve, and John, the area manager, was replaced by a new boss, Ralph. Two weeks after Ralph arrived, he called me on the intercom and said, "Ed, John has your appraisal ready. Go down to see him in his new office. Don't worry about it; we'll talk when you get back." Ralph's words and tone of foreboding made me brace for the worst.

John ushered me into his office and began by telling me that I had been his worst problem. He then proceeded to read a list of every disagreement involving me that he was aware of. These ranged from corrective actions with clerks to resource-allocation discussions with my fellow managers. It was a strange appraisal session. John wound up crossing out half of the examples cited as I rebutted his statements. At the end of the appraisal, he turned and said, "I've tried to be fair, Ed. I've tried not to be vindictive. But if someone were to ask how you're doing, I would have to say you've got room for improvement."

Discussions with Ralph, my new boss, followed as soon as I returned to my office. He advised me not to worry, that we would work out any problems. I told him that this was fine, but I also pointed out the subjectivity and dishonesty reflected in previous and current appraisals and the circumstances surrounding them.

I was bitter that a person who had just been relieved for ineffectiveness could be allowed to have such a resounding impact on my chances in the company. My predecessor had been promoted; I had improved on his results; but here I was, back in questionable status again.

THE TURNING POINT

About six weeks later, Ralph called me in and said, "Ed, I hope you make it on the job. But what are you going to do if you don't?"

At that moment, I felt as if the hands on the clock of life had reached 11:59. Time was running out very rapidly on me, and I saw myself against a wall, with my new boss about to deliver the coup de grâce. I felt that he was an honest and very capable person, but that circumstances had combined to give him the role of executioner. It seemed from his question that he was in the process of either wrestling with his own conscience or testing me to see how much resistance, if any, I would put up when he delivered the fatal blow. After all, while I had not made an issue of my ill treatment thus far in my career, no matter how unjustly I felt I had been dealt with, he was smart enough to realize that this option was still open to me.

I looked at Ralph and any thought about trying to please him went out of my mind. Sitting up straight in my chair, I met his relaxed smile with a very stern face. "Why do you care what I do if I don't make it?" I asked coldly.

"I care about you as a person," he replied.

"It's not your job to be concerned about me as a person," I said. "Your job is to evaluate my performance results. But since you've asked, it will be rough if I am fired, because I have a family and responsibilities. However, that's not your concern. You make your decision; and when you do, I'll make my decision." With that statement I returned to my office.

Several weeks after this discussion, a vice president came around to the office to discuss objectives and job philosophy with the managers. I noted at the time that while he only spent 15 or 20 minutes with the other managers, he spent over an hour talking with me. After this visit, Ralph and I had numerous daily discussions. Then Ralph called me into his office to tell me he had written a new appraisal with an improved rating. I was thrilled. I was going to make it. Later, he told me that he was writing another appraisal, stating I not only would make it but also had promotional potential.

After Ralph had changed the first appraisal, my tensions began to decrease and my effectiveness began to increase proportionately. The looser and more confident I became, the more rapidly the results improved. My assignment under Ralph became very fulfilling, and one of the best years I've spent in the company ensued. Other assignments followed, each more challenging than the previous, and each was handled satisfactorily.

Lessons from Experience

My point in relating these experiences is not to show that I was persecuted or treated unfairly by people in a large corporation. In fact, after talking to friends in the company who knew me during the period just described, I am convinced that many of the lack-of-tact and rock-the-boat statements were true. I am also convinced, however, that the problems I experienced were not uniquely attributable to me or my personality and that it is important for companies to understand what caused them.

The manager to whom I reported on my very first assignment made some informal notes which help illustrate my conviction:

"I discussed each case with Ed. As might be expected, there is as much to be said in his defense as against him. He isn't all wrong in any one case. But the cumulative weight of all those unsolicited comments and complaints clearly shows that he is causing a lot of people to be unhappy, and I must see that it stops. I don't think it is a question of what he says and does or a question of objectives. It is a question of voice, manner, approach, method—or maybe timing. No matter what it is, he must correct whatever he does that upsets so many people."

These are not the words of a scheming bigot; they are the words of a man searching for an explanation to a phenomenon that neither he nor I understood at the time. I was not knowingly insensitive to other people or intent on antagonizing them. What this man and others failed to realize was that, being a black man in a unique position in a white company, I was extremely tense and ill at ease. Levels of sensitivity, polish, and tact which were foreign to me were now necessities of life. The world of white business presented me with an elaborate sociopolitical organization that required unfamiliar codes of behavior.

Abraham Zaleznik refers to this phenomenon in *The Human Dilemmas of Leadership*:

"The anxiety experienced by the upwardly mobile individual largely comes from internal conflicts generated within his own personality. On the one hand, there is the driving and pervasive need to prove himself as assurance of his adequacy as a person; on the other hand, the standards for measuring his adequacy come from sources somewhat unfamiliar to him."[1]

My personal pride and sense of worth were driving me to succeed. Ironically, the more determined I was to succeed, the more abrasive I became and the more critical my feedback became. This in turn impelled me to try even harder and to be even more uptight. As a result, I was vulnerable to prejudgments of inability by my peers and superiors.

THE LENS OF COLOR

What most white people do not understand or accept is the fact that skin color has such a pervasive impact on every black person's life that it subordinates considerations of education or class. Skin color makes black people the most conspicuous minority in America, and all blacks, regardless of status, are subjected to prejudice. I personally was not as disadvantaged as many other blacks, but to some extent all blacks are products of separate schools, neighborhoods, and subcultures. In short, black and white people not only look different but also come from different environments which condition them differently and make understanding and honest communication difficult to achieve.

Many whites who find it easy to philosophically accept the fact that blacks will be rubbing shoulders with them experience antagonism when they realize that the difference between blacks and whites goes deeper than skin color. They have difficulty adjusting to the fact that blacks really are different. It is critical that companies understand this point, for it indicates the need for increased guidance to help blacks adjust to an alien set of norms and behavioral requirements.

THE INFORMAL ORGANIZATION

One of the phenomena that develops in every corporation is a set of behavioral and personal norms that facilitates communication and aids cohesiveness. Moreover, because this "informal organization" is built on white norms, it can reinforce the black-white differences just mentioned and thus reject or destroy all but the most persistent blacks.

1. New York, Harper & Row, Publishers, 1966, p. 111.

The informal organization operates at all levels in a corporation, and the norms become more rigid the higher one goes in the hierarchy. While this phenomenon promotes efficiency and unity, it is also restrictive and very selective. It can preclude promotion or lead to failure on the basis of "fit" rather than competence.

Chester Barnard recognized the existence of the informal organization in 1938. As he stated, "This question of fitness involves such matters as education, experience, age, sex, personal distinctions, prestige, race, nationality, faith. . . ."[2]

I believe that many of the problems I encountered were problems of fit with the informal organization. My peers and supervisors were unable to perceive me as being able to perform the job that the company hired me for. Their reaction to me was disbelief. I was out of the "place" normally filled by black people in the company; and since no black person had preceded me successfully, it was easy for my antagonists to believe I was inadequate.

I am not vacillating here from my previous statement that I was probably guilty of many of the subjective shortcomings noted in my appraisals. But I do feel that the difficulties I experienced were amplified by my lack of compatibility with the informal organization. Because of it, many of the people I had problems with could not differentiate between objective ability and performance and subjective dislike for me, or discomfort with me. I was filling an unfamiliar, and therefore uncomfortable, "space" in relation to them. Even in retrospect, I cannot fully differentiate between the problems attributable to me as a person, to me as a manager, or to me as a black man.

Toward Facilitating "Fit"

Because of the foregoing problems, I conclude that business has an obligation to even out the odds for blacks who have executive potential. I am not saying that all blacks must be pampered and sheltered rather than challenged. Nor am I advocating the development of "chosen" managers. All managers must accept the risk of failure in order to receive the satisfactions of achievement.

I do, however, advocate a leveling out of these problems of "fit" with the informal organization that operate against black managers. Here are the elements vital to this process:

□ *Unquestionable top management involvement and commitment*—The importance of this element is underscored by my discussions with the vice

2. *The Functions of the Executive* (Cambridge, Harvard University Press, 1938), p. 224.

president who visited me during my crisis period. He disclosed that his objective was to see whether I was really as bad as he was being told. His conclusion from the visit was that he couldn't see any insurmountable problems with me. This high-level interest was the critical variable that gave me a fair chance. I was just lucky that this man had a personal sense of fair play and a desire to ensure equitable treatment.

But chance involvement is not enough. If a company is truly committed to equal opportunity, then it must set up reasoned and well thought-out plans for involvement of top management.

□ *Direct two-way channels of communication between top management and black trainees*—Without open channels of communication, a company cannot ensure that it will recognize the need for a neutral opinion or the intercession of a disinterested party if a black trainee is having problems.

Clear channels of communication will also enable top management to provide empathetic sources of counsel to help the new black trainee combat the potentially crippling paranoia that I encountered. I didn't know whom to trust; consequently, I trusted no one. The counsel of mature and proven black executives will also help mitigate this paranoia.

□ *Appraisal of managers on their contributions to the company's equal opportunity objectives*—The entire management team must be motivated to change any deep beliefs about who does and doesn't fit with regard to color. Accordingly, companies should use the appraisal system to make the welfare of the black trainee coincident with the well-being of his superior. Such action, of course, will probably receive considerable resistance from middle- and lower-level management. But managers are appraised on their ability to reach other important objectives; and, more significantly, the inclusion of this area in appraisals signals to everyone involved that a company is serious. Failure to take this step signals business as usual and adds to any credibility gap between the company and black employees.

The appraisal process also motivates the trainee's superior to "school" him on the realities of the political process in the corporation. Without this information, no one can survive in an organization. After upgrading my appraisal, Ralph began this process with me. The knowledge I gained proved to be invaluable in my subsequent decision making.

□ *Avoid the temptation to create special showcase-black jobs.* They will be eyed with suspicion by the black incumbents, and the sincerity of the company will be open to question. Blacks realize that only line jobs provide the experience and reality-testing which develop the confidence required in positions of greater responsibility.

□ *Select assignments for the new black manager which are challenging, yet don't in themselves increase his chances of failure.* My assignment with John was a poor choice. He was a top-rated area manager, but had a different job orientation and was struggling to learn his new responsibilities. So naturally he would resent any inexperienced manager being assigned to him. Moreover, the fact that he had never seen a successful black manager reinforced his belief that I could not do the job.

These basic steps need not be of a permanent nature, but they should be enacted until such time as the organizational norms accept blacks at all levels and in all types of jobs. The steps will help mitigate the fact that a black person in the organizational structure must not only carry the same load as a white person but also bear the burden attributable to prejudice and the machinations of the informal organization.

Conclusion

In relating and drawing on my own experiences, I have not been talking about trials and tribulations in an obviously bigoted company. At that time, my company employed a higher percentage of blacks than almost any other business, and this is still true today. I grant that there is still much to be done as far as the number and level of blacks in positions of authority are concerned, but I believe that my company has done better than most in the area of equal opportunity. Its positive efforts are evidenced by the progressive decision to sponsor my study at the Harvard Business School, so I would be prepared for greater levels of responsibility.

There are differences in detail and chronology, but the net effect of my experiences is similar to that of other blacks with whom I have discussed these matters. While prejudice exists in business, the U.S. norm against being prejudiced precludes an admission of guilt by the prejudiced party. Thus, in my own case, my first manager and John were more guilty of naïveté than bigotry—they could not recognize prejudice, since it would be a blow to their self-images. And this condition is prevalent in U.S. industry.

My experience points out that a moral commitment to equal opportunity is not enough. If a company fails to recognize that fantastic filters operate between the entry level and top management, this commitment is useless. Today, integration in organizations is at or near the entry level, and the threat of displacement or the discomfort of having to adjust to unfamiliar racial relationships is the greatest for lower and middle managers, for they are the people who will be most impacted by this process. Therefore, companies must take steps similar to the ones I have advocated if they hope to achieve true parity for blacks.

Equal job opportunity is more than putting a black man in a white man's job. The barriers must be removed, not just moved.

Part VII

Control

Preface

In every economy and every age since economic activity began, control has been a preoccupation of alert executives. It influences organizational success and may also have a decisive bearing on a manager's style of operating. In any book on general management, therefore, management control systems need to be discussed. But advances in technology and methodology have brought other important issues under the rubric of control. One of these issues is management information systems, which in company after company have captured the attention of top executives and been a continuing topic of discussion and debate. Information systems affect both the substance and forms of management control. The second issue is forecasting, which sometimes is classified with marketing but is treated here as an aspect of control because of its vital implications for management's cost and income expectations.

The article on "What Kind of Management Control Do You Need?" deals with the importance of considering the strategy and structure of a company before designing measures of financial responsibility. "Managing the Four Stages of EDP Growth" concerns the phases of growth typically experienced by computer departments—the "life crises" they go through as well as the varying techniques needed to manage computer facilities. "How to Choose the Right Forecasting Technique" describes the strengths and limitations of various qualitative and quantitative approaches, from the Delphi method to exponential smoothing, diffusion indexes, and input-output models.

26. What Kind of Management Control Do You Need?

Richard F. Vancil

A good method of measuring a manager's financial contribution to a company must meet two criteria. It must seem fair to the manager, and it must reward him for working for the benefit of the whole company, not just his department or division. Although simple in theory, these criteria become difficult to meet in practice. The characteristics of the business may lead managers to work at cross-purposes; moreover, the strategy of a business should have a profound effect on the kinds of decisions made. In this article the requirements of designing effective management control systems are examined in both simple and complex organizations. Pointing to realities with which businessmen are familiar, the author seeks to guide executives in weighing the advantages and disadvantages of functional forms of organization, product division forms, and the so-called matrix concept of organization. He points out that profit centers are by no means a universal answer, however appealing they may be in principle to business leaders.

Profit centers are a major tool for management control in large industrial corporations. They possess important advantages:

1. Profitability is a simple way to analyze and monitor the effectiveness of a segment of a complex business. For example, a product division competes in the marketplace against several other companies in its industry, and also competes among other divisions in its company for an allocation of corporate resources for its future growth. Relative profitability in both types of competition is a useful decision criterion for top management.

2. Profit responsibility is a powerful motivator of men. Managers understand what profit is all about, and aggressive managers welcome the opportunity to have their abilities measured by the only real entrepreneurial yardstick.

Simple and powerful, profit centers sounds like a panacea, the answer to a top manager's prayer. No wonder the concept has been so widely adopted. However, as with many a miracle drug, all too often the side effects of the medicine may be worse than the illness it was intended to cure.

There is an excellent body of literature on the problems that arise in implementing the profit center concept. The question I shall discuss is a more basic one: *When* should profit centers be used? More precisely, what executives below the president of a corporation (who clearly is responsible for profits) should be held responsible for the profits from segments of the business?

Parts of this discussion will come as no surprise to corporate presidents or to their controllers. I shall stress the relevance of corporate strategy and organization structure to profit center systems—an approach that may seem obvious to such executives. But I cannot find a discussion of these considerations in the literature, and thus I am led to believe that a concise statement of the conventional wisdom may be worthwhile.

Types of Financial Responsibility

The principal types of financial responsibility can be classified as follows:

Standard cost centers are exemplified by a production department in a factory. The standard quantities of direct labor and materials required for each unit of output are specified. The foreman's objective is to minimize the variance between actual costs and standard costs. He also is usually responsible for a flexible overhead expense budget, and his objective, again, is to minimize the variance between budgeted and actual costs.

Revenue centers are best illustrated by a sales department where the manager does not have authority to lower prices in order to increase volume. The resources at his disposal are reflected in his expense budget. The sales manager's objective is to spend no more than the budgeted amounts and to produce the maximum amount of sales revenue.

Discretionary expense centers include most administrative departments. There is no practical way to establish the relationship between inputs and outputs. Management can only use its best judgment to set the budget, and the department manager's objective is to spend the budgeted amount to produce the best (though still unmeasurable) quality of service that he possibly can.

Profit centers, the focus of this article, are units, such as a product division, where the manager is responsible for the best combination of costs and revenues. His objective is to maximize the bottom line, the profit that results from his decisions. A great many variations on this theme can be achieved by defining "profit" as including only those elements of cost and revenue for which the manager is responsible. Thus a sales manager who is allowed to set prices may be responsible for gross profit (actual revenue less standard direct manufacturing costs). Profit for a product-line marketing manager, on the other hand, might reflect deductions for budgeted factory overhead and actual sales promotion expenses.

Investment centers are units where the manager is responsible also for the magnitude of assets employed. He makes trade-offs between current profits and investments to increase future profits. Stating the manager's objective as maximizing his return on investment or his residual income (profit after a charge for the use of capital) helps him to appraise the desirability of new investments.

Choice of Financial Goals

The cornerstone of every management control system is the concept of responsibility accounting. The basic idea is simple: each manager in a company has responsibility for a part of the total activity. The accounting system should be designed so that it yields a measurement of the financial effects of the activities that a manager is responsible for. This measurement can be stated in the form of a financial objective for each manager. Specifying that objective helps in delegating authority; a manager knows that the "right" decision is the course of action that moves him down the path toward his financial objective.

But this system does not go far enough. No single measurement, no matter how carefully constructed, can accurately reflect how well a manager has done his job. Part of the failure is simply due to the fact that corporations—and their managers—have multiple objectives. For instance, there is the matter of corporate social responsibility. Good performance toward that goal, even if measurable, cannot be added to the profit equation. Another major inadequacy of a single financial measurement is that it reflects performance during a particular time period, ignoring the effects that current actions may have on future performance. Every manager must make trade-offs between conflicting short-term and long-term needs; examples range all the way from the shop foreman who defers preventive maintenance in order to increase this month's output, but at the expense of a major breakdown next month, to the division manager who cuts his R&D budget in order to improve the year's profits but loses or delays the opportunity to introduce a profitable new product three years from now.

Despite these flaws, oversimplified financial measurements are almost universally used. The reason is not their value in evaluating a manager's performance—the faults noted are too obvious and important to ignore— but their effect on future performance. Specifying a financial objective can help a manager to think realistically about the tough decisions he must make, even if the objective does not always point the way to the right decision.

The selection of the right financial objective for each manager, therefore, can have an important effect on how he does his job. Although the range of *possible* objectives is very great, the financially measurable results of any manager's activities can usually be classified into one of the five categories of responsibility centers described above. As indicated, financial responsibility is simplest in the case of standard cost centers, most complex in the case of investment centers.

How should management measure the financial results achieved? It is not enough simply to say that a particular product division is a profit center; decisions are also required that specify how the profit is to be calculated, focusing in particular on how transfer prices shall be set and how the costs of services received from other organization units shall be charged against the division. Similarly, while the basic concept of an investment center is simple, it is difficult to decide which assets to include in the investment base and how they shall be valued. Therefore, although there may be only five types of financial responsibility centers, there are *many* methods of financial measurement that can be used for specific organizations.

CRITERIA FOR SELECTION

Figuring out the best way to define and measure the financial performance for each manager is the corporate controller's most challenging—and analytically demanding—task. Two types of considerations affect each choice. The first is the strategy of the company: its broad objectives, the nature of the industries in which it operates, and the niche it seeks to carve for itself in each industry on the basis of its distinctive competence. The second is the organization structure of the company—the way the total task is divided among the managers to permit delegation of authority and specialization of effort.

The controller must have a thorough knowledge of his company's strategy and organization structure. He draws on this knowledge to apply two criteria for deciding which measure of financial responsibility to use for each organization unit and how it should be calculated:

1. *Fairness*—Each manager must believe that the summary financial measurement used to report on his performance is appropriate. This means he must see all of the signals he receives about his job as consistent with each other. Moreover, he must believe that the measurement encompasses all the factors he can control and excludes those over which he has no control. And he must be convinced the measurement is calculated in such a way that a "good" decision on his part will be reflected as such by the financial measurement. The "fairness" of a financial measurement is not a fact; it is a perception through the eyes of the manager to whom it applies.

2. *Goal congruence*—The most difficult compromises that must be made in designing a management control system have to do with varying goals.

When a manager is assigned a financial objective for his activities and a fair measurement of performance is determined, ideally he should be able to pursue his objective without concern for whether or not his actions are in the best interests of the corporation. But in reality, as we know, that ideal is not easy to attain. The controller, designing a management control system with a corporatewide perspective, must ensure that managers are not working at cross-purposes. He must select objectives and measurements in such a way that a good decision by any manager is also a good decision for the corporation as a whole.

For the controller, applying these two criteria simultaneously means that he must combine the points of view of both the individual manager and the corporation. That becomes progressively more difficult as the complexity of the organization structure and the business increases. In the balance of this article I shall discuss the use of the two criteria, dealing first with relatively simple organization structures and then with more complex ones.

Use in Simple Structures

Discussing the design of a management control system for "simple" organizations is not a theoretical or academic exercise. Some small businesses have simple organization structures, and even the largest corporations progressively subdivide the management tasks to the point where an individual manager is responsible for a single functional activity. Functional units are the organizational building blocks in the most complex corporations.

What varieties of control system are possible and feasible in simple organizations? When are the criteria of fairness and goal congruence satisfied? How does a company's strategy affect the choice of a system?

PRACTICAL ALTERNATIVES

The simplified organization chart shown in *Exhibit I* is typical of a great many companies or parts of companies. The structure of the organization is simple in two respects:

1. There are only two levels of line managers in the hierarchy (the "general manager" might be thought of as the president of a small company).

2. The subordinate managers each have responsibility for a functional activity, which implies a rather natural distribution of tasks and authority between them.

Exhibit I. Functionally organized business

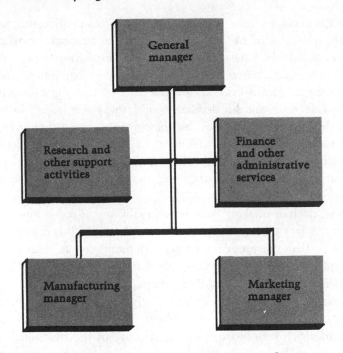

The business also requires some administrative and support activities, but the choice of financial measurements for these organizational units is less complex and will not be discussed here.

Selecting an appropriate financial measurement for this president's performance is not really a problem. He is responsible for the entire business, its profits, and the investment required. The financial responsibility of his two principal subordinates, however, is not so easily determined. The manufacturing manager, responsible for all production operations in the plant, could be charged with the responsibility of running either a standard cost center or a profit center. And the marketing manager, responsible for all sales and promotion activities, could be treated as the head either of a revenue center or of a profit center. With just two functional units, and two alternatives available for each, there are still four alternatives for the design of a management control system for this business:

Alternative	Manufacturing	Marketing
1.	Standard cost center	Revenue center
2.	Standard cost center	Profit center
3.	Profit center	Revenue center
4.	Profit center	Profit center

These four alternatives are not simply theoretical possibilities; each may be appropriate under different circumstances. The critical circumstances concern the nature of the key decisions to be made and the way decision-making authority is delegated in the organization.

As for the decisions, most of them involve choices in allocating resources. There are questions of *purpose* (e.g., whether incremental marketing expenditures should be used for advertising or for hiring more salesmen) and of *timing* (e.g., when a piece of production equipment should be replaced). In an ideal world, an all-wise and all-knowing president could make every decision, and his decision would always be "right" in the sense that it is the best course of action for the company at the time even though it may turn out to be wrong as future events unfold. The problem is that no president can make all the decisions and that, as he delegates power to subordinates, he runs the risk they will make decisions that are different from those he would make.

Effective decision making in a functionally organized business is hampered by the fact that no subordinate has the same broad perspective of the business that the president or general manager has. Many decisions, and almost all the important ones, affect more than one function in the business. They are seen differently by managers according to the functions they manage. One possible response to this problem is not to delegate authority for important decisions below the level of general manager. Another approach is to broaden the perspective of the functional manager by delegating such authority to him and then holding him responsible for the profitability of his decisions.

The implications of the second approach can best be seen by examining a series of examples. I shall describe a company situation for each of the four design alternatives mentioned.

1. No profit centers: Company A manufactures and distributes fertilizer. It buys chemicals, minerals, and other components from large suppliers and mixes them in various combinations to produce a limited variety of standard fertilizers with specified chemical properties. These are sold to farmers in bulk. Because the quality is specified and subject to verification by chemical analysis, all producers sell at the same price and offer identical volume discounts. Transportation costs are a major factor, and Company A thus enjoys a relative advantage in its local market. Its salesmen call on purchasing agents for large corporate farms and on distributors that sell to smaller farmers. Most orders are placed well in advance of the growing season, so the mixing plant is busy several months of the year, but there is still a large seasonal peak in both marketing and manufacturing.

Prices tend to fluctuate with the cost of the primary chemical components. The result is that an efficient fertilizer producer tends to earn about the same profit, as a percentage of the sales dollar, on each of the products in his line.

In this company the mission of the marketing manager is to sell as much fertilizer as he can. He has no control over product design or pricing, and promotional activities other than direct selling efforts are ineffective. His primary concern is with the effective use of his salesmen's time and with the development and maintenance of good customer relations. His stated objective is to produce as much revenue as he can with the number of salesmen currently authorized. In technical terms he is a "revenue center." He is also responsible for the expense budget for his activities.

The mission of the manufacturing manager, on the other hand, is to produce fertilizer in the required quantities as efficiently as possible. The work force is only semiskilled, and his primary concern is to ensure that they are properly trained and well supervised and that material wastage is held to a minimum. He is a "standard cost center," financially responsible for meeting the standard direct cost of each unit produced and for controlling overhead expenses against a variable budget reflecting the volume of throughput.

The president of Company A is the only man financially responsible for the profit of the company. There are a limited number of key, cross-functional decisions to be made, and he makes them. One concerns the size of the sales force; another concerns the acquisition of equipment to increase the capacity or reduce the labor costs in the mixing plant. Both of these are what are called "capacity decisions." While the evaluation of alternatives for either decision is not easy, it can be handled as well or better by the president than by either of his two subordinates.

2. Marketing profit centers: Company B produces a line of branded consumer toiletries. The products are heavily advertised and made available to consumers in drugstores, supermarkets, and other retail outlets throughout the country. The marketplace is in continual turmoil as competitors jockey for consumer attention through price promotions, premium offers, and "new" formulas and "secret" ingredients announced through both media advertising and point-of-purchase promotion. The company's field sales force is small; salesmen call on distributors and purchasing agents for large retail chains. The product itself is simple to manufacture, but consistently reliable quality is considered important to maintain customer goodwill.

Marketing is where the action is in Company B. The marketing manager is responsible for profitability, which is defined as sales revenue less standard direct manufacturing costs and all marketing costs. The president of the company is very interested in the marketing function and devotes much of his time to it. At the same time, he realizes that there are a myriad of marketing decisions to be made, many of them requiring specialized knowledge of local markets and detailed current information on competitors' actions. Therefore, he needs to delegate considerable authority to the marketing manager.

The manufacturing manager, like his counterpart in Company A, is a standard cost center, responsible for standard direct costs and a variable overhead budget.

3. Production profit centers: Company C produces a line of specialty metal products sold as semifinished components, primarily to manufacturers of high-style lighting fixtures. The company has only a few dozen customers, four of which account for over 50% of the sales volume. The business is price-competitive; Company C's equipment is not unique, and other manufacturers are frequently asked to bid against Company C on prospective contracts. Company C is renowned, however, for its technical skills in solving difficult manufacturing problems. Even on relatively routine contracts, the company is sometimes able to charge a slightly higher price because of its consistently high quality and its responsiveness in meeting its customers' "emergency" delivery requirements.

Price quotations on each contract are prepared by an estimator in the plant. The field sales force calls on old customers and prospective new ones, maintaining and developing relationships and soliciting opportunities to bid for their business.

Manufacturing is the name of the game at Company C. The manufacturing manager is responsible for profit, defined as the contribution to overhead after subtracting all direct manufacturing costs. He keeps himself informed of the backlog of orders against each type of equipment in his shop and personally reviews all bids over a nominal amount, estimating the price to quote in view of his desire for the business and his assessment of the customer's loyalty. He is also responsible for meeting his variable overhead budget.

As for the marketing manager, he is a revenue center, like his counterpart in Company A. He endeavors to use his sales force as effectively as possible to turn up attractive bidding opportunities on which the company can compete successfully.

4. Multiple profit centers: Company D is a partly integrated oil refining and marketing organization. The company's refinery purchases crude oil and refines it into gasoline, kerosene, and other products. The company also operates a regional chain of service stations, advertising its brand of gasoline to consumers. The company's strategy is to be less than self-sufficient in producing enough gasoline to meet its retail requirements. Thus the refinery is usually able to operate at capacity, and gasoline is purchased from other refiners as required.

Both the manufacturing (refinery) manager and the marketing manager are responsible for *part* of the profits earned by Company D. The refinery manager sells his gasoline to the marketing department at the same price charged by other refiners; the profit on the refinery is an important measure of the efficiency of his operations. The marketing manager, much like his counterpart in Company B, is also a profit center; he attempts to find the optimum balance and mix of marketing expenditures that will be most profitable for the company.

In this kind of situation, therefore, the president needs to delegate considerable decision-making power to not one but two subordinates. With respect to each he acts in the way described for Companies B and C.

The foregoing examples, simple as they are, show how difficult it is to generalize on the question of whether or not a functional manager should be held responsible for profit. The first, most obvious, statement is that the decision turns on the nature of the business. The tangible differences between businesses and the unique tasks they imply for management must be reflected in the management control system. The challenge for the controller is to synthesize the characteristics of the business and select a financial objective for each manager that (1) motivates him to achieve the company's objectives, and (2) minimizes unnecessary conflict between managers.

However, the characteristics of a business are not the sole determinants of financial responsibility. In fact, they are not the most important ones. This brings us to the next point: the implications of corporate strategy.

CRUCIAL ROLE OF STRATEGY

As an illustration, let us consider the situation of a franchised automobile dealership called Connelly Autos, Inc. The company sells new and used cars and auto repair services. Connelly's organization structure is simple; under the president there are two marketing managers, one for new cars and one for used cars, and a service department manager.

In this case, and in retail distribution businesses generally, it is easy to see the advantages of holding a sales manager responsible for the profits of his department. Moreover, suppose a customer with a certain amount of money to spend is undecided about buying a stripped-down new car or a more expensive model that is a year or two old. If Connelly's two sales managers compete for this customer's business, the result is probably that the customer is better served, in the sense that he has more information about the relative advantages of his two major alternatives and can ultimately make a choice that satisfies him better.

Also, the dealership is probably better off as a result of the competiton. There are many other new car and used car dealers, so if the company itself offers both choices in a manner that is as competitive as the two departments would be if they were in separate dealerships, it stands a better chance of getting a customer's business no matter which car he chooses to drive.

The difficult problem is designing a management control system for Connelly's service department manager. What is his financial responsibility? How should Connelly measure his performance in financial terms? The service department is not simply another sales department, delivering retail repair services to customers. It is also a "manufacturing" department producing services for the two automobile sales departments; it prepares new cars for delivery and services them during the warranty period, and it repairs and reconditions used cars to be sold at retail.

The real question becomes: What does Connelly want his service department manager to do? Here are several possible answers:

□ Run the service department as though it were an independent auto repair shop. With this mission, the service department manager would be responsible for profits and should probably sell his services to the new and used car departments at the regular retail price, or perhaps with a slight "dealer" discount.

□ Employ the capacity of the shop to the fullest, using renovation work on used cars as a way of absorbing slack capacity. With this mission, repair services should probably be sold to the used car department at standard direct costs. The used car manager would buy cars needing repair work, at wholesale auctions if necessary, thus providing all the volume the service department could handle. The service department would be essentially a standard cost center, and the profit on retail repairs would be de-emphasized.

□ Run the shop in such a way as to maximize customer goodwill, attempting to build a reputation that will yield regular, repeat customers for new cars. Under these circumstances, it would be very difficult to calculate a financial measurement that would appropriately reflect the performance of the service department manager. He should not be held responsible for profits, nor should he be expected to run close to capacity if he is to be responsive to customer emergencies. The shop should probably be treated as a standard cost center, but without emphasis being placed on financial performance.

Finding an answer: Thus the answer to the question of what the service department manager should do turns on Connelly's strategy for his dealership. The three alternatives outlined really characterize three different strategies. The first envisions a "balanced" dealership, the second has a strong used-car focus, and the third emphasizes new car sales.

Not all automobile dealers pursue the same strategy, nor should they. Local competitive conditions are a major factor in selecting a strategy, and the quality and type of resources available to Connelly are also critical factors in his choice. (Resources include the location of the dealership, the capital available for investment in new and used car inventories, and the competence and aggressiveness of Connelly's three subordinates.) Finally, the strategy Connelly selects will affect his image in the community as a businessman and a citizen, and his personal aspirations concerning the size and reputation of the business also have a bearing on the problem.[1]

There are thousands of automobile dealers in the United States, and they appear to be identical in terms of the characteristics of their business. Managers adopt different strategies, however, in order to differentiate their business from that of their competitors. The controller, designing a management control system, must understand both the nature of the business and the strategy being pursued if he is to create a set of financial measurements that will motivate functional managers to contribute to the achievement of company objectives. This task is not easy even in simple, functional organizations; it is more difficult still in complex organizations.

Use in Complex Structures

As a business grows and the magnitude of the management task increases, its organization structure tends to become more complex. Products come to be manufactured in more than one location and sold in more than one market; new models and lines may be added. Such multiplant, multimarket, multiproduct corporations typically have a multitier organization structure consisting of three or more layers of managers. Naturally, the management control system becomes more complex, too.

Part A of *Exhibit II* is an organization chart for a complex, functionally organized business (it may have started as the company shown in *Exhibit I*). As long as the business continues to be functionally organized, much of the discussion in the preceding section about the design of a management control system is applicable.

But an important difference should be noted. In the simple organization shown in *Exhibit I*, top management has very little choice about how to divide the functional tasks among subordinates. In many situations of the type shown in Part A of *Exhibit II*, however, reorganization along the lines shown in Part B of the same exhibit may be feasible and appropriate. In such cases, what pros and cons should be considered in deciding whether to adopt the product division approach? Except in cases where that approach seems a "natural" (for example, a conglomerate that has grown

---

1. For a more complete discussion of all the factors influencing the formulation of strategy, see Kenneth R. Andrews, *The Concept of Corporate Strategy* (Homewood, Illinois, Dow Jones–Irwin, Inc., 1971).

Exhibit II. Complex organizations

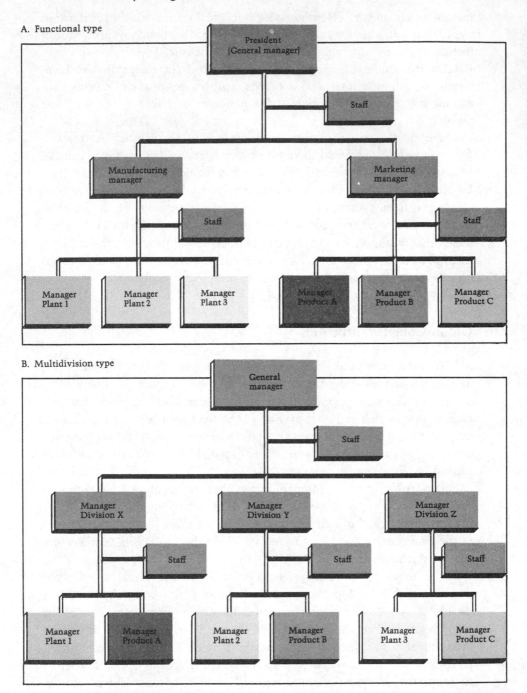

A. Functional type

President (General manager)

Staff

Manufacturing manager

Staff

Marketing manager

Staff

Manager Plant 1

Manager Plant 2

Manager Plant 3

Manager Product A

Manager Product B

Manager Product C

B. Multidivision type

General manager

Staff

Manager Division X

Manager Division Y

Manager Division Z

Staff

Staff

Staff

Manager Plant 1

Manager Product A

Manager Plant 2

Manager Product B

Manager Plant 3

Manager Product C

through the acquisition of independent businesses), the answer depends largely on how much management wants to maximize efficiency and on how much it wants to maximize responsiveness to markets. Let us consider this trade-off in some detail.

TURN TO PRODUCT DIVISIONS?

Product divisions are almost always treated as profit or investment centers. The responsibility of the division manager is usually broad enough so that he can conceive of his division as though it were an independent company. In addition, the scope and substance of his task and the objective he is to strive for may be delineated clearly. In such circumstances, the task of designing a management control system for the functional subordinates of the division manager is precisely the same as that discussed earlier; the division manager is really the general manager shown in *Exhibit I*.

Now, what can functional organizations do that product divisions cannot? Functional organizations have the potential of great efficiency. The efficiency of an activity can frequently be measured in terms of the quantity of inputs required to yield one unit of output. For a great many activities, efficiency increases as the size of the activity grows—at least, up to some point where there are no further "economies of scale" to be realized. The reason that efficiency increases is that large-scale operations permit the utilization of increasingly specialized inputs. For instance, a general-purpose machine tool and a skilled operator may be able to produce 100 parts per hour; but a specially designed piece of equipment might produce 1,000 parts per hour and require no operator at all. Also, specialization of workers can yield economies of scale, as the learning curve of production workers demonstrates.

The arguments, then, in favor of retaining the organization structure shown in Part A of *Exhibit II* might run as follows. While it is technically feasible to equip each plant so that it turns out one of the three products of the company, it would be a great waste to do so. Manufacturing costs would be much lower if each plant specialized in certain aspects of the manufacturing process, doing only a limited number of functions on all three products. Further, the quality of manufacturing supervision and technical services, such as engineering and quality control, is better when those activities are centralized under one manufacturing manager. Scattering such activities across three product divisions would both lower the quality of the personnel that could be afforded and reduce the efficiency of their services. Similar arguments might be made about the efficiency of the marketing organization.

What advantages are unique to product divisions? They hold out the promise of more *effective* management than is the case with functional organizations. (One way of contrasting effectiveness with efficiency is to say that efficiency means doing something right and effectiveness means doing the right something.) The benefits are harder to document or quantify, but the potential for improvement exists both in strategy formulation and in tactical decision making.

In a strategic sense, it is easier for a product division than a functional organization to focus on the needs of its customers, rather than on simply manufacturing or selling the current line of products. The division manager can develop a strategy for his particular business, finding a competitive niche for it that may be different from the strategy being pursued by other division managers with different product lines. Tactically, a product division can also be more responsive to current customer needs. The division manager has the authority to change the production schedule in response to the request of an important customer; in a functional organization, by contrast, such a request must "go through channels," which may be ponderous and time-consuming.

Finally, it can be argued that product divisions are an excellent training ground for young managers, fostering entrepreneurship and increasing the number of centers of initiative in a corporation.

A business organization must be both efficient and effective if it is to survive, be profitable, and grow. The fundamental choice in organizational design is not an either-or question, but one of achieving the best possible balance between the benefits from economies of scale and those from strategic and tactical responsiveness.[2] One approach that is being used increasingly in a variety of settings is the matrix form of organization.

ADOPT THE MATRIX FORM?

This relatively new form of organization apparently was developed first in the aerospace industry nearly three decades ago. Companies in that industry had massive capacity, both human and physical, for the design and manufacturing of weapons systems, and they were organized according to functional specialties. At any one moment, such a company might have had several large contracts in its shop, each at various stages of completion and each drawing on the various functional departments to a greater or lesser extent.

In these cases, management's focus was on the efficient use of each department's capacity; this meant that inadequate attention was devoted to cost and schedule performance on each contract. The solution was to

---

2. For an excellent treatise on the complex factors that must be considered in making a basic change in organization structure, see Alfred D. Chandler, Jr., *Strategy and Structure: Chapters in the History of the American Industrial Enterprise* (Cambridge, The M.I.T. Press, 1962).

Exhibit III. Concept of a matrix organization

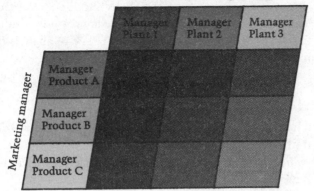

Manufacturing manager

	Manager Plant 1	Manager Plant 2	Manager Plant 3
Manager Product A			
Manager Product B			
Manager Product C			

Marketing manager

establish a new set of project managers, one for each contract, and to superimpose them across the existing functional hierarchy. A project manager's responsibility was to coordinate the inputs from each department in such a way that contractual performance requirements would be fulfilled.

Although matrix organizations, in a formal sense, are not widely used in industry, the concept has several attractive features. It holds the promise of both efficiency *and* effectiveness. Functional specialization is retained, thus permitting the efficiencies of economies of scale. But at the same time that program or product managers are viewed as the users of functional skills, they are also charged with producing a result that is competitively attractive to the customer and profitable for the company.

A matrix organization is essentially a functional organization. The six third-level managers in Part A of *Exhibit II* appear in *Exhibit III* and could still report to their respective functional superiors. However, there is an important difference: the relationships between the six managers are much more explicit in *Exhibit III*.

The matrix form of organization may be appropriate when much interaction between the functions is necessary or desirable. It can be particularly useful when one function (such as marketing) is concerned with planning for the effective combination of resources, while another function (such as manufacturing) is concerned with acquiring resources and using them efficiently. These two tasks obviously must be integrated and coordinated continuously. The matrix organization is intended to describe the interrelationships between the manufacturing and marketing functions and, without dismantling the old hierarchy, to legitimatize and encourage direct contact between the two parties concerned with any interlocking tasks or "cell" in the matrix. The matrix design does not really represent a structural change; it is simply a more realistic, comprehensive description of organizational relationships.

From the point of view of the designer of a management control system, a matrix organization poses no special problems and may offer an opportunity for a unique type of control system. Selecting the appropriate financial measurement for each functional manager may require nothing more, in some circumstances, than an application of the type of analysis described earlier. But management may need to go a step further if the nature of the business and its strategy are more complex than in those examples previously cited.

Problems in responsibility: In some businesses, both the marketing and the manufacturing functions may be highly interdependent and responsible for activities which have major effects on profits. How can the managers of the two functions be held jointly responsible?

One way is to hold each man responsible for a portion of the profits of the company, using a transfer price to permit a calculation of that profit. The determination of transfer prices in highly interdependent situations may be difficult, but it may be worth the trouble in order to motivate each manager properly.

Another approach is to use the matrix form of organization as an acknowledgment of the interdependence, and to hold each functional manager responsible for the entire profit of the business. This approach requires "double counting" of each profit dollar. In terms of *Exhibit III*, the manufacturing manager would be responsible for profit, defined as sales revenues less all manufacturing costs and all direct marketing expenses, for all products manufactured in the three plants. Each plant manager might have a similar responsibility for his plant. The sum of the defined profits for the three plants would be the total contribution to corporate overhead and net profit. Each product manager would also be responsible for profits, defined in the same way, for the products in his line. The sum of the profits for the three product managers would be the same as the total profit of the three plants.

Such a management control system may seem confusing at first, but it can be effective. The intent of double counting the profit is to make clear to all managers involved that they must work together in order to achieve their own individual objective. A profitable action which requires cooperation does not reflect to the credit of only one party, nor does it require a fictitious division of the profit between them. Both men benefit. Thus Plant Manager 1 would work with all three product managers, trying to find ways to use the facilities at his disposal in order to yield the highest profit for his plant. And Product Manager A would work with all three plant managers, attempting to utilize their resources in such a way as to maximize the profitability of his product line.

An intended effect of such a system is a certain amount of tension in the organization—an atmosphere of constructive conflict in which the managers in one function know they are working toward the same goal and must compete among themselves to cooperate with managers from the other functional area. Such conflict, if handled sensitively by a sophisticated top manager, can break down some of the parochialism of a purely functional organization without splintering it into less efficient product divisions.

Because of these potential advantages, we may see increasing use of the matrix concept in companies where functional interdependence is high and the rewards from functional specialization are too great to ignore.

Conclusion

Responsibility for the design of a management control system rests inescapably on top management. For one thing, it is top management that decides on the strategy and organization structure of a business. For another, the control system is a major tool for implementing those decisions effectively. The controller, as a member of the top management team, has an important role to play because the design of a control system is too complex a task for the chief executive to undertake without the benefit of staff support.

The president and his controller, joint designers of the management control system, face a great many choices as they try to decide (a) the type of financial objective to be specified for each organizational unit, and (b) how to calculate that measurement. There is a natural bias among corporate executives in favor of responsibility for profit. Profit is a powerful measurement; it provides a clear objective, is easily understood, and is a good motivator of such men. But not all managers are responsible for profits in any meaningful sense of that term. Creating a set of profit centers may cause more problems than it is worth.

Profit should be used as a measure of financial responsibility only when it is possible to calculate it in such a way that a manager's "profit" increases as the result of actions for which he is responsible and which he has taken in the best interests of the company.

27. Managing the Four Stages of EDP Growth

Cyrus F. Gibson and Richard L. Nolan

In all that has been said about the computer in business, there are few clues as to how the EDP department ought to grow or what management ought to be doing about the department at each stage of its growth. Here is a convenient categorization for placing the life crises of the EDP department in perspective, for developing the management techniques necessary or useful at various points, and for managing the human issues involved. These human issues, as a matter of fact, complicate the problems of growth at least as much as the hardware and software questions, which have been so well massaged in the literature; the authors show how these issues change shape as a company moves through the four stages of development. This article will be particularly helpful to the new business that is about to buy its first computer. For the company in the throes of later-stage development, it offers a framework useful for identifying issues and evaluating and controlling the growth of EDP.

From the viewpoint of the executive vice president, "The EDP manager always waffles around when he has to explain his budget." From the viewpoint of the EDP manager, "The executive vice president never seems to understand why this department needs a lot of money."

The reason for this kind of impasse is clear enough: EDP, as corporations use it today, is so complex that controlling it, or even understanding it, is almost too difficult for words. However, through our work with a number of companies, we have reached certain conclusions about how EDP departments grow and how they should fit into the company's organization. These conclusions offer a framework for communication for both the EDP manager and the senior managers to whom he reports.

There are four distinct stages in the growth of all EDP facilities, each with its distinctive applications, its rewards and its traumata, and its managerial problems. By breaking the evolution of the EDP department into four easy stages, it is possible to sort out the affairs of the department, if not into four neat, sequential packages, at least into four relatively small, sequential cans of worms.

The basis for this framework of stages is the discovery that the EDP budget for a number of companies, when plotted over time from initial investment to mature operation, forms an S-shaped curve. This is the curve that appears in the exhibits accompanying this article. The turnings of this curve correspond to the main events—often crises—in the life of the EDP function that signal important shifts in the way the computer resource is used and managed. There are three such turnings, and, consequently, four stages.

In the companies we know, there are remarkable similarities in the problems which arise and the management techniques applied to solve them at a given stage, despite variations among industries and companies, and despite ways in which EDP installations are used. Moreover, associated with each stage is a distinctive, informal organizational process. Each of these seems to play an important role in giving rise to the issues which need to be resolved if the stage is to be passed without a crisis and if the growth of the resource is to be managed to yield maximum benefit to the company.

Our purpose here is to describe the four stages in turn, listing the key characteristics of each and explaining the underlying organizational forces at work in each.

In the space of an article we can touch only on the main problems of EDP management at the different stages. Hence the view we present is bound to be somewhat simplified. Caution is advisable in another respect, too: history has not yet come to an end, and we are sure that the S-curve we describe and the stages it seems to follow do not represent the whole story. At the end of the S-curve of contemporary experience there will doubtless be more S-curves, as new EDP technologies emerge, and as companies become more ambitious in their use of EDP techniques and more sophisticated in systems analysis. However, we hope that the dynamics of later cost escalations will be clearer after the reader has finished with our description—clearer, and perhaps even predictable and controllable.

Four Stages of Growth

Three types of growth must be dealt with as an EDP department matures:
 □ A growth in computer applications—see *Exhibit I*.
 □ A growth in the specialization of EDP personnel—see *Exhibit II*.
 □ A growth in formal management techniques and organization—see *Exhibit III*.

The S-curve that overlies these three kinds of growth breaks conveniently into four segments, which represent the four stages of EDP growth:

Exhibit I. Growth of applications

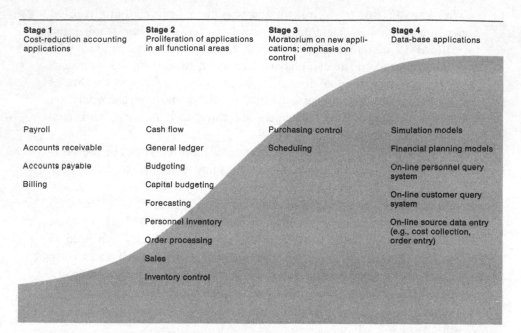

Stage 1 Cost-reduction accounting applications	Stage 2 Proliferation of applications in all functional areas	Stage 3 Moratorium on new applications; emphasis on control	Stage 4 Data-base applications
Payroll	Cash flow	Purchasing control	Simulation models
Accounts receivable	General ledger	Scheduling	Financial planning models
Accounts payable	Budgeting		On-line personnel query system
Billing	Capital budgeting		On-line customer query system
	Forecasting		
	Personnel inventory		On-line source data entry (e.g., cost collection, order entry)
	Order processing		
	Sales		
	Inventory control		

initiation, expansion, formalization, and maturity. Most notable are the proliferation of applications in Stage 2 (as reflected in *Exhibit I*) that causes the budget to increase exponentially, and the proliferation of controls in Stage 3 designed to curb this increase (as reflected in *Exhibit III*).

This sequence of stages is a useful framework for placing a company's current problems vis-à-vis EDP in perspective and helping its management understand the problems it will face as it moves forward. It is especially helpful for discussing ways to smooth out the chaotic conditions of change that have caused so many derailments in Stages 2 and 3. Even in our work with small companies, we have found the framework helpful—in obviating crises before they arise and in suggesting the kinds of planning that will induce smooth growth.

Thus one virtue of this framework is that it lays out for the company as a whole the nature of its task at each stage—whether it is a new company planning to buy its first computer, or a company in the throes of developing advanced applications, or a company with a steady, mature EDP facility.

Stage 1: Initiation

When the first computer is implanted in the organization, the move is normally justified in terms of cost savings. Rarely, at this point, does senior management assess the long-term impact of the computer on personnel,

Exhibit II. Growth of personnel specialization

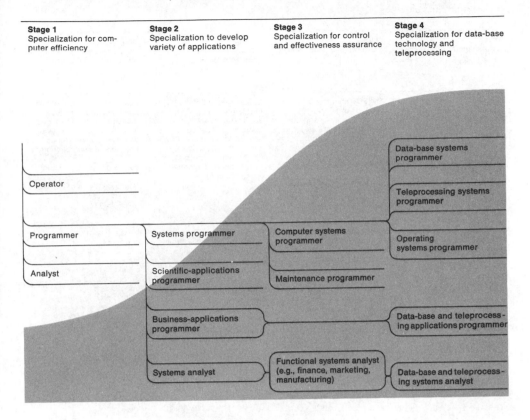

Stage 1 Specialization for computer efficiency	Stage 2 Specialization to develop variety of applications	Stage 3 Specialization for control and effectiveness assurance	Stage 4 Specialization for data-base technology and teleprocessing

Data-base systems programmer

Operator

Teleprocessing systems programmer

Programmer → Systems programmer → Computer systems programmer → Operating systems programmer

Analyst → Scientific-applications programmer → Maintenance programmer

Business-applications programmer → Data-base and teleprocessing applications programmer

Systems analyst → Functional systems analyst (e.g., finance, marketing, manufacturing) → Data-base and teleprocessing systems analyst

or on the organization, or on its strategy. Thus management can easily ignore a couple of crucial issues.

THE LOCATION QUESTION

In Stage 1, the priority management issue is to fix departmental responsibility for the computer:

□ Initially it makes economic sense to locate the computer in the department where it is first applied—very frequently, in accounting—and to hold that department responsible for a smooth introduction and a sound control of costs and benefits. The costs and benefits can be clearly stated and rigidly controlled under this approach—and they usually are.

□ However, the department where the computer will first be used—accounting, say—may not be the best location for the EDP facility later on. The later and more complex applications, such as inventory control and simulation modeling, should ideally be located in an autonomous department of computer services or management information systems which reports through a high-level manager.

But granted this longer perspective, management may decide on a less

	Stage 1 Lax management	Stage 2 Sales-oriented management	Stage 3 Control-oriented management	Stage 4 Resource-oriented planning and control
Organization	EDP is organized under the department of first-applications justification; it is generally a small department.	The EDP manager is moved up in the organization; systems analysts and programmers are assigned to work in the various functional areas.	EDP moves out of the functional area of first applications; a steering committee is set up; control is exerted through centralization; maintenance programming and systems programming become dominant activities.	EDP is set up as a separate functional area, the EDP manager taking on a higher-level position; some systems analysts and sometimes programmers are decentralized to user areas; high specialization appears in computer configuration and operation; systems design and programming take on a consulting role.
Control	Controls notably lacking; priorities assigned by FIFO; no chargeout.	Lax controls, intended to engender applications development; few standards, informal project control.	Proliferation of controls to contain a runaway budget; formal priority setting; budget justification. Programming controls: documentation, standards. Project management initiated; management reporting system introduced: project plan, project performance, customer service, personnel resources, equipment resources, budget performance. Chargeout introduced; postsystem audits. Quality control policies for computer system, systems design, programming, operations.	Refinement of management control system – elimination of ineffective control techniques and further development of others; introduction of data-base policies and standards; focus on pricing of computer services for engendering effective use of the computer.
Planning	Loose budget	Loose budget	Strong budgetary planning for hardware facilities and new applications.	Multiple 3-5 year plans for hardware, facilities, personnel, and new applications.

rigorous application of payback criteria for judging the performance of the initial application. Costs for "future development" may not be scrutinized too closely at this stage, and budgets may expand very early under this arrangement.

Many companies resolve this issue in obvious fashion. Management simply locates the facility within the department of first application for an initial period; then, when its viability has been proved and other applications develop, management creates the autonomous EDP unit.

In practice, however, this seemingly simple resolution conceals a serious trap. The department that controls the resource becomes strongly protective of it, often because a manager or a group within it wants to build up power and influence. When the time comes for computing to assume a broader role, real conflict arises—conflict that can be costly in terms of management turnover and in terms of lingering hostilities that inhibit the provision of computer services and applications across functional areas.

FEAR OF THE COMPUTER

Another priority issue is to minimize the disruption that results when high technology is injected into an organization. Job-displacement anxieties appear; some people become concerned over doing old jobs in new ways; and others fear a loss of personal identity with their work. These fears may lead to open employee resistance. While reactions of this kind may occur at any of the stages, they can be particularly destructive in Stage 1, where the very survival of the EDP concept is at stake.

In plain fact some of these fears are probably justified. For example, some employees (although usually relatively few) may indeed lose their jobs when the computer is first installed.

On the other hand, the concerns that develop from rumor or false information are usually overblown, and they are readily transformed and generalized into negative sentiments and attitudes toward management, as well as the computer itself. The wise course for management is to spike rumors with the most honest information it has, however the chips may fall. Such openness will at worst localize fears and resistances that must be dealt with sooner or later anyway.

Unless management is willing to recognize the seriousness of this anxiety, it risks a more generalized reaction in the form of unresponsive and uncreative work behavior, a broader and higher level of uncertainty and anxiety, and even sabotage, as a surprising number of cases have demonstrated.

Management can make no bigger mistake than to falsely reassure all concerned that the computer will not change their work or that it will mean no less work for everyone. Such comfort blankets lead to credibility gaps that are notoriously hard to close.

Thus the key to managing this process of initiation to the computer is to accept the fact that people's perceptions of reality and their views of the situation are what have to be understood and dealt with, rather than some "objective" reality. These perceptions will be diverse; management cannot assume that all organizational members are equally enthusiastic about introducing efficiency and reducing costs. Where you stand depends on where you sit and on who you are. In communicating its intention to introduce EDP, management should remember this and tailor its communications accordingly.

There will be variations from one situation and company to another in the manner and detail in which management releases information about future location and about the impact of the computer. Depending on circumstance, management directives may best be communicated downward by an outsider, by a department head, or by the new EDP manager. In settings where employees are rarely informed of management planning, it may even be wise to explain to the echelons why they are being given the explanation; again, in settings where the echelons have participated in planning, a formal presentation may be less effective than open group discussion.

Stage 2: Expansion

The excess computing capacity usually acquired when a company first initiates an EDP facility, combined with the lure of broader and more advanced applications, triggers a period of rapid expansion. The EDP area "takes off" into new projects that, when listed, often seem to have been selected at random. As *Exhibits I–III* show, Stage 2 represents a steady and steep rise in expenditures for hardware, software, and personnel. It is a period of contagious, unplanned growth, characterized by growing responsibilities for the EDP director, loose (usually decentralized) organization of the EDP facility, and few explicit means of setting project priorities or crystallizing plans.

It is a period, further, in which the chaotic effects of rapid development are moderated (if they are moderated at all) only by the quality and judgment of the personnel directly involved in the process. While top management may be sensitive to some of the ill effects of the computer, it tends to be attracted to and carried along with the mystique of EDP as well.

This stage often ends in crisis when top management becomes aware of the explosive growth of the activity, and its budget, and decides to rationalize and coordinate the entire organization's EDP effort. The dynamic force of expansion makes this a fairly difficult thing to do, however.

DYNAMICS OF EARLY SUCCESS

Once Stage 1 has passed, and the management and personnel of the computer area have justified and assured their permanent place in the organization, a new psychological atmosphere appears as the users from other departments (the customers) grow in number and begin to interact with the technical EDP staff. Although some users stick to economic value in judging the utility of computer applications to their particular problems and functions, other users develop a fascination with the computer and its applications as a symbol of progressive management techniques or as a status symbol for a department or individual. This fascination breeds an enthusiasm not moderated by judgment.

For their part, the technically oriented systems analysts tend to over-generalize from the successes they have achieved with transaction-oriented computer-based systems (e.g., order processing, payroll, accounts receivable) in Stage 2. They often feel that "now we can do anything"—in other words, that they have mastered problems of communication with users, that their expertise is solid, and that they are ready to select and deal with projects primarily on the basis of their technical and professional interest. In this heady atmosphere, criteria of economic justification and effective project implementation take a back seat.

When the users' exploding demands meet the technicians' euphoric urge to supply, in the absence of management constraint, exponential budget growth results. Overoptimism and overconfidence lead to cost overruns. And once this sharp growth has begun, rationales created in the mood of reinforced enthusiasm are used to justify the installation of additional capacity; this in turn provides the need for larger numbers of personnel and for more rationales for applying the now expanded resource to whatever new projects seem attractive to the crowd. So the spiral begins.

The spiral is fed by the fact that as the resource increases in size and ambition, it must have more specialists. Indeed, even without this capacity expansion, the continuing pace of technological development in the computer industry creates a constant need for new specialist talent, especially in Stage 2 and beyond. This "technological imperative" is a driving force that has caused the growth of numerous and quite diverse professional groups of computer personnel in the industrial environment. (The reader might find it helpful to review *Exhibit II* at this point.)

Many of these personnel come into the company with a primarily professional orientation, rather than an understanding of or sympathy for the long-term needs of an organization. Like the EDP specialists already employed by the company, these people will be far more interested in tackling technically challenging problems than in worrying about computer payback. If they are allowed to pursue their interests at will, the projects potentially most valuable from the company's viewpoint may never be worked on. Moreover, the chores of program maintenance and data-base development may be neglected, sowing the seeds of costly future problems.

All these factors together lead to the evolution of an informal structure among computer personnel and between computer personnel and users. The lack of clear management guidelines for project priorities, for example, often results in sympathetic wheeling and dealing between EDP systems analysts and the user groups with a preference for those projects which offer the greatest professional challenge. Without specific directives for project developments or new hardware acquisition, too, computer personnel develop expectations of a loose work environment. Some of the users, at the other end of the string, are easily enmeshed in impractical, pie-in-the-sky projects.

For short periods such an environment may be highly motivating for some, but, as we need hardly point out again, the other side of the coin is a rapidly growing budget—and a number of vocal and dissatisfied users.

In view of these informal dynamics and structures, what can management do to make this period one of controlled growth? How can control be introduced that will head off the impending crisis and dramatic cutbacks characteristic of such situations but at the same time not choke off experimentation with the resource and not turn off the motivation of specialists?

Here it is useful to compare the lists of management techniques shown for Stages 2 and 3 in *Exhibit III*. For the most part, the problems that arise toward the end of Stage 2 can be greatly alleviated by introducing right at the start of Stage 2 the techniques that companies ordinarily use in Stage 3. Before carrying out this step, however, attention should be given to two other important strategies: acquiring necessary middle-management skills and improving the company's procedures for hiring computer personnel.

ACQUIRING MANAGERS

The main key to successful management in this stage is acquiring or developing middle managers for EDP who recognize the need for priorities and criteria in project selection and who have strong administrative skills: the ability to prepare plans and stick to budgets, the ability to seek out significant projects from users who may not be demanding attention, and, generally, the ability to manage projects.

Finding such managers more often than not means going outside the company, especially since most potential middle managers among systems analysts are usually caught up in the computer growth spiral. However, where it is possible, selection from within, particularly from the ranks of systems analysts, can serve the important function of indicating that career paths exist to management ranks. This can show computer technicians and technical experts that there are career rewards for those who balance organizational needs with professional interests.

Once those at the general-management level have determined that the time has come to institute such "human controls," the EDP manager must be brought to recognize the need for them (if, indeed, he does not recognize that need already) and the fact that he has the countenance and support of top management.

For his part, the EDP manager himself must resist the tempting pressures to see his resource grow faster than is reasonable. He has a delicate and important selling job to do in communicating this to other department managers who want his services. Once he is shored up with competent subordinate managers he will be free to carry out this role.

Finally, in addition to applying administrative controls, management needs to assess continually the climate of the informal forces at work and plan growth with that assessment in mind. The formal organization of middle managers in the EDP department makes such planning, and its implementation, viable.

ACQUIRING DIVERSE PERSONNEL

Senior management must also recognize the increasing specialization of personnel within the computer department:

□ At one extreme are the highly skilled and creative professionals, such as computer systems programmers. Their motivation and interest are oriented to the technology with which they work; they have relatively little interest in organizational rewards. Their satisfaction and best performance may be assured by isolating them organizationally, to some degree.

□ At the other extreme are the analysts who work closely with functional departments of the company. These people may be expert in particular fields relevant to only a few industries or companies, performing tasks that require close interaction with both users and programmers. Their interests and value to the company can coincide when they preceive that career-path opportunities into general management are open to them.

□ There are also the operators with important but relatively low-level skills and training, with some capabilities for organizational advancement, and with relatively little direct interdependence with others.

To organize and control these diverse specialists requires decisions based on one basic trade-off: *balancing professional advancement of specialists against the need for organizational performance.*

To cater to specialist professionals, for example, a company might isolate them in a separate department, imposing few organizational checks and gearing quality control to individual judgment or peer review. Such an arrangement might motivate a systems analyst to become the world's best systems analyst.

Emphasis on organizational values, in contrast, suggests that the company locate and control the specialists in such a way as to increase the chances that short-run goals will actually be achieved on schedule. This strategy risks obsolescence or turnover among specialists, but it successfully conveys the important message that some specialists' skills can advance a management career.

However, in the early stages management is well advised to avoid the issue entirely: the highly sophisticated professional should not be hired until his expertise is clearly required. Moreover, at the time of hiring, the specialist's expectations for freedom and professional development should be explicitly discussed in the context of organizational structure and controls (these controls include those administered by the middle level of EDP management), as part of the "psychological contract."

Such discussion can go a long way toward avoiding misunderstanding during the period of rapid growth of computer applications. In effect, making clear the terms of the psychological contract is an example of the management of expectations. In this instance, it is one of the means that can be employed to introduce the organization, controls, and planning procedures that are needed to head off the crisis atmosphere of Stage 3.

Stage 3: Formalization

Let us assume that Stages 1 and 2 have run their bumpy courses without too much direct attenion from top management. More likely than not, top management becomes aware of the runaway computer budget suddenly, and it begins a crash effort to find out what is going on. Its typical question at this point is, "How can we be sure that we can afford this EDP effort?"

Top management frequently concludes that the only way to get control of the resource is through drastic measures, even if this means replacing many systems analysts and other valuable technical personnel who will choose to leave rather than work under the stringent controls that are imposed during the stage. Firing the old EDP manager is by no means an unusual step.[1]

From the perspective of computer personnel who have lived through the periods of initial acceptance and growth, but who have not developed a sense of the fit of the computer resource within company functions and objectives, the changes top management introduces at this time may seem radical indeed. Often what was a decentralized function and facility is rather suddenly centralized for better control. Often informal planning suddenly gives way to formal planning, perhaps arbitrarily. This stage frequently includes the first formalization of management reporting systems for computer operation, a new chargeout system, and the establishment of elaborate and cumbrous quality-control measures (again, see *Exhibit III*).

In short, action taken to deal with the crisis often goes beyond what is needed, and the pendulum may swing too far. In response, some computer personnel may leave. What may be worse, most will "hunker down" —withdrawing from innovative applications work, attending to short-

---

1. See Richard L. Nolan, "Plight of the EDP Manager," HBR May-June 1973, p. 143.

term goals, and following the new control systems and plans to the letter. All of this can occur at the expense of full resource utilization in the long run.

In addition, there is a parallel development that dovetails with the budget crisis to reinforce the overcontrol syndrome. Studies of computer usage show that the machines are first applied to projects that reduce general and administrative expenses—typically, replacement of clerical personnel in such tasks as accounting. Next come projects that reduce cost of goods, such as inventory control systems. The crisis atmosphere of Stage 3 roughly coincides with completion of these first two types of applications.

At this juncture the applications that have real potential for increasing revenues and profits and facilitating managerial decision making are still untouched. Financial-planning models and on-line customer service systems are two examples of such applications.

As senior management ponders the problems of Stage 3, it tends to associate the applications of the earlier stages with preexisting manual systems and straightforward cost-justification and control. In contrast, it finds projected applications for revenue-producing and decision-making projects hard to envision and define. The natural tendency is to assume that these projects will call for a faster, higher spiral of risk and cost. Thus senior management tends to introduce inappropriately strong controls that are designed, consciously or unconsciously, to put a stop to growth. This clearly may be too strong a reaction for the company's good.

THREE SOUND STEPS

In general, three control steps that are appropriate and not unduly restrictive are available for most large EDP facilities in Stage 3. First, certain of the more established and less complex operations and hardware can be centralized. Second, the increasing impacts of computer applications can be flagged and defined for the top by introducing overseer and resource-allocation mechanisms at the general-management level. Third, some parts of the systems analysis function can be decentralized and other parts centralized, depending on where the systems work can best be done (we shall say more about this shortly). Of course, this final step requires that the decentralized systems work be coordinated through a formal integrative mechanism.

But the real problem in Stage 3 is not what steps to take; it is how to take them. Management here is introducing change into a web of informal relationships and expectations. *How* the changes are managed is as important as *what* the changes should be, but more difficult to define.

That is, although there are few formal controls in the first two stages, the *informal* social structures and norms that have grown up by Stage 3 are very much a reality to the personnel involved. While it may appear that systems are replacing no systems, this will not be true:

□ Lacking guidelines for project selection, systems analysts will have projected their own sets of priorities, either individually, as a group within the company, or as members of their profession.

□ They will have created criteria and standards, although these will not ordinarily have been written down or otherwise articulated for higher levels of management.

□ Without project management guidelines, systems analysts and users will have developed their own rules and procedures for dealing with each other.

On the whole, the stronger these informal controls and structures are (and the weaker the formal controls and structures are, the stronger they will be), the more resistant the personnel will be to change and the more chaotic and traumatic the introduction of formal systems will be.

In managing changes as pervasive as these there is probably nothing worse than doing the job halfway. Doing nothing at all is disaster, of course; but management action that is undertaken on a crash basis—without enough attention to execution and second- and third-order consequences—will sharpen, not resolve, the crisis.

For example, management cannot afford to be either squeamish or precipitous in making personnel changes. Trying to introduce needed formalization of controls with the same personnel and the same organizational structure more often than not encourages conflict and the reinforcement of resistance rather than a resolution of the crisis; by refusing to fire or to enforce layoffs, senior management may simply prolong the crisis, create further dissension, and further demoralize personnel. On the other hand, management must be sure that it retains the experienced personnel who have the potential to function well in the mature stages of the operation—it may not always be obvious who these people are or what their future roles will be.

Thus, although the crisis of Stage 3 calls for action, it first calls for analysis and planning—planning that sets forth clear and explicit objectives for exploitation of the computer resource vis-à-vis the user departments. Such a plan, once it is developed and understood, can turn anarchy back into evolution, while at the same time avoiding the kind of overkill control that results in underutilization and underrealization of the potential of the resource. Here are our suggestions for general plan direction.

1. Reposition the established components of the resource.

Whether or not EDP has been carefully managed in the past, most companies need to centralize some parts and decentralize other parts of the computer resource at about this point.

The issue arises here because the company reaches a turning point in the way it uses the resource. As the EDP function evolves from the early cost-reduction applications of initiation and early growth toward projects aimed at improving operations, revenues, and the quality of unprogrammed and strategic decisions, the influence of the computer will begin to move up and spread out through the organization. The function may truly be called "MIS" instead of "EDP" from this stage forward.

We have already discussed the need for middle managers' involvement in this stage or an earlier stage. The internal structure they represent reinforces the desirability of making the MIS department autonomous and having it report to a senior level of management. At this point, also, it becomes imperative to reexamine and make explicit the rationales for existing applications that have proved beneficial and to routinize them, so that expensive specialist skills can be turned to new applications.

The pressures of new applications ventures, maturing management, specialist personnel, and increasing routine make centralization of the company's core hardware resources just about mandatory at this stage. Too, the centralization eases the tasks of maintenance of data and programs, data-base development, and some of the applications that will be coming up in Stage 4.

The very creation of a central "MIS division," however, creates additional problems.

2. Provide for top-management direction.

While centralization goes a long way toward placing the longer lead times, the greater complexity, and the higher development costs of new applications in perspective, it does not automatically help senior management to control the direction the resource takes.

Effective control derives from understanding, and some device is needed to educate senior management so that it can track and evaluate the department's progress sensibly. The device must also let the resource know what senior management's policies are and what is expected of it operationally and strategically.

This communications device becomes vital in Stage 3 because the resource has grown to a size and a power whereby its applications can affect the strategy and structure of the company as a whole. In a company where a working data base can be used to back up the corporate planning process, for example, corporate planning assumes a somewhat different shape from what it does in a company that has no such data base available. This is clearly a point at which a person at the vice-presidential level (or even the presidential level) must accept responsibility for directing the evolution of the resource.

An active, high-level steering committee is one such device. It provides a means for setting project priorities. It not only brings together those who should be concerned with overall management and planning for the company; it also provides a vehicle for confronting and resolving the political problems that inevitably arise with the computer's more direct impact on managers' roles, organizational structure, and resource allocation in Stage 3.

For, from a behavioral perspective, political issues dominate at this time as never before. Managers throughout the company now see that the applications coming through the pipeline may affect their own roles directly. In the past it was their subordinates who were most affected, and it was largely their own decision to approve or not approve a project; but now a given application may be supported from above and may impinge on their established patterns of work, their decision making, and even their ideas about what it is they do for a living.

Moreover, the prospect of applications that hint at long-term changes in organizational structures and formal departmental roles raises concern within both formal and informal groups of managers—concern about the impacts these changes will have on the strengths of their positions relative to other groups.

Such political issues can only be debated fruitfully before top management, and an expert, informed steering committee provides a convenient forum for this debate.

For his part, as a member of this committee as well as the head of his own department, the MIS manager should expect to assume a stronger role in general management councils. He should not, of course, expect to be exclusively responsible for setting priorities among projects that would benefit different groups, or for implementing significant changes completely under his own initiative.

3. Reorganize the systems analysis function.

Centralization, and tight guidelines and arbitration from a steering committee, however, can create a distance between the resource and its customers throughout the company. As Stage 3 draws to a close, the company will be planning its most important, most ambitious MIS applications to date. This is hardly a point at which to divorce the users from the resource by erecting an impenetrable divisional barrier. Complete centralization of the systems analysis function would constitute such a barrier.

In fact, gearing up for this new era of applications and controlling their impacts requires that the company revise the Stage 3 concept, staffing, and organization of the systems analysis function. The concept should change from systems analysts as developers of *products for* users to systems analysts as developers of *processes affecting* users. The distinction between product and process means, among other things, that the new applications should rarely be considered bounded projects; they will require continual modification as they are integrated into user decision making.

Therefore, systems analysts themselves will necessarily become more and more a constant element in the functioning of the users' areas. As a corollary, they will act as communications conduits between the users, on the one hand, and the computer resource and its programmers, on the other.

Organizationally, this suggests that some systems analysts should be decentralized to user locations while others are retained at the core to build a research and testing facility for the company and its planners. Thus the problem boils down to a trade-off between centralization and decentralization of systems analysts.

These, then, are our best suggestions for minimizing the strains of Stage 3: centralize certain components of the resource, install a steering committee or some equivalent thereof, and spread enough of the systems analysts through the company to ensure that users' needs are met adequately. For the company wise enough to employ these suggestions at the outset of Stage 2, the trauma of Stage 3 may be almost entirely avoidable.

Stage 4: Maturity

When the dust has settled over the changes of Stage 3, the computer resource will have reached maturity in the organization, and it will have the potential to return continuing economic benefits. The applications listed for Stage 4 in *Exhibit I* suggest how very significant the contributions of the resource can be, if only they can be achieved.

THE MANAGER'S DILEMMA

At this point the MIS manager has broken into the ranks of senior management, having risen to the level of vice president or equivalent thereof. In some instances he may even enjoy more than proportional support from the president for his view of his own function within the company. He faces this integrative dilemma:

□ On the one hand, he is under pressure to maintain a steady work environment within his own unit. His line managers and specialists are now familiar with relatively formal structure and procedures; they are presumably satisfied with their career prospects, either within their professions or within the company. Thus they may well constitute a force resisting dramatic change, reorganization, or innovation. Similarly, at this point, senior management and the users probably have a general grasp of the existing technology and existing applications of the resource, and they are reluctant to see major changes.

□ On the other hand, the MIS manager, if he is doing his job well, will be heavily involved in planning for the future. He will be aware that computer technology and modes of application and organization are continuing to change.

Thus, if he chooses to maintain stability, he knowingly runs the risk that his resource will become outdated and inefficient. If he chooses to keep up with technology, he knowingly runs the risk that he will lose the integrative fabric that makes his function applicable to the user groups and the company as a whole.

The MIS manager must strike a balance between protecting an organizational entity and keeping that entity up to date in its technical environment. He has power and credibility, but he sees that these can be threatened either by too little change or by too much change.

There are no hard and fast rules for resolving this trade-off. The key, however, lies in the quality of communications between the MIS manager and top management, and between the MIS department and users.

COMMUNICATIONS WITH THE BOSS

By definition, the mature Stage 4 function is one which is being applied to the key tasks of the organization. This may well mean that most of the funding for MIS development is devoted to applications touching directly on critical business operations. This is the case of a large petrochemical firm with which we are familiar, where new applications focus on synthetic-fiber production activities.

But whether applications are for line operations or for management decision making, the computer manager in Stage 4 is, perhaps for the first time, in a position to communicate with top management in terms of meaningful, detailed plans.

Because of the nature of his dilemma, he is bound to come under fire from the users—either for allowing parts of his department to obsolesce, in the name of stability, or for introducing change, in the name of progress and the state of the art. His relationship and communications with the top must be sound enough to allow him to weather the inevitable storms —given, of course, that the balance he strikes between stability and change is indeed reasonable in broad outline.

The experience of many suggests that the MIS manager and senior management think in terms of a three-year contract for the position, with explicit recognition that there will be organizational pressures to push out the MIS manager.

With long-term support from the top founded in such a basis, the MIS manager is in a position to legislate policies internally that will exploit the computer as fully as possible.

For his part, the senior line manager to whom a mature EDP department reports can little afford not to know the language of the computer personnel—at least to the extent necessary to evaluate project proposals.

RELATIONS WITH USERS

In Stage 4, the MIS manager must also move to strengthen the bridges that have developed between the users and computer personnel. Assuming that it is well managed internally, the computer resource still has a continuing extensive interdependence with departments it serves.

The first difficulty here is that the users are many and the MIS manager only one. He cannot hope for identical relationships with all departments.

Secondly, users naturally tend to co-opt computer personnel into their organizational spheres. If this occurs to any significant extent, user parochialisms will erode the potential for the computer unit to act as an agent for innovation and change.

However, the bridges can be strengthened and the innovative capability of the unit can be increased simultaneously through a policy of "buffering" the different subunits from user influence. Specifically, performance standards and short-term control devices should be formalized for the more routine tasks (such as all machine operations and some programming) and the MIS personnel involved with these should be removed from frequent interaction with the users. A system of project management, too, serves much the same function.

Finally, the systems analysis function at the core should by this time have taken on the character of an influential research unit, controlled primarily through checks on the progress of its projects. These projects will probably not be within the direct purview of the user groups; in a mature department, they are usually focused on long-term applications not likely to be demanded spontaneously by user groups or by the systems analysts decentralized into those groups (e.g., corporate inventory control). The weight of this core group of analysts can be used to counterbalance undue user influence.

For example, when a user needs a new application, the core group might rough it out and approve the final, detailed design; but the final, detailed design itself should be the work of the systems analysts located in the user department. The decentralized analysts will be most familiar with the user's needs and best able to produce a working system for him; for their part, the systems analysts at the core can ensure that the system that is finally designed will mesh efficiently with the company's MIS efforts as a whole, to whatever extent this is possible.

The picture of EDP-user relationships that emerges here is one of considerable complexity and subtlety. Correspondingly, integrating this more specialized and internally differentiated EDP resource into the company as a whole becomes more difficult. This integration requires that the MIS manager take steps to achieve common understanding of his objectives, not only with senior management but with all other functional managers at the vice-presidential level as well. The steering committee will be important as never before, not only as a committee for determining project priorities, but also as a sounding board for new techniques, policies, and changes within the MIS department itself.

Beyond Stage 4

Some large companies have reached the tail end of the S-shaped EDP budget curve: their departments are mature, in the sense defined by the exhibits. But has EDP evolution really come to an end for these companies? What can they expect in the future?

In retrospect, the curve seems to have been primarily driven by developments in hardware technology in the second- and third-generation computer systems. One thing certain is that computer technology advancements are continuing at an unrelenting pace. More S-shaped curves are inevitable.

Now, however, the advancements seem to be taking place more in software than in hardware; and at present the breakthrough most likely to start off another S-shaped EDP budget curve is the development of data-base technology. This development is providing a way to make the data collected and retained by the organization a companywide resource; and scores of middle management applications, such as computer modeling, appear to be on the way.

In the blush of enthusiasm for this advancement in computer technology, however, it is important to remember the painful lessons of the past. To efficiently exploit the newest technology, it must be managed. It must be reconciled with the capacity of the organization to assimilate new ways of doing business better. It is our belief that the forces underlying the crises and problems of the four stages we have described will also underlie future S-curves, such as one created by the emerging data-base technology. Consequently, management may be able to anticipate the problems and resolve them before they begin. A sign of success would be a dampening of the S-curve, with budgets rising more smoothly as future needs demand continuing investments and increasing budgets.

28. How to Choose the Right Forecasting Technique

John C. Chambers, Satinder K. Mullick, and Donald D. Smith

In virtually every decision he makes, the executive today considers some kind of forecast. Sound predictions of demands and trends are no longer luxury items, but a necessity, if the manager is to cope with seasonality, sudden changes in demand levels, price-cutting maneuvers of the competition, strikes, and large swings of the economy. Forecasting can help him deal with these troubles; but it can help him more, the more he knows about the general principles of forecasting, what it can and cannot do for him currently, and which techniques are suited to his needs of the moment. Here the authors try to explain the potential of forecasting to the manager, focusing special attention on sales forecasting for products of Corning Glass Works as these have matured through the product life cycle. The authors also include a rundown of the whole range of forecasting techniques.

To handle the increasing variety and complexity of managerial forecasting problems, many forecasting techniques have been developed in recent years. Each has its special use, and care must be taken to select the correct technique for a particular application. The manager as well as the forecaster has a role to play in technique selection; and the better he understands the range of forecasting possibilities, the more likely it is that a company's forecasting efforts will bear fruit.

The selection of a method depends on many factors—the context of the forecast, the relevance and availability of historical data, the degree of accuracy desirable, the time period to be forecast, the cost/benefit (or *value*) of the forecast to the company, and the time available for making the analysis.

These factors must be weighed constantly, and on a variety of levels. In general, for example, the forecaster should choose a technique that makes the best use of available data. If he can readily apply one technique of acceptable accuracy, he should not try to "gold plate" by using a more advanced technique that offers potentially greater accuracy but that requires nonexistent information or information that is costly to obtain. This kind of trade-off is relatively easy to make, but others, as we shall see, require considerably more thought.

Furthermore, where a company wishes to forecast with reference to a particular product, it must consider *the stage of the product's life cycle for which it is making the forecast.* The availability of data and the possibility of establishing relationships between the factors depend directly on the maturity of a product, and hence the life-cycle stage is a prime determinant of the forecasting method to be used.

Our purpose here is to present an overview of this field by discussing the way a company ought to approach a forecasting problem, describing the methods available, and explaining how to match method to problem. We shall illustrate the use of the various techniques from our experience with them at Corning, and then close with our own forecast for the future of forecasting.

Although we believe forecasting is still an art, we think that some of the principles which we have learned through experience may be helpful to others.

Manager, Forecaster and Choice of Methods

A manager generally assumes that when he asks a forecaster to prepare a specific projection, the request itself provides sufficient information for the forecaster to go to work and do his job. This is almost never true.

Successful forecasting begins with a collaboration between the manager and the forecaster, in which they work out answers to the following questions.

1. *What is the purpose of the forecast—how is it to be used?*
This determines the accuracy and power required of the techniques, and hence governs selection. Deciding whether to enter a business may require only a rather gross estimate of the size of the market, whereas a forecast made for budgeting purposes should be quite accurate. The appropriate techniques differ accordingly.

Again, if the forecast is to set a "standard" against which to evaluate performance, the forecasting method should not take into account special actions, such as promotions and other marketing devices, since these are meant to change historical patterns and relationships and hence form part of the "performance" to be evaluated.

Forecasts that simply sketch what the future will be like if a company makes no significant changes in tactics and strategy are usually not good enough for planning purposes. On the other hand, if management wants a

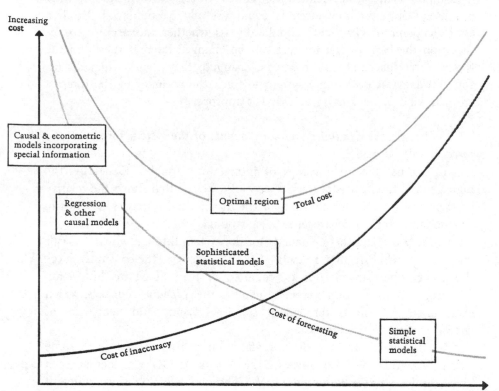

Exhibit I. Cost of forecasting versus cost of inaccuracy for a medium-range forecast, giving data availability

forecast of the effect that a certain marketing strategy under debate will have on sales growth, then the technique must be sophisticated enough to take explicit account of the special actions and events the strategy entails.

Techniques vary in their costs, as well as in scope and accuracy. The manager must fix the level of inaccuracy he can tolerate—in other words, decide how his decision will vary, depending on the range of accuracy of the forecast. This allows the forecaster to trade off cost against the value of accuracy in choosing a technique.

For example, in production and inventory control, increased accuracy is likely to lead to lower safety stocks. Here the manager and forecaster must weigh the cost of a more sophisticated and more expensive technique against potential savings in inventory costs.

Exhibit I shows how cost and accuracy increase with sophistication and charts this against the corresponding cost of forecasting errors, given some general assumptions. The most sophisticated technique that can be economically justified is one that falls in the region where the sum of the two costs is minimal.

Once the manager has defined the purpose of the forecast, the forecaster can advise him on how often it could usefully be produced. From a strategic point of view, they should discuss whether the decision to be made on the basis of the forecast can be changed later, if they find the forecast was inaccurate. If it *can* be changed, they should then discuss the usefulness of installing a system to track the accuracy of the forecast and the kind of tracking system that is appropriate.

2. What are the dynamics and components of the system for which the forecast will be made?

This clarifies the relationships of interacting variables. Generally, the manager and the forecaster must review a flow chart that shows the relative positions of the different elements of the distribution system, sales system, production system, or whatever is being studied.

Exhibit II displays these elements for the system through which CGW's major component for color TV sets—the bulb—flows to the consumer. Note the points where inventories are required or maintained in this manufacturing and distribution system—these are the *pipeline elements*, which exert important effects throughout the flow system and hence are of critical interest to the forecaster.

All the elements in gray directly affect forecasting procedure to some extent, and the color key suggests the nature of CGW's data at each point, again a prime determinant of technique selection since different techniques require different kinds of inputs. Where data are unavailable or costly to obtain, the range of forecasting choices is limited.

The flow chart should also show which parts of the system are under the control of the company doing the forecasting. In *Exhibit II*, this is merely the volume of glass panels and funnels supplied by Corning to the tube manufacturers.

In the part of the system where the company has total control, management tends to be tuned in to the various cause-and-effect relationships, and hence can frequently use forecasting techniques that take causal factors explicitly into account.

The flow chart has special value for the forecaster where causal prediction methods are called for because it enables him to conjecture about the possible variations in sales levels caused by inventories and the like, and to determine which factors must be considered by the technique to provide the executive with a forecast of acceptable accuracy.

Once these factors and their relationships have been clarified, the forecaster can build a causal model of the system which captures both the facts and the logic of the situation—which is, after all, the basis of sophisticated forecasting.

Exhibit II. Flow chart of TV distribution system

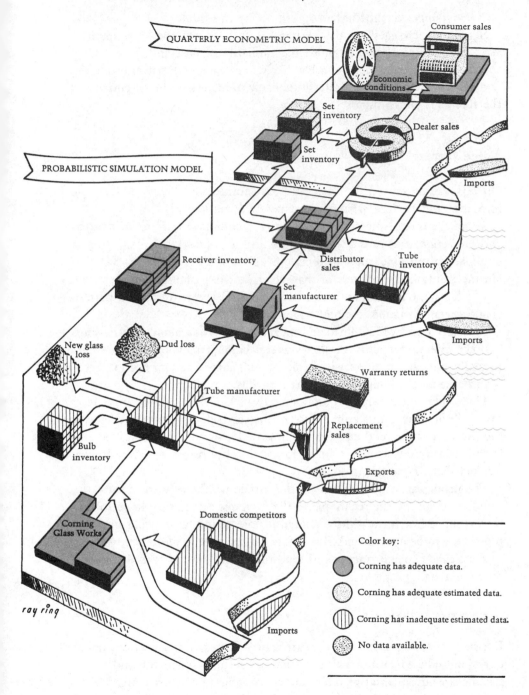

QUARTERLY ECONOMETRIC MODEL

Consumer sales

Economic conditions

Set inventory

Set inventory

Dealer sales

Imports

PROBABILISTIC SIMULATION MODEL

Receiver inventory

Distributor sales

Tube inventory

Set manufacturer

Imports

New glass loss

Dud loss

Warranty returns

Tube manufacturer

Bulb inventory

Replacement sales

Exports

Corning Glass Works

Domestic competitors

Imports

ray ring

Color key:

Corning has adequate data.

Corning has adequate estimated data.

Corning has inadequate estimated data.

No data available.

3. *How important is the past in estimating the future?*

Significant changes in the system—new products, new competitive strategies, and so forth—diminish the similarity of past and future. Over the short term, recent changes are unlikely to cause overall patterns to alter, but over the long term their effects are likely to increase. The executive and the forecaster must discuss these fully.

Three General Types

Once the manager and the forecaster have formulated their problem, the forecaster will be in a position to choose his method.

There are three basic types—*qualitative techniques, time series analysis and projection*, and *causal models*. The first uses qualitative data (expert opinion, for example) and information about special events of the kind already mentioned, and may or may not take the past into consideration.

The second, on the other hand, focuses entirely on patterns and pattern changes, and thus relies entirely on historical data.

The third uses highly refined and specific information about relationships between system elements, and is powerful enough to take special events formally into account. As with time series analysis and projection techniques, the past is important to causal models.

These differences imply (quite correctly) that the same type of forecasting technique is not appropriate to forecast sales, say, at all stages of the life cycle of a product—for example, a technique that relies on historical data would not be useful in forecasting the future of a totally new product that has no history.

The major part of the balance of this article will be concerned with the problem of suiting the technique to the life-cycle stages. We hope to give the executive insight into the potential of forecasting by showing how this problem is to be approached. But before we discuss the life cycle, we need to sketch the general functions of the three basic types of techniques in a bit more detail.

QUALITATIVE TECHNIQUES

Primarily, these are used when data are scarce—for example, when a product is first introduced into a market. They use human judgment and rating schemes to turn qualitative information into quantitative estimates.

The objective here is to bring together in a logical, unbiased, and systematic way all information and judgments which relate to the factors being estimated. Such techniques are frequently used in new-technology areas, where development of a product idea may require several "inventions," so that R&D demands are difficult to estimate, and where market acceptance and penetration rates are highly uncertain.

The gatefold chart facing page 502 presents several examples of this type (see the first section), including market research and the now-familiar Delphi technique. In this chart we have tried to provide a body of basic information about the main kinds of forecasting techniques. Some of the techniques listed are not in reality a single method or model, but a whole family. Thus our statements may not accurately describe all the variations of a technique and should rather be interpreted as descriptive of the basic concept of each.

A disclaimer about estimates in the chart is also in order. Estimates of costs are approximate, as are computation times, accuracy ratings, and ratings for turning-point identification. The costs of some procedures depend on whether they are being used routinely or are set up for a single forecast; also, if weightings or seasonals have to be determined anew each time a forecast is made, costs increase significantly. Still, the figures we present may serve as general guidelines.

The reader may find frequent reference to this gatefold helpful for the remainder of the article.

TIME SERIES ANALYSIS

These are statistical techniques used when several years' data for a product or product line are available and when relationships and trends are both clear and relatively stable.

One of the basic principles of statistical forecasting—indeed, of all forecasting when historical data are available—is that the forecaster should use the data on past performance to get a "speedometer reading" of the current rate (of sales, say) and of how fast this rate is increasing or decreasing. The current rate and changes in the rate—"acceleration" and "deceleration"—constitute the basis of forecasting. Once they are known, various mathematical techniques can develop projections from them.

The matter is not so simple as it sounds, however. It is usually difficult to make projections from raw data since the rates and trends are not immediately obvious; they are mixed up with seasonal variations, for example, and perhaps distorted by such factors as the effects of a large sales promotion campaign. The raw data must be massaged before they are usable, and this is frequently done by time series analysis.

Now, a *time series* is a set of chronologically ordered points of raw data —for example, a division's sales of a given product, by month, for several years. Time series *analysis* helps to identify and explain:

□ Any regularity or systematic variation in the series of data which is due to seasonality—the "seasonals."

□ Cyclical patterns that repeat any two or three years or more.

□ Trends in the data.

□ Growth rates of these trends.

(Unfortunately, most existing methods identify only the seasonals, the combined effect of trends and cycles, and the irregular, or chance, component. That is, they do not separate *trends* from *cycles*. We shall return to this point when we discuss time series analysis in the final stages of product maturity.)

Once the analysis is complete, the work of projecting future sales (or whatever) can begin.

We should note that while we have separated analysis from projection here for purposes of explanation, most statistical forecasting techniques actually combine both functions in a single operation.

A future like the past: It is obvious from this description that all statistical techniques are based on the assumption that existing patterns will continue into the future. This assumption is more likely to be correct over the short term than it is over the long term, and for this reason these techniques provide us with reasonably accurate forecasts for the immediate future but do quite poorly further into the future (unless the data patterns are extraordinarily stable).

For this same reason, these techniques ordinarily *cannot* predict when the rate of growth in a trend will change significantly—for example, when a period of slow growth in sales will suddenly change to a period of rapid decay.

Such points are called *turning points*. They are naturally of the greatest consequence to the manager, and, as we shall see, the forecaster must use different tools from pure statistical techniques to predict when they will occur.

CAUSAL MODELS

When historical data are available and enough analysis has been performed to spell out explicitly the relationships between the factor to be forecast and other factors (such as related businesses, economic forces, and socio-economic factors), the forecaster often constructs a *causal model*.

A causal model is the most sophisticated kind of forecasting tool. It expresses mathematically the relevant causal relationships, and may include pipeline considerations (i.e., inventories) and market survey information. It may also directly incorporate the results of a time series analysis.

The causal model takes into account everything known of the dynamics of the flow system and utilizes predictions of related events such as competitive actions, strikes, and promotions. If the data are available, the model generally includes factors for each location in the flow chart (as illustrated in *Exhibit II*) and connects these by equations to describe overall product flow.

If certain kinds of data are lacking, initially it may be necessary to make assumptions about some of the relationships and then track what is happening to determine if the assumptions are true. Typically, a causal model is continually revised as more knowledge about the system becomes available.

Again, see the gatefold for a rundown on the most common types of causal techniques. As the chart shows, causal models are by far the best for predicting turning points and preparing long-range forecasts.

Methods, Products and the Life Cycle

At each stage of the life of a product, from conception to steady-state sales, the decisions that management must make are characteristically quite different, and they require different kinds of information as a base. The forecasting techniques that provide these sets of information differ analogously. *Exhibit III* summarizes the life stages of a product, the typical decisions made at each, and the main forecasting techniques suitable at each.

Equally, different products may require different kinds of forecasting. Two CGW products that have been handled quite differently are the major glass components for color TV tubes, of which Corning is a prime supplier, and CORNING WARE® cookware, a proprietary consumer product line. We shall trace the forecasting methods used at each of the four different stages of maturity of these products to give some firsthand insight into the choice and application of some of the major techniques available today.

Before we begin, let us note how the situations differ for the two kinds of products:

□ For a consumer product like the cookware, the manufacturer's control of the distribution pipeline extends at least through the distributor level. Thus he can affect or control consumer sales quite directly, as well as directly control some of the pipeline elements.

Many of the changes in shipment rates and in overall profitability are therefore due to actions taken by the manufacturer himself. Tactical decisions on promotions, specials, and pricing are usually at his discretion as well. The technique selected by the forecaster for projecting sales therefore

Stage of life cycle	Product development	Market testing & early introduction	Rapid growth	Steady state
Typical decisions	Amount of development effort Product design Business strategies	Optimum facility size Marketing strategies, including distribution & pricing	Facilities expansion Marketing strategies Production planning *Sales*	Promotions, specials Pricing Production planning Inventories
Forecasting techniques	Delphi method Historical analysis of comparable products Priority pattern analysis Input-output analysis Panel consensus	Consumer surveys Tracking & warning systems Market tests Experimental designs	Statistical techniques for identifying turning points Tracking & warning systems Market surveys Intention-to-buy surveys	Time series analysis & projection Causal & econometric models Market surveys for tracking & warning Life-cycle analysis

should permit incorporation of such "special information." One may have to start with simple techniques and work up to more sophisticated ones that embrace such possibilities, but the final goal is there.

□ Where the manager's company supplies a component to an OEM, as Corning does for tube manufacturers, the company does not have such direct influence or control over either the pipeline elements or final consumer sales. It may be impossible for the company to obtain good information about what is taking place at points further along the flow system (as in the upper segment of *Exhibit II*), and, in consequence, the forecaster will necessarily be using a different genre of forecasting from that he uses for a consumer product.

Between these two examples, our discussion will embrace nearly the whole range of forecasting techniques. As necessary, however, we shall touch on other products and other forecasting methods.

1. PRODUCT DEVELOPMENT

In the early stages of product development, the manager wants answers to questions such as these:

□ What are the alternative growth opportunities to pursuing product X?

□ How have established products similar to X fared?

□ Should *we* enter this business; and if so, in what segments?

□ How should we allocate R&D efforts and funds?

□ How successful will different product concepts be?

□ How will product X fit into the markets five or ten years from now?

Forecasts that help to answer these long-range questions must necessarily have long horizons themselves.

A common objection to much long-range forecasting is that it is virtually impossible to predict with accuracy what will happen several years into the future. We agree that uncertainty increases when a forecast is made for a period more than two years out. However, at the very least, the forecast and a measure of its accuracy enable the manager to know his risks in pursuing a selected strategy and in this knowledge to choose an appropriate strategy from those available.

Systematic market research is, of course, a mainstay in this area. For example, priority pattern analysis can describe the consumer's preferences and the likelihood he will buy a product, and thus is of great value in forecasting (and updating) penetration levels and rates. But there are other tools as well, depending on the state of the market and the product concept.

For a defined market: While there can be no direct data about a product that is still a gleam in the eye, information about its likely performance can be gathered in a number of ways, provided the market in which it is to be sold is a known entity.

First, one can compare a proposed product with competitors' present and planned products, ranking it on quantitative scales for different factors. We call this *product differences measurement.*

If this approach is to be successful, it is essential that the (in-house) experts who provide the basic data come from different disciplines—marketing, R&D, manufacturing, legal, and so on—and that their opinions be unbiased.

Second, and more formalistically, one can construct *disaggregate market models* by separating off different segments of a complex market for indivdual study and consideration. Specifically, it is often useful to project the S-shaped growth curves for the levels of income of different geographical regions.

When color TV bulbs were proposed as a product, CGW was able to identify the factors that would influence sales growth. Then, by disaggregating consumer demand and making certain assumptions about these factors, it was possible to develop an S-curve for rate of penetration of the household market that proved most useful to us.

Third, one can compare a projected product with an "ancestor" that has similar characteristics. In 1965, we disaggregated the market for color television by income levels and geographical regions and compared these sub-markets with the historical pattern of black-and-white TV market growth. We justified this procedure by arguing that color TV represented an advance over black-and-white analogous to (although less intense than) the advance that black-and-white TV represented over radio. The analyses of black-and-white TV market growth also enabled us to estimate the variability to be expected—that is, the degree to which our projections would differ from actual as the result of economic and other factors.

The prices of black-and-white TV and other major household appliances in 1949, consumer disposable income in 1949, the prices of color TV and other appliances in 1965, and consumer disposable income for 1965 were all profitably considered in developing our long-range forecast for color-TV penetration on a national basis. The success patterns of black-and-white TV, then, provided insight into the likelihood of success and sales potential of color TV.

Our predictions of consumer acceptance of CORNING WARE® cookware, on the other hand, were derived primarily from one expert source, a manager who thoroughly understood consumer preferences and the house-wares market. These predictions have been well borne out. This reinforces our belief that sales forecasts for a new product that will compete in an existing market are bound to be incomplete and uncertain unless one culls the best judgments of fully experienced personnel.

For an undefined market: Frequently, however, the market for a new product is weakly defined or few data are available, the product concept is still fluid, and history seems irrelevant. This is the case for gas turbines, electric and steam automobiles, modular housing, pollution measurement devices, and time-shared computer terminals.

Many organizations have applied the Delphi method of soliciting and consolidating experts' opinions under these circumstances. At CGW, in several instances, we have used it to estimate demand for such new products, with success.

Input-output analysis, combined with other techniques, can be extremely useful in projecting the future course of broad technologies and broad changes in the economy. The basic tools here are the input-output tables of U.S. industry for 1947, 1958, and 1963, and various updatings of the 1963 tables prepared by a number of groups who wished to extrapolate the 1963 figures or to make forecasts for later years.

Since a business or product line may represent only a small sector of an industry, it may be difficult to use the tables directly. However, a number of companies are disaggregating industries to evaluate their sales potential and to forecast changes in product mixes—the phasing out of old lines and introduction of others. For example, Quantum-Science Corporation (MAPTEK) has developed techniques that make input-output analyses more directly useful to today's electronics businessmen. (Other techniques, such as panel consensus and visionary forecasting, seem less effective to us, and we cannot evaluate them from our own experience.)

2. TESTING AND INTRODUCTION

Before a product can enter its (hopefully) rapid penetration stage, the market potential must be tested out and the product must be introduced —and then more market testing may be advisable. At this stage, management needs answers to these questions:

◻ What shall our marketing plan be—which markets should we enter and with what production quantities?

◻ How much manufacturing capacity will the early production stages require?

◻ As demand grows, where should we build this capacity?

◻ How shall we allocate our R&D resources over time?

Significant profits depend on finding the right answers, and it is therefore economically feasible to expend relatively large amounts of effort and money on obtaining good forecasts, short-, medium-, and long-range.

A sales forecast at this stage should provide three points of information: the date when rapid sales will begin, the rate of market penetration during the rapid-sales stage, and the ultimate level of penetration, or sales rate, during the steady-state stage.

Using early data: The date when a product will enter the rapid-growth stage is hard to predict three or four years in advance (the usual horizon). A company's only recourse is to use statistical tracking methods to check on how successfully the product is being introduced, along with routine market studies to determine when there has been a significant increase in the sales rate.

Furthermore, the greatest care should be taken in analyzing the early sales data that start to accumulate once the product has been introduced into the market. For example, it is important to distinguish between sales to *innovators,* who will try anything new, and sales to *imitators,* who will buy a product only after it has been accepted by innovators, for it is the latter group that provides demand stability. Many new products have initially appeared successful because of purchases by innovators, only to fail later in the stretch.

Tracking the two groups means market research, possibly via opinion panels. A panel ought to contain both innovators and imitators, since innovators can teach one a lot about how to improve a product while imitators provide insight into the desires and expectations of the whole market.

The color TV set, for example, was introduced in 1954, but did not gain acceptance from the majority of consumers until late 1964. To be sure, the

Exhibit IV. Expenditures on appliances versus all consumer goods
[In billions of dollars]

[In billions of dollars]

Year (1)	All consumer goods* (2)	Household appliances† (3)	Radio, TV & other† (4)	Totals of columns 3 & 4 (5)	Column 5 ÷ Column 2 (6)	Column 4 ÷ Column 2 (7)
1947	110.9	3.18	1.43	4.61	4.16%	1.29%
1948	118.9	3.47	1.48	4.95	4.16	1.23
1949	119.1	3.13	1.70	4.83	4.06	1.43
1950	128.6	3.94	2.46	6.40	4.98	1.91
1951	138.4	3.87	2.26	6.13	4.43	1.63
1952	143.3	3.82	2.37	6.19	4.32	1.65
1953	150.0	3.99	2.61	6.60	4.40	1.74
1954	151.1	4.02	2.74	6.77	4.48	1.81
1955	162.9	4.69	2.79	7.48	4.59	1.71
1956	168.2	4.89	2.87	7.76	4.61	1.71
1957	176.4	4.63	3.00	7.63	4.33	1.70
1958	178.1	4.44	3.07	7.51	4.22	1.72
1959	190.9	4.86	3.42	8.28	4.34	1.79
1960	196.6	4.74	3.62	8.36	4.25	1.84
1961	200.1	4.77	3.76	8.53	4.26	1.88
1962	212.1	5.01	3.94	8.95	4.22	1.86
1963	222.5	5.24	4.54	9.78	4.40	2.04
1964	237.9	5.74	5.41	11.15	4.69	2.27
1965	257.4	6.03	6.01	12.04	4.68	2.33
1966	277.7	6.77	6.91	13.68	4.93	2.49
1967	288.1	7.09	7.41	14.50	5.03	2.57
1968	313.9	7.80	7.85	15.65	4.99	2.50

*Data obtained from Survey of Current Business, Personal Consumption Expenditure Tables (U.S. Department of Commerce, July issues).

† Data obtained from the Survey of Current Business Statistics (U.S. Department of Commerce, 1969 Biennial Edition).

color TV set could not leave the introduction stage and enter the rapid-growth stage until the networks had substantially increased their color programming. However, special flag signals like "substantially increased network color programming" are likely to come after the fact, from the planning viewpoint; and in general, we find, scientifically designed consumer surveys conducted on a regular basis provide the earliest means of detecting turning points in the demand for a product.

Similar-product technique: Although statistical tracking is a useful tool during the early introduction stages, there are rarely sufficient data for statistical forecasting. Market research studies can naturally be useful, as we have indicated. But, more commonly, the forecaster tries to identify a similar, older product whose penetration pattern should be similar to that of the new product, since overall markets can and do exhibit consistent patterns.

Again, let's consider color television and the forecasts we prepared in 1965.

For the years 1947-1968, *Exhibit IV* shows total consumer expenditures, appliance expenditures, expenditures for radios and TVs, and relevant percentages. Column 4 shows that total expenditures for appliances are relatively stable over periods of several years; hence, new appliances must compete with existing ones, especially during recessions (note the figures for 1948-1949, 1953-1954, 1957-1958, and 1960-1961).

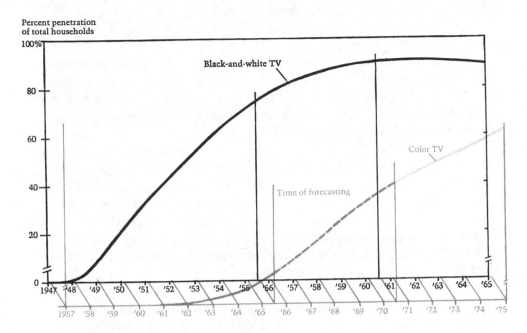

Certain specific fluctuations in these figures are of special significance here. When black-and-white TV was introduced as a new product in 1948-1951, the ratio of expenditures on radio and TV sets to total expenditures for consumer goods (see column 7) increased about 33% (from 1.23% to 1.63%), as against a modest increase of only 13% (from 1.63% to 1.88%) in the ratio for the next decade. (A similar increase of 33% occurred in 1962-1966 as color TV made its major penetration.)

Probably, the acceptance of black-and-white TV as a major appliance in 1950 caused the ratio of all major household appliances to total consumer goods (see column 5) to rise to 4.98%; in other words, the innovation of TV caused the consumer to start spending more money on major appliances around 1950.

Our expectation in mid-1965 was that the introduction of color TV would induce a similar increase. Thus, although this product comparison did not provide us with an accurate or detailed forecast, it did place an upper bound on the future total sales we could expect.

The next step was to look at the cumulative penetration curve for black-and-white TVs in U.S. households, shown in *Exhibit V*. We assumed color-TV penetration would have a similar S-curve, but that it would take longer for color sets to penetrate the whole market (that is, reach steady-state sales). Whereas it took black-and-white TV 10 years to reach steady state, qualitative expert-opinion studies indicated that it would take color twice that long—hence the more gradual slope of the color-TV curve.

At the same time, studies conducted in 1964 and 1965 showed significantly different penetration sales for color TV in various income groups, rates that were helpful to us in projecting the color-TV curve and tracking the accuracy of our projection.

With these data and assumptions, we forecast retail sales for the remainder of 1965 through mid-1970 (see the dotted section of the lower curve in *Exhibit* V). The forecasts were accurate through 1966 but too high in the following three years, primarily because of declining general economic conditions and changing pricing policies.

We should note that when we developed these forecasts and techniques, we recognized that additional techniques would be necessary at later times to maintain the accuracy that would be needed in subsequent periods. These forecasts provided acceptable accuracy for the time they were made, however, since the major goal then was only to estimate the penetration rate and the ultimate, steady-state level of sales. Making refined estimates of how the manufacturing-distribution pipelines will behave is an activity that properly belongs to the next life-cycle stage.

Other approaches: When it is not possible to identify a similar product, as was the case with CGW's self-cleaning oven and flat-top cooking range (COUNTERANGE™), another approach must be used.

For the purposes of initial introduction into the markets, it may only be necessary to determine the minimum sales rate required for a product venture to meet corporate objectives. Analyses like input-output, historical trend, and technological forecasting can be used to estimate this minimum. Also, the feasibility of not entering the market at all, or of continuing R&D right up to the rapid-growth stage, can best be determined by sensitivity analysis.

Predicting rapid growth: To estimate the date by which a product will enter the rapid-growth stage is another matter. As we have seen, this date is a function of many factors: the existence of a distribution system, customer acceptance of or familiarity with the product concept, the need met by the product, significant events (such as color network programming), and so on.

As well as by reviewing the behavior of similar products, the date may be estimated through Delphi exercises or through rating and ranking schemes, whereby the factors important to customer acceptance are estimated, each competitor product is rated on each factor, and an overall score is tallied for the competitor against a score for the new product.

As we have said, it is usually difficult to forecast precisely when the turning point will occur; and, in our experience, the best accuracy that can be expected is within three months to two years of the actual time.

It is occasionally true, of course, that one can be certain a new product will be enthusiastically accepted. Market tests and initial customer reaction made it clear there would be a large market for CORNING WARE® cookware. Since the distribution system was already in existence, the time required for the line to reach rapid growth depended primarily on our ability to manufacture it. Sometimes forecasting is merely a matter of calculating the company's capacity—but not ordinarily.

3. RAPID GROWTH

When a product enters this stage, the most important decisions relate to facilities expansion. These decisions generally involve the largest expenditures in the cycle (excepting major R&D decisions), and commensurate forecasting and tracking efforts are justified.

Forecasting and tracking must provide the executive with three kinds of data at this juncture:

◻ Firm verification of the *rapid-growth rate forecast* made previously.

◻ A hard date when sales will level to "normal," *steady-state growth*.

◻ For component products, the deviation in the growth curve that may be caused by characteristic *conditions along the pipeline*—for example, inventory blockages.

Forecasting the growth rate: Medium- and long-range forecasting of the market growth rate and of the attainment of steady-state sales requires the same measures as does the product introduction stage—detailed marketing studies (especially intention-to-buy surveys) and product comparisons.

When a product has entered rapid growth, on the other hand, there are generally sufficient data available to construct *statistical* and possibly even *causal* growth models (although the latter will necessarily contain assumptions that must be verified later).

We estimated the growth rate and steady-state rate of color TV by a crude econometric-marketing model from data available at the beginning of this stage. We conducted frequent marketing studies as well.

The growth rate for CORNING WARE® cookware, as we explained, was limited primarily by our production capabilities; and hence the basic information to be predicted in that case was the date of leveling growth. Because substantial inventories buffered information on consumer sales all along the line, good field data were lacking, which made this date difficult to estimate. Eventually we found it necessary to establish a better (more direct) field information system.

As well as merely buffering information, in the case of a component product, the pipeline exerts certain distorting effects on the manufacturer's demand; these effects, although highly important, are often illogically neglected in production or capacity planning.

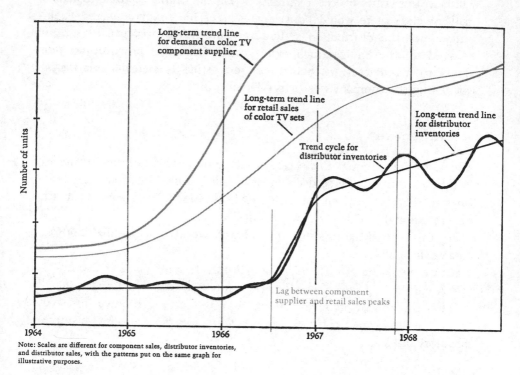

Exhibit VI. *Patterns for color-TV distributor sales, distributor inventories, and component sales*

Long-term trend line for demand on color TV component supplier

Long-term trend line for retail sales of color TV sets

Long-term trend line for distributor inventories

Trend cycle for distributor inventories

Number of units

Lag between component supplier and retail sales peaks

1964   1965   1966   1967   1968

Note: Scales are different for component sales, distributor inventories, and distributor sales, with the patterns put on the same graph for illustrative purposes.

Simulating the pipeline: While the ware-in-process demand in the pipeline has an S-curve like that of retail sales, it may lag or lead sales by several months, distorting the shape of the demand on the component supplier.

Exhibit VI shows the long-term trend of demand on a component supplier other than Corning as a function of distributor sales and distributor inventories. As one can see from this curve, supplier sales may grow relatively sharply for several months and peak before retail sales have leveled off. The implications of these curves for facilities planning and allocation are obvious.

Here we have used components for color TV sets for our illustration because we know from our own experience the importance of the long flow time for color TVs that results from the many sequential steps in manufacturing and distribution (recall *Exhibit* II). There are more spectacular examples; for instance, it is not uncommon for the flow time from component supplier to consumer to stretch out to two years in the case of truck engines.

To estimate total demand on CGW production, we used a retail demand model and a pipeline simulation. The model incorporated penetration rates, mortality curves, and the like. We combined the data generated by the model with market-share data, data on glass losses, and other information to make up the corpus of inputs for the pipeline simulation. The simulation output allowed us to apply projected curves like the ones shown in *Exhibit VI* to our own component-manufacturing planning.

Simulation is an excellent tool for these circumstances because it is essentially simpler than the alternative—namely, building a more formal, more "mathematical" model. That is, simulation bypasses the need for analytical solution techniques and for mathematical duplication of a complex environment and allows experimentation. Simulation also informs us how the pipeline elements will behave and interact over time—knowledge that is very useful in forecasting, especially in constructing formal causal models at a later date.

Tracking and warning: This knowledge is not absolutely "hard," of course, and pipeline dynamics must be carefully tracked to determine if the various estimates and assumptions made were indeed correct. Statistical methods provide a good short-term basis for estimating and checking the growth rate and signaling when turning points will occur.

In late 1965 it appeared to us that the ware-in-process demand was increasing, since there was a consistent positive difference between actual TV bulb sales and forecasted bulb sales. Conversations with product managers and other personnel indicated there might have been a significant change in pipeline activity; it appeared that rapid increases in retail demand were boosting glass requirements for ware-in-process, which could create a hump in the S-curve like the one illustrated in *Exhibit VI*. This humping provided additional profit for CGW in 1966 but had an adverse effect in 1967. We were able to predict this hump, but unfortunately we were unable to reduce or avoid it because the pipeline was not sufficiently under our control.

The inventories all along the pipeline also follow an S-curve (as shown in *Exhibit VI*), a fact that creates and compounds two characteristic conditions in the pipeline as a whole: initial overfilling and subsequent shifts between too much and too little inventory at various points—a sequence of feast-and-famine conditions.

For example, the simpler distribution system for CORNING WARE® cookware had an S-curve like the ones we have examined. When the retail sales slowed from rapid to normal growth, however, there were no early indications from shipment data that this crucial turning point had been reached. Data on distributor inventories gave us some warning that the pipeline was overfilling, but the turning point at the retail level was still not identified quickly enough, as we have mentioned before, because of lack of good data at that level. We now monitor field information regularly to identify significant changes, and adjust our shipment forecasts accordingly.

Main concerns: One main activity during the rapid-growth stage, then, is to check earlier estimates and, if they appear incorrect, to compute as accurately as possible the error in the forecast and obtain a revised estimate.

In some instances, models developed earlier will include only "macro-terms"; in such cases, market research can provide information needed to break these down into their components. For example, the color-TV forecasting model initially considered only total set penetrations at different income levels, without considering the way in which the sets were being used. Therefore, we conducted market survey to determine set use more precisely.

Equally, during the rapid-growth stage, submodels of pipeline segments should be expanded to incorporate more detailed information as it is received. In the case of color TV, we found we were able to estimate the overall pipeline requirements for glass bulbs, the CGW market share factors, and glass losses, and to postulate a probability distribution around the most likely estimates. Over time, it was easy to check these forecasts against actual volume of sales, and hence to check on the procedures by which we were generating them.

We also found we had to increase the number of factors in the simulation model—for instance, we had to expand the model to consider different sizes of bulbs—and this improved our overall accuracy and usefulness.

The preceding is only one approach that can be used in forecasting sales of new products that are in a rapid growth.

4. STEADY STATE

The decisions the manager makes at this stage are quite different from those he has made earlier. Most of the facilities planning has been squared away, and trends and growth rates have become reasonably stable. It is possible that swings in demand and profit will occur because of changing economic conditions, new and competitive products, pipeline dynamics, and so on, and the manager will have to maintain his tracking activities and even introduce new ones. However, by and large, he will concentrate his forecasting attention on these areas:

□ Long- and short-term production planning.

□ Setting standards to check the effectiveness of marketing strategies.

□ Projections designed to aid profit planning.

He will also need a good tracking and warning system to identify significantly declining demand for the product (but hopefully that is a long way off).

To be sure, the manager will want margin and profit projection and long-range forecasts to assist planning at the corporate level. However, short- and medium-term sales forecasts are basic to these more elaborate undertakings, and we shall concentrate on sales forecasts.

Adequate tools at hand: In planning production and establishing marketing strategy for the short and medium term, the manager's first considerations are usually an accurate estimate of the present sales level and an accurate estimate of the rate at which this level is changing.

The forecaster thus is called on for two related contributions at this stage:

□ He should provide estimates of *trends* and *seasonals*, which obviously affect the sales level. Seasonals are particularly important for both overall production planning and inventory control. To do this, he needs to apply time series analysis and projection techniques—that is, *statistical* techniques.

□ He should relate the future sales level to factors that are more easily predictable, or have a "lead" relationship with sales, or both. To do this, he needs to build *causal models.*

The type of product under scrutiny is very important in selecting the techniques to be used.

For CORNING WARE® cookware, where the levels of the distribution system are organized in a relatively straightforward way, we use statistical methods to forecast shipments and field information to forecast changes in shipment rates. We are now in the process of incorporating special information—marketing strategies, economic forecasts, and so on—directly into the shipment forecasts. This is leading us in the direction of a causal forecasting model.

On the other hand, a component supplier may be able to forecast total sales with sufficient accuracy for broad-load production planning, but the pipeline environment may be so complex that his best recourse for short-term projections is to rely primarily on salesmen's estimates. We find this true, for example, in estimating the demand for TV glass by size and customer. In such cases, the best role for statistical methods is providing guides and checks for salemen's forecasts.

In general, however, at this point in the life cycle, sufficient time series data are available and enough causal relationships are known from direct experience and market studies so that the forecaster can indeed apply these two powerful sets of tools. Historical data for at least the last several years should be available, and he will use all of it, one way or another.

We might mention a common criticism at this point. People frequently object to using more than a few of the most recent data points (such as sales figures in the immediate past) for building projections, since, they say, the current situation is always so dynamic and conditions are changing so radically and quickly that historical data from further back in time have little or no value.

We think this point of view has little validity. A graph of several years' sales data, such as the one shown in *Part A* of *Exhibit VII*, gives an impression of a sales trend one could not possibly get if one were to look only at two or three of the latest data points.

In practice, we find, overall patterns tend to continue for a minimum of one or two quarters into the future, even when special conditions cause sales to fluctuate for one or two (monthly) periods in the immediate future.

For short-term forecasting for one to three months ahead, the effects of such factors as general economic conditions are minimal, and do *not* cause radical shifts in demand patterns. And because trends tend to change gradually rather than suddenly, statistical and other quantitative methods are excellent for short-term forecasting. Using one or only a few of the most recent data points will result in giving insufficient consideration of the nature of trends, cycles, and seasonal fluctuations in sales.

Granting the applicability of the techniques, we must go on to explain how the forecaster identifies precisely what is happening when sales fluctuate from one period to the next and how he forecasts such fluctuations.

A trend and a seasonal are obviously two quite different things, and they must be handled separately in forecasting.

Consider what would happen, for example, if a forecaster were merely to take an average of the most recent data points along a curve, combine this with other, similar average points stretching backward into the immediate past, and use these as the basis for a projection. He might easily overreact to random changes, mistaking them for evidence of a prevailing trend; he might mistake a change in the growth rate for a seasonal; and so on.

To avoid precisely this sort of error, the moving average technique, which is similar to the hypothetical one just described, uses data points in such a way that the effects of seasonals (and irregularities) are eliminated.

Furthermore, the executive needs accurate estimates of trends *and* accurate estimates of seasonality to plan broad-load production, to determine marketing efforts and allocations, and to maintain proper inventories—that is, inventories that are adequate to customer demand but are not excessively costly.

Before going any further, it might be well to illustrate what such sorting-out looks like. *Parts A, B,* and *C* of *Exhibit* VII show the initial decomposition of raw data for factory sales of color TV sets between 1965 and mid-1970. *Part A* presents the raw data curve. *Part B* shows the seasonal factors that are implicit in the raw data—quite a consistent pattern, although there is some variation from year to year. (In the next section we shall explain where this graph of the seasonals comes from.)

Part C shows the result of discounting the raw data curve by the seasonals of *Part B*; this is the so-called deseasonalized data curve. Next, in *Part D*, we have drawn the smoothest or "best" curve possible through the deseasonalized curve, thereby obtaining the *trend cycle*. (We might further note that

Exhibit VII. Data plots of factory sales of color TV sets

Part A. Raw data for factory sales of color TV sets

Sets (thousands)

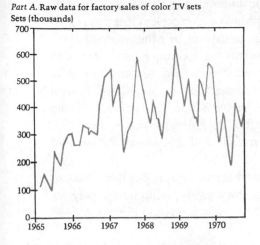

Part B. Seasonals for factory sales of color TV sets

Seasonal (Percent of average
monthly sales rate)

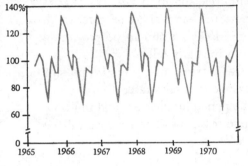

Part C. Factory sales of color TV sets (deseasonalized)

Sets (thousands)

Part D. Final trend cycle of factory sales of color TV sets

Sets (thousands)

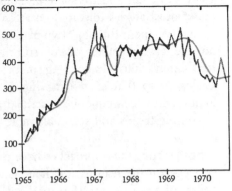

Part E. Changes in final trend cycle (growth rate)
of factory sales of color TV sets

Sets (thousands)

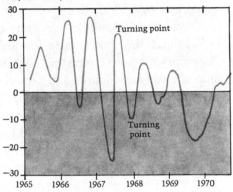

the differences between this trend-cycle line and the deseasonalized data curve represent the irregular or nonsystematic component that the fore-caster must always tolerate and attempt to explain by other methods.)

In sum, then, the objective of the forecasting technique used here is to do the best possible job of sorting out trends and seasonalities. Un-fortunately, most forecasting methods project by a smoothing process analogous to that of the moving average technique, or like that of the hypothetical technique we described at the beginning of this section, and separating trends and seasonals more precisely will require extra effort and cost.

Still, sorting-out approaches have proved themselves in practice. We can best explain the reasons for their success by roughly outlining the way we construct a sales forecast on the basis of trends, seasonals, and data derived from them. This is the method:

□ Graph the rate at which the trend is changing. For the illustration given in *Exhibit VII*, this graph is shown in *Part E*. This graph describes the successive ups and downs of the trend cycle shown in *Part D*.

□ Project this growth rate forward over the interval to be forecasted. Assuming we were forecasting back in mid-1970, we should be projecting into the summer months and possibly into the early fall.

□ Add this growth rate (whether positive or negative) to the present sales rate. This might be called the unseasonalized sales rate.

□ Project the seasonals of *Part B* for the period in question, and multiply the unseasonalized forecasted rate by these seasonals. The product will be the forecasted sales rate, which is what we desired.

In special cases where there are no seasonals to be considered, of course, this process is much simplified, and fewer data and simpler techniques may be adequate.

We have found that an analysis of the patterns of change in the growth rate gives us more accuracy in predicting turning points (and therefore changes from positive to negative growth, and vice versa) than when we use only the trend cycle.

The main advantage of considering growth change, in fact, is that it is frequently possible to predict earlier when a no-growth situation will occur. The graph of change in growth thus provides an excellent visual base for forecasting and for identifying the turning point as well.

X-11 technique: The reader will be curious to know how one breaks the seasonals out of raw sales data and exactly how one derives the change-in-growth curve from the trend line.

One of the best techniques we know for analyzing historical data in depth to determine seasonals, present sales rate, and growth is the X-11 Census Bureau Technique, which simultaneously removes seasonals from raw information and fits a trend-cycle line to the data. It is very comprehensive: at a cost of about $10, it provides detailed information on seasonals, trends, the accuracy of the seasonals and the trend cycle fit, and a number of other measures. The output includes plots of the trend cycle and the growth rate, which can concurrently be received on graphic displays on a time-shared terminal.

Although the X-11 was not originally developed as a forecasting method, it does establish a base from which good forecasts can be made. One should note, however, that there is some instability in the trend line for the most recent data points, since the X-11, like virtually all statistical techniques, uses some form of moving average. It has therefore proved of value to study the changes in growth pattern as each new growth point is obtained.

In particular, when recent data seem to reflect sharp growth or decline in sales or any other market anomaly, the forecaster should determine whether any special events occurred during the period under consideration —promotion, strikes, changes in the economy, and so on. The X-11 provides the basic instrumentation needed to evaluate the effects of such events.

Generally, even when growth patterns can be associated with specific events, the X-11 technique and other statistical methods do not give good results when forecasting beyond six months, because of the uncertainty or unpredictable nature of the events. For short-term forecasts of one to three months, the X-11 technique has proved reasonably accurate.

We have used it to provide sales estimates for each division for three periods into the future, as well as to determine changes in sales rates. We have compared our X-11 forecasts with forecasts developed by each of several divisions, where the divisions have used a variety of methods, some of which take into account salesmen's estimates and other special knowledge. The forecasts using the X-11 technique were based on statistical methods alone, and did not consider any special information.

The division forecasts had slightly *less* error than those provided by the X-11 method; however, the division forecasts have been found to be slightly biased on the optimistic side, whereas those provided by the X-11 method are unbiased. This suggested to us that a better job of forecasting could be done by combining special knowledge, the techniques of the division, and the X-11 method. This is actually being done now by some of the divisions, and their forecasting accuracy has improved in consequence.

The X-11 method has also been used to make sales projections for the immediate future to serve as a standard for evaluating various marketing strategies. This has been found to be especially effective for estimating the effects of price changes and promotions.

As we have indicated earlier, trend analysis is frequently used to project annual data for several years to determine what sales will be if the current trend continues. Regression analysis and statistical forecasts are sometimes used in this way—that is, to estimate what will happen if no significant changes are made. Then, if the result is not acceptable with respect to corporate objectives, the company can change its strategy.

Econometric models: Over a long period of time, changes in general economic conditions will account for a significant part of the change in a product's growth rate. Because economic forecasts are becoming more accurate and also because there are certain general "leading" economic forces that change before there are subsequent changes in specific industries, it is possible to improve the forecasts of businesses by including economic factors in the forecasting model.

However, the development of such a model, usually called an econometric model, requires sufficient data so that the correct relationships can be established.

During the rapid-growth state of color TV, we recognized that economic conditions would probably affect the sales rate significantly. However, the macroanalyses of black-and-white TV data we made in 1965 for the recessions in the late 1940's and early 1950's did not show any substantial economic effects at all; hence we did not have sufficient data to establish good econometric relationships for a color TV model. (A later investigation did establish definite losses in color TV sales in 1967 due to economic conditions.)

In 1969 Corning decided that a better method than the X-11 was definitely needed to predict turning points in retail sales for color TV six months to two years into the future. Statistical methods and salesmen's estimates cannot spot these turning points far enough in advance to assist decision making; for example, a production manager should have three to six months' warning of such changes if he is to maintain a stable work force.

Adequate data seemed to be available to build an econometric model, and analyses were therefore begun to develop such a model for both black-and-white and color TV sales. Our knowledge of seasonals, trends, and growth for these products formed a natural base for constructing the equations of the models.

The economic inputs for the model are primarily obtained from information generated by the Wharton Econometric Model, but other sources are also utilized.

Using data extending through 1968, the model did reasonably well in predicting the downturn in the fourth quarter of 1969 and, when 1969 data were also incorporated into the model, accurately estimated the magnitude of the drop in the first two quarters of 1970. Because of lead-lag relationships and the ready availability of economic forecasts for the factors in the model, the effects of the economy on sales can be estimated for as far as two years into the future.

In the steady-state phase, production and inventory control, group-item forecasts, and long-term demand estimates are particularly important. The interested reader will find a discussion of these topics on the reverse of the gatefold.

Finally, through the steady-state phase, it is useful to set up quarterly reviews where statistical tracking and warning charts and new information are brought forward. At these meetings, the decision to revise or update a model or forecast is weighed against various costs and the amount of forecasting error. In a highly volatile area, the review should occur as frequently as every month or period.

Forecasting in the Future

In concluding an article on forecasting, it is appropriate that we make a prediction about the techniques that will be used in the short- and long-term future.

As we have already said, it is not too difficult to forecast the immediate future, since long-term trends do not change overnight. Many of the techniques described are only in the early stages of application, but still we expect most of the techniques that will be used in the next five years to be the ones discussed here, perhaps in extended form.

The costs of using these techniques will be reduced significantly; this will enhance their implementation. We expect that computer time-sharing companies will offer access, at nominal cost, to input-output data banks, broken down into more business segments than are available today. The continuing declining trend in computer cost per computation, along with computational simplifications, will make techniques such as the Box-Jenkins method economically feasible, even for some inventory-control applications. Computer software packages for the statistical techniques and some general models will also become available at a nominal cost.

At the present time, most short-term forecasting uses only statistical methods, with little qualitative information. Where qualitative information is used, it is only used in an external way and is not directly incorporated into the computational routine. We predict a change to total forecasting systems, where several techniques are tied together, along with a systematic handling of qualitative information.

Econometric models will be utilized more extensively in the next five years, with most large companies developing and refining econometric models of their major businesses. Marketing simulation models for new products will also be developed for the larger-volume products, with tracking systems for updating the models and their parameters. Heuristic programming will provide a means of refining forecasting models.

While some companies have already developed their own input-output models in tandem with the government input-output data and statistical projections, it will be another five to ten years before input-output models are effectively used by most major corporations.

Within five years, however, we shall see extensive use of man-machine systems, where statistical, causal, and econometric models are programmed on computers, with man interacting frequently. As we gain confidence in such systems, so that there is less exception reporting, human intervention will decrease. Basically, computerized models will do the sophisticated computations, and man will serve more as a generator of ideas and a developer of systems. For example, man will study market dynamics and establish more complex relationships between the factor being forecast and those of the forecasting system.

Further out, consumer simulation models will become commonplace. The models will predict the behavior of the consumer and forecast his reactions to various marketing strategies such as pricing, promotions, new product introductions, and competitive actions. Probabilistic models will be used frequently in the forecasting process.

Finally, most computerized forecasting will relate to the analytical techniques described in this article. Computer applications will be mostly in established and stable product businesses. Although the forecasting techniques have thus far been used primarily for sales forecasting, they will be applied increasingly to forecasting margins, capital expenditures, and other important factors. This will free the forecaster to spend most of his time forecasting sales and profits of new products. Doubtless, new analytical techniques will be developed for new-product forecasting, but there will be a continuing problem, for at least 10 to 20 years and probably much longer, in accurately forecasting various new-product factors, such as sales, profitability, and length of life cycle.

Final Word

The decision maker can help the forecaster formulate the forecasting problem properly, and he will have more confidence in the forecasts provided to him and use them more effectively, if he understands the basic features and limitations of the techniques. The forecaster, for his part, must blend the techniques he uses with the knowledge and experience of the managers.

The need today, we believe, is not for better forecasting methods, but for better application of the techniques at hand.

Part VIII

Production and Operations

Preface

One way to think of management is as the art of measuring. A successful manager is one who knows, among other things, which yardsticks to use in his or her job, and how to use them appropriately.

There are four "yardsticks" in the five articles in this section that the manager may find useful in evaluating certain elements of his organization's production and operations functions. For the operating manager, the articles can serve as measures with which he can better determine which new methods and ideas can be profitably applied in his own situation and how he can go about implementing them. The articles can also help provide the general manager with insights into what key tasks confront those within these functions today, and how to integrate these tasks with the rest of the organization's strategy.

In the first article, "Manufacturing—Missing Link in Corporate Strategy," the yardstick presented attempts to measure manufacturing's potential to strengthen or weaken a company's competitive ability. In focusing on such imprecise measures of success as "efficiency," "low cost," or "productivity," top management too often overlooks that potential, the author asserts. He discusses the fundamental trade-offs inherent to the function that the manager must weigh in order to avoid such oversight.

The next two articles, "Production Planning and Control Integrated" and "Requirements Planning for Inventory Control," together present a yardstick by which the manager can take the measure of his organization's adaptation to modern technological practices. The first details how computer-based approaches can aid managers in solving such problems as unbalanced capacity, unrealistic sales forecasting, poor master and short-term scheduling, and inadequate inventory control. The second one takes a closer look at specific situations in which one such approach—requirements planning—provides for better parts management than do statistical methods such as "safety stocks," "reorder points," and "economic order quantities."

"Sweeping Changes in Distribution" covers new thinking and new ventures to provide a yardstick that marks an era in the redevelopment and restructuring of business logistics industries and services. The author predicts that further improvements in logistics will come about as a result of institutional changes

rather than as a result of technological changes as they have in the past.

Finally, "Production-Line Approach to Service" illustrates how the yardstick used for products "in the factory" applies equally well for services "in the field." The author suggests that a production-type systemic orientation toward the efficient production of results must replace the antequated conception that service is simply something performed by individuals directly for other individuals. Only by measuring by this yardstick, he maintains, can meaningful improvements in quality and productivity be forthcoming for service industries.

29 Manufacturing—Missing Link in Corporate Strategy

Wickham Skinner

The thesis of this article is that manufacturing has too long been dominated by experts and specialists. For many years these were the industrial engineers; now they are the computer experts. As a result, top executives tend to avoid involvement in manufacturing policy making, manufacturing managers are ignorant of corporate strategy, and a function that could be a valuable asset and tool of corporate strategy becomes a liability instead. The author shows how top management can correct this situation by systematically linking up manufacturing with corporate strategy.

A company's manufacturing function typically is either a competitive weapon or a corporate millstone. It is seldom neutral. The connection between manufacturing and corporate success is rarely seen as more than the achievement of high efficiency and low costs. In fact, the connection is much more critical and much more sensitive. Few top managers are aware that what appear to be routine manufacturing decisions frequently come to limit the corporation's strategic options, binding it with facilities, equipment, personnel, and basic controls and policies to a noncompetitive posture which may take years to turn around.

Research I have conducted during the past few years reveals that top management unknowingly delegates a surprisingly large portion of basic policy decisions to lower levels in the manufacturing area. Generally, this abdication of responsibility comes about more through a lack of concern than by intention. And it is partly the reason that many manufacturing policies and procedures developed at lower levels reflect assumptions about corporate strategy which are incorrect or misconstrued.

Millstone Effect

When companies fail to recognize the relationship between manufacturing decisions and corporate strategy, they may become saddled with seriously noncompetitive production systems which are expensive and time-consuming to change. Here are several examples:

□ Company A entered the combination washer-dryer field after several competitors had failed to achieve successful entries into the field. Company A's executives believed their model would overcome the technical drawbacks which had hurt their competitors and held back the development of any substantial market. The manufacturing managers tooled the new unit on the usual conveyorized assembly line and giant stamping presses used for all company products.

When the washer-dryer failed in the market, the losses amounted to millions. The plant had been "efficient" in the sense that costs were low. But the tooling and production processes did not meet the demands of the marketplace.

□ Company B produced five kinds of electronic gear for five different groups of customers; the gear ranged from satellite controls to industrial controls and electronic components. In each market a different task was required of the production function. For instance, in the first market, extremely high reliability was demanded; in the second market, rapid introduction of a stream of new products was demanded; in the third market, low costs were of critical importance for competitive survival.

In spite of these highly diverse and contrasting tasks, production management elected to centralize manufacturing facilities in one plant in order to achieve "economies of scale." The result was a failure to achieve high reliability, economies of scale, or an ability to introduce new products quickly. What happened, in short, was that the demands placed on manufacturing by a competitive strategy were ignored by the production group in order to achieve economies of scale. This production group was obsessed with developing "a total system, fully computerized." The manufacturing program satisfied no single division, and the serious marketing problems which resulted choked company progress.

□ Company C produced plastic molding resins. A new plant under construction was to come on-stream in eight months, doubling production. In the meantine, the company had a much higher volume of orders than it could meet.

In a strategic sense, manufacturing's task was to maximize output to satisfy large, key customers. Yet the plant's production control system was set up—as it had been for years—to minimize costs. As a result, long runs were emphasized. While costs were low, many customers had to wait, and many key buyers were lost. Consequently, when the new plant came on-stream, it was forced to operate at a low volume.

The mistake of considering low costs and high efficiencies as the key manufacturing objective in each of these examples is typical of the oversimplified concept of "a good manufacturing operation." Such criteria frequently get companies into trouble, or at least do not aid in development of manufacturing into a competitive weapon. Manufacturing affects corporate strategy, and corporate strategy affects manufacturing. Even in an apparently routine operating area such as a production scheduling system, strategic considerations should outweigh technical and conventional industrial engineering factors invoked in the name of "productivity."

SHORTSIGHTED VIEWS

The fact is that manufacturing is seen by most top managers as requiring involved technical skills and a morass of petty daily decisions and details. It is seen by many young managers as the gateway to grubby routine, where days are filled with high pressure, packed with details, and limited to low-level decision making—all of which is out of the sight and minds of top-level executives. It is generally taught in graduate schools of business administration as a combination of industrial engineering (time study, plant layout, inventory theory, and so on) and quantitative analysis (linear programming, simulation, queuing theory, and the rest). In total, a manufacturing career is generally perceived as an all-consuming, technically oriented, hectic life that minimizes one's chances of ever reaching the top and maximizes the chances of being buried in minutiae.

In fact, these perceptions are not wholly inaccurate. It is the thesis of this article that the technically oriented concept of manufacturing is all too prevalent; and that it is largely responsible for the typically limited contribution manufacturing makes to a corporation's arsenal of competitive weapons, for manufacturing's failure to attract the top talent it needs and *should* have, and for its failure to attract more young managers with general management interests and broad abilities. In my opinion, manufacturing is generally perceived in the wrong way at the top, managed in the wrong way at the plant level, and taught in the wrong way in the business schools.

These are strong words, but change is needed, and I believe that only a more relevant concept of manufacturing can bring change. I see no sign whatsoever that we have found the means of solving the problems mentioned. The mathematically based "total systems" approaches to production management offer the promise of new and valuable concepts and techniques, but I doubt that these approaches will overcome the tendency of top management to remove itself from manufacturing. The years of development of quantitative techniques have left us each year with the promise of a "great new age" in production management that lies "just ahead." The promise never seems to be realized. Stories of computer and "total systems" fiascoes are available by the dozen; these failures are always expensive, and in almost every case management has delegated the work to experts.

I do not want to demean the promise—and, indeed, some present contributions—of the systems/computer approach. A few years ago I felt more sanguine about it. But, since then, close observation of the problems in U.S. industry has convinced me that the "answer" promised is inadequate. The approach cannot overcome the problems described until it does a far better job of linking manufacturing and corporate strategy. What is needed is some kind of integrative mechanism.

Pattern of Failure

An examination of top management perceptions of manufacturing has led me to some notions about basic causes of many production problems. In each of six industries I have studied, I have found top executives delegating excessive amounts of manufacturing policy to subordinates, avoiding involvement in most production matters, and failing to ask the right questions until their companies are in obvious trouble. This pattern seems to be due to a combination of two factors:

1. A sense of personal inadequacy, on the part of top executives, in managing production. (Often the feeling evolves from a tendency to regard the area as a technical or engineering specialty, or a mundane "nuts and bolts" segment of management.)

2. A lack of awareness among top executives that a production system inevitably involves trade-offs and compromises and so must be designed to perform a limited task well, with that task defined by corporate strategic objectives.

The first factor is, of course, dependent in part on the second, for the sense of inadequacy would not be felt if the strategic role of production were clearer. The second factor is the one we shall concentrate on in the remainder of this article.

Like a building, a vehicle, or a boat, a production system can be designed to do some things well, but always at the expense of other abilities. It appears to be the lack of recognition of these trade-offs and their effects on a corporation's ability to compete that leads top management to delegate often-critical decisions to lower, technically oriented staff levels, and to allow policy to be made through apparently unimportant operating decisions.

In the balance of this article I would like to . . .

—sketch out the relationships between production operations and corporate strategy;

—call attention to the existence of specific trade-offs in production system design;

—comment on the inadequacy of computer specialists to deal with these trade-offs;

—suggest a new way of looking at manufacturing which might enable the nontechnical manager to understand and manage the manufacturing area.

Strategic Implications

Frequently the interrelationship between production operations and corporate strategy is not easily grasped. The notion is simple enough—namely, that a company's competitive strategy at a given time places particular demands on its manufacturing function, and, conversely, that the company's manufacturing posture and operations should be specifically designed to fulfill the task demanded by strategic plans. What is more elusive is the set of cause-and-effect factors which determine the linkage between strategy and production operations.

Strategy is a set of plans and policies by which a company aims to gain advantages over its competitors. Generally a strategy includes plans for products and the marketing of these products to a particular set of customers. The marketing plans usually include specific approaches and steps to be followed in identifying potential customers, determining why, where, and when they buy, and learning how they can best be reached and convinced to purchase. The company must have an advantage, a particular appeal, a special push or pull created by its products, channels of distribution, advertising, price, packaging, availability, warranties, or other factors.

CONTRASTING DEMANDS

What is not always realized is that different marketing strategies and approaches to gaining a competitive advantage place different demands on the manufacturing arm of the company. For example, a furniture manufacturer's strategy for broad distribution of a limited, low-price line with wide consumer advertising might generally require:

□ Decentralized finished-goods storage.
□ Readily available merchandise.
□ Rock-bottom costs.

The foregoing demands might in turn require:

□ Relatively large lot sizes.
□ Specialized facilities for woodworking and finishing.
□ A large proportion of low- and medium-skilled workers in the work force.
□ Concentration of manufacturing in a limited number of large-scale plants.

In contrast, a manufacturer of high-price, high-style furniture with more exclusive distribution would require an entirely different set of manufacturing policies. While higher prices and longer lead times would allow more leeway in the plant, this company would have to contend with the problems implicit in delivering high-quality furniture made of wood (which is a soft, dimensionally unstable material whose surface is expensive to finish and easy to damage), a high setup cost relative to running times in most wood-machining operations, and the need to make a large number of nonstandardized parts. While the first company must work with these problems too, they are more serious to the second company because its marketing strategy forces it to confront the problems head on. The latter's manufacturing policies will probably require:

□ Many model and style changes.
□ Production to order.
□ Extremely reliable high quality.

These demands may in turn require:

□ An organization that can get new models into production quickly.
□ A production control group that can coordinate all activities so as to reduce lead times.
□ Technically trained supervisors and technicians.

Consequently, the second company ought to have a strong manufacturing-methods engineering staff; simple, flexible tooling; and a well-trained, experienced work force.

In summary, the two manufacturers would need to develop very different policies, personnel, and operations if they were to be equally successful in carrying out their strategies.

IMPORTANT CHOICES

In the example described, there are marked contrasts in the two companies. Actually, even small and subtle differences in corporate strategies should be reflected in manufacturing policies. However, my research shows that few companies do in fact carefully and explicitly tailor their production systems to perform the tasks which are vital to corporate success.

Instead of focusing first on strategy, then moving to define the manufacturing task, and next turning to systems design in manufacturing policy, managements tend to employ a concept of production which is much less effective. Most top executives and production managers look at their production systems with the notion of "total productivity" or the equivalent, "efficiency." They seek a kind of blending of low costs, high quality, and acceptable customer service. The view prevails that a plant with reasonably modern equipment, up-to-date methods and procedures, a cooperative work force, a computerized information system, and an enlightened management will be a good plant and will perform efficiently.

But what is a "good plant"? What is "efficient performance"? And what should the computer be programmed to do? Should it minimize lead times or minimize inventories? A company cannot do both. Should the computer minimize direct labor or indirect labor? Again, the company cannot do both. Should investment in equipment be minimized—or should outside purchasing be held to a minimum? One could go on with such choices.

The reader may reply: "What management wants is a combination of both ingredients that results in the lowest *total* cost." But that answer, too, is insufficient. The "lowest total cost" answer leaves out the dimensions of time and customer satisfaction, which must usually be considered too. Because cost *and* time *and* customers are all involved, we have to conclude that what is a "good" plant for Company A may be a poor or mediocre plant for its competitor, Company B, which is in the same industry but pursues a different strategy.

The purpose of manufacturing is to serve the company—to meet its needs for survival, profit, and growth. Manufacturing is part of the strategic concept that relates a company's strengths and resources to opportunities in the market. Each strategy creates a unique manufacturing task. Manufacturing management's ability to meet that task is the key measure of its success.

Trade-offs in Design

It is curious that most top managements and production people do not state their yardsticks of success more precisely, and instead fall back on such measures as "efficiency," "low cost," and "productivity." My studies suggest that a key reason for this phenomenon is that very few executives realize the existence of trade-offs in designing and operating a production system.

Yet most managers will readily admit that there are compromises or trade-offs to be made in designing an airplane or a truck. In the case of an airplane, trade-offs would involve such matters as cruising speed, takeoff and landing distances, initial cost, maintenance, fuel consumption, passenger comfort, and cargo or passenger capacity. A given stage of technology defines limits as to what can be accomplished in these respects. For instance, no one today can design a 500-passenger plane that can land on a carrier and also break the sonic barrier.

Much the same thing is true of manufacturing. The variables of cost, time, quality, technological constraints, and customer satisfaction place limits on what management can do, force compromises, and demand an explicit recognition of a multitude of trade-offs and choices. Yet everywhere I find plants which have inadvertently emphasized one yardstick at the expense of another, more important one. For example:

□ An electronics manufacturer with dissatisfied customers hired a computer expert and placed manufacturing under a successful engineering design chief to make it a "total system." A year later its computer was spewing out an inch-thick volume of daily information. "We know the location of every part in the plant on any given day," boasted the production manager and his computer systems chief.

Nevertheless, customers were more dissatisfied than ever. Product managers hotly complained that delivery promises were regularly missed—and in almost every case they first heard about failures from their customers. The problem centered on the fact that computer information runs were organized by part numbers and operations. They were designed to facilitate machine scheduling and to aid shop foremen; they were not organized around end products, which would have facilitated customer service.

How had this come about? Largely, it seemed clear, because the manufacturing managers had become absorbed in their own "systems approach"; the fascination of mechanized data handling had become an end in itself. As for top management, it had more or less abdicated responsibility. Because the company's growth and success had been based on engineering and because top management was R&D-oriented, policy-making executives saw production as a routine requiring a lower level of complexity and brainpower. Top management argued further that the company had production experts who were well paid and who should be able to do their jobs without bothering top-level people.

RECOGNIZING ALTERNATIVES

To develop the notion of important trade-off decisions in manufacturing, let us consider *Exhibit I*, which shows some examples.

In each decision area—plant and equipment, production planning and control, and so forth—top management needs to recognize the alternatives and become involved in the design of the production system. It needs to become involved to the extent that the alternative selected is appropriate to the manufacturing task determined by the corporate strategy.

Making such choices is, of course, an on-going rather than a once-a-year or once-a-decade task; decisions have to be made constantly in these trade-off areas. Indeed, the real crux of the problem seems to be how to ensure that the continuing process of decision making is not isolated from competitive and strategic facts, when many of the trade-off decisions do not at first appear to bear on company strategy. As long as a technical point

Exhibit I. Some important trade-off decisions in manufacturing—or "you can't have it both ways"

Decision area	Decision	Alternatives
PLANT AND EQUIPMENT	Span of process	Make or buy
	Plant size	One big plant or several smaller ones
	Plant location	Locate near markets or locate near materials
	Investment decisions	Invest mainly in buildings or equipment or inventories or research
	Choice of equipment	General-purpose or special-purpose equipment
	Kind of tooling	Temporary, minimum tooling or "production tooling"
PRODUCTION PLANNING AND CONTROL	Frequency of inventory taking	Few or many breaks in production for buffer stocks
	Inventory size	High inventory or a lower inventory
	Degree of inventory control	Control in great detail or in lesser detail
	What to control	Controls designed to minimize machine downtime or labor cost or time in process, or to maximize output of particular products or material usage
	Quality control	High reliability and quality or low costs
	Use of standards	Formal or informal or none at all
LABOR AND STAFFING	Job specialization	Highly specialized or not highly specialized
	Supervision	Technically trained first-line supervisors or nontechnically trained supervisors
	Wage system	Many job grades or few job grades; incentive wages or hourly wages
	Supervision	Close supervision or loose supervision
	Industrial engineers	Many or few such men
PRODUCT DESIGN/ ENGINEERING	Size of product line	Many customer specials or few specials or none at all
	Design stability	Frozen design or many engineering change orders
	Technological risk	Use of new processes unproved by competitors or follow-the-leader policy
	Engineering	Complete packaged design or design-as-you-go approach
	Use of manufacturing engineering	Few or many manufacturing engineers
ORGANIZATION AND MANAGEMENT	Kind of organization	Functional or product focus or geographical or other
	Executive use of time	High involvement in investment or production planning or cost control or quality control or other activities
	Degree of risk assumed	Decisions based on much or little information
	Use of staff	Large or small staff group
	Executive style	Much or little involvement in detail; authoritarian or nondirective style; much or little contact with organization

of view dominates manufacturing decisions, a degree of isolation from the realities of competition is inevitable. Unfortunately, as we shall see, the technical viewpoint is all too likely to prevail.

Technical Dominance

The similarity between today's emphasis on the technical experts—the computer specialist and the engineering-oriented production technician— and yesterday's emphasis on the efficiency expert—time-study man and industrial engineer—is impossible to escape. For 50 years, U.S. management relied on efficiency experts trained in the techniques of Frederick W. Taylor. Industrial engineers were kings of the factory. Their early approaches and attitudes were often conducive to industrial warfare, strikes, sabotage, and militant unions, but that was not realized then. Also not realized was that their technical emphasis often produced an inward orientation toward cost that ignored the customer, and an engineering point of view that gloried in tools, equipment, and gadgets rather than in markets and service. Most important, the cult of industrial engineering tended to make top executives technically disqualified from involvement in manufacturing decisions.

Since the turn of the century, this efficiency-centered orientation has dogged U.S. manufacturing. It has created that image of "nuts and bolts," of greasy, dirty, detail jobs in manufacturing. It has dominated "production" courses in most graduate schools of business administration. It has alienated young people with broad management educations from manufacturing careers. It has "buffaloed" top managers.

Several months ago I was asked by a group of industrial engineers to offer an opinion as to why so few industrial engineers were moving up to the top of their companies. My answer was that perhaps a technical point of view cut them off from top management, just as the jargon and hocus-pocus of manufacturing often kept top management from understanding the factory. In their isolation, they could gain only a severely limited sense of market needs and of corporate competitive strategy.

ENTER THE COMPUTER EXPERT

Today the industrial engineer is declining in importance in many companies. But a new technical expert, the computer specialist, is taking his place. I use the term "computer specialist" to refer to individuals who specialize in computer systems design and programming.

I do not deny, of course, that computer specialists have a very important job to do. I do object, however, to any notion that computer specialists have more of a top management view than was held by their predecessors, the industrial engineers. In my experience, the typical computer expert has been forced to master a complex and all-consuming technology, a fact which frequently makes him parochial rather than catholic in his views. Because he is so preoccupied with the detail of a total system, it is necessary for someone in top management to give him objectives and policy guidance. In his choice of trade-offs and compromises for his computer system, he needs to be instructed and not left to his own devices. Or, stated differently, he needs to see the entire corporation as a system, not just one corner of it—i.e., the manufacturing plant.

Too often this is not happening. The computer is a nightmare to many top managers because they have let it and its devotees get out of hand. They have let technical experts continue to dominate; the failure of top management truly to manage production goes on.

How *can* top management begin to manage manufacturing instead of turning it over to technicians who, through no fault of their own, are absorbed in their own arts and crafts? How can U.S. production management be helped to cope with the rising pressures of new markets, more rapid product changes, new technologies, larger and riskier equipment decisions, and the swarm of problems we face in industry today? Let us look at some answers.

Better Decision Making

The answers I would like to suggest are not panaceas, nor are they intended to be comprehensive. Indeed, no one can answer all the questions and problems described with one nice formula or point of view. But surely we can improve on the notion that production systems need only be "productive and efficient." Top management can manage manufacturing if it will engage in the making of manufacturing policy, rather than considering it a kind of fifth, independent estate beyond the pale of control.

The place to start, I believe, is with the acceptance of a theory of manufacturing which begins with the concept that in any system design there are significant trade-offs (as shown in *Exhibit I*) which must be explicitly decided on.

DETERMINING POLICY

Executives will also find it helpful to think of manufacturing policy determination as an orderly process or sequence of steps. *Exhibit II* is a schematic portrayal of such a process. It shows that manufacturing policy must stem from corporate strategy, and that the process of determining

Exhibit II. The process of manufacturing policy determination

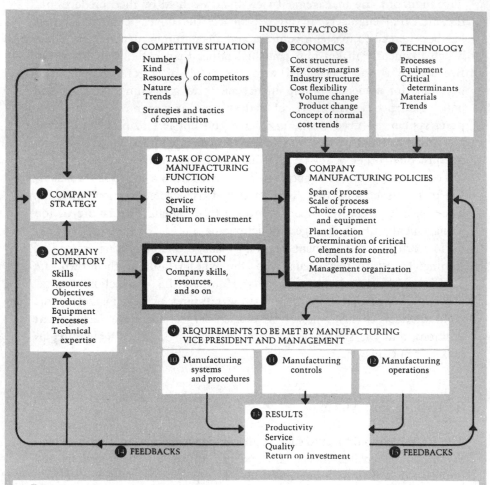

INDUSTRY FACTORS

① COMPETITIVE SITUATION
Number ⎫
Kind ⎪
Resources ⎬ of competitors
Nature ⎪
Trends ⎭

Strategies and tactics
of competition

⑤ ECONOMICS
Cost structures
Key costs-margins
Industry structure
Cost flexibility
Volume change
Product change
Concept of normal
cost trends

⑥ TECHNOLOGY
Processes
Equipment
Critical
determinants
Materials
Trends

④ TASK OF COMPANY
MANUFACTURING
FUNCTION
Productivity
Service
Quality
Return on investment

③ COMPANY
STRATEGY

② COMPANY
INVENTORY
Skills
Resources
Objectives
Products
Equipment
Processes
Technical
expertise

⑦ EVALUATION
Company skills,
resources,
and so on

⑧ COMPANY
MANUFACTURING POLICIES
Span of process
Scale of process
Choice of process
and equipment
Plant location
Determination of critical
elements for control
Control systems
Management organization

⑨ REQUIREMENTS TO BE MET BY MANUFACTURING
VICE PRESIDENT AND MANAGEMENT

⑩ Manufacturing
systems
and procedures

⑪ Manufacturing
controls

⑫ Manufacturing
operations

⑬ RESULTS
Productivity
Service
Quality
Return on investment

⑭ FEEDBACKS

⑮ FEEDBACKS

Key

1. What the others are doing

2. What we have got or can get to compete with

3. How we can compete

4. What we must accomplish in manufacturing in order
to compete

5. Economic constraints and opportunities common to
the industry

6. Constraints and opportunities common to the technology

7. Our resources evaluated

8. How we should set ourselves up to match resources,
economics, and technology to meet the tasks required
by our competitive strategy

9. The implementation requirements of our
manufacturing policies

10. Basic systems in manufacturing (e.g., production
planning, use of inventories, use of standards, and
wage systems)

11. Controls of cost, quality, flows, inventory, and time

12. Selection of operations or ingredients critical to success
(e.g., labor skills, equipment utilization, and yields)

13. How we are performing

14. Changes in what we have got, effects on competitive
situation, and review of strategy

15. Analysis and review of manufacturing operations and
policies

Exhibit III. Illustrative constraints or limitations which should be studied

---

A. Economics of the industry

Labor, burden, material, depreciation costs
Flexibility of production to meet changes in volume
Return on investment, prices, margins
Number and location of plants
Critical control variables
Critical functions (e.g., maintenance, production control, personnel)
Typical financial structures
Typical costs and cost relationships
Typical operating problems
Barriers to entry
Pricing practices
"Maturity" of industry products, markets, production practices, and so on
Importance of economies of scale
Importance of integrated capacities of corporations
Importance of having a certain balance of different types of equipment
Ideal balances of equipment capacities
Nature and type of production control
Government influences

B. Technology of the industry

Rate of technological change
Scale of processes
Span of processes
Degree of mechanization
Technological sophistication
Time requirements for making changes

---

this policy is the means by which top management can actually manage production. Use of this process can end manufacturing isolation and tie top management and manufacturing together. The sequence is simple but vital:

□ It begins with an analysis of the competitive situation, of how rival companies are competing in terms of product, markets, policies, and channels of distribution. Management examines the number and kind of competitors and the opportunities open to its company.

□ Next comes a critical appraisal of the company's skills and resources and of its present facilities and approaches.

□ The third step is the formulation of company strategy: How is the company to compete successfully, combine its strengths with market opportunities, and define niches in the markets where it can gain advantages?

□ The fourth step is the point where many top executives cut off their thinking. It is important for them to define the implications or "so-what" effects of company strategy in terms of specific manufacturing tasks. For example, they should ask: "If we are to compete with an X product of Y price for Z customers using certain distribution channels and forms of advertising, what will be demanded of manufacturing in terms of costs, deliveries, lead times, quality levels, and reliability?" These demands should be precisely defined.

□ The fifth and sixth steps are to study the constraints or limitations imposed by the economics and the technology of the industry. These factors are generally common to all competitors. An explicit recognition of them is a prerequisite to a genuine understanding of the manufacturing problems and opportunities. These are facts that a nontechnical manager can develop, study, understand, and put to work. *Exhibit III* contains sample lists of topics for the manager to use in doing his homework.

□ The seventh and eighth steps are the key ones for integrating and synthesizing all the prior ones into a broad manufacturing policy. The question for management is: "Given the facts of the economics and the technology of the industry, how do we set ourselves up to meet the specific manufacturing tasks posed by our particular competitive strategy?" Management must decide what it is going to make and what it will buy; how many plants to have, how big they should be, and where to place them; what processes and equipment to buy; what the key elements are which need to be controlled and how they can be controlled; and what kind of management organization would be most appropriate.

□ Next come the steps of working out programs of implementation, controls, performance measures, and review procedures (see Steps 9-15 in *Exhibit II*).

Conclusion

The process just described is, in my observation, quite different from the usual process of manufacturing management. Conventionally, manufacturing has been managed from the bottom up. The classical process of the age of mass production is to select an operation, break it down into its elements, analyze and improve each element, and put it back together. This approach was contributed years ago by Frederick W. Taylor and other industrial engineers who followed in his footsteps.

What I am suggesting is an entirely different approach, one adapted far better to the current era of more products, shorter runs, vastly accelerated product changes, and increased marketing competition. I am suggesting a kind of "top-down" manufacturing. This approach starts with the company and its competitive strategy; its goal is to define manufacturing policy. Its presumption is that only when basic manufacturing policies are defined can the technical experts, industrial and manufacturing engineers, labor relations specialists, and computer experts have the necessary guidance to do their work.

With its focus on corporate strategy and the manufacturing task, the top-down approach can give top management both its entrée to manufacturing and the concepts it needs to take the initiative and truly manage this function. When this is done, executives previously unfamiliar with manufacturing are likely to find it an exciting activity. The company will have an important addition to its arsenal of competitive weapons.

30. Production Planning and Control Integrated

William K. Holstein

Although much has been written about the individual segments of production planning and control systems, little has appeared in the literature to help practitioners develop an integrated view of the whole process. Many complaints about department overloads or poor delivery performances—particularly in fabrication and assembly operations—focus on scheduling or control. Actually, the basic cause may be unbalanced capacity or an unrealistic sales commitment made months previously. Thus managers must not only look at decision making at all levels, but must also recognize that good short-term performances result from an integrated set of decisions made over a long time span.

□ Where did that huge pile of work in the turret lathe department come from?

□ Why can't we get the Ajax Bearing job done before next week?

□ Should we accept such a large order for delivery in eight weeks?

□ We're up to our armpits in castings on the shop floor. What can be done to reduce this congestion?

□ Why in the devil are we still working overtime in the assembly area?

These questions are representative of real and pressing questions that many production managers face. They are also symptomatic of basic management problems in running numerous production operations.

In this article I shall discuss the contributions that modern, computer-based production planning and control systems can make to aid in the solution of these kinds of problems. I am particularly interested in identifying and tying together the various parts of a production planning and control system, and in so doing I shall focus on tasks to be fulfilled rather than on detailed methods. The systems I shall discuss are applicable to a broad range of industries, but apply most directly to fabrication and assembly operations that make a large number of parts in relatively small lots either for assembly into finished products or for sale to outside customers.

Much has been written about individual segments of production planning and control systems and the specific analytical tools and techniques for handling these separate parts. However, little has been done to help the practitioner use the many tools and techniques that are applicable to his situation in such a way that they relate to one another. Managers are frequently heard to complain about department overloads or poor delivery performances and to blame these on "poor scheduling" or "poor control." The real cause, however, may be unbalanced capacity or an unrealistic sales commitment that was made months ago.

This article is designed, therefore, to help the manager relate the various parts of production planning and control, and to develop an integrated view of the whole process. I shall present the parts in a sequence that begins with long-term planning and ends with day-to-day control of shop floor activity, using exhibits to clarify the individual parts and the way they relate to one another. I shall also cite examples of companies that have made excellent progress on one specific part of a production planning and control system and those that have been successful in tying together two or more of the parts. All of the examples are based on actual situations.

Toward Better Control

Webster's dictionary definition of a system includes "a regularly interacting or interdependent group of items forming a unified whole." The items or parts in a production planning and control system fit together in a time dimension and interact in a certain way. Long-term strategic plans that commit the company to a configuration of manpower, skills, plant, and equipment are based on very crude information and analysis. Moreover, these plans constrain the development of more complete, detailed plans closer to actual production dates. Long-term plans are made by high-level management, and, as the time span shortens and the time of actual production approaches, decision making is passed down to lower-level managers. Within the guide-lines formed by long-term plans, tactical control must be exercised over the "uncontrollable" variation in product mix and productivity in the short term.

In the very short term this control involves putting men in the right places, working on the right jobs, and regulating inventory levels. The criteria against which management's production planning and control performance is measured include inventory investment, labor cost, manufacturing cycle time (time to get work through the shop), equipment utilization, and meeting delivery deadlines.

In my view, the most important task in designing any production planning and control system which will measure up well against these criteria is to ensure that the plans and guidelines from higher levels guide, but do not unduly restrict, decision making at lower levels. Flexibility to react to new information and significant deviations from higher-level plans must be built into the system at all levels. Also, feedback information on actual conditions and performance must flow upward through the system to ensure that long-term plans are based on a realistic assessment of the production organization's ability to produce.

Production managers usually do not see their job roles in these clear, general terms. Since the "moment of truth"—that is, when poor performance becomes obvious—occurs at the time of actual production, there is a tendency to find fault in the shortest time dimension and thus focus largely on problems at the lowest level. Many production managers spend their time in a continuous, and at times frantic, search for information. In the face of a stream of demanding problems calling for immediate attention and decisions, and because of the sometimes chaotic nature of work flow and clerical decision making on the shop floor, production managers often find themselves chained to an endless sequence of routine decision making.

The consequence is little time to think about next week's or next month's possible problems and to lay plans for solving those problems. Nor is there time to evaluate recent performance and to seek ways of improving it. Despite the fact that managers often spend a great deal of time in the short term, because of the tremendous number of jobs in process, they still must delegate many seemingly small, detailed decisions to their first-line supervisors, clerical assistants, or even to the workers themselves. Management thus loses control over decisions which, taken together, may have a great impact on how efficiently the plant is run.

But things can be much better. Recently, many production managers have changed the way they manage, utilizing new systems for production planning and control. New systems do not eliminate all the crises, but they do point the way toward better control with less management involvement at the detail level. Thus they are making it possible for management to plan, redesign, and execute in a more rational manner.

Long-Term Capacity Planning

Plant facilities, equipment, skilled labor, and working capital to support inventory investments usually cannot be made available to production managers on short notice. Consequently, most organizations must be concerned with laying long-term plans for future capacities. In a sense, long-term planning is the starting point for production planning and control; thus it is the logical starting point for our consideration of production planning and control systems.

The production organization competes with engineering and marketing for the company's limited resources, so production plans must be developed, refined, and defended. The long lead times on new construction and equipment acquisition require that some major expansion plans be developed years in advance of actual installation. Analyses of future market conditions and forecasts of future demands thus become important inputs in long-term planning. Even in make-to-order shops where no formal forecasts of future demands are developed, top management's collective hunch about the state of the economy and its impact on the company's future business is a vital ingredient in plans for the future. In some cases the forecasted demand will exceed existing production capacity. When this occurs, sales forecasts must be predicated on capacity plans.

Generation of long-term forecasts of demand, sales, and economic activity is often the responsibility of marketing. The approach utilized by one major U.S. appliance manufacturing company provides a case illustration:

□ The marketing research manager spends two or three days a month reviewing the economic indicators that might aid him in projecting cyclical turning points, predicting the economic climate likely to prevail during the forecast period, and factoring in industry information on inventories, product innovations, and so on, to yield a forecast of industry sales. His forecast is then compared and reconciled with the forecast developed by a senior marketing manager who generates company sales forecasts from detailed company information on consumer surveys; product, marketing, and pricing plans; and estimates of competitors' activities.

As another example of such forecasting, a large food products company is obtaining excellent results with a computer model which generates forecasts for grocery product sales:

□ Forecasts are developed that show expected sales by regions for existing products and new products not yet on the market. As the time period covered by the forecasts approaches, more and more detail is added.

For instance, the program used to generate quarterly forecasts contains information about planned advertising promotions and seasonal consumer habits. The computer-generated forecasts are carefully scrutinized by marketing managers and production planners, who may revise them to reflect such things as expected price trends, or perhaps a conviction that a given product will have a particularly strong regional appeal.

Subsequent computer runs reorganize the revised forecasts to provide a breakdown of sales by warehouse territories. These warehouse territory forecasts form the basis of comprehensive production planning for the company's manufacturing plants, pointing up situations where additional capacity will be needed in the future.

While forecasts come in many varieties (e.g., some cover different time periods, others contain different levels of detail), they are used by manufacturing mainly in setting future capacities. Examples of long-term capacity decisions based on forecasts are plant expansion, equipment acquisition, large work force additions, and major changes in inventory investment. (Inventory is included here, since it can be viewed as comprising stored capacity. A part on the shelf represents so many hours of capacity from a past period and eliminates the need for holding the same number of hours ready to serve a future demand.)

CONTINUAL ADJUSTMENT

Given forecasts of future demand, planning of capacity is not a one-shot problem that calls for one decision per year, but, rather, a problem that calls for constant review, fiddling, and adjusting. A well-designed system will provide many buffers to soften the impact of variations in demand, but even the best buffered systems will require basic adjustment from time to time through the purchase of plant and equipment, changes in the size of the work force, and major changes in inventory investment.

For a given company, a review of its recent history and current forecasts can often provide the guidelines for future action. A shop that has been choked with work for several months, which is having increasing difficulties meeting delivery deadlines, but nevertheless still has good labor efficiencies and control procedures, probably needs a boost in capacity. Well-organized information from a production planning and control system can provide a clue as to where the capacity is most needed, and the data can even aid in analyzing the effectiveness of alternative courses of action for providing capacity.

A large Connecticut company keeps details on its purchasing requirements and shop loads as far as three years ahead. This information enables management to consider carefully the long-range planning of inventory investment as well as production capacity. The use of shop load forecasts for inventory planning is an excellent example of what I referred to

Exhibit I. Information flows for long-term capacity planning

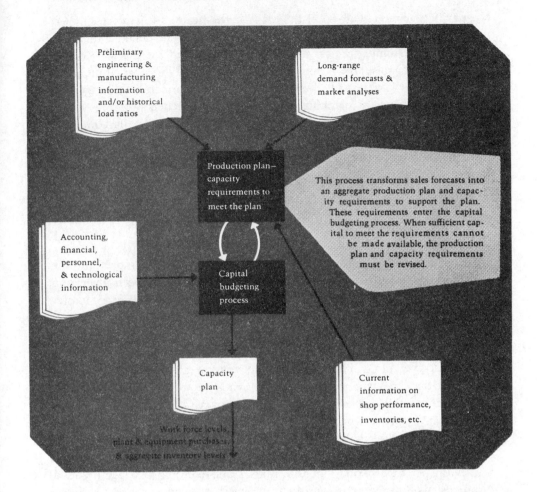

earlier as fitting together the parts of a production planning and control system.

Inventory control, when considered as a separate function, deals largely with individual item levels, order quantities, safety stocks, reorder points, and so forth. Yet one of the most important aspects of inventory management concerns the control of aggregate investment in all finished goods, subassemblies, work in process, and raw materials. The manager who understands the relationship of aggregate inventory investment to capacity, and who also has access to meaningful information on forecasted capacity requirements, can do a more effective capacity planning job than the manager who views the task as unrelated to other parts of the system.

The information flows in the capacity planning process are shown in *Exhibit I.* Capacity planning is a high-level, long-term planning activity which involves not only production managers, but also marketing, financial, and engineering managers. The element labeled "Production plan—

capacity requirements to meet the plan" is the heart of this process of (a) developing long-term production plans on the basis of demand forecasts, and (b) determining the capacity required to support the plans.

At present, this task is normally not performed by a computer, but the computer can provide some of the input information. The general problem of capacity planning has attracted researchers working at the theoretical level, and it seems likely that within a few years computer-oriented approaches will be available for many practical situations.

The next section concerns the development of rough production plans from sales forecasts and capacity plans.

Master Scheduling

This is the activity that determines the overall production plan for the next several months. After forecasts of future sales have been given and capacity and aggregate inventory levels have been pretty well fixed, master scheduling assigns productive capacity to individual end products or customer orders. Space terminology provides an analogy. A space rocket, if it is to hit the moon, must be launched within a "window" of a few hours and miles per hour. The limits on the window at launching are much rougher than they are at the other end, when the rocket nears the moon; if the launch falls outside the window, the target will be missed.

Similarly, master scheduling is done within coarse limits, but the objective is to ensure that the actual load in the shop two or three months hence will fall within rather narrow limits. Shop load is usually expressed in hours per time period, but the limits I am referring to have an added dimension. An example should help to clarify this concept.

In a two-machine shop that works a regular 40-hour week, the optimum load scheduled for a given week should be 80 machine-hours of work. If more than 80 machine-hours of work are scheduled, overtime can be used, or some of the current week's work can be pushed ahead into the following week. If less than 80 machine-hours of work are scheduled, some work can be pulled back from the next week's schedule to fill up the currently available capacity. Importantly, since master scheduling is done considerably ahead of the time of production, the actual load in the shop will not fit the shop's capacity exactly, and some "push-ahead" or "pull-back" will inevitably exist.

If, on the one hand, considerable push-ahead is required because the master schedule calls for more production in a given time period than the shop is able to produce, work in process will build up, most jobs will fall behind schedule, and almost all work in the shop will become "rush" or high priority. On the other hand, if the shop is not scheduled to capacity, pull-back will result in some jobs being completed ahead of schedule and may result in subsequent unused capacity.

Thus the lower limit on a master schedule should be a load which in hours of work and delivery date requirements will keep the shop's capacity efficiently utilized on current jobs that are neither far ahead nor behind schedule. The upper limit should be the highest load in hours and the tightest load in delivery requirements that can be handled by the shop and still allow for the inevitable rush job from a highly regarded customer, the last minute engineering change or rerun because of scrap losses, and the other occurrences which cannot be predicted in advance.

ESTIMATING SHOP LOADS

The key to successful master scheduling lies in the ability to forecast the lead times that will translate existing or prospective orders into an approximate shop load and delivery schedule. Often this is done by management intuition based, for example, on the knowledge that the shop cannot produce more than 20 model A machines per month, or that the shop load generated by a model B machine is approximately equal to the load created by 2 model A's. Intuitive planning is adequate for many situations, but the computer is making possible more sophisticated approaches.

Existing shop loads, or the forecasted load for orders already on the books, can often be a helpful input for determining the lead times required for master scheduling. The computer's ability to store a tremendous amount of detailed information in many instances means that approximate measures of aggregate shop load can be replaced with more detailed estimates of department, work center, or even machine load. To illustrate:

▢ A Midwestern manufacturer of metalworking presses has a program which compiles—from the master schedule for finished presses—weekly estimates of the total load in each work center that will be contributed by the individual component parts. This load information gives management a "20-week peek into the future, an ample length of time for problem solving." With such an advance notice, not only can future master schedules be planned on the basis of recent actual performance, but potential capacity bottlenecks can be spotted and avoided through subcontracting or other capacity adjustments.

▢ To assist in developing master schedules, a manufacturer of complex electronic and mechanical measuring equipment has a computer program that converts sales information on new or proposed orders into shop load long before detailed manufacturing information is available. The program is the result of a careful statistical analysis of the shop load contributed per sales dollar by various product classes. While not 100% reliable in predicting the load consequences of a given order, this program is of great

Exhibit II. Information flows for master scheduling

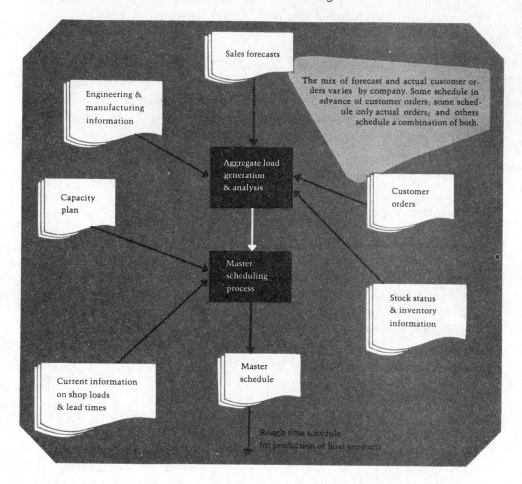

value in narrowing the limits on master scheduling and in making better estimates of the actual load hours and tightness in delivery times that the shop will encounter.

Master scheduling is graphically portrayed in *Exhibit II* as a two-step process. Sales forecasts and orders already on hand are first broken down into approximate shop loads, and then compared with the capacity plan and current shop information. The feedback information shown coming up from lower levels is a vital input to master scheduling.

One illustration of the importance of this information is its application in modifying the standard lead times used to convert orders into shop load. Lead times vary directly with shop loads. Thus, on the one hand, a master scheduling system that overlooks actual shop loads and simply uses standard lead times may make commitments which exceed the shop's capacity to produce. On the other hand, the increasing of lead times when shop loads go up and no capacity adjustments are made may cause total manufacturing cycle times to rise beyond the point where the company can compete effectively. Here, again, we see a relationship between two elements of a system that calls for careful managment consideration.

Inventory Control

Thus far inventories have been mentioned several times, and this is as it should be. Inventory control is not a separate entity but, rather, a pervasive factor that runs throughout any production planning and control system. A common system for the control of item inventories involves ordering replenishments in economic lots calculated according to one of a number of well-known "square root" formulas.[1] The lot is ordered when the stock on hand reaches a previously determined reorder point based both on estimates of the lead time required to fill the replenishment order and on the expected variability in demand during the lead time.

EOQ-REORDER POINT SYSTEM . . .

Not long ago, I had a conversation with a machine tool company manager who said, "If we are in error on the economic order quantity [EOQ] figure, we are in no great trouble; but, if we are in error on our reorder point, we can be in serious difficulty. We'll run out of parts needed to meet our assembly schedule, or, equally bad, we will be carrying an unnecessary inventory of parts."

Unfortunately, because the reorder point is directly related to what is going on in the shop, it is difficult to get straight. A typical development occurs at a time of sharply rising sales, when stock items hit their reorder points sooner than normal, resulting in an increased load on the shop. As shop load rises, lead times go up. Longer lead times, in turn, yield higher reorder points that trigger replenishment orders still faster. If all such orders are allowed to get onto the shop floor, a spiraling situation can develop where nothing gets through the shop on time. When sales drop, the reverse spiral is just as bad, or even worse, to deal with.

. . . VS. TIME-PHASED REQUIREMENTS

An alternative to the EOQ-reorder point system is time-phased requirements planning; this ties the control of piece parts and subassemblies to the assembly schedule of final products. With this system, parts can be manufactured in economic lots; but the timing of parts orders is based on

1. See, for example, John F. Magee, "Guides to Inventory Policy: I. Functions and Lot Sizes," HBR January-February 1956, p. 49.

Exhibit III. Example of time-phased requirements planning

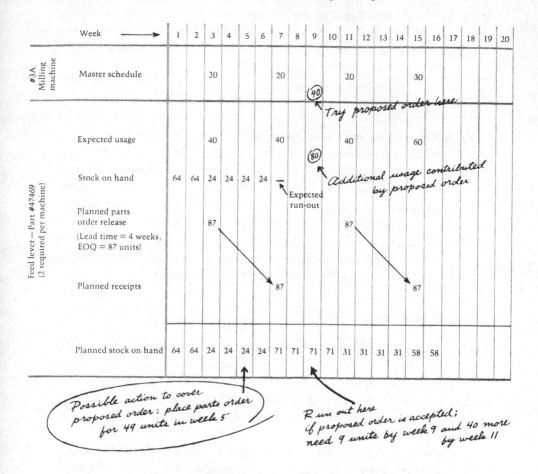

a date that is exploded back from the date of the final product assembly, rather than on a reorder point.

In the simplest version of time-phased requirements planning, a parts order is placed a standard lead time ahead of the time when assembly is expected to deplete the stock on hand. As shown in *Exhibit III*, the current supply of part #47469 is expected to run out during week 7 if no new replenishment orders are placed for the part. To prevent this stock-out and still allow the standard 4-week lead time for parts manufacturing, an order must be placed during week 3. This replenishment order for an economic lot of 87 units, along with a similar order during week 11, is shown in the exhibit.

Exhibit III also illustrates what can be accomplished when systems that support requirements planning, such as a bill-of-material processor and an inventory record system, are automated. The circled figures show how the system could handle the question: "What action is necessary if we accept an order for 40 #3A milling machines to be delivered in week 9?" Working through the bill of material for these milling machines, the system could identify all the parts required, check on-hand and on-order inventory status, and determine what action would be necessary to have the parts ready in time.

The action to handle the addition of the proposed order is triggered by an expected shortage of part #47469 in week 9. To cover this shortage, a parts order would have to be placed in week 5. More sophisticated logic could explore other alternatives, such as increasing the parts order placed in week 3, or moving the assembly lot in week 11 to a later week.

The automated bill-of-material handling also makes possible time-phased requirements planning by assembly level. Here, the due date for each component part of the final assembly is not the same, but reflects the actual time during the assembly and subassembly process when the part will be required. Thus a component part for a low-level (early in the assembly sequence) subassembly would be noted as being required several weeks ahead of an attachment to be installed late in the assembly process.

REPLENISHMENT PROBLEM

A major difficulty with any inventory system is the variability of the load placed on the production facility. Replenishment orders—whether determined by assembly schedules, reorder points, or other rules—tend to arrive without regard to the shop's capacity to handle them. Because these orders represent shop load, the inventory system is linked directly to master scheduling and lower-level systems. Although most companies attempt to provide some protection against variable demand by providing buffer inventories and safety factors in lead time estimates, a more direct approach which ties inventory control to master scheduling and short-term scheduling can greatly assist in smoothing out the load caused by inventory replenishment orders.

An example of such an approach, which squarely faces the problem of tying together the control of item inventories and shop loads, is that developed by a Wisconsin industrial goods manufacturer:

□ Working from forecasts, shop load reports, and other information, company managers develop a monthly manpower plan that extends six months into the future. The manpower plan sets the basic capacity, while detailed machine load reports provide information for short-term capacity adjustments through personnel shifts and overtime. When the inventory system does not generate enough orders to maintain production at the planned rate, the company's computer can identify jobs which will bring the plant's load up to desired levels and still maintain a well-balanced inventory.

This is a good example of how the computer has helped with shop load planning for the intermediate time range between long-term capacity planning and short-term scheduling. Later we will see how the computer, by focusing attention on critical jobs on the shop floor, can also provide help during actual production.

Short-term Scheduling

As we have seen, master scheduling entails an aggregate plan which ensures that the demands on the shop's capacity will be reasonable. I use the phrase "short-term scheduling" to describe the activity which develops the detailed plans necessary to meet the delivery commitments represented by the master schedule.

The result of short-term scheduling is a set start and completion time for every component part for final products. If, for example, a particular lot of 20 milling machines is to be assembled during week 15, 40 feed levers may be scheduled to start in the shop at the beginning of week 11 and to be completed by the end of week 14. Parts for stock would be scheduled for completion by the time the current supply is expected to be depleted.

One other important output of short-term scheduling is an estimate of the load for the next few weeks or months for each machine or work center in the shop. Indeed, *machine loading* is a term often used for the activity I call short-term scheduling. Machine load estimates can be used to assist management in (a) assigning men to machines to balance the capacities of various work centers, (b) spotting and reducing bottlenecks in work flow, and (c) planning activities on the shop floor.

Short-term scheduling is an activity that is very much like master scheduling, but it has a shorter time horizon and involves considerably more detail. The distinction between master and short-term scheduling is academic in some companies, especially those specializing in made-to-order items or products with short manufacturing cycle times. Also, the computer's ability to make large quantities of detailed information easily available tends to encourage the use of detailed information at higher levels and thus blur the distinction even more.

The foregoing discussion brings us to a level in the production planning process where the information required is often extensive and detailed. The data generally include such things as a bill of materials, showing all component parts and assembly sequences; routings or operations sheets for all parts to be manufactured; lists of raw materials, tools, and fixtures required, as well as information on their availability and their condition; estimates of existing loads already scheduled against machines or work centers in the shop, or estimates of expected lead times or delays to be encountered as work moves through the shop; and estimates of the machining and setup time for each operation on each part.

The concern here is with developing a schedule for each component part and subassembly so that (a) all raw materials arrive on time, and (b) all parts and subassemblies arrive at the appropriate assembly or stock area in time to ensure that the final product will be ready for shipment on schedule. Short-term scheduling is usually accomplished by one of two basic approaches—capacity loading and loading to infinite capacity. I will discuss each of these approaches in turn.

CAPACITY LOADING . . .

This fundamental approach begins with the specification of capacity for the scheduling period. Usually, capacity loading involves stating the number of machines to be manned in each department or work center and the number of shifts to be worked. (At a later date, individual decisions on overtime and so on may change these capacities slightly, but a reasonable estimate is good enough to start.) In the process of capacity loading, component parts requirements are exploded from a bill of materials, and the due date for each part is determined by backdating from the master schedule's due date for the final product.

After a due date has been assigned for each part, standard times for the individual manufacturing operations on the components are scheduled (loaded) in the appropriate work centers, starting with the last operation and allowing for normal material movement and delays. As each job's machining and setup time is added to a particular work center's load, a check is made to ensure that the addition of that job does not cause the total load to exceed the capacity of the work center. If the capacity is exceeded, the job is moved to another time period. If no available capacity can be found within the time required to get the job done on time, either the due date must be changed or capacity adjustments must be made through subcontracting or overtime.

While this capacity loading approach is simple to describe, it is in fact quite difficult to implement. What about the important job that cannot find room because other less important jobs have been loaded ahead of it? How do you shift the loads around when capacity is exceeded? A point to keep in mind is that it is not necessarily the last job (the cause of the overload) which should be shifted to another week.

Several companies have developed imaginative approaches to capacity loading that deal with problems of this kind. One of the best programs reported is used by a large electronics company. Its computer program loads to actual work-center capacity by scheduling backward, but the person using the program can exert considerable control over how the schedules are developed. Rush jobs can be specially coded, and instructions can be varied from "use full move and wait times" to "use no move and wait times," or even to "use more than one machine where possible." The program develops a provisional timetable according to the rules given by th᠎ scheduler, and prints a brief report that shows the scheduler whether the job can be handled within the time period he originally specified.

However, if the job cannot be accommodated as desired, the scheduler has several alternative courses of action available. He can:

☐ Try another priority.

☐ Cut the lot size (i.e., break the job into two lots).

☐ Try an earlier start time (if tools, material, and so on are available).

☐ Negotiate a later delivery date.

☐ Allow the program to overload one or more work centers after agreeing with the manufacturing superintendent and the foreman on an overtime plan or other capacity adjustment to handle the overload.

. . . VS. INFINITE CAPACITY

The second common approach to short-term scheduling is a method whereby jobs are scheduled forward, beginning with the first operation at the earliest start date. Using standard move and delay times, load is accumulated as in capacity loading. The load is allowed to fall where it may, and no consideration is given to overloads that may develop. Such overloads are called to the attention of production planners, who attempt to adjust shop capacity to handle the work as scheduled or to rework the schedule to eliminate the overloads.

Loading to infinite capacity is definitely easier to program and implement than capacity loading schemes. There are other advantages, too. Infinite capacity loading focuses attention on bottlenecks and forces action when problems develop. Furthermore, scheduled manufacturing cycle times normally have less variance because the lead times used in developing the schedules never change. If actual manufacturing cycle times are to have low variance as well, however, the shop must have good procedures for adjusting capacity to handle overloads.

Capacity loading, on the other hand, usually presents the shop with a more level load and cuts down on the need for continual capacity adjustments. The price, however, is variance in the manufacturing cycle time or poorer delivery performance that will occasionally result from smoothing the peaks and valleys in demand. The feedback from capacity loading is better than that from infinite capacity schedules because the actual lead times accurately reflect what is likely to develop in the shop. This information on expected lead times can be passed upward to revise master schedules and other higher-level plans.

One problem with any loading approach is that unloading is a difficult task when plans are changed. When a customer cancels an order for a large machine, for example, all the individual loads contributed by the hundreds of piece parts already scheduled must be erased. This may leave idle capacity in several work centers, and questions then arise as to what to do with that capacity. A similar problem crops up when a customer changes the desired delivery date on a large order. These kinds of problems can be overcome only with great difficulty with manual systems, but the versatility of the computer makes possible the rapid readjustment of shop loads when changes are required.

A STATISTICAL VIEW

It is one thing to develop schedules, but quite another to run the shop so work will be accomplished according to schedule. I shall say more about this in the next section, dispatching and shop floor control, but for the time being let me state that the schedules resulting from the kinds of loading programs just described are usually not sufficient to determine how work will be done in the shop. This is so because of machine breakdowns, engineering changes, delivery promise changes, personnel absences, missing tooling, missing raw materials, and other roadblocks to following the schedule exactly as planned.

Thus the short-term schedule is at best a close approximation of what will transpire in the shop itself. This leads one to think about the level of detail required in short-term scheduling and to wonder whether rough, approximate procedures might be used to generate schedules, especially if production is carefully controlled on the shop floor.

Stanley Reiter, a former Purdue University economics professor now at Northwestern University, and I have developed a short-term scheduling program which takes a statistical view of the shop and attempts to ensure that promised delivery dates on new orders take into account the congestion the job is going to encounter as it works its way through the shop. The program was developed as part of a larger production planning and control system for a gear company whose scheduling problem differs somewhat from other problems I have described here in that virtually all work in the shop is for a specific customer order. Master scheduling to forecasts is not done. Instead, a promise date must be generated for each order accepted.

The program works from two basic data files: (1) estimated load by work center (about 200) and by week (six months ahead), and (2) estimated delay (waiting time) that a job will encounter in each work center for each week. The delays are calculated from both the load estimates and manpower (capacity) plans by mathematical formula. When a new order is received, the promise date is determined by (a) estimating the start

Exhibit IV. Information flows for short-term scheduling

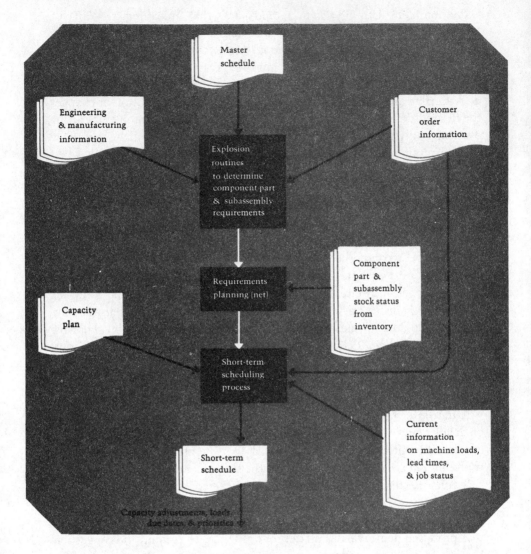

date for the job, and (b) adding the setup, machining, and delay times for each operation in the job. The delay estimates are taken from the computer file for the appropriate work center and week, and—as the job is scheduled —the setup and machine hours are added to the existing load already in the file.

Every week new delay estimates are calculated on the basis of updated load estimates. If an order is loaded and then subsequently canceled, no unloading is done. While this introduces known error into the system, there are probably other, unknown errors that are at least as important. This does not mean that accuracy is unimportant. Rather, my point is that a quick, approximate approach to setting promise dates is useful if the basic sentiments of the approach are in the right direction. To me, "in the right direction" means that a scheduling program lengthens delivery times when shop loads increase, and the output of the program gives management information for making capacity adjustments when necessary.

The delays generated by the program just described can provide management with a picture of where overloads are likely to develop. Thus management can take corrective action before the overload occurs. In fact, management can test the effect of adding capacity through overtime or extra shifts by recalculating the delays on the basis of proposed capacity additions in bottleneck work centers. Again—just so this point is not overlooked—general approximating methods may be adequate in some situations if the methods are properly designed and controlled, and if the shop is not constrained so tightly that it cannot respond to occasional errors in scheduling.

The general process of short-term scheduling is shown in *Exhibit IV*. While the information flows may appear to be similar to those shown in *Exhibit II*, the short-term scheduling process is based on considerably more detail than the master scheduling process and requires the handling of more supporting data. For example, the combining of master schedule information and customer order detail with engineering, manufacturing, and inventory information to yield data on net component parts requirements for short-term scheduling requires the processing of vast amounts of information. Although this supporting data processing task is large and complex, it should not draw management's eyes away from the main management task that is being supported—namely, the generation of a time schedule for the processing of orders in the shop to make efficient use of the company's capacity and to meet customer demands.

Dispatching and Shop Control

The scheduling and control of work actually on the shop floor is a complex and demanding task. In most large shops there are thousands, or even tens of thousands, of job orders in process at any given time. Thus there is not only the problem of limited capacity, but also the problem of what individual operation can be done next, due to sequence constraints and material, tool, and machine availability. Even though every job order in the shop may have a scheduled start and finish time, the particular sequence for the individual machine operations remains to be determined.

Many management problems are caused by a lack of up-to-date information on the status of jobs in the shop. Often even the location of a job is not known, let alone whether it is ahead of or behind schedule and what work remains to be done. In this section we shall see how a well-designed dispatching and shop floor control system can help to organize and rationalize the flow of work through the shop, and to ensure that the right jobs are being worked on at all times. We shall also see how timely reports can greatly assist management in the continuous decision-making process that is required to keep a shop going—that is, in controlling the level of in-process inventory, tracking down troublesome jobs, and spotting difficult situations before they develop.

IMPORTANCE OF TIMING

Dispatching is the shortest-term scheduling activity performed, because the scheduling takes place right in the shop where the decision has to be made on what job to do next. Some companies with good short-term scheduling or loading systems develop start dates for each individual operation to be performed on the job, and then dispatch on the basis of these scheduled start dates. In other words, when a machine becomes available, then, out of all the jobs waiting for it, the one with the earliest scheduled start time is chosen to be worked on next.

This approach works well if (a) the shop is able to follow the schedule with reasonable accuracy—that is, the jobs move through the shop without holdups for such things as missing material, tools, documents, or machine breakdowns; or if (b) the delay, move, processing, and setup times used to generate the schedule accurately reflect what is happening in the shop. Usually this is difficult, however, and the shop "drifts" off the short-term schedule between the time the schedule was generated and the time the job is actually run. This drift is caused by changes in the specification or timing of the job that may not have been rerun in the short-term schedule, the addition of last-minute rush work not included in the original schedule, and the previously cited random occurrences in the shop that prevent jobs from being run exactly according to the schedule.

To state it simply, time is the all-important ingredient in a production schedule. When timing of a schedule reflects the up-to-the-minute condition of the shop, materials flow smoothly through the shop, in-process work is completed and leaves the shipping dock at the right time, and machines are utilized efficiently.

Because of the vital importance of proper timing in the execution of work in the shop, dispatching has received considerable attention, and several companies have automated this function. All dispatching programs schedule work from a preplanned priority scheme that allows each job in queue for an available machine to be given a priority ranking relative to all other jobs competing for the same capacity.

The particular method for determining priority can vary from a simple

```
                              ORDER STATUS REPORT
                              MACHINE GROUP 62-01
                             MANUFACTURING DAY 212

   PRIORITY        PART      PREVIOUS   ARRIVAL    ORDER  PROCESSING  OPERATIONS  PROCESSING
                  NUMBER     LOCATION    TIME       QTY      TIME        LEFT      TIME LEFT

        (ORDERS IN STATION)

   HOT -3.8       324409     61-03      INSTA      212       2.3         03          8.6
   HOT  1.9       448305     60-06      INSTA      172       3.4         02         12.3
       -5.5       104961     72-08      INSTA       53       1.3         13        147.2
       -2.3       665128     61-11      INSTA       87       2.4         06         38.9
        1.2       401759     72-08      INSTA      200      12.1         00           .0

       (INCOMING ORDERS)

   HOT -9.2       489618     61-03       8-30      137       2.9         02         12.6
   HOT -1.6       393474     72-07       9-00       52       0.8         01          5.5
   HOT  0.3       506632     60-03       8-30      217      13.1         00           .0
       -2.1       170300     72-08      10-30       62       3.2         06         24.2
              463218        60-03       4-30       72                    09        126.
```

ranking by due date to complex rankings that consider not only the scheduled completion date, but also the calendar and processing time remaining, the time required for the next operation, future congestion likely to be encountered, priority codes imposed by management, and even the current inventory status of the part (see page 576 for examples of dispatching rules).

The use of any dynamic dispatching rule—that is, one in which priorities change with the passage of time or the completion of work—requires that up-to-date information be maintained to keep priorities current. This inevitably means that data on each job must be maintained in computer files. With current information on job status and priority available in machine-readable form, dispatchers or foremen can be provided with lists showing the current location and priority of all jobs in the shop. If these lists are sorted by work center, the man on the shop floor has not only a picture of all the work in each work-center queue, but also information that will enable him to make good decisions on which job to run next. Some companies are already going beyond supplying queue lists in particular work centers. I shall discuss two examples.

DAILY STATUS SYSTEM

A West Coast company which manufactures electronic systems has a dispatching system that captures up-to-the-minute information on job status and works ahead to predict what will happen during the next shift. Two daily reports are prepared. The first (simplified in *Exhibit* V) shows the jobs that are already in each work center at the beginning of the day and

Exhibit VI. Sample report of operations to be performed on "hot" jobs during the day

```
                         HOT ORDER REPORT
                        DEPARTMENT 62-00
                      MANUFACTURING DAY 212
       PART                    ARRIVAL  PREVIOUS ORDER PROCESSING OPERATIONS PROCESSING PRIORITY
       NUMBER    LOCATION      TIME     LOCATION  QTY    TIME       LEFT      TIME LEFT
  HOT  324409    62-01         INSTA    61-03    212    2.3         03        8.6      -3.8
                 68-02         8-30     62-01            6.5         02        2.1      -4.2
                 72-08         1-00     68-02            1.8         01         .3      -6.8
  HOT  432186    62-02         INSTA    68-03     57    1.2         06       13.4      -2.1
                 72-08         1-30     62-02            1.4         05       12.0      -6.3
  HOT  448305    67-01         INSTA    60-06    172    3.4         02        5.8       1.9
                 61-03         9-00     62-01            3.2         01        2.6      -0.2
                 72-02         2-30             .7             2.6         00        0.0      -3.6
```

the jobs which are expected to arrive during the day. Jobs classified as "hot" or "rush" are listed before regular jobs. Within these categories, jobs are listed by priority (minimum slack per remaining operation).

Knowing what orders he already has on hand and their relative priorities, and what jobs to expect throughout the day, the foreman can plan his work in an orderly fashion rather than simply react to a continuous stream of requests and demands from expediters, engineers, project managers, and other interested parties. As he plans his day, the foreman can sequence the work in terms of efficiently matching the capacity and skill of his work center to the demands and the priorities of the individual job orders.

The second daily report (simplified in *Exhibit* VI) shows the operations to be performed on "hot" jobs that the computer's dispatching program predicts will be completed during the day. With this "hot order report" in hand, personnel from production control can identify and locate orders that should be expedited, assess their actual versus planned progress throughout the day, and ensure that the high-priority work at the top of the queues moves as rapidly as possible.

In order to generate reports similar to those shown in *Exhibits* V and VI, a dispatching program must actually simulate the operation of the shop for one day, keeping track of what jobs are assigned to which machines, move times, queues, priorities, and so forth. This is necessary, since the program must predict not only which orders will arrive in a given work center, but also when during the day they will actually arrive.

JOB SEQUENCE SCHEDULE

The gear company that I mentioned earlier, in the section on short-term scheduling, also has an interesting dispatching system. Its program develops a schedule that specifies a detailed sequence of jobs by simulating the

Exhibit VII. Sample of schedule that specifies detailed sequence of jobs

```
                            SCHEDULE
                       WORK CENTER 1612
                          4/10/68
                                              PREVIOUS          NEXT
     PART     ORDER     START     FINISH PROCESSING  WORK CENTER    WORK CENTER
    NUMBER     QTY      TIME       TIME    TIME    + FINISH TIME   + START TIME
   ADH1722      53    W  7-40A   W  9-00A   1.33    2483 W  8-00A   3053 W  8-50A
   822185R     126    W 10-00A   W 11-00A   1.0     2514 M 10-30A   3024 TH 4-20P
   AV859       235    W 10-00P   W 11-40P   1.67    2482 W 10-30P   3031 F  3-10P
   51619Y      525    TH 5-10P   TH 9-40P   4.5     2632 W  9-20P   3053 F  8-20A
   ASF8231      27    F  1-50P   F  2-20P    .5     2483 F  9-30A   3023 F  4-00P
   5908          9    F  2-20P   F          4.33    24            40P
```

operation of the shop three days ahead, according to a minimum-slack dispatching rule. In most of the company's work centers, average setup times are used to develop the schedule, but in certain other work centers, where setup sequences are critically important (e.g., continuous heat treating furnaces), the program develops a schedule that takes into account the cost, in time, of going from one setup to another.

A simplified example of the output of this dispatching program is shown in *Exhibit* VII. Although the foreman can work directly from the schedule without having to sequence the jobs on the available machines, there may be times when he wishes to change the suggested work sequence. If he can obtain savings on setup time, or can better match man or machine capabilities to the available jobs by changing the suggested sequence, he is encouraged to do so.

The question is: How much will such a change affect other parts of the schedule for this job? To answer that question, the foreman is provided with information on where the job is coming from, when it is expected to be completed in the previous work center, where the job is going, and when it is expected to start at the next work center. With these data, the foreman can negotiate backward and forward along the job's route, if necessary, or make a change based on the information at hand that will not affect the scheduling in other work centers.

The sharp-eyed reader may have noted a seeming discrepancy in the first line of the sample schedule in *Exhibit* VII. The job is not only scheduled to start in work center 1612 before it finishes its previous operation in work center 2483, but it is scheduled to start the next operation before it finishes in work center 1612. This is the result of a "line scheduling" feature whereby the first pieces in the lot of a high-priority job are allowed to move ahead to the next operation before the last pieces in the lot are completed in the current operation. This feature requires no outside control and ensures that high-priority work will move through the shop quickly.

In conversations with production managers who have installed successful new production control systems, one big advantage is invariably mentioned: the ability to keep constant tabs on job location and status. The tighter schedules, better delivery performances, and more efficient uses of men and machines that result from such systems are acknowledged and appreciated, but the big breakthrough for most managers is the readily available current information on job location and status.

However, this information does not come at zero cost, and again a supporting system must be considered. Job location and status information is obtained in many companies through the use of remote data-collection devices on the shop floor. Data are entered into a remote device and transmitted to a central location, where they are usually punched into cards or paper tape which can then be read by a computer at frequent intervals to update the job information in the computer's files. While such collection devices speed the process of data acquisition, they are not necessarily essential in all applications. Many companies obtain job location and status information from handwritten cards or forms from the shop that are key punched before entering the computer.

PROFITABLE PAYOFFS

A well-designed dispatching system can:

□ Greatly reduce the amount of clerical work required to maintain current records.

□ Implement dynamic priorities which can be updated without laborious hand calculation, sorting, and refiling.

□ Improve the expediting function.

Nonetheless, the large dollar payoff often comes not from these advantages, but from other areas of activity on the shop floor. One important saving is the control of in-process inventory. Work in process consists largely of jobs in queues waiting for an available machine. These waiting lines are desirable for two reasons: (1) to provide a pool of work from which good setup sequences can be developed; and (2) to provide a cushion of work to prevent machine idleness. But, when the queues get too long, unnecessary investment in inventory is tied up, and the time required to get work through the shop rises.

A study at the New England plant of a large manufacturing company has shown that careful control of the amount of work in waiting lines can have a dramatic impact on overall shop performance. The analysts who conducted the study convinced the shop's management and work force that a backlog on paper is just as real as a backlog in iron on the shop floor. (Several authors have stressed the importance of this step.) Then, many jobs were removed from waiting lines in the shop and later were rereleased to the shop a short time ahead of their due date. In addition, all new work was released in tight relation to due date. This control of work releasing and the use of a shortest-processing-time dispatching rule resulted in a one-third reduction in work-in-process inventory levels. Moreover, manufacturing cycle times were cut in half, much more reliable delivery time performance was obtained, and less finished goods inventory was required to satisfy the customer demand.

Another New England company which uses critical ratios for dispatching decided to hold back on releasing all new orders until the ratio indicated that the job was behind schedule. This action forced priority work ahead of jobs that were already on the shop floor and which were ahead of schedule because of early releasing under the old system, or because of due date and engineering changes. Although, at first, it may seem unwise to hold job orders until they are behind schedule, the critical ratio priorities and the considerably reduced work-in-process inventories have enabled the company to follow and expedite jobs, and still maintain a satisfactory performance on deliveries.

Another area of big payoff as a result of improved dispatching is capacity control. Reliable information on the work and priority content of waiting lines in the shop, and the current location and status of individual jobs, can greatly improve management's ability to make short-term capacity adjustments. The control of overtime is perhaps the best example. One company president recently stated that the yearly cost of the computer required to implement a new production planning and control system in his company has been easily paid by the savings in cutting excess overtime.

Other capacity adjustments that can be made more efficiently with good location and job status information include moving a man from one work center to another, routing a job to an alternate work center for a given operation, and changing the sequence in which the various job operations are performed. All these alternatives are designed to balance the flow of work through the shop and to minimize the number of bottlenecks in work flow at machines where large backlogs have piled up.

We should have clearly in mind, however, that the short-term capacity adjustments under discussion here are the finest of the fine-tuning operations. Remember that initial capacity plans should be laid months, and even years, ahead of actual production, and that opportunities to update and revise those plans to fit actual conditions better should exist at several levels above the shop floor control level.

Viewed in this manner, short-term capacity adjustment becomes a management opportunity (a) to make small moves in reacting to occasional mishaps and requests for unusual service, and (b) to remedy, in some degree, errors in higher-level planning and scheduling. In other words, the

Exhibit VIII. Information flows in a production planning and control system

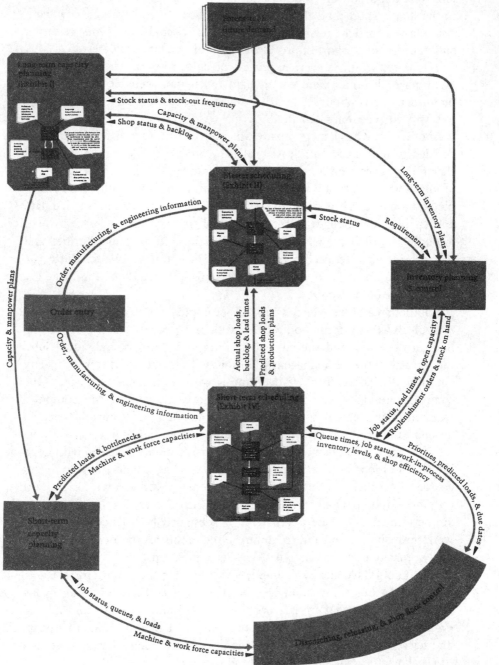

shop will have the flexibility to move a few important jobs quickly, but not enough leeway to overcome the major shortcomings in plans from higher levels.

The Integrated System

At the beginning of this article, I emphasized the goal of tying together the component parts of production planning and control systems. This is done in *Exhibit VIII*, which not only shows the various elements of a production planning and control system (and their relation to the enlarged parts previously illustrated in *Exhibits I, II, and IV*), but also highlights the major information flows that tie the parts together. In studying *Exhibit VIII*, keep in mind my early statement about high-level plans providing guidelines for lower-level planning and the importance of an upward flow of information to ensure that high-level plans are realistic.

Starting at the top of *Exhibit VIII*, long-range forecasts are transformed into capacity plans to guide master scheduling. I use the term "guide" in this instance to mean the setting of approximate limits within which master schedules can be developed. As an example, consider a company whose capacity plans involve an expansion of facilities for turning large work pieces, such as generator shafts or steel mill rolls, with a simultaneous contraction in the milling and heat treating of small forged parts:

□ Master scheduling would be expected to begin to supply a load for the new facilities and gradually build up that load to utilize the new equipment efficiently. At the same time, master scheduling would act as a filter to keep some of the milling and heat treating work out of the system.

If the demand for milling and heat treating job orders continued, strong action would be needed. Either subcontracting could be used, or marketing could be urged to discourage some orders, so as to keep actual production within the guidelines of the capacity plan. In the opposite direction, information describing growing backlogs, lengthening manufacturing cycle times, and increasing difficulty in maintaining adequate inventories could signal the need for more capacity.

Toward the bottom of *Exhibit VIII*, scheduling, dispatching, capacity adjusting, and inventory control are shown to be highly interrelated. Loads from short-term scheduling provide an advance warning of conditions that may develop in the shop, which releasing and short-term capacity planning may be able to heed. Dispatching information on the length, work content, and priority content of queues, and on the status of individual jobs, can signal situations where previous planning has not taken care of all bottlenecks and where immediate action is called for. In addition, dispatching information can be used in short-term scheduling to compare lead times, loads, and the shop's efficiency or actual performance against planned processing times or output expectations, and then to revise them as necessary.

SIGNIFICANT PROGRESS

At this point in the discussion, some managers may well be thinking: If a production planning and control system is so fine a management tool, then why doesn't every production operation use an integrated approach like this?

Actually, from what I can see, recent progress has been significant, and many companies have made great strides in production planning and control. Much of this progress has been due (a) to the development of computer hardware and software that can handle vast quantities of information rapidly and inexpensively, and (b) to practical developments on parts of the system, such as forecasting, capacity planning, and dispatching.

Despite the impressive progress in fixing up the parts, however, few companies have developed systems that tie the parts together as well as they might. There are roadblocks to overcome. The information requirements for a comprehensive system are a major problem. Data on routings, standards, tooling, materials, and engineering changes must be not only available, but also reliable and accurate. The production planning and control system exists in relationship to other systems—financial, accounting, engineering, quality control, material handling, purchasing—and the coordination and standardization required to tie into these other systems is substantial.

But, again based on what I see, progress in the design and implementation of systems that support production planning and control is proceeding faster than progress on production planning and control systems themselves. Thus, as the pressures mount for better planning and tighter control, the roadblocks to a good system are getting easier to overcome.

Conclusion

At the beginning of this article, I stated that the approaches I would discuss would relate to fabrication and assembly operations. Since this term encompasses a variety of organizations, some readers may have found significant differences between my charts and their own operations. Although there are differences in individual situations, each must deal with the basic problems of planning for capacity, such as setting delivery or due dates, developing and interpreting information on shop loads, scheduling the flow of work through the shop, and providing continuous, timely, and accurate reports for the comparison of planned and actual results.

My major point is that managers must look at decision making at all levels in seeking solutions to these problems. They must also recognize that good short-term performance results from an integrated and coherent set of decisions made over a long time span and not solely from more attention to short-term detail. The manager who translates general ideas and approaches into concrete specifications for his plant, and who then launches a well-planned and well-directed systems development effort, will be able to report such things as "on-time delivery performance up from 10% to 90%," "overtime savings which more than pay for the computer," "number of expediters decreased from nine to three," and "productivity jump of one third."

Here are representative examples of the many different dispatching rules currently in use. In each case the rule is used to select the particular job to run next out of a group of jobs waiting for an available machine. Each rule is accompanied by a brief statement about the properties of the schedules that will result from its use.

Simple rules

1. *Earliest Due Date*—Run the job with the earliest due date. Results in good due date performance.
2. *First Come, First Served*—Run the job which arrived in the waiting line first. Results in low variance of manufacturing cycle time.
3. *Shortest Processing Time*—Run the job which has the shortest setup plus machining time for the current work center. One of the best of the simple rules. Results in low in-process inventory, low average manufacturing cycle times, and good due date performance.

Combination rules

1. *Minimum Slack*—Slack equals calendar time remaining minus processing time remaining; or, slack equals due date minus present time minus setup and machining time for all remaining operations. Run the job with the least slack. Results in a very good due date performance.
2. *Critical Ratio*—The critical ratio for made-to-order work is a slack-type rule. Critical ratio equals due date minus present time, divided by number of days required to complete the job order. (The figure for days required to complete the job includes setup, machining, move, and wait times.)

The rule for parts manufactured for inventory is critical ratio equals available stock over reorder point quantity, divided by standard lead time remaining over total manufacturing lead time.

This ratio compares the rate at which stock on hand is being depleted with the rate at which total lead time is being used up. The inventory part ratio is consistent with the made-to-order part ratio; one of its great advantages is that it allows a relative ranking of both kinds of work in any queue.

31. Requirements Planning for Inventory Control
Philip H. Thurston

Specialists on inventory and scheduling and also line managers have succumbed to the lure of statistical tools in managing parts inventories. But, argues this author, the statistically based approach has shortcomings in a number of situations, and its glamour is wearing off. Requirements planning or a combination of the two can lead to substantial savings.

The phrases "safety stock," "reorder point," and "economic order quantity" are commonplace in the management of parts inventories at manufacturing companies. These terms signify that inventory is being controlled on a statistical basis. Certainly, statistics have important applications in inventory management, but during the past two decades specialists on inventory and scheduling and line managers alike have gone overboard—incurring considerable costs—in the excessive use of statistically based tools. An alternate approach called "requirements planning" can, in a number of manufacturing situations, make very substantial savings.

Basically, requirements planning sets aside the "averaging process" of statistics in managing inventory and substitutes a specific enumeration of what parts to place in inventory and when. I shall describe how this is done and offer a more complete definition of requirements planning a little further on. But first, since statistically based tools are so commonly used, let us consider, using an example, what their shortcomings are in a significant number of situations.

My example is that of a company manufacturing machine tools, which had a precise schedule of what machines were to be assembled over the ensuing 15-month period by quantities and weeks. This schedule could be translated, by using bills of material and lead times, into just what parts had to be completed in the factory or purchased in specific quantities and by specific dates. Furthermore, the marketing personnel agreed with the manufacturing personnel on the schedule. Thus uncertainty about what parts to manufacture and purchase for assembly was eliminated.

But, in using the conventional statistical approach to inventory man-

AUTHOR'S NOTE: I acknowledge with thanks the contributions to this article of Robert T. Lund, of the Harvard Business School.

Exhibit I. Actual stock level for one part using statistical approach

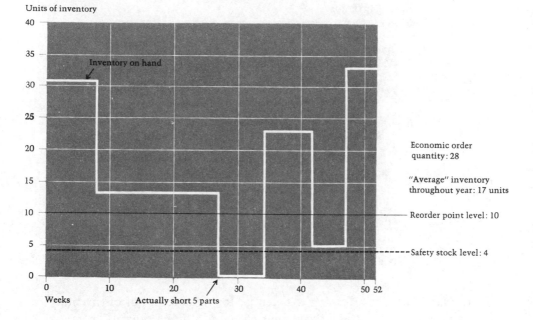

Units of inventory

Economic order
quantity: 28

"Average" inventory
throughout year: 17 units

Reorder point level: 10

Safety stock level: 4

Weeks

Actually short 5 parts

agement, what did the company's production control system do? It set safety stocks for parts at four weeks' historical average usage, presumably to allow for variations between actual and average usage rates; it set reorder points to cover safety stocks and to allow for average usage during replenishment lead time; and it established economic order quantities based on historical usage rates.

Implicit in this company's system were the assumptions that (a) the specific demand for parts in any week was unknown, (b) the forces which created the demand in one week could not be distinguished from the forces creating demand in other weeks, and (c) the demand for one part was not tied in a predictable fashion to the demand for other parts. If true, these assumptions would have justified the statistical approach used. The fact is that none of these assumptions was valid; there was a precise schedule of what to manufacture for the following 15 months.

"Statistics" Disadvantages

A little reflection—aided by specific numbers—shows the shortcomings of the *statistical* approach in situations such as in the foregoing example. If lots of, say, 18 milling machines each are scheduled to start assembly in the 8th, 27th, and 42nd weeks of the year, only 18 complete sets of parts and subassemblies are needed at the beginning of each of these weeks. That is all. No stocks are needed for assembly in any of the other 49 weeks of

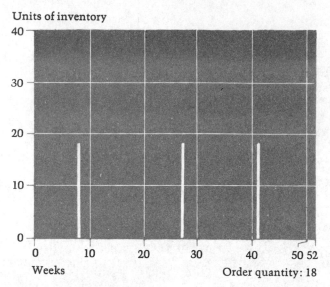

the year. This fact represents a potential for tighter control of inventory and for more purposeful commitment of manufacturing capacity than any statistical system makes possible. Under the conventional approach of using the statistical tools of economic order quantity and reorder point, the stock level for one milling machine part looked like that shown in *Exhibit I*.

Conversely, by working from the 15-month schedule, the inventory of the part could have been greatly reduced. The part *requirements* for the lots of 18 milling machines could be *planned* (hence the name *requirements planning*) to enter inventory just before their need. And the inventory of the part depicted in *Exhibit I* could have approached the pattern illustrated in *Exhibit II*.

Note that under the statistically based system (*Exhibit I*) there was a "stockout." Five parts had to be expedited, delaying assembly. And note particularly that it was not faulty operations within the system that led to the stockout, but the design of the system itself. Further, the average weekly inventory throughout the year was 17—an inventory of parts which was powerless to prevent the stockout. In contrast, the inventory shown in *Exhibit II* can be seen as nearly zero, on an average weekly basis, within a system potentially free of stockouts.

"Requirements" Advantages

It is time now for a more complete definition of *requirements planning*. It covers materials and parts which are not end products themselves, but are fabricated and assembled to become major assemblies and end products.

Requirements planning is the process of working backward from the scheduled completion dates of end products or major assemblies to determine the dates and quantities when the various component parts and materials are to be ordered. Each subassembly level and each part is considered in terms of lead time and scrap expected. The result is a schedule that puts each part or subassembly into stock shortly ahead of the need for that item in the next higher order of assembly.

This approach may seem very logical. Indeed, it is. Requirements planning has been used for more than 40 years by a manufacturer of large electrical motors. Each motor is manufactured to order. The customer and manufacturer agree on the motor specifications and the delivery date, setting the latter by gross yardsticks of factory load. Then the production control department calculates backward from the delivery date to assign the specific requirements for manufactured components to the various factory departments. This takes into consideration lead times and previously assigned work loads, and combines similar parts needed at about the same time. Thus every part is planned and timed for a specific known requirement.

Whereas this manufacturer of electrical motors works from specific, known customers' orders, some manufacturers start with forecasts of demand for *major assemblies*. In the automobile industry, for example, it is virtually impossible to predict the sales of specific end products. The choices given to customers are too numerous. But it is possible to forecast the demand for major assemblies such as a six-cylinder motor.

Other manufacturers start with forecasts of demand for *end products* and work backward from such estimates in requirements planning. A manufacturer of industrial hand tools uses this approach. The company manufactures in anticipation of orders; if its tools are not available on the distributors' shelves, sales are lost. Accordingly, the manufacturer projects sales on a statistical basis, modifies this projection by judgment, and uses this estimate of future demand to decide when lots of each of the hand tools will be assembled. The resulting assembling schedule, showing quantities and dates, is further broken down into the required components to be manufactured with suitable lead times. Thus the original statistical projection becomes the basis for requirements planning.

Earlier, I said that requirements planning is logical; however, this is not the same as saying it is easy. The approach depends on a high order of accuracy in engineering bills of material, in inventory records, in routing and leadtime information, in records of sales and purchase commitments, and in the factory load schedule. Some companies do not appreciate the value of discipline and accuracy in these records. Perhaps it is just as well when such a company controls inventory and manufacturing on a part-by-part basis (using reorder points and lot sizes). Lack of record discipline leads to less trouble there. And the book of accounts at the company with poor control never specifically records two types of hidden but quite substantial costs: those of basing decisions on poor records and those of using a less efficient system for inventory and production control.

Return now, if you will, to the case of the manufacturer of machine tools I described in the example at the outset of this article. If requirements planning is adopted there, the calculations of both the reorder point and the economic order quantity will continue to have some relevance—the reorder point in allowing for uncertainty in demand for repair parts; and the economic order quantity in deciding if some parts should be made in multiples of 18 units.

Reorder point and economic order quantity calculations may also be used for the large number of low-cost parts utilized broadly in the manufacture of many items—e.g., inexpensive hardware and cheap stamped parts—designated "C" in an A-B-C classification of parts. Far outnumbering the expensive items, the "C" items can be stocked more liberally with relatively little investment and controlled by inexpensive means. The tighter control of requirements planning, incurring somewhat greater paper-work costs, is applied to the fewer, more expensive components.

Three men—Joseph A. Orlicky, George W. Plossl, and Oliver W. Wight—who have done much to publicize and help companies with requirements planning have combined their ideas in a single publication entitled *Material Requirements Planning Systems*.[1] In his section of the publication, Orlicky contrasts a statistically based system with requirements planning:

"Order Point is part-based, whereas Requirements Planning is [end] product-oriented. Order Point utilizes data on the historical behavior of a part, while Requirements Planning ignores history and instead works with data on the relationship of components (the bill of material) that make up a product. Order Point looks at the past. Requirements Planning looks toward the future (as defined by a manufacturing master schedule)."

In the same publication, Orlicky also gives his evaluation of requirements planning by calling it "Cinderella's bright prospects for the future."

Critical Indictments

Requirements planning is basically not new. The manufacturer of motors cited earlier and others have used this approach for years. Using various designations for their systems, manufacturers had relied on detailed enumerations of parts to be manufactured and purchased long before statistical approaches to inventory management became widely known.

1. Reproduced by International Business Machines Corporation, Data Processing Division, in publication number G320-1170-0.

Why, then, was the enumeration approach seemingly lost at some companies? What happened? Simply this: the statistical approaches were and still are oversold. Who oversold? Who are the villains? Are they the specialists who sharpen their analytical tools and then point them at what they judge to be appropriate targets?

For working from known statistical tools rather than from understood problems, the specialists are greatly at fault. But the real villains are the line managers who abdicate their responsibilities, not only of understanding the real nature of their scheduling and inventory problems, but also of assessing fully the implications of analytical tools proposed by the specialists.

The (erroneous) substitution of statistically based tools for requirements planning received a big boost from the sheer difficulty that line managers encountered in breaking out and keeping track of thousands of required parts. This necessitated a strong commitment and a high order of information-processing discipline to effectively operate requirements planning systems which used manual or punched card data processing. But for more than a decade now the computer, well suited for the job, has been available to handle the details of requirements planning. The cost is down; the accuracy and speed are up.

Now that I have painted *all* specialists on inventory and scheduling, as well as *all* line managers, with a critical brush, I hasten to qualify these indictments. Some line managers to my knowledge have accurately and steadfastly discriminated between those applications where statistics are useful and those where the statistical approach is not. Likewise, some specialists have not succumbed to the glamorous, faddish, mystical, broad-front shift to statistics.

For instance, at a company manufacturing electrical generating equipment, the line supervisors and specialists jointly installed one of the early computers to improve requirements planning. The former manual system hectographed, from the bills of material and manufacturing planning, thousands of sets of 3x5 shop paper work used in loading the factory with specific parts and assemblies for planned final products. Important parts of this system were computerized. One supervisor described the change in this way:

"Under the manual system, we could load the shop just once with the parts required for each new order. Thereafter, it was too difficult to reschedule a whole job or any major part of a job. We simply had too many pieces of paper. This meant that we sometimes used machining capacity for parts which the passage of time had made less important than other parts. Then we put all our requirements on computer tapes. We could change priorities, our accuracy went up, and we could better pinpoint discrepancies between load and capacity."

It is not within the scope of this Management Memo to cover the planning of factory capacity and load. Suffice it to say that the adoption of requirements planning can be coupled to advantage with improved planning in shop loading.

The glamour of statistics is wearing off just as the glamour of the computer has. We understand both better. And I predict an increasing willingness (a) to chuck the statistical approach in those cases where the requirements planning approach is better suited, or (b) to employ a tailored combination of the two.

32. Sweeping Changes in Distribution

J. L. Heskett

We are at the end of a significant era of technological change in transportation, warehousing, inventory control, and order processing. Now a new era is evolving —one that will be marked by institutional rather than technological change. Greater gains are now possible through such change, in part resulting from the realization of promises made but unfulfilled by technology. This article discusses the nature of institutional change and suggests methods of achieving inter-organizational solutions which will be central to continued improvement of productivity in logistics.

Near the conclusion of World War II, the wartime T-2 tanker, with a rating of 15,600 tons, was thought by many to be too large for expected peacetime petroleum needs and also too large to be handled safely in most ports. Yet just 20 years later, marine architects were designing ships 20 times larger than the T-2, ships exceeding 300,000 deadweight tons which have since been built and now sail the world's oceans.

Only 25 years ago, a respectably advanced rate at which to handle bulk materials was about 500 tons per hour. Recently, a number of installations have been built capable of handling bulk materials at 40 times that rate.

Just a generation ago, there were three basic alternatives for transporting most commodities: rail, water, and truck. Since then, we have witnessed a vast increase in opportunities for transporting commodities other than petroleum by pipeline. Airfreight has become a viable alternative for many shippers. And the development of unitized freight handling and co-ordinated methods of transporting freight has produced a number of new modal combinations, including piggyback and trailers and containers on ships which, for all practical purposes, did not exist 20 years ago.

Since the inauguration of modern-day containerized service, ocean transportation to and from the United States has seen an enormous growth of containerized freight in the general cargo sector. In the North Atlantic trade, it is estimated that 60% of all containerizable freight now moves in containers.

As late as 1950, the Interstate Highway System, although conceived, had yet to be financed for construction.

The computer, whose rapid development was another by-product of World War II, has made possible only within the past 15 years the application of techniques and managerial models so vital to the successful management of logistics activities.

Clearly, the generation just ended has produced remarkable technological advances in transportation, materials handling, and information processing.

Partly in response to technological change, industrial, commercial, and governmental organizations have reorganized to improve the management of logistics activities and to make intelligent use of the newly available technology. Increased breadth, in terms of both the backgrounds of individuals attracted to the field and the scope of responsibilities which they have been given, has facilitated a trend toward the purchase of carrier services, physical facilities, and logistics equipment as elements in a broader system of related activities.

In this sense, the past decade can fairly be termed an era of organizational as well as technological change in logistics.

Toward Institutional Change

If we have witnessed significant technological and organizational change in the recent past, what does the foreseeable future hold? What are the implications of the fact that the U.S. population, and to some degree the size of the market that it represents, appears to be leveling out as emphasis on birth control increases? What will be the effect if pressures for new products and product individuality continue?

Similarly, what types of responses will be required by the growing congestion in city centers and the continuing dispersion and rapid growth of suburban markets? Will new technology continue to provide the primary means with which to deal with logistics problems arising from all these and other trends?

There are signs which suggest that the answer to my last question is *no*. While technological and organizational change will, of course, continue, major challenges will be met primarily by institutional change involving the spatial reordering of functions and facilities within an organization and among cooperating organizations.

This represents a logical progression in logistics from emphasis on decision making based on *internal cost analyses* to emphasis on *internal profit analyses* and on *interorganizational cost and profit analyses* of the sort suggested in *Exhibit I.*

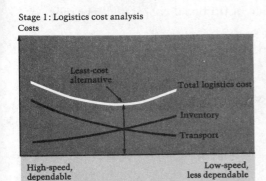
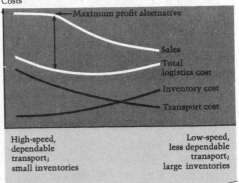
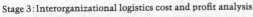

Exhibit I. Stages in the scope of analyses for logistics decision making

Stage 1: Logistics cost analysis

Costs

Least-cost alternative

Total logistics cost

Inventory

Transport

High-speed, dependable transport; small inventories

Low-speed, less dependable transport; large inventories

Range of logistics configurations, Supplier A

Stage 2: Logistics profit analysis

Costs

Maximum profit alternative

Sales

Total logistics cost

Inventory cost

Transport cost

High-speed, dependable transport; small inventories

Low-speed, less dependable transport; large inventories

Range of logistics configurations, Supplier A

Stage 3: Interorganizational logistics cost and profit analysis

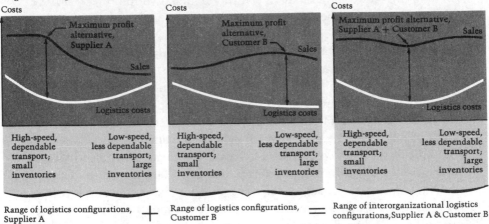

Costs

Maximum profit alternative, Supplier A

Sales

Logistics costs

High-speed, dependable transport; small inventories

Low-speed, less dependable transport; large inventories

Range of logistics configurations, Supplier A

Costs

Maximum profit alternative, Customer B

Sales

Logistics costs

High-speed, dependable transport; small inventories

Low-speed, less dependable transport; large inventories

Range of logistics configurations, Customer B

Costs

Maximum profit alternative, Supplier A + Customer B

Sales

Logistics costs

High-speed, dependable transport; small inventories

Low-speed, less dependable transport; large inventories

Range of interorganizational logistics configurations, Supplier A & Customer B

FACTORS IN SHIFT OF EMPHASIS

We will turn our interest during the foreseeable future to institutional (as opposed to technological) change, for a variety of reasons. Included among these are the seven possibilities that:

1. There are physical constraints on certain methods of transportation and materials handling, as well as restrictive public attitudes toward the further technological development of others.

2. Certain technological developments appear to be "topping out," at least for the time being.

3. Existing technologies, to an increasing extent, require for their success a rationalization of activity which can be brought about largely through institutional cooperation and new types of institutions.

4. Technological advances have made institutional cooperation not only possible, but in some cases necessary.

5. There are changing attitudes toward interorganizational coordination among individuals in business as well as government.

6. Continued emphasis on logistics management will yield information necessary to justify institutional change.

7. Perhaps of greatest importance, the economic benefits from institutional coordination and change will far exceed any that foreseeable technological developments can offer.

I shall consider each of these factors in the shift of emphasis to institutional change in the course of this article.

1. Constraints on technology: Certain transportation modes, such as rail and highway, have natural constraints imposed on them by the existing physical facilities. The height of a rail car can be increased to the point where any further increase would require massive expenditures for greater clearances at bridges, tunnels, and underpass or overpass intersections that have replaced grade-level railroad crossings.

Truckers now speak in terms of a 6-inch increase in the width of a vehicle instead of a 10-foot increase in length, which was more feasible when highway carriers were operating with 27- and 30-foot trailers. And they will have difficulty getting even that small increase in width.

Public attitude now comprises a growing constraint on the further development of other transportation technologies. The refusal to support the development of the supersonic transport, however temporary a victory for such forces it may represent, was an important indicator. It may be significantly more difficult in the future to obtain funds for the development of an ecologically and economically uncertain device such as the SST than for, say, an expanded system of bicycle paths for urban commuters.

When we throw in the growing opposition to supertankers and the fear of the potential disasters they could create, and the issues and arguments over possible ecological impacts of pipelines in the tundra of the Far North, we have a clear indication that technology in the late 1970's and 1980's may be in for close scrutiny.

2. Temporary "topping out": Several years ago, it was popular to look ahead to the "era of the 747," the great hope of airfreight advocates. These "boxcars of the sky" were to eliminate the economic barriers to the use of airfreight. Closer analysis at the time could have shown that the most significant development, the introduction of the DC-8-63F airplane, already had occurred. Furthermore, few anticipated the problems of assembling a sufficient volume of freight in one place at one time to meet the 747's vastly greater requirements for efficient operation. Finally, with their attention diverted to developments in the sky, most airfreight advocates paid too little heed to the significant improvements needed in the problem area of handling airfreight on the ground.

The same marine architects who produced the 300,000-ton ship designs now tell us that, although designs of 1,000,000 tons are possible, the economics of building and operating such ships quite likely precludes their construction in the foreseeable future, public attitude aside. Certain diseconomies of scale begin to assert themselves.

While ingenious devices for introducing automation in the warehouse have been developed in recent years, the promise of automated warehousing is yet to be realized. In fact, the requirements which it imposes on freight flow for effective utilization may in many cases be achieved only through the type of institutional cooperation I shall discuss later.

We now have the computers and the concepts to achieve significant savings through effective control of inventories. More important, economical computer and communication capacity will make possible the use of models offering more individual attention to product-line items, inventory locations, and customers. But the gains which improved technology in this area could make possible are small compared with the improvements in operations that could be achieved through proper application of currently available machines and methods.

3. *Rationalization of activity*: Typified by improved allocation of effort and responsibility among cooperating and even competing institutions, rationalization of activity has been required by the introduction of certain technologies. Conversely, technological advances have so badly outstripped institutional changes that the absence of the latter now imposes significant constraints on the former.

Perhaps the best example of this is the introduction of containerization on a wholesale basis in North Atlantic shipping several years ago.

Prospective container-ship operators planned for massive capital investment in fast, expensive ships, and the containers they would carry. Even the most forward-looking ship operators, however, did not provide for the numbers of containers which would ultimately be required for the service. They did not properly anticipate the problems of controlling container usage in the hinterlands surrounding the ports which they would serve. And they paid dearly for their traditional lack of interest in, and institutional separation from, freight before it arrived and after it left the docks.

In response to this problem, operators are making extensive efforts to: (a) acquire freight-forwarding, trucking, and other organizations which control freight in the hinterlands; (b) seek out arrangements under which containers can be jointly owned; (c) collect and transmit information in such a way that more effective control can be maintained over container usage.

4. Necessity for institutional cooperation: We have already noted that effective utilization of the 747 jetliner requires the assembly of large quantities of freight at a given place and time for shipment to a common destination. It is quite possible that, until airfreight volume increases significantly on a general front, self-organized groups of shippers with common origins and destinations may offer the best potential for providing this kind of volume.

In view of current computer capabilities and concepts, perhaps the most acute need in inventory control activities has been for more accurate data on which to base forecasts of future demand. As we have seen, the data have always existed. They needed to be collected and transmitted in a timely way. This has led to the establishment of direct lines of communications between customers and suppliers.

Production technologies have made possible smaller, lighter products that perform jobs better than their larger, heavier predecessors. At the same time, improvements in our intercity transportation systems have made it easier and less expensive to transport larger quantities of these smaller products, at least to the outskirts of large metropolitan areas.

Yet, in a growing number of cities, we have congestion and chaos.

This is clearly a case in which technology has contributed to a problem that will be solved either by more technological development, perhaps in the form of subterranean freight-access routes, or by institutional cooperation to create more efficient freight flows.

5. Changing attitudes: Many forms of organizational coordination not only are legal, but are becoming more and more attractive as problem-solving means to businessmen and government officials alike. The growing interest in coordinating inbound freight movements to congested city centers is just one example of a response by government and industry leaders to a difficult problem. This has led to the organization of the first symposium in this country to explore approaches to the problem of urban freight movements.[1]

Efforts in other countries are more advanced. For example, a recent study of freight movements into Utrecht, Holland, disclosed that the consolidation and systematic delivery of certain types of freight moving typically in small shipments could reduce the number of delivery vehicles in the city center from over 600 to 6.

1. Results of this symposium were reported in *Urban Commodity Flow*, Special Report 120 (Washington, D.C., Highway Research Board, National Academy of Sciences, 1971).

The Supermarket Institute has supported investigation into the feasibility of consolidated distribution facilities which might be operated as a joint venture by competing grocery product manufacturers and chain food-store organizations utilizing the same regional distribution centers. Essentially, such facilities would enable manufacturers and retailers to eliminate duplicated warehouse space.

In commenting on the concept of consolidated distribution facilities, the president of a large retail food chain recently remarked that "the idea may not be so farfetched, and it might have advantages to both segments of the industry." Of course, the concept will have arrived when a manufacturer or a store organization closes all or a part of its own warehouse facility to take advantage of a consolidated distribution service.

6. *Continued organizational development*: In the past 15 years there has been a rebirth in the concern for coordinated management of transportation, warehousing, materials handling, inventory-control, order-processing, and procurement activities. Evidence for this can be found in the rapidly increasing number of job titles like Physical Distribution Manager, Materials Manager, and Manager of Logistics, particularly in larger corporations. Further, the growth in membership in organizations such as the 10-year-old National Council of Physical Distribution Management (NCPD) and the even younger Society of Logistics Engineers (SOLE) has mushroomed.

Explanations for this concern and interest range from the competitive advantage that the effective management of logistics activities provides to organizational "me-too" faddism in certain industries. But an analysis of the roster of the NCPD suggests that the base of membership has spread from a few large companies in different industries to many more organizations in those same industries and then to other industries as well. Included among these are grocery and chemical product manufacturers, and manufacturers and distributors of products requiring extensive parts distribution activities. Other industries in which substantial costs of logistics, compared with sales, must be balanced against rigorous demands for customer service will see organizational change and emphasis on logistics.

As a further development in this area, managements will devote more attention to, and change the nature of, responsibility for coordinated product flow. For example, expansions in product lines without commensurate increases in sales produce higher inventory carrying costs as a percentage of sales.

As a result, in order to maintain a given level of customer service, retailers and wholesalers are limiting their speculative risk by reducing stocks of any one item (or by investing a commensurate amount of money in inventory for a broader product line) while at the same time expecting, and in fact depending on, manufacturers making speedy responses to their orders. This customer expectation, stated in the form of a willingness to substitute one manufacturer's product for another's in the event of the latter's inability to meet the customer's demands, in effect raises the incentive for speculation by manufacturers.

Thus caught in a squeeze between broader product lines and increasing demands for faster service from channel institutions, a number of manufacturers have responded by holding larger quantities of stock in semifinished form closer to markets, typically in distribution centers. There they can be cut, assembled, or packaged to order, thus postponing the company's commitment to specific stock-keeping unit locations until the last possible moment while reducing speculation (measured in terms of the elapsed time between customer order and delivery) for the customer.

To an increasing degree, logistics management will involve the operation of light manufacturing as well as distribution facilities. Perhaps the automobile assembly plant offers the most extreme example of this phenomenon. It is the closest thing to a distribution center in the channel of distribution for automobiles produced in the United States; it also houses light manufacturing activities. Because of the complexity of the latter, however, these plants typically fall under the responsibility of production management.

However, in other industries with less complex field requirements—such as the cutting to order of plate glass, paper products, lumber, and so on, and the packaging to order of common commodities—light manufacturing in the field will to an increasing extent fall within the purview of those concerned with logistics.

7. *Increased economic benefits*: Technological change can enable a company in a channel of distribution to perform its functions more efficiently. Typically, institutional change can eliminate the cost of performing a function by shifting the function to another point in the channel, where it can be integrated into other activities. Only occasionally, as with momentous developments such as containerization, can technology accomplish as much. And even then, it can do this only with the institutional change necessary to implement its introduction and growth.

Institutional Responses

Basic functions performed in a channel of distribution, such as selling, buying, storing, transporting, financing, providing information, and others, can only be shifted, not eliminated. They must be performed by some institution at some point in a channel. Distribution opportunities can be pinpointed by identifying the basic functions which can be performed most effectively by each institution in the channel, and the types of institutional change needed to accommodate efficient product flow.

The types of institutional change called for include at least four, arrayed in terms of their organizational impact on companies in a channel of distribution:

1. The coordination of policies and practices to enable cooperating channel members to perform their existing functions more effectively.

2. The shift of functions and responsibilities from one institution to another in a channel.

3. The creation of joint-venture or third-party institutions to eliminate duplication of the performance of functions in such channels.

4. The vertical integration of channel functions which are currently performed by different organizations.

It may be useful to take a closer look at each of these four types of institutional change prompted by the forces I have discussed.

1. COORDINATION OF PRACTICES

The unitized handling of products by means of such devices as pallets is one example of a technological development that has had a profound effect on interorganizational coordination. In order to reap the maximum benefits of palletization, buyers and sellers have to coordinate their materials handling systems to make use of the same size pallet, or at least pallet sizes with modular compatibility.

Thus industry standards for pallet sizes have been established for the shipment of such things as tin cans and paper products. Where standards have not been established, certain wholesalers have adapted their materials handling systems to conform with those of a dominant supplier. Companies electing not to abide by such standards do so at a price which is reflected in increased costs for handling goods.

2. SHIFTING OF RESPONSIBILITIES

A large distributor of personal care and houseware products that employed a network of direct sales personnel desired recently to gain greater control over product delivery to its distributors without actually going into the trucking business. It offered truckers an interesting proposition: a guaranteed, high profit on their investment in return for the full authority to schedule and control their trucks, reductions of up to 40% in existing charges, and access to the truckers' books to verify profit levels.

This case suggests the tremendous potential benefits made possible by a shift of functions between organizations.

A shift of stock-keeping responsibility from inventory-conscious retailers to wholesalers and manufacturers has taken place in recent years. This has resulted in part from the desire of retailers to reduce speculation and unsalable stocks in an age of expanding product lines as well as a realization that warehousing and materials handling costs may be significantly lower per unit for manufacturers and wholesalers than for their retailer customers.

In this case, the shift of responsibility for the performance of these functions in the channel of distribution is a logical result of interorganizational analysis and management.

3. THIRD-PARTY ARRANGEMENTS . . .

Cooperative interorganizational approaches in the form of joint ventures or third parties can provide the objectivity and "arm's length" management often needed when large, proud organizations wish to create a product or service requiring inputs from several participating companies. They are particularly attractive in a field that has been typified by fragmented, duplicated services—logistics.

. . . *in distribution utilities*: We are now seeing joint ventures and third-party arrangements used in the creation of so-called distribution utilities—companies that are capable of providing a complete range of warehousing, transportation, order-processing, and inventory-control services to shipper customers. A distribution utility contracts with a small to medium-sized manufacturer or a division of a larger company to remove finished stock from the end of the latter's production line and make it available for sale—when, where, and in the quantities desired—with some pre-agreed-on level of customer service. This allows the manufacturer's marketing organization to concentrate on selling.

The distribution utility, to the extent that it takes possession of a product without taking title to it, is the converse of what, in common marketing parlance, is termed a broker—one who buys and sells goods without ever taking possession of them.

However, substantial resources are required to (a) construct or acquire a network of distribution centers (warehouses), (b) support the design and installation of extensive communication and information-processing facilities, and (c) create an organization in which naturally skeptical manufacturer-customers can have confidence. The joint venture provides a convenient means of assembling such resources.

. . . *in consolidated regional centers*: The movement of carload quantities of stocks directly from the production lines of competing manufacturers into

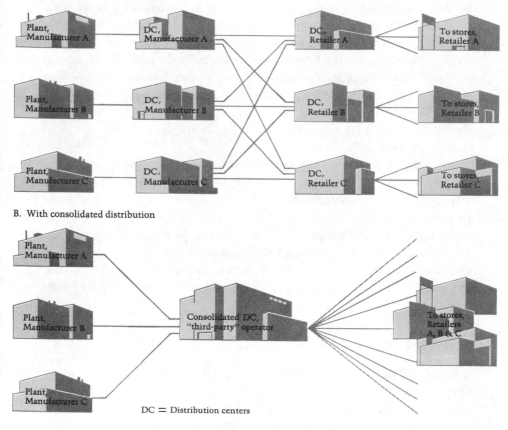

Exhibit II. *Impact of consolidated distribution on product flow to regional markets*

A. Without consolidated distribution

B. With consolidated distribution

DC = Distribution centers

common regional distribution centers for consolidated delivery direct to retail stores has been under discussion for some time, particularly in the grocery products industry. Until now, objections regarding loss of control over the product, possible disclosure of competitive information, and the elimination of an area of potential competitive advantage have overruled the economic benefits of eliminating the manufacturer-operated and the retailer-operated distribution center as shown in *Exhibit II*. But consolidated distribution of this type is now a reality.

The concept has been recently implemented in Canada with the creation of a distribution center in Vancouver, shared jointly by leading manufacturers and their chain-store customers. The success of this experiment, conducted by a task force of the Canadian Grocery Manufacturers Association, which reports that it has reduced the cost of dry grocery distribution by at least 10%, has led to its rapid expansion to two other provinces of Canada.

. . . *in central cooperative facilities*: The benefits of consolidating out-
bound freight can usually be enjoyed by a well-managed, medium-sized or
large manufacturer. However, companies typically receiving small shipments from many sources have found that they must establish cooperative
arrangements to enjoy similar benefits.

Thus far, such arrangements have been confined to the formation of
shippers' cooperatives for the consolidation of merchandise purchased by
several companies for delivery to the same destination (a metropolitan
area). Transportation cost savings, in the form of pro rata rebates, from
the replacement of small package shipments by carload and truckload
shipments have been remarkable.

Now, at the urging of city officials, these same companies are beginning to explore the creation of consolidated storage and merchandise-
processing facilities, located in low-cost suburban areas, as well as the
coordination of delivery to retail store sites.

An unpublished feasibility study in which I participated several years
ago indicated that central distribution facilities could be operated at a
satisfactory profit by a third party at a cost to retailer customers of only
80% of their current costs of receiving, processing, and delivering such
goods themselves.

4. VERTICAL INTEGRATIONS

The possibilities I have discussed thus far are interorganizational alternatives to the vertical integration of logistics operations in a channel of distribution by one powerful channel member through the merger with, or
acquisition of, companies with which it deals.

Vertical integration in logistics flourished during the late 1960's as industrial manufacturers began acquiring companies offering complementary
services, such as trucking and warehousing. Interestingly, transportation
companies were not leaders in this trend, possibly because of the Interstate
Commerce Commission's historic tendency to impose stringent controls
on the acquisition of companies offering competing modes of service. Indicators point to more active participation by transport and other companies in ventures involving the vertical integration of logistics services.

However, the rate at which this takes place will depend, among other
things, on (a) the level of pressure exerted on the ICC to relax its control,
(b) the rate at which legal means, such as financial holding companies, are
found for accomplishing vertical integration, and (c) the level of prosperity
in the logistics industries themselves. In the latter regard, adversity may
help rather than hinder the trend.

Implementation Approaches

Perhaps the three most important factors in implementing creative approaches to interorganizational problems and institutional change in logistics are management practices, labor attitudes, and regulatory policies.

MANAGEMENT PRACTICES

Clearly, individuals and companies that can adopt the attitudes and practices necessary to foster creative approaches to interorganizational problems will have an edge on their competitors. What are these attitudes and practices? Early research in the field of interorganizational management has suggested some.[2]

Companies likely to be recognized as leaders during an era of institutional change and interorganizational problem solving will be characterized by:

□ A *tendency to seek what bargaining theorists have termed "nonzero-sum results from negotiations."*

Essentially, a nonzero-sum result is one which reduces the total cost of the negotiating organizations regardless of how they divide the resulting benefits. Nonzero-sum results can be achieved only through a basic change in procedure, such as the design of quantity discounts to reflect efficient handling and shipping or the implementation of incentives to encourage the faster unloading and turnaround of transportation equipment.

In contrast, zero-sum results produce no such net benefits. Price changes made without accompanying changes in procedure only transfer costs and profits from one company's P&L statement to another's, with no net economic benefit to the channel system.

□ A *willingness to absorb risks for the mutual benefit of participants in a channel system.*

A 1968 study examined the common problem of congestion at shippers' truck docks.[3] Its authors estimated that the addition of extra truck bays in several cases would reduce truck waiting time significantly, thereby producing high rates of return on investment.

Unfortunately, to implement these programs, shippers would have to make the investment to alter their facilities, while the benefits would accrue to truckers supplying pickup and delivery services.

Presumably, such situations could be resolved if one or more truckers

2. Much of this section is based on J. L. Heskett, Louis W. Stern, and Frederick J. Beier, "Bases and Uses of Power in Interorganization Relations," in *Vertical Marketing Systems*, edited by Louis P. Bucklin (Glenville, Illinois, Scott, Foresman and Company, 1970), p. 75.

3. Karl M. Ruppental and D. Clay Whybark, "Some Problems in Optimizing Shipping Facilities," *The Logistics Review*, Vol. 4, No. 20, 1968, p. 5.

could reduce rates selectively to encourage the necessary investment, a practice frowned on by the Interstate Commerce Commission. Or the trucker might make the investment with some assurance that he would continue to receive business from the shipper at least over a period sufficient to pay him back for his investment. Again, this practice could be looked on with disfavor by the ICC or a state regulatory body.

Perhaps the only feasible course of action would be for the shipper to absorb the uncertainty by constructing the bay. In return, he might obtain an informal agreement that future consideration, in the form of a rate reduction based on cost improvement, would be given by the carrier. This would only work if one carrier provided all or at least a significant portion of the service.

□ *A willingness to innovate on behalf of the channel.*

Some companies are known as innovators in their respective business spheres, in the testing of new technologies, organizational relationships, or contractual relationships. A company that is first to establish a pool of pallets for the economic handling of goods in a channel of distribution is likely to be regarded as such an innovator, with resulting long-term rewards for successful experiments (and perhaps losses for unsuccessful ones).

□ *The establishment of a mechanism for collecting and transmitting information and skills throughout a channel.*

Information that provides an early warning of inventory build-ups at the retail level can be of use to all participants in a channel system. Manufacturers of such diverse products as drugs and fertilizers have not only provided their distributors with inventory-control systems, but also educated them in the use of these systems. Expectations of long-term improvements in distributor profitability and loyalty motivate such manufacturers with enlightened interorganizational practices.

□ *The exchange of personnel with other parties to interorganizational relationships.*

A factor which distinguishes management in the United States from that in most other parts of the world is executive mobility. U.S. executives expect to make frequent moves; rarely do they expect to spend a lifetime working for a single firm. The exchange of personnel between "business partner" organizations can set the stage for important interorganizational achievements by executives in cooperating organizations who understand each other's problems and economic constraints.

LABOR ATTITUDES

Unionism is typically held up by management as the greatest obstacle to beneficial changes of the type I have discussed. And yet, in situations where managements have recognized the value of providing job (and union membership) security in return for freedom to redesign jobs and introduce technological improvements, labor's attitudes have been positive.

Perhaps the best example of labor's cooperative attitude was reflected in an agreement some years ago between the Pacific Maritime Association, representing ship operating managements, and the International Longshoremen's and Warehousemen's Union. Under the terms of the agreement, the PMA established a trust fund to protect until retirement the salaries of ILWU members expected to be displaced.

As a result of the technology introduced subsequent to the agreement, volume increases made possible by operating economies actually created jobs, leaving the union with a trust fund that it had limited immediate need for. Thus both parties found this transaction beneficial.

REGULATORY POLICIES

The fear of undue advantage or discrimination in dealings between carriers and shippers has proved to be a deterrent to interorganizational problem solving in logistics.

For example, the proposed introduction a few years ago of "Big John" hopper cars with several times the capacity of their predecessors, significantly higher minimum shipping quantities, and rate reductions of 60% on grain transportation from the Midwest to the Southeast by the Southern Railway was delayed for months by the ICC. This period of time was necessary to investigate the effects of the proposed innovation on the traffic of competing inland waterway barge operators. The litigation involved, among other things, a dispute over the question of whether the proposal exaggerated the magnitude of cost reductions which Southern could achieve with the innovation.

In spite of regulatory deterrents, there appears to be a trend toward more creative interorganizational problem solving on the part of carriers and shippers. The trend would be accelerated if, for example, regulatory agencies would emphasize this question in their investigations of carrier rate or service proposals: To what extent will changes resulting from such proposals produce procedural changes necessary to achieve non-zero-sum benefits for negotiants? With this shift in emphasis, proposals scoring high would have a greater chance of being approved and expedited by the concerned regulatory agency.

Conclusion

Institutional changes will, to an increasing extent, replace technological changes as the major sources of continued productivity increases in transportation, warehousing, inventory-control, and order-processing activities in the intermediate future. They both make possible, and are being fostered by, the application of interorganizational management thinking which attempts to produce operating efficiencies for two or more cooperating institutions in a channel of distribution.

This shift in emphasis in logistics threatens to envelop a number of shippers, carriers, and companies in associated industries in problems with which they are not equipped to deal. Significant competitive advantages already have accrued to those fully aware of the favorable competitive positions to be gained by shifting responsibilities for logistics activities from one company to another, creating third-party joint ventures to facilitate the consolidation and coordination of product flows, and seeking non-zero-sum results from interorganizational negotiations.

Such changes promise to inject additional dimensions of excitement to match those provided by recent significant technological developments in logistics. They also promise continued rewards to the executive of sufficiently broad view and flexible mind who is able to change to meet the needs of his chosen field. Clearly, they offer unexplored frontiers in the redevelopment and restructuring of logistics services.

33. Production-Line Approach to Service

Theodore Levitt

We think about service in humanistic terms; we think about manufacturing in technocratic terms. This, according to the author, is why manufacturing industries are forward-looking and efficient while service industries and customer service are, by comparison, primitive and inefficient. He argues that if companies stop thinking of service as servitude and personal ministrations, they will be able to effect drastic improvements in its quality and efficiency. Then he shows companies how to take a manufacturing approach to this activity, one that substitutes "technology and systems for people and serendipity."

The service sector of the economy is growing in size but shrinking in quality. So say a lot of people. Purveyors of service, for their part, think that they and their problems are fundamentally different from other businesses and their problems. They feel that service is people-intensive, while the rest of the economy is capital-intensive. But these distinctions are largely spurious. There are no such things as service industries. There are only industries whose service components are greater or less than those of other industries. Everybody is in service.

Often the less there seems, the more there is. The more technologically sophisticated the generic product (e.g., cars and computers), the more dependent are its sales on the quality and availability of its accompanying customer services (e.g., display rooms, delivery, repairs and maintenance, application aids, operator training, installation advice, warranty fulfillment). In this sense, General Motors is probably more service-intensive than manufacturing-intensive. Without its services its sales would shrivel.

Thus the service sector of the economy is not merely comprised of the so-called service industries, such as banking, airlines, and maintenance. It includes the entire abundance of product-related services supplied by manufacturers and the sales-related services supplied by retailers. Yet we confuse things to our detriment by an outdated taxonomy. For example:

□ The First National City Bank (Citibank) is one of the biggest worldwide banks. Over half of its employees deal directly with the public, either selling them things (mostly money and deposit services) or helping them with things they have already bought (cashing checks, taking additional deposits, writing letters of credit, opening lockboxes, managing corporate cash). Most of the other employees work back in what is called "the factory"—a massive congeries of people, paper, and computers that processes, records, validates, and scrutinizes everything the first group has done. All the corporate taxonomists, including the U.S. Bureau of the Census, classify Citibank as a service company.

◻ IBM is the biggest worldwide manufacturer of computers. More than half of its employees deal directly with the public, either selling them things (mostly machines) or helping them with the things they have already bought (installing and repairing machines, writing computer programs, training customers). Most of the other employees work back in the factory —a massive congeries of wires, microminiature electronic components, engineers, and assemblers. All the corporate taxonomists, including the U.S. Bureau of the Census, classify IBM as a manufacturing company.

Something is wrong, and not just in the Bureau of the Census. The industrial world has changed more rapidly than our taxonomies. If only taxonomy were involved, the consequences of our contradictory classifications would be trivial. After all, man lives perfectly well with his contradictions: his simultaneous faith, for instance, in both God and science; his attachment to facts and logic when making important business decisions, but reliance on feelings and emotion when making far more important life decisions, like marriage.

I hope to show in this article that our contradictory notions about service may have malignant consequences. Not until we clarify the contradictions will companies begin to solve problems that now seem so intractible. In order to do so, they must think of themselves as performing manufacturing functions when it comes to their so-called "service" activities. Only then will they begin to make some significant progress in improving the quality and efficiency of service in the modern economy.

Field vs. Factory

People think of service as quite different from manufacturing. Service is presumed to be performed by individuals for other individuals, generally on a one-to-one basis. Manufacturing is presumed to be performed by machines, generally tended by large clusters of individuals whose sizes and configurations are themselves dictated by the machines' requirements. Service (whether customer service or the services of service industries) is performed "out there in the field" by distant and loosely supervised people working under highly variable, and often volatile, conditions. Manufacturing occurs "here in the factory" under highly centralized, carefully organized, tightly controlled, and elaborately engineered conditions.

People assume, and rightly so, that these differences largely explain why products produced in the factory are generally more uniform in features and quality than the services produced (e.g., life insurance policies, machine repairs) or delivered (e.g., spare parts, milk) in the field. One cannot as easily control one's agents or their performance out there in the field. Besides, different customers want different things. The result is that service and service industries, in comparison with manufacturing industries, are widely and correctly viewed as being primitive, sluggish, and inefficient.

Yet it is doubtful that things need be all that bad. Once conditions in the field get the same kind of attention that conditions inside the factory generally get, a lot of new opportunities become possible. But first management will have to revise its thinking about what service is and what it implies.

LIMITS OF SERVITUDE

The trouble with thinking of oneself as providing services—either in the service industries or in the customer-service sectors of manufacturing and retailing companies—is that one almost inescapably embraces ancient, pre-industrial modes of thinking. Worse still, one gets caught up in rigid attitudes that can have a profoundly paralyzing effect on even the most resolute of rationalists.

The concept of "service" evokes, from the opaque recesses of the mind, time-worn images of personal ministration and attendance. It refers generally to deeds one individual performs personally for another. It carries historical connotations of charity, gallantry, and selflessness, or of obedience, subordination, and subjugation. In these contexts, people serve because they want to (as in the priestly and political professions) or they serve because they are compelled to (as in slavery and such occupations of attendance as waiter, maid, bellboy, cleaning lady).

In the higher-status service occupations, such as in the church and the army, one customarily behaves ritualistically, not rationally. In the lower-status service occupations, one simply obeys. In neither is independent thinking presumed to be a requisite of holding a job. The most that can therefore be expected from service improvements is that, like Avis, a person will try harder. He will just exert more animal effort to do better what he is already doing.

So it was in ancient times, and so it is today. The only difference is that where ancient masters invoked the will of God or the whip of the foreman to spur performance, modern industry uses training programs and motivation sessions. We have not in all these years come very far in either our methods or our results. In short, service thinks humanistically, and that explains its failures.

PROMISE OF MANUFACTURING

Now consider manufacturing. Here the orientation is toward the efficient production of results, not toward attendance on others. Relationships are strictly businesslike, devoid of invidious connotations of rank or self.

When we think about how to improve manufacturing, we seldom focus on ways to improve our personal performance of present tasks; rather, it is axiomatic that we try to find entirely new ways of performing present tasks and, better yet, of actually changing the tasks themselves. We do not think of greater exertion of our animal energies (working physically harder, as the slave), of greater expansion of our commitment (being more devout or loyal, as the priest), or of greater assertion of our dependence (being more obsequious, as the butler).

Instead, we apply the greater exertion of our minds to learn how to look at a problem differently. More particularly, we ask what kinds of tools, old or new, and what kinds of skills, processes, organizational rearrangements, incentives, controls, and audits might be enlisted to greatly improve the intended outcomes. In short, manufacturing thinks technocratically, and that explains its successes.

Manufacturing looks for solutions inside the very tasks to be done. The solution to building a low-priced automobile, for example, derives largely from the nature and composition of the automobile itself. (If the automobile were not an assembly of parts, it could not be manufactured on an assembly line.) By contrast, service looks for solutions in the *performer* of the task. This is the paralyzing legacy of our inherited attitudes: the solution to improved service is viewed as being dependent on improvements in the skills and attitudes of the performers of that service.

While it may pain and offend us to say so, thinking in humanistic rather than technocratic terms ensures that the service sector of the modern economy will be forever inefficient and that our satisfactions will be forever marginal. We see service as invariably and undeviatingly personal, as something performed by individuals directly for other individuals.

This humanistic conception of service diverts us from seeking alternatives to the use of people, especially to large, organized groups of people. It does not allow us to reach out for new solutions and new definitions. It obstructs us from redesigning the tasks themselves; from creating new tools, processes, and organizations; and, perhaps, even from eliminating the conditions that created the problems.

In sum, to improve the quality and efficiency of service, companies must apply the kind of technocratic thinking which in other fields has replaced the high-cost and erratic elegance of the artisan with the low-cost, predictable munificence of the manufacturer.

The Technocratic Hamburger

Nowhere in the entire service sector are the possibilities of the manufacturing mode of thinking better illustrated than in fast-food franchising. Nowhere have manufacturing methods been employed more effectively to control the operation of distant and independent agents. Nowhere is "service" better.

Few of today's successful new commercial ventures have antecedents that are more humble and less glamorous than the hamburger. Yet the thriving nationwide chain of hamburger stands called "McDonald's" is a supreme example of the application of manufacturing and technological brilliance to problems that must ultimately be viewed as marketing problems. From 1961 to 1970, McDonald's sales rose from approximately $54 million to $587 million. During this remarkable ascent, the White Tower chain, whose name had theretofore been practically synonymous throughout the land with low-priced, quick-service hamburgers, practically vanished.

The explanation of McDonald's thundering success is not a purely fiscal one—i.e., the argument that it is financed by independent local entrepreneurs who bring to their operations a quality of commitment and energy not commonly found among hired workers. Nor is it a purely geographical one—i.e., the argument that each outlet draws its patronage from a relatively small geographic ring of customers, thus enabling the number of outlets easily and quickly to multiply. The relevant explanation must deal with the central question of why each separate McDonald's outlet is so predictably successful, why each is so certain to attract many repeat customers.

Entrepreneurial financing and careful site selection do help. But most important is the carefully controlled execution of each outlet's central function—the rapid delivery of a uniform, high-quality mix of prepared foods in an environment of obvious cleanliness, order, and cheerful courtesy. The systematic substitution of equipment for people, combined with the carefully planned use and positioning of technology, enables McDonald's to attract and hold patronage in proportions no predecessor or imitator has managed to duplicate. Consider the remarkable ingenuity of the system, which is worth examining in some detail:

To start with the obvious, raw hamburger patties are carefully prepacked and premeasured, which leaves neither the franchisee nor his employees any discretion as to size, quality, or raw-material consistency. This kind of attention is given to all McDonald's products. Storage and preparation space and related facilities are expressly designed for, and limited to, the predetermined mix of products. There is no space for any foods, beverages, or services that were not designed into the system at the outset. There is not even a sandwich knife or, in fact, a decent place to keep one. Thus the owner has no discretion regarding what he can sell—not because of any contractual limitations, but because of facilities limitations. And the employees have virtually no discretion regarding how to prepare and serve things.

Discretion is the enemy of order, standardization, and quality. On an automobile assembly line, for example, a worker who has discretion and latitude might possibly produce a more personalized car, but one that is highly unpredictable. The elaborate care with which an automobile is designed and an assembly line is structured and controlled is what produces quality cars at low prices, and with surprising reliability considering the sheer volume of the output. The same is true at McDonald's, which produces food under highly automated and controlled conditions.

FRENCH-FRIED AUTOMATION

While in Detroit the significance of the technological process lies in production, at McDonald's it lies in marketing. A carefully planned design is built into the elaborate technology of the food-service system in such a fashion as to make it a significant marketing device. This fact is impressively illustrated by McDonald's handling of that uniquely plebeian American delicacy, french-fried potatoes.

French fries become quickly soggy and unappetizing; to be good, they must be freshly made just before serving. Like other fast-food establishments, McDonald's provides its outlets with precut, partially cooked frozen potatoes that can be quickly finished in an on-premises, deep-fry facility. The McDonald's fryer is neither so large that it produces too many french fries at one time (thus allowing them to become soggy) nor so small that it requires frequent and costly frying.

The fryer is emptied onto a wide, flat tray adjacent to the service counter. This location is crucial. Since the McDonald's practice is to create an impression of abundance and generosity by slightly overfilling each bag of french fries, the tray's location next to the service counter prevents the spillage from an overfilled bag from reaching the floor. Spillage creates not only danger underfoot but also an unattractive appearance that causes the employees to become accustomed to an unclean environment. Once a store is unclean in one particular, standards fall very rapidly and the store becomes unclean and the food unappetizing in general.

While McDonald's aims for an impression of abundance, excessive overfilling can be very costly for a company that annually buys potatoes almost by the trainload. A systematic bias that puts into each bag of french fries a half ounce more than is intended can have visible effects on the company's annual earnings. Further, excessive time spent at the tray by each employee can create a cumulative service bottleneck at the counter.

McDonald's has therefore developed a special wide-mouthed scoop with a narrow funnel in its handle. The counter employee picks up the scoop and inserts the handle end into a wall clip containing the bags. One bag adheres to the handle. In a continuous movement the scoop descends into the potatoes, fills the bag to the exact proportions its designers intended, and is lifted, scoop facing the ceiling, so that the potatoes funnel through the handle into the attached bag, which is automatically disengaged from the handle by the weight of the contents. The bag comes to a steady, non-wobbling rest on its flat bottom.

Nothing can go wrong—the employee never soils his hands, the floor remains clean, dry, and safe, and the quantity is controlled. Best of all, the customer gets a visibly generous portion with great speed, the employee remains efficient and cheerful, and the general impression is one of extravagantly good service.

MECHANIZED MARKETING

Consider the other aspects of McDonald's technological approach to marketing. The tissue paper used to wrap each hamburger is color-coded to denote the mix of condiments. Heated reservoirs hold pre-prepared hamburgers for rush demand. Frying surfaces have spatter guards to prevent soiling of the cooks' uniforms. Nothing is left to chance or the employees' discretion.

The entire system is engineered and executed according to a tight technological discipline that ensures fast, clean, reliable service in an atmosphere that gives the modestly paid employees a sense of pride and dignity. In spite of the crunch of eager customers, no employee looks or acts harassed, and therefore no harassment is communicated to the customers.

But McDonald's goes even further. Customers may be discouraged from entering if the building looks unappealing from the outside; hence considerable care goes into the design and appearance of the structure itself.

Some things, however, the architect cannot control, especially at an establishment where people generally eat in their parked cars and are likely to drop hamburger wrappings and empty beverage cartons on the ground. McDonald's has anticipated the requirement: its blacktop parking facilities are dotted like a checkerboard with numerous large, highly visible trash cans. It is impossible to ignore their purpose. Even the most indifferent customer would be struck with guilt if he simply dropped his refuse on the ground. But, just in case he drops it anyway, the larger McDonald's outlets have motorized sweepers for quick and easy cleanup.

What is important to understand about this remarkably successful organization is not only that it has created a highly sophisticated piece of technology, but also that it has done this by applying a manufacturing style of thinking to a people-intensive service situation. If machinery is to be viewed as a piece of equipment with the capability of producing a predictably standardized, customer-satisfying output while minimizing the operating discretion of its attendant, that is what a McDonald's retail outlet is. It is a machine that produces, with the help of totally unskilled machine tenders, a highly polished product. Through painstaking attention to total design and facilities planning, everything is built integrally into the machine itself, into the technology of the system. The only choice available to the attendant is to operate it exactly as the designers intended.

Tooling Up for Service

Although most people are not aware of it, there are many illustrations of manufacturing solutions to people-intensive service problems. For example:

◻ Mutual funds substitute one sales call for many; one consultation for dozens; one piece of paper for thousands; and one reasonably informed customer choice for numerous, confused, and often poor choices.

◻ Credit cards that are used for making bank loans substitute a single credit decision (issuing the card in the first place) for the many elaborate, costly, people-intensive activities and decisions that bank borrowing generally entails.

◻ Supermarkets substitute fast and efficient self-service for the slow, inefficient, and often erratic clerks of the traditional service store.

In each of these examples a technological device or a manufacturing type of process has replaced what had been resolutely thought of as an irrevocably people-requiring service. Similar devices or processes can be used to modify and alleviate the customer-repelling abrasions of other people-intensive service conditions.

Consider the airlines. This industry is highly unusual. It is exceedingly capital-intensive in the creation of the facilitating product (the airplane), but it is extremely people-intensive in the delivery of the product (travel arrangements and the customer's flight experience). The possibilities for revenue production that a $20-million airplane represents are quickly vitiated by a surly or uncooperative reservations clerk. The potentials of repeat business that the chef so carefully builds into his meals can be destroyed by a dour or sloppy stewardess.

In fact, stewardesses have a particularly difficult job. A hundred passengers, having paid for reasonable service, understandably expect to be treated with some care. While three young ladies are there to serve them, a number of these passengers must inevitably get their drinks and meals later than others. Most experienced travelers are understanding and tolerant of the rushed stewardesses' problems, but a few usually harass them. The pressure and abuse can easily show in the stewardesses' personal appearance and behavior, and are likely to result in nearly all passengers being reciprocally mistreated. This is human. Besides, the ladies may have been on their feet all day, or may have slept only a few hours the night before.

"More and better training" is not likely to help things very much. When the pressure is on, service deteriorates. And so does a stewardess's cheerful manner and appearance, no matter how well schooled she is in personal care and keeping her cool or how attractively her clothes are designed.

But it might help to put mirrors in the airplane galley, so that each time a stewardess goes in she sees herself. There is some reason to expect that she'll look into the mirror each time she passes it, and that she'll straighten her hair, eliminate that lipstick smudge, put on a more cheerful face. Improvement will be instantaneous. No training needed.

Here is another possibility: the stewardess makes a quick trip down the aisle, passing out rum-flavored bonbons and explaining, "For those who can't wait till we get the ice out." This breaks the tension, produces an air of cheerfulness, acknowledges the passengers' eagerness for quick service, and says that the ladies are trying their hurried best. Further, it brings the stewardess into friendly personal contact with the passenger and reduces the likelihood of her being pressured and abused. She, in turn, is less likely to irritate other passengers.

From the manufacturing point of view, these two modest proposals represent the substitution of tools (or, as I prefer, technology) for motivation. Mirrors are a tool for getting self-motivated, automatic results in the stewardesses' appearance and personal behavior. Bonbons are a tool for creating a benign interpersonal ambience that reduces both the likelihood of customer irritation and the reciprocal and contagious stewardess irritation of others. They are small measures, but so is a company president's plant tour.

In each case there is considerable presumption of solid benefits. Yet to get these benefits one must think, as the factory engineer thinks, about what the problems are and what the desired output is; about how to redesign the process and how to install new tools that do the job more automatically; and, whenever people are involved, about how to "control" their personal behavior and channel their choices.

HARD AND SOFT TECHNOLOGIES

There are numerous examples of strictly "hard" technologies (i.e., pieces of equipment) which are used as substitutes for people—coffee vending machines for waitresses, automatic check-cashing machines for bank tellers, self-operated travel-insurance-policy machines for clerks. Although these devices represent a manufacturing approach to service, and while their principles can be extended to other fields, even greater promise lies in the application of "soft" technologies (i.e., technological systems). McDonald's is an example of a soft technology. So are mutual funds. Other examples are all around us, if we just think of them in the right way. Take the life insurance industry:

A life insurance salesman is said to be in a service industry. Yet what does he really do? He researches the prospect's needs by talking with him, designs several policy models for him, and "consumer-use tests" these models by seeking his reactions. Then he redesigns the final model and delivers it for sale to the customer. This is the ultimate example of manufacturing in the field. The factory is in the customer's living room, and the producer is the insurance agent, whom we incorrectly think of as being largely a salesman. Once we think of him as a manufacturer, however, we begin to think of how best to design and manufacture the product rather than how best to sell it.

The agent, for example, could be provided with a booklet of overlay sheets showing the insurance plans of people who are similar to the customer. This gives the customer a more credible and informed basis for making a choice. In time, the agent could be further supported by similar information stored in telephone-access computers.

In short, we begin to think of building a system that will allow the agent to produce his product efficiently and effectively by serving the customer's needs instead of performing a manipulative selling job.

MANUFACTURERS OUTSIDE THE FACTORY

The type of thinking just described applies not only to service industries but also to manufacturing industries. When the computer hardware manufacturer provides installation and maintenance services, debugging dry-runs, software programs, and operator training as part of his hardware sales program, he acknowledges that his "product" consists of considerably more than what he made in the factory. What is done in the field is just as important to the customer as the manufactured equipment itself. Indeed, without these services there would generally be no sale.

The problem in so many cases is that customer service is not viewed by manufacturers as an integral part of what the customer buys, but as something peripheral to landing the sale. However, when it is explicitly accepted as integral to the product itself and, as a consequence, gets the same kind of dedicated attention as the manufacture of the hardware gets, the results can be spectacular. For example:

☐ In the greeting card industry, some manufacturer-provided retail display cases have built-in inventory replenishment and reordering features. In effect, these features replace a company salesman with the willing efforts of department managers or store owners. The motivation of the latter to reorder is created by the visible imminence of stockouts, which is achieved with a special color-coded card that shows up as the stock gets low. Order numbers and envelopes are included for reordering. In earlier days a salesman had to call, take inventory, arrange the stock, and write orders. Stockouts were common.

The old process was called customer service and selling. The new process has no name, and probably has never been viewed as constituting a technological substitute for people. But it is. An efficient, automatic, capital-intensive system, supplemented occasionally by people, has replaced an inefficient and unreliable people-intensive system.

☐ In a more complex situation, the A.O. Smith Company has introduced the same kind of preplanning, routinizing, people-conserving activity. This company makes, among other things, grain storage silos that must be locally sold, installed, serviced, and financed. There are numerous types of silos with a great variety of accessories for loading, withdrawing, and automatically mixing livestock feed. The selling is carried out by local distributor-erectors and is a lengthy, difficult, sophisticated operation.

Instead of depending solely on the effective training of distributors, who are spread widely in isolated places, A. O. Smith has developed a series of sophisticated, colorful, and interchangeable design-module planning books. These can be easily employed by a distributor to help a farmer decide what he may need, its cost, and its financing requirements. Easy-to-read tables, broken down by the size of farm, numbers and types of animals, and purpose of animals (cattle for meat or cows for milk), show recommended combinations of silo sizes and equipment for maximum effectiveness.

The system is so thorough, so easy to use and understand, and so effective in its selling capability that distributors use it with great eagerness. As a consequence, A.O. Smith, while sitting in Milwaukee, in effect controls every sales presentation made by every one of its far-flung distributors. Instead of constantly sending costly company representatives out to retrain, cajole, wine-and-dine, and possibly antagonize distributors, the supplier sends out a tool that distributors *want* to utilize in their own self-interest.

PRODUCT-LINE PRAGMATICS

Thinking of service as an integral part of what is sold can also result in alteration of the product itself—and with dramatic results. In 1961, the Building Controls and Components Group of Honeywell, Inc., the nation's largest producer of heating and air conditioning thermostats and control devices, did a major part of its business in replacement controls (the after-market). These were sold through heating and air conditioning distributors, who then supplied plumbers and other installation and repair specialists.

At that time, Honeywell's product line consisted of nearly 18,000 separate catalog parts and pieces. The company had nearly 5,000 distributor accounts, none of which could carry a full line of these items economically, and therefore it maintained nearly 100 fully stocked field warehouses that offered immediate delivery to distributors. The result was that, in a large proportion of cases, distributors sold parts to plumbers that they did not themselves have in stock. They either sent plumbers to nearby Honeywell warehouses for pickup or picked up parts themselves and delivered them directly to the plumbers. The costs to Honeywell of carrying these inventories were enormous, but were considered a normal expense of doing business.

Then Honeywell made a daring move—it announced its new Tradeline Policy. It would close all warehouses. All parts would have to be stocked by the distributors. The original equipment, however, had been redesigned into 300 standard, interchangeable parts. These were interchangeable not only for most Honeywell controls, but also for those of its major competitors. Moreover, each package was clearly imprinted to show exactly what Honeywell and competing products were repairable with the contents.

By closing its own warehouses, Honeywell obviously shifted the inventory-carrying costs to its distributors. But instead of imposing new burdens on them, the new product lines, with their interchangeability features, enabled the distributors to carry substantially lower inventories, particularly by cutting down the need for competitive product lines which the distributors could nonetheless continue to service. Thus they were able to offer faster service at lower costs to their customers than before.

But not all distributors were easily persuaded of this possibility, and some dropped the line. Those who were persuaded ultimately proved their wisdom by the enormous expansion of their sales. Honeywell's replacement market share almost doubled, and its original equipment share rose by nearly 50%. Whereas previously nearly 90% of Honeywell's replacement sales were scattered among 4,000 distributors, within ten years after Tradeline's introduction the same proportion (of a doubled volume) was concentrated among only about 900 distributors. Honeywell's cost of servicing these fewer customers was substantially less, its trade inventory carrying costs were cut to zero, and the quality of its distributor services was so substantially improved that only 900 of its distributors captured a larger national market share than did the nearly 4,000 less efficient and more costly distributors.

Again, we see a people-intensive marketing problem being solved by the careful and scrupulous application of manufacturing attitudes. Motivation, hard work, personalization, training, and merchandising incentives were replaced with systematic programming, comprehensive planning, attention to detail, and particularly with imaginative concern for the problems and needs of customers (in this case, the company's distributors).

Stopgaps: Complexity . . .

Exaggeration is not without its merits, especially in love and war. But in business one guards against it with zeal, especially when one tries to persuade oneself. The judicious application of the manufacturing mentality may help the service industries and the customer-service activities of others. Yet this does not necessarily mean the more technology, the better.

Entrepreneurial roadsides are littered with the wrecks of efforts to install Cadillac technologies for people who cannot yet handle the Model T. This point is illustrated by the failure of two exceedingly well-financed joint ventures of highly successful technology companies. These joint ventures attempted to provide computerized medical diagnostic services for doctors and hospitals. The companies developed console hookups to central diagnostic computers, so that everybody could stop sending off samples to pathology laboratories and agonizingly poring through medical texts to diagnose the patients' symptoms.

The ventures failed because of hospital and doctor resistance, not for want of superior or reliable products. The customer was compelled suddenly to make an enormous change in his accustomed way of doing things, and to employ a strange and somewhat formidable piece of equipment that required special training in its use and in the interpretation of its output.

Interactive teaching machines are meeting a similar fate. The learning results they achieve are uniformly spectacular. The need for improved learning is a visible reality. The demand for greater individualization of teaching is widespread. But the equipment has not sold because technologists have created systems employing equipment that is at the cutting edge of technological progress. The teachers and school systems that must use them are far behind, and already feel badly bruised by their failure to comprehend even simple new technologies. For them, the new Cadillac technologies do not solve problems. They create problems.

. . . AND COMPROMISE

On the other hand, failure to exploit technological possibilities can be equally destructive. When a major petroleum company with nearly 30,000 retail outlets in the United States was persuaded to pioneer a revolutionary automobile repair and servicing system, compromises of the original plan ensured the system's failure.

The theory was to build a gigantic service and repair system that could handle heavy volumes of continuous activity by using specialized diagnostic and repair equipment. With this equipment (rather than a harried and overworked man at a gas station) pinpointing the exact problems, cars could be shuttled off to specific stations in the repair center. Experts would work only on one kind of problem and section of a car, with newly designed, fast-action tools. Oil changes would be made in assembly-line fashion by low-paid workers, electrical work would be performed by high-paid technicians doing only that, and a post-diagnostic checkup would be made to guarantee success.

Since profitability would require high volume, the center would have to draw on a vast population area. To facilitate this, the original proposal called for a specially constructed building at a center-city, old warehouse location—the land would be cheaper, the building would be equally accessible throughout the entire metropolitan area, the service center's technological elegance and see-through windows for customers would offset any run-down neighborhood disadvantages, and volume business would come from planned customer decisions rather than random off-street traffic.

The original concept also called for overnight pickup and delivery service; thus a car could be repaired at night while its owner slept, rather than during the day when he would need it. And because the required promotion of this service would tend to alienate the company's franchised service station dealers, perhaps driving them into the hands of competitors, it was recommended that the first center be installed in a major city where the company had no stations.

This sounds like an excellent manufacturing approach to a service situation; but the company made three fatal compromises:

1. It decided to place the center in a costly, high-traffic suburban location, on the grounds that "if the experiment fails, at least the building will be in a location that has an alternative use." The results were an awkward location, a land-acquisition cost five times higher than the original center-city location, and, therefore, a vastly inflated break-even point for the service center.

2. It decided not to offer overnight service, on the grounds that "we'd better crawl before we walk. And besides, we don't think people will leave their cars overnight in a strange and distant garage." The fact that the results would be guaranteed by a reputable, nationally known petroleum company operating an obviously sophisticated new type of consumer service facility was not persuasive to the corporate decision makers.

3. It decided to put the first center in a city occupied by its own franchised dealers, on the grounds that "we know it better." To offset the problem of not being able to advertise aggressively for business, the company offered its dealers a commission to send their repair jobs to the center.

The dealers did this, but only with jobs they could not, or did not want to, do themselves. As a result, the traffic at the big, expensive center was miserably low.

Companies that take a manufacturing approach to service problems are likely to fail if (a) they compromise technological possibilities at the conception and design stage, or (b) they allow technological complexity to contaminate the operating stage. The substitution of technology and systems for people and serendipity is complex in its conception and design; only in its *operation*, as at McDonald's, is it simple.

It is the simplicity of mutual funds that, after all, accounts for their success. But the concept is in fact much more complex than that of selling individual stocks through a single customer man sitting at a desk. Mutual funds are the financial community's equivalent of McDonald's. They are a piece of technology that not only simplifies life for both the seller and the buyer but also creates many more buyers and makes production more profitable.

Mass merchandising is similar. It substitutes a wide selection and fast, efficient self-service for a narrow selection and slow, incompetent salesclerk service. The mass merchandising retail store (e.g., general merchandise supermarket) is a new technology, incorporating into retailing precisely the thinking that goes into the assembly line, except that the customer does his own assembling.

Why Things Go Wrong

The significance of all this is that a "product" is quite different from what it is generally assumed to be. When asked once what he did, Charles Revson, head of Revlon, Inc., made the now well-known reply, "In the factory we make cosmetics, in the store we sell hope." He defined the product in terms of what the consumer wanted, not in terms of what the manufacturer made. McDonald's obviously does the same—not just hamburgers but also speed, cleanliness, reassurance, cheerfulness, and predictable consistency. Honeywell defined it not in terms of replacement parts but, rather, in terms of those needs of its distributors which, if met, would result in substantially larger proportions of patronage for Honeywell. Thus a product is not something people buy, but a tool they use—a tool to solve their problems or to achieve their intentions.

So many things go wrong because companies fail to adequately define what they sell. Companies in so-called service industries generally think of themselves as offering services rather than manufacturing products; hence they fail to think and act as comprehensively as do manufacturing companies concerned with the efficient, low-cost production of customer-satisfying products.

Moreover, manufacturing companies themselves do not generally think of customer service as an integral part of *their* products. It is an afterthought to be handled by the marketing department.

The marketing department, in turn, thinks of itself as providing customer services. There is a hidden and unintentional implication of giving something away for free. One is doing something extra as a favor. When this is the underlying communication to one's own organization, the result is about what one would expect—casual, discretionary attitudes and little attention to detail, and certainly no attention to the possibilities of substituting systems and preplanning for people and pure effort. Hence products are designed that cannot be easily installed, repaired, or modified.

(Motorola's "works in a box" television set, which has been promoted so successfully on the basis of its easy replacement and repairability, is an outstanding example of the sales-getting potential of proper care in design and manufacturing.)

CHILL WINDS FROM ICE CREAM

An excellent example of the confusion between what a company "makes" and what a customer "buys" is provided by a producer of private-label ice cream products for supermarket chains. Since supermarkets need to create low-price impressions in order to attract and hold customers, selling successfully to them means getting down to rock-bottom prices. The company (call it the Edwards Company) became extraordinarly good at producing a wide line of ice cream products at rock-bottom costs. It grew rapidly while others went bankrupt. It covered ten states with direct deliveries to stores out of its factory and factory warehouse, but continued growth eventually required establishing plant, distribution, and marketing centers elsewhere. The result was disaster, even though the company manufactured just as efficiently in the new locations as it did in the old.

Under the direct and constant supervision of the president in the original Edwards location, an exceedingly efficient telephone ordering and delivery system had been working to meet the supermarkets' rather stringent requirements. Because of limited storage and display space, they required several-times-a-week delivery at specified, uncrowded store hours. To make up for low volume in slow periods, they needed regular specials as well as holiday and summer specials. Over time, these needs had become so automatically but efficiently supplied from the original Edwards factory location that this delivery service became routinized and therefore taken for granted.

In building the new plant, the president and his compact management team focused on getting manufacturing costs down to rock bottom. After all, that is what made the sale—low prices. Not being very conscious of the fact that they had created in the original location an enormously customer-satisfying, efficient, automatic ordering and delivery system, they did not know exactly what to look for in evaluating how well they were working out these "service" details at the new plant, distribution, and marketing centers.

In short, they did not know what their product really was (why Edwards had become so successful) and they failed to expand Edwards' success. Service was not considered an integral part of the company's product. It was viewed merely as "something else" you do in the business. Accordingly, service received inadequate attention, and that became the cause of the Edwards Company's failure.

Conclusion

Rarely is customer service discretionary. It is a requisite of getting and holding business, just like the generic product itself. Moreover, if customer service is consciously treated as "manufacturing in the field," it will get the same kind of detailed attention that manufacturing gets. It will be carefully planned, controlled, automated where possible, audited for quality control, and regularly reviewed for performance improvement and customer reaction. More important, the same kinds of technological, labor-saving, and systems approaches that now thrive in manufacturing operations will begin to get a chance to thrive in customer service and service industries.

Once service-industry executives and the creators of customer-service programs begin seriously to think of themselves as actually manufacturing a product, they will begin to think like product manufacturers. They will ask: What technologies and systems are employable here? How can things be designed so we can use machines instead of people, systems instead of serendipity? Instead of thinking about better and more training of their customer-service representatives, insurance agents, branch bank managers, or salesmen "out there," they will think about how to eliminate or supplement them.

If we continue to approach service as something done by individuals rather than by machines or systems, we will continue to suffer from two distortions in thinking:

1. Service will be viewed as something residual to the ultimate reality—to a tangible product, to a specific competence (like evaluating loans, writing insurance policies, giving medical aid, preparing on-premises foods). Hence it will have residual respectability, receive residual attention, and be left, somehow, for residual performers.

2. Service will be treated as purely a human task that must inevitably be

diagnosed and performed by a single individual working alone with no help or, at best, with the rudimentary help of training and a variety of human-engineering motivators. It will never get the kind of manufacturing-type thinking that goes into tangible products.

Until we think of service in more positive and encompassing terms, until it is enthusiastically viewed as manufacturing in the field, receptive to the same kinds of technological approaches that are used in the factory, the results are likely to be just as costly and idiosyncratic as the results of the lonely journeyman carving things laboriously by hand at home.

Part IX

Expanding Horizons

Preface

After describing the intricacies of the multidimensional organization at Dow Corning Corporation, William Goggin, former chairman of the company, concludes his contribution to this section of HBR—On Management with these words: "Perhaps the single most pressing problem that faces any industrial organization is how to cope effectively with change. . . . Since change is constant, so must our organization be continually flexible and adaptive to changing conditions on all fronts."

In the mid-1960s top management of Dow Corning, perceiving that the organization had become bureaucratic, ingrown, and shortsighted, changed its structure from a traditional one to a matrix form, and then to a so-called multidimensional form. The benefits were pervasive and tangible, according to Mr. Goggin, including a more vigorous, communicative, and responsive work force, as well as improved profits.

Dow Corning is one company that was sufficiently innovative and daring to adapt radically to changing circumstances, once the necessity of adaptation became clear. The necessity to adapt to the demands of high technology or competition (domestic or from abroad) are clear, and the steps to be taken are not always difficult to determine. But the same cannot be said for what Larry E. Greiner calls the problem of "psychological saturation" of workers "who grow emotionally and physically exhausted by the intensity of teamwork and the heavy pressure for innovative solutions." This, Greiner says, happens in companies that have reached an advanced stage of development where employees work in teams and where social control, rather than formal discipline, operates.

Most corporate organizations have not come close to reaching such a "far-out" stage. But many are worrying about trends and developments that heretofore have been beyond their ken. Consider the growing nationalistic sentiment, and consequently a rising tide of restrictions on foreign business, not only in developing countries like Nigeria but also in historically "friendly" countries like Canada. Or consider the heightened expectations of U.S. consumers—quickly reflected in pressure and legislation from representatives they elect—in product quality, reliability, and safety. Or consider the well-known disaffection of blue-

collar workers toward the rigors of the assembly line. The malaise has spread to white-collar workers and even the managerial ranks; there is serious talk that middle managers may form unions!

For corporate executives, the outcome is the need to look beyond the everyday exigencies of their operations. The more knowledgeable and the more far-sighted persons in those ranks would agree with the dictum of Alfred North Whitehead: "The rate of change in our time is so swift that an individual of ordinary length of life will be called on to face novel situations which have no parallel in the past. The fixed person for the fixed duties who in the old society was such a godsend will in the future be a public danger." If not a public danger, a danger to his organization.

This section is a sampling of the many articles which the Harvard Business Review *has published over the years designed to stretch the minds of its readers and alert them to problems and issues beyond the immediate ones they face from day to day. The authors include:*

Peter F. Drucker, describing new, more adaptable structures formed to fit around the organization's objectives and strategies.

Larry E. Greiner, outlining the five stages of organizational maturation, each one culminating in a managerial crisis.

William C. Goggin, showing how Dow Corning reorganized around its various businesses and pushed decision making down the managerial ladder and out into groups formed around the businesses.

Douglas S. Sherwin, his thesis based on the employee's need to be committed, suggesting four kinds of structures to make the organism more responsive, adaptive, and dynamic.

Kenneth R. Andrews, insisting that, whatever the good intentions of "a few good guys" at the top, social responsibility cannot be made a reality until it becomes an integral part of the corporation's strategy and policy and is translated into specific, measurable objectives.

O. A. Ohmann, pleading for enlightened corporate leadership that encourages employees to exercise their ability to make decisions and assume responsibility.

It is not a question of whether corporate managers need expansion of their horizons; the question is whether they will gain the scope and vision to adapt quickly enough and accommodate to inevitable change.

34. New Templates for Today's Organizations

Peter F. Drucker

Today's businesses are increasingly complex and diverse. In this article, a well-known organization theorist describes new principles of organization design now in use and their applications to today's businesses and institutions. It is his position that not only must the new principles make it possible for organizations to function and perform, but they must also serve the higher goals of human endeavor. (This article is a consolidation of several chapters from Mr. Drucker's book Management: Tasks, Responsibilities, Practices, *published in 1974 by Harper & Row.)*

Organization structures are becoming increasingly short-lived and unstable.

The "classical" organization structures of the 1920s and 1930s, which still serve as textbook examples, stood for decades without needing more than an occasional touching up. American Telephone & Telegraph, General Motors, DuPont, Unilever, and Sears, Roebuck maintained their organizational concepts, structures, and basic components through several management generations and major changes in the size and scope of the business. Today, however, a company no sooner finishes a major job of reorganizing itself than it starts all over again.

General Electric, for instance, finished a tremendous organization overhaul around 1960, after almost a decade of hard work; since then it has revamped both its structure and its overall strategies at least twice. Similarly, Imperial Chemicals in Great Britain is restructuring an organization design that is barely 10 years old. And the same restlessness and instability afflict organization structures and concepts in the large U.S. commercial banks, in IBM, and in U.S. government agencies. For instance, the Health, Education and Welfare Department has been subjected to a "final" reorganization almost every year in its history.

To some extent this instability is a result of gross overorganizing. Companies are resorting to reorganization as a kind of miracle drug in lieu of diagnosing their ailments. Every business observer can see dozens of cases where substantial, even massive organization surgery is being misapplied to take care of a fairly minor procedural problem, or—even more often—to avoid facing up to personnel decisions. Equally common is the misuse of reorganization as a substitute for hard thinking on objectives, strategies, and priorities. Few managers seem to recognize that the right organization structure is not performance itself, but rather a prerequisite of performance. The wrong structure is indeed a guarantee of nonperformance; it produces friction and frustration, puts the spotlight on the wrong issues, and makes mountains out of trivia. But "perfect organization" is like "perfect health": the test is the ills it does not have and therefore does not have to cure.

Even if unnecessary organization surgery were not as rampant in our institutions as unnecessary appendectomies, hysterectomies, and tonsillectomies are said to be in our hospitals, there would still be an organization crisis. Twenty years ago many managers had yet to learn that organization design and organization structure deserve attention, thinking, and hard work. Almost everyone accepts this today; indeed, organization studies have been one of the true "growth industries" of the past twenty years. But while a few years ago organization theory had "the answers," today all is confusion.

The crisis is simultaneously a crisis of organization theory and of organization practice. Ironically, what is happening is not at all what organization theorists like Chris Argyris, Warren Bennis, Douglas McGregor (and I myself) have been predicting for at least 10 years: pressures for a more free-form and humanistic organization that provides greater scope for personal fulfillment play almost no part in the present organization crisis. Instead the main causes of instability are *changes in the objective task*, in the kind of business and institution to be organized. This is at the root of the crisis of organization practice.

The organization theorists' traditional answer to "organization crisis"—more organization development—is largely irrelevant to this new problem. Sometimes they seem to be pushing old remedies to cure a disease that no one has heard of before, and that inhabits a totally unfamiliar type of body. The kind of business and institution to be organized today is an enormously different beast from that of 20 years ago.

These changes in the objective task have generated new design principles that do not fit traditional organization concepts. And therein lies the crisis of theory. On the other hand, the past 20 years have also seen the emergence of new understandings of which organization needs require the most attention, and of how to go about the job of analyzing organization needs and designing organization structures. Only when we have an idea of what the new "body" looks like can we begin to treat its ills.

In what follows I compare old models with new realities and describe the new design principles. These principles can be matched to the tasks of modern management as well as to the formal needs of all organizations, independent of their purpose. In exploring these relationships, we can discern a way to avoid the organization crisis that affects so many businesses and institutions.

The Early Models

Twice in the short history of management we have had the "final answer" to organization problems.

The first time was around 1910 when Henri Fayol, the French industrialist, thought through what were, to him, the universally valid functions of a manufacturing company. (I am using the word "function" in the common, management sense, not in the way Fayol used it to describe administrative concerns.) Of course, at that time the manufacturing business presented the one truly important organization problem.

Then in the early 1920s Alfred P. Sloan, Jr., in organizing General Motors, took the next step. He found "the answer" for organizing a large, multidivisional manufacturing company. The Sloan approach built the individual divisions on the functional structure that Fayol had specified for a manufacturing business, that is, on engineering, manufacturing, selling, and so on; but it organized the business itself by the concept of federal decentralization, that is, on the basis of decentralized authority and centralized control. By the mid-1940s GM's structure had become the model for larger organizations around the world.

Where they fit the realities that confront organization designers and implementers today, the Fayol and Sloan models are still unsurpassed. Fayol's functional organization is still the best way to structure a small business, especially a small manufacturing business. Sloan's federal decentralization is still the best structure for the big, single-product, single-market company like GM. But more and more of the institutional reality that has to be structured and organized does not "fit." Indeed the very assumptions that underlay Sloan's work—and that of Fayol—are not applicable to today's organization challenges.

GM MODEL VS. PRESENT REALITIES

There are at least six ways in which the GM structure no longer serves as a model for present organization needs.

1. General Motors is a manufacturing business. Today we face the challenge of organizing the large nonmanufacturing institution. There are not only the large financial businesses and the large retailers, but also, equally, there are worldwide transportation, communications, and customer service companies. The latter, while they may manufacture a product, have

their greatest emphasis on outside services (as most computer businesses do). Then there are, of course, all the nonbusiness service institutions, e.g., hospitals, universities, and government agencies. These "nonmanufacturing" institutions are, increasingly, the true center of gravity of any developed economy. They employ the most people, and they both contribute to and take the largest share of the gross national product. They present the fundamental organization problems today.

2. General Motors is essentially a single-product, single-technology, single-market business. Even accounting for the revenues of its large financial and insurance subsidiaries, four fifths of its total revenue are still produced by the automobile. Although Frigidaire and Electromotive are large, important businesses and leaders in the consumer appliance and locomotive markets, respectively, they are but minor parts of GM. Indeed, GM is unique among large companies in being far less diversified today than it was 30 or 40 years ago. Then, in the late 1930s and early 1940s, General Motors had major investments in the chemical industry (Ethyl), in the aircraft industry (North American Aviation), and in earth-moving equipment (Euclid). All three are gone now and have not been replaced by new diversification activities outside the automotive field.

The cars that General Motors produces differ in details, such as size, horsepower, and price, but they are essentially one and the same product. A man who came up the line in, say, the Pontiac Division, will hardly find Chevrolet totally alien—and even Opel in Germany will not hold a great many surprises for him.

By contrast, the typical businesses of today are multiproduct, multitechnology, and multimarket. They may not be conglomerates, but they are diversified. And their central problem is a problem General Motors did not have: the organization of complexity and diversity.

There is, moreover, an even more difficult situation to which the GM pattern cannot be applied: the large single-product, single-technology business that, unlike GM, cannot be subdivided into distinct and yet comparable parts. Typical are the "materials" businesses such as steel and aluminum companies. Here belong, also, the larger transportation businesses, such as railroads, airlines, and the large commercial banks. These businesses are too big for a functional structure; it ceases to be a skeleton and becomes a straitjacket. They are also incapable of being genuinely decentralized; no one part on its own is a genuine "business." Yet as we are shifting from mechanical to process technologies, and from making goods to producing knowledge and services, these large, complex, but integrated businesses are becoming more important than the multidivisional businesses of the 1920s and 1930s.

3. General Motors still sees its international operations as organizationally separate and outside. For 50 years it has been manufacturing and selling overseas, and something like one quarter of its sales are now outside North

America. But in its organization structure, in its reporting relationships, and above all in its career ladders, GM is a U.S. company with foreign subsidiaries. Rather than leaning toward an international, let alone a multinational operation, GM's top management is primarily concerned with the U.S. market, the U.S. economy, the U.S. labor movement, the U.S. government, and so on. This traditional structure and viewpoint of GM's top management may, in large part, explain the substantial failure of GM to take advantage of the rapid expansion and growth of such major non-U.S. automobile markets as Europe, where GM's share has actually been dropping, or Brazil, where GM failed to anticipate a rapidly emerging automobile market.[1]

In contrast, during the last 20 years many other companies have become multinational. For these companies, a great many cultures, countries, markets, and governments are of equal, or at least of major, importance.

4. Because GM is a one-product, one-country company, information handling is not a major organization problem and thus not a major concern. At GM everyone speaks the same language, whether by that we mean the language of the automotive industry or American English. Everyone fully understands what the other one is doing or should be doing, if only because, in all likelihood, he has done a similar job himself. GM can, therefore, be organized according to the logic of the marketplace, and the logic of authority and decision. It need not, in its organization, concern itself a great deal with the logic and flow of information.

By contrast, multiproduct, multitechnology, and multinational companies have to design their organization structure to handle a large flow of information. At the very least they have to make sure that their organization structure does not violate the logic of information. And for this task, GM offers no guidance—GM did not have to tackle the problem.

5. Four out of every five GM employees are either manual production workers or clerks on routine tasks. In other words, GM employs yesterday's rather than today's labor force.

But the basic organization problem today concerns knowledge work and knowledge workers. They are the fastest growing element in every business; in service institutions, they are the core employees.

6. Finally, General Motors has been a "managerial" rather than an "entrepreneurial" business. The strength of the Sloan approach lay in its ability to manage, and manage surperbly, what was already there and known.

Today's organizer is challenged by an increasing demand to organize entrepreneurship and innovation. But for this undertaking, the General Motors model offers no guidance.

1. For a discussion of these developments, see the epilogue to the 1972 edition of my book, *Concept of the Corporation* (New York, John Day).

New Design Principles

We do not know how to handle these new organization realities or how to satisfy their structural demands. Nevertheless, the organizing task has not waited. To tackle the new realities, we have in the past 20 years improvised ad hoc design solutions to supplement the Fayol and Sloan models. As a result, the organization architect now has available five so-called design principles, i.e., five distinct organization structures. The two traditional ones already mentioned have been known as principles of organization design for many years:

□ Henri Fayol's functional structure.
□ Alfred P. Sloan's federal decentralization.

Three are new; indeed they are so new that they are not generally known, let alone recognized, as design principles:

□ Team organization.
□ Simulated decentralization.
□ Systems structure.

In team organization, a group—usually a fairly small one—is set up for a specific task rather than for a specific skill or stage in the work process. In the past 20 years we have learned that whereas team design was traditionally considered applicable only to short-lived, transitory, exceptional task-force assignments, it is equally applicable to some permanent needs, especially to the top-management and innovating tasks.

In an organization that is both too big to remain functionally organized and too integrated to be genuinely decentralized, simulated decentralization is often the organization answer. It sets up one function, one stage in the process, or one segment as if it were a distinct business with genuine profit and loss responsibility; it treats accounting fictions, transfer prices, and overhead allocations as if they were realities of the marketplace. For all its difficulties and frictions, simulated decentralization is probably the fastest growing organization design around these days. It is the only one that fits, albeit poorly, the materials, computer, chemical, and pharmaceutical companies, as well as the big banks; it is also the only design principle suited for the large university, hospital, or government agency.

Finally, in systems structure, team organization and simulated decentralization are combined. The prototype for this design principle was NASA's space program, in which a large number of autonomous units—large government bodies, individual research scientists, profit-seeking businesses, and large universities—worked together, organized and informed by the needs of the situation rather than by logic, and held together by a common goal and a joint top management. The large transnational company, which is a mix of many cultures, governments, businesses, and markets, is the present embodiment of an organization based on the systems concept.

None of the new design principles is easy or trouble-free. Compared to the traditional designs of functionalism and federal decentralization, they are indeed so difficult, complex, and vulnerable that many organization theorists maintain that they are not principles at all, but abominations. And there is no question that wherever the traditional principles can be used, they should be; they are infinitely easier. The traditional principles are, however, far more limited in their scope than the new ones, and when misapplied they can cause even greater problems.

DESIGN LOGICS

Each of the five design principles expresses or embodies a logic that makes that principle the appropriate one to apply when one or another task of management requires a structure. In this discussion we can identify three, or maybe four, logics upon which the five principles are based. For instance, although they do it differently, the functional and team design principles both embody *work* and *task* are thus appropriate designs to consider when faced with work- or task-oriented management problems.

Historically these two design principles have been viewed as antithetical, but actually they are complementary. In the functionally organized structure, the work skills—manufacturing, accounting, and so on—are designed to be static; the work moves from one stage to others. In team structure, the work is conceived as static, with skills moving to meet the requirements of the task. Because of their complementary nature, these two design principles are the only possible choices for dealing with, say, the structure of knowledge. For if you need a specific task performed and a team effort would do it best, then you need static functions as bases from which persons, and their expertise, can be moved to form a team.

Two other design logics, corresponding to those involving work and task, can also be defined. Simulated decentralization and Sloan's federal decentralization both deal with *results* and *performance*. They are result-focused designs. Unlike functional and team structures, however, they are not complementary; they are not even alternatives. Federal decentralization is an "optimum," simulated decentralization a "lesser evil" to be resorted to only when the stringent requirements of federal decentralization cannot be met.

The last of the available design principles, systems design, is focused on *relationships*, another dimension of management. Because relations are inevitably both more numerous and less clearly definable than either work and task or results, a structure focused on relations will present greater difficulties than either a work-focused or a result-focused design. There are, however, organization problems, as in the true multinational business, in which the very complexity of relationships makes systems design the only appropriate design principle.

This rough classification indicates that at least one additional design principle might yet be developed. *Decision* is as much a dimension of management as are work and task, results and performance, and relations. Yet, so far, we know of no decision-focused design principle of organization structure, but should one ever be developed, it might have wide applicability.

Ideally, an organization should be multiaxial, that is, structured around work and task, *and* results and performance, *and* relationships, *and* decisions. It would function as if it were a biological organism, like the human body with its skeleton and muscles, a number of nervous systems, and with circulatory, digestive, immunological, and respiratory systems, all autonomous yet interdependent. But in social structures we are still limited to designs that express only one primary dimension.

So, in designing organizations, we have to choose among different structures, each stressing a different dimension and each, therefore, with distinct costs, specific and fairly stringent requirements, and real limitations. There is no risk-free organization structure. And a design that is the best solution for one task may be only one of a number of equally poor alternatives for another task, and just plain wrong for yet a third kind of work.

Major Tasks of Management

A somewhat different way of viewing the relationships between the design logics and principles is to identify the principal tasks of management that the principles can structure. We have learned that, in a very general analysis, organization design should simultaneously structure and integrate three different kinds of work: (1) the operating task, which is responsible for producing the results of today's business; (2) the innovative task, which creates the company's tomorrow; and (3) the top-management task, which directs, gives vision, and sets the course for the business of both today and tomorrow. No one organization design is adequate to all three kinds of work; every business will need to use several design principles side-by-side.

In addition, each organization structure has certain formal specifications that have nothing to do with the purpose of the structure but are integral parts of the structure itself. Just as a human body can be described as having certain characteristics, regardless of the occupation of its inhabitant, so can an organization structure. Bodies have arms and legs, hands and feet, all related to each other; similarly, organizations are structured to satisfy the need for:

□ *Clarity*, as opposed to simplicity. (The Gothic cathedral is not a simple design, but your position inside it is clear; you know where to stand and where to go. A modern office building is exceedingly simple in design, but it is very easy to get lost in one; it is not clear.)

□ *Economy* of effort to maintain control and minimize friction.

□ *Direction of vision* toward the product rather than the process, the result rather than the effort.

□ *Understanding* by each individual of his own task as well as that of the organization as a whole.

□ *Decision making* that focuses on the right issues, is action-oriented, and is carried out at the lowest possible level of management.

□ *Stability*, as opposed to rigidity, to survive turmoil, and *adaptability* to learn from it.

□ *Perpetuation and self-renewal*, which require that an organization be able to produce tomorrow's leaders from within, helping each person develop continuously; the structure must also be open to new ideas.

Even though every institution, and especially every business, is structured in some way around all the dimensions of management, no one design principle is adequate to all their demands and needs. Nor does any one of the five available design principles adequately satisfy all of the formal specifications. The functional principle, for instance, has great clarity and high economy, and it makes it easy to understand one's own task. But even in the small business it tends to direct vision away from results and toward efforts, to obscure the organization's goals, and to sub-optimize decisions. It has high stability but little adaptability. It perpetuates and develops technical and functional skills, that is, middle managers, but it resists new ideas and inhibits top-management development and vision. And every one of the other four principles is similarly both a "good fit" against some formal organization specifications and a "misfit" against others.

One conclusion from this discussion is that organization structures can either be pure or effective, but they are unlikely to be both. Indeed, even the purest structure we know of, Alfred Sloan's GM, was actually mixed. It was not composed just of decentralized divisions, with functional organization within the divisions. It also contained, from the beginning, some sizable simulated decentralization. For instance, Fisher Body had responsibility for all body work but not for any final product. And top management was clearly structured as a team, or rather as a number of interlocking teams.

This does not mean that an organization structure must by necessity be unwieldy or a confused mixture. The tremendous vitality of some older structures—Sears, Roebuck and GM, for instance—shows that a dynamic balance can be achieved. One implication is clear, however, and that is that pure structure *is* likely to end up badly botched. (This tendency may explain the difficulties that both GE and Imperial Chemicals—each trying for pure decentralization—have been experiencing.) Above all, our observations lead us to conclude that organization design is a series of risk-taking decisions rather than a search for the "one best way." And by and large, organization theorists and practitioners have yet to learn this.

Building the New Structure

There are a number of important lessons to be learned from the previous discussion and from the experiences of the past 20 years. Some concern new ideas or conclusions we have not recognized before, while others involve rethinking old concepts and relationships that we thought were settled years ago.

The first thing we can conclude is that Fayol and Sloan were right: good organization structures will not just evolve. The only things that evolve by themselves in an organization are disorder, friction, and malperformance. Nor is the right structure—or even the livable one—intuitive, any more than Greek temples or Gothic cathedrals were. Traditions may indicate where the problems and malfunctions are, but they are of little help in finding solutions. Organization design and structure require thinking, analysis, and a systematic approach.

Second, we have learned that designing an organization structure is not the first step, but the last. The first step is to identify and organize the building blocks of organization, that is, the key tasks that have to be encompassed in the final structure and that, in turn, carry the structural load of the final edifice. This is, of course, what Fayol did with his functions of a manufacturing company, when he designed them according to the work to be done.

We now know that building blocks are determined by the kind of contribution they make. And we know that the traditional classification of the contributions, e.g., the staff-and-line concept of conventional U.S. organization theory, is more of a hindrance to understanding than a help.

Designing the building blocks or tasks is, so to speak, the "engineering phase" of organization design. It provides the basic materials. And like all materials, these building blocks have their specific characteristics. They belong in different places and fit together in different ways.

We have also learned that "structure follows strategy." Organization is not mechanical. It is not done by assembly, nor can it be prefabricated. Organization is organic and unique to each individual business or institution.

We realize now that structure is a means for attaining the objectives and goals of an institution. And if a structure is to be effective and sound, we must start with objectives and strategy.[2]

This is perhaps the most fruitful new insight we have in the field of organization. It may sound obvious, and it is. But some of the worst mistakes in organization building have been made by imposing on a living business a mechanistic model of an ideal organization.

Strategy—that is, the answer to the questions: "What is our business? What should it be? What will it be?"—determines the purpose of structure. It thereby determines the key tasks or activities in a given business or service institution. Effective structure is the design that makes these key activities function and produce results. In turn the key activities are the load-bearing elements of a functioning structure. Organization design is, or should be, primarily concerned with the key activities; other purposes are secondary.

Some of the new insights into organization design require us to unlearn old ideas. A few of the noisiest and most time-consuming battles in organization theory and practice are pure sham. They pose an either/or dichotomy when the correct answer is "both—in varying proportions."

The first of these sham battles that had better be forgotten is between task-focus and person-focus in job design and organization structure. Structure and job design have to be task-focused. But assignments have to fit both the person and the needs of the situation. There is no point in confusing the two, as the old and tiresome discussion of the nonproblem insists on doing. Work is always objective and impersonal; the job itself is always done by a person.

Somewhat connected with this old controversy is the discussion of hierarchical versus free-form organization.

Traditional organization theory knows only one kind of structure, applicable alike to building blocks and whole buildings. It is the so-called scalar organization, that is, the hierarchical pyramid of superior and subordinates.

Today another—equally doctrinaire—organization theory is becoming fashionable. It maintains that shape and structure are what we want them to be—they are, or should be, free form. Everything—shape, size, and apparently tasks—derive from interpersonal relations. Indeed, it is argued, the purpose of the structure is to make it possible for each person "to do his thing."

It is simply not true, however, that one of these forms represents total

---

2. The fundamental work on this topic, an in-depth study of the design of modern organization in pioneering American companies such as DuPont, General Motors, and Sears, was done by Alfred D. Chandler in his book *Strategy and Structure* (Cambridge, M.I.T. Press, 1962).

regimentation and the other total freedom. The amount of discipline required in both is the same; they only distribute it differently.

Hierarchy does not, as the critics allege, make the person at the top of the pyramid more powerful. On the contrary, the first effect of hierarchical organization is to protect the subordinate against arbitrary authority from above. A scalar or hierarchical organization does this by defining a sphere within which the subordinate has authority, a sphere within which the superior cannot interfere. It protects the subordinate by making it possible for him to say, "This is *my* assigned job." Protection of the subordinate also underlies the scalar principle's insistence that a man have only one superior. Otherwise, the subordinate is likely to find himself caught between conflicting demands, commands, interests, and loyalties. There is a lot of truth in the old proverb, "Better one bad master than two good ones."

At the same time, the hierarchical organization gives the most individual freedom. As long as the incumbent does whatever the assigned duties of his position are, he has done his job. He has no responsibility beyond it.

We hear a lot of talk these days about the individual's right to do his own thing. But the only organization structure in which this is remotely possible is a hierarchical one. It makes the least demands on the individual to subordinate himself to the goals of the organization or to gear his activities into the needs and demands of others.

Teams, by contrast, demand, above all, very great self-discipline from each member. Everybody has to do the team's "thing." Everybody has to take responsibility for the work of the entire team and for its performance. The one thing one cannot do on a team is one's own "thing."

Organization builders (and even organization theorists) will have to learn that sound organization structure needs both (a) a hierarchical structure of authority, and (b) a capacity to organize task forces, teams, and individuals for work on both a permanent and a temporary basis.

THE "ONE-WAY" MYTH

Organization theory and organization practice still assume that there is "one final answer," at least for a particular business or institution. In itself, this belief is a large part of today's organization crisis. It leads to doctrinaire structures that impose one template on everybody and everything—e.g., operating and innovating components; manufacturing and service units; single-product and multimarket businesses. And if any person or process, no matter how insignificant, seems out of place, a total root-and-branch reorganization has to be done to accommodate it.

Maybe there is one right answer—but if so, we do not yet have it. Indeed for certain businesses and institutions, such as a large airline or government agency, we do not even have one poor answer—all we have are a multitude of equally unsatisfactory approaches. But, as remarked before, the organizing task will not wait; it will by necessity continue to be a central preoccupation of managers. Therefore, they had better learn to understand the design principles we already have. They must also learn the formal specifications of organization, and the relationships between the tasks of a business and the structures available to it.

The true lesson of the organization crisis is, however, quite different. It is that the traditional quest for the one right answer—a quest pursued as wholeheartedly by the new "heretics" of free-form organization as by the most orthodox classicists—pursues the wrong quarry. It misconceives an organization as something in itself rather than as a means to an end. But now we can see that liberation and mobilization of human energies—rather than symmetry, harmony, or consistency—are the purpose of organization. Human performance is both its goal and its test.

35. Evolution and Revolution as Organizations Grow

Larry E. Greiner

This author maintains that growing organizations move through five distinguishable phases of development, each of which contains a relatively calm period of growth that ends with a management crisis. He argues, moreover, that since each phase is strongly influenced by the previous one, a management with a sense of its own organization's history can anticipate and prepare for the next developmental crisis. This article provides a prescription for appropriate management action in each of the five phases, and it shows how companies can turn organizational crises into opportunities for future growth.

A small research company chooses too complicated and formalized an organization structure for its young age and limited size. It flounders in rigidity and bureaucracy for several years and is finally acquired by a larger company.

Key executives of a retail store chain hold on to an organization structure long after it has served its purpose, because their power is derived from this structure. The company eventually goes into bankruptcy.

A large bank disciplines a "rebellious" manager who is blamed for current control problems, when the underlying cause is centralized procedures that are holding back expansion into new markets. Many younger managers subsequently leave the bank, competition moves in, and profits are still declining.

The problems of these companies, like those of many others, are rooted more in past decisions than in present events or outside market dynamics. Historical forces do indeed shape the future growth of organizations. Yet management, in its haste to grow, often overlooks such critical developmental questions as: Where has our organization been? Where is it now? And what do the answers to these questions mean for where we are going? Instead, its gaze is fixed outward toward the environment and the future —as if more precise market projections will provide a new organizational identity.

Companies fail to see that many clues to their future success lie within their own organizations and their evolving states of development. Moreover, the inability of management to understand its organization development problems can result in a company becoming "frozen" in its present stage of evolution or, ultimately, in failure, regardless of market opportunities.

My position in this article is that the future of an organization may be less determined by outside forces than it is by the organization's history. In stressing the force of history on an organization, I have drawn from the legacies of European psychologists (their thesis being that individual behavior is determined primarily by previous events and experiences, not by what lies ahead). Extending this analogy of individual development to the problems of organization development, I shall discuss a series of developmental phases through which growing companies tend to pass. But, first, let me provide two definitions:

1. The term *evolution* is used to describe prolonged periods of growth where no major upheaval occurs in organization practices.

2. The term *revolution* is used to describe those periods of substantial turmoil in organization life.

As a company progresses through developmental phases, each evolutionary period creates its own revolution. For instance, centralized practices eventually lead to demands for decentralization. Moreover, the nature of management's solution to each revolutionary period determines whether a company will move forward into its next stage of evolutionary growth. As I shall show later, there are at least five phases of organization development, each characterized by both an evolution and a revolution.

Key Forces in Development

During the past few years a small amount of research knowledge about the phases of organization development has been building. Some of this research is very quantitative, such as time-series analyses that reveal patterns of economic performance over time. The majority of studies, however, are case-oriented and use company records and interviews to reconstruct a rich picture of corporate development. Yet both types of research tend to be heavily empirical without attempting more generalized statements about the overall process of development.

A notable exception is the historical work of Alfred D. Chandler, Jr., in his book *Strategy and Structure*.[1] This study depicts four very broad and general phases in the lives of four large U.S. companies. It proposes that

1. *Strategy and Structure: Chapters in the History of the American Industrial Enterprise* (Cambridge, M.I.T. Press, 1962).

outside market opportunities determine a company's strategy, which in turn determines the company's organization structure. This thesis has a valid ring for the four companies examined by Chandler, largely because they developed in a time of explosive markets and technological advances. But more recent evidence suggests that organization structure may be less malleable than Chandler assumed; in fact, structure can play a critical role in influencing corporate strategy. It is this reverse emphasis on how organization structure affects future growth which is highlighted in the model presented in this article.

From an analysis of various studies,[2] five key dimensions emerge as essential for building a model of organization development:

1. Age of the organization.
2. Size of the organization.
3. Stages of evolution.
4. Stages of revolution.
5. Growth rate of the industry.

I shall describe each of these elements separately, but first note their combined effect as illustrated in *Exhibit I*. Note especially how each dimension influences the other over time; when all five elements begin to interact, a more complete and dynamic picture of organizational growth emerges.

After describing these dimensions and their interconnections, I shall discuss each evolutionary/revolutionary phase of development and show (a) how each stage of evolution breeds its own revolution, and (b) how management solutions to each revolution determine the next stage of evolution.

AGE OF THE ORGANIZATION

The most obvious and essential dimension for any model of development is the life span of an organization (represented as the horizontal axis in *Exhibit I*). All historical studies gather data from various points in time and then make comparisons. From these observations, it is evident that the same organization practices are not maintained throughout a long time span. This makes a most basic point: management problems and principles are rooted in time. The concept of decentralization, for ex-

2. I have drawn on many sources for evidence: (a) numerous cases collected at the Harvard Business School; (b) *Organization Growth and Development*, edited by William H. Starbuck (Middlesex, England, Penguin Books, Ltd., 1971), where several studies are cited; and (c) articles published in journals, such as Lawrence E. Fouraker and John M. Stopford, "Organization Structure and the Multinational Strategy," *Administrative Science Quarterly*, Vol. 13, No. 1, 1968, p. 47; and Malcolm S. Salter, "Management Appraisal and Reward Systems," *Journal of Business Policy*, Vol. 1, No. 4, 1971.

Exhibit I. Model of organization development

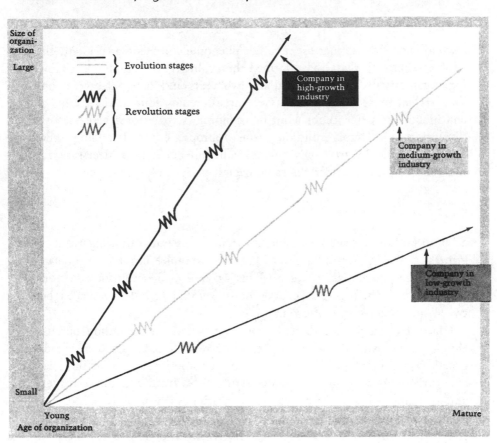

Size of organization

Large

Evolution stages

Revolution stages

Company in high-growth industry

Company in medium-growth industry

Company in low-growth industry

Small

Young

Mature

Age of organization

ample, can have meaning for describing corporate practices at one time period but loses its descriptive power at another.

The passage of time also contributes to the institutionalization of managerial attitudes. As a result, employee behavior becomes not only more predictable but also more difficult to change when attitudes are outdated.

SIZE OF THE ORGANIZATION

This dimension is depicted as the vertical axis in *Exhibit I*. A company's problems and solutions tend to change markedly as the number of employees and sales volume increase. Thus, time is not the only determinant of structure; in fact, organizations that do not grow in size can retain many of the same management issues and practices over lengthy periods. In addition to increased size, however, problems of coordination and communication magnify, new functions emerge, levels in the management hierarchy multiply, and jobs become more interrelated.

STAGES OF EVOLUTION

As both age and size increase, another phenomenon becomes evident: the prolonged growth that I have termed the evolutionary period. Most growing organizations do not expand for two years and then retreat for one year; rather, those that survive a crisis usually enjoy four to eight years of continuous growth without a major economic setback or severe internal disruption. The term evolution seems appropriate for describing these quieter periods because only modest adjustments appear necessary for maintaining growth under the same overall pattern of management.

STAGES OF REVOLUTION

Smooth evolution is not inevitable; it cannot be assumed that organization growth is linear. *Fortune*'s "500" list, for example, has had significant turnover during the last 50 years. Thus we find evidence from numerous case histories which reveals periods of substantial turbulence spaced between smoother periods of evolution.

I have termed these turbulent times the periods of revolution because they typically exhibit a serious upheaval of management practices. Traditional management practices, which were appropriate for a smaller size and earlier time, are brought under scrutiny by frustrated top managers and disillusioned lower-level managers. During such periods of crisis, a number of companies fail—those unable to abandon past practices and effect major organization changes are likely either to fold or to level off in their growth rates.

The critical task for management in each revolutionary period is to find a new set of organization practices that will become the basis for managing the next period of evolutionary growth. Interestingly enough, these new practices eventually sow their own seeds of decay and lead to another period of revolution. Companies therefore experience the irony of seeing a major solution in one time period become a major problem at a later date.

GROWTH RATE OF THE INDUSTRY

The speed at which an organization experiences phases of evolution and revolution is closely related to the market environment of its industry. For example, a company in a rapidly expanding market will have to add employees rapidly; hence, the need for new organization structures to accommodate large staff increases is accelerated. While evolutionary periods tend to be relatively short in fast-growing industries, much longer evolutionary periods occur in mature or slowly growing industries.

Exhibit II. The five phases of growth

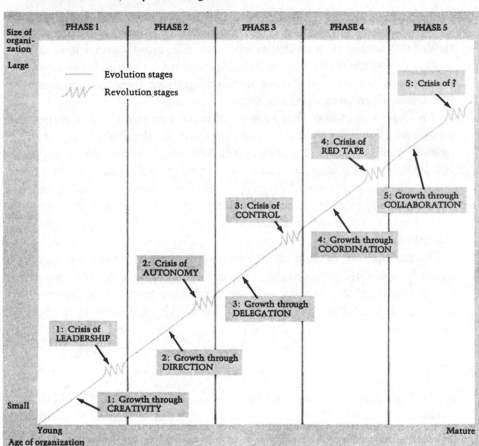

Evolution can also be prolonged, and revolutions delayed, when profits come easily. For instance, companies that make grievous errors in a rewarding industry can still look good on their profit and loss statements; thus they can avoid a change in management practices for a longer period. The aerospace industry in its infancy is an example. Yet revolutionary periods still occur, as one did in aerospace when profit opportunities began to dry up. Revolutions seem to be much more severe and difficult to resolve when the market environment is poor.

Phases of Growth

With the foregoing framework in mind, let us now examine in depth the five specific phases of evolution and revolution. As shown in *Exhibit II*, each evolutionary period is characterized by the dominant *management style* used to achieve growth, while each revolutionary period is characterized by the dominant *management problem* that must be solved before growth can continue. The patterns presented in *Exhibit II* seem to be typical for companies in industries with moderate growth over a long time period; companies in faster growing industries tend to experience all five phases more rapidly, while those in slower growing industries encounter only two or three phases over many years.

It is important to note that *each phase is both an effect of the previous phase and a cause for the next phase.* For example, the evolutionary management style in Phase 3 of the exhibit is "delegation," which grows out of, and becomes the solution to, demands for greater "autonomy" in the preceding Phase 2 revolution. The style of delegation used in Phase 3, however, eventually provokes a major revolutionary crisis that is characterized by attempts to regain control over the diversity created through increased delegation.

The principal implication of each phase is that management actions are narrowly prescribed if growth is to occur. For example, a company experiencing an autonomy crisis in Phase 2 cannot return to directive management for a solution—it must adopt a new style of delegation in order to move ahead.

PHASE I: CREATIVITY . . .

In the birth stage of an organization, the emphasis is on creating both a product and a market. Here are the characteristics of the period of creative evolution:

□ The company's founders are usually technically or entrepreneurially oriented, and they disdain management activities; their physical and mental energies are absorbed entirely in making and selling a new product.

□ Communication among employees is frequent and informal.

□ Long hours of work are rewarded by modest salaries and the promise of ownership benefits.

□ Control of activities comes from immediate marketplace feedback; the management acts as the customers react.

. . . *and the leadership crisis*: All of the foregoing individualistic and creative activities are essential for the company to get off the ground. But therein lies the problem. As the company grows, larger production runs require knowledge about the efficiencies of manufacturing. Increased numbers of employees cannot be managed exclusively through informal communication; new employees are not motivated by an intense dedication to the product or organization. Additional capital must be secured, and new accounting procedures are needed for financial control.

Thus the founders find themselves burdened with unwanted management responsibilities. So they long for the "good old days," still trying to act as they did in the past. And conflicts between the harried leaders grow more intense.

At this point a crisis of leadership occurs, which is the onset of the first revolution. Who is to lead the company out of confusion and solve the managerial problems confronting it? Quite obviously, a strong manager is needed who has the necessary knowledge and skill to introduce new business techniques. But this is easier said than done. The founders often hate to step aside even though they are probably temperamentally unsuited to be managers. So here is the first critical developmental choice—to locate and install a strong business manager who is acceptable to the founders and who can pull the organization together.

PHASE 2: DIRECTION . . .

Those companies that survive the first phase by installing a capable business manager usually embark on a period of sustained growth under able and directive leadership. Here are the characteristics of this evolutionary period:

◻ A functional organization structure is introduced to separate manufacturing from marketing activities, and job assignments become more specialized.

◻ Accounting systems for inventory and purchasing are introduced.

◻ Incentives, budgets, and work standards are adopted.

◻ Communication becomes more formal and impersonal as a hierarchy of titles and positions builds.

◻ The new manager and his key supervisors take most of the responsibility for instituting direction, while lower-level supervisors are treated more as functional specialists than as autonomous decision-making managers.

. . . and the autonomy crisis: Although the new directive techniques channel employee energy more efficiently into growth, they eventually become inappropriate for controlling a larger, more diverse and complex organization. Lower-level employees find themselves restricted by a cumbersome and centralized hierarchy. They have come to possess more direct knowledge about markets and machinery than do the leaders at the top; consequently, they feel torn between following procedures and taking initiative on their own.

Thus the second revolution is imminent as a crisis develops from demands for greater autonomy on the part of lower-level managers. The solution adopted by most companies is to move toward greater delegation. Yet it is difficult for top managers who were previously successful at being directive to give up responsibility. Moreover, lower-level managers are not accustomed to making decisions for themselves. As a result, numerous companies flounder during this revolutionary period, adhering to centralized methods while lower-level employees grow more disenchanted and leave the organization.

PHASE 3: DELEGATION . . .

The next era of growth evolves from the successful application of a decentralized organization structure. It exhibits these characteristics:

□ Much greater responsibility is given to the managers of plants and market territories.

□ Profit centers and bonuses are used to stimulate motivation.

□ The top executives at headquarters restrain themselves to managing by exception, based on periodic reports from the field.

□ Management often concentrates on making new acquisitions which can be lined up beside other decentralized units.

□ Communication from the top is infrequent, usually by correspondence, telephone, or brief visits to field locations.

The delegation stage proves useful for gaining expansion through heightened motivation at lower levels. Decentralized managers with greater authority and incentive are able to penetrate larger markets, respond faster to customers, and develop new products.

. . . and the control crisis: A serious problem eventually evolves, however, as top executives sense that they are losing control over a highly diversified field operation. Autonomous field managers prefer to run their own shows without coordinating plans, money, technology, and man-power with the rest of the organization. Freedom breeds a parochial attitude.

Hence, the Phase 3 revolution is under way when top management seeks to regain control over the total company. Some top managements attempt a return to centralized management, which usually fails because of the vast scope of operations. Those companies that move ahead find a new solution in the use of special coordination techniques.

PHASE 4: COORDINATION . . .

During this phase, the evolutionary period is characterized by the use of formal systems for achieving greater coordination and by top executives taking responsibility for the initiation and administration of these new systems. For example:

□ Decentralized units are merged into product groups.

□ Formal planning procedures are established and intensively reviewed.

◻ Numerous staff personnel are hired and located at headquarters to initiate company-wide programs of control and review for line managers.

◻ Capital expenditures are carefully weighed and parceled out across the organization.

◻ Each product group is treated as an investment center where return on invested capital is an important criterion used in allocating funds.

◻ Certain technical functions, such as data processing, are centralized at headquarters, while daily operating decisions remain decentralized.

◻ Stock options and companywide profit sharing are used to encourage identity with the firm as a whole.

All of these new coordination systems prove useful for achieving growth through more efficient allocation of a company's limited resources. They prompt field managers to look beyond the needs of their local units. While these managers still have much decision-making responsibility, they learn to justify their actions more carefully to a "watchdog" audience at headquarters.

. . . and the red-tape crisis: But a lack of confidence gradually builds between line and staff, and between headquarters and the field. The proliferation of systems and programs begins to exceed its utility; a red-tape crisis is created. Line managers, for example, increasingly resent heavy staff direction from those who are not familiar with local conditions. Staff people, on the other hand, complain about uncooperative and uninformed line managers. Together both groups criticize the bureaucratic paper system that has evolved. Procedures take precedence over problem solving, and innovation is dampened. In short, the organization has become too large and complex to be managed through formal programs and rigid systems. The Phase 4 revolution is under way.

PHASE 5: COLLABORATION . . .

The last observable phase in previous studies emphasizes strong interpersonal collaboration in an attempt to overcome the red-tape crisis. Where Phase 4 was managed more through formal systems and procedures, Phase 5 emphasizes greater spontaneity in management action through teams and the skillful confrontation of interpersonal differences. Social control and self-discipline take over from formal control. This transition is especially difficult for those experts who created the old systems as well as for those line managers who relied on formal methods for answers.

The Phase 5 evolution, then, builds around a more flexible and behavioral approach to management. Here are its characteristics:

◻ The focus is on solving problems quickly through team action.

◻ Teams are combined across functions for task-group activity.

▢ Headquarters staff experts are reduced in number, reassigned, and combined in interdisciplinary teams to consult with, not to direct, field units.

▢ A matrix-type structure is frequently used to assemble the right teams for the appropriate problems.

▢ Previous formal systems are simplified and combined into single multipurpose systems.

▢ Conferences of key managers are held frequently to focus on major problem issues.

▢ Educational programs are utilized to train managers in behavioral skills for achieving better teamwork and conflict resolution.

▢ Real-time information systems are integrated into daily decision making.

▢ Economic rewards are geared more to team performance than to individual achievement.

▢ Experiments in new practices are encouraged throughout the organization.

. . . and the ? crisis: What will be the revolution in response to this stage of evolution? Many large U.S. companies are now in the Phase 5 evolutionary stage, so the answers are critical. While there is little clear evidence, I imagine the revolution will center around the "psychological saturation" of employees who grow emotionally and physically exhausted by the intensity of teamwork and the heavy pressure for innovative solutions.

My hunch is that the Phase 5 revolution will be solved through new structures and programs that allow employees to periodically rest, reflect, and revitalize themselves. We may even see companies with dual organization structures: a "habit" structure for getting the daily work done, and a "reflective" structure for stimulating perspective and personal enrichment. Employees could then move back and forth between the two structures as their energies are dissipated and refueled.

One European organization has implemented just such a structure. Five reflective groups have been established outside the regular structure for the purpose of continuously evaluating five task activities basic to the organization. They report directly to the managing director, although their reports are made public throughout the organization. Membership in each group includes all levels and functions, and employees are rotated through these groups on a six-month basis.

Other concrete examples now in practice include providing sabbaticals for employees, moving managers in and out of "hot spot" jobs, establishing a four-day workweek, assuring job security, building physical facilities for relaxation *during* the working day, making jobs more interchangeable, creating an extra team on the assembly line so that one team is always off

Category	PHASE 1	PHASE 2	PHASE 3	PHASE 4	PHASE 5
MANAGEMENT FOCUS	Make & sell	Efficiency of operations	Expansion of market	Consolidation of organization	Problem solving & innovation
ORGANIZATION STRUCTURE	Informal	Centralized & functional	Decentralized & geographical	Line-staff & product groups	Matrix of teams
TOP MANAGEMENT STYLE	Individualistic & entrepreneurial	Directive	Delegative	Watchdog	Participative
CONTROL SYSTEM	Market results	Standards & cost centers	Reports & profit centers	Plans & investment centers	Mutual goal setting
MANAGEMENT REWARD EMPHASIS	Ownership	Salary & merit increases	Individual bonus	Profit sharing & stock options	Team bonus

for reeducation, and switching to longer vacations and more flexible working hours.

The Chinese practice of requiring executives to spend time periodically on lower-level jobs may also be worth a nonideological evaluation. For too long U.S. management has assumed that career progress should be equated with an upward path toward title, salary, and power. Could it be that some vice presidents of marketing might just long for, and even benefit from, temporary duty in the field sales organization?

Implications of History

Let me now summarize some important implications for practicing managers. First, the main features of this discussion are depicted in *Exhibit III*, which shows the specific management actions that characterize each growth phase. These actions are also the solutions which ended each preceding revolutionary period.

In one sense, I hope that many readers will react to my model by calling it obvious and natural for depicting the growth of an organization. To me this type of reaction is a useful test of the model's validity.

But at a more reflective level I imagine some of these reactions are more hindsight than foresight. Those experienced managers who have been through a developmental sequence can empathize with it now, but how did they react when in the middle of a stage of evolution or revolution?

They can probably recall the limits of their own developmental understanding at that time. Perhaps they resisted desirable changes or were even swept emotionally into a revolution without being able to propose constructive solutions. So let me offer some explicit guidelines for managers of growing organizations to keep in mind.

Know where you are in the developmental sequence.

Every organization and its component parts are at different stages of development. The task of top management is to be aware of these stages; otherwise, it may not recognize when the time for change has come, or it may act to impose the wrong solution.

Top leaders should be ready to work with the flow of the tide rather than against it; yet they should be cautious, since it is tempting to skip phases out of impatience. Each phase results in certain strengths and learning experiences in the organization that will be essential for success in subsequent phases. A child prodigy, for example, may be able to read like a teenager, but he cannot behave like one until he ages through a sequence of experiences.

I also doubt that managers can or should act to avoid revolutions. Rather, these periods of tension provide the pressure, ideas, and awareness that afford a platform for change and the introduction of new practices.

Recognize the limited range of solutions.

In each revolutionary stage it becomes evident that this stage can be ended only by certain specific solutions; moreover, these solutions are different from those which were applied to the problems of the preceding revolution. Too often it is tempting to choose solutions that were tried before, which makes it impossible for a new phase of growth to evolve.

Management must be prepared to dismantle current structures before the revolutionary stage becomes too turbulent. Top managers, realizing that their own managerial styles are no longer appropriate, may even have to take themselves out of leadership positions. A good Phase 2 manager facing Phase 3 might be wise to find another Phase 2 organization that better fits his talents, either outside the company or with one of its newer subsidiaries.

Finally, evolution is not an automatic affair; it is a contest for survival. To move ahead, companies must consciously introduce planned structures that not only are solutions to a current crisis but also are fitted to the *next* phase of growth. This requires considerable self-awareness on the part of top management, as well as great interpersonal skill in persuading other managers that change is needed.

Realize that solutions breed new problems.

Managers often fail to realize that organizational solutions create problems for the future (i.e., a decision to delegate eventually causes a problem of control). Historical actions are very much determinants of what happens to the company at a much later date.

An awareness of this effect should help managers to evaluate company problems with greater historical understanding instead of "pinning the blame" on a current development. Better yet, managers should be in a position to *predict* future problems, and thereby to prepare solutions and coping strategies before a revolution gets out of hand.

A management that is aware of the problems ahead could well decide *not* to grow. Top managers may, for instance, prefer to retain the informal practices of a small company, knowing that this way of life is inherent in the organization's limited size, not in their congenial personalities. If they choose to grow, they may do themselves out of a job and a way of life they enjoy.

And what about the managements of very large organizations? Can they find new solutions for continued phases of evolution? Or are they reaching a stage where the government will act to break them up because they are too large?

Concluding Note

Clearly, there is still much to learn about processes of development in organizations. The phases outlined here are only five in number and are still only approximations. Researchers are just beginning to study the specific developmental problems of structure, control, rewards, and management style in different industries and in a variety of cultures.

One should not, however, wait for conclusive evidence before educating managers to think and act from a developmental perspective. The critical dimension of time has been missing for too long from our management theories and practices. The intriguing paradox is that by learning more about history we may do a better job in the future.

36. How the Multidimensional Structure Works at Dow Corning

William C. Goggin

In 1967 Dow Corning Corporation, which is jointly owned by the Dow Chemical Company and Corning Glass Works, reorganized from a conventional divisionalized type of organization into a matrix form of organization. As top management continued to experiment and innovate, the matrix form turned into what the company now calls a multidimensional organization. Judging from employees' reactions to the new pattern, as well as from impressive gains in sales, profits, productivity, and exports, the multidimensional organization is a striking success. This article examines the underlying philosophy of this organization pattern, its working parts, its use by management, and its advantages and disadvantages.

Although Dow Corning was a healthy corporation in 1967, it showed symptoms of difficulty that troubled many of us in top management. These symptoms were, and still are, common ones in U.S. business and have been described countless times in reports, audits, articles, and speeches. Our symptoms took such form as:

□ Executives did not have adequate financial information and control of their operations. Marketing managers, for example, did not know how much it cost to produce a product. Prices and margins were set by the division managers.

□ Cumbersome communications channels existed between key functions, especially manufacturing and marketing.

□ In the face of stiffening competition, the corporation remained too internalized in its thinking and organizational structure. It was insufficiently oriented to the outside world.

□ Lack of communication between divisions not only created the antithesis of a corporate team effort but also was wasteful of a precious resource —people.

□ Long-range corporate planning was sporadic and superficial; this was leading to overstaffing, duplicated effort, and inefficiency.

Fearing that our problems would become worse instead of better in the

Exhibit I. *Evolution of a new organization concept*

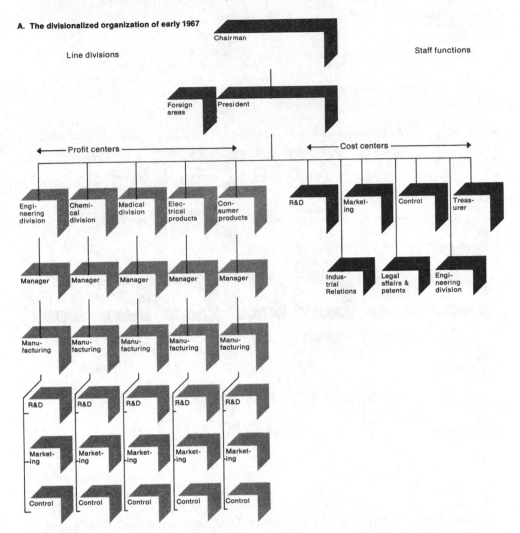

future, we undertook major changes in our organizational structure. We turned to a matrix concept of organization—what we later came to call the multidimensional organization.

We made this revolutionary and novel move with our fingers crossed. For one thing, we knew of no case where a full-fledged, permanent matrix organization was in successful operation. We knew that the matrix structures pioneered by the aerospace industry in the late 1950s and the 1960s had been successful, but they had been project expedients, not designs for permanent organizations. For another, the new pattern bore little resemblance to the existing one (see Part A of *Exhibit I*); we were committing ourselves to a drastic overhaul, not a modification.

This overhaul meant that communicating the purpose and nature of the

Exhibit I. (continued)

**B. Two-dimensional
concept – profit and
cost centers**

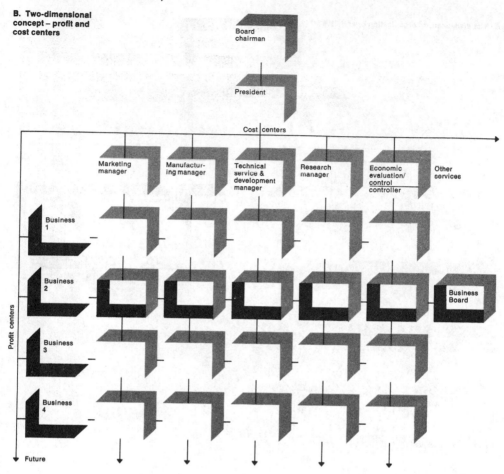

change to employees would be very difficult and sometimes nearly impossible. However, we were confident that in the long run the matrix form would stimulate innovation and lead to increased emphasis on opportunities for profit rather than preoccupation with problems. And we were determined to make it succeed.

Four-Dimensional System

As we first thought of it, the matrix organization was to be two-dimensional. As Part B of *Exhibit I* suggests, the different businesses in Dow Corning were seen as:

1. *Profit centers*—These were the different businesses the company was in. Businesses were defined along product lines—for instance, rubber, encapsulants and sealants; resins and chemicals; fluids, emulsions, and

Exhibit I. (continued)

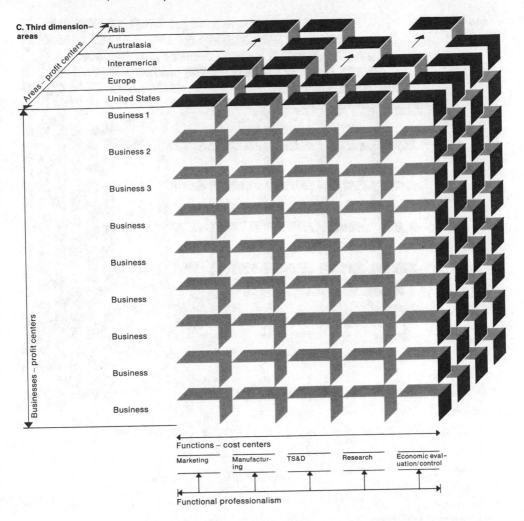

C. Third dimension—areas

Areas – profit centers

Asia
Australasia
Interamerica
Europe
United States

Business 1
Business 2
Business 3
Business
Business
Business
Business
Business
Business

Businesses – profit centers

Functions – cost centers

| Marketing | Manufactur-ing | TS&D | Research | Economic eval-uation/control |

Functional professionalism

compounds; specialty lubricants; and consumer, medical, and semi-conductor products. In most of the cases each business's product line served a related group of industries, markets, or customers.

2. *Cost centers*—These were functional activities and included marketing, manufacturing, technical service and development, and research, as well as a number of supportive activities, such as corporate communications, legal and administrative services, economic evaluation, the controller's office, the treasurer's office, and industrial relations.

But soon we came to see further dimensions of the system:

3. *Geographical areas*—Business development varied widely from area to area, and the profit-center and cost-center dimensions could not be carried out everywhere in the same manner. Part C of *Exhibit I* shows this

Exhibit I. (continued)

**D. Fourth dimension –
space & time**

Business | Marketing | Manu-facturing | Technical service & development | Research | Economic evaluation/control

Functions

Areas

Business

Growth through planning & time

dimension. Note that each area is considered to be *both* a profit and a cost center. Dow Corning area organizations are patterned after our major U.S. organization. Although somewhat autonomous in their operation, they subscribe to the overall corporate objectives, operating guidelines, and planning criteria. During the annual planning cycle, for example, there is a mutual exchange of sales, expense, and profit projections between the functional and business managers headquartered in the United States and the area managers around the world.

4. *Space and time*—A fourth dimension of the organization denotes fluidity and movement through time (see Part D). The multidimensional organization is far from rigid; it is constantly changing. Unlike centralized or decentralized systems that too often are rooted deep in the past, the multidimensional organization is geared toward the future. Long-term planning is an inherent part of its operation.

Keys to Effectiveness

In a multidimensional organization like the one we developed, decision making tends to be flattened out or spread across the organization. No longer is the chief executive or the president required to pass judgment on every important issue. Most of the decisions are made at the middle management level, but not unilaterally; the intent is to push decision making as far down into the organization as possible and encourage group consensus.

What are the requirements of making such a system work?

The first requirement is that communications within the corporation be thorough and complete. Timely and relevant data must go to all who have a *need to know*. A risk is attached to this: sensitive information often must be distributed well beyond the executive suite, leading to the ever-present danger that some data will find their way out of the corporation. Offsetting this concern is the fact that business conditions change so rapidly that today's confidential information may be virtually worthless tomorrow.

The second requirement is that those in charge of projects be able to understand and use the available data.

To appreciate what these requirements mean for managerial structure and reporting relationships, let us see how the Business Boards operate at Dow Corning.

BUSINESS BOARD OPERATION

There is a Business Board for each of the company's ten businesses. The only full-time board member is the manager of the business. His position

Exhibit II. The Business Board

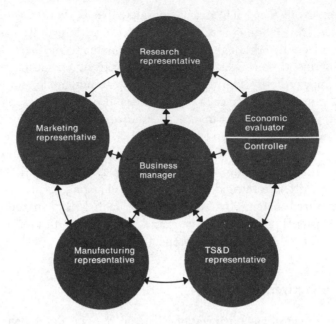

in the organization is at once critical and tenuous. It is critical because his direct responsibility is the profit yield generated from the business he is charged with managing. It is tenuous because on paper he does not have direct control of the resources needed to accomplish his task. His operative body, his total resource, comprises representatives from the marketing, technical service and development, research, manufacturing, and economic evaluation/control functions (see *Exhibit II*). These are the Business Board members. They report *directly* to their functional group heads (vice president of marketing and distribution, director of technical service and development, and so on).

Organizationally, there is a strong dotted-line relationship running from the board member to the board manager. More important than organizational lines, however, is the clear understanding of where the profit responsibility lies. *Exhibit II* illustrates the structure and communications pattern of a board. Its manager reports directly to Dow Corning's top management. His primary task—to generate profits—is accomplished through the total and combined support of his board members.

At the outset, this setup created a stress-strain situation. Prior to 1968 the functional specialist at Dow Corning had concerned himself exclusively with maintaining and improving the professionalism of his function. Now, in addition, he was asked to lead in developng profits for his business. However, as his understanding of business goals increased and his comprehension of the workings of other functions increased, the stress began to dissipate.

The operation of each Business Board produces a healthy and invigorating power balance. The business manager must be a *leader,* not a dictator. He must work diligently toward sound economic decisions. Harmonious and productive Business Board activity is a tall order and does not happen automatically. Our experience is that teamwork rapidly improves with practice.

Cross-functional communications play a big part in the process. Since 1968, we have seen important changes in perspective. For example, in the early 1960s, an aggressive Dow Corning marketing manager would typically consider the generation of, say, 18% more sales dollars as *the* single most critical objective for the corporation. In line with this priority, he would make a strong case for allocating heavy marketing expenses to support sales objectives.

Today, the aggressive marketing manager who is on a Business Board is still concerned with the generation of increased sales dollars. But his overriding aim is generating the *most profitable* sales dollar. In order to know and evaluate intelligently the profitability of products he is responsible for, he seeks to use the inputs of his functional colleagues in manufacturing, technical service and development, research, and economic evaluation. Our history with the multidimensional organization indicates that similar advances in understanding have occurred among all the other functional representatives on each board.

TWO-BOSS SYSTEM

A majority of the company's professional personnel work in dual authority relationships (see *Exhibit III*). While it may seem schizoid for a person to be responsible to two bosses, that is exactly what happens in a successful multidimensional operation—and it works well. Of course, the person must not become involved in a tug-of-war between his functional and Business Board bosses, or be given cause to despair over who is really appraising his day-to-day performance. To prevent that kind of situation, the functional and business managers are jointly responsible for periodic performance reviews that let the individual know exactly where he stands and what is expected of him.

Top management must also ensure that both the functional and the Business Board managers are given the authority, responsibility, and accountability for successfully attaining their objectives. The ultimate measurement is the long- and short-term rate of profit growth.

Making the two-boss system workable depends on the establishment of an environment of trust and confidence. Nurturing and perpetuating this environment must begin at the very top of the organization. Corporate goals and objectives must be seen by every employee as good, proper,

Exhibit III. The two-boss system

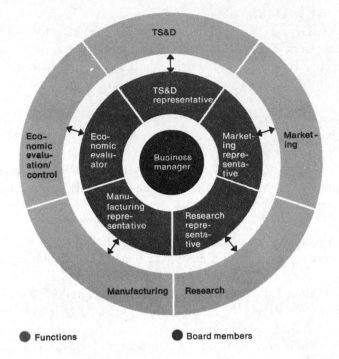

potentially achievable, and worthy of strong commitment. Only then can an individual commit himself with a clear conscience to achieving the goals while working in a complex system of interlocking responsibilities.

SUPPORTING SUBSYSTEMS

Another type of organization is the product management group (PMG). This is essentially a small Business Board devoted to long- and short-term planning for individual product families, or what we call business planning units (BPUs). A PMG comprises functional representatives, as does a Business Board, but its members may come from lower organizational levels. It is responsible for profits in its product area and is vested with the authority to bring its requests for resources to the appropriate Business Board. Once a request is approved, the PMG is fully responsible for wise investment of its resources so that corporate goals can be achieved. PMG managers often attend Business Board meetings, which is evidence of the vital contribution these people make to the company.

PMGs are usually permanent. However, the chairmanship of such a group is not a full-time responsibility, as it is on a Business Board. Personnel shifts within the PMGs are common, serving to bring fresh blood to the groups and to train lower-level management people for greater responsibilities.

Industry management teams are yet another subsystem. While the PMG concentrates its efforts on the management of individual product families, the industry management teams are concerned with the marketing of many products to a single major market or industry, such as the automotive market or the electronics industry.

In addition to the foregoing subsystems, Dow Corning has occasional need for short-term ad hoc task forces. Typical task force projects might be solving a product or processing problem, streamlining order entry and delivery procedures, resolving inventory problems, or developing a corporate safety promotion.

CORPORATE BUSINESS BOARD

I have described the flattened-out or egalitarian style of management and decision making that is built into the multidimensional organization. In order to keep the overall corporate direction well balanced and to prevent the potential splinter effect of several semiautonomous businesses zealously seeking to accomplish their individual goals and objectives, we have a guiding body called the Corporate Business Board. It comprises the chairman, president, vice presidents, and other functional heads; it is similar to executive committees in many corporations. As the top decision-making body in the corporation, this group provides cross-communications between businesses, functions, and areas. It influences and approves long- and short-range corporate objectives.

The Corporate Business Board meets at least once a month to review the sales and profit progress of each business against its projected plans. Progress in each geographical area is reviewed quarterly on the same basis. The board also meets as needed to review or initiate critical corporate projects and programs.

Area Management

At this point in our organizational evolution, the geographical areas are at different stages of development. Within the next two to four years, however, all will be patterned closely after the U.S. organization. Each area has its own management, though corporate "ground rules" apply uniformly to all. Area managers must decide when modifications of these ground rules are absolutely necessary because of local customs and business practices, government regulations, and other considerations.

Close communication is maintained between area managers and the U.S. organization. The former must not function independently; at the same time the businesses and functions cannot do their jobs without intimate knowledge of area operations. The area managers work according to a plan for sales, expenses, and profits. The plan for each area is integrated into the plan for each business and function. Thus the area plan is viewed as a part of a larger corporate whole. This two-way system allows each area to maintain a viable cost-center/profit-center balance and to operate with a sufficient degree of autonomy.

Twice each year the area managers meet with the executive management to plan, review, and coordinate global plans and programs.

Crucial Support Systems

The basic charter for each function at Dow Corning is clear and unequivocal:

□ *Marketing*—generation of sales volume, with a sharp eye on profitability.

□ *Technical service and development*—new product commercialization and old-product maintenance.

□ *Manufacturing*—volume and efficiency in production, engineering, and technology.

□ *Research*—assurance of a steady flow of new products that can be commercialized.

□ *Economic evaluation, control, and planning*—development of a common corporate economic language and a uniform analytical system for evaluating capital expenditures and all strategic programs having an economic impact.

These functions are found in nearly all large U.S. corporations. In a multidimensional organization, however, they are perhaps more closely related, and it is especially important that they work together smoothly and productively. Consistent and uniform standards are essential.

To help achieve such coordination, our company maintains a number of support systems. Here I shall describe only six of them; the order of description is not intended to suggest relative priorities or importance. *Exhibit IV* lists the support systems and the operating entities they are designed to support.

MANAGEMENT BY OBJECTIVES

One pillar of a multidimensional organization is MBO. At Dow Corning, MBO involves (a) a hierarchy of objectives, and (b) employee *involvement, participation,* and *accountability* at all levels.

The objectives of each business, function, or support group are established on the basis of overall corporate objectives. A condensed version of

Exhibit IV. Role of support systems

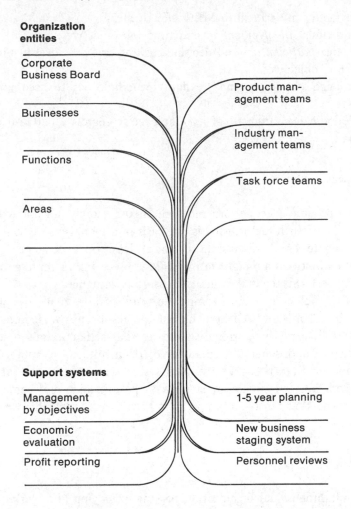

Organization entities

Corporate Business Board

Product management teams

Businesses

Industry management teams

Functions

Task force teams

Areas

Support systems

Management by objectives

1-5 year planning

Economic evaluation

New business staging system

Profit reporting

Personnel reviews

our corporate objectives for one recent year, with the confidential data excluded, appears in the Appendix on page 668. Note that these objectives are simply stated, clear, and, for the most part, quantifiable. (Even Objective VIII will be stated in measurable terms before long, we hope; work toward that end is under way.) These objectives constitute the sum total of results that must be accomplished by members of the organization within given time periods, generally one year and five years.

To develop objectives in this way in every business, function, and area, a great amount of communication must go on throughout the planning cycle. For example, each Business Board must know what the marketing function's sales projections and expense requirements are. And marketing cannot make its projections without specific inputs from each business and area. Also, a PMG must develop its set of objectives in accordance with the goals of the parent business.

Four factors are critical to MBO effectiveness:

1. Individual *involvement* in preparing job objectives.

2. Active *participation* and decision making at every level in pursuit of established objectives.

3. Enough *autonomy* and *freedom* for employees to accomplish the goals set.

4. Periodic *measurement* of an employee's progress in attaining his or her goals.

PERSONNEL REVIEWS

Reviews of employee performance are linked closely to the MBO approach. The fourth factor listed is the basis of a manager's discussion with a subordinate (such discussions occur at least once a year). For professional employees a 5-point rating scale is used, with 1 representing outstanding performance and 5 unsatisfactory performance.

Ideally, each professional employee understands that his rating is largely based on how well he achieved the results he was committed to achieve. Our experience strongly indicates that self-appraisals tend to be more critical and demanding than imposed, or autocratic, appraisals.

As one might expect, the two-boss system comes into play at review time. Both bosses evaluate an employee's performance and agree on the single rating that most fairly represents their judgment of his work.

PLANNING PROCESS

The multidimensional organization has many moving and working parts, and planning how they are to fit together is a major activity. Our corporate planning department develops the format and planning cycle that guides the activities of the businesses, functions, and areas.

The planning department does not *do* the planning. It simply develops, administers, and communicates the corporate ground rules. Each business, function, and area must do its own planning. The total effort is funneled into one- and five-year corporate plans that are reviewed and approved by the Corporate Business Board before they are presented to the board of directors for final approval.

ECONOMIC EVALUATION

Another extremely important support system is economic evaluation. This involves evaluating capital expenditures as well as any proposed strategic program that carries economic impact. Economic evaluation provides us with a common economic language. Each Business Board is staffed with an economic evaluator whose primary job is to measure the value of a new investment or new strategy to his business and to the corporation. The economic evaluator is generally the business's controller as well.

In a dynamic organization many options for new business development are considered, options which can originate from any source. Potentially, they must meet the ROI criteria set forth in the corporate objectives. It is up to the economic evaluator to assess objectively the investment proposals put before his business or the Corporate Business Board. His analysis includes the probable ROI, discounted cash flow, and net present value of the proposed investment. He is also expected to present alternatives to the proposed solution along with the appropriate economic justification.

Economic evaluation does not stifle thinking about new business opportunities; what it does do is vastly reduce the chance for error. It replaces investment decisions based on emotions and "gut feel" with economically sound and objective investment decisions.

PROFIT REPORTING

All sales and expenditures are identified or assigned to a business or business planning unit. This allows the company's total profit before tax to be clearly identified by each geographic area as well as by each of the ten businesses. In the marketing function, for example, field salesmen are assigned specific business planning units or product lines for which they have sales responsibility. Selling costs are directly assigned to the business planning units of the products sold. The other cost center functions operate in a like manner.

In this direct-costing system we identify and separate both variable and fixed costs. This allows area and business managers to separate the planning and control of those costs which vary with volume from those which are fixed or subject to management decision. The system thereby provides a sure and uncluttered approach to profit determination. It also eliminates "hidden" expenses and greatly facilitates businesslike financial management.

NEW BUSINESS STAGING

A company that stresses advanced technology naturally places much emphasis on new-product development and commercialization. Before the development of our multidimensional organization, an average of nearly eight years elapsed from the time a new product was conceptualized until

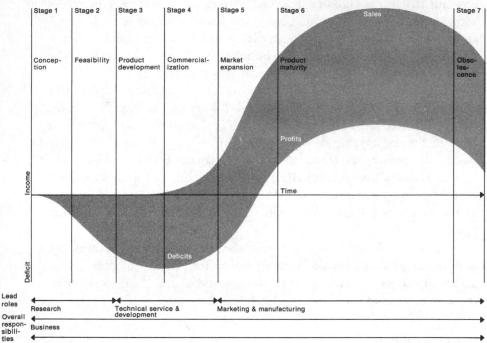

Exhibit V. *Product life cycle and management responsibilities*

Stage 1	Stage 2	Stage 3	Stage 4	Stage 5	Stage 6	Stage 7
Conception	Feasibility	Product development	Commercialization	Market expansion	Product maturity	Obsolescence

Lead roles

Research   Technical service & development   Marketing & manufacturing

Overall responsibilities

Business

Product management team

---

it reached commercialization (if it ever did). In the light of encroaching competitive pressures, we realized we needed to reduce the commercialization time. As a result, our new business staging system was born.

This system provides a disciplined and organized approach to new product commercialization. As *Exhibit V* shows, seven stages of the product life cycle are identified, ranging from conception (Stage 1) through product obsolescence (Stage 7). The task is to identify and coordinate the efforts of many people. In each stage one function has the major role to play and acts as the project quarterback. For example, in Stage 2 (feasibility), research is the prime mover. When a product moves to Stage 4 (commercialization), technical service and development assumes ball control. In Stage 5 (market expansion), it is marketing's ballgame.

But in no stage does the lead function have the only input. For instance, marketing is often much involved in Stage 4 commercialization projects, just as technical service and development is instrumental in keeping Stage 5 products properly maintained and free from operating defects.

The new business staging system is designed to produce a team effort, with clearly identified functional responsibilities. Using this system, the corporation hopes to reduce by 50%, before the end of this decade, the time that is traditionally required for the commercialization of a new product.

Conclusion

The advantages and disadvantages of a system such as Dow Corning's can be realistically evaluated only after management has taken a rather exhaustive internal audit. I can personally attest to the difficulty of this task; it requires management to criticize a structure that many of its members have spent years developing.

By all quantitative and qualitative measurements, it can be stated, after our years of experience, that our multidimensional organization is successful. At the same time, however, even though I am an enthusiastic proponent of the system, I must be the first to caution that the multidimensional technique is not a panacea for all organization problems. And the dedication that top management must maintain during the long and arduous years of restructuring should not be underestimated.

What kinds of companies might benefit from a multidimensional organization? Those that meet all or most of the following conditions should be good prospects:

□ Developing, manufacturing, and marketing many diverse but interrelated technological products and materials.

□ Having market interests that span virtually every major industry.

□ Becoming multinational with a rapidly expanding *global* business.

□ Working in a business environment of rapid and drastic change, together with strong competition.

Conversely, a company with a limited product line, operating mostly in the United States, and serving a single industry or a limited number of customers would not have much use for this system. Nor would many service-oriented industries or manufacturing companies with nontechnical commodity-type products. I believe, however, that certain forward-thinking service-oriented industries (e.g., health management, education, and financial service) might use a modified version of the multidimensional organization quite effectively. My own experience and knowledge of service-related companies lead me to believe that many of the principles of multidimensional organization can be applied to nonmanufacturing operations.

COSTS AND BENEFITS

The initiation fee to the multidimensional organization group is very high. Some costs to consider are:

1. Willingness to cope with resistance to change.

2. Top management dedication for years—and this means not one, but essentially all, top executives.

3. A highly intelligent and motivated middle management anxious to see the whole corporation progress—no freeloaders.

4. Determination to minimize internal politics—no empire builders.

5. An abundance of patience on the part of the board of directors, top management, and middle management.

At the outset, much of the existing organization may be uprooted, with functions and businesses redefined and realigned, and new geographic areas established. People movement soars to a high peak as many activities and jobs are phased out and new ones are created. At all levels, especially middle management, there is uncertainty and serious questioning of the "new" system.

Once operational, the system is surprisingly flexible, but at the outset it *appears* to be rigid. This is so because on paper a matrix structure clearly defines lines of authority. What cannot be clearly written into the scheme at the start is how free-flowing communication tends to soften the rigid-looking organizational lines once the system becomes operative. Also, in our own case, a number of subsystems that were not built into the original structure, such as the product management groups and the new business staging system, have tended to add flexibility and cross-communications throughout the entire corporation.

There is one final condition that should be considered by corporations desiring to explore the multidimensional concept further: the basic orientation of the *entire* organization must be psychologically attuned to results. Managers who have grown accustomed to rationalizing failure and near misses will find the climate of a dynamic multidimensional organization very uncomfortable because it is so results-oriented and facts-conscious. Those who prefer "telling it like it is" will find the system exciting and rewarding.

The break-in period for our new system was three to four years. The company did not suffer unduly as a result of the organizational upheaval. In fact, the economic downturn during 1970-1971 served to reinforce the system's potential for coping with difficulty.

What advantages stand to be gained from a multidimensional organization? Our experience points to the following:

□ Higher profit generation, even in an industry (silicones) price-squeezed by competition. (Much of our favorable profit picture seems due to a better overall understanding and practice of expense controls throughout the company.)

□ Increased competitive ability based on technological innovation and product quality without a sacrifice in profitability.

□ Sound, fast decision making at all levels in the organization, facilitated by stratified but open channels of communication and by a totally participative working environment.

□ A healthy and effective balance of authority among the businesses, functions, and areas.

□ Progress in developing short- and long-range planning with the support of all employees.

□ Resource allocations that are proportionate to expected results.

□ More stimulating and effective on-the-job training.

□ Accountability that is more closely related to responsibility and authority.

□ Results that are visible and measurable.

□ More top-management time for long-range planning and less need to become involved in day-to-day operations.

Perhaps the single most pressing problem that faces any industrial organization is how to cope effectively with change. The multidimensional organization is designed to combat that problem. Since change is constant, so must our organization be continually flexible and adaptive to changing conditions on all fronts. We perceive our organization to be a dynamic one, and, to date, our experience indicates that we do indeed have the ability to manage change rather than be managed by it.

Appendix to Chapter 36

Corporate Objectives for One Recent Year

    I. *Profits*—Maintain rate of growth of pretax profits of at least A% per year.

    II. *Sales*—Increase worldwide sales by at least B%.

    III. *Share of market*—Increase market share by C%.

    IV. *Productivity*—Improve productivity (total cost of employees divided by sales) by D%.

    V. *Return on investment*—Increase ROI to E% after taxes and maintain it at that level.

    VI. *New capital*—Expected return on new capital investment should be at least F% after taxes.

    VII. *New products*—Products less than five years old should contribute a minimum of G% of total sales.

    VIII. *Quality of life*—In all countries, Dow Corning should continue to fulfill its social responsibilities as a leading corporate citizen.

    IX. *Safety*—Both corporate frequency and severity rates should be among the ten best reported to the Manufacturing Chemists Association each year.

37. Strategy for Winning Employee Commitment

Douglas S. Sherwin

This article originated with one businessman's concern that employees' lack of commitment to work and to the organization deprived the employees of their right to satisfaction on the job, and deprived business of important benefits. Here he describes an approach for eliciting commitment. It calls for management to rely not on power, which is rapidly becoming an impotent tool of direction, but on a philosophy of leadership emphasizing shared objectives. The author also suggests several new forms of organization to take the place of outworn concepts.

Lack of commitment by employees is behind much of the behavior blamed for high costs and poor service. Students of the management art, therefore, have devoted themselves to understanding the causes of commitment and alienation among employees. Their insights have resulted in persuasive new approaches aimed at gaining commitment and changing behavior. Participative management, Theory Y styles of supervision, management by objectives, sensitivity training, job enrichment, leadership and human relations training are some of the products of this creative effort.

Business executives are anxious to see employee attitudes improved. Appreciating that the results they get come from existing behavior, and that better results require different behavior, they doggedly—though perhaps not always hopefully—try out new ideas for altering attitudes and behavior. But the results are often disappointing. When the training has been given and the employee returns to his job, managers usually find the employee backsliding to his old habits, attitudes, and behavior. They end up feeling disillusionment and lack of conviction toward training programs and other techniques designed to change personality, attitudes, or behavior.

What is the explanation? It lies, I believe, in the most basic assumptions of organization. Commitment, far from being something that has to be created in employees, is a natural, psychological need of every person. But we in management frustrate it at the source by assumptions and practices that we apply in the organizing process. Because these assumptions are intrinsic to organizing and are made prior to any functioning of the organization, their influence is always present and maintains a kind of irreducible level or core of employee alienation. So when the employee returns to his job after training, he comes again under their influence and eventually resumes the behavior observed before the training.

According to contemporary thought, organization is a strategy for achieving goals.[1] Based on this criterion, our strategy has to be judged incomplete; the organization has not permitted its members to satisfy their psychological and social needs. In this article I shall first describe how our prevailing concept of management power frustrates employee commitment, and how a new approach to leadership can cope with this problem. In the second part of the discussion I shall describe three more obstructions to commitment—the divisionalization of functions; the one-man, one-boss, principle; and permanent work arrangements. In the third part I shall suggest four quite different organizational forms for achieving employee commitment: (1) modular structures, (2) temporary assignments, (3) nonlinear structures, and (4) temporary structures.

Power or Leadership?

The organization hires, separates, changes duties, transfers, penalizes, promotes or does not promote, sets and resets pay, changes locations, and may even sell itself, or part of itself along with its employees, to some other organization. But it is less the actual exercise of power than the *concept* itself that discourages commitment. That concept can be stated simply. Power is an innate right of the organization. It is not only inherent but indispensable. For without it, how can the organization accomplish its mission, viz., make money for the owners?

This concept of power divides employees into two classes with apparently divergent interests. It places the organization unmistakably on the side of the owners' interests and *opposed to the employees' interests.* What else is power for if not to control employees? They are simply to be managed along with the other factors of all production to produce a residual payment of adequate size for the entrepreneurial factor of production—risk. This orientation of the organization and its management employees to the owners' purpose separates the other employees from that purpose. Thus the organization in effect *renounces* any employee commitment to the organization.

Power, to the employee, is clearly the differentiating quality between the

---

1. See, for example, Alfred D. Chandler, Jr., *Strategy and Structure* (Cambridge, M.I.T. Press, 1962).

organization and himself. The organization has it; he does not. His reaction to this fact is ambivalent.

□ On the one hand, he resents it; and when the organization is unresponsive, frustration and impotence can escalate his resentment to hostility. Resentful employees, consciously or unconsciously, may do the organization harm in large or small ways. They certainly do not identify with it.

□ On the other hand, the employee never questions that power is inherently a right of the organization or doubts that it is indispensable to the organization's task. For, plainly, it must have power to deal with him. Otherwise, he reasons, lack of discipline, anarchy, chaos, unfairness, and failure would follow. These he does not want.

Thus the astonishing thing is that the employee totally accepts the organization's concept of power. Still, he senses unpleasant implications. If the organization needs power to deal with him in order to secure its purpose, then his interests must somehow be at odds with the organization's interests, and vice versa. The objectives of the organization must not be his. As he sees it, therefore, it is a case of "them and us"—or even "them and me": two classes. Rejected by the organization, the employee rejects *it*. He "decommits." He perceives himself as excluded and subordinate—an object.

But he accepts this condition as a price he has to pay to earn his bread. Thus, work becomes a means to an end instead of a worthy end in itself, and he makes no commitment to it or to his organization. For when people commit themselves, in my observation, it is to ends, not means. Without a commitment to the organization, the job and its wages are simply a commodity to the employee—undifferentiated from another job. One employment opportunity resembles another. Loyalty has no basis.

IMPENDING BANKRUPTCY

Having exercised power for so long, we managers seldom wonder at its origin. We merely take it for granted as the natural state of things. Still, thinking about its origin can be revealing.

Perhaps unconsciously we suppose power is bestowed on the organization by the owners. Yet that assumption does not stand up when we reflect on it. Owners have an objective: to receive income and profit from risking the diminution or even entire loss of their ownership. When they select a board of directors, they delegate to it the authority to decide and act for them on certain matters. The directors delegate further to the officers. Through this process, the management becomes the owners' agent.

But that is the be-all and end-all of authority. While managers receive authority from owners to act for them, nothing in this itself invests them with authority over employees. The owners' purpose is not to organize people; not to hire, pay, or fire people; not to punish or reward; not to use power over anyone. These are *means* selected by the owners' agents, the management, to achieve the owners' purpose. Power is not really a necessary attribute of management; it is a recourse that management chooses.

Later I hope to demonstrate why we do not need power and are actually better off without it. Now I want to illustrate that we hardly have power. Let us consider the sources of it and what is happening to them.

If the organization does not derive power from ownership, then from where is it derived? Without running abstract discussions of terms into the ground, I think it helps to make one distinction between authority and power—terms which share many meanings:

□ I see *authority* as something passed on to others in the interest of efficiency. It is passed on freely, as a pragmatic thing, to get things done. It can be delegated down, as in the process just described, or up, as in the case of citizens' delegating authority to representatives to make the laws.

□ On the other hand, *power* connotes something arrogated to oneself. It is taken, rather than given. It is primarily for the benefit of those who possess it rather than those from whom it has been taken.

Power seems always to be associated with the ability to make someone choose between alternatives—one of which is to be avoided. Some of the alternatives we read about are hard indeed, e.g., liquidation for the Mafia soldier who does not keep the oath, excommunication for the cleric who disobeys church doctrine, and doing without for those refusing to buy at the monopoly price.

One source of power in business is economic. Do what the organization asks, or face an undesirable economic alternative; choose between doing the job satisfactorily or separation, between obeying the rules or receiving penalties, between average performance at average pay or superior performance with increased pay and perquisites.

A second source, surprisingly, has nothing to do with the organization. It comes directly from what we might call the work ethic. It is the particular system of values held by our *employees* that says having a job is good, that hard work is good, cooperating and doing your part are good, loyalty is good, obeying the rules is good, and so on. In other words, employees do what the organization asks, not solely because of the difficult economic alternatives, but because to do otherwise is to make themselves outlaws of their own value system. Thus, they themselves have been a source of the organization's power.

Drying up of sources: Now, what is happening to the two sources of organizational power? We already see the near-bankruptcy of economic power. For one thing, the organization's ability to make the employee face alternatives has been narrowly circumscribed. Government has limited the organization's actions by legislation, regulation, and court judgment. Organized labor presents countervailing power. Penalties and separations are subject to grievance procedures or strikes. Promotions are subject to seniority. Wages are set for the contract period, making rewards for superior performance unavailable as means of influencing performance. Where there is no contract, management's actions are still influenced by the union, waiting in the wings to promote itself from a real or imagined abuse of power.

What is more, the economic alternatives have become less severe. The government's commitment to a full employment policy has lessened the impact of separation, so that loss of a job no longer signifies extended unemployment. Pay is also comparable for similar work in a given area; benefits vest earlier; unemployment benefits are substantial. Finally, the employee's own view of work as a commodity is a factor: if he regards one employment like another, he is not going to be so much influenced by penalties or the threat of being fired.

Actually, there is reason to suspect that corporate economic power has not been very effective for some time. We have really been operating on employees' acceptance of the work ethic—and therefore on their sufferance. But a changing ethic now threatens this source too. Despite radicals at the fringe of society, the great majority of people do not deny the work ethic. But they are questioning and *qualifying* it. Having a job is good, but not any job; hard work is good, but not necessarily of itself; making money is good, but how it is made is important; sacrifice for family is good, but doing your thing is important too; loyalty is good, if to a worthy cause; doing your best is good, but does the end justify it? More than ever before, work is going to be on the employee's terms.

How far will values change? Businesses have so far been spared revolts against power such as witnessed in church and university. But conditions in the business situation make it vulnerable to a changing ethic. Employee dissatisfaction with management exists in almost every business—dissatisfaction with the investment results of pension plans, with incentive plans whose value is affected by management's performance, with the business philosophy of management, and with loss of employment when management fails to do its job well enough. Such dissatisfaction can crystallize, given the right spark of activism from employees seeking involvement or recourse, and result in opposition to, and eventual neutralization of, the organization's power.

However we add it up, it is scary from a management standpoint. The power of the organization coming from its ability to make the employee choose between economic alternatives has been blunted if not entirely lost, while the power derived from the system of popular values gives every

sign of disappearing with changing values. Power thus seems more in tune
with the way things have been than with the way they are going to be.
With only a little bit of it in our future, how are we going to get our job
done?

We have a choice: we can defend every inch of the way to conserve what
economic power remains—in the end losing it anyway to angry and in-
dignant employees. We can be keepers of the gate, so to speak, enjoying
while they last the prerogatives fortuitously accorded us by the work ethic.
Or we can accept the decline of organization power and start developing
a concept that lets us accomplish things without the threat of arrogated
power. I advocate the latter. The alternative I propose is a concept of
leadership.

When we think about leadership, we usually think of special *qualities*
that make managers more effective. So leadership is conventionally regarded as an ingredient of good managing. There is, of course, no "right"
view, but I find it helpful to turn the relationships around—to think not
of leadership as an aspect of managing, but managing as a tool of leadership.
And to look not to qualities of leadership, but to the requirements of
followership.

Leadership, in this broader view, means enlisting all members of the
organization in the purpose of the organization. Therefore it is inextricably
bound with purpose. Leadership without purpose has no meaning; purpose
exists only because a leadership formulated it. Like the mountain and valley
of the philosophers' ancient puzzle, one concept cannot exist without
the other. Leadership is prior to purpose and purpose is prior to managing
—both chronologically and logically. It is just this priority that gives
leadership primacy over managing.

Leadership is also a relationship between leader and follower. It cannot
exist by itself; it exists only *if* followership is produced. Doubtless there are
special qualities of leadership. But looking beyond this, it is plainly something that elicits a positive response from those led. Followership then
becomes not a happy accident of certain qualities of the manager but the
essential meaning of leadership itself. Leadership really begins, therefore,
not with the leader, but with the follower.

What creates in a follower a desire to follow a leader? The key to followership is that every individual is always striving to meet his own psychological needs. What leadership does is enable the individual to satisfy his
psychological needs by his own actions, which are the very actions sought
by the leader to achieve the purpose of the organization.

Leadership not only replaces power; it is made *possible* by disregarding power. For power is anathema to leadership. Power does not produce followership; it antagonizes it. Power is the root of the managing group's attitude as enforcer, driver, superior, privileged, and causative. But attitudes beget attitudes, and this one creates a negative response from employees.

THE MANAGERIAL JOB

Power has always been the main pillar and most visible aspect of managing. Maxims like: "management is cause, all else effect," "managers must manage," "managing is creating pressure in the most constructive way" —all attest to the prominent role of power in concepts of managing. What happens to the meaning of managing if we remove power from the concept?

We can give managing new meaning and importance by conceiving it as the *tool* of leadership to achieve the organization's purpose. Managing, in this view, becomes art, technique, systematization, method, and economics. And where leadership is emotions, feelings, spirit, and purpose, managing is cool, impersonal, objective, and imaginative; it connotes professional *action* for getting results—including followership. If we embrace this view, we would think of ourselves at every level of management first and primarily as leaders—and then as practitioners of the art and science of managing.

Thus, it becomes every manager's responsibility to enlist the people in the organization's cause and to provide the requirements of followership. We do not know what all these requirements are. We have to assume that work can satisfy many of them if, by creative managing, we introduce psychological satisfiers into the work situation and eliminate, neutralize, or compensate for nonsatisfiers already present. We want followership not to depend on accidental or even instinctive qualities in a manager. We want it produced by rational, conscious, purposive managing that *understands* the requirements of followership as it understands the requirements of manufacturing, marketing, or finance; and that creates conditions for followership as it creates conditions for success in these other areas.

Every major project requires certain inputs to achieve its objectives. Management is *one* of the necessary inputs. It may be a scarcer and more expensive resource than others, but it is not sufficient; it is not above the other inputs, nor is it better than they. In the concept proposed here, it is simply equal to the other necessary inputs.

Supplying the management input now becomes simply the duty of the appointed manager. It is not a nobler duty; it is but one function cooperating with other functions to achieve the purpose of the enterprise.

What is described is a humble concept of managing. But no inference should be made that management operates with a low profile, that it is a mere facilitator, or that its decisions can be determined by vote, consensus, or democratic process. It must be tough. It must do its duty, contribute its input without vacillation, apology, or guilt, and *in spite of* sympathy and empathy for individuals adversely affected, although managers most certainly will have such feelings. Otherwise the management input is anti-leadership, failing everyone.

HOW MUCH DIFFERENCE?

Pragmatist philosopher William James once observed, "A difference that *makes* no difference *is* no difference." So what *is* the difference if after all the manager continues—as he must—to hire, fire, transfer, promote, penalize, and direct much as he did before, using power?

The difference is in the way that employees interpret management actions. As things stand, employees tend to view managers' actions as self-serving and for the benefit of the owners—only incidentally and indirectly in the interests of the employees. They see the purpose of the organization as the owners' purpose and achieving it as management's objective.

The subordination of power, on the other hand, makes it possible for nonmanagement employees to share in the purpose and objectives of the organization. For without power, managers must *enlist*, rather than force, the contribution of employees. Enlisting their contribution (which is of course only another way of saying "securing their followership") implies that a process must take place. In that process information and judgments are exchanged and an understanding of conditions is built. Out of the process come objectives and means—different, perhaps, and hopefully better than they otherwise would be, but in any case deserving of support by employees because the employees shared in making them. The employee becomes more involved in the social system of the company and thereby satisfies certain of his psychological needs. And as a result of the process, managers' actions can be *accepted* by employees as the necessary input that managers make as their obligation.

If management does its job, enlisting the commitment of all employees to the shared objectives, there is less need for discipline. Where that need nevertheless arises, the employee's peers can be expected to support disciplinary action, and the employee himself is more disposed to accept it.

Other Obstructions

Although power and the negative attitudes it evokes are the greatest impediment to employee commitment and followership, they are not the only ones. Let us look briefly at several other obstacles. (Ironically, they were created, for the most part, by management itself in the name of scientific management.)

1. FUNCTIONAL DIVISION

Divisionalization of functions begins when the board of directors elects a management as its agent to produce income and profits from the owners' investment. It consists of dividing up the tasks involved in producing that income. The whole is divided into divisions, divisions into departments, departments into groups, and so on—each unit being a finer collection of tasks, activities, and functions, until at last every job is defined.

While the concept of power erodes commitment by evoking negative emotions, the fragmentation of the work prevents commitment by driving emotion right out of the organization. The whole effort is preoccupied with classifying, defining, and ranking jobs, duties, and functions. Feelings, emotion, and attitudes are not considered in the process. For the process really has nothing to do with people; it is the work that is being organized.

It is only *after* jobs are classified, ranked, and staffed, and after results fall short of expectations, that we turn our thoughts to the motivation of the humans who operate the organization machine. Motivation, of course, is an emotion-related concept. Emotion is a mysterious ingredient of performance that pushes it beyond what would be expected from the state of skill, technique, or virtuosity of the performer. It is a common enough phenomenon in athletic competition, where individuals and teams that are "up" or have "desire" perform beyond normal expectations.

When emotion is not present in an organization, there can be no commitment either. For commitment is in fact an emotion. An organizing process that simply divides the work up into little bitty pieces and ignores emotion, leaving it to chance, necessarily leaves commitment to chance also.

2. ONE-MAN, ONE-BOSS CONCEPT

Governing the divisionalization of functions is the convention that each individual should have but one supervisor. Managing is a pragmatic art, and this principle, born of the common-sense observation that a person is confused by instructions from two people, is one of its best-accepted tenets.

Just as the divisionalization of functions has nothing to do with people, the one-man, one-boss principle really has nothing to do with the work. It fixes the people-to-people relationships and establishes the hierarchy of the organization. It limits the organization to one structure, and one structure only, to achieve the purposes of the organization. And it provides but a single path for communication up or down.

The one-man, one-boss principle affects commitment by exerting a direct, negative effect on communication (also, as we shall see later, it precludes some organizational arrangements that might increase commitment). Communication is the lifeline for the survival of employee commitment. When employees cannot communicate upward, they conclude that the organization does not care what they think and they turn themselves off. It is by accident, not intent, that the organization system silences the employee. The *purpose* of the organization system is not to achieve communication but to get the work done.

The work is accomplished through a system of power and authority flowing through the single, linear path that the one-man, one-boss structure provides. Communication is the vehicle for power and authority; hence it takes the same direction through the organization's single structure that they do. Decisions, ideas, policies, procedures, and instructions flow down relatively easily. But communication up is labored. Every supervisor is a potential terminus. Each one must say "yes" for an idea to survive. If communication up fails to navigate the single channel available, it fails altogether.

The result? Though managements are usually truly interested in ideas and feedback from throughout the organization and establish systems and programs to get them, they gather little that is significant. Yet throughout the organization employees have ideas and opinions which they cannot express. In the end they turn themselves off because they "know" the organization does not really care what they think. What lies between but the organization system?

3. PERMANENT ASSIGNMENTS

Another convention attending the divisionalization of functions is that job assignments are more or less permanent. By "permanent" I mean open-ended: at the time the assignment is made, no plan exists for ending it. Because this keeps the managers' options open, it seems eminently sensible.

Nevertheless, the practice produces a static organization. Movement depends ultimately on openings created by separations, quittings, retirements, deaths, and newly created jobs. These events are infrequent in relation to the total number of employees. Therefore most employees are in their jobs for long periods and have limited job experiences in a career. A fast-advancing employee may have only half a dozen or so job experiences in a 25-year span.

Glenn A. Bassett illustrates the dilemma in reporting the startling outcome of a study at General Electric:

A study group examining the utilization of manpower in one of GE's divisions perceived that, besides payroll turnover, another very important kind of turnover was involved. This was position turnover—opportunities to move within the organization. The group found that one of the factors causing payroll turnover was a lack of position turnover. In the end it "came to the realization that, to a point at least, losses from our payrolls were essential to provide a sufficient number of openings to permit us to move people flexibly into developmental assignments."[2]

In other words, the organization had to lose people accidentally in order to get openings in which to develop those who remained! Losing people is certainly an undiscriminating way to achieve movement in the organization. But in fact we do little on purpose to relieve the organization's static character. On the contrary, we ensure this character by our practice of essentially permanent assignments.

A work career that follows a pattern of long periods per job and few jobs per career stifles emotion and commitment. An employee can be ruined by the ease and familiarity of a job held too long. His development curve flattens from the absence of new things to learn. He loses his stomach for new challenges. He begins to doubt his ability to master new things, shrinks from the unknown, avoids new jobs and different locations. His job becomes dull, routine, and automatic—easy but unpleasant, and to be gotten out of the way with as little involvement as possible so that he can get on with the "real" stuff of life. Deprived of fulfillment on the job, he looks elsewhere for it—the stock market, church, family, sports, hobbies, union—not necessarily ever finding it.

In the hierarchy of an employee's needs is the need to make a commitment. But too often he does not make it to the company; he sublimates this drive outside the organization. Such employees may stay on the payroll, but they have quit their jobs.

More Flexible Forms

Dividing up the work, permanent assignments, and the one-boss, one-job principle thus add to the agency of power in suppressing positive emotion, which is crucial because it is intrinsically bound in the nature of followership. Leadership elicits followership by causing followers to *want* to do what the leader asks. "Wanting" is an emotion. So emotion is a condition for followership; it must be present for followership to exist. *How* leadership elicits its presence is, as pointed out earlier, a problem for managing.

What organization forms and practices can we create to reintroduce and preserve the positive emotion indispensable for followership and commit-

2. "Personnel Systems in Business," *The Conference Board Record*, August 1970, p. 58.

ment? I want to suggest four quite different organizational forms for managers to experiment with in order to diversify the organization and make it more dynamic, flexible, and responsive. Only rudiments of these structures appear in business today. The fact that they are present in any form implies that the traditional assumptions are not absolute and invariable.

Each of these structures is based on some modification or contradiction of the traditional assumptions. But they must not be considered exceptions to the traditional concepts. They must appear as useful alternatives in their own right. Otherwise it is unlikely that their use will expand sufficiently to alter the character of today's typical organization.

MODULAR STRUCTURES

The term "modular structure" is intended to express the idea of a unit that is complete but small, autonomous yet united with other units, and whose mission is explicitly stated. The purpose of using such structures is to repair the emotion-neglecting effect of divisionalization of functions. *Emotion is practically the whole objective of modular structuring.* We observe that the president of a company or division is more emotionally involved and committed than other employees; it is no coincidence that his job also has the clearest and most acutely felt accountability and is the only one not divided. So modular structuring aims for many wholes, many "presidents," and more keenly felt accountability throughout the organization.

On the other hand, structuring in modules is by no means proposed as an alternative to dividing up tasks. It is supplementary. We do not want to forgo the demonstrated benefits of specialization. So let us specialize the work, but collect the fragments, not in divisions, but in small organic, complete, mission-oriented groupings.

In such groupings members can more easily grasp and identify with the mission and individually influence the results. Each employee can more keenly feel the necessity of carrying his load. Failure stands out and so does success. Peer respect becomes a powerful motivator. The employee experiences his function as organic to the whole. And accountability becomes a factor for all employees, not solely management employees. These are all strong social and psychological forces that engage the employee's emotional being.

Smallness, completeness, autonomy, and union are clearly competing objectives. Small organizations, to be complete, have to be large enough to include the necessary functions. Autonomy of the unit in achieving *its* mission must not compromise the purpose of the whole. Organizing in modular structures, therefore, involves an optimizing process that balances requirements among these competing ends.

How does this approach differ from the well-known profit center approach? Profit centers resemble modular structures because their mission is explicit. Profit centers are heralded as a superior organizational form, but results have sometimes been disappointing. Various explanations are possible. Profit centers are often not small; they may be incomplete; they may have too much or too little autonomy; and their relationships to each other and to the larger whole may be poorly defined. The mission itself perhaps should not be simply profitability but objectives compounded of profits, adaptation, diversification, development, and other ends.

But I think the most important reason of all is that there are still relatively so few profit center structures in our organizations that, when they are established, there is an undersupply of men trained to run them. Before a man becomes a profit center manager, he usually has spent years climbing the ladder of the traditional organization. Despite the depth of that experience, it often leaves him ill-prepared to manage a profit center. He learns that job in the crucible, while his employer pays for his education. Good plant managers, on the other hand, can be quickly located because there are many plants and plant organizations. Hence the paradox that until we have lots of mission- or contribution-centered modular structures, results may be disappointing.

TEMPORARY ASSIGNMENTS

Generally speaking, when a person is assigned to a position in business, he and others consider the job to be permanent unless management changes its mind. We have grown so accustomed to this convention that we forget that the custom *could* well be just the opposite. That is, the job could be considered *temporary* unless management changes its mind.

Most of us are likely to recoil from this radical idea. No one wants to give up his job while someone else takes a crack at it. And is it not hard enough to get an established team without disrupting it on purpose? Nevertheless, however disturbing it may be, if permanent assignments contribute to a lack of movement that stifles commitment, we have to consider its alternative seriously.

Understanding the nature of the problem makes it familiar. The problem is one of balancing means between competing, deserving ends. One deserving end is to get the immediate job done well; the other, to provide for employee renewal and development so that jobs *continue* to be done well. The first end is served by leaving a competent man in his job until an opening occurring elsewhere affects him. The second end is served by moving him before that happens.

So far we have resolved the question mostly in favor of doing the immediate job. The result is the static organization. But once we decide it is sufficiently important to inject movement into the organization, we will plan for the temporary assignment as we do for other objectives. We will lay out the position's objectives, strategies, economics, language, problem areas, restraints, management systems, and whatever else a new incumbent needs to know to grasp its parameters quickly and contribute— then select employees for it whose experience and personality equip them to contribute quickly while growing in their jobs from the opportunity.

While those of us brought up on traditional practice might understandably shrink from the idea of temporary assignments, newcomers to a system already using them might like them. Indeed, some day employees may scoff at the "best man" syndrome of the earlier tradition—the fiction that the most qualified man or woman for a job is the one selected. They may think that assigning a man a job permanently because he got to it first makes less sense than giving others who are qualified a chance at it too.

Temporary assignments would of course increase position turnover. Boredom with jobs that have become dull, routine, and automatic from having been held too long would doubtless decrease. The additional job experiences would sustain a rising learning and development curve. Most important, giving an employee opportunities to master successive challenges would increase his self-confidence.

NONLINEAR STRUCTURES

The one-man, one-boss principle is a pragmatic principle—good because it has worked. But suspending it when circumstances warrant may be just as pragmatic. Certainly, the rule does not stand up to scrutiny as an exclusive principle. Around us are many examples of persons acting under the direction of different managements. Men moonlight, work for political action under a party leader, build a church under a committee chairman, do community work for a businessmen's service organization.

Breach of the rule is already observed in business organizing. In the office of the president, where authorities and responsibilities are shared by executives, rather than divided among them, the employee can get direction or approval from any available member of the office. Since he has two bosses, the structure becomes nonlinear.

Exposing the executives in the president's office to the broader responsibilities of the top man multiplies their job experiences. It also multiplies paths of communication for their men. We should propagate such benefits by extending the concept to lower levels of the organization. But a more radical departure from the one-boss principle can expand the benefits still further. In the office-of-the-president concept, the employee has more than one supervisor, but he himself has only one set of purposes, objectives, and duties—one job, that is. He is a member of but one group. Why not give the employee, say, *two* sets of purposes, objectives, and duties, having him report for each set to a different supervisor and making sure he has sufficient time to perform both jobs? This would make him a member of two groups. When men have more than one job and report to more than one supervisor, the result is no longer the single-structured pyramid but a *network* of jobs and job relationships.

Occasionally suspending the one-boss rule would permit us to introduce diversity into the organization. Employees would have more opportunities for development, involvement, and fulfillment at work. Communication would be made easier by the increased number of reporting relationships. Commitment, in these circumstances, would be more readily given.

TEMPORARY STRUCTURES

When nonlinear structures are also temporary, they offer, I think, a special opportunity to organize for change. The staff has largely inherited the burden of causing change. But the staff is part of the organization's permanent structure. What makes change difficult to organize for is precisely that no one can predict when or from where the next idea will come, or what kind of repsonse will be needed.

Because survival demands change, students of management have sought a flexible alternative to the permanent staff structure—one in which the organization can be exactly engineered to fit each challenge. Project management, task forces, management cells, project clusters, and what Warren G. Bennis has called "organic populism" are examples of such ad hoc organizations to cause change. Bennis predicts that organizations of the future "will be adaptive, rapidly changing *temporary systems*, organized around problems-to-be-solved by groups of relative strangers with diverse professional skills. . . . they will evolve in response to problems rather than to programmed expectations. . . ."[3]

A wonderful concept! Why then has it made hardly a dent in the traditional organization? The administrative problems have proved too great an obstacle. They are rooted in traditional assumptions of organizing. When the functions of a management group are divided up, nothing is supposed to be left over. Therefore, it is reasoned, the permanent structure is *the* organization. Ad hoc structures are messy expedients—necessary only because some idiosyncrasy of the regular organization prevents it from achieving the desired end.

In view of this, we have given little thought to the generalized use of ad hoc structures. Left to their own devices, managers are thwarted by the rigidities of the permanent organization. The specialization of work,

3. "Post-Bureaucratic Leadership," *Trans-Action*, July-August 1969, p. 45; and T. George Harris, "A Conversation with Warren G. Bennis," *Psychology Today*, February 1970, p. 48.

the one-man, one-boss principle, and permanent assignments establish a single, fixed, strong relationship of people-to-people and people-to-work. So strong are these relationships that, as we see it, the work *belongs* to the employee and the employee *belongs* both to his supervisor and to his department.

A manager who wants to use a temporary or ad hoc structure utilizing people outside his jurisdiction must get the concurrence of too many of his fellow managers, convincing them of their mutual interest in the problem, and achieving some kind of consensus with them on the team's charter and chairmanship. And after the temporary group is formed, he must contend with the independence of the members, who remain oriented toward their supervisors in their permanent departments.

Suggestions for action: What can we in management do to overcome these deterrents to ad hoc groups, assuming we want to experiment with greater use of them?

The first step is to recognize that our organizations are now dominated by the requirements of performing systematized functions. Then we should redress the balance. Perhaps little more is needed than to give standing to temporary structures by preparing guidelines for their use and encouraging managers to utilize them.

The much more difficult step is to loosen the bonds tying people to their work and to their departments. Here we need a new concept of employees; we need to regard them as discrete, versatile resource *units*, able to make contributions where needed in the organization, rather than as fixed components of particular divisions and hierarchies. The more we practice departures from the one-boss principle and from permanent assignments, so as to become accustomed to the concept of the employee as an individual contributor, the more freely we will utilize him or her in temporary systems organized to evaluate, decide, and bring about changes without involving the regular hierarchy. Members of temporary organizations would not operate as representatives of their functional departments, but, as individuals, would do the work for which the structure is organized.

Temporary structures can multiply job experiences, increase the number of interpersonal relationships, introduce flexibility into an otherwise static system, and expand opportunities for communication. Most important, they can ease the way for change. People just naturally want to improve things. So when one thinks about it, it is strange that "resistance to change" is what is reported by observers of organizational behavior when actually "change" presents the best chance employees have to satisfy their psychological needs! The key to this paradox is that change is great when you are its agent; it is only bad when you are its object. Temporary structures can make more people the agent.

Conclusion

What will happen if we do not find a way to let our employees meet their psychological needs on the job? How long will we be permitted to keep the present industrial system if we do not? These are frightening questions. Let us dream a little and imagine what matters might be like if we *do* meet the need.

A committed man is a Theory Y man. It will be remembered that Douglas McGregor used the now familiar categories of Theory X and Theory Y to refer to assumptions about people which he thought underlay contrasting styles of managing. Theory Y people have integrity, work hard toward objectives, assume responsibility, desire to achieve, want their organization to succeed, and will make decisions; on the other hand, Theory X people are not very interested in the organization, its performance, on-the-job achievement, assumption of responsibility, or hard work. What manager would not be excited to think what he could accomplish if his department were filled with Theory Y people!

Unfortunately, Theory Y remains but a potential. I remember once counseling one of our general managers, who was then having a lot of people problems, not to regard his hourly employees as Theory X. "But Doug," he said, "they *are* Theory X." And he was right!

Theory X behavior is what we observe all around. This may be due in part to employees' earlier environments in the home and school. But the working environment, I believe, makes a final contribution. Can we really expect much from a Theory Y style of managing if it is simply overlaid onto assumptions of organizing that prevent the employee from meeting his psychological needs? Environment *selects* behavior, and the business organization selects Theory X behavior. Until the basic assumptions of organizing are adapted to the Theory Y hypothesis of man's nature, Theory Y behavior is likely to remain only a matter of faith.

Suppose we could wave a wand and instantly introduce the changes proposed in this article. Would we get greatly increased commitment from our employees? Perhaps not immediately. Followership (like leadership) is weak. The cause is lack of exercise. Our employees have been conditioned by experience to suppress their feelings and withhold commitment. To change that behavior, management will need to provide employees with a very different body of experience on the job. Adapting our organizing concepts to human needs is certainly the first imperative. In addition, employees must be allowed to experience the attraction and excitement of pursuing a shared mission. Finally—and this is crucial—every instance and demonstration of employee commitment, even when critical of management, has to produce an affirmative and supportive reaction from managers. When this happens, we will know we are making progress.

38. Can the Best Corporations Be Made Moral?

Kenneth R. Andrews

"The overriding master problem now impeding the further progress of corporate responsibility is the difficulty of making credible and effective, throughout a large organization, the social component of a corporate strategy originating in the moral convictions and values of the chief executive." So asserts this author, who then adds that the source of the difficulty is the nature and impact of narrowly designed measurement and reward-and-penalty systems. In this article, he discusses the issue of public responsibility in a private corporation, and suggests the outlines of a management program of action.

The concept of corporate social responsibility has made steady progress during the past few decades. The words mean in part voluntary restraint of profit maximization. More positively, they mean sensitivity to the social costs of economic activity and to the opportunity to focus corporate power on objectives that are possible but sometimes less economically attractive than socially desirable. The term includes:

□ The determination of a corporation to reduce its profit by voluntary contributions to education and other charities.

□ The election of an ethical level of operations higher than the minimum required by law and custom.

□ The choice between businesses of varying economic opportunity on grounds of their imputed social worth.

□ The investment for reasons other than (but obviously still related to) economic return in the quality of life within the corporation itself.

This doctrine of corporate social responsibility is vigorously opposed honestly and openly by conservative lawyers and economists and covertly by the adherents of business as usual. Milton Friedman, the conservative economist of the University of Chicago, denounces the concern for responsibility as "fundamentally subversive" to a free society. He argues that "there is one and only one social responsibility of business—to use its resources and engage in activities designed to increase its profits so long as it . . . engages in open and free competition without deception or fraud."[1]

Thus, for example, the manager who makes decisions affecting immediate profit by reducing pollution and increasing minority employment more than present law requires is in effect imposing taxes upon his stockholders and acting without authority as a public legislative body.

Other critics of the doctrine like to point out:

□ How much easier are the platitudes of virtue than the effective combination of profitable and socially responsive corporate action.

□ How little experience with social questions businessmen immersed in their narrow ambitions and technology can be expected to have.

□ How urgent are the pressures of survival in hard times and against competition.

□ How coercive of individual opinion in an organization is a position on social issues dictated by its management.

□ How infrequently in the entire population occur the intelligence, compassion, knowledge of issues, and morality required of the manager presumptuous enough to factor social responsibility into his economic decisions.

Given the slow rate at which verbalized good intentions are being converted into action, many critics of the large corporation suspect that for every chief executive announcing pious objectives there are a hundred closet rascals quietly conducting business in the old ways and taking immoral comfort in Friedman's moral support.

The interventionists question the effectiveness of the "invisible hand" of competition as the ethical regulator of great corporations capable of shaping in significant degree their environments. Interventionists think also that regulation by government, while always to some degree essential under imperfect competition, is not sufficiently knowledgeable, subtle, or timely to reconcile the self-interest of corporate entrepreneurship and the needs of the society being sore-tried and well served by economic activity.

The advocates of public responsibility for a so-called "private" enterprise assert that, in an industrial society, corporate power, vast in potential strength, must be brought to bear on certain social problems if the latter are to be solved at all. They argue that corporate executives of the integrity, intelligence, and humanity required to run companies whose revenues often exceed the gross national product of whole nations cannot be expected to confine themselves to economic activity and ignore its consequences, and that henceforth able young men and women coming into business will be sensitive to the social worth of corporate activity.

To reassure those uneasy about the dangers of corporate participation in

1. *Capitalism and Freedom* (Chicago, University of Chicago Press, 1962), p. 133.

public affairs, the social interventionists say to the economic isolationists that these hazards can be contained through professional education, government control and self-regulation.

This is not the place to argue further against Friedman's simplistic faith in the powers of the market to purify self-interest. We must observe, however, that the argument for the active participation of corporations in public affairs, for responsible assessment of the impact of economic activity, and for concern with the quality of corporate purposes is gaining ground, even as uneasiness increases about the existence of corporate power in the hands of managers who (except in cases of crisis) are answerable only to themselves or to boards of directors they have themselves selected.

Criticism of corporate activity is manifest currently in consumerism, in the movement to introduce social legislation into stockholder meetings and to reform board memberships, and (more dangerously) in apathy or antipathy among the young. The most practicable response to this criticism by those holding corporate power is to seek to justify limited government by using power responsibly—the ultimate obligation of free persons in any relatively free society.

We need the large corporation, not for its size but for its capability. Even the vivisectionists of the Justice Department who seek a way to divide IBM into smaller parts presumably have no illusion that the large corporation can or should be eliminated from the world as we know it.

On the assumption, then, that corporate social responsibility is not only here to stay, but must increase in scope and complexity as corporate power increases, I suggest that we look forward to the administrative and organizational consequences of the incursion of private corporations into public responsibility.

Nature of the Problem

Among the many considerations confronting the executive who would make social responsibility effective, there are some so well known that we can quickly pass them by. Hypocrisy, insincerity, and hollow piety are not really dangerous, for they are easily detected.

In fact, it is much more likely that genuinely good intentions will be thought insincere than that hypocritical protestations of idealism will be mistaken for truth. "Mr. Ford (or Mr. Kaiser or Mr. Rockefeller) doesn't really mean what he says," as an organization refrain is more Mr. Ford's or Mr. Kaiser's or Mr. Rockefeller's problem than what he should say. Cynicism, the by-product of impersonal bureaucracy, remains one of the principal impediments to the communication of corporate social policy.

I would like to set aside also the problem of choice of what social contribution should be attempted—a problem which disparity between the infinite range of social need and the limits of available corporate resources always brings to mind.

The formulation of specific corporate social policy is as much a function of strategic planning as the choice of product and market combinations, the establishment of profit and growth objectives, or the choice of organization structure and systems for accomplishing corporate purposes.

Rather than wholly personal or idiosyncratic contributions (like supporting the museum one's wife is devoted to) or safe and sound contributions like the standard charities, or faddist entry into fashionable areas, corporate strategic response to societal needs and expectations makes sense when it is closely related to the economic functions of the company or to the peculiar problems of the community in which it operates.

For a paper company, it would seem a strategic necessity to give first priority to eliminating the poisonous effluents from its mills rather than, for example, to support cultural institutions like traveling art exhibits. Similarly, for an oil company it would seem a strategic necessity to look at its refinery stacks, at spillage, and at automobile exhaust.

The fortunate company that is paying the full social cost of its production function can make contributions to problems it does not cause—like juvenile delinquency, illiteracy, and so on—or to other forms of environmental improvement more appropriate to corporate citizenship than directly related to its production processes.

As leaders of business move beyond conventional philanthropic contributions to strategy-related investments in social betterment, they begin to combine the long-run economic interests of their companies with the priorities (as for pollution) becoming evident in pubic concern, seeking those points where indeed what is good for the country is good for General Motors.

Once the conscious planning which a fully developed corporate strategy requires is understood, the practical alternatives before any company are not impossibly difficult to identify and to rank according to relevance to economic strategy or to organization needs and resources.

The outcome is an integrated self-consistent strategy embodying defined obligations to society relevant to but not confined to its economic purposes. The top management of a large company, once it elects to, can be expected to have less difficulty in articulating such a strategy than in dealing with the problems of organization behavior to which I now turn.

The advance of the doctrine of corporate social responsibility has been the apparent conversion of more and more chief executive officers. Change toward responsible behavior and the formulation of strategic intentions are obviously not possible without their concern, compassion, and conviction.

So long as the organization remains small enough to be directly influenced by the chief executive's leadership, certain results can be traced to his determination that they occur—as in centrally decided investments, specific new ventures, cash contributions to charity, and compensation, promotion, and other personnel policies.

But as an organization grows larger and as operations become more decentralized, the power and influence of the chief executive are reinterpreted and diffused. For example:

If a large company is to be sufficiently decentralized to make worldwide operations feasible, power must be distributed throughout a hierarchy inhabited by persons (a) who may not share their chief executive's determination or fervor, (b) who may not believe (more often) that he means what he says, and (c) who may be impelled to postpone action on such problems as management development, pollution, or employment and advancement of minority representatives.

At this point, the overriding master problem now impeding the further progress of corporate responsibility is the difficulty of making credible and effective, throughout a large organization, the social component of a corporate strategy originating in the moral convictions and values of the chief executive.

Quantifiable results: The source of the difficulty is the nature and impact of our systematic planning processes, forms of control, systems of measurement, and pattern of incentives, and the impersonal way all these are administered. The essence of the systematic rational planning we know most about is quantitative information furnished to the process and quantitative measures of results coming out.

Once plans are put into effect, managers are measured, evaluated, promoted, shelved, or discharged according to the relation of their accomplishments against the plan. In the conventions of accounting and the time scale of exact quantification, performance becomes short-run economic or technical results inside the corporation. Evaluation typically gives full marks for current accomplishment, with no estimate of the charges against the future which may have been made in the effort to accomplish the plan.

Since progress in career, dependent on favorable judgments of quantifiable performance, is the central motivation in a large organization, general and functional managers at divisional, regional, district, and local levels are motivated to do well what is best and most measured, to do it now, and to focus their attention on the internal problems that affect immediate results.

In short, the more quantification and the more supervision of variance, the less attention there will be to such intangible topics as the social role of Plant X in Community Y or the quality of corporate life in the office at Sioux City.

The leaner the central staff of a large organization is kept, the more stress there will be on numbers; and, more importantly, the more difficulty there will be in making qualitative evaluation of such long-term processes as individual and management development, the steady augmentation of organizational competence, and the progress of programs for making work meaningful and exciting, and for making more than economic contributions to society.

The small headquarters group supervising the operations of a conglomerate of autonomous organizations hitherto measured by ranking them with respect to return on equity would not expect to have before it proposals from the subsidiaries for important investments in social responsibility. Such investments could only be made by the corporate headquarters, which would not itself be knowledgeable about or much motivated to take action on opportunities existing throughout the subsidiaries.

Corporate amorality: One colleague of mine, Joseph L. Bower, has examined the process by which corporate resources are allocated in large organizations.[2] Another, Robert W. Ackerman, has documented through field studies the dilemmas which a financially oriented and present-tense accounting system pose for the forward progress of specific social action, like pollution abatement and provision of minority opportunity.[3] Still a third, Malcolm S. Salter, has studied the impact of compensation systems in multinational corporations.[4]

It appears that the outcome of these and other research studies will establish what we have long suspected—that good works, the results of which are long term and hard to quantify, do not have a chance in an organization using conventional incentives and controls and exerting pressure for ever more impressive results.

It is quite possible then, and indeed quite usual, for a highly moral and humane chief executive to preside over an "amoral organization"—one made so by processes developed before the liberalization of traditional corporate economic objectives. The internal force which stubbornly resists efforts to make the corporation compassionate (and exacting) toward its own people and responsible (as well as economically efficient) in its

2. *Managing the Resource Allocation Process* (Boston, Division of Research, Harvard Business School, 1969).
3. "How Companies Respond to Social Demands," HBR July-August 1973, p. 88.
4. "Tailor Incentive Compensation to Strategy," HBR March-April 1973, p. 94.

external relationships is the incentive system forcing attention to short-term quantifiable results.

The sensitivity of upward-oriented career executives at lower and middle levels to what quantitative measures say about them is part of their ambition, their interest in their compensation, and their desire for the recognition and approval of their superiors. When, as they usually do, they learn how to beat the system, the margin of capacity they reserve for a rainy day is hoarded for survival, not expended in strengthening their suborganization's future capability or in part-time participation in corporate good works or responsible citizenship on their own time.

With individuals, as with organizations, survival takes precedence over social concern. All we need do to keep even experienced, capable, and profit-producing managers on the ropes of survival is to focus the spotlight on their day-to-day activities and exhaust their ingenuity in outwitting the system by increasing the level of short-term results they are asked to attain.

The isolationists should be quite content with the amorality of an organization motivated by career-oriented responsiveness to narrowly designed measurement and reward-and-penalty systems. The interventionists are not. They look for solutions in the experience, observation, and research I have been drawing on in describing the set of problems a new breadth of vision reveals to us.

Thus the art of using the two-edged sword of contribution to society and of stimulation to creative achievement within the corporation becomes even more sophisticated when that institution must not only relate to the societies of different countries and cultures but also attract and keep the dedication of men and women with values and desires not typically American.

Program of Action

Inquiry into the nature of the problem suggests the outlines of a program of action. It begins with the incorporation into strategic and operating plans—of subsidiaries, country or area organizations, or profit centers—of specific objectives in areas of social concerns strategically related to the economic activity and community environment of the organization unit.

Since the executive in New York cannot specify the appropriate social strategy for the company in Brazil or the branch in Oregon, or even know what the people there want to work on, intermediate managers who are aware of the social and organization policy of the company, must elicit (with staff help if necessary) proposals for investment of money, energy, time, or concern in these areas.

The review of plans submitted may result in reduction or increase in commitments in all areas; it is essential that the negotiation include attention to social and organization objectives, with as much quantification as reasonable but with qualitative objectives where appropriate.

The development of such strategic and operating plans turns critically on the initiative of responsible corporate individuals, who must be competent enough to accomplish demanding economic and social tasks and have time as well for their families and private affairs.

Financial, production, and sales requirements may be transmitted down rather than drawn upward in an efficient (though often sterilizing) compaction of the planning process. The top-down promulgation of an imaginative and community-centered social and organization strategy, except in terms so general as to be ineffective, is not only similarly unwise in stifling creativity and commitment but also virtually impossible.

QUALITATIVE ATTENTION

Once targets and plans have been defined (in the negotiation between organization levels), the measurement system must incorporate in appropriate proportion quantitative and qualitative measures. The bias to short-term results can be corrected by qualitative attention to social and organization programs. The transfer and promotion of managers successful in achieving short-term results is a gamble until their competence in balancing short- and long-term objectives is demonstrated.

Incidentally, rapid rotation virtually guarantees a low level of interest in the particular city through which the manager is following his career; one day it will be seen to be as wasteful as an organization-building and management-development device as it is useful in staffing a growing organization. The alternative—to remain in a given place, to develop fully the company's business in a given city assisted by knowledge and love of the region—needs to become open to executives who do not wish to become president of their companies.

When young middle managers fall short of their targets, inquiry into the reasons and ways to help them achieve assigned goals should precede adverse judgment and penalty. Whenever measurement and control can be directed toward ways to correct problems observed, the shriveling effects of over-emphatic evaluation are postponed. In addition, managers learn that something is important to their superiors other than a single numerical indicator of little significance when detached from the future results to which it relates.

Internal audit: The curse of unquantifiability which hangs over executive action in the areas of corporate responsibility may someday be lifted by the "social audit," now in very early stages of development. In its simplest form, this is a kind of balance sheet and operating statement. On it are listed the dollar values of such corporate investments as training programs, individual development activities, time devoted by individuals to community projects, contributions to pollution abatement, transportation, taxes, and the like. All of these investments call the attention of a company and community to the cumulative dollar worth of corporate functions ancillary to production and sales.

But the further evolvement of the social audit, which one day may develop the conventions that make comparison possible, is not essential to immediate qualitative attention to progress being made by managers at all organizational levels toward their noneconomic goals. Consider, for example:

▢ Internal audit groups, necessarily oriented to examining what the public accounting firm must ultimately certify, can be supplemented by adding to their auditors and accountants permanent or temporary personnel, public relations, or general management persons who are qualified to examine, make comment on, and counsel with managers on their success and difficulties in the areas of social contribution and organization morale.

▢ The role in the community of a local branch office, the morale of the work force, clerical and functional staffs, and the expertise and enthusiasm of the salesmen are all capable of assessment, not in hard numbers but nevertheless in valid and useful judgments.

▢ The public relations and personnel staffs of organizations are all too often assigned to superficial and trivial tasks. The employment of such persons in the internal audit function, especially if they have—without necessarily the qualifications or temperament of high-spirited doers—the experience, perspective, and judgment of long service in the organization, would raise the importance of these functions by increasing their usefulness.

Maturity of judgment: Every large corporation develops unintentionally a group of highly experienced but, after a time, uncompulsive managers who are better assigned to jobs requiring maturity of judgment rather than the ability to sprint. The internal qualitative audit, combined with a parallel inquiry by a committee of outside directors, to which I shall allude in a moment, could be an internal counseling, review, and support function epitomizing effective staff support of line operations. It could also provide opportunity for the cadre of older managers no longer motivated by primitive incentives.

Men with executive responsibility, including accountants and controllers, often exercise judgment only distantly affected by numbers; this is not a new requirement or experience. To the extent that managers in the hierarchy are capable of interpreting numbers intelligently, they must be capable of relating results produced to those in gestation and of judging the significance of a profit figure (not to be found in the figure itself) at a given point of time.

Incentive modification: If measurement of performance is to be broad and knowledgeable enough to encompass progress under a strategy containing social and organizational objectives, then the incentive system in a company or organization unit must reward and penalize accomplishments other than those related to economic efficiency.

Moreover, it must become well known in such an organization that persons can be demoted or discharged for failure to behave responsibly toward their subordinates, for example, even if they are successful in economic terms. Career-oriented middle managers must learn, from the response that their organization leadership and community activities receive, how to appreciate the intrinsic worth and how to estimate the value to their own future of demonstrated responsibility.

MANAGEMENT DEVELOPMENT

Besides liberating the evaluation process by adding qualitative judgment to numbers, the activity which needs expansion in making an organization socially effective and internally healthy is management development—not so much in terms of formal training programs (although I should be the last person to demean the importance of these) as in planned careers.

If organizations elect, as interesting organizations will, high standards of profit and social contribution to be achieved simultaneously, then much is required of the character, general education, and professional competence of managers who must show themselves—whatever their schooling—as liberally educated.

It follows from the argument I am making that, in moderating the amorality of organizations, we must expect executive mid-career education to include exposure to the issues of responsibility raised here and to the invaluable experience of participating in nonprofit community or government organizations. Under short-term pressures, attention to development is easily postponed, either as a cost that should be avoided for now or as a process requiring more attention to persons than is convenient or possible.

The management action so far suggested does not constitute innovation so much as reemphasis: it requires not heroic action but maturity and breadth of perspective. Once the aspiration to reach beyond economic to social and human objectives is seen to require extending conventional incentive and performance measurement systems, it is not difficult to avoid imbalance and the unintended organizational consequences of which I have spoken. Awareness of the problem generates its solution.

AUDIT BY DIRECTORS

But the current move toward revitalization of the board of directors does provide a formal resource to the chief executive who is secure enough and interested enough to avail himself of it. Committees of outside directors are now being formed in a number of companies to meet regularly with the internal audit and outside audit staffs to look closely at the thoroughness and adequacy of the procedures used to ensure that the true condition of the company is reflected in its published accounting statements.

The Penn Central debacle, in the midst of which the board of directors was apparently unaware of approaching disaster, has given considerable impetus to this trend.

If internal audit teams were to extend their counsel, nonpunitive inspection, and recommendations for improvement to social performance and to the quality of organization life as felt by its members, the information they would gather and the problems they would encounter could be summarized for the board committee in the same way as the more conventional subjects of their scrutiny.

In any case, the pervasiveness of the chief executive's posture on social responsibility can be inquired into, and the quality of the management across the organization can be reported on. The board of directors, supposed to provide judgment and experience not available inside the organization, can be—in its proper role of constructive inquiry into the quality of the corporation's management and its support for investment in improving it—a potent force in moderating the management's understandable internal interest in day-to-day achievement.

Conclusion

Nothing will happen, either inward or outward, to further advance the doctrine of social responsibility unless those in charge of the corporation want it to happen and unless their associates share their values and put their backs into solving the organization's master problem. There must be desire and determination first. It must be embodied in a strategy that makes a consistent whole of private economic opportunity and public social responsibility, planned to be implemented in an organization which will be humanely and challengingly led and developed.

A few good guys cannot change the course of a large corporation by their personal influence, but they can arrange that the systems of implementation are appropriate in scope to the breadth of corporate economic and social purpose. Now that enlightened chief executives have made this commitment, it would be tragic to have their will subverted, their determination doubted, and their energy dissipated by bureaucratic organization.

The giant corporation, which in small numbers does half the work of our economic system, is here to stay. It is the dominant force of our industrial society. In its multinational forms it has no higher sovereignty to which it reports; in its national forms it is granted wide latitude. Thus it is important to all of us that its affairs be responsibly conducted and that limited knowledge of the art of managing a large organization not be permitted to thwart us.

If organizations cannot be made moral, the future of capitalism will be unattractive—to all of us and especially to those young people whose talents we need. It is not the attack of the muckrakers we should fear but the apathy of our corporate citizenry.

39. "Skyhooks": With Special Implications for Monday Through Friday

O. A. Ohmann

Every human being, this observer of organizational behavior asserts, needs "skyhooks"—something that he can believe in and trust and that gives meaning to his activities. (Some say it is God manifesting Himself.) In recent years our industrialized society has engendered certain trends that have made the need for skyhooks more important and the possession of skyhooks less accessible: abundance without satisfaction, disillusionment with the notion that science represents the whole truth, and the trend toward bigness. The author calls on managers to meet employees' needs by giving them maximum opportunity to use their talents and take on responsibility. Originally published in 1955, Ohmann's article was reissued in 1970 as an "HBR Classic," with a retrospective commentary by the author.

During the last several years, while my principal job assignment has been management development, I have become increasingly impressed with the importance of intangibles in the art of administration. With the managerial revolution of the last generation and the transition from owner-manager to professional executive, there has appeared a growing literature on the science and art of administration. A shift in emphasis is noticeable in these writings over the past 30 years.

Following the early engineering approach typified by the work of Frederick Taylor and others, there next developed a search for the basic principles of organization, delegation, supervision, and control. More recently, as labor relations became more critical, the emphasis has shifted to ways of improving human relations. The approach to the problems of supervisory relationships was essentially a manipulative one. Textbooks on the techniques of personnel management mushroomed. Still later it became more and more apparent that the crux of the problem was the supervisor himself, and this resulted in a flood of "how to improve yourself" books. Meanwhile the complexities of the industrial community increased, and the discontents and tensions mounted.

It seems increasingly clear, at least to me, that while some administrative practices and personnel techniques may be better than others, their futility arises from the philosophical assumptions or value judgments on which this superstructure of manipulative procedure rests. We observe again and again that a manager with sound values and a stewardship conception of his role as boss can be a pretty effective leader even though his techniques are quite unorthodox. I am convinced that workers have a fine sensitivity to spiritual qualities and want to work for a boss who believes in something and in whom they can believe.

This observation leads me to suspect that we may have defined the basic purposes and objectives of our industrial enterprise too narrowly, too selfishly, too materialistically. Bread alone will not satisfy workers. There are some indications that our people have lost faith in the basic values of our economic society, and that we need a spiritual rebirth in industrial leadership.

Certainly no people have ever had so much, and enjoyed so little real satisfaction. Our economy has been abundantly productive, our standard of living is at an all-time peak, and yet we are a tense, frustrated, and insecure people full of hostilities and anxieties. Can it be that our *god of production* has feet of clay? Does industry need a new religion—or at least a better one than it has had?

I am convinced that the central problem is not the division of the spoils, as organized labor would have us believe. Raising the price of prostitution does not make it the equivalent of love. Is our industrial discontent not in fact the expression of a hunger for a work life that has meaning in terms of higher and more enduring spiritual values? How can we preserve the wholeness of the personality if we are expected to worship God on Sundays and holidays and mammon on Mondays through Fridays?

I do not imply that this search for real meaning in life is or should be limited to the hours on the job, but I do hold that the central values of our industrial society permeate our entire culture. I am sure we do not require a bill of particulars of the spiritual sickness of our time. The evidences of modern man's search for his soul are all about us. Save for the communist countries there has been a world-wide revival of interest in religion. The National Council of Churches reports that 59% of our total population (or 92 million) now claim church affiliation. The November 22, 1954 issue of *Barron's* devoted the entire front page to a review of a book by Barbara Ward, *Faith and Freedom*.[1]

Perhaps even more significant is the renaissance in the quality of religious thought and experience. Quite evidently our religion of materialism, science, and humanism is not considered adequate. Man is searching for anchors outside himself. He runs wearily to the periphery of the spider web of his

1. New York, W. W. Norton & Company, Inc., 1954.

own reason and logic, and looks for new "skyhooks"—for an abiding faith around which life's experiences can be integrated and given meaning.

Perhaps we should assume that this need for "skyhooks" is part of man's natural equipment—possibly a function of his intelligence—or, if you prefer, God manifesting Himself in His creatures. It seems to me, however, that the recent intensification of this need (or perhaps the clearer recognition of it) stems in part from certain broad social, economic, political, and philosophical trends. I shall not attempt a comprehensive treatment of these, but shall allude to only a few.

I have already indicated that on the economic front we have won the battle of production. We have moved from an economy of scarcity to one of abundance. We have become masters of the physical world and have learned how to convert its natural resources to the satisfaction of our material wants. We are no longer so dependent and so intimately bound to the world of nature. In a way we have lost our feeling of being part of nature and with it our humble reverence for God's creation.

While the industrialization of our economy resulted in ever-increasing production, it also made of individual man a production number—an impersonal, de-skilled, interchangeable production unit, measured in so many cents per hour. For most employees, work no longer promotes the growth of personal character by affording opportunities for personal decision, exercise of judgment, and individual responsibility. *Nation's Business* quoted the modern British philosopher, Alexander Lindsay, on this point as follows:

"Industrialism has introduced a new division into society. It is the division between those who manage and take responsibility and those who are managed and have responsibility taken from them. This is a division more important than the division between the rich and poor."[2]

Certainly the modern industrial worker has improved his material standard of living at the cost of becoming more and more dependent on larger and larger groups. Not only his dignity but also his security has suffered. And so he reaches out for new "skyhooks"—for something to believe in, for something that will give meaning to his job.

2. John Kord Lagemann, "Job Enlargement Boosts Production," December 1954, p. 36.

Appendix to Chapter 39

Retrospective Commentary

It's time I level with HBR readers about how "Skyhooks" came about. In a very real sense, I did not write it. It came as a stream of consciousness—but only after I had worked very hard for several weeks at putting my ideas together. I wrote the paper mainly to clear my own thinking, and to try it out for criticism on the Cleveland Philosophical Club. After much reading and thinking, I got absolutely nowhere. In desperation I was about to abandon the idea and write on a different subject. Deep inside my consciousness I said in effect to my silent partner within, "Look, if you want me to do this, you better help." About 2 a.m. that morning the ideas flowed in a continuous stream, and I put them down in shorthand notes as fast as I could.

The word "Skyhooks" for the title came in the heat of a discussion with a group of business executives attending the Institute of Humanistic Studies at Aspen, Colorado. As we debated the limits of the rational and scientific approach to life, it occurred to me that science appears rational on the surface, but at its very foundation typically lies a purely intuitive, non-rational assumption made by some scientist. He just hooked himself on a "piece of sky out there" and hung on. It was a complete leap of faith that led him.

In my studies of exceptional executives I had found a mystery not easily explainable by rational elements. These men, too, were hanging on sky-hooks of their own—hidden and secret missions which went way beyond their corporate business objectives. Sometimes the mission was a "nutsy" one. Often it had long roots back in the executive's childhood and was emotional, intuitive, beyond rationality, selfless—but it stuck. For example, it might be like John F. Kennedy's determination to become President; reportedly he was doing it for his older brother, who had the ambition to be President but never made it because he was a war casualty.

Or perhaps the mission was like that of the president of one of our largest corporations. When he was 12 years old, his father died. He promised his mother he would help her work the farm in the hills so that his eight younger brothers could go through school. This is what he continued to do all of his life—helping other young men to make something of themselves. He was a great developer of managers.

I could fill a book with such examples. Many great executives I have known have something deep inside that supports them; something they trust when the going gets tough; something ultimate; something personal; something beyond reason—in short, a deep-rooted skyhook which brings them calm and confidence when they stand alone.

There is another interesting aspect to this question. In our rational, analytical, and highly successful Western culture, we have come to place great value on the material gains which represent the end results of our achievements. This is what our kids are complaining about: that we have gone overboard on material values and made a culture of *things*. But the *results* of our strivings are dead works; the life is in the *process* of achieving, in the leap of faith. David was great not when he slew Goliath, but when he decided to try.

So it seems to me that the skyhooks mystique is also characterized by a commitment to value the *process*, the working relationships with others, the spiritual bonds growing out of the faith in the God-potential deep within another person, and the basis of genuine community. The rest is the means, not the end.

In 1955, when my article was published, the generation gap had not been invented, and Marshall McLuhan had not alerted us to the fact that "the medium is the message." Yet a quick look backward reveals the considerable impact of youth and "McLuhanism" on our history and our future. The "McCarthy Kids" have ousted a President and his party, halted the military domination of our foreign policy, radically changed our educational and religious institutions, revised industry's approach to management recruiting, and made the Peace Corps type of job competitive with the "goodies" offered by business. Generalizing about the medium having greater impact than the message, they have pointed out that our values are dictated by our social systems—especially the technological, political, and managerial systems. More important than the things we create in industry, they say, is the *way* we create them—the kind of community we establish in our working together.

Without debating the merits of "pot" versus liquor, or anarchy versus order, I believe their emphasis on social process is introducing a new dimension into our corporate life and values.

"Skyhooks" was written for myself and not for publication. For a while I refused to give anybody a copy, but under pressure I duplicated a small number of copies for my friends, and they wanted copies for their friends. When the Editor of HBR got his copy and asked, "How about publishing it?" I answered, "Only if you take it as it is; I don't want to revise it." I see little need for revising it now—except perhaps the reference to the increase in membership in the institutional church. The search for ultimate values and meanings is keener than in 1955, but it is apparently no longer satisfied merely by church affiliation.

Disillusionment with science: A second trend which seems to bear some relation to our urgent need for a faith grows out of our disillusionment with science. As a result of the rapid advance of science, the curtains of ignorance and superstitition have been pulled wide on all fronts of human curiosity and knowledge. Many of the bonds of our intellectual enslavement have been broken. Reason and scientific method were called on to witness to the truth, the whole truth, and nothing but the truth. We were freed from the past—its traditions, beliefs, philosophies, its mores, morals, and religion. Science became our religion, and reason replaced emotion.

However, even before the atom bomb there was a growing realization that science did not represent the whole truth, that with all its pretensions it could be dead wrong, and, finally and particularly, that without proper moral safeguards the truth did not necessarily make men free. Atomic fission intensified the fear and insecurity of every one of us who contemplated the possibility of the concentration of power in the hands of men without morals. We want science to be in the hands of men who not only recognize their responsibility to man-made ethical standards (which are easily perverted) but have dedicated themselves to the eternal and absolute standards of God. Thus, while the evidence of material science has been welcomed, our own personal experiences will not permit us to believe that life is merely a whirl of atoms without meaning, purpose, beauty, or destiny.

Trend toward bigness: A third factor contributing to our insecurity is the trend toward bigness and the resulting loss of individuality. This is the day of bigger and bigger business—in every aspect of life. The small is being swallowed by the big, and the big by the bigger. This applies to business, to unions, to churches, to education, to research and invention, to newspapers, to our practice of the professions, to government, and to nations. Everything is getting bigger except the individual, and he is getting smaller and more insignificant and more dependent on larger social units. Whether we like it or not, this is becoming an administrative society, a planned and controlled society, with ever-increasing concentration of power. This is the day of collectivism and public-opinion polls. It is the day when the individual must be *adjusted to the group*—when he must above all else be sensitive to the feelings and attitudes of others, must get an idea of how others expect him to act, and then react to this.

This is the insecure world which David Riesman has described so well in his book, *The Lonely Crowd*.[3] He pictures man as being no longer "tradi-

3. New Haven, Yale University Press, 1950.

tion directed" as was primitive man, nor as in Colonial days is he "inner directed" as if by the gyroscope of his own ideals, but today he is "outer directed" as if by radar. He must constantly keep his antenna tuned to the attitudes and reactions of others to him. The shift has been from morals to morale and from self-reliance to dependence on one's peer group. However, the members of one's peer group are each responding to each other. Obviously these shifting sands of public opinion offer no stable values around which life can be consistently integrated and made meaningful. The high-water mark of adjustment in such a society is that the individual be socially accepted and above all else that he appear to be *sincere*.

This is certainly not a favorable environment for the development of steadfast character. It is essentially a neurotic and schizophrenic environment which breeds insecurity.

This socially dependent society also offers an ideal market for the wares of the "huckster," the propagandist, and the demagogue. Lacking a religious interpretation of the divine nature of man, these merchants in mass reaction have sought the least common denominator in human nature and have beamed the movies and newspapers at the ten-year mental level. One wonders if this approach to people does not make them feel that they have been sold short and that they are capable of much better than is expected of them. Has this demoralizing exposure of the cheapness of our values not intensified our search for something better to believe in?

On top of all these disturbing socioeconomic trends came the war. This certainly was materialism, science, and humanism carried to the logical conclusion. The war made us question our values and our direction. It left us less cocksure that we were right, and more fearful of ourselves as well as of others. It made us fearful of the power which we had gained, and led us to search our soul to determine whether we had the moral strength to assume the leadership role that had been given to us. We have been humbled in our efforts to play god and are about ready to give the job back. Note, however, that this is not a characteristic reaction to war. Typically wars have been followed by a noticeable deterioration of moral standards, of traditional values, and of social institutions.

Perhaps none of these rationalizations for our return to religion is entirely valid. I suspect that the search for some kind of overarching integrative principle or idea is the expression of a normal human need. Certainly history would indicate that man's need for a god is eternal even though it may be more keenly sensed in times of adversity. A religion gives a point of philosophical orientation around which life's experiences can be organized and digested. Without the equivalent, a personality cannot be whole and healthy. Short-term goals which need to be shifted with the changing tide do not serve the same integrative function as do the "skyhooks" which are fastened to eternal values. I do not personally regard the current religious revival as a cultural hangover, nor as a regression. Being a mystic I prefer instead to view the need for such a faith as the spark of the Creator in us to drive us on to achieve His will and our own divine destiny.

Why Monday Through Friday?

If we may grant for the moment that modern man *is* searching for deeper meanings in life, we may then ask: What has this to do with industry? If he needs "skyhooks," let him get them in church, or work out his own salvation. The business leaders of the past insisted that "business is business" and that it had little bearing on the individual's private life and philosophy.

There are several reasons why "skyhooks" must be a primary concern of the business administrator:

□ For the individual the job is the center of life, and its values must be in harmony with the rest of life if he is to be a whole and healthy personality.

□ This is an industrial society, and its values tend to become those of the entire culture.

□ The public is insisting that business leaders are in fact responsible for the general social welfare—that the manager's responsibilities go far beyond those of running the business. They have delegated this responsibility to the business executive whether he wishes to play this role or not.

□ Even if the administrator insists on a narrow definition of his function as merely the production of goods and services as efficiently as possible, it is nevertheless essential that he take these intangibles into account, since they are the real secrets of motivating an organization.

□ Besides all this the administrator needs a better set of "skyhooks" himself if he is to carry his ever-increasing load of responsibility without cracking up. The fact that so many administrators are taking time to rationalize, defend, and justify the private enterprise system is an outward indication of this need for more significant meanings.

Anything Wrong with Capitalism?

We may ask, then: What specifically is wrong with our capitalistic system of private enterprise? What is wrong with production or with trying to improve our present standard of living? What is wrong with a profit, or with private ownership of capital, or with competition? Is this not the true American way of life?

Nothing is necessarily wrong with these values. There are certainly worse motives than the profit motive. A refugee from communism is reported to have observed: "What a delight to be in the United States, where things are produced and sold with such a nice clean motive as making a profit."

I am not an economist, and it is beyond the scope of this article to attempt a revision of our economic theory. I am tempted, however, to make a couple of observations about these traditional economic concepts:

1. That while the values represented by them are not necessarily wrong, they are certainly pretty thin and do not challenge the best in people.

2. That many of the classical economic assumptions are outmoded and are no longer adequate descriptions of the actual operation of our present-day economy.

For example, the concept of economic man as being motivated by self-interest not only is outmoded by the best current facts of the social sciences, but also fails to appeal to the true nobility of spirit of which we are capable.

The concept of the free and competitive market is a far cry from the highly controlled and regulated economy in which business must operate today. General Motors does not appear to want to put Chrysler out of business, and apparently the union also decided to take the heat off Chrysler rather than to press its economic advantage to the logical conclusion. The assumption that everyone is out to destroy his competitors does not explain the sharing of technology through trade associations and journals. No, we also have tremendous capacity for cooperation when challenged by larger visions. We are daily denying the Darwinian notion of the "survival of the fittest"—which, incidentally, William Graham Sumner, one of the nineteenth-century apologists for our economic system, used for justifying unbridled self-interest and competition.

Certainly the traditional concept of private ownership of capital does not quite correspond to the realities of today's control of large blocks of capital by insurance companies and trusteed funds.

The notion of individual security through the accumulation of savings has largely given way to the collectivist means of group insurance, company annuities, and Social Security.

The concept that all profits belong to the stockholders is no longer enthusiastically supported by either the government or the unions, since both are claiming an increasing cut.

And so, while we may argue that the system of private enterprise is self-regulatory and therefore offers maximum individual freedom, the simple, cold fact is that it is in ever-increasing degree a managed or controlled economy—partly at the insistence of the voters, but largely as the result of the inevitable economic pressures and the trend toward bigness.[4]

4. See John Kenneth Galbraith, *American Capitalism* (Boston, Houghton Mifflin Company, 1952).

Regardless of the rightness or wrongness of these changes in our system of enterprise, the changes have been considerable, and I doubt that classical economic theory can be used as an adequate rationale of its virtues. I am therefore not particularly optimistic about the efficacy of the current campaign to have businessmen "save the private enterprise system and the American way of life" by engaging in wholesale economic education, much of which is based on outmoded concepts.

Much as economic theory needs revision, I fear that this is not likely to cure our ills. Nor do I believe that profit-sharing or any other device for increasing the workers' cut (desirable as these efforts may be) will give us what we really want. It is, rather, another type of sharing that is needed, a sharing of more worthy objectives, a sharing of the management function, and a sharing of mutual respect and Christian working relationships.

Goals and purposes: What is wrong is more a matter of goals and purposes—of our assumptions about what we are trying to do and how we can dignify and improve ourselves in the doing. There is nothing wrong with production, but we should ask ourselves: *Production for what?* Do we use people for production or production for people? How can production be justified if it destroys personality and human values both in the process of its manufacture and by its end use? Clarence B. Randall of Inland Steel, in his book, *A Creed for Free Enterprise*, says:

"We have come to worship production as an end in itself, which of course it is not. It is precisely there that the honest critic of our way of life makes his attack and finds us vulnerable. Surely there must be for each person some ultimate value, some purpose, some mode of self-expression that makes the experience we call life richer and deeper."[5]

So far, so good, Mr. Randall. But now notice how he visualizes industry making its contribution to this worthy objective:

"To produce more and more with less and less effort is merely treading water unless we *thereby release time and energy for the cultivation of the mind and the spirit* and for the achievement of those ends for which Providence placed us on this earth."

Here is the same old dichotomy—work faster and more efficiently so that you can finish your day of drudgery and cultivate your soul on your own time. In fact he says: "A horse with a very evil disposition can nevertheless pull the farmer's plow." No, I am afraid the job *is* the life. *This* is what must be made meaningful. We cannot assume that the end of production justifies the means. What happens to people in the course of producing may be far more important than the end product. Materialism is not a satisfactory "skyhook." People are capable of better and want to do better.

5. Boston, Little, Brown and Company, 1952, p. 16.

(Incidentally, I have the impression that Mr. Randall's practices line up very well with my own point of view even if his words do not.)

Perhaps we should ask: What is the really important difference between Russian communism and our system? Both worship production and are determined to produce more efficiently, and do. Both worship science. Both have tremendously improved the standard of living of their people. Both share the wealth. Both develop considerable loyalties for their system. (In a mere 40 years since Lenin started the communist revolution a third of the world's people have come to accept its allegiance.) True, in Russia capital is controlled by the state, while here it is theoretically controlled by individuals, although in actual practice, through absentee ownership, it is controlled to a considerable extent by central planning agencies and bureaus, both public and private.

No, the real difference is in the philosophy about people and how they may be used as means to ends. It is a difference in the assumptions made about the origin of rights—whether the individual is endowed with rights by his Creator and yields these only voluntarily to civil authority designated by him, or whether rights originate in force and in the will of the government. Is God a myth, or is He the final and absolute judge to whom we are ultimately responsible? Are all standards of conduct merely man-made and relative, or absolute and eternal? Is man a meaningless happenstance of protoplasm, or is he a divine creation with a purpose, with potential for improvement, and with a special destiny in the overall scheme of things? These are some of the differences—or at least I hope that they still are. And what a difference these intangible, perhaps mythical "skyhooks" make. They are nevertheless the most real and worthwhile and enduring things in the world. The absence of these values permitted the Nazis to "process" people through the gas chambers in order to recover the gold in their teeth.

The Administrator Contributes

This, then, is part of our general cultural heritage and is passed on to us in many ways. However, it really comes to life in people—in their attitudes, aspirations, and behaviors. And in a managerial society this brings us back to the quality of the individual administrator. He interprets or crystallizes the values and objectives for his group. He sets the climate within which these values either *do* or *do not* become working realities. He must define the goals and purposes of his group in larger and more meaningful perspective. He integrates the smaller, selfish goals of individuals into larger, more social and spiritual, objectives for the group. He provides the vision without which the people perish. Conflicts are resolved by relating the immediate to the long-range and more enduring values. In fact, we might say this *integrative function* is the core of the administrator's contribution.

The good ones have the mental equipment to understand the business and set sound long-term objectives, but the best ones have in addition the philosophical and character values which help them to relate the overall goals of the enterprise to eternal values. This is precisely the point at which deep-seated religious convictions can serve an integrative function, since they represent the most long-range of all possible goals. Most really great leaders in all fields of human endeavor have been peculiarly sensitive to their historic role in human destiny. Their responsibility and loyalty are to some distant vision which gives calm perspective to the hot issues of the day.

This function of the administrator goes far beyond being a likable personality, or applying correct principles of organization, or being skillful in the so-called techniques of human relations. I am convinced that the difficulties which so many executives have with supervisory relationships cannot be remedied by cultivation of the so-called human relations skills. These difficulties spring, rather, from one's conception of his function or role as a boss, his notion about the origin and nature of his authority over others, the assumptions he makes about people and their worth, and his view of what he and his people are trying to accomplish together. To illustrate:

If, for example, my personal goal is to get ahead in terms of money, position, and power; and if I assume that to achieve this I must best my competitors; that the way to do this is to establish a good production record; that my employees are means to this end; that they are replaceable production units which must be skillfully manipulated; that this can be done by appealing to the lowest form of immediate selfish interest; that the greatest threat to me is that my employees may not fully recognize my authority or accept my leadership—if these are my values, then I am headed for trouble—all supervisory techniques notwithstanding.

I wish I could be quite so positive in painting the picture of the right values and approaches to management. I suspect there are many, many different right answers. No doubt each company or enterprise will have to define its own long-term purposes and develop its own philosophy in terms of its history, traditions, and its real function in our economy. I am also certain that no one philosophy would be equally useful to all managers. The character of an organization is, to a large extent, set by the top man or the top group, and it is inevitable that this be the reflection of the philosophy of these individuals. No one of us can operate with another's philosophy. I have also observed that in most enterprises the basic faith or spirit of the organization is a rather nebulous or undefined something which nevertheless has very profound meaning to the employees.

A *successful executive*: Recognizing then the futility of advocating any one pattern of values, it occurs to me that it might, however, be suggestive

or helpful if I told you something of the philosophy of one extremely successful executive whom I have pumped a good deal on this subject (for
he is more inclined to live his values than to talk about them):

As near as I can piece it together, he believes that this world was not an
accident but was created by God and that His laws regulate and control the
universe and that we are ultimately *responsible to Him*. Man, as God's
supreme creation, is in turn endowed with creative ability. Each individual
represents a unique combination of talents and potentials. In addition, man
is the only animal endowed with freedom of choice and with a high capacity
for making value judgments. With these gifts (of heredity and cultural
environment) goes an obligation to give the best possible accounting of
one's stewardship in terms of maximum self-development and useful service
to one's fellows in the hope that one may live a rich life and be a credit to
his Creator.

This executive also assumes that each individual possesses certain God-
given rights of self-direction which only *the individual* can voluntarily
delegate to others in authority over him, and that this is usually done in
the interest of achieving some mutual cooperative good. The executive
therefore assumes that his *own* authority as boss over others must be
exercised with due regard for the attendant obligations to his employees
and to the stockholders who have temporarily and voluntarily yielded
their rights in the interest of this common undertaking. (Notice that he
does not view his authority as originating with or derived from his immediate superior.) This delegated authority must, of course, be used to
advance the common good rather than primarily to achieve the selfish
ambitions of the leader at the expense of the led.

He further assumes that the voluntary association of employees in
industry is for the purpose of increasing the creativity and productivity of
all members of the group and thus of bringing about increased benefits to
all who may share in the ultimate use of these goods and services. What
is equally important, however, is that in the course of this industrial
operation each individual should have an opportunity to develop the
maximum potential of his skills and that the working relationships should
not destroy the individual's ability to achieve his greatest maturity and
richness of experience. As supervisor he must set the working conditions
and atmosphere which will make it possible for his employees to achieve
this dual objective of increasing productivity and maximizing self-development.

These goals can best be achieved by giving employees maximum opportunity to exercise their capacity for decision making and judgment
within their assigned area of responsibility. The supervisor is then primarily
a coach who must instruct, discipline, and motivate all the members of the
group, making it possible for each to exercise his special talent in order to

maximize the total team contribution. Profits are regarded as a measure of the group's progress toward these goals, and a loss represents not only an improper but even an immoral use of the talents of the group.

There is nothing "soft" about his operation. He sets high quality standards and welcomes stiff competition as an additional challenge to his group. He therefore expects and gets complete cooperation and dedication on the part of everyone. Incidentally, he views the activity of working together in this manner with others as being one of life's most rewarding experiences. He holds that this way of life is something which we have not yet fully learned, but that its achievement is part of our divine destiny. He is firmly convinced that such conscientious efforts *will* be rewarded with success. He manages with a light touch that releases creativity, yet with complete confidence in the outcome.

This is probably a poor attempt at verbalizing the basic philosophy which this man lives so easily and naturally. I hope, however, that it has revealed something of his conception of his role or function as an executive, and his view of what he and his organization are trying to do together. With this account of his values I am sure that you would have no difficulty completing the description of his administrative practices and operating results. They flow naturally from his underlying faith, without benefit of intensive training in the principles and art of administration.

As you would suspect, people like to work for him—or with him. He attracts good talent (which is one of the real secrets of success). Those with shoddy values, selfish ambitions, or character defects do not survive— the organization is self-pruning. Those who remain develop rapidly because they learn to accept responsibility. He not only advocates but practices decentralization and delegation. His employees will admit that they have made mistakes, but usually add with a grin that they try not to make the same one twice. People respond to his leadership because he has faith in them and expects the best in them rather than the worst. He speaks well of the members of his organization, and they appear to be proud of each other and of their record of performance. He takes a keen interest in developing measurements of performance and in bettering previous records or competitive standards. He feels that no one has a right to "louse up a job"—a point on which he feels the stockholders and the Lord are in complete agreement.

While he does not talk much about "employee communications" or stress formal programs of this type, his practice is to spend a large proportion of his time in the field with his operating people rather than in his office. He is "people oriented," and he does a particularly good job of listening. The union committee members have confidence in his fairness, yet do a workmanlike job of bargaining. In administering salaries he seems to be concerned about helping the individual to improve his contribution so that a pay increase can be justified.

In his general behavior he moves without haste or hysteria. He is typically well organized, relaxed, and confident, even under trying circumstances. There is a high degree of consistency in his behavior and in the quality of his decisions because his basic values do not shift. Since he does not operate by expediency, others can depend on him; and this consistency makes for efficiency in the discharge of delegated responsibility. Those operating problems which do come to him for decision seem to move easily and quickly to a conclusion. His long-term values naturally express themselves in well-defined policies, and it is against this frame of reference that the decisions of the moment easily fall into proper perspective.

In policy-level discussions his contributions have a natural quality of objectivity because "self-concern" does not confuse. Others take him at face value because his motives are not suspect. When differences or conflicts do arise, his approach is not that of compromise; rather, he attempts to integrate the partisan views around mutually acceptable longer-range goals. The issues of the moment then seem to dissolve in a discussion of the best means to the achievement of the objective. I have no doubt that he also has some serious problems, but I have tried to give a faithful account of the impression which he creates. There is a *sense of special significance* about his operation which is shared by his associates.

This Is the Key

It is precisely this "sense of special significance" which is the key to leadership. We all know that there are many different ways of running a successful operation. I am certainly not recommending any particular set of administrative practices—although admittedly some are better than others. Nor am I suggesting that his set of values should be adopted by others, or for that matter could be. What I am saying is that a man's real values have a subtle but inevitable way of being communicated, and they affect the significance of everything he does.

These are the vague intangibles—the "skyhooks"—which are difficult to verbalize but easy to sense and tremendously potent in their influence. They provide a different, invisible, fundamental structure into which the experiences of every day are absorbed and given meaning. They are frequently unverbalized, and in many organizations they defy definition. Yet they are the most real things in the world.

Jacob D. Cox, Jr., late president of Cleveland Twist Drill Company, told a story that illustrates my point:

Jimmy Green was a new union committee member who stopped in to see Mr. Cox after contract negotiations had been concluded. Jimmy said that every other place he had worked, he had always gone home grouchy; he never wanted to play with the children or take his wife to the movies. And then he said, "But since I have been working here, all that has changed. Now when I come home, the children run to meet me and we have a grand romp together. It is a wonderful difference and I don't know why, but I thought you would like to know."[6]

As Mr. Cox observed, there must be a lot of Jimmy Greens in the world who want an opportunity to take part freely in a cooperative effort that has a moral purpose.

6. *Material Human Progress* (Cleveland, Cleveland Twist Drill Company, 1954), p. 104.

Bibliography: The Well-Read Manager

John B. Bennett and Ronald L. Weiher

As change continues to accelerate, so does the manager's quest for relevant information that will allow him to keep pace. The problem is, how does one find his way in the vast and growing body of management literature? This article not only tells where to obtain assistance but also presents a sampling of books, periodicals, and literature guides for the manager who wants to remain generally informed and functionally competent.

In an average week, as many as 60 new books relevant to business may reach large university libraries. Along with the books come the current issues of some 900 serial publications relating to business, ranging from *The Wall Street Journal* and *Business Week* to such exotica as *Fertilizer Trends* and *Business in Nebraska*. In one way or another, each of these books and serials is of potential value to the manager. But how can he know what is being published—let alone decide what is useful?

The easy solution, of course, is simply to read those few new books on management that become best sellers or crop up in cocktail conversation and to skim the periodicals that are boardroom standbys. Unfortunately, this approach is scarcely calculated to keep the manager abreast of the advances in theory and practice that are relevant to his role.

Of all the circumstances in which a manager must rely on the literature, the most common is the most demanding—the need to know current information. In the early stages of his career, he must keep up with advances in his particular area of expertise and be aware of developments that affect his company. As he progresses in the organization, he also needs to know about his subordinates' specialties.

In addition to remaining generally up to date, a manager may need to familiarize himself with particular activities that are currently of concern to his company (for example, divestiture or the responsibilities of directors). Or perhaps he wants to develop a general background in an emerging field. How can he find out what information is available—and not just in books, but in trade and professional periodicals as well?

In short, managers must know the literature in their profession if they wish to keep abreast of current developments and have ready access to published information on specific topics. In this article, we shall identify what we call the "literature of management" and suggest where to find it. At the end of the article, we shall present a sampling of books, periodicals, and guides to further reading and information.

Literature of Management

Near the turn of the century, the first collegiate schools of business were founded, and books were written to teach students what management and business were all about. These early books did little more than describe practices and institutions. As management studies became more professional in the academic setting, management literature became more analytical and was based less on ad hoc "principles."

Today, much of the literature of management is directed to the active practitioner and aims to bridge the gap between theory and practice. It is not dry, dusty, or esoteric. Some of the literature is addressed to the manager as decision maker. Some is focused on the psychology of management. Other parts of the literature examine the organization and structure of business institutions. A large segment is devoted to management activities in such areas as finance, marketing, control, and planning.

The majority of this knowledge is available in the form of books (450,000 volumes, for example, in Baker Library at the Harvard Business School, with more than 3,000 new titles added every year). This exploding body of business information is augmented by serial publications of all sorts—periodicals, newspapers, statistical annuals, directories, and the reports of a host of conferences and government agencies. (By conservative estimate, 2,500 different periodicals of management interest are published in the United States each year.) A variety of indexes and guides enable the business researcher to find what he wants in this mass of print.

Where to Look

In the most literal sense, all of these books and periodicals might just as well have never been published unless the manager knows where to find them. There are, in fact, a number of places he can go for guidance.

The best of these sources is the nearest library. The nearest library is very often the corporate library in the manager's own organization. Virtually all major companies operate specialized libraries or information centers as a part of their organization (for example a business library at headquarters, a scientific library in the R&D area, and engineering libraries in various sectors of the organization). The manager who keeps his company librarian informed about his and the organization's information needs will be pleasantly surprised at the cooperation he will receive. If the company does not have its own library, he can request assistance from the Consultation Service of the Special Libraries Association (235 Park Avenue South, New York, N.Y. 10003) or review the Strable book on special libraries cited in the reading list.

In addition to in-house libraries, some of the larger cities in the United States have outstanding business collections. (A notable example is the Brooklyn Public Library. The public libraries in Boston, Cleveland, and Newark also have substantial business collections.) Even a small public library will have some management books, periodicals, and reference sources. And, although there may be some restrictions on its use, the library of a college with a program of business administration is another likely source of help. In such collections the manager can expect to find—

. . . recent management-oriented books from the major publishers;

. . . common business directories, like Dun & Bradstreet's *Million Dollar Directory* and *Poor's Register of Corporations, Directors and Executives;*

. . . local city and state directories of businesses and manufacturers;

. . . the more popular business magazines and newspapers;

. . . the major periodical indexes;

. . . a selection of U.S. government documents and statistical reports relevant to business;

. . . investment-information references, such as Moody's *Investor Service* and Standard & Poor's *Corporation Records;*

. . . tax service publications such as those produced by Prentice-Hall, Inc. and Commerce Clearing House, Inc.

In addition to the various sources of information just mentioned, a library may have reading lists and bibliographies on topics of current management interest. (Those items that are not in the library may be available through interlibrary loan.) The large metropolitan libraries provide staffs with the specialized skills to handle business information requests. However, any librarian can usually respond to factual questions as well as help in the use of the collection.

While a library is usually the best repository of management literature, there are numerous other sources to which a manager can turn. For example:

□ More than 15,000 trade associations, professional societies, and other groups with voluntary membership exist in the United States. Many of these groups are business-oriented and can often provide information that is not available in libraries or elsewhere. Moreover, a number of them have publishing programs of considerable magnitude. (For example, the American Management Association is the publisher of 200 books and 6 periodicals.)

A manager might know about the more important associations; he probably does not know about them all. The *Encyclopedia of Associations*, and the *Directory of National Trade and Professional Associations*, both cited later in this article, are standard sources of identification. They can be found in most libraries.

□ Bookstores, particularly those which service a university with its own school of business, can also be of assistance. The smaller stores understandably carry a limited selection. Nevertheless, almost every bookstore will have *Books in Print* and *Paperbound Books in Print*. (The latter lists over 350 titles under the heading "Business—Management.") Of course, almost all bookstores will place orders for books they do not have in stock.

□ Publishers themselves can provide considerable guidance. Should a manager wish, a publisher will mail him regular information about new titles. In addition, he will fill mail orders for individual titles. Among the major publishers of management books are Richard D. Irwin, Inc., McGraw-Hill Book Company, Inc., and Prentice-Hall, Inc.

MONITORING NEW PUBLICATIONS

To remain up to date, a manager should help himself as much as possible. This is particularly relevant for learning about new literature. An inquiry that is directed to a library, a special-interest group, or a publisher will yield information about material already in print. In some instances, as in the case of a publisher's mailing list, the inquiry will serve as a basis for continuing information. Yet these sources do not cover the broader range of new business material.

To learn about significant new publications in special fields, a manager can subscribe to the lists of new business books published from time to time by some of the business libraries. (Among these are Baker Library and the Newark and Cleveland public libraries.) He should also systematically check the popular business periodicals which carry reviews of new books.

Two publications are particularly helpful in keeping abreast of the current literature. The first is *Management Review*, a monthly compilation of feature articles, book surveys, and condensations and summaries from business magazines. The second is *Management Abstracts*, a quarterly publication that reviews books and abstracts a wide range of articles for management; photocopies of the abstracted articles are available. (Both of the foregoing publications are included in the periodicals section of the list that accompanies this article.)

Finally, a manager should not overlook the opportunity to browse in a good library whenever possible. This is one of the best ways to become familiar with the materials that make up the literature of management.

The remainder of this article is a sampling for managers who wish to explore what has been published about their profession. Our list is divided into three sections: (1) books, (2) periodicals, and (3) guides to information. There is no such thing as a list of the "best" books about management, but we have attempted to make this one as representative as possible.

1. Books

Under each heading in this section of the list, we have made it a point to include:

At least one up-to-date textbook. This should provide a place to start if an individual needs an overall view; a textbook's purpose is not as much to provide new knowledge as to record the state of the art. (Textbooks are indicated by an asterisk.)

At least one book of readings. This should give a feel for different points of view on a single subject and help an individual to delve into the periodical literature, which is a common source of such readings. (Books of readings are indicated by a dagger.)

A small selection of general books. These provide a representative sample of the literature. Each is written from its author's individual viewpoint with the purpose of advancing the state of management knowledge.

The books were chosen by a variety of methods. Many titles came from a perusal of the manuscript of Lorna M. Daniells' forthcoming book, *Business Information Sources* (cited below). Faculty members of the Harvard Business School suggested some of the titles. For others, we examined reserve-book and business-course reading lists and scanned published bibliographies. Then a look at the most heavily used books in Baker Library's Core Collection (a group of 4,000 titles that emphasize recent and representative books on business and related subjects) turned up still more titles. The final choices were made with our own idiosyncratic and fallible judgment.

GENERAL MANAGEMENT

Chester I. Barnard, *The Functions of the Executive* (Cambridge, Harvard University Press, 1968).

Patrick E. Connor and others, editors, *Dimensions in Modern Management* (Boston, Houghton Mifflin, 1974).†

Peter F. Drucker, *Management: Tasks, Responsibilities, Practices* (New York, Harper & Row, 1974).

Fremont E. Kast and James E. Rosenzweig, *Organization and Management: A Systems Approach*, 2nd edition (New York, McGraw-Hill, 1974).*

Harold Koontz and Cyril O. O'Donnell, *Principles of Management: An Analysis of Managerial Functions*, 5th edition (New York, McGraw-Hill, 1972).*

Harwood F. Merrill, editor, *Classics in Management*, revised edition (New York, American Management Association, 1970).†

BUSINESS POLICY AND CORPORATE PLANNNING

Russell L. Ackoff, *A Concept of Corporate Planning* (New York, Wiley-Interscience, 1970).

Kenneth R. Andrews, *The Concept of Corporate Strategy* (Homewood, Illinois, Dow Jones-Irwin, 1971).

David W. Ewing, editor, *Long-Range Planning for Management*, 3rd edition (New York, Harper & Row, 1972).†

Harry Jones, *Preparing Company Plans; A Workbook for Effective Corporate Planning* (New York, Wiley, 1974).

Robert J. Mockler, *Business Planning and Policy Formulation* (New York, Appleton-Century-Crofts, 1972).*

George A. Steiner, *Top Management Planning* (New York, Macmillan, 1969).

BUSINESS IN SOCIETY

Melvin Anshen, editor, *Managing the Socially Responsible Corporation* (New York, Macmillan, 1974).†

Neil W. Chamberlain, *The Place of Business in America's Future: A Study in Social Values* (New York, Basic, 1973).

Arthur Dahlberg, *How to Save Free Enterprise* (Old Greenwich, Connecticut, Devin-Adair, 1974).

Keith Davis and Robert L. Blomstrom, *Business and Society: Environment and Responsibility*, 3rd edition (New York, McGraw-Hill, 1975).*

Richard N. Goodwin, *The American Condition* (New York, Doubleday, 1974).

George C. Lodge, *The New American Ideology* (New York, Knopf, 1975).

S. Prakash Sethi, editor, *The Unstable Ground: Corporate Social Policy in a Dynamic Society* (Los Angeles, Melville, 1974)†

MULTINATIONAL BUSINESS

Richard J. Barnet and Ronald E. Müller, *Global Reach: The Power of the Multinational Corporations* (New York, Simon and Schuster, 1974).

William A. Dymsza, *Multinational Business Strategy* (New York, McGraw-Hill, 1972).

Richard Eells, *Global Corporations, the Emerging System of World Economic Power* (New York, Interbook, 1972).

Raymond Vernon, *Manager in the International Economy*, 2nd edition (Prentice-Hall, 1972)*

Raymond Vernon, *Sovereignty at Bay: The Multinational Spread of U.S. Enterprise* (New York, Basic Books, 1971).

S. Prakash Sethi and Jagdish N. Sheth, editors, *Multinational Business Operations* (Pacific Palisades, California, Goodyear, 1973). 4 volumes†

HUMAN BEHAVIOR IN ORGANIZATIONS

David A. Kolb and others, editors, *Organizational Psychology: A Book of Readings*, 2nd edition (Englewood Cliffs, New Jersey, Prentice-Hall, 1974).†

Harold J. Leavitt, *Managerial Psychology*, 3rd edition (Chicago, University of Chicago Press, 1972).

Fred Luthans, *Organizational Behavior; A Modern Behavioral Approach to Management* (New York, McGraw-Hill, 1973).*

Douglas M. McGregor, *The Human Side of Enterprise* (New York, McGraw-Hill, 1960).

F. J. Roethlisberger, *Man-in-Organization* (Cambridge, Harvard University Press, 1968).

Edgar H. Schein, *Organizational Psychology*, 2nd edition (Englewood Cliffs, New Jersey, Prentice-Hall, 1972).

QUANTITATIVE METHODS

Harold Bierman and others, *Quantitative Analysis for Business Decisions*, 4th edition (Homewood, Illinois, Irwin, 1973).*

Robert L. Childress, *Mathematics for Managerial Decisions* (Englewood Cliffs, New Jersey, Prentice-Hall, 1974).*

Edwin Mansfield, editor, *Managerial Economics and Operations Research: Techniques, Applications, Cases*, 3rd edition (New York, Norton, 1975).†

Robert Schlaifer, *Analysis of Decisions Under Uncertainty* (New York, McGraw-Hill, 1969).*

Nicolai Siemens and others, *Operations Research; Planning, Operating, and Information Systems* (New York, Free Press, 1973).*

ACCOUNTING/CONTROL

Robert N. Anthony and others, *Management Control Systems: Text, Cases and Readings*, revised edition (Homewood, Illinois, Irwin, 1972).*†

James A. Gentry and Glenn L. Johnson, *Finney and Miller's Principles of Accounting: Introductory*, 7th edition (Englewood Cliffs, New Jersey, Prentice-Hall, 1970). (The 8th edition scheduled for publication in 1976).*

Robert J. Mockler, *Information Systems for Management* (Columbus, Ohio, Merrill, 1974).*

Clarence B. Nickerson, *Accounting Handbook for Nonaccountants* (Boston, Cahners, 1975).

Alfred Rappaport, editor, *Information for Decision Making: Quantitative and Behavioral Dimensions*, 2nd edition (Englewood Cliffs, New Jersey, Prentice-Hall, 1975).†

Donald H. Sanders, *Computers in Business: An Introduction*, 3rd edition (New York, McGraw-Hill, 1975).*

FINANCE

Harold Bierman and Seymour Smidt, *The Capital Budgeting Decision: Economic Analysis and Financing of Investment Projects*, 4th edition (New York, Macmillan, 1975).*

Eugene F. Brigham, editor, *Readings in Managerial Finance* (New York, Holt, 1971).†

Royce Diener, *How to Finance a Growing Business*, revised edition (New York, Fell, 1974).

Donald P. Jacobs and others, *Financial Institutions*, 5th edition (Homewood, Illinois, Irwin, 1972).*

Robert Lekachman, *Inflation: the Permanent Problem of Boom & Bust* (New York, Random House, 1973).

James C. Van Horne, *Fundamentals of Financial Management*, 2nd edition (Englewood Cliffs, New Jersey, Prentice-Hall, 1974).*

MARKETING

Steuart H. Britt and Harper W. Boyd, editors, *Marketing Management and Administrative Action*, 3rd edition (New York, McGraw-Hill, 1973).†

James M. Carman and Kenneth P. Uhl, *Phillips and Duncan's Marketing: Principles and Methods*, 7th edition (Homewood, Illinois, Irwin, 1973).*

Ben M. Enis and Keith K. Cox, editors, *Marketing Classics; A Selection of Influential Articles* (Boston, Allyn and Bacon, 1969).†

Ross Lawrence Goble and Roy T. Shaw, editors, *Controversy and Dialogue in Marketing* (Englewood Cliffs, New Jersey, Prentice-Hall 1975).†

Theodore Levitt, *Marketing for Business Growth* (New York, McGraw-Hill, 1973).

George Risley, *Modern Industrial Marketing* (New York, McGraw-Hill, 1972).

PRODUCTION AND OPERATIONS MANAGEMENT

Harold T. Amrine and others, *Manufacturing Organization and Management*, 3rd edition (Englewood Cliffs, New Jersey, Prentice-Hall, 1975).*

Charles H. Becker, *Plant Manager's Handbook* (Englewood Cliffs, New Jersey, Prentice-Hall, 1974).

Elwood S. Buffa, *Basic Production Management*, 2nd edition (New York, Wiley, 1975).*

Richard I. Henderson and Waino W. Suojanen, *The Operating Manager; An Integrative Approach* (Englewood Cliffs, New Jersey, Prentice-Hall, 1974).*

M. K. Starr, editor, *Management of Production; Selected Readings* (Baltimore, Penguin, 1970).†

LABOR AND INDUSTRIAL RELATIONS

Derek C. Bok and John T. Dunlop, *Labor and the American Community* (New York, Simon and Schuster, 1970).

Roy P. Fairfield, editor, *Humanizing the Workplace* (Buffalo, Prometheus, 1974).†

Andrew Levison, *The Working-Class Majority* (New York, Coward, McCann & Geohegan, 1974).

C. Northcote Parkinson, editor, *Industrial Disruption* (London, Leviathan House, 1973).†

Lloyd G. Reynolds, *Labor Economics and Labor Relations*, 6th edition (Englewood Cliffs, New Jersey, Prentice-Hall, 1974)*

Bertram Silverman and Murray Yanowitch, editors, *The Worker in "Post-Industrial" Capitalism; Liberal and Radical Responses* (New York, Free Press, 1974).†

PERSONNEL

Douglas C. Basil, *Women in Management* (New York, Dunellen, 1972).

Herbert J. Chruden and Arthur W. Sherman, editors, *Readings in Personnel Management* (Cincinnati, South–Western, 1972).†

William F. Dowling and Leonard R. Sayles, *How Managers Motivate: The Imperatives of Supervision* (New York, McGraw-Hill, 1971).*

H. G. Kaufman, *Obsolescence and Professional Career Development* (New York, AMACOM, 1974).

Harold Koontz, *Appraising Managers as Managers* (New York, McGraw-Hill, 1971).

Paul Pigors and Charles A. Myers, *Personnel Administration; A Point of View and a Method*, 7th edition (New York, McGraw-Hill, 1972). (8th edition to be published in spring 1976).*

2. Periodicals

Our primary source for this section of the list was the *Business Periodicals Index (BPI)*, a major bibliographic tool of business research that indexes titles widely held by U.S. libraries. To the titles selected from *BPI*, we added some others that seemed particularly noteworthy.

Because of the variety and volume of special-purpose periodicals, we have included only those dealing with management in general. The interested reader should consult *Ulrich's International Periodical Directory* (cited later) for specialized areas. Most periodical publishers will send a sample issue on request. Their addresses, as well as information on subscription costs, can be found in *Ulrich's*.

Business and Society Review, 870 Seventh Avenue, New York, New York 10019 (quarterly, $34).

Business Horizons, School of Business, Indiana University, Bloomington, Indiana 47401 (bimonthly, $10).

California Management Review, Graduate School of Business Administration, University of California, Berkeley, California 94720 (quarterly, $10).

The Columbia Journal of World Business, 407 Uris, Columbia University, New York, New York 10027 (quarterly, $12).

Fortune, 541 North Fairbanks Court, Chicago, Illinois 60611 (monthly, $14).

Harvard Business Review, Subscription Service Dept., Soldiers Field, Boston, Massachusetts 02163 (bimonthly, $18).

The International Executive, 64 Ferndale Drive, Hastings-on-Hudson, New York 10706 (3 issues a year, $21).

International Management, McGraw-Hill House, Shoppenhangers Road, Maidenhead, Berkshire, England (monthly, $26).

Management Review, AMACOM, Saranac Lake, New York 12983 (monthly, members $13.50; non-members $16.50).

MSU Business Topics, Graduate School of Business Administration, Michigan State University, East Lansing, Michigan 48823 (quarterly, free).

S.A.M. Advanced Management Journal, Society for Advancement of Management, 135 West 50th Street, New York, New York 10020 (quarterly, members $10; non-members $13).

Sloan Management Review, Sloan School of Management, Massachusetts Institute of Technology, Cambridge, Massachusetts 02139 (3 issues a year, $12).

University of Michigan Business Review, Graduate School of Business Administration, University of Michigan, Ann Arbor, Michigan 48104 (bimonthly, $6).

3. Guides to Information

This category, like the others, is a compromise with size. A compilation of all the sources, from the volumes of the U.S. Census to the *Sugar Year Book*, would be impossibly long. Therefore, we settled for those items that point to the wide range of available information. However, the indexes to periodicals and newspapers that appear in this section represent more than a sampling. They are the key bibliographic controls providing access to the literature of management.

Anbar Management Services (Wembley, England, Anbar Publications)

In five sections: *Top Management Abstracts, Accounting and Data Processing Abstracts, Marketing and Distribution Abstracts, Personnel & Training Abstracts, Work Study and O & M Abstracts*. Each section published eight times per year.

K.G.B. Bakewell, *How to Find Out: Management and Productivity*, 2nd edition (Oxford, England, Pergamon, 1970).
Useful for its inclusion of British and European information sources.

Business Periodicals Index (New York, H. W. Wilson Co., 1958-to date).
A subject guide to a wide range of management, business, and trade periodicals. Monthly with periodic cumulations.

Core Collection: An Author and Subject Guide (Boston, Baker Library, Harvard Business School, annual).
Approximately 4,000 titles in the library's browsing collection, with emphasis on recent representative books in business and related fields. Published annually.

Lorna M. Daniells, *Business Information Sources* (Berkeley, University of California Press, to be published early 1976).
Will be the standard guide to business literature.

Encyclopedia of Associations (Detroit, Gale Research Co., latest edition).
Vol. 1: Addresses, executive officers, membership, activities, and publications of national organizations of the U.S.; Vol. 2: Geographic and executive index; Vol. 3: New Associations (quarterly).

Encyclopedia of Business Information Sources (Detroit, Gale Research Co., 1970).
Bibliographies, associations, periodicals, directories, handbooks and manuals, statistics sources, and general books.

F&S Index of Corporations and Industries (Cleveland, Predicasts, Inc., 1960-to date).
Information about U.S. companies, products, and industries in periodicals, business newspapers, and special reports.

F&S International Index (Cleveland Predicasts, Inc., 1967-to date).
Similar information for the rest of the world.

National Trade and Professional Associations of the United States and Labor Unions (Washington, D.C., Columbia Books, annual).
Addresses, executive officers, membership, budgets, publications, meeting dates.

Predicasts (Cleveland, Predicasts, Inc., 1960-to date).
Abstracts U.S. forecast statistics for economic indicators and specific products and commodities. Quarterly with annual cumulations.

Public Affairs Information Services (New York, Public Affairs Information Service, Inc., 1915-to date).
Includes business and economic affairs. Indexes books, periodical articles, and government and private agency reports. Weekly with periodic cumulations.

Statistics Sources; A Subject Guide to Data on Industrial, Business, Social, Educational, Financial, and Other Topics for the United States and Internationally (Detroit, Gale Research Co., latest edition).

Edward G. Strable, editor, *Special Libraries: A Guide for Management*, revised edition (New York, Special Libraries Association, 1975).
  Information on establishing a corporate library.

Ulrich's International Periodicals Directory; A Classified Guide to Current Periodicals, Foreign and Domestic (New York, Bowker, latest edition).
  Latest edition includes 55,000 periodicals.

Wall Street Journal Index (Princeton, New Jersey, Dow Jones Books, 1957-to date).
  Monthly with annual cumulations.

The Wall Street Review of Books (Pleasantville, New York, Docent Corporation, 1973-to date).
  Lengthy reviews of books in business and finance. Quarterly.

World Guide to Trade Associations (New York, Bowker, 1973-74).
  In two volumes, provides addresses and telephone numbers of 26,000 associations.

Worldcasts (Cleveland, Predicasts, Inc., 1964-to date).
  Abstracts foreign forecasts by geographic region and product. 8 times a year.

The Contributors

B. Charles Ames, formerly a Managing Partner in the Cleveland office of McKinsey & Company, is now president—CEO of Reliance Electric Company in Cleveland. He has specialized in marketing management, with emphasis on organization and planning.

Kenneth R. Andrews, who is Donald K. David Professor of Business Administration at the Harvard Business School, is also a director of four corporations and chairman of the editorial board of the *Harvard Business Review*. His current research focuses on improving the effectiveness of boards of directors.

Chris Argyris, for twenty years associated with Yale University, has been James Bryant Conant Professor of Education and Organizational Behavior at the Graduate School of Education, Harvard University, since 1971. He is the author of numerous articles and books dealing with the individual and the organization, the latest of which is *Behind the Front Page: Organizational Self-Renewal in Metropolitan Newspapers* (1974).

Fernando Bartolomé is Associate Professor of Business Administration, specializing in organizational behavior, at the Institut Européan d'Administration des Affaires (INSEAD) in Fontainebleau, France. He concluded the study on which his article in this book is based while he was a doctoral student at the Harvard Business School.

John B. Bennett is Lecturer in oral communications at the Harvard Business School, where he also serves as Editorial Consultant for Educational Programs.

John C. Chambers is Manager, Management Science at Xerox Corporation, and was previously associated with the Ford Motor Company, North American Aviation, and Corning Glass Works. His research interests center on strategic planning for new products and development of improved forecasting methods.

Gordon Donaldson is Willard Prescott Smith Professor of Corporate Finance at the Harvard Business School. Besides *Corporate Debt Capacity* (1961), on which his contribution to this book is based, he has written other books and articles on finance.

Peter F. Drucker is Clarke Professor of Social Science at the Claremont Graduate School, Claremont, California. He is a well-known consultant and writer who has published many books, most recently *Management: Tasks, Responsibilities, Practices* (1974). Mr. Drucker has been the recipient of many awards for his work in the area of management.

Cyrus F. Gibson is Associate Professor of Business Administration at the Harvard Business School. He has recently been studying behavioral and social forces that affect efficient use of computer models in various organizational settings.

Frank F. Gilmore, a pioneer in analyzing executives' planning problems, is now retired. Formerly he was a professor in the Graduate School of Business and Public Administration at Cornell University and director of the Executive Development Program there.

William C. Goggin recently retired as Board Chairman and Chief Executive Officer of Dow Corning. In 1967, after serving for nine years as general manager of Dow Chemical's several hundred million dollar plastics business, he joined Dow Corning as its president. He holds several patents, has written various technical papers, and is trustee or director of a number of organizations.

Larry E. Greiner is a Professor of Organizational Behavior at the University of Southern California, where he specializes in organizational development.

John S. Hammond III is Associate Professor of Business Administration at the Harvard Business School. He was formerly employed in the Electronics Division of National Cash Register Company, and he holds a patent on circuitry. He is the author of technical publications on electronics and on decision making.

Roger Harrison is Vice President of Development Research Associates, Inc. of Newton Centre, Massachusetts. He is concerned with the design and building of organizations to cope with unusual stresses and with the development of initiative and autonomy through experienced-based learning processes.

Robert H. Hayes is Professor of Business Administration at the Harvard Business School, where he teaches manufacturing policy, production and operations management, and computer applications. Formerly he held positions at IBM and McKinsey & Company.

Frederick Herzberg is University Distinguished Professor of Management at the College of Business, the University of Utah, and was formerly chairman of the psychology department at Case Western Reserve. He is a well-known authority on motivation and the nature of work, and he is one of the major proponents of job enrichment as a motivator. His books include *Work and the Nature of Man* (1966) and *The Motivation to Work* (1959).

James L. Heskett is 1907 Foundation Professor of Business Logistics at the Harvard Business School. He is the coauthor of *Business Logistics* (1964, 2nd ed. 1973), *Highway Transportation Management* (1963), and *Case Problems in Business Logistics* (1973). He is conducting research in inventory location strategy and interorganizational problem solving.

William K. Holstein is Dean of the School of Business at the State University of New York at Albany. His field of interest has been production management, and he has specialized in the development and installation of production scheduling systems. He is the coauthor of *Liberal Education and Engineering* (1960).

Edward W. Jones, Jr., is a division manager with New York Telephone. He is presently on a special assignment to the president of the company with responsibility to help organize and improve manpower training and utilization within the New York City business community. He is expected to return to a line assignment shortly with direct responsibility for divisional telephone operations and management of several thousand employees.

Robert L. Katz has had broad experience in both business and education. He heads a consulting firm specializing in corporate strategy and is a director of a number of publicly held corporations. He previously taught in the graduate schools of business at Dartmouth, Harvard, and Stanford. He has also published three books and has helped found five industrial or financial companies.

Philip Kotler is Harold T. Martin Professor of Marketing at Northwestern University. He has been interested in the development and application of marketing principles in market analysis, new product development, competitive marketing strategies, promotional planning, and information systems. He has written a number of influential books, among them *Marketing Management: Analysis, Planning, and Control* (2nd edition, 1972), and he has received many awards for his contributions to advertising and marketing management.

Paul R. Lawrence is Wallace Brett Donham Professor of Organizational Behavior at the Harvard Business School. He is currently studying the process of improving communication, performance, and the quality of work life in mass-production assembly plants. His most recent book, in which he focuses on relationships among groups of organizations with regard to issues of power and dependence, is *Mayors in Action* (1974), written with John P. Kotter.

Harry Levinson, a psychologist, is President of the Levinson Institute and Lecturer in the Laboratory of Community Psychiatry, Harvard Medical School. He was previously associated with the Menninger Foundation as Director of the Division of Industrial Mental Health. He also has taught at the Harvard Business School. He is the author of the award-winning book, *The Exceptional Executive* (1968), as well as other books and articles.

Theodore Levitt is Professor of Business Administration at the Harvard Business School. He has written many articles for the *Harvard Business Review* and several books, the latest of which is *Marketing for Business Growth* (1974). His articles have won three McKinsey Awards and a John Hancock Award for Excellence.

Sidney J. Levy is Professor of Behavioral Science in Management at Northwestern University. He has also been staff psychologist since 1948 and director of psychological research since 1952 at Social Research, Inc., where he has been concerned primarily with consumer behavior. His most recent book is *Promotional Behavior* (1970).

Jay W. Lorsch is Professor of Organizational Behavior and chairman of the area at the Harvard Business School. In their most recent book *Organizations and Their Members: A Contingency Approach* (1974), he and John J. Morse have expanded the ideas in "Beyond Theory Y." His research interests lie in applying behavioral science knowledge to the improvement of organizational effectiveness.

John C. McLean taught at the Harvard Business School for sixteen years before joining Continental Oil Company in 1954 as assistant to the president. He became President and Chief Executive Officer at Continental in 1969 and was chairman and chief executive until his death in 1974.

Myles L. Mace is currently a professional corporate director. He has had a long career as corporate executive, teacher, and observer of top management behavior. He was vice president of Litton Industries, Inc. and Professor of Business Administration at the Harvard Business School. His most recent publication was *Directors: Myth and Reality* (1972).

John J. Morse is Associate Professor of Behavioral Science at the Graduate School of Business Administration of the University of California at Los Angeles. He is the coauthor of *Organizations and Their Members: A Contingency Approach*, which is based on the article that appears in this collection.

Satinder K. Mullick is a Project Manager in the Operations Research Department of Corning Glass Works. He specializes in strategic and tactical planning for new products.

Derek A. Newton is Professor of Business Administration at the University of Virginia. He has considerable experience in sales, as a representative, training manager, and sales manager. A book based on the research for the article printed here, *Sales Force Performance and Turnover*, was published in 1970.

Edward G. Niblock was a financial planner with Xerox Corporation when he died at the age of thirty-two, shortly before his article appeared in *HBR*.

Richard L. Nolan is Associate Professor of business at the Harvard Business School. His recent research has focused on controlling computer resources through internal pricing, and he has been investigating the conceptual and technical problems of designing internal pricing systems. He has published many articles on EDP issues.

O. A. Ohmann, now retired, was Assistant to the President of the Standard Oil Company of Ohio and worked on problems and programs for management development. Earlier in his career he was head of the Department of Psychology at the Cleveland College of Western Reserve University.

William T. Sandells, Jr. is assistant treasurer and assistant controller of Baystate Corporation, a bank holding company. He is a certified public accountant and is currently involved in a broad spectrum of financial work, ranging from the development of systems to the analysis of results.

John K. Shank is Associate Professor of Business Administration at the Harvard Business School, where he is currently engaged in empirical research on corporate responsiveness and the development of a new approach to measuring Affirmative Action programs.

Benson P. Shapiro is Associate Professor of Business Administration at the Harvard Business School, where he teaches courses in sales management and creative marketing strategy. He has done extensive work in the sales management field through consulting and case study preparations.

Douglas S. Sherwin is Vice President and General Manager of Phillips Products Company (a subsidiary of Phillips Petroleum Company). He is also a Director of the company.

William W. Sihler is Professor of Business Administration and Associate Dean for Academic Affairs at the Graduate School of Business Administration of the University of Virginia. He specializes in corporate finance and is currently at work on a book in that area.

Wickham Skinner is Associate Dean for the M.B.A. program and James E. Robison Professor of Business Administration at the Harvard Business School, where he has been since 1958. From 1948 to 1958 he was with Honeywell, Inc., serving in production control, manufacturing management and project supervision, as well as in marketing and general administration.

Donald D. Smith is a Senior Project Leader in the Operations Research Department at Corning Glass Works. His current interests are the area of time series analysis and econometrics.

Louis W. Stern is Professor of Marketing at Northwestern University. His primary interest has been in public policy as it applies to antitrust matters, and he is presently studying interorganization management in marketing. He has written on potential competition theory and conglomerate mergers and has published many books and articles, among them *Distribution Channels: Behavioral Dimensions* (1969).

Philip H. Thurston is Professor of Business Administration at the Harvard Business School, where he teaches courses in strategy formulation and manufacturing management in the Program for Management Development.

Richard F. Vancil, Professor of Business Administration at the Harvard Business School, is also chairman of the control area. He recently completed a seven-year-long study of formal corporate planning systems. He is the author of books and articles on finance, control, and organization.

Richard E. Walton is Edsel Bryant Ford Professor of Business Administration at the Harvard Business School and is Director of its Division of Research. His field is organizational behavior, and he has been studying organizational innovations that have the dual purpose of upgrading the quality of work life and increasing productivity.

Ronald L. Weiher is Associate Librarian in charge of public services for Baker Library at the Harvard Business School. In addition to planning and coordinating the services available to the library's users, he reviews microprint publications for *Microform Review*.

H. Edward Wrapp is Associate Dean for Management Programs and Professor of Business Policy at the University of Chicago's Graduate School of Business. In addition to once having been a corporate executive himself, he has worked on a variety of consulting assignments in business and has written numerous cases on management.

Index

Account, management of, 242–247
Accounting and control, books on, 721–722
Ackerman, Robert W., 691
Ackoff, Russell L., 156
Adaptability, and organization, 631
Administrator
  conceptual skill, 23–25
  human skill, 21–23
  and skyhooks, 708–712
  and resistance to change, 404–405
  technical skill, 20–21
  relative importance of skills, 25–28
  skills, and executive development, 29–30
Advertising vs. personal selling, 240
Age
  missionary salesmen, 226
  new-business salesmen, 233
  and organization development, 638–639
  and performance, sales force, 218–220
  technical salesmen, 229
Airfreight, 585, 588–589
Airlines, stewardesses' job, 608–609
Allocation
  and distribution, 72–73
  and temporary shortages, 254–255
Alternatives
  in developing strategy for smaller
    company, 167–169
  in manufacturing, 540–542
  in marketing planning, 201–202
Aluminum industry, customer orientation,
  177–178
American Petroleum Institute Quarterly,
  193
American Telephone and Telegraph Co.,
  623
Ames, B. Charles, 197

Analysis
  decision tree, 87–89, 112, 113
  in developing strategy for smaller
    company, 158–160
  in grass roots market research program,
    268–270
  input-output, 512
  investment, 16–17
  with preferences, 104–108
  of present operations, in corporate
    planning, 124
  probability, 338–346
  trend, 525
Andrews, Kenneth R., 686
Anheuser-Busch, 253
Ansoff, H. Igor, 13
Appraisal
  of appraisers, MBO, 65–66
  of black manager, 452–453, 454–455
  of capital investments, 309–310
Area management, matrix organization,
  659–660
Argyris, Chris, 27, 412, 425, 624
Assessment
  in grass roots market research program,
    270–271
  in obtaining preliminary preference
    curve, 100–101
Asset positions, in value analysis, 90–91
Assets, and capital structure, 288
Assignments
  permanent, and employee commitment,
    678–679
  temporary, 681–682
Audit of social responsibility action,
  693–694, 696
Authority vs. power, 672

Automation, and McDonald's french fries, 606–607
Automobile industry, production orientation, 186–187
Autonomy crisis and direction, organization, 643–644
Avon products, 241
Awareness, executive lack of, 433–435

Bales, Robert F., 30
Barnard, Chester I., on conceptual skill, 24
Barron's, 699
Bartolomé, Fernando, 412, 413
Barzun, Jacques, 178
Bassett, Glenn A., 678
Baumer, Elmer F., 268n
Behavior, contrasting patterns of, 396
Beier, Frederick J., 597n
Benefits and costs, matrix organization, 665–667
Bennett, John B., 715
Bennis, Warren, 624
  on organic populism, 683
Bias, in market research, 278–279
Bierman, Harold Jr., 303n
Blacks
  early on-the-job experience, 451–454
  and informal organization, 457–458
  lessons from experience, 456–457
  managerial challenges, 454–456
  offer of managerial job to, 449–450
  and problems of "fit," 458–460
  as trainees, 450
Blind spots, executive, 435–436
Books for managers, 719–723
Books in Print, 718
Boulding, Kenneth, on hierarchy, 6
Bower, Joseph L., 691
Bucklin, Louis P., 597n
Budget and long-range plan, design of, 144–147
Budgeting and planning, equilibrium, 151–154
Burns, Tom, 378n
Business board, matrix organization, 655–657
  corporate, 659
Business Information Sources (Daniells), 719

Business in Nebraska, 715
Business in society, books on, 720
Business Periodicals Index (BPI), 723
Business planning units (BPUs), matrix organization, 658
Business policy, books on, 720
Business Week, 715

Campanella, Roy, 449
Canadian Grocery Manufacturers Association, 595
Capacity loading, 561–562
Capital. See also Capital investments
  cost of, 299–301
  estimating cost of, 301–303
  vs. income, 298
Capital investments, 303–306
  appraisal of, 309–310
  bench marks in evaluating, 323–324
  management concern over, 308–309
  payout vs. return in judging, 310–312
Capitalization standard, 335–336
Capital structure, and assets, 288
Cash. See also Cash flow; Discounted cash flow
  adequacy, vs. cash solvency, 347–348
  inadequacy, 328–329
Cash flow
  and debt policy, 338–341
  decision diagram with, 90
Causal models, forecasting, 508–509
Certainty equivalent, 98, 102
Chambers, John C., 501
Chandler, Alfred D. Jr., 478, 633n, 637, 638, 670n
Change, exploitation of, 12–13. See also Resistance to change
Change orientation, and viability, 47
Channel system, distribution, 597–598
Chief executive, role and skills, 37–38. See also Administrator; Executive; Top Management
Cincinnati Milacron, plan-budget linkages, 148–154
Clarke, D. A. Jr., 268n
Cleveland Philosophical Club, 701
Climate, organizational, 382–385
Closing, in selling process, 243
Coch, Lester, 391, 393, 396, 397
Collaboration, in organization, 645–647

Commerce Clearing House, Inc., 717
Commitment, restricted, 430–431
Communication
and decision curves, 112–113
in matrix organization, 655
and motivation, 364–365
quantitative analysis in facilitating, 71, 73
Company, account management role, 246
Compensation
missionary salesman, 226–227
new-business salesman, 233
and quality of work life, 357
technical salesman, 229–230
trade salesman, 222
and turnover, sales force, 218
Competence motivation, 385–386
Computer department. See EDP department
Computer expert, and manufacturing, 542–543
Conceptual skill
administrator, 23–25
development of, 32–33
innate vs. trained, 636
and management level, 27–28
Conflict resolution, and organizational ideology, 50–53
Constitutionalism, and quality of work life, 358
Consultants, in creating corporate goals, 132–133
Containerization, 585, 589–590
Continental Oil Co., evaluation of capital investments, 308–309
Contingency theory, 379, 386–388
Control(s). See also Dispatching and shop control; Management control; Production planning and control
books on, 721–722
contradictory, and preference curves, 111–112
crisis, and delegation, organization, 644
decentralized, and grass roots market research, 281
and financial responsibility, types, 465–466
of grass roots market research program, 273–276

Controls (cont'd)
of in-process inventory, 570–571
and profit center, 464–465
Convertible issues, cost of, 301
Coordination
interfunctional, and marketing planning, 205–206
planning and budgeting, 149–150
and red-tape crisis, organization, 644–645
Core elements in developing strategy for smaller company, 166–167
Corning Glass Works, 650
forecasting, 501–528 passim
marketing, 177
Corporate business board, matrix organization, 659
Corporate Debt Capacity (Donaldson), 292
Corporate morality. See Social responsibility
Corporate objectives
and marketing planning, 203
matrix organization, 668
Corporate planning. See also Plan-budget design; Planning; Production planning and control
administrative focus, 119–120
analyzing present in, 124
books on, 720
corporate objectives in, 122–124
creating goals in, 130–133
evaluating program in, 126–130
five-year forecast outline, 139–142
planners' problems, 136–138
predicting future in, 124–125
realistic evaluation in, 121–122
staff, 133–135
president's involvement in, 120–121
Corporate staff, and grass roots market research, 281
Corporate strategy, and manufacturing, 537–539
Corporate Strategy (Ansoff), 13
Corporation
amorality, 691–692
social responsibility, 686–688
Corridors of comparative indifference, 8, 16
Cost(s)
and accuracy, forecasting, 503

Cost(s) (cont'd)
  and benefits, matrix organization,
    665–667
  of capital, 299–303
  of fixed obligations, 301
  of grass roots market research, 279
  long-run, of MBO, 61–63
  of selling, 247–250
Cost center
  matrix organization, 653
  standard, 465
Cox, Jacob D. Jr., 712
Creativity and leadership crisis,
  organization, 642–643
A Creed for Free Enterprise (Randall),
  707
Criterion, in decision tree, 91
Critical ratio, dispatching rule, 576–577
Cultural beliefs, executives, 416–418
Customer orientation, vs. product
  orientation, 176–178, 194–196
Cyert, Richard M., 14

Daily status system, in dispatching and
  shop control, 567–568
Daniells, Lorna M., 719
Data availability, in grass roots market
  research, 278
Data collection, in grass roots market
  research, 272–273
Data processing department. See EDP
  department
Debt/equity decision. See also Debt
  policy
  factors, 289–292
  impact on value, 293–294
  limits, 294–295
  rules of thumb, 292–293
Debt policy. See also Debt/equity decision
  and capitalization standard, 335–336
  conventional approaches, 329–334
  and decision making, 346–349
  and earnings-coverage standard,
    336–337
  probability analysis, 341–346
  and risk, 326–329
  trends, 349–351
Decentralization
  federal, 628, 629
  simulated, 628, 629

Decision making, 14–15
  contrasting views of, 13–14
  and debt policy, 346–349
  decentralized, and market research,
    267–268
  and executive blind spots, 435–436
  and executive lack of awareness,
    433–435
  and interpersonal relationships, 425–
    426
  logistics, 587
  manufacturing, 543–546
  and organization, 631
  in person-oriented organization, 45
  and restricted commitment, 430–431
  and risks, 86–88
  and subordinate gamesmanship,
    431–433
  words vs. actions, 426–428
Decision tree, 71
  preference curve with, 104
Decision-tree analysis, 87–89
  and preference curve, 112, 113
Delegation, and control crisis, organization, 644
Delphi technique, forecasting, 507, 512,
  516
Demand
  containment of, 253–254
  forecasts, in long-term capacity
    planning, 551–552
  and lot size, 71–72
Demarketing. See also Marketing
  defined, 251–253
  general, 252–256
  ostensible, 258–259
  questions, 259–260
  selective, 256–258
Dependence vs. independence, 418
Dewey, John, 163
Direction and autonomy crisis, organization, 643–644
Direct mail advertising, 240
Directors, audit of social responsibility
  actions, 696
Directory of National Trade and Professional Associations, 718
Disaggregate market model, 511
Discounted cash flow
  bench marks, 323–324

Discounted cash flow (*cont'd*)
  in calculating return on investment,
    312–313
  and declining income, 319–321
  in evaluating capital investments,
    308–312
  and increasing income, 318–319
  and irregular cash flow, 321–323
  simple application, 315–324
  and uniform income, 315–318
Discretion, vs. standardization, 605–606
Discretionary expense center, 465
Discussion, open, in improving inter-
    personal relations, 445
Dispatching, rules, 576–577
Dispatching and shop control. *See also*
    Distribution
  daily status system, 567–568
  job sequence schedule, 568–570
  payoffs, 570–573
  in production planning and control,
    565–566
  timing, 566–567
Distance dimensions, and market research,
    265–266
Distribution. *See also* Dispatching and
    shop control
  and allocation, 72–73
  central cooperative facilities, 595–596
  consolidated regional centers, 594–595
  constraints on technology, 588
  coordination of practices, 593
  factors in shift of emphasis, 587–592
  implementation approaches, 597–599
  institutional change, 586–592
  institutional responses, 592–596
  logistics management, 591–592
  need for institutional cooperation in,
    590
  shifting of responsibilities, 593–594
  technological changes, 585–586
  and temporary shortages, 254–255
  third-party arrangements, 594–596
  utilities, 594
  vertical integrations, 596
Distrust and antagonism toward top
    management, 437–438
Dividend policy, 295–299
Donaldson, Gordon, 286, 289, 292, 326
Dow Chemical Co., 650

Dow Corning Corp., 621
  corporate objectives, 668
  multidimensional structure, 650–667
Drucker, Peter F., 160, 623
Dry cleaning, obsolescence, 178–179
Dun & Bradstreet's *Million Dollar
    Directory*, 717
Du Pont (E. I.) de Nemours & Co., Inc.,
    182, 623
  grass roots market research, 267
  marketing, 177

Earliest due date, dispatching rule, 576
Earnings coverage ratio, 335
Earnings coverage standard, 336–337
Earnings per share, and debt/equity
    decision, 289, 290–291
Eastman Kodak Co., 253
Econometric models in forecasting,
    526–527
Economic evaluation, matrix organization,
    662–663
Economy of effort, and organization, 631
EDP department
  expansion, 488–490
  and fear of computer, 487–488
  formalization, 492–497
  future of, 500
  growth stages, 483–484
  initiation, 484–485
  location, 485–487
  manager's dilemma, 497–498
  maturity, 497–500
  relations with users, 499–500
Ego concepts, and MBO, 66–68
Electrical circuits and inventory, transfer
    of insight, 71–72
Electrical engineering analogies in organi-
    zation structure and control, 75–77
Electric utilities, obsolescence, 179
Electronics industry, marketing vs. R&D,
    191–192
Employee(s). *See also* Employee com-
    mitment; Personnel
  diversity, and quality of work life,
    359–360
  motivation with KITA, 361–366
  and skyhooks, 698–700
Employee commitment, 669–700. *See also*
    Motivation

Employee commitment (*cont'd*)
  and flexible organizational forms,
    679–684
  and management power vs. leadership,
    670–676
  obstructions to, 676–679
Employee counseling and motivation, 365
Encyclopedia of Associations, 718
End products, demand forecasts, and
  requirements planning, 581
Energy, focusing of, 7
EOQ reorder point system, 557
Equilibrium, planning and budgeting,
    151–154
Equity, costs of, 301
Evaluation, realistic, in corporate planning,
    121–122
Executive(s). *See also* Administrator;
    Management; Manager(s); Social
    responsibility; Top Management
  blind spots, 435–436
  cultural beliefs, 416–418
  development, and administrative skills,
    28–30
  distrust and antagonism toward,
    437–438
  effects of fear on, 418–421
  expression of feelings, 415–416
  improving interpersonal relationships,
    439–445
  influence of values on operations,
    428–429
  interpersonal relations, 413–415
  job characteristics, 421
  lack of awareness of behavior patterns,
    433–435
  personal relationships and fear, 419–421
  relationships at home, 423–424
  as restive achievers, 421–423
  successful, 709–712
  words vs. actions, 426–428
Expectations and choices, value analysis,
    91–93
Expense center, discretionary, 465
Experience, and debt policy, 331
Expression of feelings, executives, 415–416

Fairless, Benjamin F., on coaching, 33
Fairness, in selection of financial goals,
    467–468

Faith and Freedom (Ward), 699
Fayol, Henri, 411, 625, 628, 632
Federal decentralization, 628, 629
Feedback
  in appraisal of MBO appraisers, 65
  in improving interpersonal relations,
    442–444
Fertilizer Trends, 715
Finance, books on, 722
Financial goals, choice of, 466–468
Financial responsibility, types of, 465–
    466
First come, first served, dispatching rule,
    576
First National City Bank (Citibank)
    service orientation, 601–602
Fixed costs of selling, 248–250
Fixed obligations, cost of, 301
Flexibility
  and debt/equity decision, 292
  in production planning and control, 550
Flow chart, and forecasting, 504–506
Ford, Henry, marketing genius, 187–188
Ford, Robert, 361n
Forecast(s)
  in corporate planning, 124–126
  of demand, in long-term capacity
    planning, 551–552
  five-year, 139–142
  purpose, 502–504
  and system flow chart, 504–506
Forecaster, collaboration with manager,
    502–506
Forecasting, 501–502
  causal models, 508–509
  econometric models, 526–527
  manager, forecaster, and method,
    502–506
  and product development, 510–512
  of product growth rate, 517–520
  and product's rapid growth stage,
    517–520
  and product's steady state, 520–527
  and product testing and introduction,
    513–517
  qualitative techniques, 506–507
  similar-product technique, 514–516
  time series analysis, 507–508
  X-11 technique, 524–526
Forrester, Jay W., 76, 77

Fortune, 30, 198
  on profit squeeze, 78
Fouraker, Lawrence E., 638
French, John R. P. Jr., 391, 393, 396, 397
Friedman, Milton, 686, 687, 688
Fringe benefits, and motivation, 364
Fuller Brush Co., 241
Functional division, and employee commitment, 677
Functional structure, 628
Functions, planning staff, 134–135

Galbraith, John Kenneth, 185, 706n
Gamesmanship, subordinates, 431–433
General Cable, 165, 168, 169
General Electric Co.
  grass roots market research, 267
  organization, 623, 632
General management, books on, 719–720
General Mills, plan-budget linkages, 148–154
General Motors Corp., 182, 623
  organization structure, 625–627, 632
  service orientation, 601
General Public Utilities Corp., study of shareholders and dividend policy, 296–298
General systems analogies, in organization structure and control, 77–78
General Telephone and Electronics, 165, 167
Geographical areas, in matrix organization, 653, 655
Gestalt Therapy (Perls, Hefferline, and Goodman), 424
Gibson, Cyrus F., 482
Gilmore, Frank, 117, 118, 156
Goals
  congruence, in selection of financial goals, 467–468
  and purposes, and skyhooks, 707–708
Goggin, William, 621, 650
Goodman, Paul, 424
Greiner, Larry E., 621, 636
Grocery stores, obsolescence, 179–180
Group, working with, in improving interpersonal relationships, 441–442
Group action, MBO, 64–65

Growth
  phases, organization, 641–647
  and quality of work life, 358
Growth industry, self-deception, 180–181

Hammond, John S. III, 4, 86
Harris, T. George, 683n
Harrison, Roger, 3, 39
Harvard Business School, 716
Hawthorne effect, 371
Hawthorne experiments, 355, 365
Hayes, Robert H., 4, 70
Health, Education and Welfare Department, U.S., reorganization, 623
Hefferline, Ralph F., 424
Herzberg, Frederick, 356, 361
Heskett, J. L., 261, 585, 597n
Hierarchical organization, 633–634
Hierarchy, and information transmittal, 6
Hobbes, Thomas, 355
Holstein, William K., 548
The Human Dilemmas of Leadership (Zaleznik), 457
Honeywell, Inc., product-line policy, 611–612
Human behavior in organizations, books on, 721
Human relations
  administrator's skill in, 21–23
  development of skills, 31–32
  and executive development, 29
  intragroup vs. intergroup, 35–36
  management level and skill in, 26–27
  training, and motivation, 364
Hunt, Pearson, 289n, 304n
Hygiene factors, vs. motivators, 366–373

IBM Corp., 623
  service orientation, 602
Ideology, organizational, 39–40. See also Organization
  and conflict resolution, 50–53
  and external viability, 46–48
  and internal viability, 48–50
  and values, 41
Imperial Chemicals Ltd., organization, 623, 632
Implementation, grass roots market research program, 273

Incentive modification and social responsibility, 695
Income
vs. capital, 298
and debt/equity decision, 289
uniform, in evaluating capital investments, 315–318
Independence vs. dependence, 418
Indispensability, delusion of, 183–185
Industrial companies, marketing planning pitfalls, 198–202
Industrial engineering and manufacturing, 542
Industrial relations, books on, 723
Industry
growth, and organization development, 640–641
management teams, matrix organization, 659
practice, and dividend policy, 297
Infinite capacity scheduling, 562–563
Influence, distribution of, 383
Informal organization, and blacks, 457–458
Information. *See also* Information flows; MIS
defined, 79–80
guides to, 724–726
manager's need for, 6–7
new insights into, 78–79
predicting value of, 82–83
value of, 80–82
Information flows
for long-term capacity planning, 553
for master scheduling, 556
for production planning and control, 572
for short-term scheduling, 564
In-process inventory, payoff in control of, 570–571
Input-output analysis, 512
Institute of Humanistic Studies, 701
Internal audit of social responsibility action, 693–694
International Longshoremen's and Warehousemen's Union, 599
Interorganizational management, and distribution, 597
Interpersonal relationships
and decision making, 425–426

Interpersonal relationships (*cont'd*)
executives, 413–415
at home, 423–424
improving, 439–445
and organizational climate, 383–384
and organization structure, 633–634
Interstate Commerce Commission and distribution changes, 596, 598, 599
Introspection, superior, and MBO, 68
Inventory. *See also* Inventory control
and electrical circuits, transfer of insight, 71–72
in-process, payoff in control of, 570–571
in long-term capacity planning, 552–553
replenishment problem, 559–560
time-phased requirements, 557–559
Inventory control
critical indictments, 582–584
and requirements planning, 580–582
statistical approach, 578–580
Investment analysis, 16–17
Investment center, 465–466
Irwin, Richard D., Inc., 718

James, William, 676
Job characteristics, executives, 421
Job descriptions, and MBO, 55, 56
Job enrichment, 369, 370–373
steps to, 374–375
Job loading, 369–370
Job participation, and motivation, 365
Job requirements, planning staff, 135
Job sequence schedule, in dispatching and shop control, 568–570
Jones, Edward W. Jr., 412, 448

Kaiser Aluminum & Chemical Corp., marketing, 177–178
Katz, Robert L., 3, 19
Key accounts, and grass roots market research, 281
Key people, in creating corporate goals, 131
KITA, motivation with, 361–366
Know-how, and resistance to change, 399–400
Kotler, Philip, 251

Labor attitudes, and distribution, 598–599
Laboratory training, in improving interpersonal relations, 444–445

Labor relations, books on, 723
Lagemann, John Kord, 700n
Land, Rex, 128
Lawrence, Paul R., 356, 378n, 390
Leadership, vs. power, 670–676
Leadership crisis, and creativity, organization, 642–643
Leavitt, Harold J., 13n, 378n
Levinson, Harry, 4, 54
Levitt, Theodore, 176, 601
Levy, Sidney J., 251
Life insurance industry, soft technology, 610
Lilly, David M., 152
Lindblom, Charles, on muddling through, 13
Lindsay, Alexander, on social division, 700
Logistics decision making, stages in scope of analysis for, 587
Logistics management, distribution, 591–592
and vertical integration, 596
The Lonely Crowd (Riesman), 703
Long-range planning
appropriate equilibrium, 151–154
and market research, 277
plan-budget design in, 144–147
plan-budget linkage examples, 147–151
Lorsch, Jay W., 356, 377, 378n
Luce, R. Duncan, 88n
Lund, Robert T., 578n

Mace, Myles L., 118, 119
MacFarland, James P., 153–154
Machiavelli, Niccolò, 355
Magee, John F., 87, 557n
Major assemblies, demand forecasts, and requirements planning, 581
Management. See also Management control; Manager(s); MBO; Sales management; Social responsibility
general, books on, 719–720
interorganizational, and distribution, 597
literature of, 716–719
logistics, 591–592, 596
major tasks, 630–632
myths, 5
power vs. leadership, 670–676
practices, and distribution, 597–598
and resistance to change, 400–404

Management Abstracts, 718
Management by objectives. See MBO
Management control
in complex structures, 475–481
and financial goal choice, 466–468
in simple structures, 468–475
Management development, and social responsibility, 695
Management information system. See MIS
Management Review, 718
Manager(s)
black, 448–460
books for, 719–723
collaboration with forecaster, 502–506
as conceptualizer, 12
defined, 18
EDP department, 490–491
implications of contingency theory for, 388
and imprecision, art of, 9–11
information guides for, 724–726
information need, 6–7
MIS, 497–498
periodicals for, 723–724
and power game, 7–9
reading matter for, 715–719
time and energy, focusing of, 7
views on appraisals, 56–57
Managerial job, and employee commitment, 675–676
Managerial style, and organizational climate, 384
Manufacturer, service role outside factory, 610–611
Manufacturing. See also Dispatching and shop control; Distribution; Production; Production planning and control
and corporate strategy, 537–539
decision making, 543–546
millstone effect, 533–535
pattern of failure, 536–537
vs. service, 604–605
shortsighted views of, 535–536
technical dominance, 542–543
trade-offs in design, 539–542
March, James G., 14
Marginal funds, 302
Market changes, and market research, 264

Marketing. *See also* Demarketing; Marketing planning; Market research; Selling
  books on, 722
  customer-oriented vs. product-oriented, 176–178
  mechanized, at McDonald's, 607–608
  and obsolescence, 178–181
  and population myth, 181–182
  and production pressures, 185–191
  profit centers, in simple organizations, 471–472
  vs. R&D, 191–195
  vs. selling, 185–186
Marketing planning
  direction and definition in, 202–209
  practitioners' pitfalls, 198–202
  and programming, 211–213
  strategies founded in facts, 209–211
Marketing research, vs. market research, 262–263
Market research
  benefits, 276–278
  case example, 268–276
  centralized, 260–262
  criteria, 280–282
  and decentralized decision making, 267–268
  and forecasting, 511
  grass roots, 263–266
  vs. marketing research, 262–263
  pitfalls, 278–280
  sales force involvement in, 266–267
  and statistical tracking, in new product testing and introduction, 513–514
Martineau, 262
Master scheduling, 554–555
  and estimating shop loads, 555–557
Material Requirements Planning Systems (Orlicky, Plossl, and Wight), 582
Mathematical programming, and transfer of insight, 73–74
Matrix organization. *See also* Organization
  area management, 659–660
  corporate objectives, 668
  costs and benefits, 665–667
  Dow Corning's need for, 650–652
  crucial support systems, 660–664
  four-dimensional system, 652–655
  and internal viability, 48–49

Matrix organization (*cont'd*)
  keys to effectiveness, 655–659
  and management control, 478–481
Maturity of judgment, and social responsibility programs, 694–695
MBO (management by objectives)
  appraisal of appraisers, 65–66
  and ego concepts, 66–68
  failure causes, 54–55
  group action, 64–65
  "ideal" process, 55–58
  long-run costs, 61–63
  matrix organization, 660–662
  missed point in, 58–59
  motivational assessment, 63–64
  and personal goals, 59–60
  and policy straitjackets, 11
  and psychological needs, 60–61
  and task orientation, 44–45
McCormick Multiple Management plan, 33
McDonald's
  production-line approach to service, 605–607
  mechanized marketing, 607–608
McGraw-Hill Book Co., 718
McGregor, Douglas, 56, 377, 378, 386, 624, 685
McKinsey & Co., 198
McLean, John G., 286, 308
McLuhan, Marshall, 702
Mencken, H. L., 285
Mergers, 17
Merritt, A. J., 304n
Milk industry, grass roots market research, 268–276
Miller, Merton H., 293
Minimum slack, dispatching rule, 576
MIS (management information system)
  and growth of EDP department, 495
  manager's dilemma, 497–498
Missionary selling, 224–227
Modigliani, Franco, 293
Modular structures, and employee commitment, 680–681
Money, time value of, 324
Montgomery, George G. Jr., 120
Moody's *Investor Service*, 717
Morale, and grass roots market research, 279–280

Morgenstern, Oskar, 88n
Morse, John J., 356, 377
Motivation
    competence, 385–386
    vs. hygiene factors, 366–373
    with KITA, 361–363
    myths about, 363–366
    and organizational orientation, 49–50
Motivational assessment, MBO, 63–64
Motives
    hidden, in evaluating corporate plans, 128
    and risk, 83–85
Muddling with a purpose, 11–15
Mullick, Satinder K., 501
Multilevel selling, 243–244
Multinational business, books on, 720–721
Multiple profit centers, in simple organizations, 472–473

National Council of Churches, 699
National Council of Physical Distribution Management (NCPD), 591
National Training Laboratory, 444
National Wholesale Grocers Association, 179
Nation's Business, 700
New-business selling, 232–235
New business staging, matrix organization, 663–664
New Jersey Retail Grocers Association, 179
Newton, Derek A., 214
Niblock, Edward G., 143
Nolan, Richard L., 482, 483n, 492n
Nonlinear structures, and employee commitment, 682–683
Nonzero-sum results, 597
North, Harper O., 507n

Objectives
    in corporate planning, 122–124
    open-ended, 16
Objectivity and MBO, 57–58
Obsolescence
    in former growth industries, 178–180
    shadow of, 178–181
Ohmann, O. A., 698
Oil industry
    decline in, 181–182
    and indispensability delusion, 183–185

Oil industry (cont'd)
    product provincialism, 188–191
    R&D vs. marketing in, 192–194
One-man, one-boss concept, and employee commitment, 677–678
Opening, in selling process, 243
Operations, influence of values on, 429
Operations management, books on, 722–723
Operations research (OR)
    savings from, 75
    vs. strategy for smaller company, 162–163
Opinion panels, 513–514
Organic populism, 683
Organization(s). See also Ideology, organizational; Matrix organization; Structure
    arrangements, and marketing planning, 203–205
    books on human behavior in, 721
    building new structure, 632–635
    buyer-seller interaction, 242–243
    climate characteristics, 382–385
    complex, management control in, 475–481
    coordination, in plan-budget linkages, 149–150
    development forces, 637–641
    development model, 637–641
    dimensions, 380
    early models, 625–630
    fit of characteristics, 379
    flexible forms, and employee commitment, 679–684
    formal characteristics, 381–382
    growth phases, 641–647
    implications of history, 647–649
    informal, and black manager, 457–458
    and major management tasks, 630–632
    new design principles, 628–630
    person orientation, 45–46
    power orientation, 42–43
    pure vs. effective, 631–632
    relationships, and plan-budget design, 146
    role orientation, 43
    scalar, 633
    simple, management control in, 468–475

Organizations (cont'd)
  social responsibility behavior, 689–692
  task orientation, 43–45
  values and ideologies, 41
Organization chart
  complex organization, 476
  functionally organized business, 469
Organization structure and control
  electrical engineering analogies, 75–77
  general systems analogies, 77–78
Orlicky, Joseph A., 582
Overpopularity, and demarketing, 255–256

Pacific Maritime Association, 599
Padberg, Daniel I., 268n
Paperback Books in Print, 718
Participation, and resistance to change, 391–393
Payoffs, dispatching and shop control, 570–573
Payout vs. return in judging capital investments, 310–312
Performance, sales force
  and age, 219–220
  and turnover, 217–219
Periodicals for managers, 723–724
Perls, Frederick, 424
Permanent assignments, and employee commitment, 678–679
Personal fears, in evaluating corporate plans, 129
Personal goals, and MBO, 59–60
Personal relationships and fear, executives, 419–421
Personal selling
  vs. advertising, 240–241
  assistance in missionary selling, 224
Personnel. See also Employee(s): Employee commitment; Motivation
  books on, 723
  EDP department, 491–492
  management philosophies, 368–369
  reviews, matrix organization, 662
Person orientation, organization, 45–46
PERT network, 71
Petrochemical industry, 184–185
Pipeline simulation, in forecasting, 518–519

Placement, executive, and administrative skills, 30
Plan(s), unplanned, 137–138
Plan-budget design. See also Planning
  financial features, 144–145
  organizational relationships, 146
  timing considerations, 146–147
Plan-budget linkage
  content-related, 148–149
  organization coordination, 149–150
Planner, corporate planning problems, 136–138
Planning. See also Corporate planning; Marketing planning; Plan-budget design; Production planning and control
  books on, 720
  long-term capacity, 550–554
  in matrix organization, 662
  realism and reach in, 143–144
  requirements, and inventory control, 580–582
  staff, 133–135
Plossl, George W., 582
Policy
  books on, 720
  determination, manufacturing, 543–546
  straitjackets, avoiding, 10–11
Pondy, Louis R., 13n
Poor's Register of Corporations, Directors and Executives, 717
Population and marketing, 181–182
Power, vs. leadership, 670–676
Power game, playing, 7–9
Power orientation, organization, 42–43
Preference(s), analysis with, 104–108
Preference curve, 98–99
  benefits, 103–104
  and better communication, 112–113
  characteristics, 99–100
  company vs. individual, 111
  contradictory controls, 111–112
  with decision trees, 104
  decreasing risk aversion, 108, 109–110
  limitations on use, 113
  obtaining, 100–101
  procedure summarized, 101–102
  verification, 102–103
  zero illusion, 110–111
Preference theory, 86

Prentice-Hall, Inc., 717, 718
Presentation, in selling process, 243
Probability analysis, 341–346
    and cash flow, 338–341
Problem identification, in developing
        strategy for smaller company,
        164–166
Problem solving, in technical selling, 231
Product
    elimination, 256
    provincialism, oil industry, 188–191
Product development, 510–511
    for defined market, 511–512
    for undefined market, 512
Product differences measurement, 511
Product divisions, and management
        control, 477–478
Production. *See also* Dispatching and shop
        control; Distribution; Manufacturing;
        Production planning and control
    and operations management, books on,
        722–723
    pressures, and marketing, 185–191
    trade-offs in design of system, 539–542
Production planning and control, 548–550
    dispatching and shop control, 565–573
    integrated system, 573–574
    inventory control, 557–560
    long-term capacity planning, 550–554
    master scheduling, 554–557
Production profit centers, in simple
        organizations, 472
Productivity, and quality of work
        life, 358–359
Product life cycle
    and forecasting, 509–527
    product development, 510–512
    rapid growth, 517–520
    steady state, 520–527
    testing and introduction, 513–517
Product management group (PMG),
        matrix organization, 658
Product orientation
    automobile industry, 186–187
    vs. customer orientation, 176–178,
        194–196
    railroads, 176, 178
Profit center
    defined, 465
    and management control, 464–465

Profit center (*cont'd*)
    matrix organization, 652–653
    vs. modular structure, 681
    in simple organizations, 470–473
Profit reporting, matrix organization, 663
Profit squeeze, 78
Programming, and market planning,
        211–213
Promotional assistance, and trade selling,
        219
Promotion practices, 17
Psychological needs, and MBO, 60–61
Publications, monitoring, 718–719
Pyke, Donald L., 507n
Pyrrhic selling, 245

Quaker Oats, plan-budget linkages,
        148–154
Qualification(s)
    in selling process, 243
    planning staff, 134–135
Qualitative techniques, forecasting,
        506–507
Quality of work life
    and accommodating to diversity,
        359–360
    defined, 357–358
    and productivity, 358–359
Quantitative analysis, 70–71
    and transfer of insight, 71–74
Quantitative methods, books on, 721
Quantum-Science Corp. (MAPTEK), 512
Questions, in improving interpersonal
        relationships, 440–441

Raiffa, Howard, 88n
Railroads, product orientation, 176, 178,
        195
Ramsey, F. P., 88
Randall, Clarence B., on goals and
        purposes, 707
Raytheon, plan-budget linkages, 148–154
Realism and reach, in planning, 143–144
Recession behavior, cash flows, 338–345
Red-tape crisis and coordination, organiza-
        tion, 644–645
Reference consequences, 99–100
Regression analysis, 525
Regulatory policies, and distribution, 599
Reiter, Stanley, 563–565

Rejection, fear of, 419
Requirements planning, and inventory
    control, 580–582
Research and development, vs. marketing,
    191–195
Resistance to change, 390–391
    administrator's role, 404–405
    causes, 394–400
    management action and, 400–404
    and participation, 391–393
    retrospective commentary, 406–408
Responsibility, in matrix organization,
    480–481
Responsibility accounting, 466
Return on investment
    discounted cash flow in calculating,
        312–313
    in evaluating capital investments,
        310–312
Revenue center, 465
Revson, Charles, 615
Reynolds Metals Co., marketing, 178
Riesman, David, 703
Risk
    of cash inadequacy vs. cash insolvency,
        347–348
    and debt/equity decision, 289, 292
    and debt policy, 326–329
    and decisions, 86–88
    and motive, 83–85
Risk attitude, defining, 96–98
Risk aversion, decreasing, preference curve
    for, 108, 109–110
Risk premium, in preference theory, 101
Robinson, Jackie, 449
Rockefeller, John D., 182
Rogers, Carl, 418
Role orientation, organization, 43
Rothschild, Nathan, 82
Rousseau, Jean Jacques, 355
Ruppental, Karl M., 597n

SAGE Air Defense Computer System, 76
Sales, to innovators vs. imitators, 513
Sales force
    capability, and market research, 281–282
    deployment of, 241–242
    market research involvement, 266–267
    performance and turnover, 217–219
    turnover rate, 217–218

Sales management
    and missionary selling, 224–227
    and new-business selling, 232–235
    and technical selling, 228–232
    and trade selling, 219–224
Sales Management's Annual Survey of
    Buying Power, 271
Sales manager, account management role,
    246–247
Salesperson, account management role,
    245–246
Salter, Malcolm S., 638, 691
Sandalls, William T. Jr., 143
Saturday Review, 12
Savage, Leonard J., 88
Scalar organization, 633
Scheduling
    master, in production planning and
        control, 554–557
    short-term, 560–565
Schlaifer, Robert O., 88
Science, disillusionment with, and
    skyhooks, 703
"The Science of Muddling Through"
    (Lindblom), 13
Sears, Roebuck & Co., 623, 632
Security, and quality of work life, 358
Selection, executive, and administrative
    skills, 30
Self-examination, and MBO, 67–68
Self-preoccupation, and resistance to
    change, 398–399
Selling
    costs of, 247–250
    vs. marketing, 185–186, 194–195
    missionary, 224–227
    new-business, 232–235
    personal, 240–241
    process of, 243–245
    Pyrrhic, 245
    technical, 228–232
    trade, 219–224
    types, 215
Sensitivity training (T-groups), 444–445
    and motivation, 364
Service
    field vs. factory, 602–603
    hard and soft technologies, 609–610
    Honeywell's product-line policy,
        611–613

Service (*cont'd*)
  manufacturer's role outside factory,
    610–611
  vs. manufacturing, 604–605
  McDonald's production-line approach
    to, 605–608
  in selling process, 243
  vs. servitude, 603–604
  stopgaps, complexity and compromise,
    613–615
  tooling up for, 608–609
  why things go wrong, 615–617
Shank, John K., 143
Shapiro, Benson P., 238
Shareholders, and dividend policy,
    295–299
Share repurchase, 306
Sherwin, Douglas W., 669
Shop loads, estimating, and master
    scheduling, 555–557
Shortages, temporary, and demarketing,
    253–255
Shortest process time, dispatching rule,
    576
Short-term scheduling, 560–561
  capacity loading, 561–562
  infinite capacity, 562–563
  statistical view, 563–565
Sihler, William W., 286, 287
Similar-product technique, forecasting,
    514–516
Simulated decentralization, 628, 629
Simulation, in forecasting, 518–519
Size, and organization development, 639
Skills
  of administrator, 20–28
  and executve development, 29–30
  and role, chief executive, 37–38
Skinner, Wickham, 533
Skyhooks
  and administrator, 708–712
  and capitalist values, 705–708
  and disillusionment with science,
    703
  and trend toward bigness, 703–705
Sloan, Alfred P. Jr., 625, 627, 628, 629,
    632
Smidt, Seymour, 303n
Smith, Donald D., 501
Smith (A. O.) Co., 611

Social change, resistance to, 395–396
Social relationships, and resistance to
    change, 395–397
Social relevance, and quality of work life,
    358
Social responsibility
  action program, 692–696
  organization behavior, 689–692
  self-consistent strategy, 689
  and skyhooks, 698–700
Society of Logistics Engineers (SOLE),
    591
Southern Railway, 599
Space and time, in matrix organization,
    655
Special Libraries Association, 717
Split needs, and market research,
    263–264
Stability, and organization, 631
Stages of evolution, in organization
    development, 640
Stages of revolution, in organization
    development, 640
Stalker, G. M., 378n
Standard & Poor's *Corporation Records*,
    717
Standard cost center, 465
Standardization vs. discretion, 605–606
Starbuck, William H., 638
Statement of corporate goals, 133
Statistical approach, inventory control,
    578–580
Statistical decision theory, 79
Statistical tracking
  in new product testing and introduction,
    513–514
  and warning, in forecasting, 519
Steiner, Gary, 14
Steiner, George A., 118, 128n
Steinkraus, Herman W., on administrative
    skills, 27–28
Stern, Louis W., 261, 597n
Stopford, John M., 638
Strategy
  fact founded, in marketing planning,
    209–211
  in management control of simple
    organization, 473–475
  and management science, 162–163
  and manufacturing, 537–539

Strategy (*cont'd*)
   practical planning method, 163–170
   for smaller company, evolution of
      approach, 157–162
   and structure, 632–633
Strategy and Structure (Chandler), 637
Structure. *See also* Organization and
      interpersonal relations, 633–634
   modular, and employee commitment,
      680–681
   nonlinear, 682–683
   perception of, 382–383
   temporary, 683–684
Stryker, Perrin, 20n
Subordinates, gamesmanship, 431–433
Sumner, William Graham, 706
Supermarket Institute, 591
Supertankers, 585, 589
Support systems, matrix organization,
      660–664
Swalm, Ralph O., 84, 87, 100, 110, 111
Sykes, Allen, 304n
Sylvania Electric, grass roots market
      research, 267
System
   overemphasis, in marketing planning,
      201
   parameters, and transfer of insight, 72
   structure, 628–630
Systems analysis function, and EDP
      department growth, 496–497

Task forces, 44
   in matrix organization, 659
Task orientation, organization, 43–45
Taylor, Frederick W., 54, 542, 546
Team organization, 628, 629
Team selling, 244–245
Technical selling, 228–232
Technical skill
   of administrator, 20–21
   development of, 31
   and management level, 25–26, 36–37
Technological imperative, and EDP
      department growth, 489
Technology
   constraints on, 588
   hard and soft, in production-line
      approach to service, 609–610
Telephone selling, 240

Temporary assignments, and employee
      commitment, 681–682
Temporary structures, and employee
      commitment, 683–684
Terminology, and resistance to change,
      401–402
Territorial differences, and market
      research, 264–265
Testing and executive selection, 30
Theory Y
   and contingency theory, 378–379,
      386–387
   and employee commitment, 685
   and Theory X, 377–378
Third-party arrangements, distribution,
      594–596
Threat, and organizational orientation,
      47–48
Thurston, Philip H., 578
Time
   and energy, focusing of, 7
   and grass roots market research, 279
   and space, matrix organization, 655
Time horizons, planning and budgeting,
      150–151
Time orientation, and organizational
      climate, 384
Time-phased requirements planning,
      557–559
Time series analysis in forecasting,
      507–508
Timing
   in dispatching and shop control,
      566–567
   in plan-budget design, 146–147
   value of sense of, 8–9
Top management. *See also* Executives(s);
      Management; Manager(s); Social
      responsibility
   contribution to marketing plans,
      206–207
   direction of EDP department, 495–496
   distrust and antagonism toward,
      437–438
Toro, plan-budget linkages, 148–154
Total systems approach to manufacturing,
      535–536
Trade selling, 219–224
Training
   blacks, 450

Training (cont'd)
  technical salesmen, 229
  new-business salesmen, 233
  trade salesmen, 223
Trend analysis, 525
Trend cycle, 522, 524
TRW Systems, 44, 49
Turning points, in forecasting, 508
Turnover
  and performance, sales force, 217–219
  position, 678–679
Two-boss system, matrix organization,
  657–658

Ulrich's International Periodicals
  Directory, 723–724
Uncertainty, 84
  and value analysis, 94
Unilever, 623
Unions, and market research, 279
Utilities
  distribution, 594
  obsolescence, 179

Value(s), 428–429
  and debt/equity decision, 293–294
  and ideologies, organization, 41
  influence on operations, 429
  of information, 80–83
Value analysis, 89–90
  computing asset positions, 90–91
  expectations and choices, 91–93
  questionable alternatives, 94–96
Vancil, Richard F., 464
Variable costs of selling, 248–250

Verification, preference curve, 102–103
Vertical integration and logistics
  management, 596
Viability
  imprecision in maintaining, 10
  and organizational ideology, 46–50
Von Neumann, John, 88

Wages and motivation, 363–364
Wagner, Harvey M., 75
The Wall Street Journal, 715
Walton, Richard E., 356, 357
Ward, Barbara, 699
Warehousing, automated, 589
Warnaco, plan-budget linkages, 148–154
Weiher, Ronald L., 715
Western Electric Co., Hawthorne
  experiments, 355, 365
Wharton Econometric Model, 526
White, Robert W., 379n
Whybark, D. Clay, 597n
Wight, Oliver W., 582
Wilkinson Sword, 253
Williams, Charles, 289n
Woodward, Joan, 378n
Work habits, in creating corporate goals,
  130–131
Workweek reduction, and motivation,
  363
Worth and certainty equivalent, 97–98
Wrapp, H. Edward, 3, 5

X-11 Census Bureau Technique, 524–526

Zaleznik, Abraham, 457
Zero illusion, preference curve, 110–111